The Angelic Life

A Vision of
Orthodox Monasticism

The Angelic Life

Contents

«Ἰσάγγελος γίνεται μοναχὸς
διὰ τῆς ἀληθοῦς προσευχῆς»
—Ὁσίου Νείλου Ἀγκύρας

*A monk becomes equal to the angels
through true prayer.*
—*St. Neilos of Ancyra*

About This Book

WHEN ELDER EPHRAIM of Arizona suggested to me that I establish my own monastic community, it occurred to me that a crucial element for the success of such an undertaking would be to have a clear vision of what our monastic life is all about. Having this vision would not only keep our community connected to its purpose and deeper values but would also help new members grasp our mindset. Therefore, I began to put down in writing precisely what this vision was that I had acquired after studying the Bible and the holy Fathers, after my years of living on Mount Athos, and after being Elder Ephraim's cell attendant in Arizona for more than two decades and closely witnessing a contemporary, living example of holy monastic life.

When I had completed writing several dozen pages, I translated them into Greek for Elder Ephraim to examine. He was delighted to see the direction this book was heading and encouraged me to continue writing. In the years that have passed since then, I expanded this book considerably.

Being aware of my many shortcomings and how difficult it is to write a comprehensive book on a topic with such breadth and complexity as the monastic life, I shared rough drafts of this book with many people around the world (especially monastics) who have more experience and wisdom than me in order to receive constructive criticism. Both the monastics and laymen who read it found tremendous benefit and inspiration from what I had written. Several of them began reading it at their monasteries during meals; others gave it to their novices as a monastic primer; some expressed regret for not having had such a book when they were beginners; one of them began translating it into Russian, and others into Romanian and German; and many urged me to publish it.

I hesitated to publish this book, fearing that my limited experience and failures to live up to the ideals presented in it would mar my attempt to teach others. Furthermore, I am constantly finding new ways to expand and improve this text, and I would not want to publish something incomplete or erroneous. I certainly don't consider myself wiser than St. Basil the Great who was dissatisfied with the original drafts of his monastic rules and saw the need to revise them continually, or than St. Caesarius of Arles who destroyed the first draft of his monastic rule after revising it for twenty-two years. I also hesitated to publish my personal vision of monasticism as if it were a definitive exposition of Orthodox monasticism in general, bearing in mind the wide variety of approaches that can be found among holy monasteries. But since my fellow monastics convinced me that there is a great need for such a book today—and since 90% of this book is not my own poor words but simply verbatim quotes from the holy Fathers (some of which would be appearing in English for the first time)—I proceeded to publish this labor of love.

My hope and prayer are that many more monastics and laymen will find benefit and inspiration from this attempt of mine to capture the beauty and heart of Orthodox monasticism—the angelic life.

Hieromonk Ephraim
St. Nilus Skete, Alaska

Introduction

MONASTERIES ARE THE "nerves and support of the Church"[1] as well as her boast[2] and adornment[3] because they directly contribute to the Church's primary work, which is to save souls. Monasteries accomplish this in several ways:

1) They provide a place conducive for salvation for people who want to dedicate themselves to God in the traditional, Orthodox way.[4]

---

[1] St. Theodore the Studite, *Κατηχήσεις, Λόγος ριδ΄* [114], (PG 99:657). St. Theodore also calls monks "the salt of the earth and the light of the world," "a light for them that sit in darkness," and "an example and a declaration." Fr. Alexander Schmemann observed: "According to St. Theodore the monks must be in the Church her active inner kernel, a perpetual reminder of the Christian's ultimate calling, the 'support and affirmation' of the Church" ("Byzantium, Iconoclasm and the Monks," *St. Vladimir's Seminary Quarterly,* 3.3 (1959): 30).

[2] See St. Isaac the Syrian, *Ascetical Homily* 11: "The boast of the Church of Christ is the monastic way of life" (*The Ascetical Homilies of Saint Isaac the Syrian,* Revised Second Edition, [Boston: Holy Transfiguration Monastery, 2011], 196).

[3] "Monasticism is the glory of the Church, and the monastics—as St. Gregory of Nyssa teaches—are the hair of the head of the body of the Church and are a real adornment of the head. For monastics are dead to the world as strands of hair are dead, yet they shine and radiate the light of Christ" (in Metropolitan Hierotheos Vlachos, «Ὁ Ὑγιὴς καὶ ὁ Ἄρρωστος Μοναχισμός», *Ἐνιαύσιον 2013,* [2014]: 41). [Note: Quotations taken from books written in Greek or Russian are presented here in our own English translation.]

[4] As St. Sophrony of Essex said: "To me, a monastery is a place where our entire life is dedicated to following Christ, to attaining the mind of Christ Himself, Who bears within Himself all of mankind.... As monastics we put caring for anything in the material realm off to the side. This does not mean that we do not help our fellow men materially; we do that constantly. But our primary concern does not lie in this but in our abiding in God" (Ἀρχιμανδρίτου Σωφρονίου, *Οἰκοδομώντας τὸν Ναὸ τοῦ Θεοῦ: μέσα μας καὶ στοὺς ἀδελφούς μας,* τομ. Α΄ [Ἔσσεξ: Ἱερὰ Μονὴ Τιμίου Προδρόμου, 2014], 143, 154).

2) They offer a warm, peaceful, and theocentric place of pilgrimage for laypeople who have been drained by the cold, noisy, and egocentric world, and who feel the need to "recharge their batteries."[5]

3) St. John of Sinai wrote: "Angels are a light for monks, and the monastic life is a light for all men. Hence monks should spare no effort to become a shining example in all things."[6] Monastics who are devoted to God and focused on the spiritual life will naturally inspire others by their good example.[7]

4) A monastery with a priest can serve the Divine Liturgy daily, bringing great benefit to those attending[8] as well as to the many souls commemorated, both living and

---

[5] Archimandrite George Kapsanis, the former abbot of Gregoriou Monastery, explained how a theocentric place touches people: "When one is on the Holy Mountain [or in any monastery], one has the sense of being in another world with different criteria with other goals, and the sense of another kingdom: the kingdom to come. One tastes and communes with this kingdom. Then one realizes that the egocentric criteria and goals of the world cannot be correct, and one feels the need to conform one's life to the criteria of the Holy Mountain, which are none other than the theanthropic criteria of Orthodoxy. This explains the transformation in the life of many pilgrims, who after their pilgrimage to the Holy Mountain begin to live a pious life in a more ecclesiastical, traditional, and Orthodox manner" (Ἀρχιμανδρίτου Γεωργίου, Ὀρθόδοξος Μοναχισμὸς καὶ Ἅγιον Ὄρος, [Ἅγιον Ὄρος: Ἱερὰ Μονὴ Ὁσίου Γρηγορίου, 1998], 40). Fr. Theodoros Zeses observed: "St. John Chrysostom repeatedly admonishes the faithful to visit monasteries so that they might see for themselves that the application of Christianity's ascetic principles is not some utopian dream, but rather something entirely possible" (Protopresbyter Theodoros Zisis, *Following the Holy Fathers,* trans. Rev. Dr. John Palmer [Columbia: New Rome Press, 2017], 40).

[6] *John Climacus: The Ladder of Divine Ascent,* Classics of Western Spirituality, trans. Colm Luibhéid, Norman Russell (New York: Paulist Press, 1982), 234. Similarly, St. John Chrysostom called monks "lights of the world" (*A Select Library of the Nicene and Post-Nicene Fathers of the Christian Church: St. Chrysostom: Homilies on the Gospel of St. Matthew,* Philip Schaff, ed. [New York: Christian Literature Company, 1895], 400).

[7] St. Athanasios of Athos began his *Canonical Rule* for monks with the importance of inspiring laymen: "Those who exert themselves in journeying along the single-minded way of the solitary life and who do not deviate in striving to attain its holy goal, who by purity of mind and soul and body have conditioned themselves for the brilliant enlightenment which comes from the Holy Spirit, end up by suffusing not only themselves with light, or, to put it more correctly, a godlike appearance, but also everyone in the world with whom they converse. They enlighten other people of any rank or calling whatever. They challenge them and incite them on to a like goal, drawing and attracting them as the light of a beacon fire or a magnet" (*Byzantine Monastic Foundation Documents,* John Thomas and Angela Constantinides Hero, ed. [Washington, D.C.: Dumbarton Oaks, 2000], 250). And as St. Nicodemos of the Holy Mountain wrote: "Through their ascetical struggles and monastic way of life, first they purified themselves and then set out to purify others; first they were enlightened and afterwards enlightened others; first they were perfected and then perfected others. To put it succinctly, first they became holy and afterwards made others holy" (Νικοδήμου τοῦ Ἁγιορείτου, Συμβουλευτικὸν Ἐγχειρίδιον [Ἀθήνα: Ἔκδοσις Βιβλιοπωλείου Νεκτάριου Παναγόπουλου, 1999], 30).

[8] St. Gregory the Dialogist said: "We need, then, to eschew the present life with our whole mind, looking upon it as already lost to us, and to offer up each day the sacrifice of the Flesh and Blood of the Lord. For only this sacrifice has the power to protect the soul from eternal death" (*The Evergetinos, A Complete Text, Book IV,* ed. Archbishop Chrysostomos and Hieromonk Patapios [Etna: Center for Traditionalist Orthodox Studies, 2008], 346–48).

departed.[9] The priests can also offer the Mystery of Confession to pilgrims, which can be helpful especially for people who would otherwise not go to confession.[10]

5) Because monastics are free from the burdens of the married life, they typically have more time to help the world through prayer, and can also use their talents to do God-pleasing activities, such as writing books, painting icons, composing hymns, etc. Larger monasteries have also been known for their effective social work in the form of caring for orphans, the elderly, the poor, the sick, etc.[11]

6) The spiritual focus of monasteries has enabled them to preserve authentic Christianity in times when other Christians have been overcome by the spirit of this world.[12]

---

[9] St. Gregory the Dialogist also said: "Is it not then obvious that if the Bloodless Sacrifice [i.e., the Divine Liturgy], when offered for those who have reposed, is of such benefit, as we have elsewhere said, that it has even greater power to benefit the living?" (Archbishop Chrysostomos, *The Evergetinos*, vol. 4, 346). St. Cyril of Jerusalem taught: "We commemorate … all who in past years have fallen asleep among us, believing that it will be a very great advantage to the souls, for whom the supplication is put up, while that Holy and most Awful Sacrifice is presented" (F. L. Cross, ed., *St. Cyril of Jerusalem's Lectures on the Christian Sacraments* [New York: St. Vladimir's Seminary Press, 1995], 74). And St. John Chrysostom said: "Not in vain did the Apostles order that the remembrance should be made of the dead in the dreadful Mysteries. They know that great gain resulteth to them, great benefit" (Philip Schaff, ed., *The Nicene and Post-Nicene Fathers*, vol. 13, *Chrysostom: Homilies on Galatians, Ephesians, Philippians, Colossians, Thessalonians, Timothy, Titus, and Philemon* [New York: Christian Literature Company, 1889], 197).

[10] Archimandrite George Kapsanis noted: "It often happens on the Holy Mountain that many people who came without the intention of confessing [in its monasteries] end up confessing. And others who do confess in the world, when they visit the Holy Mountain, they confess sins that they had either been unaware of or lacked the courage to confess" (Ἀρχιμανδρίτου Γεωργίου, Ὀρθόδοξος Μοναχισμὸς καὶ Ἅγιον Ὄρος, 33).

[11] St. Basil the Great taught that a monk should "admonish the undisciplined, encourage the faint-hearted, minister to the sick, wash the feet of the saints, and be mindful of the duties of hospitality and fraternal charity" (*Saint Basil: Ascetical Works*, vol. 9, trans. Sister M. Monica Wagner, C. S. C. [Washington, D.C.: Catholic University of America Press, 1962], 34). Following this injunction, St. Theodosios the Cenobiarch built a monastery with "hostels and hospitals for monks, for worldly visitors, and for the poor; a home for the aged; and a 'monastery within a monastery' for monks mentally afflicted after excessive or ill-judged asceticism" (Derwas J. Chitty, *The Desert a City*, (New York: St. Vladimir's Seminary Press, 1966], 109). Bearing this and other examples in mind, Elder Ephraim said: "If we examine various time periods in history, we will observe the role of monasteries in society. With schools, homes for the elderly, and hospitals, monks and nuns rallied all their material and spiritual abilities to alleviate their neighbor's pain" (from the manuscript of a homily "What Does Monasticism Offer to Society?"). Nevertheless, despite these natural expressions of love for one's neighbor by monastics, social work has never been the focus of Orthodox monasticism. This point is elaborated in chapter 6) section 11) on page 327.

[12] Fr. Theodoros Zeses wrote: "Authentic Christianity, Christianity in its fullness, is cultivated in the monasteries, and the preservation of this is the greatest contribution to the world and to society imaginable.... Should it ever become impossible, or at least very difficult, for the Gospel to be applied in the world, it will be far from the world in monasteries and sketes that authentic, ascetical, heavenly-minded, eschatological Christianity will be preserved... where both authentic man, man according to the image of Christ, and the natural environment, so cruelly ravaged by industrialization, are both safeguarded.... A Christianity lacking asceticism, continual struggle, afflictions, hardships, self-mortification, the renunciation of a worldly manner of life and thought, is a Christianity which has lost its true character" (Zisis, *Following the Holy Fathers*, 30, 31, 40).

7) Last (and certainly not least), throughout the history of the Church, time and time again it was the monasteries and the monastic hierarchs that preserved the Orthodox faith in its purity.[13] St. Ignatius Brianchaninov taught that even faith itself will disappear without the presence of monasteries,[14] which act as "barometers"[15] of the Church. St. Barsanuphius of Optina added: "The whole world is upheld by this monasticism. When monasticism will no longer exist, then will come the Dread Judgment."[16]

+ + +

The Focus and Aim

The focus of all Christians is to love God with all one's heart, soul, and mind, and to love one's neighbor as oneself.[17] This central role of love is even more pertinent for monastics, who are called to be exemplary Christians. This is why St. Paisios of the Holy Mountain declared: "The whole work of a monk is love."[18] Elder Aimilianos said: "What kind of life

---

[13] The long list of monastic saints who helped safeguard Orthodoxy includes Sts. Anthony the Great, Macarios the Great, Basil the Great, Efthymios, Ephraim the Syrian, Melanie, Theodosios the Cenobiarch, Symeon the Stylite, Savas the Sanctified, Maximos the Confessor, John the Damascene, Stephen the New, Theodore and Theophan the Branded, Gregory Palamas, and Mark of Ephesus. At the Seventh Ecumenical Council, 136 of the 350 fathers participating were abbots and monks. As St. Amphilochios Makris of Patmos said: "Monks guard the castle walls of our Church and protect her from her enemies, who like wolves are pouncing to tear her up in this contemporary materialistic era of ours. Alienation from the Orthodox mindset will only occur when the monasteries—the castles of Orthodoxy—are empty" (Ὁ Γέροντας τῆς Πάτμου Ἀμφιλόχιος Μακρῆς [1889–1970], Βίος - Ὑποθῆκαι - Μαρτυρίαι, [Πάτμος: Ἱερᾶς Μονῆς Εὐαγγελισμοῦ, 2007], 202). St. Theodore the Studite declared: "The work of a monk is not to bear the slightest innovation in the Gospel, so that they will not give laymen an example of heresy" (Θεοδώρου Στουδίτου, Ἐπιστολὴ λθ΄, Θεοφίλῳ Ἡγουμένῳ, PG 99:1049).

[14] According to St. Sophrony: "St. Ignatius Brianchaninov (1807–1867) said that without the monasteries, the world will not be able to keep even faith. Which faith? The faith that God Himself, the Creator of the world, came on earth, became man, spoke with us, and made known to us the plan He has for us—His plan from before the ages" (Σωφρονίου, Οἰκοδομώντας τὸν Ναὸ τοῦ Θεοῦ, Τόμος Α΄, 418).

[15] "Monasticism is a barometer that stands in a secluded room, closed from every side, showing an exact condition of the weather outside" (*Игнатий Брянчанинов, свт. Полное собрание писем*: В 3 томах. Т. 1: Переписка с архиереями Церкви и настоятелями монастырей / Сост. О. И. Шафранова. — М.: Паломник, 2011. С. 127). Archimandrite Ambrose explained this statement of St. Ignatius as follows: "The height or decline of the spiritual life of the Church in each epoch is defined by the condition of monasticism in that period" (Archbishop Antony of San Francisco, *The Young Elder: a biography of blessed Archimandrite Ambrose of Milkovo* [Jordanville: Holy Trinity Monastery, 1974], 15).

[16] Victor Afanasiev, *Elder Barsanuphius of Optina* (Platina: St. Herman of Alaska Brotherhood, 2000), 264.

[17] Cf. Lk. 10:27.

[18] Γέροντος Παϊσίου Ἁγιορείτου, *Πνευματικὴ Ἀφύπνηση, Λόγοι Β΄* [Σουρωτὴ Θεσσαλονίκης: Ἱερὸν Ἡσυχαστήριον "Εὐαγγελιστὴς Ἰωάννης ὁ Θεολόγος," 1999], 319.

is monastic life? First of all, as we live it and feel it, it is a life of love."[19] When Elder Paisius of Sihla was asked: "How must monks live in order to save their souls?" he replied: "Live in love, for the Savior says, 'By this shall all men know that ye are My disciples, if ye have love one to another' (Jn. 13:35)."[20]

St. Paul warned: "Even if we speak with the tongues of men and of angels, have the gift of prophecy, know all mysteries and all knowledge, have all faith to move mountains, give away all our possessions, and surrender our body to be burned but have not love, we are nothing."[21] In the same spirit, St. Athanasios the Great said: "No matter how hard a person labors, if he lacks love for his neighbor he has labored in vain,"[22] and St. Maximos the Confessor taught: "Every ascesis lacking love is foreign to God."[23] St. Achard of Jumièges (in seventh-century Gaul) on his deathbed warned his monastic disciples: "You have borne the yoke of penance and are grown old in the exercise of religious duties in vain if you do not sincerely love one another."[24] St. Anthony the Great became the greatest monk in Egypt not by being the most ascetical monk but by loving God the most.[25] St. Sophrony of Essex remarked: "If in our monastic life we do not learn to love, how can the meaning of monasticism be esteemed?"[26] Thus, the most serious accusation we could ever hear—assuming the accusation has some basis in reality, of course—is that we lack love, whether collectively or individually.

Since we are called not only to love God with our whole heart but also to love our neighbor as ourselves, a monastery not only should be dedicated to worshipping God, but

---

[19] Γέροντος Αἰμιλιανοῦ, «Μοναχισμός, Πορεία πρὸς τὸν Θεόν», ἐν *Σύναξις Εὐχαριστίας· Χαριστήρια εἰς Τιμὴν τοῦ Γέροντος Αἰμιλιανοῦ* (Ἀθῆναι: Ἰνδίκτος, 2003), 53.

[20] Archimandrite Ioanichie Bălan, *A Little Corner of Paradise: The Life and Teaching of Elder Paisius of Sihla,* trans. the Sisters of St. Nilus Skete (Platina: St. Herman of Alaska Brotherhood, 2016), 204.

[21] Cf. 1 Cor. 13:1–3.

[22] PG 28:277A.

[23] PG 90:941D.

[24] Rev. Alban Butler, *The Lives of the Fathers, Martyrs, and Other Principal Saints,* vol. 9 (Derby: Richardson and Son, 1866), 153.

[25] "Abba Amoun of Nitria came to see Abba Anthony and said to him, 'Since my rule is stricter than yours how is it that your name is better known amongst men than mine is?' Abba Anthony answered, 'It is because I love God more than you'" (Benedicta Ward, *The Sayings of the Desert Fathers* [Kalamazoo: Cistercian Publications, 1975], 67).

[26] Σωφρονίου, *Οἰκοδομῶντας τὸν Ναὸ τοῦ Θεοῦ, Τόμος Α΄*, 22. St. Sophrony also wrote: "I understand monasticism as a special form of love. Love can take various forms. Sometimes it brings joy and makes life with other people pleasant and rewarding. But there can also be another form of love: love which torments and burdens people and makes life unbearably hard until its last desire for the salvation of all others is satisfied; and the paths which lead to the attainment of this love are out of the ordinary" (Archimandrite Sophrony Sakharov, *Striving for Knowledge of God: Correspondence with David Balfour* [Essex: Monastery of St. John the Baptist, 2016], 252–53).

also should care for others: by offering advice and hospitality to pilgrims, by giving material and spiritual alms to the needy, and especially by praying for the entire world. For as the Theotokos revealed, a monk is someone "who prays for the whole world."[27]

Abba Moses taught: "The aim of our [monastic] profession is the Kingdom of God, … but our [temporal] objective is a clean heart, without which it is impossible for anyone to reach our aim."[28] Thus, our primary work is to attain a clean heart by uprooting the passions and cultivating the virtues: love, obedience, humility, chastity, prayer, fear of God, silence, repentance, patience, watchfulness, fasting, self-denial, authenticity, detachment, simplicity, seriousness, forcefulness, zeal, transforming anger, self-reproach, remembrance of death, etc.

St. Basil the Great taught: "The ascetical life has one aim—the soul's salvation—and all that can contribute to this end must be observed with much fear as a divine command."[29] Thus, the purpose of a monastery is the salvation of souls, and in this book we shall attempt to outline "all that can contribute to this end." This spiritual typikon summarizes our understanding and application of the monastic life, based on the Bible and on the writings and lives of the saints of the Church. Special attention is given to the mindset and traditions we have received from our holy spiritual forefathers (namely, Elder Ephraim of Arizona and St. Joseph the Hesychast). In the spirit of the Three Hierarchs, St. Nicodemos of the Holy Mountain, and many other Church Fathers, the findings of contemporary scientific studies and historical details have been included wherever they are relevant and helpful. Also following the example of St. Nicodemos, we have included many lengthy footnotes. These asides were relegated to the bottom of the page not because they are unimportant but simply to avoid interrupting the flow of the main text.

---

[27] St. Silouan the Athonite wrote: "The Lord chooses out men to pray for the whole world. When [Saint] Parthenios, the ascetic of Kiev, [in the 19th century after receiving the schema] sought to know what the strict monastic observance was, the Mother of God told him, 'The monk who wears the schema is a man who prays for the whole world'" (Archimandrite Sophrony Sakharov, *Saint Silouan the Athonite* [New York: St. Vladimir's Seminary Press, 1991], 493). Likewise, St. Symeon of Thessalonica declared that for monks, "this is what should be done above all: to pray. Through prayer, these [monks] are like fire in their yearning and become partakers of the age to come" (D. Balfour, Ἁγίου Συμεὼν Θεσσαλονίκης: Ἔργα Θεολογικά [Θεσσαλονίκη: Πατριαρχικὸν Ἴδρυμα Πατερικῶν Μελεῶν, 1981], κεφ. 26, στ. 574–82, 450). Elder Ephraim also said: "Monasticism's greatest offering is its testimony that Jesus is Christ and its prayer for the world" (from the manuscript of a homily "What Does Monasticism Offer to Society?").

[28] *John Cassian: Conferences,* Colm Luibhéid, ed. (New York: Paulist Press, 1985), 39 (Conference 1). St. Sophrony of Essex also reminds us that correcting our ethical behavior is merely the means to an end: "The goal of asceticism is the accomplishment of the will of God. Our goal, eternal life, consists in knowing God (Jn. 17:3), and not in correcting our ethical behavior. This does not of course mean that we do not have to grow in moral rectitude. But the first and greatest commandment is to love God (Mt. 22:37). When we lose touch with the memory of God, when we forget God, we sin against this commandment" (Sakharov, *Striving for Knowledge of God,* 289)

[29] Wagner, *Saint Basil: Ascetical Works,* vol. 9, 217.

As pertaining to non-dogmatic matters, we have not limited ourselves to extracting benefit and inspiration from the wise sayings of Orthodox Christians only, since we agree with the consensus of the holy Fathers that the heterodox also have helpful insights that the Orthodox should take advantage of.[30] Furthermore, we have drawn from the wisdom of monastic saints and rules of Western Europe that were Orthodox (that is, from well before the Great Schism), even though historically the rest of the Orthodox Church has unfortunately been neglecting them merely out of ignorance until just recently.[31]

We are hopeful that this book will prove to be beneficial not only for monastics but also for laymen, because the spiritual principles in this book apply to all people, both monastics and laymen. St. John Chrysostom taught: "When Christ orders us to follow the narrow path, He addresses Himself to all. The monastics and the lay person must attain the same heights…. Those who live in the world, even though married, ought to resemble the monks in everything else. You are entirely mistaken if you think that there are some things required of ordinary people, and others of monks."[32]

If *all* the writings of the holy Fathers on monasticism were collected into one place, they would easily fill dozens of volumes. Rather than doing such an exhaustive task, we have attempted here instead to capture only the *essence* of what they have said. This book could have been a fraction of its current size if we had simply summarized in our own words what the holy Fathers taught instead of quoting them verbatim. However, we chose not to do this because we perceive much grace in their inspired words. Besides, there already exist many such "monastery typika" nowadays which summarize the teachings of the holy Fathers on monasticism. The drawback of many of these documents is that they come across as a cold set of rules because they usually focus on answering only the practical questions: "What?" "Who?" "When?" "Where?" and "How?" while underemphasizing the most important question for us rational human beings: "Why?" We believe that the most effective way to address all those questions and especially the latter existential question, is to let the holy Fathers speak for themselves.

---

[30] Since quoting the heterodox in a book about Orthodox monasticism might seem inappropriate to some readers, we have included an appendix (see page 451) to demonstrate that this approach is indeed patristic.

[31] A zealous supporter and catalyst of the contemporary Orthodox movement to venerate the saints of the West was St. John Maximovitch (St. Gregory of Tours, *Vita Patrum: The Life of the Fathers,* trans. Fr. Seraphim Rose [Platina: St. Herman of Alaska Brotherhood, 1988], 13).

[32] As quoted in David G. R. Keller, *Oasis of Wisdom: The Worlds of the Desert Fathers and Mothers* (Collegeville: Liturgical Press, 2005), xx. (*Epist. Ad Haeb.,* 7, 4; 7,41 and *Adv. Oppugn. Vitae monist.,* 3, 14.) Echoing this sentiment, St. Gregory Palamas said: "The commandments of the Lord are directed to all, married and celibate, without exception. The only difference is that monks pursue the more perfect application, according the words of the Lord, 'If thou wilt be perfect, go and sell that thou hast, and come and follow me' (Mt. 19:21)" (*Φιλοκαλία, Τόμος Δ΄* [Ἀθήνα: Ἀστήρ, 1976], 92).

Dedication

To our dear Elder Ephraim
whose love and humility
have touched the
hearts of us all

Preface

by Archimandrite Aimilianos[33]
Former Abbot of the Holy Monastery of Simonos Petras

a MONASTIC RULE should be an embodiment, preservation, and presentation of the canons of the Church concerning monasticism.... It should not be one more law among many, a new burden, a new order for monks to learn well—if they want to be monks today—nor a systematic and detailed inventory of duties and rights, but a living, concrete, contemporary presentation of the holy canons adopted centuries ago by the Church which nursed the problems of monasticism, as flesh of its own flesh.... It should not restrict the brotherhood, for then it will be loathsome, but should stimulate it to live.... Where there is no rule to embody the spirit of the Gospel, there is no oneness of spirit, and then the brotherhood is doomed to fall apart.

Today, most monastery regulations resemble secular rulebooks comprising matters related to the practical life. Theosis is the center around which the thought and the heart of the monk should revolve. The Regulation should therefore be a spiritual document—not a bill of law—which will awaken the hearts of the monks and rouse them to spiritual combat, so that they are drawn by the vision of the Kingdom of God and live with their gaze fixed on precisely this aim of theosis. Emphasis should be placed on the genuine cenobitic life, which manifests itself in obedience and discipline, poverty, prayer, and study, in the martyr's outlook, and in desire for Christ. It should be an aid to theological and mystical understanding and to the experience of the mystery of deification in Christ and of liturgical

---

[33] This preface consists of excerpts from Elder Aimilianos's presentation in 1973, "On the Preparation of an Internal Regulation for the Holy Monasteries of the Church of Greece," his "Regulations of the Holy Cenobium of the Annunciation Ormylia, Halkidiki," as published in *The Authentic Seal,* 36–37, 75–77, 160–61, and his commentary on the Rule of St. Macarius, as published in *Νηπτικὴ Ζωὴ καὶ Ἀσκητικοὶ Κανόνες,* 355. I am grateful to Abbess Nikodimi for her permission to include quotations from her holy elder's books.

life. The cenobium [i.e., the monastic community] should again become "a heaven on earth"[34] and "an assembly convoked by God,"[35] a likeness of the Apostolic assembly.

The aim of the foundation of the holy cenobitic community is for the sisters [or monks] to live together in one place and, with God's protection and aid, by living in perfect imitation of the life of our Lord in the flesh, and with much labor, many struggles and the continuous study of His commandments, to achieve the salvation of souls, that perfection which is elevating and pleasing to God, and blessed deification.... It shall not be mere co-habitation on the part of cold individuals, but a drawing together of souls, a common course pursued by persons united in affection in one body, "rejoicing in each other lovingly in divine delectation,"[36] venerating with one mouth and one heart the Lord "Who is the head, from Whom the whole body, joined and knit together by every joint with which it is supplied, when each part is in harmonious operation, makes increase of the body for the edification of itself in love."[37]

The Scriptures and the Fathers should have their rightful place [in the life of the monastics]. Theology should shed light on everyday problems. Dogma should be regarded as a basis for piety. The typikon of the Church should be observed in its spirit. Communion should again be taken with the frequency ordained by the sacred canons. The spirit of worship should be interpreted every day in the monastery. Continuous prayer should be regarded as the fundamental criterion for spirituality. Youth should be respected and its enthusiasm fostered. The elevated spiritual life and the vision of the glory of God should be studied as the ultimate desire for the monk.

Moreover, pre-eminence should again be given to the Patristic principle of individual training. The person should not be stifled, the personality should be cultivated, the individual understood. The manual worker as well as the labourer in spiritual matters should learn that they both serve God in like manner, though the unity of the brotherhood must be preserved, and spirituality must be cultivated by living within it. The cenobium must once again start filling the Church with saints.

---

[34] *The Ladder of Divine Ascent,* Revised Edition, (Brookline: Holy Transfiguration Monastery, 2001), 44.

[35] PG 141:740.

[36] St. Dionysius the Areopagite, PG 3:536B; *Pseudo-Dionysius: The Complete Works,* trans. Colm Luibhéid, The Classics of Western Spirituality (New York: Paulist Press, 1987), 247.

[37] Eph. 4:15–16.

Chapter One:
Becoming a Monk

1) What is a Monk?

PEAKING FROM THEIR OWN PERSONAL EXPERIENCES, different saints have found different ways to define what a monk is. Abba Zacharias stated: "He is a monk who forces himself in everything."[38] St. John of Sinai explained: "A monk is one who holds only to the commands of God in every time and place and matter. A monk is one who constantly constrains his nature and unceasingly watches over his senses. A monk is he who keeps his body in chastity, his mouth pure and his mind illumined. A monk is a mourning soul that both asleep and awake is unceasingly occupied with the remembrance of death."[39] Likewise, St. Efthymios the Great taught: "Brethren, strive for what brought you out here, and do not neglect your own salvation. You must at all times stay sober and awake. As Scripture says, 'Keep awake, and pray not to enter into temptation.'[40] … [Monks] must always await and ponder the hour of death and the dread day of judgment, fear the threat of eternal fire and desire the glory of the kingdom of heaven."[41] St. Nilus of Ancyra wrote: "It is said that a monk is

---

[38] PG 65:180A; see also Ward, *The Sayings of the Desert Fathers,* 67.

[39] Holy Transfiguration Monastery, *The Ladder of Divine Ascent,* 4.

[40] Mt. 26:41.

[41] Cyril of Scythopolis, *The Lives of the Monks of Palestine,* trans. R.M. Price (Kalamazoo: Cistercian Publications, 1991), 12–13.

an altar on which and from which pure prayers are offered to the Most High God."[42] Similarly, St. Maximos the Confessor stated: "A monk is a man who has freed his intellect from attachment to material things and by means of self-control, love, psalmody and prayer cleaves to God."[43]

St. Paisius Velichkovsky gave the following definition of a monk:

> What is a monk? A monk is a fulfiller of the commandments of Christ, a perfect Christian, an imitator of and a participant in the passion of Christ, a daily martyr, a voluntary dead man who willingly dies in spiritual struggles. A monk is a pillar of patience, a depth of humility, a fount of tears, a treasury of purity, one who laughs at all that is considered splendid, sweet, glorious, and attractive in this world. A monk is a soul that is pained, constantly meditating on the memory of death, both in wakefulness and in sleep. A monk is one who constantly forces nature, and who guards his feelings without weakening. A monk is of the order and condition of the fleshless ones, though preserved in a material body, having in mind at all times, in every place, and in every work, only what is divine.[44]

St. Nectarios of Aegina described the monastic life as follows:

> A monk's way of life consists of ceaselessly seeking God's countenance, yearning for Him, possessing a strong love for Him, and perpetually hastening toward Him. The monk offers his heart as a sacrifice to Him alone—an offering that is holy, pure, and perfected in love. Truly, he does not live for himself, but for the Lord, and the Lord visits him mystically; He mystically reveals Himself to the eyes of the soul of the monk who is devoted to Him, and such a monk receives the betrothal of the grace of the future vision of the Lord's countenance.[45]

Several saints emphasized the necessity of withdrawing from the world in order to be a monk. For example, St. Isaac the Syrian said: "A monk is he who remains outside the world and is ever supplicating God to receive future blessings."[46] And St. Eustathios of Thessalonica wrote: "A monk is primarily he who has formed (or rather renewed) his heart in solitude and understood all the works of God. This deep understanding is a manifestation of his theoretical training and virtuous life."[47]

St. Eustathios also gave the following advice to a monk to remind him of his calling:

> Bear in mind that you are an angel of light even though you are wearing black. You have been appointed to stand beside the true Light. You are now a close friend of

---

[42] *Epistle to Andreas the Presbyter,* III:32; PG 79:388A.

[43] *The Philokalia,* vol. 2, G.E.H. Palmer, Philip Sherrard, Kallistos Ware, eds. (London: Faber&Faber, 1979), 74.

[44] St. Paisius Velichkovsky, "Field Flowers," *The Orthodox Word,* no. 120 (Jan.–Feb. 1985), 25.

[45] Cleopas Strongylis, *St. Nectarios of Pentapolis and the Island of Aegina: The Monastic Ideal,* vol. 2, The Catechetical Letters, trans. Christopher Tripoulas (Brookline: Holy Cross Orthodox Press, 2012), 120 (Letter #44).

[46] Holy Transfiguration Monastery, *The Ascetical Homilies of Saint Isaac the Syrian,* 170–71 (Homily 6).

[47] PG 135:848AB.

God Himself and have vowed to acquire various virtues. Therefore, you have a great obligation, O magnificent monk, so do not delay in fulfilling your duty.[48]

A monk holds a torch from the Father of Lights, and from there he radiates light that shines and illumines, if not the whole world as the Apostles did, then at least many places of the earth. This is what is typically accomplished by lanterns perched in high places. They emit light that warns of an enemy onslaught, or as a lighthouse they show where rocks lie beneath the surface so that people avoid dangerous reefs, and they do other such salvific things.[49]

A true monk is a citizen of heaven, not of the earth, even though he dwells on the earth. His way of life is ethereal; he is celestial since he flies above everything earthly.[50]

St. Symeon the New Theologian declared that a monk is he who has withdrawn "truly from the world and the things in it" and has ascended "perceptibly to a height of spiritual theoria through the working of the Commandments," and "he clearly perceives the transformation that has taken place within him."[51] Elsewhere he added the following lofty characteristics of a true monk:

The monk is one who is not mixed with the world and always converses with God alone. Seeing he is seen, loving he is loved, and he becomes a light mysteriously shining.[52]

The one who is one with God is no longer alone, even if he lives alone or inhabits the desert or even a cave. But if he has not found Him, has not known Him, and has not received fully the Word become flesh, he is not a monk, absolutely not![53]

The real monks and solitaries are those who are alone with God and are in God, detached from every type of discursive reasoning, who see only God in a mind empty of thought, secured in light like an arrow in the wall or a star in heaven, or in any other manner which I cannot express.[54]

St. Paisius Velichkovsky encouraged monastics to be far from the world:

It is better to battle alone with the demons, and in hunger, nakedness, and every sorrow to die with a small struggle in the desert, fleeing the world, than to seek great labors for salvation in the midst of the world—for the flame of the passions of this world ignites and scorches the monk who returns to it. If one may be dispassionate,

---

[48] PG 135:905C.

[49] PG 135:904C.

[50] PG 135:838A.

[51] As quoted in Ἀρχιμανδρίτου Χριστοδούλου, *Ὀρθόδοξος Μοναχισμός: Ἐκκοσμίκευση ἢ Ἀναδρομὴ πρὸς τὸ Ἀρχαῖον Κάλλος;* (Ἱ. Μονὴ Ἁγίου Συμεὼν τοῦ Νέου Θεολόγου, 2001), 32.

[52] *Divine Eros: Hymns of Saint Symeon the New Theologian,* trans. Daniel K. Griggs (New York: St. Vladimir's Seminary Press, 2010), 48 (Hymn 3).

[53] Archbishop Basil Krivocheine, *In the Light of Christ: Saint Symeon the New Theologian (949–1022), Life-Spirituality-Doctrine,* trans. Anthony P. Gythiel (New York: St. Vladimir's Press, 1986), 150–51 (*Hymn* 27. 18–27).

[54] Ibid., 151 (*Hymn* 27. 73–81).

even such a one in the world will suffer harm. And he who is passionate will be tangled up in every sinful net....

Therefore, O monk, be sober with your mind, be sober [i.e., watchful]. Find for yourself a melancholy place which is absolutely useless to men, from where you cannot be banished, a place remote from the world. Lead there your silent life, where, even if you wish to do some kind of worldly activity, there will be no opportunity for this, thanks to the remoteness from the world. In the desert, by the sole fact of having withdrawn from the world, a man is delivered from the passions.[55]

St. Paisios of the Holy Mountain saw self-sacrifice as a key part of being a monk:

The monk is helped naturally by his whole way of life to have love and sacrifice. He has set out to die for Christ. In other words, he set out for sacrifice....

If a monastic is making slow progress in this matter [of self-sacrifice], then he is not a monastic. Then where is the spirituality? There is no spirituality when there is no sacrifice. All the spiritual disciplines which a monk does without sacrificing himself are nothing....

When someone takes seriously the struggle that must be carried out in this life, there is a divine flame in him. If this divine flame is missing, then he is useless. It is this that gives him joy, courage, *philotimo* [a sense of honor, or eager goodness]. This is what the Lord said, *I came to cast fire upon the earth.*"[56]

St. Nicephoros the Monk viewed monasticism as a lofty art and science: "The monastic life has been called the art of arts and the science of sciences, because this holy way of life does not bestow on us what is corruptible, diverting our nous from higher to lower things and completely stifling it. On the contrary, it offers us strange and indescribable good things, that 'the eye has not seen, and the ear has not heard, and man's heart has not grasped' (1 Cor. 2:9)."[57]

St. Maximos the Confessor taught that becoming a monk only outwardly is insufficient:

He who has renounced things such as marriage, possessions, etc., has made his outer self a monk but not yet his inner self. Only he who has renounced the passionate thoughts of these things has made a monk of the inner self, which is the nous. It is easy to make a monk of one's outer self if one wants to; but no small struggle is required to make one's inner self a monk.

Who, then, in this generation has been completely freed from passionate thoughts and has been granted continuous, pure, and immaterial prayer which is the mark of the inner monk?[58]

St. John Chrysostom declared that a monk is superior to a king:

---

[55] St. Paisius Velichkovsky, "Field Flowers," 26–28.

[56] Elder Paisios of the Holy Mountain, *Spiritual Counsels, Volume II: Spiritual Awakening* (Souroti: Holy Monastery "Evangelist John the Theologian," 2008), 236–37.

[57] Νικηφόρου Μονάζοντος, «Λόγος περὶ νήψεως καὶ φυλακῆς καρδίας» ἐν *Φιλοκαλία τῶν Ἱερῶν Νηπτικῶν,* τόμος δ´ (Ἀθῆναι: Ἀστήρ, 1991), 18; see also Palmer, Sherrard, Ware, *The Philokalia,* vol. 4, 194–95.

[58] Μαξίμου τοῦ Ὁμολογητοῦ, «Περὶ ἀγάπης ἑκατοντὰς τετάρτη» ἐν *Φιλοκαλία τῶν Ἱερῶν Νηπτικῶν,* τόμος β´ (1991), 46 (κεφ. ν´–να´); see also Palmer, Sherrard, Ware, *The Philokalia,* vol. 2, 106.

Unlike the king, the monk displays self-control. Too often a king is a slave to his passions. His desire for glory and wealth leads him to warfare. His love of luxurious living leads him to feast on rich food and drink and to adornment in gems and gold and fine clothing. By contrast, the monk enters battles only to overcome the wicked forces in the world. He dresses simply, eats lightly, and drinks water with more pleasure than those who drink fine wine.[59] …

If you want to examine the warfare conducted by each, you will find the one fighting and resisting and defeating demons and being crowned by Christ … but the king is [merely] fighting barbarians. Just as demons are much more fearsome than men, likewise he who resists and defeats them is much more illustrious. And if you want to determine the motivation of each for fighting, you will find them greatly unequal. One fights the demons for the sake of piety and the worship of God … whereas the other fights barbarians for the sake of seizing places or mountains or money.[60]

Several other saints also lauded the lofty state of monasticism. St. John of Karpathos wrote: "Monks should not consider anything worldly as superior to their own monastic vocation; for, without any contradiction, monks are higher and more glorious than crowned monarchs, since they are called to be in constant attendance upon God."[61] St. Theodore the Studite added: "I acknowledge that the monastic life is lofty and exalted, even angelic, purifying every sin on account of its perfect way of life."[62] St. Nectarios of Aegina elaborated:

What, indeed, is more honorable than this [monastic] way of life? What is more resplendent? It adorns our "image" (Gen. 1:27) and gives it its original beauty; it leads to blessedness; it beautifies the one who lives it; it leads to spiritual philosophy; it reveals mysteries; it teaches the truth; it makes the word of God dwell in the heart; it safely leads to the desired end; it renders man a citizen of heaven; it turns one's breath into a ceaseless melody; it makes one's entire life a harmony; it unites man with the angels; it renders man Godlike; it raises him to the Divine; it unites him with God.[63]

2) The Novitiate

i) Whom to Accept

There are three categories of people living in a monastery: postulants (ὑποψήφιοι), novices (δόκιμοι), and monks (μοναχοί). A postulant is simply a layman who has been

---

[59] Stephen K. Black, "John Chrysostom on Power and The Episcopacy in the Late Fourth Century," 3 www.firstpaloalto.com/downloads/JohnChyrsostom.pdf.

[60] John Chrysostom, *A Comparison Between a King and a Monk/Against the Opponents of the Monastic Life*, Studies in the Bible and Early Christianity, vol. 13, trans. David G. Hunter (New York: Edwin Mellen Press, 1988), 71; PG 47:389.

[61] Palmer, Sherrard, Ware, *The Philokalia*, vol. 1, 326.

[62] PG 99:1816CD and Thomas and Hero, *Byzantine Monastic Foundation Documents,* 76.

[63] Constantine Cavarnos, *Modern Orthodox Saints 7: St. Nectarios of Aegina,* Second Edition (Boston: Institute for Byzantine and Modern Greek Studies, 1988), 186; and Ἀρχιμ. Τίτου Ματθαιάκη, Ὁ Ὅσιος Νεκτάριος Κεφαλᾶς, «Ἐπιστολὴ πρὸς Μοναχόν» (Ἀθῆναι, 1955), 261.

given permission to stay at the monastery for an extended visit because he is considering monasticism.

Saint Paisios of the Holy Mountain said: "It is most important for a beginner, while still in the world, to find a spiritual father who will be a friend of monasticism, because most of the spiritual fathers in our times are *monachomachoi* ("monk-fighters") and war against monasticism in many different ways."[64]

Elder Aimilianos recommended in the *Regulations of the Holy Cenobium of the Annunciation*: "It is a good thing for postulants to visit the monastery often for a number of days or longer periods over a length of time before coming to reside there [permanently]."[65] After the seriousness of his intent to become a monk has become clear to himself and to the abbot (which is typically after one to six months), the abbot can clothe him as a novice. Only after being a novice for several years can he be tonsured a monk.

When St. Basil the Great was asked whether all applicants to the monastery are to be received, he replied:

> It is not without danger to reject those who come to the Lord through us. … Yet, it is clearly our obligation to inquire thoroughly into the past life of those who come… to ensure that they are not unstable in character and quick to change their decisions.
>
> The fickleness of such persons renders them suspect, since not only do they themselves have no benefit, but also they harm others by reviling, telling lies, and wickedly slandering our work. Inasmuch, however, as everything can be corrected through diligence, and since the fear of God overcomes all kinds of defects of the soul, we should not immediately give up on these people. Rather, they should be led to practice suitable disciplines, and if we find in them some indication of stability after their resolution has been tested by time and laborious trial, they may be safely admitted. Otherwise, they should be sent away before they are a part of the community, so that their trial period may not harm the community. It is also necessary to examine to ascertain whether a man who has previously fallen into sin confesses with deep contrition his secret shameful acts and condemns himself.…
>
> A general method of testing everyone is to ascertain whether they are prepared to bear all humiliations without false shame, so that they accept even the most menial tasks, if it seems reasonable that these tasks are useful. And after all humiliations each candidate has been proved a useful vessel for the Lord, so to speak, and ready for every good work through exhaustive scrutiny by those competent to examine such matters, let him be counted among those who have devoted themselves to the Lord.[66]

---

[64] Elder Paisios of the Holy Mountain, *Epistles,* (Thessaloniki: Holy Monastery of the Evangelist John the Theologian, 2002), 31.

[65] Archimandrite Aimilianos of Simonopetra, *The Authentic Seal: Spiritual Instructions and Discourses,* (Ormylia: Evangelismos tis Theotokou Monastery, 1999), 169.

[66] Βασιλείου Καισαρείας τοῦ Μεγάλου, *Ἅπαντα τὰ Ἔργα: Ἀσκητικὰ Α΄,* τόμος 8, μετάφρασις Κωνσταντίνου Καρακόλη, Ἑλληνικοὶ Πατέρες τῆς Ἐκκλησίας (Θεσσαλονίκη: Πατερικαὶ Ἐκδόσεις «Γρηγόριος ὁ Παλαμᾶς», 1973) 242–45; see also Wagner, *Saint Basil: Ascetical Works,* vol. 9, 259–61 (Question 10 of the *Long Rules*).

The Council in Gangra (held in AD 340) forbade people from becoming monastics if they have children to raise or elderly parents to care for.[67] Likewise, the fifth-century "Canons of Marūtā" state:

> When the *rišdairā* [i.e., the abbot] receives a brother into the monastery, there shall be an examination; he has to interrogate accurately that one who is being received, as to what his profession is and from whence he comes and regarding the reason why he wants to become a monk. If he is a slave and his master a faithful, he shall not receive him except his master permits him. If he is a freeman, and has faithful parents and these do not agree, they shall not receive him. If he is separated from his parents, is independent and dwells by himself, he shall be received. If he has a wife and his wife does not agree, he shall not receive him. If, however, he has sons and daughters, even if his wife agrees, he shall not be received. A man whom his wife persecutes and has fled from her, shall be received. A brother who has killed someone but did not hate him since yesterday and beforetime, and did not kill him willfully, shall be received.[68]

Similarly, the *Rules of Išō' Bar Nūn* declare:

> If there is a man who has a wife, and they both in common conclusion want to separate themselves for life in holiness—not that the marriage is impure in their eyes but holy and pure but since they have desired for a higher life—it is lawful to do so. If somebody wants to sanctify himself, but as husband or wife they are bound in the yoke of marriage, if one partner does not want, then the other who wants to sanctify has no authority, for not the one of them has authority over his body but his partner, says the divine apostle (vid. 1 Cor. 7:4).[69]

Quoting Abba Paphnutius, St. John Cassian taught that there are three kinds of calling to monasticism:

> The first is from God, the second comes by way of man, and the third arises from necessity. The vocation from God comes whenever some inspiration is sent into our sleepy hearts, stirring us with a longing for eternal life and salvation, urging us to follow God and to cling with most saving compunction to His commands....
>
> The second type of calling is, as I have said, that which comes through human agency when the example and the advice of holy people stirs us to long for salvation....
>
> The third kind of vocation is that which comes through necessity. Imprisoned by the riches and pleasures of this world, we are suddenly put to the test. The danger of death hangs over us. The loss or seizure of our property strikes us. The death of those

---

[67] Canon XV: "If anyone should abandon his own children, or fail to devote himself to feeding his children, and fail, as far as depends on them, to bring them up to be godly and to have respect for God, but, under the pretext of ascetic exercise, should neglect them, let him be anathema." Canon XVI: "If any children of parents, especially of faithful ones, should depart, on the pretext of godliness, and should fail to pay due honor to their parents, godliness, that is to say, being preferred with them, i.e., among them, let them be anathema" (Agapius and Nicodemus, *The Rudder,* trans. D. Cummings [Boston: The Orthodox Christian Educational Society, 1957], 528).

[68] Arthur Vööbus, *Syriac and Arabic Documents Regarding Legislation Relative to Syrian Asceticism,* (Stockholm: Etse, 1960), 142–45.

[69] Ibid., 191.

we love reduces us to sadness. And we are moved to turn in haste to the God whom we had neglected in the good times....

Of these three types of call, the first two seem to have the better beginnings. Yet I have occasionally found that some who started from the third level, that which seems the lowliest and the least committed, have turned out to be perfect men.... So it is the conclusion that counts. Someone committed by the beginnings of a glorious conversion can prove to be a lesser man because of carelessness, and someone constrained by some necessity to become a monk can, out of fear of God and out of diligence, reach up to perfection.[70]

St. Christodoulos of Patmos wrote the following in regards to whom to accept as a novice:

Whenever a layman arrives asking to be admitted on the grounds that he wishes to enter the lists for Christ [and prove his mettle] in submission, first he must be carefully interrogated by the superior, and closely examined concerning his circumstances, lest he be come to the monastery not simply out of the love of God and desire to save his soul, but constrained by earthly contingencies, creditors, perhaps, or extreme poverty and disinclination to work, or numerous children, so that he is come to the monastery as to a refuge that will furnish escape and dispense from effort. If his initiative is recognized as having this kind of basis, if these are the cracked and rotten foundations he is laying for the laborious edifice of virtue, he must be allowed as much assistance as is possible, but, with benevolence, alms and the appropriate admonition, he must be sent away.[71]

St. Seraphim of Sarov "regarded as true monks and nuns only those who had embraced the monastic life for no other reason than love for God and for the sake of the salvation of their soul."[72] In the same spirit, St. Nikolai Velimirovich wrote to someone considering monasticism:

If you have doubts, my child, know that you are more likely to be for marriage than for a monastery.... You say that you often sit with your mother by the fire and you count pros and cons together. But I tell you this—no matter how much you count up, it is not pros and cons that will decide which way you go, but attractiveness. Love is above all reasons. If love for God does not lead you to quiet monastic solitude, then love for the world will keep you in the world and lead you into marriage....

Great love for God does not tolerate the world, it does not love company, it seeks solitude. That love has moved thousands of souls to depart the wide path of the world and head for the deaf deserts in order to secretly meet with their Creator who is all love, both by name and by essence. But most of all, they head for the desert in order to make themselves worthy of that vision and that meeting....

I write to you thus, not to attract you to monastic life, but rather to turn you away from it, because if you depart the world in the spirit of doubt, I am afraid that yearning for the world will increase in you and overcome you. You will be in a monastery bodily,

---

[70] Luibhéid, *John Cassian: Conferences,* 83, 84, 85 (Conference 1).

[71] Thomas and Hero, *Byzantine Monastic Foundation Documents,* 592.

[72] Archimandrite Lazarus Moore, *St. Seraphim of Sarov: A Spiritual Biography* (Blanco: New Sarov Press, 1994), 258.

but in the world with your soul. And the world torments one more in the mirror of the soul than in reality.[73]

St. John of Sinai, however, realized that coming to a monastery with good intentions is not necessarily a prerequisite or a guarantee of success. He wrote:

> Nor let us abhor or condemn the renunciation [i.e., renouncing the world and joining a monastery] due merely to circumstances. I have seen men who had fled into exile meet the emperor by accident when he was on tour, and then join his company, enter his palace, and dine with him. I have seen seed casually fall on the earth and bear plenty of thriving fruit. And I have seen the opposite, too.[74]

The holy Fathers of the Sixth Ecumenical Council decreed that a person may choose to become a monk no matter what sins he has committed,[75] since the monastic life represents a state of repentance.[76] Likewise, St. John of Sinai wrote: "Let no one, by appealing to the weight and multitude of his sins, say that he is unworthy of the monastic vow.... Where there is much corruption, considerable treatment is needed to draw out all the impurity. The healthy do not go to a hospital."[77]

When the nuns of St. Nectarios of Aegina informed him about a young lady who was interested in joining their convent, he wrote them a letter in which he outlined the qualities that a monastic aspirant should have:

> Above all, I want to know if her love burns for the Divine; if she loves prayer with all her heart and longs for it greatly and exceedingly; if she can exercise self-denial; if she can deny her will; if she can subject herself to someone else's will; if she can perform something contrary to her will; if she does not answer back and receives orders without protest; if she is able to say to the Lord, "Not as I wish, Lord, but as You do"; if she is able to withstand temptation; if she unequivocally believes in divine help and

---

[73] *A Treasury of Serbian Orthodox Spirituality, Volume 6,* (Third Lake: New Gracanica Monastery, 2008), 14–15.

[74] Holy Transfiguration Monastery, *The Ladder of Divine Ascent,* 8.

[75] Canon XLIII: "It is permissible for a Christian to choose the ascetic mode of life and abandoning the turbulent whirl of ordinary life to enter a Monastery, and to take a tonsure in accordance with monkish habit, even though he should have been found guilty of any offense whatsoever. For our Savior God said: 'Him that cometh to me I will in no wise cast out' (John 6:37). As therefore monastic life represents to us a state of repentance as though engraved upon a pillar, we join in sympathizing with anyone that genuinely adopts it, and no one shall prevent him from accomplishing his aim" (Agapius and Nicodemus, *The Rudder,* 341). Commenting on this last sentence, Georgios Apostolakis (a canon law expert) wrote: "Since no one can prevent a legally qualified Christian from becoming a monk, it is unacceptable to claim that the bishop as the chief shepherd of his diocese has the authority to prevent a Christian from exercising this right of his by refusing to give him his approval for being tonsured" (excerpt from a personal correspondence 12/17/2014).

[76] St. Symeon of Thessalonica taught: "The most sacred schema of monks is included in this [sacrament of] repentance" (PG 155:197A).

[77] Holy Transfiguration Monastery, *The Ladder of Divine Ascent,* 8.

protection; and finally, lest I pose more questions, if she is able to forgive all that her sisters may do, before the sun goes down, for the sake of the commandment of love.[78]

St. Sophrony of Essex taught: "The authentic behavior of a person who comes and wants to be accepted in a monastery is to feel that he is unworthy to be accepted. Each person should feel his weakness, his passions, and should be full of a spirit of repentance. Without repentance, progress is impossible."[79] "The foundation of spiritual life is repentance."[80]

An ancient monastic tradition is not to accept monks who have already been tonsured elsewhere. For example, the angel who appeared to St. Pachomios instructed him: "A stranger from another monastery having another rule shall not eat or drink with them, nor enter into the monastery unless he finds himself on a journey."[81] The *Incipit Tertia Patrum Regula Ad Monachos* ("The Third Rule of the Fathers" from sixth-century Gaul) only accepts monks from another monastery under the condition that they have the blessing of their abbot.[82] Likewise, the fifth-century Syriac *Rules of Rabbūlā for the Monks* state: "No one shall receive a brother that moves from monastery to monastery without a word (assignment) of the *rišdairā* with whom he stayed."[83] St. Ferréol of Uzès (in sixth-century Gaul) wrote: "We absolutely refuse, forbid, and prohibit a monk or cleric belonging to another place or monastery to be received for any reason, exercising precaution in such matters out of zeal for charity, in case he introduces some novelty, thus giving rise to the sordidness of scandal."[84]

These rules excluding previously tonsured monks were written because every monastery has its own mindset, and a person from another monastery will already have grown accustomed to a particular approach to the monastic life. It is unlikely that he will be both willing and able to renounce his previous understanding of monasticism in order to conform to the new brotherhood's understanding. Thus, these conflicting outlooks are likely to be a constant source of friction and temptations both for him and for the rest of

---

[78] Strongylis, *St. Nectarios of Pentapolis and the Island of Aegina,* vol. 2, 73 (Letter #15).

[79] Σωφρονίου, *Οἰκοδομῶντας τὸν Ναὸ τοῦ Θεοῦ, Τόμος Α΄,* 291.

[80] Sakharov, *Striving for Knowledge of God,* 305.

[81] *Pachomian Koinonia, Volume Two: Pachomian Chronicles and Rules,* trans. Armand Veilleux, (Kalamazoo: Cistercian Publications, 1981), 127 (32:5).

[82] Vid. *Early Monastic Rules: The Rules of the Fathers and the Regula Orientalis,* Carmela Vircillo Franklin (Collegeville: Liturgical Press, 1982), 59.

[83] Vööbus, *Syriac and Arabic Documents,* 33.

[84] *Regula Ferreoli,* as translated in St. Smaragdus of Saint-Mihiel, *Commentary on the Rule of Saint Benedict,* trans. David Barry (Kalamazoo: Cistercian Publications, 2007), 493.

the brotherhood. Nevertheless, Elder Ephraim made exceptions to this rule on occasion, as did Sts. Theodore the Studite[85] and Athanasios of Athos.[86]

Even though St. Athanasios of Athos sometimes accepted monks from other monasteries, he did not want such monks to become the new superior immediately. He wrote:

> If … the superior should die … the [new] superior must be selected only from this particular community. He should not be a man who has come here from some other monastery, been formed anew in a single day, and right then and there be put in charge. For he brings with him nothing that would aid the brothers in the practice of virtue, except that he wants them to vote for him as their leader, although they know nothing of his manner of life. Let the holy assemblage of the brothers be sure of this, that we regard it as essential that a stranger coming from another monastery should not straightaway assume the superiorship.[87]

St. Nilus Sorsky was very hesitant to accept monks in his community. He wrote:

> It is proper to follow the example of the ancient and blessed Fathers, even if we are not able to equal the exploits. If anyone does not wish to follow this basic approach, let him cease harassing me, even though I also am a poor sinner. I turn away such persons and have nothing to do with them. I do not wish to be their master, and still they come and try to force me to lead them. Also for those who live together with us, if they do not care to observe our teaching which I give them from the holy Writings, I do not wish to answer for them, for I am not guilty of their self-will. But for those who really desire to live our style of life freely and without any worldly thinking, I accept such. I teach them the word of God, even though I myself do not always perfectly observe it.[88]

St. Paisios of the Holy Mountain foresaw a grim future for the next generation of monastic candidates:

> This generation [i.e., of the late 20th century] starts out for monasticism on the best of terms, with ideals, but the devil renders useless all this potential. The next generation won't be like this. Many will come to the monasteries who will not be suitable for the monastic life. They will be in such a state that they will be forced to become monks. They will be worn out and wounded by the world. Married couples will be divorced, with or without the blessing of the Church, and these spouses will go their separate ways to live in the monasteries. Young people who are weary of the worldly life will go to the monastery, some for the salvation of their soul, and others to find some peace and serenity. Others who really want to marry, but who are afraid to commit themselves to another person, will become monks. In other words, in the coming years people with mental illness and others who hesitate to start a family will perhaps come to the monasteries. They will be saying to themselves, "What will I find in married life? What will I do in the world? It's better to go and become a monk."

---

[85] Vid. Thomas and Hero, *Byzantine Monastic Foundation Documents,* 108.

[86] Ibid., 225.

[87] Ibid., 255.

[88] *Nil Sorsky: The Complete Writings,* The Classics of Western Spirituality, trans. George A. Maloney (New York: Paulist Press, 2003), 40.

In other words, some people will take monasticism to be a life of ease and idleness. Now, as to what kind of spiritual progress they may make, well, that's another matter. No one will come in a spirit of repentance. People will be in such a state that they'll be forced to become monks. Their motives won't be pure. This is the danger. It's different if someone sets out specifically to become a monk. These people will need a great deal of help, because, having tasted the pleasures of the world, the devil will oppose them more strenuously, while the rest of us will not be opposed so vigorously. With us the devil will try to prevent our spiritual work, to weaken our resolve with negligence or slothfulness, so that those who follow us will not find any spiritual yeast to ferment their own spiritual life.[89]

ii) Age Limits

In the old days, some saints would allow young children to join the monastery. For example, St. Benedict wrote: "Let children and boys take their places in the oratory [i.e., the monastery's church] and at table with all due discipline; outdoors, however, or wherever they may be, let them be under custody and discipline until they reach the age of understanding."[90] St. Caesarius of Arles wrote in his *Rule for Nuns* in the early sixth century: "If possible, never, or at best with difficulty, let little girls be received into the monastery, unless they are six or seven years old, so that they are able to learn their letters and to submit to obedience."[91] A century later, St. Donatus of Besançon paraphrased this same rule in chapter 6 of his *Regula ad Virgines.* St. Fructuosus of Braga even allowed "the tiniest children who are still in the cradle" to join the monastery along with their parents.[92] Canon XL of the Sixth Ecumenical Council sets the minimum age of submitting to the monastic yoke at ten years of age.[93]

St. Basil the Great elaborated on this matter:

> Since the Lord says: "Suffer the little children to come unto me" (Mk. 10:14), and the apostle praises him who has known the Holy Scripture from infancy (2 Tim. 3:15) and also orders that children be reared "in the discipline and correction of the Lord" (Eph. 6:4), we consider every time of life, even the very earliest, to be suitable for receiving postulants.[94]

Although St. Basil allows children to *enter* the monastery, he also makes it clear that they should not make the vow of celibacy until they have matured. For he wrote:

---

[89] Elder Paisios, *Spiritual Awakening,* 378–79.

[90] *Rule of St. Benedict,* Chapter LXIII.

[91] *The Rule for Nuns of St. Caesarius of Arles,* trans. Maria Caritas McCarthy (Washington, D.C.: Catholic University Press, 1960), 173.

[92] Vid. *The Fathers of the Church: Iberian Fathers, Braulio of Saragossa, Fructuosus of Braga,* trans. Claude W. Barlow, vol. 2, #63 (Washington, D.C.: Catholic University of America Press, 1969), 186.

[93] Agapius and Nicodemus, *The Rudder,* 336.

[94] Βασιλείου τοῦ Μεγάλου, *Ἀσκητικὰ Α΄,* ΕΠΕ 8, 252–53; see also Wagner, *Saint Basil: Ascetical Works,* vol. 9, 264 (Question 15 in the *Long Rules*).

> The name *virgin* is given to a woman who voluntarily devotes herself to the Lord, renounces marriage, and embraces a life of holiness. And we admit professions dating from the age of full intelligence. For it is not right in such cases to admit the words of mere children. But a girl of sixteen or seventeen years of age, in full possession of her faculties, who has been submitted to strict examination, and is then constant, and persists in her entreaty to be admitted, may then be ranked among the virgins, her profession ratified, and its violation rigorously punished. Many girls are brought forward by their parents and brothers, and other kinsfolk, before they are of full age, and have no inner impulse towards a celibate life. The object of the friends is simply to provide for themselves. Such women as these must not be readily received, before we have made public investigation of their own sentiments.[95] ...
>
> When reason and the ability to discern come [in a child who has reached maturity] ... permission to make the vow of virginity should be granted, inasmuch as his decision is now certain, since it comes from his own volition and judgment after reaching the age of reasoning.[96]

Despite these saints allowing children to join a monastery, most of the holy Fathers did not permit beardless youths to become novices. For example, the Emperor John Tzimiskes wrote in the "Tragos" (a typikon for the Holy Mountain): "We must strictly enjoin that boys, beardless youths, and eunuchs who journey to the Mountain to be tonsured should not be received at all."[97] Likewise, St. Nicodemos of the Holy Mountain wrote these comments in *The Rudder* on the aforementioned Canon XL of the Sixth Ecumenical Council:

> But inasmuch as this generation of ours has become prone to passions, ... those about to adopt the monastic style of life [should wait] until they reach the point of growing a beard, since this is also more to the interest of the very persons themselves who are going to become monks, in order that the judgment of their reasoning faculty may be rendered more perfect (i.e., more maturely developed), and consequently the trial likewise.[98]

This is why the Charter of the Holy Mountain states: "In order to be tonsured a monk, one must have undergone a trial for one to three years and be eighteen years old."[99]

---

[95] *Nicene and Post-Nicene Fathers, Series II, vol. 8, Basil: Letters and Select Works,* Philip Schaff, "Letter to Amphilochios Concerning the Canons," (New York: Christian Literature Company, 1895), 237 (PG 32:720).

[96] Βασιλείου τοῦ Μεγάλου, *Ἀσκητικὰ Α΄,* ΕΠΕ 8, 258–59; see also Wagner, *Saint Basil: Ascetical Works,* vol. 9, 267 (Question 15 in the *Long Rules*). Since, according to St. Basil, an individual's own choice is necessary for becoming a monk, the canon law expert P. Panagiotakis opined that a pathologically ill person whose mental illness prevents him from making rational choices should not become a monk (vid. *Σύστημα τοῦ Ἐκκλησιαστικοῦ Δικαίου κατὰ τὴν ἐν Ἑλλάδι ἰσχὺν αὐτοῦ,* Τόμος Δ΄, Τὸ δίκαιον τῶν μοναχῶν, 58, 59).

[97] Thomas and Hero, *Byzantine Monastic Foundation Documents,* 238.

[98] Agapius and Nicodemus, *The Rudder,* 338.

[99] Article 93.

A further problem with teenagers is that they rarely have the maturity and stability needed for living monastically. If a person lacks the maturity to live monastically, he is not ready to become a novice. For as St. Paisius Velichkovsky said, "He who lives in a monastery, whether he be tonsured or not [i.e., whether he is a monk or a novice], must observe the monastic way and take an example from his elders."[100]

According to St. Palladios, novices must spend three years doing the most difficult tasks before becoming monks.[101] In the *Epistle to Castor* attributed to St. Athanasios the Great, the trial period lasts only one year.[102] According to the typikon of the monastery of St. Theodore the Studite, the trial period for novices was a mere two or three weeks.[103] But the fifth canon of the First-and-Second Council imposed a three-year minimum, which could be reduced to six months under exceptional circumstances.[104] Thereafter, some typika of monasteries in the Byzantine era set the minimum at six months,[105] others set it at one year,[106] others at two years,[107] and others at three years.[108]

In the early years of St. Anthony's Monastery in Arizona, Elder Ephraim tonsured novices (making them rasophore monks) after they had been at the monastery only one or two years. But after a couple recently tonsured monks returned to the world, he realized that two years was not nearly enough for novices here in contemporary America, and he began to wait five or even ten years before tonsuring them.

As for a maximum age for accepting novices, there should be no upper limit. In the words of St. Ephraim the Syrian: "Do not disregard old men when they decide to come and labor in the monastic life.... You do not know whether this old man may be a chosen

---

[100] Schemamonk Metrophanes, *Blessed Paisius Velichkovsky, The Man Behind the Philokalia,* trans. Fr. Seraphim Rose (Platina: St. Herman of Alaska Brotherhood, 1976), 178.

[101] Παλλαδίου, *Λαυσαϊκόν,* ΕΠΕ Φ6, 216.

[102] Μεγάλου Ἀθανασίου, *Ἐπιστολὴ α΄ πρὸς Κάστορα,* PG 28:853D.

[103] Vid. Thomas and Hero, *Byzantine Monastic Foundation Documents,* 108.

[104] See footnote #2355 on page 444.

[105] Vid. "Typikon of Timothy for the Monastery of the Mother of God Evergetis," Thomas and Hero, Thomas and Hero, *Byzantine Monastic Foundation Documents,* 494–95; "Typikon of Michael VIII Palaiologos for the Monastery of the Archangel Michael on Mount Auxentios near Chalcedon," ibid., 1228.

[106] "Typikon of Athanasios the Athonite for the Lavra Monastery," ibid., 263.

[107] Vid. "Typikon of Athanasios Philanthropenos for the Monastery of St. Mamas in Constantinople," ibid., 1010.

[108] Vid. "Rule of Neilos, Bishop of Tamasia, for the Monastery of the Mother of God of Machairas in Cyprus," ibid., 1140; "Typikon of Empress Irene Doukaina Komnene for the Convent of the Mother of God Kecharitomene in Constantinople," ibid., 685; "Typikon of Nikephoros Blemmydes for the Monastery of the Lord Christ-Who-Is at Ematha near Ephesos," ibid. 1203; "Typikon of Theodora Palaiologina for the Convent of Lips in Constantinople," ibid., 1270; "Rule of Christodoulos for the Monastery of St. John the Theologian on Patmos," ibid., 593.

vessel."[109] But St. Nectarios of Aegina set the maximum age limit at forty-five for novices wishing to join his convent.[110]

A common challenge faced by older people wishing to become novices is that the non-monastic way they have been living for decades has become second nature, and they encounter great difficulties trying to conform their way of life and especially their way of thinking to that of the monastery. As St. Fructuosus of Braga (in seventh-century Portugal) explained in his *General Rule for Monasteries:*

> Some old novices regularly come to the monastery and we know that many of them promise observance of the rule out of want and weakness and not to profess the religious life. When such are found, they must be investigated very carefully, and amid the other legal questionings they are to answer only what is asked. For they have a way of never giving up their previous customs and of wandering into idle tales, as they were long trained. When they are corrected by some spiritual brother, they immediately burst into anger and, for a long time, they are urged on by the ills of spiritual weakness and they never completely cease from rancor and bitterness. And when they slip into such faults, so often and so extensively, when even their spiritual weakness leaves them, they usually lose their restraint to the extent of the telling of idle stories and in laughter.
>
> Accordingly, they are to be introduced to the monastery with this precaution, that they are not to tell idle stories day or night, but are to give themselves to sobs and tears, to ashes and sackcloth, and are with throbbing hearts to do penance for their past sins and not again to commit acts that require penance. The degree of pravity which they previously devoted to sin must be doubled in the full devotion paid to lamentation. Since for seventy and more years they have so abundantly sinned, it is fitting that they be bound in severe penance, just as a surgeon cuts into a wound more deeply when he sees rotten flesh. Such are to be corrected by true penance; if they are unwilling, then, they are to be punished immediately with excommunication [i.e., expulsion]. If they have been warned twice seven times and have not given up this vice, they are to be brought to an assembly of elders and there, for the last time, are to be examined. If they do not permit themselves to amend their ways, they must be dismissed.
>
> On the other hand, we may show mercy to them as to little children; we may honor them as fathers, if they are quiet, simple, humble, obedient, frequently in prayer, deploring their own sins as much as those of others, daily risking their lives, always keeping Christ on their lips, not being idle when they have strength to work, guided by the opinion of their elders rather than by their own, completely abandoning all family affection, giving all they have to Christ's poor rather than to their relatives, keeping nothing for themselves, with all their mind and courage observing the law of God and their neighbors, day and night meditating on the law of the Lord. They may be excused from duties in the bakery and kitchen and may be free from working in the field and on heavy jobs, except that some of the lighter tasks may be assigned to them, lest their weary years be completely broken before their time.[111]

---

[109] Chrysostomos, *The Evergetinos, Book I,* 234; Παύλου Μοναχοῦ, *Εὐεργετινός,* τόμος Α´ (Ἀθῆναι, 1977), 401 (Ἐφραὶμ Σύρου, κζ´).

[110] Vid. *The Charter of the Holy Monastery in Aegina of the Holy Trinity,* Article 5:5.

[111] Barlow, *The Fathers of the Church: Iberian Fathers,* vol. 63, 187–89.

iii) How to Evaluate a Novice

Elder Aimilianos set forth the following criteria for evaluating whether a novice is ready to be tonsured in the *Regulations of the Holy Cenobium of the Annunciation*:

> Novices shall learn the New Testament, the Psalter, the Old Testament, basic ascetic literature and the monastic way of life and shall practice guarding the intellect and participating actively in worship. Moreover, they shall learn perfect discipline in everything, deep and incontrovertible inner obedience, effacement and forgetfulness of themselves and all things, courtesy and delicacy in manner and speech, manifest and natural respect and the silence becoming to saints. They shall be instructed in the cenobitic way of life, tolerating and being tolerated, honouring others and supporting them. Their lives shall be subject to the present Typikon and to the statutes and prescriptions envisaged by it.
>
> During the period of their novitiate, which is "a test of the worth of them and their parents,"[112] the following shall be assessed:
> * Whether there is communion of spirit.
> * Whether they can abandon parents, property and their own will and opinions.
> * Whether "they are prepared to undergo without false shame all humiliations."[113]
> * Whether they have stout resistance to bodily temptations and those of the soul and spirit, especially when these are unexpected.
> * Whether they love study and value manual labor "and will accept the most humble of tasks."[114]
>
> Equally, enquiry shall be made as to whether they are perhaps "unstable and quick to judge,"[115] whether they are afflicted with serious psychological problems which strongly influence their volition or make their personalities immature and irresponsible.
>
> They shall be further tested as to: their capacity for liturgical life, their desire for Christ and the martyrs' spirit, their perseverance and ascetic struggle, their ability to remain indifferent to their thoughts (λογισμοί) or to overcome them, the purity of their intentions, the ease with which they take to the communal life and their ability to survive without the need for the support of others.
>
> Should any novice prove unable to adapt to the conditions, the tasks, the programme, the order, the life and the spirit of the Community, or if for any reason she is scandalized by it or by the sisters, is troubled, taciturn, idle or sickly, then it is not in her own best interest to stay in the monastery. The novitiate leads to the tonsure, as long as the new member is able to live in the monastic community without problems and in joy. This is to safeguard the spiritual interests and the future of the novice.
>
> Those who are slothful or suspicious, who bewail their lot, moan or judge the actions of others, who are undisciplined, importunate, disobedient, who persist in their own opinions or ideas, disrupt the unity of the Community, speak ill of the Abbess or the Administration, pervert souls, reveal secrets, cause scandal or infringe these Regulations shall never be tonsured. Should any such have received the monastic habit and persist in this state, they should be expelled from the Cenobium as vessels replete with passions and as ruins.... Lack of curiosity as to the affairs and *diakonemata* [i.e.,

---

[112] Halkin, *Sanctii Pachomii Vitae Graecae* (Brussels: Subsidia Hagiographica 19, 1932), 14,1.29–15, 1.1.

[113] Wagner, *Saint Basil: Ascetical Works,* vol. 9, 261 (Question 10 in the *Long Rules*).

[114] Ibid.

[115] Ibid., 260.

assigned tasks] of others, as well as dedication to the performance of one's own task are fundamental principles of the spirituality of the monastic profession.[116]

iv) When to Tonsure a Novice

St. Basil the Great taught that one should only take monastic vows after reaching "the age of discretion."[117] Although he set that age at sixteen or seventeen for people in the fourth century, in today's frivolous Western society (for example, the average teenager spends more than one hundred hours per month wasting time with electronic entertainment), the minimum age for tonsuring should be increased many more years. The fifth-century Synod in Carthage suggested that the minimum age for tonsuring should be twenty-five.[118] In Palestine from the fifth to seventh centuries, "the period of novitiate in the coenobium was likely to last about ten years or more, until the candidate reached maturity—roughly the age of thirty—and had become an experienced monk."[119]

St. John of Sinai warns: "Let the superior be circumspect in his reception of sheep, for in every instance God does not forbid refusal and dissuasion.... Before a man gains understanding through experience, let us not lay our hands quickly upon him [i.e., tonsure him], lest ... they make vows while they are still in ignorance, [and] they afterwards come to know our way of life, and are unable to endure its weight and burning heat, and desert us and return to the world. This will not be without danger for those who tonsure prematurely."[120] Because as St. Basil the Great warns: "If he [i.e., a monk] has consecrated himself to God and has afterward turned aside to another mode of life, he is guilty of sacrilege."[121]

Patriarch Theodore Balsamon explained that the period of the novitiate is necessary

> so that he who is to be tonsured may be nourished as with milk, come of age through obedience, grow up through prayer, become a man through abstinence, and reach full growth through humility. And in this manner, as an unassailable soldier of Christ he may stand before Him Who enlisted him as a noble, heavy-armed, javelin-throwing warrior, wearing chastity as a breastplate, repentance as a shield, obedience as a helmet, prayer as a bow, hesychia as a spear, abstinence as a sword, patience as a scabbard, and humility as a leather sack.[122]

---

[116] Elder Aimilianos, *The Authentic Seal,* 169–71, 177.

[117] Vid. Agapius and Nicodemus, *The Rudder,* 806 (Canon XVIII of St. Basil the Great).

[118] Vid. ibid., 703 (Canon 135).

[119] Joseph Patrich, *Sabas, Leader of Palestinian Monasticism* (Washington, D.C.: Dumbarton Oaks, 1995), 264.

[120] Holy Transfiguration Monastery, *The Ladder of Divine Ascent,* 244, 241.

[121] Wagner, *Saint Basil: Ascetical Works,* vol. 9, 264 (Question 14 in the *Long Rules*).

[122] Ἐπιστολὴ χάριν τῶν ρασοφόρων, PG 138:1377C.

v) The Departure of Novices

When a novice decides to leave the monastery, he may not take any of his monastic clothes with him. As St. John Cassian wrote:

> When someone has been received [into the monastery as a novice], all his former possessions are removed from him, such that he is not even permitted to have the clothing that he wore. He is brought to the Council of the brothers, stripped of what is his in their midst, and clothed in the garb of the monastery at the hands of the abba. Thus he may know not only that he has been despoiled of all his former things but also that he has put off all worldly pride and has stooped to the poverty and want of Christ....
>
> Thenceforth, knowing that he will be clothed and fed from there [i.e., from the monastery], he will learn both to possess nothing and never to be worried about the morrow, according to the words of the Gospel, and he will not be ashamed to be on a par with the poor—that is, with the body of the brotherhood....
>
> The clothing that he has taken off is deposited with the bursar and kept until, thanks to various trials and tests, he has made progress and they clearly recognize the virtue of his way of life and of his endurance. And when they see, as time goes on, that he can stay in that place and maintain the same fervor with which he began, they give it to the poor. But if they notice that he has committed the sin of complaining or is guilty of an act of disobedience, however slight, they stripped him of the garb of the monastery with which he had been clothed and, just once more in what he used to wear, which had been laid aside, they drive him out. For no one is allowed to depart with what he received, nor do they permit anyone to continue to dress as such when they see that he has even once veered away from the rule of his training.[123]

Because novices are not officially a part of the brotherhood, they may still have their own money. But since novices in a cenobium have no need to spend money (because the monastery covers all their expenses), typically they put whatever money they brought with them to the monastery in an envelope, which the abbot keeps in a safe place. If the novice chooses to leave the monastery, the abbot is obliged to return to him the contents of that envelope. But if the novice becomes a monk, then the money in the envelope is given to the monastery.

Likewise, any property that a novice owned in the world becomes the monastery's when he becomes a monk, as Blessed Augustine wrote: "Let those that had property in the world at the time of their entry into the monastery be prepared willingly to place all in common."[124] In the same vein, the *Rule of Macarius*[125] states that the entrant is to understand that "he shall not from that hour be the judge, not only of the property that he brought

---

[123] *John Cassian: The Institutes,* trans. Boniface Ramsey (New York: Newman Press, 2000), 80–81.

[124] Hugh of St. Victor, *Explanation of the Rule of St. Augustine* (United Kingdom: Forgotten Books, 1901) 12.

[125] This monastic rule was not written by St. Macarius the Great but was composed in Orthodox Gaul in the fifth century.

but even of himself."[126] The *General Rule for Monasteries* by St. Fructuosus of Braga explains that those who seek to enter the monastery must be carefully questioned "whether they have done everything which they have heard in the words of Verity in the Gospel, which says: 'He who has not renounced all that he possesses cannot be My disciple,'[127] ... and 'If thou wilt be perfect, go sell what thou hast, and give to the poor, and come, follow Me and thou shalt have treasure in heaven.'[128] ... But if any of these ... renounce falsely and leave so much as a single coin anywhere, we order him to be thrown out immediately, for we see him not in the number of the apostles, but rather a follower of Ananias and Sapphira.[129] You should know that he cannot live up to the measure of a monk in a monastery, nor stoop to the poverty of Christ, nor acquire humility, nor be obedient, nor abide there continuously."[130]

3) Renunciation of the World

The holy Apostles taught that Christianity and "the world" are incompatible. St. James wrote: "Do you not know that friendship with the world is hostility toward God? Therefore whoever wishes to be a friend of the world makes himself an enemy of God."[131] He also said: "Pure and undefiled religion in the sight of God is ... to keep oneself unstained by the world."[132] St. Peter warned: "If, after they have escaped the defilements of the world by the knowledge of the Lord and Savior Jesus Christ, they are again entangled in them and are overcome, the last state has become worse for them than the first."[133]

Since "monasticism is nothing but Christian life in its perfection,"[134] it naturally follows that a fundamental aspect of monasticism is renunciation of the world. As St. Symeon of Thessalonica explained:

> The world has nothing in common with monks, just as it has nothing in common with the crucified Savior and His disciples, who lived the same way of life [as monks] and were dead to the world.... The true monk loves Christ, and nothing can separate him from the love of Christ, as Paul says. He desires to depart and be together with

---

[126] Chapter 24 of the *Incipit Regula Macharii Abbatis,* as translated in Franklin, *Early Monastic Rules,* 49.

[127] Cf. Lk. 14:26.

[128] Mt. 19:21.

[129] Vid. Acts 5:1–11.

[130] Barlow, *The Fathers of the Church: Iberian Fathers,* vol. 63, 183.

[131] Jas. 4:4.

[132] Jas. 1:27

[133] 2 Pet. 2:20.

[134] Ἀρχιμανδρίτου Ἀθανασίου, *Ἡ Φωνὴ Ἑνὸς Μοναχοῦ* (Κύπρος: Ἱερᾶς Μονῆς Τροοδιτίσσης, 1998), 35.

Christ, and he manifests this desire in practice by fleeing to the desert, to the mountains, to solitude, for Christ's sake.[135]

Evgenia Zhoukova observed the central position that renunciation has historically held for monasticism:

> In the currently used *Service of the Great Schema,* renunciation is presented first in line among other vows of the candidate monk.... Already from the position this vow has in the modern-day service, we can get an inkling of its original importance as a vow.... We have also observed that in several Lives of the Saints of the first generation [of monks], coming to monasticism was rarely accomplished by performing some *Service of the Monastic Schema* or by tonsuring....
>
> On the contrary, the sense of renunciation—which was expressed in different ways and had various nuances—is clearly presented as the entrance to monasticism.... [In particular,] the saints proceeded to: 1) free themselves from their possessions, 2) depart from their home, and 3) go to the place of their asceticism. This renunciation of theirs is what rendered them monks and ascetics. As an external sign of their renunciation of the world, 4) changing their garments was also required....
>
> All catechisms [in the early days of monasticism] had renunciation of the world as a most fundamental theme with which they usually begin. Thus, the purpose of the catechism is to prepare the candidate for renunciation and to teach him that renunciation is the most basic aspect of monastic life.[136]

St. Basil the Great viewed renunciation as a prerequisite for pleasing God:

> The discipline for pleasing God in accordance with Christ's gospel is accomplished by detaching oneself from the cares of the world and by withdrawing completely from its distractions....
>
> If we do not estrange ourselves from both fleshly ties and worldly society, being transported, as it were, to another world in our manner of living, as the one who said, "our citizenship is in heaven" (Phil. 3:20), it is impossible for us to achieve our goal of pleasing God, inasmuch as the Lord said unequivocally: "Thus, every one of you that doth not renounce all that he possesseth cannot be my disciple" (Lk. 14:33).[137] ... Also—and this is the chief point—it is the first step toward the likeness to Christ, who, being rich, became poor for our sake (2 Cor. 8:9).[138]

St. John Chrysostom lamented that monastics have no choice but to flee society to avoid sin:

> Would that such conditions prevailed in society, that so many would not have to flee the world in order to avoid sin and vice; would that those who have fled might be able to return! However, since evil prevails in the world, criticizing those who teach and admonish young people to become monastics is like criticizing one who hastens

---

[135] Balfour, Ἁγίου Συμεὼν Θεσσαλονίκης: Ἔργα Θεολογικά, 178.

[136] Εὐγενία Β. Ζουκόβα, Γέννηση καὶ Ἐξέλιξη τῆς Ἀκολουθίας τοῦ Μοναχικοῦ Σχήματος: Κατὰ τοὺς Δ΄–Ζ΄ αἰῶνες βάσει ἁγιολογικῶν πηγῶν (Ἀθήνα, 2010), 158–59, 183, 249–50.

[137] Βασιλείου τοῦ Μεγάλου, Ἀσκητικὰ Α΄, ΕΠΕ 8, 206–7; see also Wagner, *Saint Basil: Ascetical Works,* vol. 9, 242–43 (Question 5 of the *Long Rules*).

[138] Ibid., 256 (Rule #8 of the *Long Rules*).

to get the inhabitants out of a burning house in order to save them, rather than simply letting them burn.[139]

Thus, one aspect of renouncing the world is to be geographically distant from people. As Abba Ammonas (a disciple of St. Anthony) wrote:

The soul cannot know God unless it withdraws itself from men and from every distraction. For then the soul will see the adversary who fights against it. And once it has seen the adversary and has overcome him every time he engages it in battle, then God dwells in the soul, and all the labour is changed to joy and gladness....

This is why the holy fathers also withdrew into the desert alone, men such as Elijah the Tishbite and John the Baptist. For do not suppose that because the righteous were in the midst of men it was among men that they had achieved their righteousness. Rather, having first practised much quiet, they then received the power of God dwelling in them, and then God sent them into the midst of men, having acquired every virtue, so that they might act as God's provisioners and cure men of their infirmities. For they were physicians of the soul, able to cure men's infirmities. This was the need for which they were dragged away from their quiet and sent to men. But they are only sent when all their own diseases are healed. For a soul cannot be sent into the midst of men for their edification if it has some defect of its own. And those who go before they are made perfect, go at their own will and not at God's. And God says in reproof about such, "I sent them not, but they ran of themselves" (Jer. 23:21). For this cause they are neither able to guard themselves, nor to edify another soul....

Many monks at the present time have been unable to persevere in quiet because they could not overcome their self-will. For this reason they live among men all the time, since they are unable to despise themselves and flee from the company of men, or to engage in battle. Thus they abandon quiet, and remain in the company of their neighbours, receiving their comfort thereby, all their lives. Therefore they have not been held worthy of the divine sweetness, or to have the power dwelling within them. For when that power looks down upon them, it finds that they receive their comfort in this present world and in the passions that belong to the soul and the body. As a result it cannot overshadow them any more, for love of money, human vainglory, and all the soul's sicknesses and distractions, prevent that divine power from overshadowing them.[140]

Echoing this opinion of Abba Ammonas, St. Gregory the Theologian wrote:

Elijah on Mount Carmel dedicated himself to philosophy [St. Gregory here and elsewhere speaks of monastic solitude as "philosophy"] with joy, and John [the Baptist] did so in the desert. Jesus himself did many actions for people, but in order to dedicate himself to prayer went to silent and desert places. For which reason? I think, in order to furnish us with a law according to which, for a pure association with God, one must remain in tranquillity and at least to a small degree raise one's intellect from deceitful things.[141]

[139] "Against the Opponents of the Monastic Life," PG 47:328, as translated in Zisis, *Following the Holy Fathers*, 39.

[140] *The Letters of Ammonas*, trans. Derwas J. Chitty (Oxford: SLG Press, 1979), 18–19 (Letter XII).

[141] *Oratio XXVI (Λόγος κϛ΄ Εἰς ἑαυτὸν ἐξ ἀγροῦ ἐπανήκοντα μετὰ τὰ κατὰ Μάξιμον)*, 7, 8–16 (PG 35:1237A).

Evagrios the Solitary (as well as St. Theodoros the Great Ascetic who paraphrased him)[142] encouraged monks to be far from the world:

> I tell you, love isolation from the world. It frees you from the circumstances of your own land and makes you enjoy only the benefits of quietude. Avoid tarrying in a city, and persevere dwelling in the wilderness. "Lo," says holy David, "I have fled afar off and have dwelt in the wilderness."[143] If possible, do not go to a city at all. For you will see nothing of benefit, nothing useful, nothing profitable for your way of life. The same holy man again remarks: "I have seen iniquity and gainsaying in the city."[144] Therefore, seek places that are free from distractions and solitary.[145]

In the same spirit, St. Eustathios of Thessalonica wrote:

> Are you unaware that an ascetic should live far from the world so that he is inaccessible to the crowds, or at least difficult to access? ... Since a monk comes from the world, he must transcend the world. But if a monk is in contact with the world as everyone else is, how will he live up to his calling of transcending the world? How can this ostensibly supernatural person avoid being ridiculed for depending on the world?[146]

Abba Dorotheos explained: "[The holy Fathers] have realised that by living in this world they could not attain virtue easily. So they decided to seek a separate life, a separate way. This is the monastic life. So they started to leave the world and live in the deserts; fasting, sleeping on the ground, keeping vigil and other hardships, renouncing their native land, relatives, money and possessions, they crucified the world in themselves."[147] This is why St. Gregory the Theologian stated: "Those are wiser than the majority who have separated themselves from the world and consecrated their life to God. I mean the Nazarites [i.e., monks] of our day."[148] Elder Ephraim explained: "Realizing that worldly things constitute a hindrance in overcoming their falling away from God, monks decide to withdraw from the world in order to attain salvation."[149]

Likewise, St. Isaac the Syrian wrote:

> If flight [from men] and watchfulness is profitable for Anthony and Arsenius, how much more is it for the infirm? And if God esteemed the stillness of these men—whose

---

[142] Vid. Palmer, Sherrard, Ware, *The Philokalia*, vol. 2, 24

[143] Ps. 54:7. All references to the Psalms herein are according to their numbering in the Septuagint.

[144] Ps. 54:9.

[145] Παναγιώτη Παπαευαγγέλου, *Εὐαγρίου τοῦ Ἀσκητοῦ καὶ Νείλου τοῦ Μοναχοῦ, Ἅπαντα τὰ Ἔργα,* 11Α (Θεσσαλονίκη: Γρηγόριος ὁ Παλαμᾶς, 1997), 66–69; see also Constantine Cavaros, *The Philokalia,* vol. 1 (Belmont: The Institute for Byzantine and Modern Greek Studies, 2008), 129; and Palmer, Sherrard, Ware, *The Philokalia,* vol. 1, 34.

[146] PG 135:856BC, 840A.

[147] Constantine Scouteris, *Abba Dorotheos: Practical Teaching on the Christian Life* (Athens: 2000), 76–77.

[148] *Cyril of Jerusalem, Gregory Nazianzen,* Nicene and Post-Nicene Fathers: Second Series, Volume VII, ed. Philip Schaff, (New York: Christian Literature Company, 1895), 405.

[149] From the manuscript of a homily "What Does Monasticism Offer to Society?"

words, presence, and help the whole world was in need of—higher than succor given to all the brethren, nay rather, to all mankind, how much more will this be the case with the man who is unable perfectly to guard himself?[150]

Fr. Dumitru Stăniloae explained why monks leave the world:

> Monks take one road, Christians in the world another. Monks take the surest, the most radical, the shortest way. They know that the passions have become entrenched in human nature and so man must fight the battle of controlling himself. But they also know that their own will is weakened by these passions and the battle with them is made easier by taking away from them the opportunity of getting started and being stirred up, in other words by taking from the passions the material which allows them to develop and catch on fire. So they choose to leave the world. Thus from the beginning they cut off the starting and arousal power of the passions. For monks, from here on, the problem is to persist in this withdrawal, because an appetite deprived for a long time of material to satisfy it, or of the chance to be active, withers away, and no longer becomes a passion, or at least it is weakened.[151]

Archimandrite George Kapsanis also observed: "There is an apparent contradiction: a monk strives after true sociability by withdrawing from society. This is something inexplicable with worldly logic. He flees people in order to acquire dispassion and thus loves people as God does."[152]

When St. Macarius the Great was asked which way is the easiest to be saved, he replied: "Whosoever leaves the world and goes to a quiet place and cries over his sins finds his salvation"[153] because "the thoughts of the world drag the mind away toward worldly and corruptible things and do not permit it to love God or to be mindful of the Lord."[154] Likewise, St. John Chrysostom said: "The wilderness is the mother of stillness."[155] St. Isaac the Syrian wrote: "Stillness cuts off the occasions and causes that renew thoughts, while within its walls it makes the memories of predispositions grow old and wither."[156] St.

---

[150] Holy Transfiguration Monastery, *The Ascetical Homilies of Saint Isaac the Syrian,* 353 (Homily 44).

[151] Dumitru Staniloae, *Orthodox Spirituality,* trans. Archimandrite Jerome and Otilia Kloos (South Canaan: St. Tikhon's Seminary Press, 2002), 150.

[152] Ἀρχιμανδρίτου Γεωργίου, Ὀρθόδοξος Μοναχισμὸς καὶ Ἅγιον Ὄρος, 53–54.

[153] *The Great Synaxaristes of the Orthodox Church, January* (Buena Vista: Holy Apostles Convent, 2003), 647.

[154] *Pseudo-Macarius: The Fifty Spiritual Homilies and the Great Letter,* trans. George A. Maloney, S.J. (New York: Paulist Press, 1992), 113–14.

[155] "For what purpose doth He go up into the mountain? To teach us that wilderness and solitude are good when we are to pray to God. For this reason, you see, He is continually withdrawing into the wilderness, and there often spends the whole night in prayer, teaching us earnestly to seek such quietness in our prayers, as the time and place may confer. For the wilderness is the mother of stillness; it is a calm and a harbor, delivering us from all turmoils" (*St. Chrysostom: Homilies on the Gospel of St. Matthew,* 300 (Homily L); PG 58:504).

[156] Holy Transfiguration Monastery, *The Ascetical Homilies of Saint Isaac the Syrian,* 465 (Homily 65).

Eustathios of Thessalonica concurred: "The purpose of stillness is to make the soul impassive (ἀταραξία)."[157]

In the same vein St. Basil the Great wrote:

> We must strive after a quiet mind.... The wilderness is of the greatest use for this purpose, inasmuch as it stills our passions and gives reason for leisure to cut them out of the soul. Let there then be such a place as ours, separate from intercourse with men, that the continuity of our ascesis be not interrupted from without....
>
> Quiet, then, as I have said, is the first step in our sanctification; the tongue purified from the gossip of the world; the eyes unexcited by fair color or comely shape; the ear not relaxing the tone or mind by voluptuous songs, nor by that especial mischief, the talk of light men and jesters. Thus the mind, saved from dissipation from without, and not through the senses thrown upon the world, falls back upon itself, and thereby ascends to the contemplation of God.[158]

St. Nicodemos of the Holy Mountain wrote: "The benefit of stillness is greater than money, glory, and worldly pleasures, according to St. Gregory the Theologian: 'Quiet and freedom from affairs is more precious than the splendour of a busy life.'[159] And according to the wise St. Neilos: 'The life of stillness is more splendid than a large fortune,'[160] for according to St. Basil the Great: 'Stillness is the first step in our soul's purification.'[161] St. Isidore of Pelusium also says: 'Departure into solitude has given me a fair amount of knowledge. For he who lives amidst turbulence and wants heavenly knowledge has forgotten that "whatever is sown in thorns is choked by them, and he who lacks stillness cannot know God."[162,163] This is why David said: 'Be still, and know that I am God.'[164,165] St. Joseph the Hesychast declared: "Anyone who has found grace found it in hesychia."[166]

In his commentary on the second Hymn of Ascent in first mode ("For those in the desert, divine longing becometh unending, in that they are outside the vain world."), St. Nicodemos of the Holy Mountain wrote:

---

[157] PG 135:788C.

[158] PG 32:225BC; *Basil: Letters and Select Works,* Letter 2, 110, 111.

[159] Schaff, *Cyril of Jerusalem, Gregory Nazianzen,* 478 (Letter CXXXI to Olympius).

[160] PG 79:748A; see also Palmer, Sherrard, Ware, *The Philokalia,* vol. 1, 214.

[161] *Basil: Letters and Select Works,* Letter 2, 111; PG 32:228A.

[162] Quoted from a homily attributed to St. Athanasios the Great: Λόγος διακριτικὸς, καὶ εἰς τὰς ἐντολὰς τοῦ Θεοῦ τοῖς ἀποταξαμένοις καὶ σωθῆναι θελουμένοις (PG 28:1416C).

[163] Ἐπιστολὴ ΥΒ΄ Θαυμασίῳ.

[164] Ps. 45:10.

[165] Νικοδήμου τοῦ Ἁγιορείτου, Συμβουλευτικὸν Ἐγχειρίδιον, 23–24.

[166] *Letters and Poems: St. Joseph the Hesychast,* Letter 77; Γέροντος Ἰωσὴφ τοῦ Ἡσυχαστου - Ἐπιστολὲς καὶ Ποιήματα: ἐκ τοῦ ἀρχείου τῆς Ι.Μ.Μ.Β., 60 χρόνια ἀπὸ τὴν κοίμησή του, β΄ ἔκδοση διορθωμένη καὶ ἐπαυξημένη, (Ἅγιον Ὄρος: Ἱερὰ Μεγίστη Μονὴ Βατοπαιδίου, 2019), 315.

The love and longing of monks dwelling in the desert and in stillness are not attracted by any material and vain thing.... Since God is infinite and inexpressible by nature, the hermits' longing for God never ends but is ceaseless and ever-moving, always increasing and rushing to what is above....

Those who are sitting in the desert and leading a life of stillness despise all pleasures and things desired by other people, and they gather their nous in their heart away from every worldly disturbance and thought, and there they pray without ceasing, meditating on the most desired and sweetest name of Jesus, saying with love, "Lord Jesus Christ, Son of God, have mercy on me." With this unceasing prayer and continuous meditation of the divine name of Jesus, they ignite in their heart a yearning and eros for God alone, and they extend their nous to contemplate the beauty of God. Enraptured by that exquisite beauty, they are beside themselves and are forgetful even of food and water and clothing and even the natural needs of the body.[167]

St. Basil the Great wrote the following about where he lived in seclusion as a monk:

Someone else might admire the abundant flowers or the multitudinous songbirds, but to these I do not have leisure to turn my mind. The greatest praise we can give of this place is that, besides being suited, because of its singularly apt location, for the production of every kind of fruits, it nourishes the sweetest of all fruits to me: solitude; not only because it is free from the uproar of the city, but also because it is removed from the encroachment of travelers, except for those who come to us for the purpose of hunting.[168]

When the evil thought starts up and says, "What is the good of your passing your life in this place? What do you gain by withdrawing yourself from the society of men?" ... Oppose it ... and say: ... For this reason I flee to the mountains "as a sparrow out of the snare of the fowlers."[169] For, I have been delivered as a sparrow. And I pass my life, O evil thought, in this solitude in which the Lord dwelt. Here is the oak of Mambre;[170] here is the ladder leading to heaven and the companies of angels which Jacob saw; here is the desert in which the people, having been purified, were given the laws, and, thus entering the land of promise, saw God. Here is Mount Carmel on which Elias, taking up his abode, was well-pleasing to God. Here is the plain into which Esdras withdrew and at the command of God produced his divinely inspired books. Here is the desert in which the blessed John ate locusts and preached penance to men. Here is the Mount of Olives which Christ ascended to pray, teaching us how to pray. Here is Christ, the lover of solitude. For, He says: "Where two or three are gathered together for my sake, there am I in the midst of them."[171] Here is the narrow and close

---

[167] Νικοδήμου τοῦ Ἁγιορείτου, *Νέα Κλίμακα: Ἑρμηνεία τῶν Ἀναβαθμῶν τῆς Ὀκτωήχου* (Θεσσαλονίκη: Ὀρθόδοξος Κυψέλη, 2009), 14–16.

[168] *Saint Basil: Letters, Vol. 1, Fathers of the Church,* vol. 13, 47 (Letter 14, "To Gregory His Companion"). If cities in the 4th century (which were incomparably less populous than contemporary cities) disturbed St. Basil with their "uproar" (even though this was long before the industrial revolution filled cities with noisy machines), what would he say about cities in the 21st century replete with noise pollution—not to mention their air pollution, soil pollution, light pollution, electromagnetic pollution, and water pollution?

[169] Cf. Ps. 124:7.

[170] Gen. 13:18, 18:1.

[171] Mt. 18:20.

way that leads to life.[172] Here are the teachers and prophets, "wandering in deserts, mountains, caves, and holes in the earth."[173] Here are apostles and evangelists, and monks living as citizens of the desert.[174]

St. John Chrysostom also praised the solitude of monastic living:

> This life which seems to you to be a galling and wearisome life, I mean that of the monks and of them that are crucified, is far sweeter, and more to be desired than that which seems to be easy, and more delicate.... Observe from their retreats at once the first signs of their tranquillity. For they have fled from market places, and cities, and the tumults amidst men, and have chosen the life in mountains, that which hath nothing in common with the things present, that which undergoes none of the ills of man, no worldly sorrows, no grief, no care so great, no dangers, no plots, no envy, no jealousy, no lawless lusts, nor any other thing of this kind. Here already they meditate upon the things of the kingdom, holding converse with groves, and mountains, and springs, and with great quietness, and solitude, and before all these, with God. And from all turmoil is their cell pure, and from every passion and disease is their soul free, refined and light, and far purer than the finest air.[175]

St. John Cassian declared: "The solitary life is greater and more sublime than that of the cenobia."[176] St. John of Sinai also believed that living in complete solitude can have greater benefits but also greater dangers. Since he was writing to monks in a cenobium, he admitted: "we hesitate to philosophize in our discourse about the haven of stillness"[177] because "we do not consider it permissible to talk about peace to the courageous warriors of our King who are struggling in the battle [in a cenobium]."[178] Nevertheless, he did mention a few ways in which a monk living alone in stillness is superior to a monk in a cenobium:

> A monk living with another monk is not like a monk living as a solitary.... The former is often helped by his brother; but an angel assists the latter. The noetic hosts unite in worship with him whose soul is quiet, and dwell lovingly with him.[179]
>
> Those whose mind has learned true prayer converse with the Lord face to face, as if speaking into the ear of the emperor. Those who make vocal prayer fall down before Him as if in the presence of the whole senate. But those who live in the world petition the emperor amidst the clamour of all the crowds.[180]

---

[172] Cf. Mt. 7:14.

[173] Heb. 11:38.

[174] *Saint Basil: Letters, Vol. 1,* 108–10 (Letter 42).

[175] *St. Chrysostom: Homilies on the Gospel of St. Matthew,* 399.

[176] *John Cassian: The Conferences,* Ancient Christian Writers, no. 57, trans. Boniface Ramsey, O.P. (New York: Paulist Press, 1997), 399.

[177] Holy Transfiguration Monastery, *The Ladder of Divine Ascent,* 197.

[178] Ibid., 198.

[179] Ibid., 199.

[180] Ibid., 200.

Why did the holy fathers of Tabennisi never have so many lights [i.e., saints] as those of the Scete? Those of you who can, understand this. I cannot speak, or rather, I do not want to.[181]

St. Photios the Great explained what St. John meant in that last paragraph: "This means that the work of stillness is great and results in greater progress than living in a cenobium. He did not want to say this for the sake of those who are weaker."[182] Tabennisi was where St. Pachomios had his foundation famed for its cenobitic character, whereas the desert of Scetis was a center for hesychasts.[183]

Regarding the dangers of solitary life, St. John of Sinai wrote:

He who is sick in soul from some passion and attempts stillness is like a man who has jumped from a ship into the sea and thinks that he will reach the shore safely on a plank.[184]

Stillness has received many experienced men but has rejected them by reason of their self-rule [ἰδιορρυθμία], and shown them to be lovers of pleasure. Others she has taken, and by fear and the concern for the burden of their condemnation, has made them zealous and fervent.[185]

He who has not yet known God is unfit for stillness, and exposes himself to many dangers. Stillness chokes the inexperienced; not having tasted the sweetness of God, they waste time in being taken captive, robbed, made despondent and subjected to distractions.[186]

St. Isaac the Syrian also viewed living in stillness as the loftiest monastic path. He wrote:

The commandment that says, "Thou shalt love the Lord thy God with all thy heart, and with all thy soul, and with all thy mind" [Mt. 22:37], more than the world, nature, and all that pertains thereto, is fulfilled when you patiently endure in your stillness.[187]

Do not compare those who work signs and wonders and mighty acts in the world with those who practise stillness with knowledge. Love the idleness of stillness above providing for the world's starving and the conversion of a multitude of heathen to the worship of God. It is better for you to free yourself from the shackle of sin than to free slaves from their slavery.[188]

The man who sighs over his soul for but one hour is greater than he who raises the dead by his prayer while dwelling amid many men.... The man who follows Christ in

---

[181] Ibid., 202–3.

[182] PG 88:1117C.

[183] Cf. Holy Transfiguration Monastery, *The Ladder of Divine Ascent,* 203f.

[184] Ibid., 199.

[185] Ibid., 203.

[186] Ibid., 206–7.

[187] Holy Transfiguration Monastery, *The Ascetical Homilies of Saint Isaac the Syrian,* 353–54 (Homily 44).

[188] Ibid., 144 (Homily 4).

solitary mourning is greater than he who praises Christ amid the congregations of men.[189]

True is the word of the Lord which declares that no man possessing love for the world can acquire the love of God, nor can any who has communion with the world have communion with God, nor can any who has concern for the world have concern for God.[190]

Every kind of virtue you can name, and every labor by which righteousness is accomplished, can be practised, acquired, and perfected outside of stillness; but dispassion and purity cannot be acquired outside of stillness.[191]

A man who possesses this gift in perfection [i.e., the gift of rapture in prayer and continuous tears] will not readily be found, nay, scarcely at all. For this power is a gift of the watchfulness of stillness; and because there is no one in our dispirited generation who has embraced perfect stillness and complete watchfulness, we are also devoid of its gifts.[192]

Because of all these benefits, St. Isaac advocated the solitary form of monasticism and taught monks how to live in this manner:

This is the definition of stillness: silence to all things. If in stillness you are found full of turbulence, and you disturb your body by the work of your hands and your soul with cares, then judge for yourself what sort of stillness you are practising, being concerned over many things in order to please God! For it is ridiculous for us to speak of achieving stillness if we do not abandon all things and separate ourselves from every care.[193]

We should not mix the work of stillness with care for anything at all, except for the things that are proper to stillness. Let every discipline be honored in its own place, lest we become confused in our disciplines. He who has many cares is the slave of many; but he who has forsaken all and cares only for the state of his soul, the same is a friend of God. Consider that there are many men in the world who give alms and fulfill [the commandment of] love of neighbor in matters pertaining to the body; but toilers in complete and beautiful stillness, and men entirely devoted to God, are scarcely to be found and are exceedingly few. Who among men in the world, who give alms or accomplish another form of righteousness through material things, has attained to one of the gifts which those who remain in stillness receive from God?

If you live in the world, practise virtuous disciplines suitable to laymen; but if you are a monk, distinguish yourself in the works wherein monks excel. If, however, you wish to practise both, you will quickly fall from the one and the other alike. These are the works of monks: freedom from worldly things, bodily toil in prayer, and unceasing recollection of God in the heart. So judge for yourself whether without these things the worldly virtues will suffice you.

---

[189] Ibid., 461 (Homily 64).

[190] Ibid., 428 (Homily 59).

[191] Ibid., 554 (Appendix A).

[192] Ibid., 551 (Appendix A).

[193] Ibid., 235 (Homily 21).

Question: Is it really true that a monk who endures hardship in stillness cannot acquire the two modes of virtue—the outward and the inward, I mean—to keep in his heart both care for God and solicitude for other men?

Answer: I am of the opinion that even though a man who wishes to dwell in stillness abandons all things, takes concern for his soul alone, and is without any care for the things of this life, he will still be unable perfectly to perform the work of stillness; therefore, how much more so if he has solicitude for others?[194]

We do not make our habitation alone with our soul, and practise stillness and seclusion, for the sake of the many works of the monastic ordinances and in order to accomplish these. For it is well known that fellowship with many facilitates this because of bodily vigor [i.e., the body is better sustained in a community and has more strength to complete the various regulations]. But if these works were necessary, there would not have been Fathers who abandoned the company and fellowship of men, some of whom inhabited tombs and others who chose seclusion in a solitary place. Such men greatly enfeebled their bodies in this manner, and neglected them, and could not fulfill their rules because of their weakness and the physical hardship.... They said no psalm and they did nothing else that is performed with the body. Instead of all the monastic ordinances, the infirmity of their body and their stillness sufficed them. This was their way of living all the days of their life. And in all this supposed idleness not one of them wished to forsake his cell, nor, because they did not perform any of the monastic canons, did they wish to wander about outside [their cells] or to be gladdened by the chanting in the churches and by the divine offices performed by other men.[195]

This is virtue: that in his mind a man should be unoccupied with the world. As long as the senses have dealings with external things, the heart cannot have rest from imaginations about them. Outside of the desert and solitude, the bodily passions do not abate, nor do evil thoughts cease.[196]

As a moderate way of practicing stillness, St. Isaac the Syrian mentions the practice of some monks "who have not chosen total stillness (that is, not to meet with any man), but who hold to the rule of stillness throughout the week or for periods of seven weeks."[197] He taught that such monks are imperfect and should also do good works for other people out of brotherly love:

The fulfilling of the duty of love with respect to providing for physical well-being is the work of men in the world, or even of monks, but only those who are imperfect, who do not dwell in stillness, or who combine stillness with brotherly concord and continually come and go. For such men this thing is good and worthy of admiration. Those, however, who have chosen to withdraw from the world in body and in mind so that they might establish their thought in solitary prayer by deadness to what is transitory, to concern over all affairs, and to the sight and recollection of worldly things, should not serve in the husbandry of physical things and visible righteousness.[198]

---

[194] Ibid., 232 (Homily 21).

[195] Ibid., 460–61 (Homily 64).

[196] Ibid., 113–14 (Homily 1).

[197] Ibid., 528 (Homily 76).

[198] Ibid., 230–31 (Homily 21).

St. Symeon the New Theologian praised the benefits of solitary life in his poems:

> For truly these are monks and solitaries living alone,
> these who are alone with God alone, and in God,
> stripped of considerations and all sorts of thoughts,
> seeing God alone in their mind without thoughts,
> in a mind fixed on the light like an arrow stuck in a wall,
> or like a star in heaven, or how I cannot say.
> Equally, they inhabit their cells like another shining bridal chamber
> and believe they live in heaven, or truly so do they live.[199] ...
> Being like an island in the middle of the sea,
> they ought to dwell
> and to consider the whole world
> as utterly inaccessible for settlement by themselves,
> as though a great chasm were established
> around their whole monastery,
> so as those who are in the world
> do not pass through to the monastery
> nor do those on this island go over to them in the world,
> and look upon them with strong affection,
> nor turn a memory of them in heart or mind,
> rather monks ought to be disposed like corpses to corpses,
> regarding them as not perceived by their senses,
> and they become as lambs, truly willing victims.[200]

St. Zosima Verkhovsky, a Russian hesychast, described from his own experience the joys and sorrows of living in solitude:

> [Through solitude] the soul has means for salvation in the Lord, is able to stand mentally before God, has purity of prayer, sobriety of memory, unrestrained powers of thought, motivation to please God, control of the mind which keeps it from vain wandering, sorrow and joy in the Lord: sorrow over one's own sins and careless way of life, joy at having been created a rational creature, and having been chosen from amongst the worldly multitude and led to this angelic brotherhood, and even having been granted to emulate the holy Fathers in a life of silence, established by God's Providence for His servants.[201]
>
> The inner desert, I trust, will be a teacher leading one to spiritual advancement. There are no comforts there, as in the world, with which the soul might busily pre-occupy itself; there is no need for excessive handiwork, and there is no one to visit for entertainment or idle conversation. You would have no visitors with whom you might share a comforting and fine meal except for your disciple (or a pilgrim) with whom you would eat only the strictest fast food. One must suffer the horror of demons, the loneliness and languishing of daily and continuous confinement and seclusion. The fear of death settles continuously in one's soul, frightening it with thoughts of being

---

[199] Griggs, *Divine Eros: Hymns of Saint Symeon the New Theologian,* 206–7 (Hymn 27).

[200] Ibid., 300–301 (Hymn 41).

[201] Abbess Vera Verkhovsky, *Elder Zosima: Hesychast of Siberia,* trans. Gregory Dobrov and Barbara McCarthy (Platina: St. Herman of Alaska Brotherhood Press, 1990), 96.

attacked and possibly killed by animals, snakes, and evil people. One suffers extreme need in everything, dire poverty, and lack of the most essential things, living in a meager hut which has nothing in it save a few books which are one's only joy and consolation. One hears neither of his friends and how they live, nor of the health of his relatives, nor of his loved ones. All the pleasures of his past life have departed. In a word, he has died to the world, and the world to him. There is nothing temporal over which to rejoice, thus darkening the mind, drawing it away from God. The whole mind, reason, memory and feelings, the whole person is immersed in God, ascending to Him through the contemplation and vision of His wisdom, His greatness, and His Providence in His works. Heaven and earth are as two constantly open books before him in which he reads of the greatness and wisdom of our God. To Him alone he weeps day and night, prostrating himself in supplication, begging to be strengthened and preserved till the end of his days in this way of life, the demands of which exceed his strength, but which he nevertheless undertook for God's sake. I trust that for his life of constant seclusion without exit from the desert, poverty and complete isolation from everything and everyone, the Lord will grant such a one the gift of tears, as a kind of betrothal to the joy and salvation of his soul to come.[202]

[In the deep forest,] every occasion, each object seen and heard turns one to contemplation on the omnipotence, the wisdom, the goodness of God.... We learn how much the desert-dwelling life enhances non-acquisitiveness and passionlessness. Besides, it becomes more apparent that everything which occurs in this world, all passing, corrupt and fleeting things, and even we ourselves, are actually not dwellers of this world, but involuntarily feel in our souls absolute repulsion to all that is in this world. And we only regret that up until now we have not realized what a sweet-melancholy life and what a transcendence in mind is given to those who live for God in the desert.[203]

I believe that if one departs for the inner desert overcome and persuaded by a divine love for Christ, he will truly live as if in Paradise. No longer hindered by any obstacles, he will be free to delight constantly in the thought of God and in sweet prayer of the heart and mind, with God and in his God. No longer shedding tears of grief alone, but weeping in joyful sorrow, he will dwell in the mountain heights as a heavenly bird, offering sweet songs to his Creator and Redeemer. Separated from all persons and things, as a beloved lamb of Christ, he will graze and take his fill in joy of the heart through the grace of Christ. Indeed, such a person would not trade his desert life for royal chambers that require excessive care, for living this way he may constantly contemplate the Kingdom of Heaven with ease.[204]

Contemporary studies have also found non-spiritual benefits of solitude. One recent survey of relevant literature concluded that solitude provides three crucial benefits: "new ideas, an understanding of self, and closeness to others."[205] Another study of great historical figures

[202] Ibid., 104–5.

[203] *Little Russian Philokalia, Vol. III: A Treasury of Saint Herman's Spirituality* (Platina: St. Herman of Alaska Brotherhood, 1988), 184–85.

[204] Verkhovsky, *Elder Zosima,* 107.

[205] Cal Newport, *Digital Minimalism: Choosing a Focused Life in a Noisy World* (New York: Penguin Random House, 2019), 98.

found that solitude is necessary for obtaining "clarity, creativity, emotional balance, and moral courage."[206] Sherry Turkle wrote: "In recent years, psychologists have learned more about how creative ideas come from the reveries of solitude.... Our brains are most productive when there is no demand that they be reactive."[207]

Despite the many benefits of being *geographically* removed from the world, the holy Fathers taught that being *inwardly* detached from the world is even more important. St. Nicetas Stethatos taught: "To become a monk does not mean to abandon men and the world, but to renounce the will of the flesh, to be destitute of the passions. If it was once said to a great spiritual master, 'Flee men and you will be saved,' it was said in precisely this spirit: for even after he fled, he dwelt among men and lived in inhabited regions along with his disciples. But because he so assiduously fled in a spiritual sense at the same time as he fled visibly, he suffered no harm from being with other men."[208] And St. Palladios wrote: "We are concerned not with the place where they [i.e., the exemplary monks] settled, but rather it is their way of life that we seek."[209]

St. Theoliptos of Philadelphia also emphasized the inner renunciation of the world:

> The monastic profession is a lofty and very fruitful tree whose root is detachment from all corporeal things, whose branches are the soul's freedom from passionate cravings and total alienation from the things you have renounced, and whose fruit is the acquisition of virtues, a deifying love, and the uninterrupted joy that results from these things.... Flight from the world bestows refuge in Christ. By "world" I mean attachment to sensory things and the flesh.[210]

Even St. Isaac the Syrian said: "No one can draw nigh to God save the man who has separated himself from the world. But I call separation not the departure of the body, but departure from the world's affairs."[211] And according to St. Symeon the New Theologian:

> Neither does being in the middle of a city prevent us from executing the commandments of God as long as we are eager and vigilant, nor do stillness and withdrawing from the world benefit us if we are negligent and lazy....[212]

---

[206] Raymond M. Kethledge, Michael S. Erwin, *Lead Yourself First: Inspiring Leadership Through Solitude* (New York: Bloomsbury USA, 2017), xiii.

[207] Sherry Turkle, *Reclaiming Conversation: The Power of Talk in a Digital Age* (New York: Penguin Press, 2015), 62.

[208] Palmer, Sherrard, Ware, *The Philokalia,* vol. 4, 99.

[209] Palladius, *The Lausiac History,* Ancient Christian Writers, trans. Robert T. Meyer (New York: Newman Press, 1964), 29.

[210] Θεολήπτου Μητροπολίτου Φιλαδελφείας, «Λόγος τὴν ἐν Χριστῷ κρυπτὴν ἐργασίαν διασαφῶν» ἐν *Φιλοκαλία τῶν Ἱερῶν Νηπτικῶν,* τόμος δ΄ (1991), 4; see also Palmer, Sherrard, Ware, *The Philokalia,* vol. 4, 177.

[211] Holy Transfiguration Monastery, *The Ascetical Homilies of Saint Isaac the Syrian,* 113 (Homily 1).

[212] Ἁγίου Συμεὼν τοῦ Νέου Θεολόγου, «Κατηχητικὸς λόγος κβ΄», Φιλοκαλία, ΕΠΕ (Θεσσαλονίκη: 1989), τόμος 19Δ, 256, παρ. 9, στ. 18–21.

Renunciation of the world and complete withdrawal from it—if it includes complete withdrawal from all worldly things, habits, opinions and people, and the disowning of body and will—in a very short time will bring great profit to a man who is fired with such zeal....[213]

Who would not weep for me, who would not grieve deeply, because I fled the world and the things in the world (cf. 1 Jn. 2:15), and yet I am not separated from the world in my senses? I have put on the habit of monks, yet I love the things in the world just like the worldly: glory, wealth, both pleasures and enjoyments.[214]

St. Ignatius Brianchaninov wrote that true withdrawal from the world consists of enclosing one's mind within oneself:

Outward prayer alone is not enough. God pays attention to the mind, and they are not true monks who fail to unite exterior prayer with inner prayer. Strictly defined, the word "monk" means a recluse, a solitary. Whoever has not withdrawn within himself is not yet a recluse, he is not yet a monk even though he lives in the most isolated monastery. The mind of the ascetic who is not withdrawn and enclosed within himself dwells necessarily amongst tumult and unquietness. Innumerable thoughts, having free admission to his mind, bring this about; without purpose or necessity his mind wanders painfully through the world, bringing harm upon itself. The withdrawal of a man within himself cannot be achieved without the help of concentrated prayer, especially the attentive practice of the Jesus Prayer.[215]

St. John of Sinai held renunciation in such high regard that he set it as the basis of monastic life by making it the first step in his *Ladder*. He wrote:

Those who enter this [monastic] contest must renounce all things, despise all things, deride all things, and shake off all things, that they may lay a firm foundation. A good foundation of three layers and three pillars is innocence, fasting and temperance....[216]

All who have willingly left the things of the world, have certainly done so for the sake of the future Kingdom, or because of the multitude of their sins, or for love of God. If they were not moved by any of these reasons, their withdrawal from the world was unreasonable.... The man who renounces the world from fear is like burning incense, that begins with fragrance but ends in smoke. He who leaves the world through hope of reward is like a millstone, that always moves in the same way (that is, revolves round itself, is self-centered). But he who withdraws from the world out of love for God has obtained fire at the very outset; and, like fire set to fuel, it soon kindles a larger fire.[217]

---

[213] *Writings from the Philokalia on Prayer of the Heart,* trans. E. Kadloubovsky and G.E.H. Palmer (London: Faber and Faber, 1951), 98 (Precepts #5).

[214] Griggs, *Divine Eros: Hymns of Saint Symeon the New Theologian,* 193 (Hymn #24).

[215] Igumen Chariton of Valamo, *The Art of Prayer: An Orthodox Anthology,* trans. E. Kadloubovsky, E. M. Palmer (Boston: Faber and Faber, 1966), 54.

[216] Holy Transfiguration Monastery, *The Ladder of Divine Ascent,* 6.

[217] Ibid., 4, 7.

According to St. John Cassian, Abba Paphnutius taught that there are three kinds of renunciation necessary for monks: "The first renunciation has to do with the body. We come to despise all the riches and all goods of the world. With the second renunciation we repel our past, our vices, the passions governing spirit and flesh. And in the third renunciation we draw our spirit away from the here and the visible and we do so in order solely to contemplate the things of the future. Our passion is for the unseen."[218] St. John of Sinai, however, held a different view of what the three kinds of renunciation are: "No one can enter crowned into the heavenly bridechamber without making the three renunciations. He has to turn away from worldly concerns, from men, from family; he must cut selfishness away; and thirdly, he must rebuff the vanity that follows obedience."[219]

Both Abba Dorotheos of Gaza and St. Theodoros the Great Ascetic understood monastically the verse of St. Paul: "No one engaged in warfare entangles himself with the affairs of this life, in order that he may please him who enlisted him as a soldier."[220] Abba Dorotheos commented on this: "Likewise we should also strive to be free from any concern of this world and to be occupied only with God, and, as it says, be like a virgin devoted and without distraction (1 Cor. 7:34–35)."[221] And St. Theodoros concluded:

> The monk, therefore, must be detached from material things, must be dispassionate, free from all evil desires, not given to soft living, not a drinker, not slothful, not indolent, not a lover of money, pleasure, or glory. Unless he raises himself above all these things, he will not be able to achieve this angelic way of life.... This spiritual life and its activities are full of delight, and is "the good portion that shall not be taken away" (Lk. 10:42) from the soul that has attained it.[222]

St. Peter of Damascus taught that a monk wanting to be more devoted to God will naturally reduce material cares: "A sensible person struggles intelligently to minimize, so far as he can, the needs of his body, so that he may devote himself to the keeping of the commandments with few or no material preoccupations. Indeed, the Lord Himself says, 'Do not worry about your life, what you will eat, or what you will drink, or about your body, what you will put on' (Mt. 6:25)."[223]

In order to protect the clergy and monastics from secular cares, the holy Fathers of the Fourth Ecumenical Council declared:

---

[218] Luibhéid, *John Cassian: Conferences,* 85.

[219] Luibhéid, *John Climacus: The Ladder of Divine Ascent,* 83.

[220] 2 Tim. 2:4.

[221] *Abba Dorotheos: Discourses and Sayings,* trans. Eric Wheeler (Kalamazoo: Cistercian Publications, 1977), 80.

[222] Θεοδώρου τοῦ Μεγάλου Ἀσκητοῦ, «Κεφάλαια πάνυ ψυχωφελῆ ρ΄» ἐν *Φιλοκαλία τῶν Ἱερῶν Νηπτικῶν,* τόμος α΄ (1991), 311–12 (κεφ. μθ΄); see also Palmer, Sherrard, Ware, *The Philokalia,* vol. 2, 23 (ch. 49).

[223] Palmer, Sherrard, Ware, *The Philokalia,* vol. 3, 153.

No Bishop, Clergyman, or Monk shall henceforth be allowed to farm any estate or office, or to involve himself in secular cares, unless he be unavoidably called by laws to the guardianship of minors, or the Bishop permit him to take care of the affairs of the church, or of those of orphans or widows unprovided for, and of persons in especial need of ecclesiastical assistance, for the fear of God.[224]

St. Isaac the Syrian taught: "One of the saints said: 'It does not befit the rule of your manner of life to feed the starving and to make your cell a hospice, for this is the laymen's portion and it is meet for them to practise this as something good, but not for anchorites, who are liberated from care for visible things, and keep guard on their minds through prayer.'"[225] In the same spirit, St. Paisios of the Holy Mountain said:

[Anti-monastic clergymen] in waging their war even make use of Fathers of the Church who were involved in important social work, such as Saint Basil the Great and his *Vasileiada*.[226] I don't wish to refer to the life of Saint Basil the Great before he began the *Vasileiada* [when he lived as a hermit], but simply express my thought: What would Saint Basil the Great do if he lived in our era? I am of the opinion that he would again retreat to a cave with his prayer-rope, watching the flame of love (of the social work of other holy Fathers) being spread everywhere; not only to the faithful but even to the unfaithful, who all together constitute Social Providence.... In other words, social welfare is shouting every day: "Holy Fathers of our times, leave charity to us, the lay people, who are not in a position to do something else, and look to concern yourselves with something more spiritual."

Unfortunately, however, some clergymen not only do not follow this exhortation, since they do not understand it, but they also prevent those who do understand it and want to dedicate themselves entirely to Christ, feeling intensely the inclination to depart from the world.... [Such clergymen] even make the unreasonable demand that monks leave the desert and come to the world to take up the social work and philanthropy....

The monk departs far from the world not because he hates it, but because he loves it. In this way he will, through his prayer, help the world more in those matters that are, being humanly impossible, only possible by God's intervention. This is how God saves the world.... I want to stress the great mission of the monk, which is of greater importance than human philanthropy....

External stillness combined with discerning asceticism rapidly brings internal stillness (i.e., peace of the soul), which is a necessary prerequisite for refined and exacting spiritual labour. For, the more someone becomes alienated from the world, the more the world is alienated from within him. Then, worldly thoughts are expelled and man's mind is purified and he becomes a man of God....

The undistracted nature of a hesychast's life in the desert greatly assists prayer with its many prerequisites.

Love the blessed desert and respect it, if you want the desert to assist you with its sacred seclusion and sweet serenity, that you become serene and your passions

---

[224] Agapius and Nicodemus, *The Rudder*, 248 (Canon III).

[225] Holy Transfiguration Monastery, *The Ascetical Homilies of Saint Isaac the Syrian*, 409 (Homily 54).

[226] *Vasileiada* was the name given by the successors of Saint Basil (*Vasileios* in Greek) the Great to his social and philanthropic work.

devastated, so as to draw near unto God. Be careful not to adapt the holy desert to your passionate self, for this shows great impiety. (It is like going on pilgrimage to Holy Golgotha with *bouzoukia* [i.e., guitars].) The desert is for a higher spiritual life, the angelic, and for more physical asceticism and not for more bodily comfort, as if on vacation. Therefore, love the desert with all its harsh seclusion if you want to quickly make fruitful your sterile soul and become incorporeal.[227]

When St. Paisios of the Holy Mountain was asked why monks do not stay in the world to do social work, he explained:

Aren't lighthouses supposed to be always out on the rocks? Are you saying they should go to the cities and be added to the streetlights? Lighthouses have one mission and street lights another. A monk is not a little street light to be put in the city at the side of the road to shine on pedestrians so they don't trip. A monk is an isolated lighthouse, high on the crags of a rocky shore, providing light and direction for those on the seas and the oceans to guide their ships to reach their destination: God.[228]

4) Stability

In general, a monk is obliged to remain in his "monastery of repentance" (i.e., the monastery in which he was tonsured and chose to live a life of repentance) until the end of his life, and this ideal is implicit in the vows of the great schema.[229] The *Greek* version of this vow for the great schema says: "Do you [vow to] remain in the monastery and in the ascetic life until your last breath?"[230] However, the *Slavonic* version of the same vow takes into consideration the possibility of going elsewhere under obedience: "Do you vow to abide in this monastery, or in that to which under holy obedience you will be sent, and in the ascetic life until your last breath?"[231]

St. Basil the Great explained the reason for monastic stability:

Once someone has joined and lived with a spiritual brotherhood … he has entered an agreement of spiritual cohabitation having an indissoluble and eternal connection and cannot separate and cut himself off from those with whom he has been joined.…

If he says that some of the brethren are bad and carelessly prevent what is good and neglect decorum and fail to keep the exactitude proper for ascetics, and therefore

---

[227] Elder Paisios, *Epistles,* 31–35, 55, 98, 119, 205.

[228] Elder Paisios, *Spiritual Awakening,* 320; see also Γέροντος Παϊσίου, *Πνευματικὴ Ἀφύπνηση,* 320. Likewise, St. John Chrysostom said that monasteries "are as lights shining from a lofty place to mariners afar off" (*The Nicene and Post-Nicene Fathers, Chrysostom: Homilies on Galatians, Ephesians, Philippians, Colossians, Thessalonians, Timothy, Titus, and Philemon,* vol. 13, Homily 14 on Timothy [New York: Christian Literature Company, 1895], 456).

[229] For more about the great schema and levels in monasticism, see chapter 7) section 2) on page 388.

[230] *Τάξις καὶ Ἀκολουθία τοῦ Μεγάλου καὶ Ἀγγελικοῦ Σχήματος,* 20. The first patristic mention of this vow of stability is found in the catechism of St. George of Hozeva who lived in the ninth century (vid. Ζουκόβα, *Γέννηση καὶ Ἐξέλιξη τῆς Ἀκολουθίας τοῦ Μοναχικοῦ Σχήματος,* 245).

[231] *The Great Book of Needs,* vol. 1 (South Canaan: St. Tikhon's Seminary Press, 1998), 364.

he must separate himself from them, such a person has not contrived a sufficient justification for leaving.[232]

St. Efthymios the Great warned: "Just as a tree which is continually transplanted cannot bear fruit, so the monk who moves from place to place cannot produce virtue."[233] And St. John of Sinai wrote: "If you have bound yourself by obligations and perceive that the eye of your soul is not becoming lucid, do not request leave to quit. The proven are proven everywhere, and the reverse is equally true."[234] St. Maximos the Confessor taught: "In a time of temptations do not leave your monastery but stand up courageously against the thoughts that surge over you, especially those of sorrow and listlessness. For when you have been tested by afflictions in this way, according to divine providence, your hope in God will become firm. But if you leave, you will show yourself to be worthless, unmanly and fickle."[235]

The Seventh Ecumenical Council institutionalized these teachings by decreeing: "A monk or nun must not leave his or her monastery or nunnery, respectively, and go away to another. But if this should occur, it is necessary that he or she be afforded a hospitable reception as a guest. But it is not fitting that he or she be entered without the approval of his abbot, or of her abbess, as the case may be."[236] In his interpretation of this canon, St. Nicodemos of the Holy Mountain explained that a monk or nun who has gone to another monastery "must not be held to be enrolled in the brotherhood or sisterhood there, as the case may be, without the approval and a dismissory letter from his own abbot (or from her own abbess, if it be a nun)."[237]

The First-and-Second Council also stated:

> If any monk runs away from his own monastery to another or riotously enters a worldly resort, both he himself and the one receiving him shall be excommunicated until the absconder has returned to the monastery which he has wrongly fallen out of. But if, in any particular case, the bishop should wish to send away to another monastery some of the monks of proven reverence and decorousness of life for the purpose of stocking the other monastery, or should wish to transfer them even to a mundane house for the purpose of compassing the salvation of the inmates thereof by establishing the

---

[232] Βασιλείου Καισαρείας τοῦ Μεγάλου: Ἅπαντα τὰ Ἔργα, 9, Παν. Κ. Χρήστου, Ἀσκητικαὶ Διατάξεις 21:1, 2 (Θεσσαλονίκη: ΕΠΕ, 1973), 496, 498.

[233] Chrysostomos, *The Evergetinos, Book I,* 353; *Four Great Fathers,* trans. Leo Papadopoulos (Jordanville: Holy Trinity Monastery, 2007), 16.

[234] Holy Transfiguration Monastery, *The Ladder of Divine Ascent,* 46.

[235] Μαξίμου τοῦ Ὁμολογητοῦ, «Ἑκατοντὰς πρώτη τῶν περὶ ἀγάπης κεφαλαίων» ἐν Φιλοκαλία τῶν Ἱερῶν Νηπτικῶν, τόμος β´ (1991), 8 (κεφ. νβ´); see also Palmer, Sherrard, Ware, *The Philokalia,* vol. 2, 58 (ch. 52).

[236] Agapius and Nicodemus, *The Rudder,* 450 (Canon XXI).

[237] Ibid., 451.

monks therein, or should see fit to place them elsewhere, this course shall not render either the monks or the ones receiving them subject to any penalty.[238]

Commenting on this canon, St. Nicodemos of the Holy Mountain added: "The ornament of a monastery is the condition of having monks stay in it permanently in quietude and not keep going away."[239]

However, St. Basil also taught that a monk may depart from his monastery if he is being harmed there or if he is fulfilling the Lord's command:

> He who is withdrawing from his brethren because he is being harmed should not keep his motive hidden within himself, but should censure the wrong done to him, in the manner taught by the Lord, Who said: "If thy brother sin, go and tell him his fault between thee and him alone" (Mt. 18:15), and so on. Then, if the amendment he desires is effected, he has not only gained his brethren but also has not dishonored their union. But if he sees that they persist in the evil and are not willing to correct it, he will report this to those empowered to judge in such cases, and then, after several have given testimony, he may withdraw. In this manner, he will not be separating himself from brethren but from strangers, for the Lord compares one who persists in evil to a heathen and publican: "let him be to thee as the heathen and publican" (Mt. 18:17). If, however, he leaves the society of his brethren because of his fickle nature, let him cure his own weakness, or, if he will not do this, let the brotherhoods refuse to accept him. And if, by the Lord's command, one is attracted to some other place, such do not sever their relations, but they fulfill the ministry. There is no other acceptable reason for the brethren to leave their community.[240]

The Synod of Patriarch Nicholas of Constantinople taught the same thing:

> Question VI: If perchance anyone is tonsured as a monk at whatever place he may be, and afterwards finds that he is being harmed there as respects his soul and he wishes to depart thence on account of the harm, but receives a prohibitive tether from his Superior not to leave, what ought he himself to do—ignore the harm his soul is suffering, or ignore the Superior's tether?
>
> Answer: He ought first to tell his Superior the cause of the harm he is suffering, and if that harm and the peril incurred by his soul are manifest, he ought to depart thence, and not bother about the Superior's tether.[241]

St. Nicodemos of the Holy Mountain added the following comment to this:

> It is implied here that if the Superior fails to correct the scandal and the cause of the harm, the monk ought to leave. Such being the case, however, the monk ought to take care to get the tether of his Superior untied or loosed if the latter will consent to untie it for him; but if he refuses to do so, he ought to go to the local Bishop and have it untied by the latter, and not by anyone else, just as Apostolic canon XXXII prescribes

---

[238] Agapius and Nicodemus, *The Rudder,* 459–60 (Canon IV).

[239] Ibid.

[240] Βασιλείου τοῦ Μεγάλου, *Ἀσκητικὰ Α΄*, ΕΠΕ 8, 338–41; see also Wagner, *Saint Basil: Ascetical Works,* vol. 9, 305 (Question 36 of the *Long Rules*).

[241] Agapius and Nicodemus, *The Rudder,* 972–73.

[for excommunicated presbyters and deacons]; for no one can untie himself by himself.[242]

Canon XVII of St. Nicephoros the Confessor likewise states: "A monk is permitted to leave his monastery for three reasons: 1) if perchance the abbot is a heretic; 2) if women come into the monastery; or 3) if children are learning secular letters in the monastery."[243] St. John the Prophet, however, says: "If it is determined accurately that the abba proclaims heresy, then the brother should indeed abandon him. If, however, there is only a suspicion about this, then the brother should neither abandon him nor examine what he believes. For what is concealed from people is revealed to God."[244]

St. Sophrony of Essex observed that the vow of stability

> is not an imprescriptible [i.e., inviolable] mark of monasticism, as are the other vows. The monastic life can be lived outside the monastery: in the world, in the desert. In the lives of a great many saints who were monks we read of their voluntarily or involuntarily abandoning the monastery in which their vows were made, without this being considered a fall or even any violation of the monastic state. Many of them were taken from their monasteries and set to perform some hierarchical service in the Church; many, for one reason or another, were transferred to other monasteries, many received the blessing of their superiors to leave for a good purpose; and finally, there are instances of flight from the monastery because of the "difficulty of salvation" there.[245]

St. Savas of Kalymnos demonstrated the flexibility of the vow of stability when he appeared in a vision to a nun of his monastery whose conscience was reproving her for having left her "monastery of repentance" in order to join his monastery. He drew a circle around the two monasteries and told her: "Look, my daughter; these are both ours. That one is a convent, and this one is also a convent!"[246]

Likewise, the authors of *Byzantine Monastic Foundation Documents* mentioned in their preface: "During the monastic reforms of the eleventh and twelfth centuries, when many monks sought a more austere life, [the vow of] stability was increasingly seen in

---

[242] Ibid.

[243] Agapius and Nicodemus, *The Rudder,* 452. St. Nicephoros explained that the reason why children should not be taking secular school lessons in the monastery is "because it is improper for them to reveal the good things being done in the monastery, for it says in the Gospel: 'Do not sound a trumpet before thee when thou doest good' (cf. Mt. 6:2)" (*Spicilegium Solesmense,* J. -B. Pitra, vol. 4 [Paris: 1858], 392).

[244] *Barsanuphius and John, Letters,* vol. 2, trans. John Chryssavgis (Washington, D.C.: Catholic University of America Press, 2006), 126 (letter 537).

[245] Archimandrite Sophrony Sakharov, *Truth and Life* (Essex: Monastery of Saint John the Baptist, 2014), 103–4.

[246] Ἱερομονάχου Δημητρίου Καββαδία, *Γέροντας καὶ Γυναικεῖος Μοναχισμός* (Ἅγιον Ὄρος: Ἱερᾶς Μεγίστης Μονῆς Βατοπαιδίου, 2015), 268.

terms of profession rather than of place, and transfers were not only permitted but in some cases encouraged, especially from a lower to a higher, or stricter, monastery."[247]

Elder Aimilianos made a distinction between subjective and objective reasons for wanting to leave one's monastery. He taught:

> We have cases of monastics who are no longer happy in their monastery.... Thoughts enter the monk and tell him: "The Elder is not good; he doesn't love me; I can't stand it here." Because of these thoughts his heart yields to the pressure, and since he is not living a Christian and happy life he decides (or they decide) that he should leave the monastery with the hope that elsewhere he will be able to live under circumstances that are somewhat more humane and comfortable. This is in itself an illicit divorce; it is not permitted by the Church. For the rest of his life, this person will be guilty before God.
>
> There is only one case which permits me to leave my monastery: when I am not at rest for objective reasons. The life at the monastery is such that I can neither pray nor read or keep vigil; my soul is overwhelmed and cannot survive with such a life. So why would I remain in this monastery? This could happen if the monastery becomes a tourist attraction, and I do not feel my heart thriving, or if the monastery has a propensity for working so much that afterwards I collapse out of extreme exhaustion and sleep and am unable to have a spiritual life. In this case a monk may insist many times, with courtesy and dignity, to change monastery. Especially when the Elder or the Eldress has fallen asleep to whom he had been under obedience, it is easier. Usually the spiritual fathers grant the possibility to a monk to go somewhere else.[248]

St. Benedict outlined how a monk should be received when returning to his monastery:

> If a brother, who through his own fault leaveth the monastery or is expelled, desireth to return, let him first promise full amendment of the fault for which he left; and thus let him be received in the last place, that by this means his humility may be tried. If he should leave again, let him be received even a third time, knowing that after this every means of return will be denied him.[249]

St. Waldebert expanded on this in his own rule for nuns and wrote:

> If a sister is ever lost to the Christian religion and flees from the walls of the monastery and, having fled outside, later recalls her original religion and returns full of fear of eternal judgement, she must first make all emendation to the monastery. Afterwards, if her penance is believable, then she may be received again within the monastery walls. Even if this happens two or three times, she shall be extended like piety though she will be placed in the last place among the penitents and examined for a long time until some proof of her life [sincerity] is discovered. But if after a third

---

[247] Thomas and Hero, *Byzantine Monastic Foundation Documents,* xviii.

[248] Ἀρχιμ. Αἰμιλιανοῦ Σιμωνοπετρίτου, *Νηπτικὴ Ζωὴ καὶ Ἀσκητικοὶ Κανόνες: Ἑρμηνεία στοὺς Ὁσίους Πατέρες Ἀντώνιο, Αὐγουστίνο καὶ Μακάριο* (Ὁρμύλια: Ἱερὸν Κοινόβιον Εὐαγγελισμοῦ τῆς Θεοτόκου, Ἰνδίκτος, 2011), 24–25.

[249] *Rule of St. Benedict,* Chapter XXIX.

reception she again incurs the stain of sinful flight, she should know that afterwards she will be denied all chance to return.[250]

5) The Monastic Struggle

Ever since the beginning of monasticism the first thing novices are traditionally told when they come to a monastery is how difficult monasticism is. For example, when St. Paul the Simple came to St. Anthony's cell in order to become a monk, St. Anthony did and said everything he could to discourage him.[251] Abba Pinufius (in fourth-century Egypt) warned postulants how difficult monasticism is as follows:

> According to the words of Scripture, now that you have set out "to serve the Lord, remain in the fear of God and prepare your soul" not for peace or security or pleasure but "for trials and difficulties" (Sir. 2:1). For "we must enter the kingdom of God through many tribulations" (Acts 14:21), inasmuch as "the gate is narrow and the path is strait which leads to life, and few there are who find it" (Mt. 7:14). Consider, then, that you are one of the chosen few, and do not grow cold through the example and the lukewarmness of the multitude, but live as do the few, so that with the few you may deserve to be found in the kingdom. "For many are called, but few are chosen" (Mt. 20:16). And "small is the flock" (Lk. 12:32) to whom the Father is pleased to give the inheritance.[252]

Similarly, St. Caesarius of Arles said in a homily to monks: "In this place, dearly beloved, we have gathered not to enjoy quiet, not to be secure, but rather to fight and to engage in combat. It is to struggle that we have advanced here."[253] St. Columbanus in sixth-century Ireland concluded his monastic rule with this description of the struggle:

> The monk shall live in a monastery under the rule of one father and in the company of many brethren, in order that he may learn humility from one, patience from another. One will teach him silence, another meekness. He shall not do what pleases him; he shall eat what is set before him, clothe himself with what is given him, do the work assigned to him, be subject to a superior whom he does not like. He shall go to bed so tired that he may fall asleep while going, and rise before he has had sufficient rest. If he suffers wrong, he shall be silent; he shall fear the head of the monastery as a master,

---

[250] *The Rule of a Certain Father to the Virgins,* trans. J. A. McNamara, J. Halborg, in J. A. McNamara, *The Ordeal of Community.* Peregrina Translation Series 5, 2nd ed. (Toronto: Peregrina, 1993), chapter 21.

[251] Vid. *The Great Synaxaristes of the Orthodox Church: March,* 141–43; or Chrysostomos, *The Evergetinos, Book 1,* 218–19.) Similarly, Abba Palamon also tried to intimidate St. Pachomios by telling him: "You cannot withstand the type of austerity and deprivation I go through here" (*Four Great Fathers,* 45). St. Pachomios in turn tried to discourage St. Macarios in a similar manner (vid. Palladius, *The Lausiac History,* XVIII). Others who did likewise were Helle the Ascetic (vid. *The Lives of the Desert Fathers,* trans. Norman Russell [Kalamazoo: Cistercian Publications, 1980], 91) and Abba Gregory the Anchorite (vid. John Moschos, *The Spiritual Meadow,* trans. John Wortley, Series #139 [Kalamazoo: Cistercian Studies, 1992], 73).

[252] Ramsey, *John Cassian: The Institutes,* 99.

[253] St. Caesarius of Arles, "A Homily of Saint Caesarius to Monks," chapter 1. http://www.academia.edu /1860501/Caesarius_of_Arles_On_Living_in_Community

and love him as a father, being ever convinced that what he commands is profitable to him; nor shall he criticize the words of the elders because it is his duty to obey and to do what he is bidden, as Moses says: "Attend, and hear, O Israel" (Deut. 6:4).[254]

St. Basil the Great warned:

> Do not think that all who live in a monastery are saved, the bad as well as the good, for this is not so. Many, indeed, come to the life of virtue, but few bear its yoke. The kingdom of heaven belongs to the violent and "the violent take it by force"—these are the words of the Gospel (vid. Mt. 11:12). By "violence" is meant the affliction of the body which the disciples of Christ voluntarily undergo by denying their own will, refusing respite to the body, and observing the commandments of Christ. If, then, you wish to seize the kingdom of God, become a man of violence; bow your neck to the yoke of Christ's service. Bind the strap of the yoke tightly about your throat. Let it pinch your neck. Rub it thin by labor in acquiring virtues, in fasting, in vigils, in obedience, in stillness, in psalmody, in prayer, in tears, in manual labor, in bearing all the tribulations which befall you at the hands of men and demons.[255]

These warnings and counsels were eventually formalized and included in the Service of the Great Schema as the "catechism." Ninth- and tenth-century manuscripts of this service have various texts as a catechism,[256] but in contemporary practice, the only catechism used is the one presented on page 399 of this book.

St. Sophrony of Essex also told his monastics how difficult our life is: "You all know that the loftier the goal, the more difficult it is to achieve. So we should not be surprised that the monastic life is the most difficult and grievous thing in the world.... We must have a deep awareness of the fact that monasticism is almost always a state of living in sorrow, for we monastics are crucified beside the crucified Christ. What is strange about this? When our mind is immersed in the contemplation of the eternal realities that Christ spoke about, we find ourselves by grace in a state in which we are not aware that we are suffering."[257]

Abba Pinufius outlined the stages of monastic progress for beginners as follows:

> The beginning of our salvation and the preserving of it is the fear of the Lord.[258] For by this the rudiments of conversion, the purgation of vice, and the preserving of virtue are acquired by those who are being schooled for the way of perfection. When this has penetrated a person's mind it begets contempt for all things and brings forth the forgetfulness of one's family and a horror of the world itself. By this contempt, however, and by being deprived of all one's possessions, humility is acquired. Humility, in turn, is verified by the following indications: first, if a person has put to death

---

[254] *Celtic Spirituality,* Oliver Davies and Thomas O'Loughlin, ed. (New York: Paulist Press, 1999), 256; see also: http://www.scrollpublishing.com/store/Columbanus.html

[255] Βασιλείου τοῦ Μεγάλου, *Ἀσκητικὰ Αʹ,* ΕΠΕ 8, 122–23; see also Wagner, *Saint Basil: Ascetical Works,* vol. 9, 30.

[256] Ζουκόβα, *Γέννηση καὶ Ἐξέλιξη τῆς Ἀκολουθίας τοῦ Μοναχικοῦ Σχήματος,* 248.

[257] Σωφρονίου, *Οἰκοδομώντας τὸν Ναὸ τοῦ Θεοῦ, Τόμος Αʹ,* 139, 431.

[258] Cf. Prov. 9:10.

in himself all his desires; second, if he conceals from his elder not only none of his deeds but also none of his thoughts; third, if he commits nothing to his own discretion but everything to his [elder's] judgment and listens eagerly and willingly to his admonitions; fourth, if in every respect he maintains a gracious obedience and a steadfast patience; fifth, if he neither brings injury on anyone else nor is saddened or sorrowful if anyone else inflicts it on him; sixth, if he does nothing and presumes nothing that neither the general rule nor the example of our forebears encourages; seventh, if he is satisfied with utter simplicity and, as being an unfit laborer, considers himself unworthy of everything that is offered him; eighth, if he does not declare with his lips alone that he is inferior to everyone else but believes it in the depths of his heart; ninth, if he holds his tongue and is not a loudmouth; tenth, if he is not ready and quick to laugh.[259] By such indications, and by others like them, true humility is recognized. When it is possessed in truth, it will at once bring you a step higher to love, which has no fear.[260] Then all the things that you used to do out of a certain dread of punishment you will begin to do without any difficulty, as it were naturally, and no longer with a view to punishment or fear of any kind, but out of love for the good itself and out of pleasure in virtue.[261]

Perhaps the most common pitfall for zealous beginners in a monastery is to judge the imperfections of the other monks and novices, since people typically come to monasticism with an idealized image of it. The sad reality nowadays, however, is that most (if not all) people in a monastery are still only somewhere in the beginning of their long journey towards perfection, and thus still have plenty of vices which they are struggling to overcome. Aware of this reality, Abba Pinufius continued his teaching: "In order to attain more easily to this [perfection], you should seek out, while you live in the community, examples of a perfect life that are worthy of imitation; they will come from a few, and indeed from one or two, but not from the many."[262] If in the fourth century examples of a perfect life were rare, now in the twenty-first century they should be almost non-existent. For according to the prophecies of several saints, monks in the end times would be pitifully weak compared to those in the early days of monasticism.[263]

Because of this, Abba Pinufius continued his teachings to beginners as follows:

In order to be able to lay hold of all of this [spiritual progress] and to abide permanently under this spiritual rule, you must observe the following three things in the

---

[259] For more on the matter of monastic laughter, see chapter 5) section 16) on page 234.

[260] Cf. 1 Jn. 4:18.

[261] Ramsey, *John Cassian: The Institutes,* 99–100.

[262] Ibid., 100.

[263] "Once, when the holy Fathers were making predictions about the last generation, they said, 'What have we ourselves done?' One of them, the great Abba Ischyrion replied, 'We ourselves have fulfilled the commandments of God.' The others replied, 'And those who come after us, what will they do?' He said, 'They will struggle to achieve half our works.' They said, 'And to those that come after them, what will happen?' He said, 'The men of that generation will not accomplish any works at all and temptation will come upon them; yet those who will persevere in that day will be greater than either us or our fathers'" (Benedicta Ward, *The Sayings of the Desert Fathers,* 111).

community, in accordance with the words of the Psalmist: "Like one who was deaf I did not hear, and I was like one who was mute and did not open his mouth. And I became like a man who did not hear, not having any rebukes in his mouth" (Ps. 37:13–14). Thus you too should set out as one who is deaf and mute and blind, so that, apart from looking upon him whom you have chosen to imitate by reason of his perfection, whatever you might see that is less than edifying you will not see, being as it were blind....

If you hear that anyone is disobedient, insolent, or disparaging, or that anyone is doing something differently than was taught to you, you should not stumble and be inveigled into imitating him because of such an example, but, like one who is deaf and does not hear these things in the least, you should ignore them all. If insults or injuries are inflicted on you or on anyone else, be steadfast and pay heed to a vindictive retort as would a mute person, repeating over and over again in your heart the verse of the Psalmist: "I said: I will guard my ways lest I sin with my tongue. I set a guard at my mouth when the sinner stood against me. I was dumb and was humbled and was silent even from saying good things" (Ps. 38:1–3).[264]

Yet despite the manifold hardships inherent to monasticism, this path contains a mystical and hidden joy, for the holy Fathers recognized it as the "light yoke" of which Christ spoke.[265] For example, St. Theodore the Studite said that the cenobium is our "light, our life, and our true joy, for nothing is more joyous than a soul being saved."[266] The *Rule of St. Comghall* (from sixth-century Ireland) says: "The service of the Lord is light, wonderful, and pleasant. It is an excellent thing to place oneself in the hands of a holy mentor, that he may direct one's path through life."[267] Elder Aimilianos explained this in more detail in the *Regulations of the Holy Cenobium of the Annunciation:*

The nuns shall ever have the perfect joy of Christ within them. This joy shall be accompanied by the spirit of contrition and repentance, which comes to the true believer as a visitation from the Holy Spirit. To each one, the Lord shall show "what great things she shall suffer for My name's sake."[268] Suffering for Christ, endeavoring with all her might to behold the glory of God, and her divine calling to the monastic life shall make her a participant in the ranks of the Apostles. Each nun shall thus wage her own combat in the common arena to achieve the goal of Christianity which, according to St. Basil the Great, is "the imitation of Christ according to the measure of His Incarnation, insofar as is conformable with the vocation of each individual."[269,270]

---

[264] Ramsey, *John Cassian: The Institutes,* 100–101.

[265] "Take My yoke upon you, and learn of Me; for I am meek and lowly in heart, and ye shall find rest for your souls. For My yoke is easy, and My burden is light" (Mt. 11:29–30).

[266] Θεοδώρου Στουδίτου, *Μεγάλη Κατήχησις,* 470.

[267] Uinseann Ó Maidín, *The Celtic Monk: Rules and Writings of Early Irish Monks* (Kalamazoo: Cistercian Publications, 1996), 33.

[268] Cf. Acts 9:16.

[269] Wagner, *Saint Basil: Ascetical Works,* vol. 9, 319 (Question 43 in the *Long Rules*).

[270] Cf. Elder Aimilianos, *The Authentic Seal,* 180.

Chapter Two:
The Abbot

1) His Characteristics

AINT BASIL THE GREAT believed that "instruction how to lead the Christian life depends less on words than on daily example."[271] Therefore, he taught: "The superior … should make his life a clear example of the keeping of every commandment of the Lord.… To consider first, then, that which is indeed first in importance, he should be so confirmed in humility by the love of Christ that, even if he is silent, the example of his actions may afford more effective instruction than any words.… Therefore, meekness of character and humility of heart should characterize the superior."[272] St. Basil also taught that an abbot should be "chosen in preference to the rest after a thorough examination of his life and character and consistently good conduct. Age should also be taken into consideration where special honor is to be accorded. It is somehow in keeping with man's nature that what is more aged is more worthy of respect."[273] St. Basil added that the abbot should be someone who is "skilled in guiding those who are making their way toward God, who will be an unerring director of your life. He should be adorned with virtues, bearing witness by his own works to his love for God, conversant with the Holy Scripture, undistracted from worldly matters, free from avarice, a good, quiet man, tranquil, pleasing to God, a lover of the poor, mild, forgiving, laboring hard for the spiritual advancement of those who come to him, without

[271] *Nicene and Post-Nicene Fathers: Second Series, Volume VIII, Basil: Letters and Select Works,* (New York: Christian Literature Company, 1893), 208 (Letter 150).

[272] Βασιλείου τοῦ Μεγάλου, *Ἀσκητικὰ Α΄,* ΕΠΕ 8, 370–71; see also Wagner, *Saint Basil: Ascetical Works,* vol. 9, 319 (Question 43 in the *Long Rules*).

[273] Ibid., 210.

vainglory or arrogance, impervious to flattery, not given to vacillation, and preferring God to all things else."[274]

St. Paisius Velichkovsky added to this list that the abbot should "have for everyone a true, unhypocritical love, [and] that he be meek, humble, patient."[275] St. John of Sinai emphasizes: "It is love that shows who is a true shepherd, for it was out of love that the Shepherd was crucified."[276] St. Athanasios I, the Patriarch of Constantinople, wrote in his monastic rules that the abbot "must be a God-loving man, that is, one who takes care to lead souls to God, because nothing else is more important to God than this."[277]

St. John Cassian wrote: "No one is chosen to rule over a community of brothers unless, before he himself exercises authority, he has learned by obedience how he should command those who will be subject to him and has understood from the institutes of the elders what he should pass on to the young. For they [i.e., the monks of fourth-century Egypt] declare that to rule well and to be ruled well is typical of the wise person, and they insist that this is a most lofty gift and a grace of the Holy Spirit. They say that a person cannot enjoin beneficial precepts on his subjects unless he has first been instructed in every virtuous discipline, and that someone cannot obey an elder unless he has been consumed with the fear of God and has been perfected by the virtue of humility."[278] Likewise, St. Fructuosus of Braga wrote in his *General Rule for Monasteries:* "First of all, an abbot must be sought who is seasoned by the practices of a holy life; not one who is newly professed, but who, for a long period of time has been proved by laboring hard in a monastery under an abbot in the company of many."[279]

St. Donatus of Besançon (in seventh-century Gaul) wrote that the abbess should have the following characteristics:

> The mother of the monastery, who will be first in dignity among the congregation, must always be mindful of the burden she has taken up and of Him to Whom she must give account of her stewardship. She should know better how to subordinate herself than to rule. Therefore, she must be instructed in divine law that she may know whence to "bring forth both new things and old."[280] Chaste, sober, merciful, she will often place mercy above justice so that the same will be done for her. Let her hate vice and love her sisters. Let her act prudently and not be excessive in correcting them, lest in

---

[274] Ibid., 19.

[275] Metrophanes, *Blessed Paisius Velichkovsky,* 136.

[276] Luibhéid, *John Climacus: The Ladder of Divine Ascent,* 42; Ἰωάννου Σιναΐτου, *Κλῖμαξ,* PG 88:1177.

[277] Thomas and Hero, *Byzantine Monastic Foundation Documents,* 1501.

[278] Ramsey, *John Cassian: The Institutes,* 38 (ii. 3).

[279] Barlow, *The Fathers of the Church: Iberian Fathers,* vol. 63, 181–82.

[280] Cf. Mt. 13:52. Similarly, the *Rule of the Master* states: "The abbot must be well-versed in the [divine] law so that he himself may either teach all things by bringing witness to bear [from biblical and patristic sayings] or else may assign readings pertinent to the occasion" (*The Rule of the Master,* trans. Luke Eberle [Kalamazoo: Cistercian Publications, 1977], 160).

trying to scrape out the rust she destroy the vessel. Let her always be distrustful of her own fragility and remember that the bruised reed must not be crushed. By that we do not mean that she should permit vice to flourish but that she should cut it out prudently and charitably so that she sees what may be of help and, as we say, study more to be loved than to be feared. Let her not be turbulent and anxious, neither excessive nor obstinate, neither jealous nor overly suspicious so that she never rests. Let her orders be prudent and considerate and let her distinguish whether the work she assigns is according to God or to the world and temper it accordingly. Let nothing contrary to her teaching be seen in her deeds nor anything blameworthy be found in her preaching lest God say to her error, "What hast thou to do, to declare my statutes, or that thou shouldst take my covenant in thy mouth? Seeing thou hatest instruction and castest out my words behind thee?"[281] She must make no distinction of persons in the monastery and not love one more than another, except for what she finds better in good actions or obedience.[282]

These suggestions for an abbess apply to an abbot as well, because monastic principles are identical for both genders. As St. Basil the Great taught: "Since there are convents not only for men but for women who also profess virginity, all that has been said applies to both sexes alike."[283] The First-and-Second Council supported this opinion of St. Basil by decreeing: "Whatever rules the holy Council has made in regard to men who are leading the monastic life of monks, the same rules apply also to women who are leading the monastic life of nuns."[284]

In fact, St. Basil the Great believed that nuns should be even more strict with themselves than monks should, for he wrote:

> This [monastic] way of life requires on the part of women a greater and a more signal decorum in the observance of poverty, quietude, obedience, and fraternal love, a greater strictness with regard to going about in public, more caution in the matter of acquaintances, greater care in preserving mutual affection and avoiding factional groups; for in all these respects the lives of virgins should exhibit a more excellent zeal.[285]

Commenting on this difference, Archbishop Christodoulos of Athens wrote: "This holy father, knowing the psychology of women, their sensitivity, and their rich world of feelings,

---

[281] Ps. 49:16–17.

[282] Donatus of Besançon, "Regula ad Virgines: a Working Translation," trans. Jo Ann McNamara and John E. Halborg, *Vox Benedictina: A Journal of Translations from Monastic Sources,* 2 (1985), ch. 1.

[283] Wagner, *Saint Basil: Ascetical Works,* vol. 9, 221.

[284] Agapius and Nicodemus, *The Rudder,* 461 (Canon VI).

[285] Βασιλείου τοῦ Μεγάλου, *Ἀσκητικὰ Α΄,* ΕΠΕ 8, 152–53; see also Wagner, *Saint Basil: Ascetical Works,* vol. 9, 221.

encourages them to have greater strictness and more perfect caution so that souls are not lost."[286]

Elder Aimilianos described the role of the abbess in the *Regulations of the Holy Cenobium of the Annunciation* as follows:

> Besides her spiritual and vigilant personal life, the Abbess should possess: a bold spirit, an all-embracing and limitless love without discrimination between persons that is expressed in deed, discernment of thoughts and spirits, a good education, firm prudence, a mild character, and fitting speech. She should not be possessed by excess of industry, haste or anxiety, but should be at ease in herself and in her manner....
>
> It shall be her concern to see the community progress and increase, and she shall remain within the sheepfold, leaving it [only] whenever the interests of the monastery dictate or because of its necessary relations with the outside world. She herself, "ever studying the Law of God on the one hand, while speaking not at all of the things of the earth,"[287] shall strengthen the sisters in a manner fitting to God to work with a will as if in service to the Lord, continuously speaking the word of God to them "like a scribe trained for the Kingdom of God, who brings from his store of treasure both new and old,"[288] so that "she shall be regarded not as a human being but rather an angel of God dwelling among them."[289] She shall be the link between them and God, "representing the person of the Saviour,"[290] so that when a nun sees her, "she should think she is seeing Christ Himself ... and should believe with certainty that she is joined to Him and is following Him."[291,292]

St. Theodoros the Great Ascetic explained how a monk should view his abbot:

> When you have taken up your dwelling with a spiritual father and perceive benefit from him, let no one separate you from his love and from living with him. Do not judge him in any respect; do not revile him even if he censures or strikes you; do not listen to someone who slanders him to you; do not side with anyone who reviles him, lest the Lord should be angered with you and blot you out of the book of the living (cf. Ex. 32:33).[293]

Commenting on the above patristic quotes, Elder Aimilianos said: "You can see that, in today's world, such teaching would be taken as promoting a personality cult. But the Fathers had their reasons. Theodore the Studite says that the monk who is docile is saved

[286] Μητρ. Δημητριάδος Χριστοδούλου, *Πρακτικὰ πανελληνίου μοναστικοῦ Συνεδρίου Ἁγίων Μετεώρων* (Holy Meteora: Holy Monastery of Transfiguration, 1990): 297–98.

[287] Πρβλ. *Βίος ἕτερος ἁγίου Παχωμίου* 14, Halkin, 180, στιχ. 13–14.

[288] Vid. Mt. 13:52.

[289] Πρβλ. *Βίος ἕτερος ἁγίου Παχωμίου* 14, Halkin, 193, στιχ. 19–20.

[290] St. Basil the Great, *PG* 31:1409A.

[291] St. Symeon the New Theologian, *Sources Chretiennes* 51, 47, ll. 24–26.

[292] Elder Aimilianos, *The Authentic Seal,* 164–65.

[293] Θεοδώρου τοῦ Μεγάλου Ἀσκητοῦ, «Κεφάλαια πάνυ ψυχωφελῆ ρ΄» ἐν *Φιλοκαλία τῶν Ἱερῶν Νηπτικῶν,* τόμος α΄ (1991), 310 (κεφ. μ΄); see also Palmer, Sherrard, Ware, *The Philokalia,* vol. 2, 21 (ch. 40).

through the instructions and prayers of his abbot. St. Pachomios's monks said of him: 'Therefore we die together, so that we can live together in this man, who rightly leads us to life.' Wherever the spiritual life has flourished, there has been a single person at the head. Wherever a monastery has flourished, there has been an abbot—an abbot who knew how to love, to live Christ, and to administer."[294]

Elder Aimilianos highlighted the importance of the ability of the abbot to inspire love in his disciples:

> Naturally, the abbot does not inspire respect and obedience by creating fear in his monks, but through his love. However, love is a two-edged sword; as long as it is not based on specific gifts or abilities of the elder (e.g., based on his holiness, his wisdom, his cleverness, his activeness), then there is no danger. The elder should be loved because he is the father, the abbot, in the place of God. The abbot is to be loved—not his gifts. When a monk does not love his elder and does not hold him in high esteem in his heart, then a grain of sand seems like a mountain, and his life becomes unbearable; everything seems to be cumbersome, insurmountable difficulties. Whereas love towards one's elder transforms mountains into grains of sand. The degree of a monk's genuine love for his abbot determines the monk's ease in his spiritual life, the comfort in his relationship with God, and the progress in his prayer....
>
> Certainly, the phrase: "the abbot should be loved" [in the Rule of Blessed Augustine][295] is not an exhortation towards the monks to love him, but advice to the abbot that he should be lovable. For it is not easy to love a man if the person does not inspire love. His life and behavior must be such that he is naturally loved. The monks should not have to make efforts to love him, to understand him, to devote themselves to him....
>
> If, God forbid, the abbot is unable to be worthy of being loved, will the monks not love him? Of course they will love him, for they are obliged to do so in the name of God. But they will have a terrible struggle to love an unlovable person, and life in the monastery will be a quagmire, an uphill battle. This happens as the years pass, when the [new] elder is not the select one of the brotherhood or of God but is the one elected out of necessity. When a suitable person does not exist, to avoid dissolving the monastery, someone has to be elected or someone is brought in from outside the monastery. But you understand how difficult and tiresome life is then in such a monastery. This is why St. Augustine says that monks should simultaneously fear and love the abbot, and the abbot should be loved. Then life in the monastery is intertwined with the joy of Christ, and Christ truly rests within such a monastery.[296]

St. Sophrony of Essex taught that a beginner needs a staretz [i.e., an elder] for two reasons: "1) To cut off in his disciple or novice every manifestation of personal, sinful, carnal will, and to guide his will in conformity with the will of God. 2) To nourish his disciple (by his instructions) so that he is brought up from inferior stages towards greater spiritual heights;

---

[294] Elder Aimilianos, *The Authentic Seal,* 56.

[295] Vid. *Explanation of the Rule of St. Augustine,* Catholic Classics, vol. 1 (Jasper: Revelation Insight Publishing Co., 2008), 36; and *Saint Augustine: The Monastic Rules,* trans. Sister Agatha Mary, S.P.B., Gerald Bonner (New York, New City Press, 2004), 38 (Rule 7:3).

[296] Γέροντος Αἰμιλιανοῦ, *Νηπτικὴ Ζωὴ καὶ Ἀσκητικοὶ Κανόνες,* 347–49.

to give him the tasks which correspond to his spiritual development and his strength."[297]
St. Sophrony added that the second point can be partially replaced by reading the ascetical
works of the holy Fathers of the Church, "however this cannot completely replace an ideal
and perfect staretz—though such an elder would always, in any epoch, be difficult to find,
and apart from this, present-day [in 1932] novices (self-willed, self-confident, clever,
impatient, arrogant, omniscient) are incapable of living under the authority of a true
elder."[298]

St. Paisios of the Holy Mountain advised beginners how to choose an elder: "You
should, as much as you can, seek after:

a) an Elder who is a spiritual man with virtues, more a practitioner than solely a
teacher. It is good if he has become a 'captain' after starting out as a 'deck boy,' so
that he does not apply to others a monastic life he has only learned from books. He
should have great love and discernment by nature, so he can feel sympathy for his
children.... It is very helpful if the disciple is at least eighteen to twenty years
younger than the Elder, as this creates in the disciple a natural feeling of respect.

b) The Elder should live a simple life, without cares and unnecessary worldly concerns....

c) The Elder should be a friend of stillness and of prayer, in order that he unite you
also to God through prayer so you can find the true joy of divine consolation."[299]

2) His Responsibilities

The primary responsibility of the abbot is to care for the spiritual formation of his
monks. St. Basil the Great teaches: "He who is entrusted with general supervision should
behave as one liable to give an account for each person under his care, bearing in mind that
if one of the brethren falls into sin, not having been forewarned by him of the ordinance of
God, or if, having fallen, he remains in that state, uninstructed as to the manner of making
amends, 'the blood of that one will be required at his hands,'[300] as it is written."[301] Likewise
St. Theodore the Studite warns abbots: "You must give yourself as an example [to the other
monks] of good works, for you know very well that you will give an account when Christ
is seated to judge all men."[302]

---

[297] Sakharov, *Striving for Knowledge of God,* 290.

[298] Ibid.

[299] Elder Paisios, *Epistles,* 53–54.

[300] Ez. 3:20.

[301] Βασιλείου τοῦ Μεγάλου, Ἀσκητικὰ Α΄, ΕΠΕ 8, 300–301; see also Wagner, *Saint Basil: Ascetical Works,*
vol. 9, 287 (Question 25 in the *Long Rules*).

[302] Θεοδώρου Στουδίτου, Ἴαμβοι καὶ ἐπιγράμματα, PG 99:1781.

Elsewhere, St. Basil adds: "It is necessary then that he who is over the community and gives orders to all should after strict testing be entrusted with this care and should watch over each man anxiously, as is meet, in order that he may lay down rules and issue commands for the common good in a manner well pleasing to God, due regard being paid to the abilities and strength of each."[303] "Let him establish good order among the brethren, making an allotment of tasks according to the fitness of each member."[304]

The abbot regulates the life of each monk as he sees fit. Namely, he assigns them their personal prayer rule, chooses which books they may or may not read, gives them their tasks, decides if and when they will visit a doctor, regulates their sleeping and eating schedule, permits or forbids them to do anything, assigns or cancels penances, and permits or prohibits them to receive Holy Communion.

Despite the authoritative position of the abbot, he must bear in mind that his goal is not to make the monastery run smoothly by keeping the other monks in line as slaves but to help them mature spiritually. As St. Paul wrote: "for the perfecting of the saints ... till we come ... unto perfect men, unto the measure of the stature of the fulness of Christ, that we be no more children."[305] St. Theodore the Studite said: "What is more pleasing for a father than to see his own children growing in virtue and progressing in spiritual maturity?"[306] Since being a dictator seems to be more effective and is much less painful than being a father, it will be a subtle challenge for the abbot to choose to be the *father* of his disciples and to "suffer in travail until Christ is formed in them,"[307] instead of abusing his power.

Thus, the "order" created by the abbot is not dictatorial but is in a spirit of fatherly love. Elder Aimilianos captures the challenge of this fatherly approach in his description of his vision of the formation of the individual in a monastery as follows:

> The renaissance of monasticism would also be served by an attempt to adapt the monastic life to some extent, in accordance with changes in the psychological mindset

---

[303] *The Ascetic Works of Saint Basil,* trans. W. K. L. Clarke (London: Society for Promoting Christian Knowledge, 1925), 347 (Rule 303 in the *Shorter Rules*).

[304] Wagner, *Saint Basil: Ascetical Works,* vol. 9, 320 (Question 43 in the *Long Rules*).

[305] Cf. Eph. 4:13–14.

[306] Θεοδώρου Στουδίτου, *Μεγάλη Κατήχησις,* 455. To emphasize the importance of maturing spiritually, Elder Ephraim loved to quote the saying of St. Isaac the Syrian who said: "God does not want to put into His Kingdom oxen [i.e., people who are stupid in spiritual matters]" (vid. Γέροντος Ἐφραίμ, *Πατρικαὶ Νουθεσίαι,* ἔκδοσις 3η, [Ἅγιον Ὄρος: Ἱερὰ Μονὴ Φιλοθέου, 1989], 247; see also Elder Ephraim, *Counsels from the Holy Mountain* [Florence: St. Anthony's Greek Orthodox Monastery, 1999], 190). Note: All excerpts taken from the publications I translated: *Monastic Wisdom, Counsels from the Holy Mountain,* and *My Elder Joseph the Hesychast,* have been retranslated here from the original Greek. Furthermore, I have also compared the slightly edited versions of the letters of St. Joseph the Hesychast found in *Monastic Wisdom* with the unedited publication of these letters, found in the publication I am currently translating into English: Γέροντος Ἰωσὴφ τοῦ Ἡσυχαστοῦ, *Ἐπιστολὲς καὶ Ποιήματα.*

[307] Cf. Gal. 4:19.

of modern man and the needs of the educated. The daily program should not be a steamroller, expunging people's characters and quashing their personalities. The monk should not be a spineless creature, without opinions. Labour and the system of study should help the monks, in accordance with the potential of each one, and they should have sufficient time for hesychia and study. Education should be encouraged, while obedience should be tempered with discretion, freedom, and a great deal of love.[308]

Stressing the importance of being a loving father to the monks, St. Christodoulos of Patmos wrote to the superior: "Love your brotherhood, all those who are under your rule, strive for them as for your own children, cherish them as your very bowels, give to each the direction suited and appropriate to him, to the strong, the wretched, the sagacious, the ignorant, to the young, to the old."[309] Or as Fyodor Dostoyevsky put it succinctly: "To love someone means to see him as God intended him."[310]

 St. Benedict taught that the abbot forms the monks through instruction:

> Let the abbot always bear in mind that he must give an account in the dread judgment of God of both his own teaching and of the obedience of his disciples. And let the abbot know that whatever lack of profit the master of the house shall find in the sheep, will be laid to the blame of the shepherd. On the other hand he will be blameless, if he gave all a shepherd's care to his restless and unruly flock, and took all pains to correct their corrupt manners.... The abbot ought always to remember what he is and what he is called, and to know that to whom much hath been entrusted, from him much will be required (Lk. 12:48); and let him understand what a difficult and arduous task he assumeth in governing souls and accommodating himself to a variety of characters.[311]

Likewise, St. Theodore the Studite said: "Since there are many and diverse characters, the method of instructing should also be implemented accordingly. For in the way that one person is healed, a different person might be harmed; in the manner one is benefited, another is destroyed; and with the words that someone is edified, it happens that another is damaged."[312] This is why St. Waldebert (in seventh-century Gaul) wrote in his monastic rule for nuns: "The abbess must take care on both sides lest, on the one hand, she nourish vice in the hearts of her subjects by excessive kindness, or, by excessive austerity of discipline, she cause those whom soft words might heal to be torn away by rigid correction.... She must learn the habits of each of them so that she will know how to repress the vice in each."[313] And as St. John of Sinai wrote: "Sometimes what serves as a medicine for

---

[308] Elder Aimilianos, *The Authentic Seal,* 36–7; Γέροντος Αἰμιλιανοῦ, *Σφραγὶς Γνησία,* 51.

[309] Thomas and Hero, *Byzantine Monastic Foundation Documents,* 593.

[310] As quoted by Helmut Thielicke in *The Waiting Father* (Cambridge: Lutterworth Press, 1959), 220.

[311] *Rule of St. Benedict,* Chapter II.

[312] Θεοδώρου Στουδίτου, *Μεγάλη Κατήχησις,* ὁμιλία 44.

[313] J. A. McNamara and J. Halborg, *The Rule of a Certain Father to the Virgins,* 75.

one is poison for another; and sometimes something given to one and the same person at a suitable time serves as a medicine, but at the wrong time it is a poison. I have seen an unskilled physician who, by subjecting to dishonour a sick man who was contrite in spirit, only drove him to despair. And I have seen a skilled physician who operated on an arrogant heart with the knife of dishonour, and drained it of all its evil-smelling pus."[314]

St. Basil the Great said that it is the abbot's responsibility to teach: "If the hand or foot obey not the guidance of the eye, the one will inevitably touch dangerous things to the destruction of the whole body, and the other will knock against them or be precipitated from a height.[315] … In the same way, a superior's neglect [in giving spiritual instruction] is dangerous, since he has to answer for all."[316]

Even more important than teaching by words is teaching by examples. St. Dorotheos of Gaza advised an abbot: "Teach them especially by your deeds, since an example is more effective than words."[317] St. Isidore of Seville wrote that the abbot "will show that he is to be imitated in all his work, for he will not command anyone to do anything he himself has not done."[318] St. Neilos the Ascetic wrote: "Self-appointed teachers… should learn from Abimelech and Gideon that it is not words but actions that inspire people to follow a leader. Abimelech prepared a load of wood, and after carrying it he said: 'Do what you have seen me do' (Judg. 9:48). Gideon also shared tasks with his men and by his own example showed them what to do, saying: 'Look at me, and do likewise' (Judg. 7:17)…. The Lord Himself first acted and then taught. All this shows that it is more convincing to teach through actions than through words."[319]

According to St. Basil the Great, the abbot should humbly render personal service to the monks of his community, since this teaches by example and displays fatherly love. "The brethren should accept to be served in bodily matters as well as in spiritual matters by those who seem to hold the highest positions in the brotherhood. For the principle of

---

[314] Holy Transfiguration Monastery, *The Ladder of Divine Ascent,* 166.

[315] Clarke, *The Ascetic Works of St. Basil,* 191; see also Wagner, *Saint Basil: Ascetical Works,* vol. 9, 286 (Question 24 in the *Long Rules*).

[316] Βασιλείου τοῦ Μεγάλου, *Ἀσκητικὰ Α΄,* ΕΠΕ 8, 298–99; see also Wagner, *Saint Basil: Ascetical Works,* vol. 9, 286.

[317] Wheeler, *Abba Dorotheos: Discourses and Sayings,* 261.

[318] "The Rule of Isidore" in *Monastic Studies,* no. 18, Christmas 1988, "Modern Monasticism and the Crisis of Faith," Benedictine Priory of Montreal, 9.

[319] Νείλου τοῦ Ἀσκητοῦ, «Λόγος ἀσκητικός, πάνυ ἀναγκαῖος καὶ ὠφελιμώτατος», ἐν *Φιλοκαλία τῶν Ἱερῶν Νηπτικῶν,* τόμος α΄ (Ἀθῆναι: Παναγιώτου Ἀθ. Τζελάτη, 1893), 121; see also Palmer, Sherrard, Ware, *The Philokalia,* vol. 1, 217.

humility imposes the duty of service upon the superior and shows to the lesser that to be served is not unfitting."[320]

Thus, menial tasks should be done not just by novices and the younger fathers but also by the senior fathers and even the abbot. Christ plainly said: "If I then, your Lord and Master, have washed your feet; ye also ought to wash one another's feet. For I have given you an example, that ye should do as I have done to you."[321] Countless saints of the Church did lowly tasks despite their lofty position. For example, when the monks of St. Feodosij of the Kiev Caves informed him that no one had carried water from the well or cut wood for cooking, he immediately went and did these menial tasks himself, despite being their superior.[322] And when St. Nectarios of Aegina was a bishop and the head of the Rizarios Theological Academy, he cleaned the toilets for three months when their janitor was ill.[323]

The importance of teaching disciples collectively on a regular basis has been stressed by several monastic saints. St. Pachomios ordained: "Every week, two teachings are given by the superior."[324] Abba Shenoute the Great[325] decreed: "The superiors of these abodes shall give catechesis in the gathering three times per week."[326] Likewise, St. Isidore of Seville wrote:

> Three times a week after the singing of terce, the brothers should gather together in a body to hear the abbot in conference once the signal has been given. Let them hear the senior teaching and instructing all in the teachings of salvation. They should hear the abbot with the greatest eagerness and silence, showing the intention of their minds

---

[320] Βασιλείου τοῦ Μεγάλου, *Ἀσκητικὰ Α΄*, ΕΠΕ 8, 316–17; see also Wagner, *Saint Basil: Ascetical Works,* vol. 9, 294 (Question 31 in the *Long Rules*).

[321] Jn. 13:14–15.

[322] Vid. *The Hagiography of Kievan Rus',* trans. Paul Hollingsworth (Boston: Harvard University Press, 1992), 62.

[323] Similarly, Dr. Kenneth Jernigan (the president of the National Federation of the Blind with 50,000 members) cleaned toilets. His secretary reminisced: "At the end of a very long weekend he told a departing state affiliate that he was going to go and clean the bedroom and bathroom he had used while staying at the Center. One person said in an astonished tone: 'He's the leader of the Federation, and he still cleans toilets!' Dr. Jernigan replied that it would be an irresponsible waste of the Federation's resources if he spent very much time cleaning toilets but that, if he was unwilling to spend some time cleaning, he didn't deserve to lead." Likewise, we could say that if an abbot is unwilling to spend some time doing menial tasks, he is not worthy to be the abbot. (Vid. Mary Ellen Gabias, "Reminiscences of Mary Ellen Gabias," *The Braille Monitor,* vol. 42, no. 1, January/February, 1999.)

[324] Δ. Πετρακάκου, *Μοναχικοὶ θεσμοί,* Μ. Παχωμίου «Κανόνες», (Leipzig: A. Deichert, 1907), 116.

[325] By the 5th century, Abba Shenoute the Great was regarded by those in the Thebaid as the most important representative of Egyptian monasticism, but he was virtually unknown by those abroad because he wrote only in Coptic.

[326] Bentley Layton, *The Canons of Our Fathers: Monastic Rules of Shenoute,* Oxford Early Christian Studies, (Oxford: Oxford University Press, 2014), 237.

with sighing and groaning. The conference itself either will be for the correcting of faults, the formation of character, or for other reasons to benefit the monastery.[327]

St. Theodore the Studite advised the abbot: "You shall always be on your guard to teach catechism three times a week in the evening either by your own agency or through another of your children since this is the salutary tradition of the fathers."[328] It is written in the life of St. Paisius Velichkovsky: "When the life of the brethren began to fall into decline, the brethren were to admit to themselves that one of the principal causes of this decline was the cessation of the starets' daily discussions [of patristic texts]."[329]

Elder Aimilianos emphasized the importance of teaching disciples as follows:

> The deepest and most essential means by which an elder forms a disciple and makes him of like form is through words. Through words he gives birth to him, he renews him, he saves him, he fills him with the Holy Spirit, he imparts Christ to him. It is the one thing that God expects of him. The elder may have thousands of gifts: the gift of prophecy, of working miracles, of love, of discerning spirits, of governing, etc. All these can't accomplish anything (and perhaps are even harmful), but they become useful when there are words, the seed of words, by which the elder gives birth to his son. These words are the transmission of the word of God through his teaching, through his corrections, through his advice, through his reproofs, through his jokes, and through any means by which it is expressed.[330]

3) Making Corrections

An essential part of the abbot's role as the teacher and father of his monks is to correct them. St. Basil the Great explained how an abbot should make corrections:

> Harshness is ever to be put aside, even in censuring. The more you show modesty and humility yourself, the more likely are you to be acceptable to the patient who needs your treatment.[331]

> [The superior] must be compassionate, showing long-suffering to those who through inexperience fall short in their duty, not passing sins over in silence but meekly bearing with the restive, applying remedies to them with all kindness and delicate adjustment. He must be able to find out the proper method of cure for each fault, not rebuking harshly, but admonishing and correcting with meekness.[332]

---

[327] *Monastic Studies,* no. 18, 15.

[328] Thomas and Hero, *Byzantine Monastic Foundation Documents,* 78.

[329] Fr. Sergii Chetverikov, *Starets Paisii Velichkovskii: His Life, Teachings, and Influence on Orthodox Monasticism,* trans. Vasily Lickwar and Alexander I. Lisenko (Belmont: Nordland Publishing Company, 1980), 154.

[330] Γέροντος Αἰμιλιανοῦ, *Νηπτικὴ Ζωὴ καὶ Ἀσκητικοὶ Κανόνες,* 439–40.

[331] *Basil: Letters and Select Works,* 111 (Letter 2).

[332] Clarke, *The Ascetic Works of St. Basil,* 216 (Question 43 in the *Long Rules*).

Abba Dorotheos gave similar advice to the superior:

> When mistakes do occur [by others] do not be greatly indignant, but calmly show
> the damage the mistake caused. If you are forced to reprove someone, try to find the
> right time for it. Do not be strict about small mistakes and inflexible, and do not censure
> continuously. This is annoying, and endless reproofs lead to insensibility and contempt.
> Do not give orders imperatively but in humility, taking counsel with the brother.
> Speaking like this is more effective and more persuasive and keeps your neighbor
> calm.[333]

This insight of Abba Dorotheos that continual censuring will ruin a relationship has been verified by contemporary longitudinal studies in the context of married couples. These studies concluded: "The difference between happy and unhappy couples is the balance between positive and negative interactions during conflict. There is a very specific ratio that makes love last. That 'magic ratio' is 5 to 1. This means that for every negative interaction during conflict, a stable and happy marriage has five (or more) positive interactions."[334] It would be helpful to ascertain if this same ratio is required also in a monastic setting for stable relationships. Perhaps this ratio depends somewhat on one's spiritual and psychological health, for it is evident from the lives of saints that through deep humility and self-reproach many holy disciples managed to "metabolize" in a spiritually and psychologically healthy manner a tremendous number of negative interactions to their own benefit.

An abbot must take care to find a balance between gentleness and severity. St. Benedict wrote: "In his teaching the Abbot should always observe that principle of the Apostle in which he saith: 'Reprove, entreat, rebuke' (2 Tim. 4:2), that is, alternating gentleness with severity, as the occasion may call for, let him show the severity of the master and the loving affection of a father."[335] Likewise, St. Gregory the Dialogist wrote: "Gentleness must therefore be mingled with severity. A kind of mixture in due proportion must be made from both, so that subjects may not be made worse by great harshness, or made to come undone by excessive kindness."[336] With this same understanding, Elder Ephraim told me that it is unwise to correct someone two consecutive times, but instead we should alternate corrections with pleasant words.

St. Paisios of the Holy Mountain warned against correcting a young monk too harshly:

> A young monk who is bumptious and egotistical should not be humbled too
> suddenly by his elder, because then he will push out off-shoots like a young tree which
> is full of sap when it has been pruned too hard....

---

[333] Constantine Scouteris, *Abba Dorotheos: Practical Teaching on the Christian Life,* 261.

[334] www.gottman.com/blog/the-magic-relationship-ratio-according-science/

[335] *The Rule of Saint Benedict,* Chapter II.

[336] *Regula Pastoralis* II.6; PL 77:38B (as translated in Barry, *Commentary on the Rule of Saint Benedict,* 139).

A small tree is gently tied with grass, not with wire, otherwise its bark will be injured and become stunted. Restrictions on a beginner should be gentle, too, and applied with kindness, so that he is not stunted spiritually.[337]

Nevertheless, St. John Chrysostom warned of the danger of being too gentle when correcting serious faults: "To always address one's disciples with mildness, even when they need severity, is not the part of a teacher but would be more the part of a corrupter and enemy."[338] Likewise, St. Basil the Great taught:

> There is an undeniable need to avenge those who are negligent of the divine commandments, lest we who are silent obtain the wrath of God along with them. Eli the High Priest was not silent to his sons about their transgression, but he failed to avenge or display the proper irritation against them.[339] Thus he provoked such divine wrath that his people and his sons were destroyed, the divine ark was taken by foreigners, and Eli himself died a bitter death.[340]

Many of the holy Fathers point out the danger of censuring with anger. St. Basil the Great wrote: "The superior should not administer a rebuke to wrongdoers when his own passions are aroused; for, by admonishing a brother with anger and indignation, he does not free him from his faults but involves himself in the error."[341] St. John of Sinai taught: "A fox found in the company of hens is an unseemly sight, but nothing is more unseemly than an enraged shepherd. The former agitates and destroys but hens, while the latter agitates and destroys rational souls."[342] In the same vein, Abba Macarius said: "If you are moved to anger in reproving somebody, you merely satisfy your own passion. Do not go lose your own self in order to save others."[343] Abba Dorotheos added to this: "No wise man destroys his own house in order to use the materials to build his neighbor's house,"[344] and: "It is totally foreign to a monk to become angry."[345] Moreover, as St. Joseph the Hesychast

---

[337] Elder Paisios of Mount Athos, *Athonite Fathers and Athonite Matters* (Souroti: Holy Convent of the Evangelist John the Theologian, 1993), 196–97.

[338] "Commentary on the Epistle of St. Paul to the Galatians," in *Nicene and Post-Nicene Fathers,* vol. 13 (Grand Rapids: Eerdmans Publishing Co., 1983), Chapter One, 1.

[339] Vid. 1 Sam. 2:22–25.

[340] As paraphrased by *The Monastic Rule of Iosif Volotsky,* New Revised Edition, trans. David M. Goldfrank (Kalamazoo: Cistercian Publications, 2000), 259. The precise words of St. Basil may be found in Wagner, *Sanit Basil: Ascetical Works,* vol. 9, 46–47.

[341] Wagner, *Saint Basil: Ascetical Works,* vol. 9, 327 (Question 50 in the *Long Rules*).

[342] Holy Transfiguration Monastery, *The Ladder of Divine Ascent,* 238.

[343] John Wortley, *The Alphabetical Sayings of the Desert Fathers* (New York: St. Vladimir's Seminary Press, 2014), 131 (Macarius 17).

[344] Scouteris, *Abba Dorotheos: Practical Teaching on the Christian Life,* 262.

[345] Ibid., 91.

observed, "I've never seen a person be corrected through anger but always through love; and then he will even make sacrifices."[346]

Thus, someone who has been corrected angrily is not going to make a permanent change of his behavior. At best he will behave properly only as long as he knows he is being watched; at worst, he will continue his harmful behavior out of spite.

At the end of his life, Abba Romanos revealed his secret of avoiding anger: When he was asked how to direct souls, he replied: "I cannot remember ever having told anyone to do something, before having resolved in my mind not to become angry, in case what I asked was not done. By this tactic, I was able to live peaceably with everyone at all times."[347]

When the abbot does get angry, he should not think that his position of authority prevents him from apologizing. Elder Ephraim learned this lesson after he witnessed St. Joseph the Hesychast apologizing to one of his disciples after getting angry with him. Elder Ephraim commented: "I acquired invaluable experience from this incident, so that in the future I would know that I should ask forgiveness even from my disciples."[348]

Blessed Augustine likewise believed that the superior should apologize after speaking angrily, but he also pointed out that this is unwise when dealing with younger monks. He wrote in his monastic rule:

> You must then avoid being too harsh in your words, and should they escape your lips, let those same lips not be ashamed to heal the wounds they have caused. But if the necessity of good order compels you to speak harshly in order to put minors in their place, then even if you think you have been unduly harsh in your language, you are not required to ask forgiveness lest, by practicing too great a humility toward those whose duty it is to defer to you, the authority to rule is undermined. However, you should still ask forgiveness from the Lord of all, Who knows with what deep affection you love even those whom you might happen to correct with undue severity.[349]

Elder Paisius of Sihla once explained to an abbot how important it is to know when and how to make corrections:

> There's a time for everything. There's a time for humility and a time for authority, a time for reproof and a time for comfort, a time for pardon and a time for boldness, a time for kindness and for sternness; that is, a time for all things. Sometimes it's fitting to show humility and call everyone brothers and sons in humility. At other times, when it's needed, it's proper to take and to show authority in the formation of someone, but

---

[346] Γέροντος Ἰωσὴφ τοῦ Ἡσυχαστοῦ, *Ἔκφρασις Μοναχικῆς Ἐμπειρίας*, ἔκδοσις τετάρτη, (Ἅγιον Ὄρος: Ἱερὰ Μονὴ Φιλοθέου, 1992), 62; see also Elder Joseph the Hesychast, *Monastic Wisdom* (Florence: St. Anthony's Greek Orthodox Monastery, 1998), 62.

[347] Chrysostomos, *The Evergetinos, Book IV,* 449.

[348] Ὁ Γέροντάς μου Ἰωσὴφ ὁ Ἡσυχαστὴς καὶ Σπηλαιώτης, Γέροντος Ἐφραίμ, 1η ἔκδοσις (Ἀθήνα: Ἱερὰ Μονὴ Φιλοθέου, 2008) 172; see also Elder Ephraim, *My Elder Joseph the Hesychast* (Florence: St. Anthony's Greek Orthodox Monastery, 2012), 191.

[349] Hugh of St. Victor, *Explanation of the Rule of St. Augustine*, 142.

never unto destruction. In times of consolation, it's also fitting to show kindness, and in times of severity, to show zeal toward each one. Also, it's necessary that the spiritual father judge rightly according to the canons.[350]

Corrections should always be done with love and compassion. St. Porphyrios of Kafsokalyvia taught: "Without love, prayer is of no benefit, advice is hurtful, and pointing out errors is harmful and destructive to the other person who senses whether we love him or not and reacts accordingly."[351] Fyodor Dostoyevsky observed: "Nothing is easier than to denounce the evildoer; nothing is more difficult than to understand him.... Let us not forget that the causes of human actions are usually immeasurably more complex and varied than our subsequent explanations of them."[352] Dostoyevsky also said through the mouth of Staretz Zosima:

> Above all, remember that you cannot be anyone's judge. No man on earth can judge a criminal until he understands that he himself is just as guilty as the man standing before him and that he may be more responsible than anyone else for the crime. Only when he has understood this can he become a judge. Absurd though it may sound, this is the truth.... There will be moments when you will feel perplexed, especially in the presence of human sin. You will ask yourself: "Must I combat it by force or try to overcome it by humble love?" Always choose humble love, always. Once you have chosen it, you will always have what you need to conquer the whole world. Loving humility is a powerful force, the most powerful, and there is nothing in the world to approach it.[353]

In the same spirit, Elder Arsenios Boca said: "It is better that your disciples love you rather than fear you, because fear engenders hypocrisy and lies, whereas love engenders truth."[354] Blessed Augustine basically agreed with this, although his approach was slightly more austere: "Let him [the abbot] uphold discipline while instilling fear. And though both are necessary, he should strive to be loved by you rather than feared, ever mindful that he must give an account of you to God."[355] Commenting on this statement of Blessed Augustine, Elder Aimilianos added:

> The saint is not doing away with fear. If a person is loved without inspiring fear, this means that he is not honorable and that his love is not God's kind of love but is human. A spiritual father's love is in the form of God's love; it is a love befitting God

---

[350] Bălan, *A Little Corner of Paradise,* 179–80.

[351] Holy Convent of the Life-giving Spring—Chrysopigi, *Wounded by Love: The Life and the Wisdom of Elder Porphyrios,* trans. John Raffan (Evia: Denise Harvey, 2005), 181.

[352] Fyodor Dostoyevsky, *The Idiot,* trans. Constance Black Garnett (New York: Dover, 1915), 484.

[353] Fyodor Dostoevsky, *The Brothers Karamazov,* trans. Andrew R. MacAndrew (New York: Bantam Classics, 1984), 429, 427.

[354] *Γεροντικὸ Ρουμάνων Πατέρων,* (Θεσσαλονίκη: Ὀρθόδοξος Κυψέλη, 2008), 207.

[355] St. Augustine of Hippo, *The Rule of Saint Augustine,* trans. Tarsicius J. van Bavel (United Kingdom: Image Books, 1986), ch. 7.

if it is coupled with fear towards him. Fear is an element that manifests on the one hand the authenticity of the elder and on the other hand the authenticity of disciple's obedience and love. Love towards God or towards the elder is inconceivable without the element of fear.[356]

This is why Abba Isidore the Priest taught: "Disciples must love as their fathers those who are truly their masters and fear them as their leaders; they should not lose their fear because of love, nor because of fear should love be obscured."[357]

A person in a position of spiritual authority should have motherly compassion. St. Ephraim the Syrian taught: "Have you been appointed an Abbot? Take care not to become proud. Before the brothers, with simplicity and humility, be as one of them. Keep in mind your former labors—that is, those to which you were assigned as a novice—and remember that these brothers are now at that stage of submission in which you were before. Therefore, be not heedless regarding their salvation, but look after them with motherly affection."[358] This is reminiscent of St. Seraphim of Sarov's counsel to an abbot that he should be more of a mother than a father to his disciples,[359] and of St. Gregory the Dialogist's advice: "Care must be taken that subjects know their church leader as a mother by his loving kindness, and as a father by his discipline."[360]

St. Theodore the Studite taught monks who were superiors:

> My children, make the appropriate concessions for the spiritual and bodily needs of the brethren … mixing benevolence with abruptness, gentleness with austerity, leniency with authoritativeness, meekness and sociability with modesty and a lack of bold familiarity—according to the character of each, according to what is suitable to each. For some need a goad (as the fathers teach), others a bridle; some a punishment, others forgiveness; and yet others reproving, and others overlooking.[361]

Thus, a prudent abbot will also know when *not* to make corrections. St. Gregory the Dialogist said: "Let him [i.e., the abbot] tolerantly pass over certain things as though not noticing them, yet not permit them to grow by passing over them."[362] Elder Ephraim intentionally

---

[356] Γέροντος Αἰμιλιανοῦ, *Νηπτικὴ Ζωὴ καὶ Ἀσκητικοὶ Κανόνες,* 348. St. Joseph the Hesychast inspired this mixture of love and fear in his disciples. As St. Ephraim of Katounakia related: "I've never felt more love and fear towards anyone else in the world than towards Elder Joseph" (*Γέροντας Ἐφραὶμ Κατουνακιώτης* [Ἅγιον Ὄρος, Ἱερὸν Ἡσυχαστήριον, «Ἅγιος Ἐφραίμ»], 39).

[357] Ward, *The Sayings of the Desert Fathers,* 107 (Isidore the Priest 5).

[358] Chrysostomos, *The Evergetinos, Book IV,* 452.

[359] Vid. Moore, Archimandrite Lazarus, *An Extraordinary Peace: St. Seraphim, Flame of Sarov* (Port Townsend: Anaphora Press, 2009), 232.

[360] *Regula Pastoralis* II.6; PL 77:38A (as translated in Barry, *Commentary on the Rule of Saint Benedict,* 143).

[361] Θεοδώρου Στουδίτου, *Μεγάλη Κατήχησις,* 233 (ὁμιλία 63).

[362] *Moralia* XXIV.25.54; CCSL 143B:1228 (as translated in Barry, *Commentary on the Rule of Saint Benedict,* 156).

chose not to correct the little things the other fathers did that displeased him. For example, one of the priests would cense the Arizonitissa icon without coming very close to it. Elder Ephraim told me that he considered this disrespectful, but since he didn't want to upset that priest by nitpicking, he chose not to correct him.

In general, it is more prudent to correct a person in private rather than publicly. St. John Chrysostom said: "Just as sores become more painful by being unbandaged and frequently exposed to cold air, so also the soul after having sinned, if in the presence of many it be rebuked for what it has done amiss, grows thereby more shameless. In order therefore that this might not take place, the word [of correction] administered its medicine to you covertly."[363] St. Isaac the Syrian likewise observed:

> A man who corrects his brother in his private chamber cures his evil; but a man who makes accusation against another in a public gathering worsens his wounds. He who cures his brother in secret makes manifest the strength of his love; but he who puts his brother to shame in the eyes of his companions gives a proof of the strength of his envy. A friend who rebukes another in secret is a wise physician; but he who wishes to cure in the eyes of many is in reality a reviler.[364]

4) Punishments

It is the responsibility of the abbot to assign penances and punishments to his disciples for their faults. As St. Fructuosus of Braga wrote in Spain in the seventh century in his *Rule for the Monastery of Compludo:*

> In all the excesses of the monks a suitable punishment must be applied according to the judgment of the abbot and the elders, giving attention to the type of fault, the age and character of the individual; it must be most diligently seen to that heavy punishment is not inflicted for lesser faults, or, on the other hand, that light and inconsequential punishment declared for the most serious offenses. The head of the abbey and his prior[365] must be continually known for ability to judge and weigh actions, for the sake of pious justice and commiseration, just as one takes care of the wound of a sick person in such a way as to cure rather than damage the injured member; for, just as priors judge the faults of those in their charge, so also will their wrongs be judged by God Himself.[366]

St. Easterwine had this kind of commiseration to such a great degree that "when he was compelled to reprove a fault [in his monastery], it was done with such tender sadness that

---

[363] "Against Publishing the Errors of the Brethren," The Nicene and Post-Nicene Fathers, vol. 9, *Chrysostom: On the Priesthood, Ascetic Treatises, Select Homilies and Letters, Homilies on the Statues,* Philip Schaff, ed. (New York: Christian Literature Company, 1895), 237.

[364] Holy Transfiguration Monastery, *The Ascetical Homilies of Saint Isaac the Syrian,* 363–64 (Homily 48).

[365] In Western monasticism a dean was a senior monk in charge of ten younger monks and novices, whereas the prior was the second-in-command at a monastery.

[366] Barlow, *The Fathers of the Church: Iberian Fathers,* vol. 63, 168.

the culprit felt himself incapable of any new offence which should bring a cloud over the benign brightness of that beloved face."[367]

Monastic regulations throughout the centuries included detailed lists of punishments for various transgressions committed by the monks. For example, the *Regula Orientalis* gives the following sequence of punishments:

> When a fault has been discovered, let him who is found at fault be corrected discreetly by the abbot. But if this is not sufficient for his amendment, let him be corrected by a few seniors. And if he has not amended himself, let him be chastised in front of everybody. But if he will not have amended at this, let him be excommunicated and let him not eat anything. If not even this profits him, let him be placed last after all the rest, regardless of his previous position, in the order of singing the psalms. But if he persists in his perversity, let even the right of singing the Psalms be taken from him. If this shame still does not move him, let him be held back from associating with the brothers, so that he may take part neither in meals nor in the office, nor may any of the junior brothers speak with him. He will be so constrained for as long a time as the nature of the fault the demands, according to the judgment of the abbot and the seniors, and until he humbles himself, repenting his fault from his heart, and seeks pardon for his errors before all.[368]

St. Nectarios of Aegina wrote the following list of punishments to choose from in his charter for his nuns in Aegina:

1) Advice or admonition in front of the sisterhood (preceded by the same in front of the Board of Trustees or the Abbatial Council).
2) Prohibition of eating at the Common Meal, and isolation in one's cell (according to the prevailing custom in the Holy Mountain).
3) Saying prayer-ropes (according to the prevailing custom in the Holy Mountain).
4) Prohibition of associating and talking (partial or entire) with others, reduction of food to as little as half of the regular amount, and prohibition of receiving Communion.
5) Cessation from one's monastic duties.
6) Removal from the regular hierarchical order to the basest position, and being sent away to stay in a monastery dependency or other property under supervision.
7) Expulsion from the office of Trustee or Eldress.
8) Temporary expulsion from the monastery for two to twenty-four months.
9) Expulsion from the Abbacy.
10) Permanent expulsion.

---

[367] Sabine Baring-Gould, *The Lives of the Saints* (London: John C. Nimmo, 1877), 172. St. Easterwine (or Eosterwine) lived in the seventh century and was the second Anglo-Saxon abbot of Wearmouth in England.

[368] Franklin, *Early Monastic Rules,* 79.

11) Being sent off to the proper ecclesiastical court through the proper Metropolitan for removal of the monastic garment.

St. Basil the Great advised: "Let the punishments of him who is condemned for any fault be suited to the measure of his sin: [for example,] to be prevented from taking part in psalmody, to be excluded from the common prayers, or from participation in meals; wherein the monk who is entrusted with the oversight of discipline will assign the punishment in proportion to the greatness of the fault."[369] Similarly, *The Rule of Macarius* ordered: "If, however, someone should murmur, be contentious, or resist anything with a will contrary to commands, after he has been suitably reproved according to the judgment of the superior, let him be excluded as long as the nature of the fault demands it and until he humbles himself by doing penance."[370] Commenting on this rule, Elder Aimilianos explained how such punishments are actually given out of love:

> What this rule dictates is not harshness but respect for the person's freedom. If I [as abbot] assign a task to someone, and he starts objecting: "I can't do this; I don't want to do that; this other thing tires me," if I give in, I will always have to give in because the brother will have learned to follow a new path. But by following this new path, he enters into the way of sorrow, darkness, depression. His soul and heart become a wreck, and he loses the freedom of his spirit, the ease in his spiritual journey. In order to avoid making him miserable and to secure his freedom, we treat him like this so that he will either live the way of truth or get up and leave. If he leaves, he will realize his mistake and feel the bitterness of his disobedience as Eve did.[371]

Some punishments in monastic rules were extremely harsh. For example, St. Pachomios said that monks who habitually deceive their brothers should be beaten with twigs and then be given only bread and water until they correct their behavior![372] Following the example of St. Theodore the Studite,[373] St. Athanasios of Athos admitted that he had a prison "in which, after many warnings and admonitions, the disobedient and refractory brothers are confined, put on a diet of dry food and disciplined in virtue."[374]

St. Isidore of Seville believed that the following faults merited abstention from Communion for three days:

> That person is guilty of a lesser fault who loves to be idle, comes rather late for the Office, a conference or a meal, laughs in choir or wastes time in stories; who leaves the Office or work without necessity and goes outside, loves sluggishness and sleep, swears rather often, is given to much speaking, begins to do some work of service

---

[369] Clarke, *The Ascetic Works of St. Basil,* 138.

[370] Franklin, *Early Monastic Rules,* 37.

[371] Γέροντος Αἰμιλιανοῦ, *Νηπτικὴ Ζωὴ καὶ Ἀσκητικοὶ Κανόνες,* 383.

[372] Πετρακάκου, *Μοναχικοὶ θεσμοί,* 120 (M. Παχωμίου «Κανόνες»).

[373] Vid. Thomas and Hero, *Byzantine Monastic Foundation Documents,* 108.

[374] Ibid., 225.

enjoined on him without obtaining a blessing, or on completing a task does not ask for a blessing; who negligently or tardily fulfills a task enjoined, or accidentally breaks some vessel or damages some small object, uses a book negligently, goes off somewhere on his own for a moment, secretly receives a letter or any kind of gift from someone, or on receiving a letter hides it and answers it without the abbot's consent; who sees or speaks with any relatives or with seculars without the order of a senior, is disobedient to a senior or answers him disrespectfully, and does not restrain his tongue with regard to a senior; who is lewd in speech, tends to unseemly gloating, jokes and laughs a lot; who speaks, prays or eats with an excommunicated person, or does not reveal a nocturnal illusion to his father. These and like faults are to be amended by a three days' excommunication.[375]

Several monastic rules advocate corporal punishment, but the approach used by Manuel, Bishop of Stroumitza, in his rules for the Eleousa Monastery in 11th-century Byzantium seems more appropriate for contemporary times. He advised the abbot: "Do not readily expel from the monastery those who perhaps have made a false step over something, but whip them not with a strap and rod but with a spiritual penalty."[376] Likewise, St. Theodore the Studite disapproved of corporal punishments but chose instead to reprimand monks publicly when they broke vessels.[377]

The *Rule of the Master*[378] explained why corporal punishments are to be avoided:

It is right that one who sins should repent in his heart, and not be physically whipped for it, because we live under the soul's rule and not in the body's service. Therefore, since the soul rules and the body serves, it is evident that a misdeed of the ruler is greater than that of the servant. So where there is understanding of correction, the thorns of sin must be purged from the root of the heart by excommunication,[379] since the limbs of the body should not unjustly suffer punishment for a fault not its own when, without its consent, sin has been imposed upon it by the heart's command.[380]

St. Benedict implemented the following form of punishment: "Whoever is excommunicated for graver faults from the oratory and the table, let him, at the time that the Work of God is celebrated in the oratory, lie stretched, face down in silence before the door of the

---

[375] Isidore of Seville, *Regula monachorum,* rule 16 (PL 103:568C–569B).

[376] Thomas and Hero, *Byzantine Monastic Foundation Documents,* 183.

[377] Vid. Κωνσταντῖνος Νικολάου Στεφανίδης, «Ἡ Θεολογία τῆς Κοινοβιακῆς Ζωῆς στὶς Κατηχήσεις τοῦ Ἁγίου Θεοδώρου Στουδίτου» (PhD diss., Ἀριστοτέλειο Πανεπιστήμιο Θεσσαλονίκης, 2010), 49.

[378] The "Rule of the Master" (*Regula Magistri*) was probably composed in the early sixth century near Rome. It was based on the rule of St. Benedict but is much longer.

[379] The term "excommunication" in this text does not mean being deprived of the ability to participate in the Church, nor does it mean exclusion from Holy Communion, but it means being punished with a temporary isolation from the others.

[380] Eberle, *The Rule of the Master,* 158.

oratory at the feet of all who pass out."[381] Similarly, St. Athanasios of Athos would punish his monks by making them "stand in the narthex, and after the dismissal [of the church service] would order them to prostrate themselves before each of the brethren, saying, 'Forgive me.'"[382] This tradition is still kept in some places on Mount Athos, with the difference that in contemporary practice, the monk at fault would be on his knees without making prostrations to each person passing by, and instead of saying merely, "Forgive me," he would say: "Fathers and brothers, forgive me, for I have … [gotten angry, talked idly, been selfish, etc.]." Another contemporary Athonite punishment is for the monk at fault to stand in trapeza (i.e., the refectory) holding a large prayer-rope and silently say the Jesus prayer for the duration of the meal.

Ideally, the monk who is at fault should have so much repentance that he will volunteer to be given a punishment, as in the old days. As one historian wrote about ancient Palestinian monasticism: "Discipline in any particular monastery was not the result of a system of punishments determined by the Rule, but rather issued from the free choice of each individual monk."[383] St. John of Sinai mentioned two examples of this in *The Ladder:*

> Often they applied to the great judge, I mean the shepherd, that angel among men, with requests and begged him to put irons and chains on their hands and neck, and to manacle their legs in the stocks, and not to set them free until the tomb received them, or not even the tomb….[384]

> Then when he saw that the doctor [i.e., the abbot] did not wish to make too severe an incision (because he deserved sympathy), he flung himself on the ground, embraced my feet, moistened them with abundant tears, and asked to be shut in the Prison.[385]

Nevertheless, the abbot must take care when administering punishments, so that the true spirit of monasticism is not replaced by discipline. There are four potential negative repercussions of resorting to discipline via threats and punishments in order to force disciples to do one's will:

> 1) It is foreign to the spirit of true Christian liberty;[386] As St. Sophrony of Essex warned: "If the abbot and other elders in the monastery are ever obliged to have recourse to 'discipline' to constrain the brethren, this is a sure sign of

---

[381] *Rule of St. Benedict,* Chapter XLIV.

[382] Richard P. H. Greenfield and Alice-Mary Talbot, *Holy Men of Mount Athos,* Dumbarton Oaks Medieval Library (Cambridge: Harvard University Press, 2016), 276–77.

[383] Patrich, *Sabas, Leader of Palestinian Monasticism,* 267.

[384] Holy Transfiguration Monastery, *The Ladder of Divine Ascent,* 59.

[385] Ibid., 62.

[386] See section "Obedience and Freedom" on pages 117–125 for the difference between healthy and unhealthy monastic discipline.

the debasement of monasticism and, possibly, of a total forgetting of its purpose and essence."[387]

2) Punishing indiscriminately and especially without love runs the risk of weakening the abbot's connection with his disciples.

3) Punishments are unlikely to effect a permanent change in one's disciples, since their motivation to conform would be extrinsic. As Mahatma Gandhi observed: "Victory attained by violence is tantamount to a defeat, for it is momentary."[388]

4) The reason why people in authority need to resort to threats and punishments is often because they have failed to instruct sufficiently those who are under their guidance.

When Elder Ephraim was younger, he gave somewhat severe punishments. In his later years, however, he rarely punished us. He learned from experience that extrinsically motivating his disciples through punishments might temporarily make them do *what* he wanted, but this approach would not bring about a permanent inner change in them to make them do something for the reasons *why* he wanted. For this reason, instead of resorting to punishments he would primarily try to help his disciples to understand why their behavior was harmful. Sometimes, however, he would still give punishments in conjunction with advice. This approach is supported by recent studies that have shown that the most effective way to change undesirable behavior is to combine intrinsic with extrinsic motivation.[389]

5) His Authority

Following the traditions of Orthodox monasticism, the abbot of the monastery is charged with the complete authority and responsibility for directing the brotherhood and for making all spiritual and material decisions of the monastery. As St. Athanasios of Athos put it: "After the superior's promotion and installation I firmly desire that he should have *absolute authority* [emphasis added] and dominion in every respect in both spiritual and corporal matters. He must not be disturbed or impeded by anyone at all, especially as he is carrying out his duties well, in a manner pleasing to God, and in the spirit of God."[390] Similarly, St. Neophytos, who established Docheiariou Monastery on the Holy Mountain, wrote: "I left you behind as my successor by the providence of God and you are obligated

---

[387] For the entire quotation, see the text referenced in footnote #675 on page 122.

[388] *Satyagraha Leaflet,* no. 13, May 3, 1919.

[389] Vid. Kerry Patterson, Joseph Grenny, David Maxfield, Ron McMillan, and Al Switzler, *Change Anything: The New Science of Personal Success* (New York: Grand Central Publishing, 2011), 108–9.

[390] Thomas and Hero, *Byzantine Monastic Foundation Documents,* 278.

after my passing to become lord and autocrat of the monastery of Docheiariou and to have control of all the affairs and properties."[391]

St. Christodoulos of Patmos also wrote something similar in his testament regarding his successor:

> Let our spiritual brother Theodosios have complete rule over the monastery, receiving from me full and unconditional authority, as I, the said monk Christodoulos, received it from our most powerful and sacred emperor, with this one proviso, that he is not to introduce any of his relatives into the monastery. In everything else he has full authority, within strict monastic observance, taking to himself a rigorous and discreet monk, whomever he chooses and God may send, to instruct him in the spiritual life. He is not to meet with any opposition, either from the monks or from this instructor we spoke of, but have all the authority and [right of] dominion and inalienable ownership of a master who cannot be removed.[392]

Likewise, the 11th-century typikon of the Monastery of Petritzonitissa decreed:

> All that has been laid down by the superior is law, and those subordinate to him must pay attention to all his utterances as to the divine laws themselves and consider none unimportant or make distinctions in his utterances or contradict him or oppose him in any other way. For all these things are proof of disobedience and independence and furthermore of indiscipline which is the confusion and destruction of obedience and discernment, and just judgment for these actions will come on those who practice such things.... For a monk is not allowed to utter anything in the presence of the superior other than "I have sinned, Father, pardon me."[393]

St. Basil the Great believed that democratic rule would ruin monastic tradition,[394] and he taught that the monastery should be governed by a single person rather than by several.[395] St. Benedict also wanted the abbot to have complete authority over the monastery. He disapproved of the abbot sharing the authority with someone else who is second in command (i.e., a "prior") because this situation could lead to "envy, discord, slander, quarrels, jealousy, and disorders."[396] He concluded: "We foresee, therefore, that for the preservation of

---

[391] Ibid., 1307.

[392] Thomas and Hero, *Byzantine Monastic Foundation Documents,* 595.

[393] Ibid., 538–39.

[394] "The brethren will not adopt a popular system of government as it were, to the abrogation of the rule and traditional discipline" (Wagner, *Saint Basil: Ascetical Works,* vol. 9, 322 [Question 45 in the *Long Rules*]).

[395] "There should be one [εἷς] leader appointed to command in this admirable way of life" (ibid., 210). St. Basil writes in Question 35 of the *Long Rules* that collective rule in a monastery would only work if each one of the superiors is of a lofty spiritual caliber. But since he said that finding more than one such person in the same brotherhood "is not an easy thing and we have never known it to happen [in the 4th century]," it is even less likely to happen in the 21st century when the spiritual level of monks is much lower than it was in the days of St. Basil.

[396] *Rule of St. Benedict,* Chapter LXV. St. Smaragdus of Saint-Mihiel (in ninth-century Gaul) in his commentary on this rule astutely observed that the friction might not even be between the abbot and the prior

peace and charity it is best that the government of the monastery should depend [only] on the will of the abbot."[397] In the event, however, that a monastery does have a prior, St. Benedict ordered: "Let the prior reverently do what his abbot hath enjoined on him, doing nothing against the will or the direction of the abbot."[398] The *Regula Orientalis* states: "Let all the brothers look to his [i.e., the abbot's] governance, doing nothing without his advice and decision. The abbot, who looks after the needs of the monastery, shall freely make decisions on all matters within the monastery."[399] Similarly, St. Waldebert in his rule for nuns commanded that the prioress should be in complete obedience to the abbess.[400]

Yet, despite the abbot's "absolute authority," he should discuss serious issues with the senior fathers before making his decisions, as is evident from the monastic rules of St. Basil the Great,[401] St. Pachomios,[402] St. Benedict,[403] St. Theodore the Studite,[404] and St. Paisius

---

but between their followers: "Quarrels and slander, and all these things, are produced between prior and abbot, especially through their followers" (Barry, *Commentary on the Rule of Saint Benedict,* 512).

[397] *Rule of St. Benedict,* Chapter LXV.

[398] Ibid.

[399] Franklin, *Early Monastic Rules,* 61. The *Regula Orentalis* is a collection of monastic rules from fifth-century Orthodox Gaul.

[400] "She [i.e., the prioress] must be one on whom the abbess may rely that she will in no way deviate from what she commanded; but in all things be subject and bound by the orders of her seniors; she will do nothing against the will of the abbess or order anything to be so done, but do all after asking her; according to what is written, 'Ask thy father and He will show thee; ask thy elders and they will tell thee' (Deut. 32:7)" (J. A. McNamara and J. Halborg, *The Rule of a Certain Father to the Virgins,* chapter 2).

[401] "Generally speaking, the Superior must remember what the Holy Scripture says: 'Do everything with counsel'" (Clarke, *The Ascetic Works of St. Basil,* 269, Rule 104). See also Κωνσταντίνου Μουρατίδη, Ἡ Μοναχικὴ Ὑπακοὴ ἐν τῇ Ἀρχαίᾳ Ἐκκλησίᾳ (Ἀθήνα, 1956), 87.

[402] "He [the superior] should not neglect always to consult the elders to be able to discern his thoughts" (Πετρακάκου, *Μοναχικοὶ θεσμοί,* 118 [Μ. Παχωμίου «Κανόνες»]).

[403] "Whenever weighty matters are to be transacted in the monastery, let the Abbot call together the whole community, and make known the matter which is to be considered. Having heard the brethren's views, let him weigh the matter with himself and do what he thinketh best. It is for this reason, however, we said that all should be called for counsel, because the Lord often revealeth to the younger what is best. Let the brethren, however, give their advice with humble submission, and let them not presume stubbornly to defend what seemeth right to them, for it must depend rather on the Abbot's will, so that all obey him in what he considereth best.... If, however, matters of less importance, having to do with the welfare of the monastery, are to be treated of, let him use the counsel of the seniors only" (Chapter III of the Rule of St. Benedict of Nursia [c. 480–547]). St. Donatus of Besançon in the seventh century repeated these counsels almost verbatim in his *Regula ad Virgines* ("Rules for Nuns").

[404] St. Theodore the Studite advised the abbot: "You shall not make or do anything according to your own opinion whether regarding a spiritual or a physical matter of any kind. First, you should not act without the advice and prayer of your lord and [spiritual] father; second, without the advice of those who are foremost in knowledge and prudence regarding the issue in question. For there is need of one advisor or perhaps two, three, or more as the fathers have instructed us and as we have discussed in detail" (Thomas and Hero, *Byzantine Monastic Foundation Documents,* 79).

Velichkovsky,[405] the *Rule of the Master*,[406] and following the Charter of the Holy Mountain, which calls for an Abbatial Council to help govern the monastery. Even St. Athanasios of Athos—who, when including some rules of St. Theodore the Studite for his typikon, noticeably omitted his teaching requiring the abbot to consult the other fathers—wrote: "In my own case, now, I have absolute dominion, so that not even one person can gainsay my command, and yet I have no intention of leaving my successor behind without consulting the brothers."[407]

This approach of consultative rule not only safeguards the abbot from making human mistakes, but it also increases the satisfaction of the fathers whose opinions are respected and taken into consideration. St. Anthony of Siya grasped this concept, which is why he exhorted the abbot who would be his successor "to judge concerning monastery matters with all the brethren at trapeza, and to do nothing without taking counsel of them."[408]

The degree to which the abbot will seek the counsel of the other monks should be directly proportional to their wisdom and expertise in a particular issue. Abba Dorotheos cited the verse in Proverbs: "those who have no guidance fall like leaves, but there is safety in much counsel"[409] to explain that this "does not mean taking counsel from all and sundry, but clearly from someone in whom he has full confidence."[410]

Nevertheless, it is evident from the aforementioned patristic references (in the preceding paragraphs) that even though the abbot should seek the advice of the senior fathers, the authority to make most decisions still belongs to him alone. Thus, it is his

---

[405] "[The abbot] may begin no action without the advice of the brethren who are experienced in spirituality and searching the Scriptures. If something happens which must be announced before an entire *sobor* [i.e., council] of the community, the whole *sobor* acts upon it with common knowledge and consensus. In such a way, peace, unity of mind and an indestructible bond of love are maintained among the brethren" (Chetverikov, *Starets Paisii Velichkovskii,* 134).

[406] Regarding the abbot seeking counsel the *Rule of the Master* states: "Whatever the abbot wishes to do or have done for the good of the monastery is to be done with the counsel of the brothers. When all the brothers have been called together, let there be a general discussion about the good of the monastery. However, it is not on their own initiative or against the will of abbatial authority that the brothers happen to engage in deliberation, but by the command and direction of the abbot. The counsel of all is to be sought because sometimes there are as many diverse opinions as there are people—all at once the best advice may well be given by one from whom it was least expected, and this may redound most to the common good—and from the many opinions the one to choose will be easy to find. But if none of the brothers can give apt counsel, then let the abbot, after explaining his reasons, decide as he wills, and it is right that the members follow the head" (Eberle, *The Rule of the Master,* 114).

[407] Thomas and Hero, *Byzantine Monastic Foundation Documents,* 255. The same sentiment was expressed also by Emperor Michael VIII Palaiologos in his *Typikon for the Monastery of the Archangel Michael:* "Even though the superior, because of his authority, is allowed to do what he wants without the consent of the others, still it is not a good idea, for it causes problems for many" (ibid., 1226).

[408] I. M. Kontsevich, *The Northern Thebaid,* (Platina: St. Herman of Alaska Brotherhood, 1975), 153–54.

[409] Prov. 11:14.

[410] Wheeler, *Dorotheos of Gaza: Discourses and Sayings,* 123.

opinion that will resolve disagreements. As Elder Aimilianos expressed in the *Regulations of the Holy Cenobium of the Annunciation*: "The blessing of the Elder or the Abbess shall be the force which maintains the monastery, overriding individual will, rightly dispensing the word and judgment of God and ensuring unity."[411]

Fr. Theocletos of Dionysiou believed that the reason why the Charter of the Holy Mountain gave the authority for making decisions to the Abbatial Council instead of to the abbot was because of "the decline in monasticism during the second decade of the twentieth century. In other words," he continued, "the Athonite authors took into consideration their present reality and decreed rules for the operation of the Athonite society with worldly criteria, which are necessary for every epoch that distances itself from genuine monastic life."[412]

Yet it would be erroneous to suppose that entrusting governmental authority to the Abbatial Council instead of to the abbot is a twentieth-century innovation. On the contrary, this innovation began in the last two centuries of the Byzantine Empire. For example, the typikon of St. John the Forerunner in Serres written in 1332 obliges the superior to govern in collaboration with four brothers, both for spiritual and temporal affairs.[413] The typikon of Emperor Manuel II Palaiologos for the monasteries of Mount Athos in 1406 formalized the governing role of the "preeminent monks" into an administrative council of fifteen of the leading monks and the superior. They were to meet every day or two to review the performance of the various officials of the monastery, and they were to resolve disputed

---

[411] Elder Aimilianos, *The Authentic Seal,* 175.

[412] Hieromonk Joseph of Philotheou, however, believed that the real reason why the Charter of the Holy Mountain gave that authority to the Abbatial Council was not because of a decline in monasticism but because centuries of monastic experience on the Holy Mountain had led the fathers to this concession as a practical way of preserving order. He said that a superior who founds a community can easily (and should) exercise absolute authority over the disciples who come to join him. But when a superior is chosen from an existing brotherhood to govern the rest of the fathers (and especially when a person outside the brotherhood is chosen to do so), it is only natural that they will not be willing to entrust him with absolute authority. Therefore, to avoid chaos and interminable quarrelling, the Athonite fathers deemed it wise to entrust an Abbatial Council with the authority to govern the monastery.

[413] "When aboard a ship in the middle of the sea waves a storm arises, and when the sea grows wild, stirring up on high the waves so that the boat is tossed about perilously, it is totally impossible for the helmsman alone to rescue the ship unharmed unless he should have the assistance and help of the sailors.... Now in the same manner, it is not in the natural order for the superior of the monastery to do anything right or to set affairs in order unless he has other assistants under him.... I decree that there be four brothers with this superior.... Together with the superior, these shall have the license, authority, and power to examine and judge all of the officials.... In addition, the superior will make use of these advisors both with regard to all spiritual matters as well as with regard to the most important temporal affairs. With their advice, he will deal with these issues. They, likewise, will remind the superior if something arises which ought to be set straight.... With one accord, they should unite in administering and improving the monastery, not in a manner which focuses on the spiritual aspect and on the things pleasing to God, [but which looks also] to the physical realities" (Thomas and Hero, *Byzantine Monastic Foundation Documents,* 1607–8).

issues by majority vote.[414] However, the compilers of *Byzantine Monastic Foundation Documents* made the following comments on this: "Collaborative rule had been popular from time to time in Byzantium,"[415] but "the notion of collaborative government was never carried to such an extreme (i.e., decision-making by majority vote) in the rest of our documents [which include all Byzantine monastic typika from the seventh to the fifteenth century] as it is here [i.e., in the typikon of Emperor Manuel II]."[416]

Christ clearly indicated how a Christian leader is to exercise authority: "Ye know that they which are thought to rule over the Gentiles exercise lordship over them, and their great ones exercise authority upon them. But it shall not be so among you, but whosoever will be great among you shall be your servant, and whosoever of you will be the chiefest shall be slave of all. For even the Son of Man came not to be served but to serve, and to give His life as a ransom for many."[417] St. Basil the Great uses the words of St. Paul: "Let a man so account of us, as of ministers of Christ and stewards of the mysteries of God"[418] to show that the abbot "will not exercise his knowledge as his private possession in a spirit of authority, but will fulfil it with fear and trembling towards God as an act of service to God and of care for souls bought by the blood of Christ."[419] This is why Konstantinos Mouratidis concludes: "In terms of the internal organization [of the monastery] the abbot is not the bearer of his own authority—that is, he does not operate *ipso jure*—but he has representative authority."[420]

Thus, it is not the abbot who is the head of a monastery but Christ. As St. Basil taught: "All we who are united in the one hope of our calling are one body with Christ as our Head."[421] In the same spirit, St. Pachomios said: "Just as a dead man does not say to other dead men, 'I am your head,' likewise I never considered myself the head of the brethren,

---

[414] "Everything affecting the monastery should be done with the council of the leading monks and the superior.... It would be right to have nothing affecting the monastery determined without the counsel of the leading monks. Everything, in fact, should be done with the knowledge, intention and approval of them and of the superior.... These councillors should come together for a meeting each day if possible, and definitely every two days. Together with the superior they should deliberate about what must be done; they should examine the services of the monastery and how they are provided by the appointed officials.... If there is any disagreement among them concerning what has to be done, the majority of votes should prevail" (Thomas and Hero, *Byzantine Monastic Foundation Documents*, 1620).

[415] Ibid., 1498.

[416] Ibid., 1614.

[417] Mk. 10:42–45.

[418] 1 Cor. 4:1.

[419] Clarke, *The Ascetic Works of St. Basil,* 298 (Rule 184 in the *Shorter Rules*).

[420] Μουρατίδη, Ἡ Ὑπακοὴ ἐν τῇ Ἀρχαίᾳ Ἐκκλησίᾳ, 81.

[421] Wagner, *Saint Basil: Ascetical Works,* vol. 9 (Question 7 in the *Long Rules*), 249.

but only God is."[422] St. Basil the Great also taught that the brethren are equals with the abbot and that the abbot should imitate the humility of Christ: "Superiors, therefore, should be the first to make of themselves an exact model of Him by observing the standard of humility handed down by our Lord Jesus Christ.... If the Lord was not ashamed to minister to His own servants ... what must we do to our equals [ὁμοτίμοις] that we may deem to have attained the imitation of Him?"[423]

St. Theodore the Studite furthered this concept and wrote in his rules for the superior: "It is necessary for you rather to dedicate yourself spiritually as a slave to your brothers of the same spirit, even though when appearing in public you are reckoned their lord and teacher."[424] It was because St. Theodore viewed himself "as a slave to his brothers of the same spirit" that he humbly sought their prayers[425] and would typically begin his catecheses with the phrase, "My fathers, brethren, and children."

The Desert Fathers warn the abbot not to desire authority over the brethren:

> If, with fear of God and humility, one commands a brother to complete some task, then his words, coming from God, make the brother eagerly obey and fulfill the command. If, however, someone motivated not by the fear of God but desires to command authority over a brother, then God, Who knows the secret dispositions of the heart, will not inspire him to obey or do it. For everything done for God's sake is evident, as is everything done autocratically. Autocratic commands are full of anger and disturbance, which show that they are from the evil one.[426]

A further problem with autocratic commands is on a practical level: the larger a hierarchical organization is (whether it be a monastery, a company, or a military unit), the less possible it becomes for the authority to be in touch with the details of a situation or a task. As Captain David Marquet explains: "Those at the top have all the authority and none of the information [about the details]. Those at the bottom have all the information and none of the authority. Not until those without information relinquish their control can an organization run better, smoother, and faster and reach its maximum potential."[427] In other words,

---

[422] Μουρατίδη, *Ἡ Ὑπακοὴ ἐν τῇ Ἀρχαίᾳ Ἐκκλησίᾳ*, 82. In fact, St. Pachomios not only did not view himself as the head of the brethren, but he even behaved as their servant to such an extreme that some of them treated him with contempt (vid. Veilleux, *Pachomian Koinonia: The Life of St. Pachomius*, vol. 1, 431–32).

[423] Βασιλείου τοῦ Μεγάλου, *Ἀσκητικὰ Α΄*, ΕΠΕ 8, 370–71; see also Wagner, *Saint Basil: Ascetical Works*, vol. 9, 319–20 (Question 43 in the *Long Rules*).

[424] Thomas and Hero, *Byzantine Monastic Foundation Documents*, 77.

[425] "As for me—as you see—I am poor and destitute of virtues, possessing nothing worthy of emulation to inspire you to do good. I talk about improving, and I yearn to be corrected. May this happen through the prayers of my father and of your father and also by your own supplications; for I believe that they work towards my salvation.... I am supported by your prayers" (Θεοδώρου Στουδίτου, *Μεγάλη Κατήχησις*, 209, ὁμιλία 55). Elder Ephraim also frequently asked us to pray for him.

[426] Παύλου Μοναχοῦ, *Εὐεργετινός*, τόμος Δ΄, 628; Chrysostomos, *The Evergetinos, Book IV*, 448.

[427] Simon Sinek, *Leaders Eat Last* (New York: Penguin Random House, 2014), 180.

the more an authority tries to micromanage his subordinates, the more likely it is that mistakes will happen. A further problem with micromanaging is that it decreases morale in the subordinates by disconnecting them from taking responsibility for their actions. Captain Marquet even went as far as to say: "The goal of a leader is to give no orders. Leaders are to provide direction and intent and allow others to figure out what to do and how to get there."[428] It is worth pondering to what degree this approach may be implemented in a monastery.

6) Governing Souls

The most challenging task for the abbot is to govern the souls entrusted to his care and to form Christ in them. As St. Neilos the Ascetic said: "Of all things, the governing of souls is the most toilsome."[429] This is "the art of arts and the science of sciences," in the words of St. Gregory the Theologian.[430] St. Symeon the New Theologian warned abbots from his own experience: "In this work [of the abbacy] you will have no rest for your body, no enjoyment. Your nights and days alike will be spent in concern for the souls entrusted to you, lest a single one of them become the prey of wild beasts ... lest the one mind [of the community] become many."[431]

The abbot is called to lay down his life for his disciples. St. Theodore the Studite told his monks: "Since I the wretched and unworthy one have been entrusted with this care of protecting you, I am obliged to lay down my lowly soul till bloodshed for the sake of your common salvation. For this is the characteristic—according to the words of the Lord[432]—of a good and true shepherd.... It is my duty to imitate God [i.e., Christ], whereas it is yours to imitate the Apostles [i.e., His disciples]; He loved and was loved so much that His holy disciples shed their own blood—in resemblance of Him—for the sake of confessing His name."[433] St. Basil the Great wrote that the superior should have the disposition towards the brethren "'as when a nurse cherisheth her children'[434] desiring to impart to each what

---

[428] Ibid., 183.

[429] Constantine Cavarnos, *The Philokalia, A Second Volume of Selected Readings,* (Boston: Institute for Byzantine and Modern Greek Studies, 2009), 134. Likewise, St. Theodore the Studite said: "My service [as abbot] is not trivial but arduous and difficult to bear.... I must toil and struggle in reminding my lords and fathers [i.e., the other monks] to do what is proper" (Θεοδώρου Στουδίτου, *Μεγάλη Κατήχησις,* 168 [ὁμιλία 44]).

[430] PG 35:425.

[431] *Symeon the New Theologian: Discourses,* trans. C. J. de Catanzaro, Classics of Western Spirituality (New York: Paulist Press, 1980), 221.

[432] Vid. Jn. 10:11.

[433] Θεοδώρου Στουδίτου, *Μεγάλη Κατήχησις,* 148 (ὁμιλία 38) καὶ 252 (ὁμιλία 69).

[434] 1 Thes. 2:7.

pleases God and benefits all in common, not only the Gospel of God but also his own soul, according to the commandment of our Lord and God Jesus Christ Who said: 'A new commandment I give unto you, that ye love one another, even as I have loved you.'[435] 'Greater love hath no man than this, that a man lay down his life for his friends.'[436],[437]

Even harder than guiding each soul individually is to guide the brotherhood collectively by establishing a *modus operandi* in the monastery that encourages the desired behaviors. A simple example of failing to accomplish this would be in regard to resolving differences between the fathers: If the abbot fails to implement the wise advice attributed to Phocylides, "Do not pass a judgment before you have heard the word of both parties,"[438] and makes the very common error of being biased in favor of whoever tells him his own version of the disagreement first, the fathers will soon learn that whoever finds the abbot first will be vindicated. As a result, after two fathers have an argument, both will "race" to present their side to the abbot first. An alternative way of dealing with disagreements between the fathers would be to use the Native American "talking stick."[439]

---

[435] Jn. 13:34.

[436] Jn. 15:13.

[437] Clarke, *The Ascetic Works of St. Basil,* 267 (Rule 98 in the *Shorter Rules*).

[438] P. W. van der Horst, *The Sentences of Pseudo-Phocylides* (Leiden: E. J. Brill, 1978), 173. The *Constitutions of the Holy Apostles* rephrased this maxim as a warning: "It is a dangerous thing to judge without hearing both sides" (*Ante-Nicene Fathers,* Vol. 7: *Lactantius, Venantius, Asterius, Victorinus, Dionysius, Apostolic Teaching and Constitutions, 2 Clement, Early Liturgies,* Alexander Roberts and James Donaldson, ed. [New York: Christian Literature Company, 1886], 405).

[439] Stephen Covey explains the talking stick as follows: "Whenever people meet together [to discuss a matter], the Talking Stick [which instead of a stick could be any designated object] is present. Only the person holding the Talking Stick is permitted to speak. As long as you have the Talking Stick, you alone may speak, until you are satisfied that you are understood. Others are not permitted to make their own points, argue, agree or disagree. All they may do is attempt to understand you and then articulate that understanding. They may need to restate your point to make sure you feel understood, or you may just simply feel that they understand. As soon as you feel understood, it is your obligation to pass the Talking Stick to the next person and then to work to make him feel understood. As he makes his points, you have to listen, restate and empathize until he feels truly understood. This way, all of the parties involved take responsibility for one hundred percent of the communication, both speaking and listening. Once each of the parties feels understood, an amazing thing usually happens. Negative energy dissipates, contention evaporates, mutual respect grows, and people become creative. New ideas emerge. Third alternatives appear…. Many may hesitate to buy into this process because it seems a little pedestrian, even childish and inefficient, but I'll guarantee you, it's just the opposite. It requires such self-control and draws such maturity into the communication that even though it may seem inefficient at first, it becomes highly effective—that is, it achieves the desired results in terms of both synergistic decisions and synergistic relationships, bonding and trust" (Stephen R. Covey, *The 8ᵗʰ Habit,* [New York: Free Press, 2004], 197–99). Especially when first attempting to implement this strategy, it will be helpful if a person with seniority (such as the abbot) acts as a moderator to ensure that no one speaks out of turn. Ideally, he will also be capable of translating accusations, judgmental statements, and demands into a nonviolent expression of observations, feelings, needs, and requests. This mediation of the abbot would be in line with the teachings of St. Ephraim the Syrian who wrote: "A wise abbot will not reproach a beginner when he hears that he has argued with an older father, but he will carefully examine the matter and act as the mediator between them with the fear of God" (Παύλου Μοναχοῦ, *Εὐεργετινός,* τόμος Δ΄, με΄, 2, 641).

St. Paisius Velichkovsky implemented the following strategy of dealing with severe disagreements: "If there was a misunderstanding among the brethren, a reconciliation was to follow without fail, according to the words of the Scriptures: 'Let not the sun go down on your wrath.'[440] And if any brother was so hardened as to wish to remain unreconciled, he was to be placed under suspension by the starets, being forbidden from even setting foot on the church's threshold and from reciting the Lord's Prayer[441] till he humbled himself."[442] St. Columbanus of Ireland (in the sixth century) added: "If two brothers have had an argument and come to anger, [their punishment is to pass] two days on one loaf and water."[443] Blessed Augustine wrote: "Although a brother is often tempted to anger, yet prompt to ask pardon from one he admits to having offended, such a one is better than another who, though less given to anger, finds it too hard to ask forgiveness. But a brother who is never willing to ask pardon, or does not do so from his heart, has no reason to be in the monastery, even if he is not expelled."[444]

St. John of Sinai emphasized the importance of a spiritual guide for beginners in monasticism:

> Those of us who wish to go out of Egypt, and to fly from Pharaoh, certainly need some Moses as a mediator with God and from God, who, standing between action and divine vision, will raise hands of prayer for us to God, so that guided by him we may cross the sea of sin and rout the Amalek of the passions.[445] That is why those who have surrendered themselves to God deceive themselves if they suppose that they have no need of a director.[446]

Therefore, the abbot needs to be especially vigilant with novices to ensure that they make a good beginning in their monastic life. St. Joseph the Hesychast taught: "In monasticism, a good beginning results in an excellent ending, whereas a bad beginning results in a horrible ending."[447] He also observed: "If a monk embraces from the beginning a demanding, lofty lifestyle, he will become a saint. Otherwise, if he follows a path that is a

---

[440] Eph. 4:26.

[441] Because it includes the phrase: "Forgive us our debts as we forgive our debtors."

[442] Chetverikov, *Starets Paisii Velichkovskii,* 143.

[443] G. S. M. Walker, *Sancti Columbani Opera.* (Dubin: Dublin Institute for Advanced Studies, 1957), *Scriptores Latini Hiberniae,* no. 2, 159; *Monks' Rules,* Columbanus Hibernus: http://www.ucc.ie/celt/online/T201052.html

[444] Bavel, *The Rule of Saint Augustine,* vi. 2.

[445] Vid. Ex. 17.

[446] Holy Transfiguration Monastery, *The Ladder of Divine Ascent,* 5.

[447] Γέροντος Ἐφραίμ, Ὁ Γέροντάς μου Ἰωσήφ, 239; see also Elder Ephraim, *My Elder Joseph the Hesychast,* 332. Or, as St. Ephraim the Syrian put it: "If you make a good beginning, you will also conclude your old age in a pleasing manner; and you will be as a lamp that enlightens many on the path of the Lord. Lay a strong foundation, then, so that your work may be exalted" (Chrysostomos, *The Evergetinos, Book I,* 223).

little wide, he will later go downhill. Sometimes he may even end up worse than people in the world."[448]

St. Nectarios of Aegina astutely observed that both the positive and negative moods of the superior are transmitted to the disciples. Bearing this in mind, he instructed the abbess of his monastery:

> You should know that your cheerfulness brightens the faces of the sisters and turns the convent into paradise, while your sadness and scowling passes over to the sisters, and the delight of paradise is put to flight. Know that the happiness and joy of the sisters depends on you, and you have a responsibility to keep this feeling present in their hearts. Do this even if you must force yourself on many occasions. I advise you not to give yourself over to bouts of depression, because this greatly wounds the hearts of your sisters. Your reward will be great if you become the bearer of joy to your sisters. I give you this advice because I also hold this same principle in my life.
>
> I want my disciples to hold this same principle. When you gladden the heart of your neighbor—and especially your sister who has denied herself everything and expects spiritual joy from you alone—then you may be sure that you are pleasing God much more than by making long prayers and great fasts.
>
> Understand that your current role is that of spiritual mother. You are no longer Chrysanthi, who was able to do whatever she wanted. If you uphold your moral duties to your sisters precisely, then you uphold your duties to God as well. If you supposedly ignore the former for the sake of the latter, know that such duties are not acceptable to God, either. The superior of a monastery lives not for herself, but for the sisterhood, and in living for the sisterhood she lives for God. God accepts her life as an acceptable sacrifice.[449]

7) Mistakes by the Abbot

St. Basil the Great explained how to deal with mistakes made by the abbot as follows:

> If a person does not accept the superior's decisions, he should express his objections to him either publicly or in private, if he has serious grounds that are consonant with the Scriptures; otherwise, he should keep silent and do what was ordered. But if he is too shy, let him use others as intermediaries in the matter, so that, if the command is contrary to the Scriptures, he may deliver both himself and his brethren from harm.... But if some persist in disobedience, finding fault in secret and not openly stating their grievance, thus becoming the cause of quarreling in the community and undermining the authority of the commands given, they should be expelled from the community as teachers of disobedience and rebellion.[450]

---

[448] Γέροντος Ἰωσήφ, Ἔκφρασις Μοναχικῆς Ἐμπειρίας, 262; see also Elder Joseph, *Monastic Wisdom,* 226.

[449] Strongylis, *St. Nectarios of Pentapolis and the Island of Aegina,* vol. 2, 181 (Letter #99); see also Μητροπολίτου Τίτου Ματθαιάκη, Ἅγιος Νεκτάριος Πενταπόλεως, Κατηχητικαὶ Ἐπιστολαί (Ἀθῆναι, 1984), 193 (Ἐπιστολὴ 99).

[450] Βασιλείου τοῦ Μεγάλου, Ἀσκητικὰ Α΄, ΕΠΕ 8, 382–83; see also Wagner, *Saint Basil: Ascetical Works,* vol. 9, 325 (Question 47 in the *Long Rules*).

Elder Ephraim usually advised his monks to obey any decisions of the abbot that seemed unwise to him for the sake of keeping the peace. St. Sophrony of Essex taught the same thing, and explained why:

> The abbot is the one who has a general overseeing of things. But it is possible that among the brethren there are some who are more capable than he in some matters, which is something that can create a very touchy situation. Nevertheless, this does not mean that the abbot will submit himself to them. In the life of Patriarch Barnabas of Yugoslavia we have the following example: He entrusted various tasks to other people, but he was the one who made the final decisions. It was up to him to choose the guidelines, whether in the sector of canon law or in the liturgical or practical life. In this way, he assigned to his various subordinates the work of preparing the necessary facts in regard to what he had to accomplish. He had a better look at the details, thought about it, and made the decision. This is necessary for preserving unity of life.
>
> All things are relative, and the organization does not have an absolute character. Due to this relativity, one can always say "yes" or "no." In monasticism, however, we should say "yes" in order to keep the line that the abbot has chosen. He might know less than others for a particular matter, but even so, it is up to him to make the decision. The disciple contributes by working together with the abbot and not breaking the unity of life, so that the coordinated efforts that everyone is making are always preserved.
>
> This is a very sensitive issue in the life of a monastery. Each one of us might have the opinion that the abbot has not chosen the best line and might start resisting, disobeying, disagreeing with him, etc. Even in the event that the brother is right, the result will be negative. In things regarding this life we might suffer some loss. But this is not so serious as that which is caused by a struggle of wills when this appears within a monastery. This unity of wills and unity regarding guidelines is mandatory.
>
> We read in *Saint Silouan* that if the abbot, as the elder, has some flaws, we must pray for him; God needs to be with him and to protect him by His grace. Thus, we must find ways to avoid conflicts. In other words, we should take a stance that leads to salvation with prayer, and the life of the monastery will preserve its desired unity. This is very important.[451] ... When there is a disagreement over worldly matters, finances, or a problem with the typikon, etc., the spiritual life is destroyed.[452]

St. Christodoulos of Patmos in his rule described how a superior should be corrected if he does not carry out his duties properly:

> If the superior should ever, in any way, set at nought any of these our dispositions in the present document, whether those above that we began with or those that we may add between here and the end, or if he should be seen corrupting the severity of the cenobitic way of life, perhaps out of his own fondness for pleasure, or if he should wish to misappropriate the monastery's revenues, and be convicted of stealing, I do not wish everyone immediately to stand up against him in a disorderly manner. The more preeminent brothers, those vested with authority, the steward, the ecclesiarch and the priests, may, with great mildness and suitable respect, draw his attention to his fault and point out the value of filial and brotherly love, in a generalized attempt to reform him; and this, not once but repeatedly, in a pleasant way with great gentleness. If he

---

[451] Σωφρονίου, *Οἰκοδομῶντας τὸν Ναὸ τοῦ Θεοῦ, Τόμος Α΄*, 38–40.

[452] Ibid., 50.

comes to himself and abstains from the forbidden activity, he shall be as before and remain superior, but if, even when they have exhorted him, both individually and in a body, he sticks obstinately to his evil ways and is completely incorrigible, I command that he be removed from his office without confusion or strife, and another elected and chosen in the manner prescribed.[453]

Similarly, St. Fructuosus of Braga wrote in his monastic pact that novices are expected to sign:

We [the novices] remind you, our master [i.e., the abbot], that if you should treat any of us unjustly—which it is unreasonable to believe and which may God not allow to happen—if you should treat any of us with pride or anger, or should love one and show hatred and rancor for another, or should dominate one but revere another, as people often do, then we shall have the right also granted to us by God to take our complaint without pride and without anger through the dean to the prior, and the prior shall humbly kiss the feet of you our lord and lay before you the details of our complaint, and you must be willing to listen patiently and to bend your neck humbly to the common Rule and correct and reform yourself. If you are not willing to correct yourself, then we may also have the power of consulting other monasteries, or else a bishop who lives under the Rule, or a Catholic[454] count who is a defender of the Church, and of inviting them to meet with us, that, in their presence, you may correct yourself and fulfill the tenets of the Rule. We must be as your disciples, subjects, or adopted children, humble, obedient in all necessary things; and when we die you must offer us to Christ spotless and unharmed. Amen.[455]

Likewise, St. Basil the Great wrote that if the superior commits a fault, "those who are eminent by reason of age and sagacity should be entrusted with the task of giving [him] the admonition."[456] He also said: "No one is to concern himself with the superior's method of administration or make curious inquiries about what is being done, with the exception of those who, by reason of their rank and sagacity, are closely associated with the superior.

---

[453] Thomas and Hero, *Byzantine Monastic Foundation Documents,* 588–89.

[454] St. Fructuosus was using the term "Catholic" not in contrast to the term "Orthodox" (since he was writing four centuries before the Great Schism) but in contrast to heresies prevalent in his day.

[455] Barlow, *The Fathers of the Church: Iberian Fathers,* vol. 63, 209.

[456] The full quotation is: "Just as the superior is responsible for guiding all the brotherhood, so also it is incumbent on the rest to admonish him, if any offence is suspected with reference to him. That good order be not impaired, however, such admonishment should be entrusted to those who are pre-eminent both as regards years and wisdom. If there be anything that needs reformation, we have both benefited our brother, and through him ourselves, for we have brought back to the right path one who is, so to speak, the rule of our life and should by his own rectitude correct our perversity. If, on the other hand, any are baselessly disturbed on his account, they will be disabused of the bad opinion they had entertained of him, when full information is supplied by a clarification of the matter which had caused groundless suspicions to arise" (PG 31:988; see also Clarke, *The Ascetic Works of Saint Basil,* 193 [Question 27 in the *Long Rules*]). Note that St. Basil (speaking on behalf of the rest of the monks) calls the abbot merely "our brother" and says, "it is incumbent **on the rest**" to admonish the abbot, and that it is only for the sake of good order that this admonition is limited to being given by the senior monks. In other words, this gives further evidence that St. Basil views the abbot not as someone above the law or even above the other monks but merely as the first among equals.

He, in turn, on his part, is bound to take counsel with these and to deliberate with them on community matters, in obedience to the advice of Him who said: 'Do all things with counsel' (Eccl. 32:24)."[457]

The holy Fathers warn monks not to judge their elder. For example, St. Basil the Great wrote: "In order that no one may fall easily into this vice of doubting [the superior's orders] to his own detriment and that of others, this must be the general rule in the brotherhood ... that the superior's actions should not be curiously scrutinized, but everyone should concern himself with his own work."[458] Likewise St. John of Sinai wrote:

> Once we have entered the arena of piety and obedience [i.e., the monastery], we must no longer judge our good manager [i.e., the abbot] in any way at all, even though we may perhaps see in him some slight failings, since he is only human. Otherwise, by sitting in judgment we shall get no profit from our subjection.
>
> It is absolutely indispensable for those of us who wish to retain undoubting faith in our superiors to write their good deeds indelibly in our hearts and constantly remember them, so that when the demons sow among us lack of faith in them, we may be able to silence them by what is preserved in our memory.... The moment any thought of judging or condemning your superior occurs to you, leap away from it as from fornication.... Give that snake no place.... Say to that serpent: "Listen, deceiver, I have no authority to judge my superior, but he has been appointed to sit in judgment on me."[459]

St. Symeon the New Theologian added: "If you live in the midst of the brethren of a monastery, refuse to set yourself in opposition to the father who has tonsured you, even if you should see him commit fornication or be drunk and, in your opinion, badly conducting the affairs of the monastery, even if he strikes you and insults you and you suffer many other troubles at his hand."[460] St. Theodoros the Great Ascetic wrote: "Do not be the judge of the actions of your spiritual father, but be one who fulfills his commands. For the demons are in the habit of showing you his defects, so that your ears may be deaf to his words. They aim either to drive you from the arena as a feeble and cowardly fighter, or simply to terrify you with thoughts that undermine your faith, and so to make you sluggish in performing every kind of virtue."[461] St. Theodore the Studite—despite his own tremendous sagacity and holiness—saw the benefit of being corrected by the other fathers of his monastery, even though he was their

---

[457] Ibid., 326 (Question 48).

[458] Βασιλείου τοῦ Μεγάλου, *Ἀσκητικὰ Α´,* ΕΠΕ 8, 384–85; see also Wagner, *Saint Basil: Ascetical Works,* vol. 9, 326 (Question 48 in the *Long Rules*).

[459] Holy Transfiguration Monastery, *The Ladder of Divine Ascent,* 22–23.

[460] C. J. de Catanzaro, *Symeon the New Theologian: Discourses,* 213; Συμεὼν τοῦ Νέου Θεολόγου, *Κατήχησις 18,* Sources Chrétiennes 104, 276. ΕΠΕ Φ19Δ, 176.

[461] Θεοδώρου τοῦ Μεγάλου Ἀσκητοῦ, «Κεφάλαια πάνυ ψυχωφελῆ ρ´» ἐν *Φιλοκαλία τῶν Ἱερῶν Νηπτικῶν,* τόμος α´ (1991), 310 (κεφ. μβ´); see also Palmer, Sherrard, Ware, *The Philokalia,* vol. 2, 21 (ch. 42).

abbot and spiritual father. He said: "I rejoice because God has given me not only children but also lords and masters and fathers, so that when I fall they raise me up, and when I slip they rectify me, and when I am not being useful they make me such."[462] This shows that St. Theodore had attained the third and highest degree of humility, which, according to St. John of Sinai, "is a true distrust of one's good qualities and a constant desire to learn [of one's faults]."[463] St. John also observed that "the Lord has arranged in His providence that no one can see his own faults as well as his neighbour does. So we are bound to give thanks for our healing not to ourselves but to our neighbour and to God."[464]

Metropolitan Kallistos Ware explained why the elder also learns from the disciple:

> The relation between starets and spiritual child ... is not one-sided, but mutual. Just as the starets enables the disciples to see themselves as they truly are, so it is the disciples who reveal the starets to himself.... Both of them, the spiritual father as well as the disciple, have to learn as they go.
>
> The mutuality of their relationship is indicated by stories in the *Sayings of the Desert Fathers* where an unworthy abba is saved through the patience and humility of his disciple. A brother, for example, has an elder who is given to drunkenness, and is sorely tempted to leave him; but, instead of doing so, he remains faithfully with his abba until the latter is eventually brought to repentance. As the narrator comments, "Sometimes it is the young who guide their elders to life."[465] The disciple may be called to give as well as to receive; the teacher may often learn from his pupils. As the Talmud records, "Rabbi Hanina used to say, 'Much have I learnt from my teachers, more from my fellow-students, but from my pupils most of all.'"[466]
>
> In reality, however, the relationship is not two-sided but triangular, for in addition to the abba and his disciple there is also a third partner, God. Our Lord insisted that we should call no one "father," for we have only one Father, Who is in heaven.[467] The abba is not an inerrant judge or an ultimate court of appeal, but a fellow-servant of the living God; not a tyrant, but a guide and companion on the way.[468]

St. Fructuosus of Braga wrote in his *General Rule for Monasteries* that it is the responsibility of the rest of the brotherhood to correct an abbot if he falls into heresy:

> They [i.e., the abbots] must inquire into and study the past sayings of the Fathers in their writings, in order to know from them what they should do themselves, so that, inside and out, before and behind, they have a mind full of eyes, lest they fall into some

---

[462] Θεοδώρου Στουδίτου, *Μεγάλη Κατήχησις,* 216–17 (ὁμιλία 58).

[463] Holy Transfiguration Monastery, *The Ladder of Divine Ascent,* 152.

[464] Ibid., 158.

[465] Benedicta Ward, *The Wisdom of the Desert Fathers* (United Kingdom: Lion, 1998), §209 (56–57).

[466] *A Rabbinic Anthology,* C. G. Montefiore and H. Loewe, ed. (Cambridge: Cambridge University Press, 1938), §494.

[467] Mt. 23:8–10.

[468] "The Spiritual Guide in Orthodox Christianity," Metropolitan Kallistos Ware of Diokleia http://churchmotherofgod.org/articleschurch/articles-about-the-orthodox-church/2348-the-spiritual-guide-in-orthodox-christianity.html?showall=1&limitstart=

heresy—heaven forbid—and perish. For this, they must always stand in the council of the brothers on balanced scales as though being weighed, that, by recalling the past, foreseeing the future, and examining the present, they may avoid the goads of heresy.[469]

8) Hearing Confessions

St. Basil taught that a fundamental prerequisite for making "any progress worth mentioning"[470] is that a monk "reveal the secrets of his heart to those of his brethren whose office it is to exercise a compassionate and sympathetic solicitude for the weak,"[471] since "a vice kept secret is a festering wound in the soul."[472] This practice of revealing thoughts was embraced by most monastic saints.

For example, St. John Cassian wrote:

> In order to be able to arrive easily at this [humility], they [i.e., novices] are then taught never, through a hurtful shame, to hide any of the wanton thoughts in their hearts but to reveal them to their elder as soon as they surface, nor to judge them in accordance with their own discretion but to credit them with badness or goodness as the elder's examination discloses and makes clear.... Indeed, the devil in all his slyness will not be able to deceive or cast down a young man unless he inveigles him, either by haughtiness or by embarrassment, into covering up his thoughts. For they declare that it is an invariable clear sign that a thought is from the devil if we are ashamed to disclose it to an elder.[473]

Likewise, it was written about St. Lazaros of Mt. Galesion: "To all those who came to him and chose to make their abode with him, he taught one thing above all else, making it the preliminary foundation and a favorable starting point for progress and amelioration: that they do not hide their thoughts from him, neither having nor doing anything without his approval, following their own wishes."[474] Similarly, St. Benedict wrote: "The fifth degree of humility is, when one hideth from his Abbot none of the evil thoughts which rise in his heart or the evils committed by him in secret, but humbly confesseth them."[475] Abba Isaiah said: "Do not conceal any of your thoughts, sorrows, or desires.... Do not be ashamed to confess to your elder every thought that troubles you and you will be alleviated of it, for nothing gives greater joy to the evil spirits than a person who keeps silent about his thoughts,

---

[469] Barlow, *The Fathers of the Church: Iberian Fathers,* vol. 63, 192.

[470] Wagner, *Saint Basil: Ascetical Works,* vol. 9, 289 (Question 26 in the *Long Rules*).

[471] Ibid.

[472] Ibid., 325 (Question 46).

[473] Ramsey, *John Cassian: The Institutes,* 82 (iv. 9).

[474] Thomas and Hero, *Byzantine Monastic Foundation Documents,* 158–59.

[475] *Rule of St. Benedict,* Chapter VII.

whether these are good or evil."[476] St. Savas of Serbia wrote in his charter for Hilandar Monastery on the Holy Mountain: "I advise all of you, brethren, as soon as an abbot is appointed over you, be quick to tell him about every movement of your soul and to confess to him all your thoughts that are harmful to your soul, so that your love and your disposition would be imprinted in him."[477] St. Joseph the Hesychast wrote: "No one can be purified without frank confession; ... I have never seen a soul make progress in the prayer without the sincere confession of hidden thoughts."[478]

St. Symeon the New Theologian emphasized the importance of frequent confession: "You should also confess the thoughts of your heart to your spiritual father every hour, if possible. But if not, do not put it off till evening, but after the morning Office examine yourself and confess all that has befallen you."[479]

St. Fructuosus of Braga taught in his *Rule for the Monastery of Compludo* that even things that are not sinful should be revealed to one's elder: "None shall conceal his thoughts, his visions, his dreams, and his own negligences from an elder, nor the occasions when he is moved by shame or the desire to harm or his being driven by stubbornness."[480]

The typikon of the Monastery of Evergetis decreed that the abbot may appoint other monks to hear confessions of the others, even if they are not priests:

> He [the superior] is to be allowed, if perhaps he cannot act in person since the brotherhood is numerous, to authorize whichever priests and deacons he wishes, and even some of the more reverent brothers, to hear the thoughts of the more uneducated majority, the thoughts that trouble us day by day and hour by hour which must always be easy to absolve and not have caused more deep-seated trouble, and to remit them and grant forgiveness. But the thoughts that require some healing and care must be referred to the superior by those who hear them, and he is to bring about the appropriate healing.[481]

Likewise, St. Symeon of Thessalonica also believed that monks without the priesthood may confess the other monks if the bishop blesses this. He wrote:

> Bishops are giving permission to monks to listen to people's thoughts [as in confession], and the monks, disregarding the fact that they are not priests, bless and forgive them. Is this good? ... I will say my opinion, and I think it is Patristic. Since this is the work of the priesthood, it must be done by bishops and priests. It should not be done at all by laymen unless somewhere there is an urgent need where there is no

[476] *Abba Isaiah of Scetis: Ascetic Discourses,* trans. John Chryssavgis and Pachomios Penkett (Kalamazoo: Cistercian Publications, 2002), 41, 59–60.

[477] *Charter of Hilandar Monastery,* Article 17.

[478] Γέροντος Ἰωσήφ, Ἔκφρασις Μοναχικῆς Ἐμπειρίας, 49, 305; see also Elder Joseph, *Monastic Wisdom,* 52, 262.

[479] C. J. de Catanzaro, *Symeon the New Theologian: Discourses,* 283.

[480] Barlow, *The Fathers of the Church: Iberian Fathers,* vol. 63, 166.

[481] Thomas and Hero, *Byzantine Monastic Foundation Documents,* 476–77.

priest, in which case the bishop should appoint a pious monk who knows the law of God—that is, the holy canons. However, he should only listen to their thoughts in order to relay the matter to the bishop or in order to discern what is beneficial to the soul of the person confessing, but by no means should he forgive and remit sins. For if he does, he will be acting as a priest without the priesthood, baptizing and blessing, etc., which is foreign to Church practice.[482]

Monks often claim to want "confession of thoughts," whereas in reality they simply want to complain about others. The typikon of the Monastery of Evergetis warned against this:

But make your confession without accusing each other when perhaps a violent dispute or some other argument occurs. Do not make your confession if you consider yourselves blameless and you are looking really for condemnations, nor should you speak about the bodily needs which afflict you. For there is always a time for them, but this is a time for making confession and obtaining healing for spiritual passions. If you must speak of some violent dispute, be keen to ascribe and assign to yourselves all the blame and reason for the fault, whatever it is. But if you speak about some other passions, reveal these completely so that you can gain double benefit from this, by both attaining sound health of soul and clothing yourself in exalting humility, for possessing this we will actually be like God Who says, "Learn from me that I am gentle and lowly in heart" (Mt. 11:29). What else would be a clearer proof of gentleness and humility in heart than clearly to bear all affliction nobly and blame oneself in everything? The true confession without which I do not think anyone gains salvation is the cause of so many good things.[483]

Confession is so important that the typikon of the Monastery of Evergetis added that a monk who does not confess should be excommunicated and expelled:

Then we order that a person who does not make confession should be excommunicated from the Lord God Ruler of All until, coming to his senses and thinking of higher things, he confesses all his faulty and harmful thoughts. Thus it would be necessary also to expel such a person from the monastery and cut him off like a rotten limb, and as a wound that is hard to heal or completely incurable to remove him and cast him away, but the uncertainty of the future and the expectation that perhaps one day he may come to his senses held us back from this purpose. However, for him to be liable to the penalty of excommunication is very useful since it is very effective. Indeed, what benefit does he obtain from remaining at the monastery? What benefit comes from not making confession, or rather does not harm and ruin follow and a continued practice of evil and everything whatsoever that brings destruction to the soul? So then, as it is difficult for someone who is sick or has wounds to return to health when he hides these from the doctor, so it is much more difficult for the person who does not make confession ever to gain health of soul....

So then, by acting in this way, my brothers, we will not only be rescued from our own faults but we will possess later on something that is more sure; for the author of *The Ladder* says "Stripes that are exposed will not become worse," and again, "A soul

---

[482] PG 155:884D–885A.

[483] Thomas and Hero, *Byzantine Monastic Foundation Documents,* 477.

that thinks about confession is held back by it from sinning as if by a rein." So the revelation of one's own faults is very useful. In future let us all run eagerly to it.[484]

Ever since the beginning of monasticism, the holy Fathers taught that we should not reveal our thoughts to just anyone but only to the abbot and to the other monk or monks who are appointed to give advice. The rules attributed to St. Anthony the Great instruct monastics: "Do not reveal your thoughts to all but only to those who are able to save your soul."[485] Abba Isaiah taught: "Do not reveal your thoughts before everyone, lest you scandalize your neighbor."[486] Likewise, St. Ephraim the Syrian wrote: "You must not reveal your thoughts to just anyone, but only to those whom you know to be spiritual, taking no note of their appearance or whether the hair of their head and beard is white."[487] Abba Silouanos warned: "There is great danger in entrusting one's thoughts to persons without experience and spiritual discretion."[488] Likewise, St. John Cassian taught: "We must not entrust the hidden things of our hearts to just anyone, but to spiritual Elders who have discernment and to whose worthiness many have testified—and not just by the number of years they have had gray hair. For many, attending only to age and external appearances, have entrusted their thoughts to inexperienced and undiscerning men, and in this way have fallen into despair on account of their Elders' inexperience."[489]

St. Basil the Great taught that we are obliged to reveal to the superior not only our own sins but also the sins of the other fathers, if we have not managed to convince them to reveal them to the abbot on their own. He said: "Every sin must be made known to the superior, either by the sinner himself or by those who have become aware of the sin, if they cannot cure it themselves.... It is obvious that concealing sin contributes to the death of the sick man; 'for the sting of death is sin' (1 Cor. 15:56), says the Scripture, and also, 'open rebukes are better than hidden love' (Prov. 27:5). So let no one conceal a sin in behalf of another, lest we become slayers of our brethren rather than their friends."[490] Likewise, Nikon of the Black Mountain wrote: "It is said in the *Gerontikon:* 'An elder said: "If you see a brother doing a bad thing and you do not tell the one with the authority to correct him,

[484] Ibid., 477–78.

[485] PG 40:1069C, Rule #41, as cited in Γέροντος Αἰμιλιανοῦ, *Νηπτικὴ Ζωὴ καὶ Ἀσκητικοὶ Κανόνες,* 99.

[486] Chryssavgis and Penkett, *Abba Isaiah of Scetis,* 96.

[487] Chrysostomos, *The Evergetinos, Book I,* 171.

[488] Ibid., 170.

[489] Ibid., 173.

[490] Βασιλείου τοῦ Μεγάλου, *Ἀσκητικὰ Α΄,* ΕΠΕ 8, 380–83; see also Wagner, *Saint Basil: Ascetical Works,* vol. 9, 324 (Question 46 in the *Long Rules*).

you have obviously demonstrated that you hate your brother. To love a brother is to desire his profit as if it were your own, and his success as if it were your own."""[491]

St. Basil even warned that if we conceal someone else's serious sin, we are to receive the same penance as the one who actually committed the sin: "As for one who has been aware of their having committed any of the aforesaid [serious] sins, and has failed to confess it, but they have been detected or exposed, and convicted of it, he shall do the same time that is done by the perpetrator of the evils, and he himself shall be subject to the same penalty."[492]

Elder Ephraim explained that this does not mean that we are to tattle on the other fathers for every little transgression they commit. Moreover, informing the superior requires some caution lest we fall into the mistake of focusing on other people's sins instead of our own. When Elder Ephraim found out that a novice was informing his abbot every time he noticed the other fathers doing something wrong, Elder Ephraim warned that novice that his soul would suffer great harm if he continued to do so. He was concerned that tattling would ruin the spirit of the monastery. Nevertheless, he did appreciate it when he was informed of the more serious mistakes made by other monks.

Aware that knowing when to reveal the sins of others to the abbot requires discretion, St. Anatoly (Zertsalov) of Optina, who was the proctor, "in general ... would always ask Father Amvrosy's advice before informing the superior of misdemeanors on the part of the brethren."[493]

The person hearing confessions in a monastery must be careful not to reveal what was said during confession. As St. Waldebert wrote in his rule for nuns:

> The abbess or prioress or whoever of the senior sisters the abbess had entrusted with receiving confessions, should in no way reveal either minor or serious crimes except to the just judge who washes away all confessed crimes. For she whose wounds have been confessed in shame not for the receiving of blame but for the restoration of health has confessed and has God as just witness from whom she expects to be healed.[494]

Summarizing the teachings of St. Nectarios of Aegina on confession in women's monasteries, Elder George of Gregoriou Monastery explained: "Just as the abbot must be the spiritual father of the monks in men's monasteries, likewise in women's monasteries the abbess is the spiritual mother. She is responsible for examining the thoughts of the nuns

---

[491] Nikon of the Black Mountain, *Pandektes* 10:70 as quoted in Goldfrank, *The Monastic Rule of Iosif Volotsky,* 261.

[492] Agapius and Nicodemus, *The Rudder,* 833 (Canon LXXI of St. Basil).

[493] Saint Anatoly (Zertsalov) of Optina, *A Collection of Letters to Nuns,* trans. Holy Nativity Convent (Jordanville: Holy Trinity Monastery, 1993), 261.

[494] J. A. McNamara and J. Halborg, *The Rule of a Certain Father to the Virgins,* chapter 7.

and guiding them spiritually. The presence of a spiritual father/confessor is an aid to the work of the abbess."[495]

Elder Ephraim taught that a confessor should not limit the confession merely to what a person confesses but should also ask the person questions, since some people fail to confess thoroughly either due to ignorance of what is sinful or due to shame. The same teaching is found in the *Rule of the Master:* "The deans themselves [i.e., the monks in a monastery who are appointed to hear the confessions of the other monks] should on their own initiative interrogate their charges [i.e., the monks under their charge] about this, lest perhaps because of the simplicity of some of them or indeed for very shame brought on by what is evil the brother is too shy to confess depraved and obscene things."[496] Nevertheless, some caution is needed since an indiscreet confessor can do harm by being psychologically violent in forcing a person to confess sins. Besides, confession without repentance has little value.

9) Seniority

It is an ancient monastic tradition to determine the sequential order of monks in a monastery by their time in the monastery. St. Jerome wrote that the fourth-century monastic tradition of St. Pachomios dictated that "the order in which the monks walked, sat, intoned psalms, were served food at table, and took Communion was based on the date of entrance to the community."[497] Likewise, the monastic *Rule of St. Ailbe* (who lived in sixth-century Ireland) taught: "Whenever anything is to be distributed, this should be done according to each person's rank in seniority."[498] St. Fructuosus of Braga also said: "He who was first to enter the monastery shall walk first, sit first, be first to receive a devout token, first to communicate in church, first to speak when the brothers are questioned on any matter, first to say a psalm, first to sit down in choir, first to do a week of duty, and first to extend his hand at table."[499] St. Donatus of Besançon (paraphrasing St. Benedict)[500] wrote: "The order of precedence in the monastery is determined by the time of their conversion and the merit of their lives."[501] St. Benedict added: "In no place whatever let age determine the order or be a disadvantage.... Thus, for instance, let him who came into the monastery at the second

---

[495] Ἀρχιμανδρίτου Γεωργίου, *Ὀρθόδοξος Μοναχισμὸς καὶ Ἅγιον Ὄρος,* 159.

[496] Eberle, *The Rule of the Master,* 159.

[497] Marilyn Dunn, *The Emergence of Monasticism* (United Kindgom: Blackwell Publishing, 2000), 121.

[498] Maidín, *The Celtic Monk,* 25.

[499] Fructuosus of Braga, *Regula Complutensis,* 23; PL 87:1110B (as translated in Barry, *Commentary on the Rule of Saint Benedict,* 496).

[500] *Rule of St. Benedict,* Chapter LXIII.

[501] Donatus of Besançon, "Regula ad Virgines: a Working Translation," ch. 66.

hour of the day, know that he is younger than he who came at the first hour, whatever his age or dignity may be."[502] Although St. Benedict believed that monks who have been ordained to the priesthood or diaconate should not automatically be given seniority over the rest of the monks,[503] the Athonite tradition is to give them such seniority.

St. Benedict taught that the younger should treat the older with respect: "Wherever the brethren meet each other, let the younger ask the blessing from the older; and when the older passeth by, let the younger rise and give him place to sit; and let the younger not presume to sit down with him unless his elder biddeth him to do so, that it may be done as it is written: 'In honor preferring one another' (Rom. 12:10)."[504] Likewise, *The Rule of Tarn* (from sixth-century Gaul) states: "If any senior is present, a junior should not presume to talk too much; but as often happens if the senior is less experienced, let the junior in his turn speak of those things which he is ordered."[505] *The Rule of Paul and Stephen* (written in sixth-century Italy) advises: "The seniors should offer the affection of a father to the juniors and, when it is necessary to issue a command, they should not become puffed-up and rash or shout, but with confidence, quiet simplicity, and the authority coming from a good life, they should impose whatever is fitting in pursuit of the common good."[506]

The spirit of seniority in a monastery has been explained as follows by Elder Aimilianos in the *Regulations of the Holy Cenobium of the Annunciation:* "The virtue of obedience shall be expressed within a voluntarily acknowledged climate of seniority within the community, through the respect accorded to the elder sisters by the younger and by the discipline shown by the latter in all things. They shall all be servants of each other, not through any necessity or constraint, but rather by their own free choice.... All nuns shall be required to behave with refinement, politeness and respect to all others, without exception."[507]

The application of seniority among the fathers in a monastery is a delicate issue because it can be easily abused by those with seniority. Specifically, they can fall into two temptations: *demanding* special treatment and treating their "inferiors" with *disrespect*. In

---

[502] *Rule of St. Benedict,* Chapter LXIII.

[503] "Let the one who hath been ordained be on his guard against arrogance and pride, and let him not attempt to do anything but what is commanded him by the Abbot, knowing that he is now all the more subject to the discipline of the rule.... Let him, however, always keep the place which he had when he entered the monastery, except when he is engaged in sacred functions, unless the choice of the community and the wish of the Abbot have promoted him in acknowledgment of the merit of his life" (*Rule of St. Benedict,* Chapter LXII).

[504] Ibid.

[505] Benedictine Priory of Montreal, "The Rule of Tarn" (*Regula Tarnantensis*), On the Trinity, *Monastic Studies,* no. 17, Christmas (1986): 224.

[506] Barry Hagan, "The Rule of Paul and Stephen: A Translation and Commentary," *The American Benedictine Review,* vol. 58, no. 3 (2007): 329 (chapter 2).

[507] Elder Aimilianos, *The Authentic Seal,* 176.

some monasteries novices are intentionally treated with disrespect as a way of testing them. Nevertheless, caution and vigilance must be exercised in doing so, lest their disrespectful treatment of novices stems not out of a desire to help them acquire humility but out of their own unchecked egotism.

St. Sophrony of Essex taught that seniority should not become a pretext for superiority but merely an aid to orderliness. He told his monastics: "I don't want you to form the notion that because someone came to the monastery before the others he acquires a position of precedence according to the date of his arrival. Of course, we do implement this for the sake of keeping some orderliness. But we must not view this order as a law to be enforced in everything…. We keep a certain order—for example regarding the abbot, the spiritual fathers, the stewards, etc.—but in our conscience there is no hierarchical order in life. We respect everyone. In fact, we ought to obey not only our monastic brothers and sisters but also the laymen that come to us…. God is pleased when each one of the brothers, fathers, and novices thinks: 'I who am so unworthy of God have been accepted by His elect.'"[508]

It was probably this understanding of equality (in terms of mutual respect) that led St. Basil the Great to view *equality* as something a person comes to the monastery to learn,[509] and led St. Eustathios of Thessalonica to say to a passionate monk: "You are out of control because you have neither brotherly love nor friendship or cenobitic living or any communication (and I'm not talking about spiritual communication but any other kind) in which there is a rational equality and the corresponding equality in speaking. For wherever there is dissimilarity and inequality, there disturbances prevail."[510]

In the same spirit, St. John Chrysostom described the equality in monasteries as follows:

> No one can be heard insulting there, nor seen insulted, nor commanded, nor giving commands; but all are devoted to those that are waited on, and every one washes the strangers' feet, and there is much contention about this. And he doeth it, not inquiring who it is, neither if he be a slave, nor if he be free; but in the case of every one fulfills this service. No man there is great nor lowly. What then? Is there confusion? Far from it, but the highest order. For if any one be lowly, he that is great seeth not this, but hath accounted himself again to be inferior even to him, and so becomes great. There is one table for all, both for them that are served, and for them that serve; the same food, the same clothes, the same dwellings, the same manner of life. He is great there, who eagerly seizes the lowly task.[511]

---

[508] Σωφρονίου, *Οἰκοδομῶντας τὸν Ναὸ τοῦ Θεοῦ, Τόμος Β′*, 29–30.

[509] See footnote #562 on page 100.

[510] PG 135:773B.

[511] *St. Chrysostom: Homilies on the Gospel of St. Matthew*, 420 (Homily 72:3).

The equality of the brethren in a monastery is based on a sublime theological principle. St. Sergius of Radonezh said that he wanted his brethren to be one as the Holy Trinity is one.[512] St. Sophrony of Essex developed this idea theologically to a greater degree by writing in his *Testament:* "In the monastic community the purpose is the acquisition of unity … in the image of the oneness of the Holy Trinity.… In this amazing unity, each one of us is, in a sense, in his hypostasis the center of all: everyone and everything is for him. And he offers everything that is his and his entire being for all and for each. There is no one greater, no one lesser."[513]

It is an ancient monastic tradition that the abbot appoint someone to run the monastery in his absence. St. Pachomios taught: "When the father of the monastery is away, let the second in order have the authority to give orders for everything until he returns."[514] Nowadays, however, with the prevalence of cell phones, this rule has become nearly obsolete because the abbot can still be reached no matter how far away he goes. Nevertheless, since St. Basil the Great pointed out[515] that there are still some other circumstances (such as bodily illness) that could temporarily prevent the abbot from making decisions and speaking with the guests even when he is not absent, he should appoint a deputy who is capable of fulfilling the abbot's duties when he is not able to do so himself. But St. Theodore the Studite advises abbots: "You should not go out frequently or roam about unnecessarily, leaving your own flock. For, it is desirable that you have time to spend with the flock and be able to save these sheep endowed with reason, but most wily and given to straying."[516]

A frequent cause of tension among monastics is when one of them tries to correct another or even just makes a suggestion. Ideally, a younger monk should never correct an older one, since it is not his place to do so but the abbot's. As St. Iosif Volotsky wrote: "Neither the young nor the novices shall rebuke or forbid, but shall attend only to themselves and censure themselves from every standpoint. If they see someone doing something improper and not according to the norms of reverent brothers, they shall not forbid or rebuke, but each one quietly and alone shall report to the elder with whom that other

---

[512] cf. Hieromonk Nikolai Sakharov, "St. Sophrony's 'Testament': The Trinity as a model for monastic community," *Analogia: The Pemptousia Journal for Theological Studies* 11 (2020): 63.

[513] Σωφρονίου, *Οἰκοδομώντας τὸν Ναὸ τοῦ Θεοῦ, Τόμος Β΄,* 166–67.

[514] Μ. Παχωμίου, F. Halkin, SPVG, 18–19; see also: Veilleux, *Pachomian Koinonia,* vol. 2, 5–6, 9; 181–82.

[515] "Since it often happens, either through bodily infirmity, or the necessity of travel, or for some other reason, that the superior is absent from the community, some other person approved by him and by others who are competent to judge should be selected to take charge of the brethren in his absence.… This will ensure that, when the superior is away, the brethren will not adopt a democratic system of government as it were, violating the rule and the traditional discipline.… By this arrangement there will also be a person to give wise answers to visitors" (Βασιλείου τοῦ Μεγάλου, *Ἀσκητικὰ Α΄,* ΕΠΕ 8, 376–77; see also Wagner, *Saint Basil: Ascetical Works,* vol. 9, 322 [Question 45 in the *Long Rules*]).

[516] Thomas and Hero, *Byzantine Monastic Foundation Documents,* 78.

lives."[517] Likewise, *The Rule of Tarn* states: "Let no junior here dare to criticize a senior, but if he knows that something is being done or has been done in violation of the rule, it must be reported to the abbot or the prior, to be corrected by the reproach of the rule which is required."[518] The "Rules for the Monks in Persia" wanted only the abbot to make corrections, since they declared: "A monk shall take care of the correction of himself only, and not of that of his brothers."[519]

Nevertheless, for practical reasons it is sometimes necessary for a younger monk to correct an older one. In general, monastics should only correct each other if the following four qualifications are met:

1) The abbot or a more senior monk is not present to make the correction;
2) Damage that is not insignificant will be done if a correction is not made immediately;
3) There is a good chance that the monk being corrected will not be offended; and
4) The person making the correction can do so with humility and love.[520]

---

[517] Goldfrank, *The Monastic Rule of Iosif Volotsky,* 261.

[518] *Monastic Studies,* no. 17, 226.

[519] Vööbus, *Syriac and Arabic Documents,* 91.

[520] When it is necessary to give someone a message that may be interpreted as criticism, it is invaluable to be able to implement the principles of nonviolent communication—as explained in chapter 5) section 13) on page 211.

Chapter Three:
Obedience

1) Reason for Obedience

HE EXPERIENCE OF CENTURIES of Orthodox monasticism has shown that the fundamental virtue for monastic progress is obedience. As St. Diadochos of Photiki said: "It is well known that obedience is the chief among the initial virtues, for first it displaces pride and then it engenders humility within us"[521] Likewise, St. Synkletike taught: "It seems to me that for those who live in monasteries obedience is a higher virtue than chastity, however perfect. Chastity is in danger of pride, obedience has the promise of humility."[522] Similarly, St. Efthymios the Great taught: "Above all recognize this: those who renounce this life must not have a wish of their own but in first place acquire humility and obedience."[523] And according to Abba Or, "Humility is the crown of a monk."[524]

Abba Poemen explained: "A person's will is a brazen wall (cf. Jer. 1:18) and an immoveable rock between him and God. If a person abandons it, he too says: 'In my God I will leap over the wall' (Ps. 18:30)."[525] Thus, it is through renouncing our own will in obedience to our elder that we may approach God.

St. Columbanus viewed mortification of one's will as central to monastic life:

> The main part of the monks' rule is mortification [of self-will] since they are indeed commanded by scripture: "Do nothing without counsel" (Sir. 32:24). Thus if nothing is done without counsel, then everything is to be asked for by counsel. Thus we are commanded by Moses also: "Ask your father and he will show you, your elders and they will tell you" (Dt. 32:7). But although this discipline may seem hard to those who are hard of heart, namely, that we should always hang upon the words of another, to those who are secure in their fear of God it will seem sweet and safe if it is kept

---

[521] Φιλοκαλία, τόμος α΄ (1991), 246; see also Palmer, Sherrard, Ware, *The Philokalia,* vol. 1, 265.

[522] Benedicta Ward, *The Desert Fathers: Sayings of the Early Christian Monks* (New York: Penguin Classics, 2003), 143.

[523] Cyril of Scythopolis, *Lives of the Monks of Palestine,* 12–13.

[524] Γεροντικόν (Ἀθῆναι: ἔκδοσις Α.Ε. Παπαδημητρίου, 1960), 126 (κεφ. θ΄); see also Ward, *The Sayings of the Desert Fathers,* 247.

[525] Wortley, *The Alphabetical Sayings of the Desert Fathers,* 236 (Poemen 54).

wholly and not just in part, since nothing is sweeter than security of conscience and nothing safer than exoneration of the soul, which no one can achieve through their own efforts since it properly belongs to the estimation of others.[526]

Lauding the benefits of obedience, Abba Rufus exclaimed: "O obedience, salvation of the faithful! O obedience, mother of all the virtues! O obedience, discloser of the kingdom! O obedience opening the heavens, and making men to ascend there from earth! O obedience, food of all the saints, whose milk they have sucked, through you they have become perfect! O obedience, companion of the angels!"[527]

Obediently cutting off one's will is the ultimate form of renunciation. As St. Symeon the New Theologian taught: "Many people have renounced this world and the things of the world, but few are they who renounce their own wills. Regarding them, the word of God aptly says: 'Many are called but few are chosen'(Mt. 22:14)."[528] St. Theodore the Studite said: "We will attain glory not through abstinence, nor through vigil, or by sleeping on the ground, or with any other ascesis, but rather through cutting off our will, thus demonstrating the martyrdom of struggle in the cenobitic life."[529] Furthermore, St. Symeon wrote: "They who with fear and trembling lay the foundation of faith and hope upon the rock of obedience to spiritual fathers, receiving their commands as from the mouth of God, build on this foundation of unhesitating obedience and immediately accomplish self-denial. For by fulfilling not their own but their spiritual father's will for the sake of God's commandment and for exercise in virtue, they not only achieve self-denial but also mortification towards everything in the world."[530]

In the same spirit, St. Symeon's elder, St. Symeon the Pious, said: "Consider, brother, that what is called perfect retirement from the world is the complete mortification of self-will."[531] The purpose of this renunciation and mortification of our self-will through obedience is to acquire humility. For St. John of Sinai taught that obedience leads to humility,[532]

---

[526] Oliver Davies and Thomas O'Loughlin, *Celtic Spirituality,* 254.

[527] PG 65:392A; see also Ward, *The Sayings of the Desert Fathers*, 211.

[528] Συμεὼν τοῦ Νέου Θεολόγου, ΕΠΕ Φ19Α, 520.

[529] Ἁγίου Θεοδώρου τοῦ Στουδίτου, *Μικρὰ Κατήχησις,* 112. Elsewhere St. Theodore wrote: "May no one tell me: 'I chant and recite so many hymns and say so many prayers. I eat and drink very little. I sleep in a chair and do so many prostrations. I lift my hands up to heaven in prayer for many hours.' All those things are acceptable—and why wouldn't they be? But let him tell me if he has a lowly spirit and cuts off his will so that he is always obedient and never objects or grumbles at all or argues ever" (Θεοδώρου Στουδίτου, *Μεγάλη Κατήχησις,* 144).

[530] Συμεὼν Νέου Θεολόγου, *Ἠθικὸς Δ´,* SC, τ. 129 (Paris, 1967), 18–20.

[531] C. J. de Catanzaro, *Symeon the New Theologian: Discourses,* 126.

[532] "The ever-memorable Fathers laid down that the way to humility, and its foundation, is bodily toil; but I would say obedience and honesty of heart [are], because they are naturally opposed to self-esteem" (Holy Transfiguration Monastery, *The Ladder of Divine Ascent,* 160). St. Theodoros the Great Ascetic also saw the connection between obedience and humility: "He who has embraced obedience and slain his own will with

and Abba Dorotheos of Gaza taught that humility is the indispensable "mortar" for holding together all the other virtues when building the house of the soul.[533]

St. John Cassian gave the following explanation of the value of obedience:

> The chief concern and instruction of this man [i.e., the elder], whereby the young man [i.e., the novice] who was brought to him may be able to ascend even to the loftiest heights of perfection, will be, first of all, to teach him to conquer his desires. In order to exercise him assiduously and diligently in this respect, he will purposely see to it that he always demands of him things that he would consider repulsive. For, taught by numerous experiences, they declare that a monk, and especially the younger men, cannot restrain their yearning for pleasure unless they have first learned to mortify their desires through obedience. And so they assert that someone who has not first learned to overcome his desires can never extinguish anger or sadness or the spirit of fornication, nor can he maintain true humility of heart or unbroken unity with his brothers or a solid and enduring peace, nor can he even stay in the cenobium for any length of time.[534]

In the same spirit, St. Nectarios of Aegina wrote: "[These are] the rules of monastic life: First: self-denial. Following this is the cutting-off of the will and submission. Second: patience and humility, and everything that follows these virtues. And third: watchfulness and discernment."[535]

St. Basil the Great gave another reason for obedience:

> A wise abbot knows how to examine with precision the character and the passions and the soul's impulses, and he arranges accordingly whatever each person needs. This is why one should certainly not resist his orders but should be convinced that the knowledge and therapy of his own self is the most difficult thing of all because self-love naturally exists in people, and every person lacks true judgment due to his passionate attachment to himself. But the knowledge and therapy from another person is easier because the passion of self-love in those judging others does not prevent a correct diagnosis.[536]

St. Joseph the Hesychast viewed perfect obedience as means by which a disciple acquires the love and virtues of his elder. He wrote: "The main reason why a disciple should attach

---

the sword of humility has indeed fulfilled the things he promised to Christ in the presence of many witnesses" (Θεοδώρου τοῦ Μεγάλου Ἀσκητοῦ, «Κεφάλαια πάνυ ψυχωφελῆ ρ΄» ἐν *Φιλοκαλία τῶν Ἱερῶν Νηπτικῶν*, τόμος α΄ (1991), 310 (κεφ. μγ΄); see also Palmer, Sherrard, Ware, *The Philokalia*, vol. 2, 21 [ch. 43]).

[533] "The person that desires to build a house must also place mortar between the stones [of virtues] since without it, the stones rub against one another and the house would fall down. Mortar represents humility because it comes from the earth and is under the feet of all. Therefore, *The Sayings of the Desert Fathers* say: 'Every virtue that is done without humility is not a virtue.' 'As it is impossible to build a boat without nails, so it is impossible to be saved without humility'" (Scouteris, *Abba Dorotheos: Practical Teaching on the Christian Life*, 215).

[534] Ramsey, *John Cassian: The Institutes*, 82.

[535] Strongylis, *St. Nectarios of Pentapolis and the Island of Aegina*, vol. 2, 154; Ἅγιος Νεκτάριος Πενταπόλεως, *Κατηχητικαὶ Ἐπιστολαί*, 160 (Ἐπιστολὴ 75).

[536] Μ. Βασιλείου, *Ἀσκητικαὶ διατάξεις*, ΕΠΕ 9, κεφ. κβ΄, 519.

himself to an elder and is perfectly obedient is this: the elder, who is on fire with the love of Christ, transmits the talent of his virtue's riches. The disciple, in turn, enjoys bountiful grace from his spiritual father, because he cuts off his own will and has complete self-denial and obedience."[537]

The holy Fathers, however, warn that this struggle is very difficult. For example, St. Theodore the Studite says that living in a cenobium under obedience demands "denying our will regarding work, orders, food, drink, clothes, shoes, location, and manner of submission."[538] Although one's freedom is severely limited, if one realizes that this sacrifice is the means to achieving a heavenly goal, then "that which seemed grievous becomes joyful with the joy of the Holy Spirit because of the hope of things laid up in heaven."[539] A truly obedient disciple will justifiably be full of hope for reaching heaven, since St. John of Sinai taught that he will escape judgment.[540]

The Rule of the Master describes both the difficulty and the reward for this great struggle of obedience:

> Now, it may be said that such as these travel the narrow way, because their own desires are never slightly put into effect and they do not do what they wish. But bearing the yoke of another's judgment, they are restrained from going where their own pleasure would lead them, and what they themselves would choose to do or achieve is denied them by the master. In the monastery their will is daily thwarted for the sake of the Lord, and in the spirit of martyrdom they patiently endure whatever commands they receive to test them. In the monastery they will assuredly say to the Lord, with the prophet: "For your sake we are being slain all the day; we are looked upon as sheep to be slaughtered" (Ps. 43:23). And later on, at the judgment, they will likewise say to the Lord: "You tested us, God, you refined us like silver. You let us fall into the net. You laid heavy burdens on our backs. You have set men over our heads" (Ps. 65:10–11). Therefore, when they say, "You have set men over our heads," it is evident that they are to have over them as God's representative a superior, whom they fear in the monastery. And continuing with what is stated, they will rightly say to the Lord again, this time in the next world: "But now the ordeal by fire and water is over, and you brought us out into refreshment" (Ps. 65:12), that is, "We have gone through the thwarting of our own will and by serving in obedience we have come to the enjoyment of your love."[541] ...

> To say, "I want this and I reject that; I like this and I hate that," is allowed to no one in the monastery, so that self-will be not chosen and indulged. And let him know that whoever wishes to live the religious life perfectly in the monastery will more than

---

[537] Γέροντος Ἰωσήφ, Ἔκφρασις Μοναχικῆς Ἐμπειρίας, 431; see also Elder Joseph, *Monastic Wisdom*, 367.

[538] Νικολάου, «Ἡ Θεολογία τῆς Κοινοβιακῆς Ζωῆς»,75–76.

[539] Ibid.

[540] "If anyone has his conscience in the utmost purity in the matter of obedience to his spiritual father, then he daily awaits death as if it were sleep, or rather life, and is not dismayed, knowing for certain that at the time of his departure, not he, but his director, will be called to account" (Holy Transfiguration Monastery, *The Ladder of Divine Ascent*, 39).

[541] Eberle, *The Rule of the Master*, 123–24.

likely not be permitted what he desires according to his own will. Why? Because "there are ways which men think right, but whose end plunges into the depth of hell" (Prov. 16:25). And what he does not want, this will be enforced, in order to root out his self-will, which is the enemy of God."[542]

St. Symeon the New Theologian stated: "the complete deadening of one's own will is a cross and death."[543] But he also called it a "life-giving deadening"[544] because "through this deadening, a monk is spiritually brought to life in a paradoxical way."[545]

A further benefit of complete obedience is freedom from cares, which in turn facilitates pure prayer. As Archimandrite Zacharias put it: "By obedience accomplished in God's name, the monk concentrates his spirit on the advice or commandment given him, and thus, freed from every care over transient matters, he directs his mind uninterruptedly to prayer."[546] Abba Dorotheos of Gaza had such inner peace due to his obedience that he worried that something was wrong with himself. As he once told his monks:

> You are inexperienced with "unconditional" obedience, nor do you know the peace that it bestows. I once inquired of the Elder Abba John, the disciple of Abba Barsanouphios, saying to him: "Master, since Holy Writ says that 'we must through much tribulation enter into the kingdom of God' (Acts 14:22), and I see that I have not a single tribulation, what ought I do, lest I lose my soul?" ...
>
> He said to me: "Do not be concerned. You have no reason to be troubled, for all those who place themselves under obedience to their spiritual Fathers have this freedom from care and find peace."[547]

St. Silouan the Athonite saw numerous fruits of obedience. He wrote:

> Rare are they who know the mystery of obedience. The obedient man is great in the sight of God. He follows in the footsteps of Christ, Who in Himself gave us the pattern of obedience. The Lord loves the obedient soul and affords her His peace, and then all is well and the soul feels love towards all men.
>
> The obedient man has put his whole trust in God, wherefore his soul dwells continually in God, and the Lord gives him His grace; and this grace instructs him in every good thing, and gives him the strength to abide in goodness. He sees evil but evil does not approach his soul, for the grace of the Holy Spirit is with him, which preserves him from all sin, and he is at peace, and prays to God unburdened.

---

[542] Ibid., 260–61.

[543] Ἁγίου Συμεὼν Νέου Θεολόγου, *Κατηχητικὸς Λόγος 20,* τόμ. 104, (Paris: Krivochéine, «Sources Chrétiennes», 1964), 332.

[544] Ἁγίου Συμεὼν Νέου Θεολόγου, *Ἠθικὸς Λόγος 6,* τόμ. 129 (Paris: Darrouzès, «Sources Chrétiennes», 1967), 124.

[545] Ἀρχιμανδρίτου Ἐφραίμ, «Ἡ Ὑπακοὴ κατὰ τὸν Γέροντα Ἰωσὴφ τὸν Ἡσυχαστή», ἐν *Σύναξις Εὐχαριστίας· Χαριστήρια εἰς Τιμὴν τοῦ Γέροντος Αἰμιλιανοῦ,* 254.

[546] Archimandrite Zacharias, *Christ, Our Way and Our Life* (South Canaan: Saint Tikhon's Seminary Press, 2003), 136.

[547] *Our Holy Father Dorotheos of Gaza: Various Soul-Profiting Instructions to His Disciples,* trans. Metropolitan Chrysostomos (Etna: Center for Traditionalist Orthodox Studies, 2017), 51.

The obedient soul is beloved of the Holy Spirit, and soon knows the Lord and receives the gift of prayer of the heart.

The obedient man has surrendered himself to God's will, wherefore he is given the gifts of freedom and rest in God, and he prays with mind untrammelled [i.e., unhindered]; but the proud and disobedient cannot pray with a single mind, however austerely they may live. They know neither the manner of the working of grace nor whether the Lord has forgiven them their sins. But the obedient man is conscious without a shadow of doubt that his sins are forgiven him, because he feels the presence of the Holy Spirit in his soul.[548]

His disciple, St. Sophrony of Essex, explained the benefits of obedience in more detail:

Obedience is the basis of monasticism … and obedience is both sacrament and life in the Church. At first sight the abdication of free will and the power of reason might appear to run counter to God's design for man, whom He has endowed with a freedom like His own and whom, in virtue of that freedom, He calls to reign eternally with Him. Putting their free will and ability to reason into the hands of another, even though this other be a priest, would cause many people to feel as if the ground had gone from under their feet. Such a step would be like hurling themselves into a black abyss, losing their personalities and delivering themselves into the worst of slaveries. It would be self-annihilation. But to those who by faith have followed the teaching of the Church, and have renounced themselves in the spirit of that teaching, obedience is revealed as an inexpressibly great gift from on high. The "obedient" man may be compared to the eagle who rises on strong wings into the heavens and there serenely surveys the space which separates him from the earth, enjoying his safety and mastery over heights inaccessible and fatally terrifying to others. With confidence, love and joy the novice [or monk] readily submits his will and jurisdiction over himself to his spiritual father, thereby releasing himself from the heavy burden of earthly cares and arriving at something the value of which it is impossible to define—*purity of the mind in God.*

Monasticism above all means purity of the mind, which is unattainable without obedience. That is why there can be no monasticism without obedience, and the man who lacks obedience is not a monk in the true sense. It is possible to receive great gifts of God—even the perfection of martyrdom—outside the monastic condition; but purity of mind is a special gift of monasticism, unknown on other paths, and the monk can only reach this state through obedience. That is why I consider obedience to be the hard core of monasticism and to include the other two vows as a natural corollary. St. John Climacus, for instance, speaks thus: "… the mother of purity is inner silence (hesychasm) and obedience. The freedom from passions acquired through inner silence does not remain unshakeable when in constant contact with the world; but when this freedom is born of obedience it remains in all circumstances tried and steadfast."[549] And of voluntary poverty he says: "Will he who has relinquished his very soul still think to acquire possessions?" Thus obedience "by will … like two wings of gold lightly bears one up to the sky"[550] of freedom from passion.

…

---

[548] Sakharov, *Saint Silouan the Athonite,* 420.

[549] PG 88:888C.

[550] Ibid., 667C.

The educated man of the present day, with his developed critical approach, is incomparably less fitted for the ascetic exercise of obedience than the man of a simple turn of mind who is not seduced by intellectual curiosity. The cultured man, enamoured of his own critical intelligence, which he is accustomed to consider his principal dignity and the one solid foundation of "his" personal life, has to renounce this wealth of his before becoming a novice, or it will be difficult for him to enter into the Kingdom. But how is this to be done? Is not the man into whose hands we must put our will just another human being like ourselves—one, indeed, who may sometimes seem to us to stand lower than we do? The disciple begins to argue within himself: "Is this *staretz* an oracle, then? And how does he know God's will? God gave us our reason and we must do our reasoning ourselves. For instance, there is no sense at all in what the *staretz* has just told me. It is all rubbish." And so on. This sort of attitude makes the novice doubtful and hesitant about his spiritual father's every word, his every directive; and so he forgets that God's will in this world expresses itself in the very same outward forms as serve to manifest both the natural will of man and the demonical will, when this last is made manifest through man. He judges by outward appearances, after the manner of the "reasoning" man, and therefore does not find the path to the living faith.

St. John Climacus says that the novice who "voluntarily delivers himself into servitude receives *true freedom* in exchange."[551] Thus it is, finally, that the experience of obedience becomes the experience of authentic freedom in God.

In the presence of divine truth the novice finds himself profoundly convinced of the imperfection of his own reasoning powers. This marks an important stage in his ascetic life. In mistrusting his intelligence the monk frees himself from the nightmare in which all mankind lives.

...

By this renunciation of his will and judgment, for the sake of cleaving to the divine will which surpasses any human wisdom, the novice is in fact renouncing nothing else than his own egocentric will, the product of the passions, and his feeble little intelligence, and thereby showing true wisdom and superior will. In this manner the novice lightly—and imperceptibly to himself—advances to a height which men of the greatest intellectual culture cannot attain, or even apprehend. This height is purity of mind in God, as we have said earlier.[552]

St. Sophrony's disciple, Archimandrite Zacharias, added:

When the monk fulfills his obedience, he is imitating Christ. He sets himself on the path of the Lord's will. Only a psychologically healthy soul can undertake obedience. Psychological health is demonstrated by the monk's awareness that he himself is unfit for immediate knowledge of the great and perfect will of God. He follows the wise exhortation of the Scriptures: "Ask thy father and he will show thee; thine elders and they will tell thee" (Deut. 32:7). He holds to the general rule of monastic ascesis: "Do not trust in yourself." He thus has recourse to his spiritual father, confident that to him has been given to know God's will more clearly. In this way, he recognizes that the true God is the God of his father (cf. Gen. 31:5 et al.; Ex. 18:4) as well as the God of our Fathers, and he overcomes the disorder of "double-minded" (Jas. 1:8) fallen man, who cannot discover a sure path of life. Having this humble

---

[551] PG 88:630C.

[552] Sakharov, *Truth and Life,* 83–84, 86–87, 88.

predisposition the monk becomes fit enough to put his hand to the salutary plough of obedience (cf. Lk. 9:62).[553]

The abbot will also need to have the humility and discernment to know when to be "obedient" to his own disciples. For example, when a disciple feels very strongly about doing something his own way and lacks the self-denial to cut off his own will, it can be a mistake for the abbot to demand obedience from him, especially if the issue is inconsequential. This is why Abba Mark teaches the abbot: "He who does not attend to your recommendations from the very first word, do not compel him to carry out what you have proposed to him by entering into a disputatious war of words with him; rather, take care to reap gain from that which he rejected; for you will benefit more from your forgiveness [of your disciple's disobedience] than from his correction."[554]

This type of scenario is likely to happen frequently, considering that St. Paisios of the Holy Mountain[555] and Elder Ephraim have observed that nowadays due to the general spiritual decline in people, most novices lack the fortitude to cut off their will, and therefore the abbot and the rest of the brotherhood need to deal very patiently with them for years until they gradually learn to live monastically. As St. Barsanuphius the Great wrote: "If a person wants to bend a tree or a vine branch, then that person bends them gradually so that they do not break. However, if a person pulls them suddenly and forcefully, the thing breaks at once. Understand what I am saying."[556] St. Sophrony of Essex taught: "Demonstrating sympathy and understanding will help all who are beginning this [monastic] path to bear their cross. Ridicule and reproach are beneficial only to older monks."[557] St. Paisius Velichkovsky made a similar observation:

> It is a fact that everyone who lives in our monastery has not yet attained the same level of spiritual growth, but this cannot be otherwise. Some have succeeded in mortifying their egos through obedience, patiently suffering insults, abuses, reproaches and various forms of temptations, and this they do with such joy.... There are those monks too, who ... are able to tolerate reproaches and temptations only with great difficulty but they mature in spiritual strength.... Finally, there are those monks who are still too immature to be fed solid food, as the Bible states it. In simple terms, they are not able to patiently endure reproaches, abuses and temptations. They must still be fed the milk of human love and condescension, until they spiritually mature into the patience that is demanded of them. They try to replace their faults and weaknesses with continual self-reproach and sincere desire for salvation. In spite of their varying levels

---

[553] Zacharias, *Christ, Our Way and Our Life,* 134.

[554] Chrysostomos, *The Evergetinos, Book IV,* 453.

[555] See footnote #89 on page 12.

[556] *Barsanuphius and John, Letters,* vol. 1, trans. John Chryssavgis (Washington, D.C.: Catholic University of America Press, 2006), 45 (letter 25).

[557] Ἁγίου Σωφρονίου τοῦ Ἀθωνίτου, *Πνευματικὰ Κεφάλαια,* μετάφραση ἀπὸ τὰ ρωσικὰ Ἀρχιμανδρίτου Ζαχαρία (Ἔσσεξ: Ἱερὰ Πατριαρχικὴ καὶ Σταυροπηγιακὴ Μονὴ Τιμίου Προδρόμου, 2021), 121 (κεφ. 37).

of spiritual maturity, all the monks are equally penetrated by the desire to keep God's commandments firmly because they are mutually united in that indissoluble bond of His love.[558]

St. John of Sinai elaborated on this in his epistle *To the Shepherd:*

> Before all things, O venerable father, we have need of spiritual strength, so that by taking their hands, as though they were small children, we should be able to free those whom we endeavour to bring within the Holy of Holies ... whenever we should behold them afflicted and straitened by a throng of thoughts that would hinder them (and this comes to pass especially at the threshold of the entrance). If some are very childlike or very weak, we are obliged to raise them up upon our shoulders and carry them until they have passed through the door of that truly strait entrance, for here it is that every sort of stifling and straitness generally occur.[559]

Nevertheless, St. Ephraim the Syrian warned against being too patient with beginners:

> If you are entrusted with the spiritual guidance of a beginner, do not show sympathy toward him more than the Creator requires ... so as not to be dragged down together with him. For one must not be negligent of the ship when the lifeboat has broken away.... A spark, however small, when it falls onto the threshing floor, is capable of incinerating an entire year's harvest. Each of us must then tolerate the weaknesses of his neighbor to the extent that reason demands, and not above measure.[560]

Elder Aimilianos explained how to condescend to those who have weaknesses:

> The weaker a monk is, the more beautifully the monastery will treat him. For a person loves his weak member; it becomes a part of his flesh. A weakness is a fearsome passion, and if a person does not satisfy it, he will neither be able to pray nor to be at peace. He will keep grumbling his whole life; he will keep complaining and thinking he is right. For the sake of the monastery's peace, St. Augustine says to give the weak brethren what they want....
>
> After someone enters the monastery and finds warmth and a warm welcome and becomes a monk, then he begins to kick, to have demands and objections: "You don't love me; you don't pay attention to me; you never say 'yes' to me." In this case, the abbot should give him what he wants so that the whole monastery is not disturbed....
>
> If you don't treat him who has a weak character well, he will always be an inept and useless person. But if you behave properly towards him and train him correctly, after some time he will reach the point of being able to offer something to God. Whereas if a strong person does not hunger and suffer hardships, all the riches and gifts that God has given him—his spiritual health and balance—will go to waste.[561]

---

[558] Chetverikov, *Starets Paisii Velichkovskii,* 117–18.

[559] Holy Transfiguration Monastery, *The Ladder of Divine Ascent,* 244.

[560] Chrysostomos, *The Evergetinos, Book IV,* 478–79.

[561] Γέροντος Αἰμιλιανοῦ, *Νηπτικὴ Ζωὴ καὶ Ἀσκητικοὶ Κανόνες,* 235, 254.

2) Requirement for Complete Obedience

The obedience that the holy Fathers expect monks to have towards their abbot is complete. St. Basil the Great wrote:

> Just as God—Who is the Father of all and has the right to be called such—demands unquestioning obedience from His servants, likewise he who is a spiritual father among men and aligns his orders with the laws of God demands obedience without objections. For, if one who is devoted to learning a craft that is useful for this present life obeys the craftsman in everything and does not object at all to his orders, nor does he even distance himself from him momentarily but is always observed by his teacher and accepts the food and drink and the lifestyle that he dictates, how much more will they who come to learn piety and equality (after convincing themselves that they will be able to acquire this knowledge from the abbot) offer to the abbots complete submission and absolute obedience in everything, and they will not demand an explanation for the orders but will execute the work they are ordered to do.[562]

It was in this same spirit that St. Nectarios of Aegina wrote to his nuns: "Because God has placed me as your leader, I shall give orders without giving an explanation, so that your loyalty and patience may be tested. I will tolerate no questioning, no asking why. 'He who is able to accept this, let him accept it' (Mt. 19:12)."[563]

St. Basil also added:

> Let him [i.e., a monk] surely realize that he does not oppose or obey man but the Lord Who said: 'He that heareth you heareth Me, and he that rejecteth you rejecteth Me' (Lk. 10:16)....[564]
>
> The abbot is nothing but he who has the place of the Savior and has become a mediator between God and men.[565]

St. Benedict likewise wrote that the abbot "is believed to hold the place of Christ in the monastery."[566] In the same spirit, *The Rule of the Master* states: "See to it, brothers, that no one take this appointment [of a new abbot] with ill-will and despise Christ, whose representative in the monastery this man will be for you."[567]

With this understanding, St. Joseph the Hesychast said to Elder Ephraim when he was a novice: "Do you know what Athonite monasticism teaches? This: 'Have you pleased

---

[562] Μ. Βασιλείου, *Ἀσκητικαὶ διατάξεις,* ΕΠΕ 9, κεφ. ιθ΄, 486–88.

[563] Strongylis, *St. Nectarios of Pentapolis and the Island of Aegina,* vol. 2, 138; *Ἅγιος Νεκτάριος Πενταπόλεως, Κατηχητικαὶ Ἐπιστολαί, Ἐπιστολὴ* 59.

[564] Clarke, *The Ascetic Works of St. Basil,* 243 (Rule 38 in the *Shorter Rules*). In the same vein, St. Columbanus began his monastic rule by stating: "At the first word of a senior, all on hearing should rise to obey, since their obedience is shown to God, as our Lord Jesus Christ says: 'He who hears you hears Me'" (Oliver Davies and Thomas O'Loughlin, *Celtic Spirituality,* 246).

[565] Μ. Βασιλείου, *Ἀσκητικαὶ Διατάξεις,* ΕΠΕ 9, 516; PG 31:1409A.

[566] *Rule of St. Benedict,* Chapter II.

[567] Eberle, *The Rule of the Master,* 276.

your elder? You have pleased God. Have you not pleased your elder? Neither have you pleased God.' This is because you don't see God; you do, however, see your elder, who is God's representative. Therefore, whatever you do to him passes on to God."[568] Elder Aimilianos wrote: "The abbot administers by divine right and is able to demand absolute obedience, which is transferred directly to God. [As St. Athanasios the Great said:] 'They endeavor to carry out his commands as if they had received them from God.'[569]"[570]

St. Symeon the New Theologian declared:

> He who has acquired absolute faith in his spiritual father, when he looks at him, he thinks that he is looking at Christ Himself.... He shows his living faith in him by venerating as holy the very place where his father and guide stood....
>
> When he [the disciple] uses something that is his [of his spiritual father], he does so with fear and reverence, judging himself unworthy not only to look at him and serve him but even to enter his cell.[571]

In the same vein, Sts. Callistus and Ignatius Xanthopoulos taught:

> Cleave to him [i.e., your elder] with body and spirit like a devoted son to his father and from then onwards obey all his commands implicitly, accord with him in everything, and see him not as a mere man, but as Christ Himself.
>
> Follow his [the abbot's] orders with all your strength faithfully, looking to him as if to Christ Himself and not as if to a mere man. Cast far away from yourself all disbelief and doubt, as well as your own opinions and insistence on your own will. Thus, follow the teacher at every step with simplicity and without examining his orders. Have your conscience as a mirror that clearly shows you that you are being perfectly obedient to your spiritual guide without judging what he says.[572]

St. John Cassian instructed that a monk should obey without questioning orders:

> Above all ... take care to make yourself an idiot and a fool in this life, according to the saying of the apostle[573] in order to become wise. That is, be obedient with simplicity and faith without examining your orders or hesitating to execute them....[574]

---

[568] Γέροντος Ἐφραίμ, *Ὁ Γέροντάς μου Ἰωσήφ*, 232; see also Elder Ephraim, *My Elder Joseph the Hesychast*, 323.

[569] Μεγάλου Ἀθανασίου, *Πρὸς Κάστορα, Περὶ τῶν κανονικῶν τῶν κοινοβίων διατυπώσεων 5* (ἀμφ.), PG 28:856C.

[570] Elder Aimilianos, *The Authentic Seal*, 57.

[571] Συμεὼν Ν. Θεολόγου, *Κεφάλαια Θεολογικὰ πνευματικά*, (Paris: Sources Chrétiennes, 1942), 51, 48. ΕΠΕ Φ19Α, 408–10.

[572] Καλλίστου καὶ Ἰγνατίου Ξανθοπούλων, *Μέθοδος καὶ κανὼν ἀκριβής*, PG 147:652. *Φιλοκαλία*, τ. Δ´, Ἀστήρ, 206; see also E. Kadloubovsky and G. E.H. Palmer, *Writings from the Philokalia on Prayer of the Heart*, 174.

[573] "If any man among you seemeth to be wise in this world, let him become a fool, that he may be wise" (1 Cor. 3:18).

[574] Κασσιανοῦ τοῦ Ῥωμαίου, *Πρὸς Κάστορα, περὶ τῶν Κανονικῶν τῶν Κοινοβίων διατυπώσεων*, ΒΕΠΕΣ 35, 181; see also Ramsey, *John Cassian: The Institutes*, 101.

That is true obedience which, even though something difficult is commanded it, endeavors to carry it out without any discussion or hesitation. There is no murmuring about the thing being impossible, but with complete faith and devotion he receives whatever has been said not as coming from a man but as commanded him by God. For obedience must be preferred to all the virtues, so that everything is put after it; and a monk should be content to endure all possible loss, provided that he does not seem to violate this good thing in any way.[575]

St. Basil the Great also wrote:

Just as sheep obey the shepherd and turn to whichever direction he leads them, likewise godly ascetics should obey the abbots without inquiring too inquisitively into the orders when they are free of sin, but should execute them with all eagerness and zeal....

If this kind of agreement is established in the ascetical system, peace will easily prevail among the ascetics, and salvation will be attained with the love and concord of all.[576]

St. Theodore the Studite urged his monks when he was about to die: "Stick to the race of obedience until the end so that you will 'obtain the unfading crown of righteousness' (cf. 1 Pet. 5:4 and 2 Tim. 4:8). Led by humility, you should always deny your own will and pattern yourselves only after the judgments of your superior."[577]

St. Nicodemos of the Holy Mountain wrote:

Submit to him [i.e., your elder] not just every will of yours—which is easier—but even every opinion of yours, which is more difficult. For there are many disciples who do cut off their will and do the will of their elder, but they do not renounce their opinions, especially if they are very educated. They always have the thought deeply rooted in their heart that whatever opinions and thoughts they themselves have regarding anything is better and wiser than the opinions and thoughts of their elder.[578]

In the same spirit, St. Joseph the Hesychast taught: "Genuine obedience is not merely a matter of executing an order externally and as a formality. Genuine obedience means training yourself to think and believe exactly as your elder thinks and believes.... Obedience entails subordinating your soul's convictions so that you may be freed from your evil self."[579] (And this is why an opinionated person will have difficulty progressing in monasticism.)

---

[575] *Regula Cassiani* 31:1–2 (as translated in Barry, *Commentary on the Rule of Saint Benedict,* 525).

[576] Μ. Βασιλείου, *Ἀσκητικαὶ Διατάξεις, κβ΄* PG 31:1407, 1409D; (ΕΠΕ 9, 516, 518).

[577] Thomas and Hero, *Byzantine Monastic Foundation Documents,* 80.

[578] As quoted in the presentation delivered by Archimandrite George Kapsanis "Orthodox Monasticism According to St. Nicodemos of the Holy Mountain" during the First Conference "St. Nicodemos of the Holy Mountain: His Life and Teaching," September 21–23, 1999 (http://www.pigizois.net/pneumatikoi_logoi/ orthodojos_monaxismos.htm).

[579] Γέροντος Ἐφραίμ, *Ὁ Γέροντάς μου Ἰωσήφ,* 238, 105; see also Elder Ephraim, *My Elder Joseph the Hesychast,* 330, 97–98.

Elder Aimilianos told his monks how crucial this kind of spiritual obedience is:

> The job of a disciple is to receive the mind-set of his elder. Monasticism consists in handing down and receiving this mind-set. It is not possible for there to be an assimilation of God nor cooperation or cohesion in a monastic family if there is not only one mind-set. In order that we may live and survive, each one of us must stop having his own ideologies....
>
> Due to the fall of man, in a monastic community the individual ideologies—which are the castles that separate the soul from God—cannot fall if there is no knowledge and receiving of the mind-set of the elder. In other words, the disciple must completely sacrifice everything that seems holy and perfect, everything strong and beautiful, everything spiritual and material that conflicts with this mind-set.[580]

St. Ephraim of Katounakia taught: "Real obedience—blind obedience—is considered to be genuine by the Fathers because it alone can crush self-absorption, self-love, and ego-centricity."[581] Abba Isaiah taught: "Let us be obedient to our fathers in everything, removing our every will, to be submissive to them so that their blessing rests upon us, as it did with Elisseus [i.e., the Prophet Elisha]."[582]

St. Barsanuphius the Great taught that a disciple who disobeys is destroying his own soul:

> If anyone is a true disciple, that person will obey his abbot in everything until death. Everything the abbot does is for our edification; so one should not dare to disagree with his words or to say: "What is this? Why is this?" Otherwise, one is not a disciple but a judge of one's abbot. All these things happen only as a result of a truly evil human will. Therefore, if someone's abbot asks for something to be done and the disciple resists, then it is clear that this disciple wants to impose his own opinion and invalidate the abbot's word. So the disciple can discern who is actually the abbot here: is it the one whose word was abolished, or the one whose word was applied? Whoever wants to impose his own will is a son of the devil; and whoever does the will of such a person is doing the will of the devil. Therefore, if anyone follows one's own will, that same person will not find rest in this way. What are the consequences of this? None other than disobedience, which is the destruction of the soul.[583]

St. Ephraim the Syrian reminds disciples that the obedience they have towards their elder does not depend on how virtuous he is:

> Those who live the monastic life, brethren, should not be disobedient or in any way contradict their teachers in the Lord, but should behave with great humility before God and men. If it so happens that an elder preaches virtue by words alone, but neglects to put them into practice, let us not for this reason give the devil the opportunity to divert our souls from this end, but let us call to mind the Lord, Who said: "The scribes

---

[580] Γέροντος Αἰμιλιανοῦ, *Νηπτικὴ Ζωὴ καὶ Ἀσκητικοὶ Κανόνες*, 433–34, 435.

[581] Elder Joseph of Vatopaidi, *Obedience Is Life: Elder Ephraim of Katounakia,* (United Kingdom: Pemptousia, 2003), 106.

[582] Chryssavgis and Penkett, *Abba Isaiah of Scetis: Ascetic Discourses,* 201.

[583] Chryssavgis, *Barsanuphius and John, Letters,* vol. 2, 135–36 (letter 551).

and the Pharisees sit in Moses' seat; all therefore whatsoever they bid you do, that … do; but do not ye after their works, for they say, and do not" (Mt. 23:2–3).[584]

One potential pitfall associated with obedience (whether the obedience is to the orders of one's elder or even to the canons of Church law) is to execute it in a cold and legalistic manner—that is, following the letter of the law while sacrificing its spirit. For example, executing specific orders sometimes unintentionally inconveniences someone else. A cold way to deal with this would be to disregard the other person's difficulty and blindly obey orders. A much kinder way to deal with this would be to discuss the problem with him and try to find a way to execute the order in a way that will not create difficulties for him. Or, in the event that no such solution can be found and we do not have the opportunity to verify that the elder wants us to execute the command despite the difficulties it creates, then at least we could genuinely apologize to the other person with compassion for the difficulty our obedience is causing him.

Since obedience is a natural expression of humility, a humble person will be obedient to everyone. St. Ephraim the Syrian wrote:

> The beginning of the fruit is the flower, and the beginning of humility is submission to the Lord. For he who is submissive is obedient to everyone; he is forbearing and shows respect to the young and old. If his superior gives him an order he obeys, telling himself: "He is my Lord." If some other brother gives him an order he will obey him, too, telling himself: "He is the brother of my Lord." And even if a little child gives him an order he will still obey him, telling himself: "This child is the child of my Lord."[585]

In the same spirit, Abba Dorotheos taught that there are three degrees of humility: obeying our superiors, obeying our equals, and obeying our inferiors. St. Benedict taught: "The brethren must render the service of obedience not only to the abbot, but they must thus also obey one another, knowing that they shall go to God by this path of obedience."[586] St. John the Prophet, however, qualified this as follows: "If those who gave you the order are brothers, and you see that the matter will bring you harm or else is beyond your ability, again ask your abbot and do whatever he tells you."[587]

This is why the monastic vows include obedience not just to the abbot but also to the entire brotherhood: "Do you vow to preserve, even unto death, obedience to the Igumen,

---

[584] Chrysostomos, *The Evergetinos, Book I,* 313.

[585] As quoted in Ἀρχιμανδρίτου Ἀθανασίου, *Ἡ Φωνὴ Ἑνὸς Μοναχοῦ* (Λευκωσία: Ἱερᾶς Μονῆς Τροοδιτίσσης, 1998), 346.

[586] *Rule of St. Benedict,* Chapter LXXI.

[587] Chryssavgis, *Barsanuphius and John, Letters,* vol. 1, 283 (letter 288).

and to all the Brethren (*Sisters*) in Christ?"[588] Commenting on this, Metropolitan Hierotheos Vlachos explained:

> It is clearly evident here that obedience to the superior, the abbot, is linked inseparably with obedience to the brotherhood, since the abbot cannot act autonomously and arbitrarily in the monastery. It goes without saying that the abbot must obey Orthodox Tradition as well as the Bishop. For an obedience associated with obedience to the elder that is independent of Church Tradition and the Bishop is an individualistic and psychological kind of obedience.[589]

3) Harm of Partial Obedience

St. Basil the Great wrote: "If you have found a teacher of good works, … take heed to yourself that you do nothing contrary to his judgment; for whatever is done without his consent is a kind of theft and sacrilege leading not to your profit but to your death, even if it seems good to you. For, if it is good, why is it done secretly and not in the open?"[590] St. Mark the Ascetic warned: "A disciple under obedience who secretly mingles his own will [with the will of his elder] is an adulterer."[591] Likewise, St. Barsanuphius the Great wrote:

> Every good deed that is not performed for—and only for—the love of God, but rather for one's own will, is found to be something polluted and causes God to flee….[592]
>
> If you cut off your will in one matter but do not do the same in another, it is clear that even in the one where you did cut it off, you still have another will. Indeed, a submissive person submits in everything; and such a person is carefree about salvation, since someone else will give account for him, namely, the one to whom one has submitted and to whom one has confided oneself.[593]

St. Basil also said (and was quoted by St. Athanasios of Athos in his own rule[594]): "True and perfect obedience of subordinates to their abbot is shown in this: not only in refraining from what the abbot regards as improper, but also by not doing what is praiseworthy

---

[588] *The Great Book of Needs,* vol. 1, 364.

[589] Μητροπολίτου Ἱεροθέου, *Ὁ Ὀρθόδοξος Μοναχισμός* (Βοιωτία: Ἱερὰ Μονὴ Γενεθλίου τῆς Θεοτόκου–Πελαγίας, 2002), 525; Metropolitan of Nafpaktos Hierotheos, *Orthodox Monasticism as the Way of Life of Prophets, Apostles and Martyrs* (Levadia: Birth of the Theotokos Monastery, 2011), 470.

[590] Βασιλείου τοῦ Μεγάλου, *Ἀσκητικὰ Α΄,* ΕΠΕ 8, 102–5; see also Wagner, *Saint Basil: Ascetical Works,* vol. 9, 20.

[591] Μάρκου τοῦ ἀσκητοῦ, *Περὶ πνευματικοῦ νόμου,* PG 65:921; see also Palmer, Sherrard, Ware, *The Philokalia,* vol. 1, 118.

[592] Chryssavgis, *Barsanuphius and John, Letters,* vol. 2, 39 (letter 401).

[593] Ibid., 202–3 (letter 614).

[594] Vid. Thomas and Hero, *Byzantine Monastic Foundation Documents,* 260.

without his approval."[595] Along the same lines, St. Neophytos of Docheiariou later wrote: "Heed your superior and obey him as Christ Himself our master.... Do not resist him, nor contradict him at all if possible even in the slightest matter, since, indeed, he who resists or objects or contradicts him in any way whatever or causes him grief in some matter, or provokes him to anger, does all [these things] to God, inasmuch as he did it to the one given him by God in his stead to rule and shepherd you."[596] Similarly, St. Benedict wrote: "Obedience will be acceptable to God and agreeable to men then only, if what is commanded is done without hesitation, delay, lukewarmness, grumbling or complaint, because the obedience which is rendered to Superiors is rendered to God. For He Himself hath said: 'He that heareth you heareth Me.'[597] And it must be rendered by the disciples with a good will, 'for the Lord loveth a cheerful giver.'[598] For if the disciple obeyeth with an ill will, and murmureth, not only with lips but also in his heart, even though he fulfil the command, yet it will not be acceptable to God, who regardeth the heart of the murmurer."[599] Likewise, St. Columbanus wrote: "He who does something by himself without asking, or who contradicts and says, 'I am not doing it,' or who murmurs, if it is a serious matter, let him do penance with three impositions [i.e., punishments], if a slight one, with one."[600]

St. Symeon the New Theologian warns:

> Whoever falls into such mistakes—I mean, of course, talking back to and lacking faith in his spiritual father and guide—is ruined horribly, and while he is still alive he descends into the deepest parts of Hades, and as a son of disobedience and destruction he becomes the dwelling place of Satan and all his unclean power....
>
> All of you together, both young and old, both the first and last, endeavor to preserve your subjection to the abbot unadulterated, obeying his words in every matter. For he who resists his commands resists the orders of God.[601]

St. Athanasios of Athos wrote in his typikon: "Preserve a good disposition, humility, and obedience to your superior until death, not contradicting or annoying him in any respect."[602]

In his *General Rule for Monasteries,* St. Fructuosus of Braga with a biblical allegory elaborated on the damage suffered by monks who complain:

---

[595] Βασιλείου τοῦ Μεγάλου, *Ἀσκητικὰ Α΄,* ΕΠΕ 8, 146–47; see also Wagner, *Saint Basil: Ascetical Works,* vol. 9, 218–19.

[596] Thomas and Hero, *Byzantine Monastic Foundation Documents,* 1309.

[597] Lk. 10:16.

[598] 2 Cor. 9:7.

[599] *Rule of St. Benedict,* Chapter V.

[600] *Sancti Columbani Opera,* 170–71 (Penitential 9).

[601] *Μικρὰ Κατήχησις,* 327. Πρβλ. Μοναχοῦ Νικοδήμου Μπιλάλη, μν. ἔργ., 202

[602] Thomas and Hero, *Byzantine Monastic Foundation Documents,* 265.

And whatever they do they must do without complaint, lest—and may this never happen—by their complaints, they perish like those who perished in the desert (vid. Num. 11, 14, 16, 20). Those complainers in the desert perished by eating manna, while these in the monastery die daily mouthing the scriptures. Those because of their complaints did not enter the land of promise, and these because of their complaints do not enter the land of promise of Paradise. What a terrible loss to leave Egypt, to have crossed the sea, to have played upon the tambourine with Moses and Mariam when Pharaoh drowned (vid. Ex. 15:20), to have eaten manna and yet not to have entered the land of promise; how much greater a misfortune to leave the Egypt of this world, to pass daily through the sea of baptism with the bitterness of penitence, to beat upon the drum, that is, to crucify the flesh with Christ, and to eat the manna which is heavenly grace, and yet not to enter the land of the heavenly kingdom.[603]

The monastic rules attributed to St. Anthony the Great state: "Do not undertake any task, whatever it may be, without the advice of the father of the monastery."[604] Commenting on this, Elder Aimilianos told his monks:

The saint is saying not to undertake any task without a blessing. Thus, you should neither increase your prayer rule, nor change your diet, or extend your vigil, or read an additional book, or create a new friendship, or enter discussions with others, or write or become interested in something, or change your manners. For example, you might read the *Life of St. Pachomios the Great,* and something in it makes an impression on you. So you say to yourself: 'I will also implement this.' No. Whatever is not blessed is nonexistent, in the sense that it does not exist as something good before God. On the contrary, it is material for the evil one, a denial of goodness....

With this rule, St. Anthony the Great does not want to constrict the heart of a monk, nor does he want to make his life difficult or to strangle his personhood. He made this rule so that there would be a balance in the monastery and the blessing of God....

St. Anthony the Great wants to create a spirit of unity, a family mindset. In a family, one does not do whatever he wants.... The cohesion of the brotherhood is lost if the elder is not consulted for everything.[605]

St. Paisius Velichkovsky taught:

The disciples for their part should be in the hands of the superior like an instrument in the hands of a master, or like clay in the hands of a potter; they should do nothing without his blessing, should have nothing of their own, but should have everything—books, bed, and the rest—by the blessing of their father; they should not trust their own mind, and in a word, they should be like dead men before their death, having no will or understanding of their own. Such should be the rule of true novices.[606]

Likewise, St. Symeon the New Theologian wrote: "Listen only to the admonitions of your [spiritual] father, give to him humble answers, and tell him your thoughts as to God, even

---

[603] Barlow, *The Fathers of the Church: Iberian Fathers,* vol. 63, 184–85.

[604] Rule #32, PG 40:1069A.

[605] Γέροντος Αἰμιλιανοῦ, *Νηπτικὴ Ζωὴ καὶ Ἀσκητικοὶ Κανόνες,* 69–71.

[606] Metrophanes, *Blessed Paisius Velichkovsky,* 137.

mere temptations, and may you hide nothing from him, nor do anything without his opinion, neither go to sleep, nor eat, nor drink!"[607] In the same spirit, Elder Aimilianos stated in the *Regulations of the Holy Cenobium of the Annunciation:* "Nothing shall be decided, said, done, taken, promised or offered without her [i.e., without the Abbess' blessing]."[608] St. Sophrony of Essex explained:

> We should begin every action by asking for a blessing, to give our every undertaking the character of a divine work. All the trivialities of everyday life, as well as the big things, require a knowledge of the will of God, for in the life of man *everything is important.* Through his blessing the whole of life acquires a sacred character, for only that which is accomplished in the name of the Lord is inscribed in eternity.[609]

Even though the abbot has the right to demand perfect obedience of his disciples, he must have the discernment to make this demand sparingly and only when absolutely necessary, as did Elder Ephraim. This requirement of obedience, however, does not mean that a disciple cannot humbly tell his abbot that he foresees difficulties in executing an order, as St. Benedict taught:

> If, perchance, any difficult or impossible tasks be enjoined on a brother, let him nevertheless receive the order of him who commandeth with all meekness and obedience. If, however, he see that the gravity of the task is altogether beyond his strength, let him quietly and seasonably submit the reasons for his inability to his Superior, without pride, protest, or dissent. If, however, after his explanation the Superior still insisteth on his command, let the younger be convinced that so it is good for him; and let him obey from love, relying on the help of God.[610]

Thus, a disciple is expected to explain this, since the abbot cannot be all-knowing. Elder Ephraim said that a disciple may even voice his objections twice without this being viewed as disobedience. But if the abbot still insists, then the disciple is obliged to be obedient despite whatever difficulties he foresees.

4) Disobeying Harmful Orders

When the orders of the abbot go against the commandments of God, however, a monk not only has the right to disobey but is obliged to do so. As St. Ephraim the Syrian taught: "The disciple who obeys in such circumstances will *himself* not go unpunished by God."[611]

---

[607] Griggs, *Divine Eros: Hymns of Saint Symeon the New Theologian,* 50 (Hymn 4).

[608] Elder Aimilianos, *The Authentic Seal,* 175–76.

[609] Sakharov, *Truth and Life,* 90.

[610] *Rule of St. Benedict,* Chapter LXVIII.

[611] Chrysostomos, *The Evergetinos, Book IV,* 451.

Abba Poemen taught that if a monk sees that he is losing his soul by living with a bad elder, he should leave him without even waiting to ask anyone for permission:

> A brother questioned Abba Poemen, saying, "I am losing my soul through living near my abba; should I go on living with him?" The old man knew that he was finding this harmful and he was surprised that he even asked if he should stay there. So he said to him, "Stay if you want to." The brother left him and stayed on there. He came back again and said, "I am losing my soul." But the old man did not tell him to leave. He came a third time and said, "I really cannot stay there any longer." Then Abba Poemen said, "Now you are saving yourself; go away and do not stay with him any longer," and he added, "When someone sees that he is in danger of losing his soul, he does not need to ask advice. It is right to ask about secret thoughts and then it is up to the old man to test them; but with visible faults, do not ask; cut them off at once."[612]

Regarding this incident with Abba Poemen, St. Ignatius Brianchaninov wrote:

> Evidently this meant that the elder in question was breaking the moral tradition of the Church. It is another matter when no harm is done to the soul, and one is only disturbed by thoughts. Disturbing thoughts are obviously diabolic. We must not yield to them. They operate just where we receive spiritual profit, which is what the demons want to snatch from us.[613]

St. Basil the Great wrote about God-pleasing disobedience in more detail:

> But if we are ordered to do something opposed to the commandments of the Lord or something that appears to corrupt or adulterate it, it is time then to say: "We ought to obey God rather than men,"[614] and to be mindful of the Lord who says, "They do not follow the voice of a stranger, but flee from him, because they do not recognize the voice of strangers."[615] And we ought to be mindful of the Apostle, who, for our reassurance, dared to hold to account even the angels when he said: "Though we ourselves or an angel from heaven should proclaim a gospel to you other than the one we have already proclaimed to you, let him be anathema."[616] From these sayings we are taught that even if someone is very genuine, maybe even of exalted status and held in admiration, yet who hinders us from doing what the Lord has prescribed, or who orders us to do what the Lord has forbidden, such a one ought to be avoided and execrated [i.e., loathed] by all who love the Lord....[617]
>
> But his [i.e., the abbot's] subjects—discipline being preserved and subjection recognising the limits imposed upon it—must remember the Lord's words: "My sheep hear My voice, and I know them and they follow Me, and I give unto them eternal life"[618] ... and the apostle's words too: "If any man teacheth a different doctrine and

---

[612] Ward, *The Sayings of the Desert Fathers,* 193.

[613] St. Ignatius Brianchaninov, *The Arena* (Jordanville: Holy Trinity Monastery, 1991), 47. All quotations herein from this publication are used by permission.

[614] Acts 5:20.

[615] Jn. 10:5.

[616] Gal. 1:8.

[617] Clarke, *The Ascetic Works of St. Basil,* 272–73 (Rule 114 in the *Shorter Rules*).

[618] Jn. 10:27–28.

consenteth not to sound words, even the words of our Lord Jesus Christ, and to the doctrine which is according to godliness, he is puffed up, knowing nothing."[619] Then after enumerating the consequences he added: "Flee such things."[620,621] ...

"Despise not prophesyings; test all things; hold fast that which is good; abstain from every form of evil."[622] So that if any thing is said according to the commandment of the Lord, or is directed towards the commandment of the Lord, we must obey, though it should seem to involve death; but if anything is contrary to the commandment or injures the commandment, though an angel from heaven or one of the apostles enjoins it, whether it promises life or threatens death, we must in no wise listen to it.[623]

Following St. Basil, St. Symeon the New Theologian wrote:

In all those matters in which there is no deviation from God's commandment or from the apostolic canons and regulations, you must absolutely obey him [i.e., your abbot] in them all and trust in him as you would in the Lord. But in those matters in which the Gospel of Christ and the laws of His church are jeopardized, you must not only not follow the orders of the person who suggests this to you or orders it, but must not do so even if an angel has come down from heaven and is preaching something to you contrary to what those who were eyewitnesses to the Word have preached.[624]

Likewise, St. Eustathios of Thessalonica advised a rasophore monk:

Ignore your abbot when he simply tells you to do worldly things that are sinful. For you have not been appointed to be a real slave of his but to be a brother and fellow-servant, or rather to be a disciple. And no disciple who knows what Christ wants will be persuaded by a teacher who thinks differently. Likewise, no honest servant of a good master will obey a fellow-servant ordering him to do things that would grieve his master. Similarly, a prudent brother would be above all reproach if he disobeys his foolish brother inciting him to do something detrimental to the father they both have in common.

Therefore, you, too, O beginner monk, if you love our Father in heaven, if you are truly His honest servant, if your mind is attached to the Great Teacher, follow your abbot in everything he teaches that is right as a good servant, since he has been appointed as your master, and you should love him deeply as your gentle father. But if he leads you astray from the right path and guides you off course, away from the path taken by those with a correct understanding, then you must boldly but respectfully object.

However, this bold objection should be made carefully so that no one can repudiate it. Entreat him and explain your stance spiritually. He might respect your boldness or your entreaties or your explanations. But if he tells you that you are forbidden to speak boldly like that, explain to him that the kind of boldness he as a great-schema monk

---

[619] 1 Tim. 6:3–4.

[620] 1 Tim. 6:5.

[621] Clarke, *The Ascetic Works of St. Basil,* 347 (Rule 303 in the *Shorter Rules*).

[622] 1 Thes. 5:20–22.

[623] Clarke, *The Ascetic Works of St. Basil,* 347 (Rule 303 in the *Shorter Rules*).

[624] Niketas Stethatos, *The Life of Saint Symeon the New Theologian,* trans. Richard P. H. Greenfield (London: Dumbarton Oaks, 2003), 151.

said he forbids is different from the boldness you are showing towards him. In the former case, the boldness reveals an irrational audacity, but in this case it is trying to avoid something evil. If he continues to threaten you, citing the saying: "A son should die even if he is justifiably objecting to his father's orders," attempting to condemn anyone who objects to him of fratricide, let him rave as someone no longer sane but delirious, and whatever he says will be nonsense. Such a person is not a father, since he does not allow his son to raise any objections, nor do your words qualify as objections to a father. After all, the greatest Father of all, although He gives commandments, does not tire of listening to our demands for exemption, nor does He kill us or reject us. On the contrary, He persuades the one entreating Him to be obedient, even when his entreaties are not justifiable.

So do not obey orders that lead you to do wicked things, but object freely and sincerely. If your spiritual father continues to pressure you, flee from him as from a fire and proceed to renounce him publicly. Rise up against him and disown him as one who is deranged. Henceforth have as your only father the first Father of all, and put your trust in Him.[625]

In more recent times, St. Ignatius Brianchaninov wrote essentially the same thing to monks: "Obey all the fathers and brethren in matters that do not conflict with the Law of God, or with the rule and order of the monastery, or with the management of the monastic authorities. But on no account obey what is evil, even though you have to put up with a certain amount of trouble and suffering for your firmness and your refusal to please men."[626] Likewise, St. Daniel of Katounakia wrote to the nuns whom he inherited from St. Nectarios of Aegina:

I do not mean, my children in the Lord, that you should be blindly and irrationally obedient as some are to those who teach and supposedly assume spiritual authority for the sake (even if only slightly) of their ego and self-interest. No! But be careful, and if you see from us advice and counsels that are not consistent with the pure spirit of paternal discernment and the unerring prescriptions of the holy Church Fathers, you should not obey.[627]

Ivan Kontzevitch warned of pseudo-elders:

In pseudo-eldership, the will of one person is enslaved by the will of another, contrary to the point made by the Apostle Paul: "Ye are bought with a price, be not ye the servants of men" (1 Cor. 7:23), and this situation entails a feeling of oppression, despondency or an unhealthy partial attitude to the "elder." A true grace-filled attitude to an elder, although based on unconditional obedience, does not deprive a person of the feeling of joy and freedom in God, because he is not in submission to the will of man, but through it to the will of God. He knows from his experience that the elder shows him the best way out of any given external difficulty, or offers him the best cure

---

[625] PG 135:872C–873B.

[626] Brianchaninov, *The Arena,* 49.

[627] Γέροντος Δανιὴλ Κατουνακιώτου, *Μοναχικὰ Ἐντρυφήματα* (Ἅγιον Ὄρος: Ἔκδοσις Μοναστικῆς Ἀδελφότητος Δανιηλαίων, 1982), 49.

of his spiritual illness. While the grace-filled elder is the bearer of God's will, the pseudo-elder overshadows God.[628]

There are conflicting opinions regarding what exactly is meant by the phrases "blind obedience" and "obedience until death."[629] Demetrios Petrakakos held the opinion[630] that since the holy Fathers teach that a monk is expected to disobey his abbot whenever the latter goes against the commandments of God, the phrase "blind obedience" inaccurately describes the nature of his obedience (since a disciple blindly obeying his abbot's commands would not notice if any of them go against the commandments of God). Petrakakos concluded that "the phrase 'obedience until death' refers not to the *nature* of obedience [i.e., being obedient even if it results in his death] but to the magnitude of the monk's efforts as well as to the *duration* of it [i.e., until he dies]."

Further evidence that seems to support Petrakakos's conclusion that the phrase "until death" refers to duration is the fact that the same phrase is also used in the Slavonic great-schema vows of keeping virginity and poverty "until death" (since maintaining virginity cannot cause death). Likewise, Mouratidis, after agreeing with those statements of Petrakakos, adds: "The required 'obedience until death' applies to the monk's offering of his own volition but not of his own [rational] judgment. Proof of the monk's freedom to judge is his right [according to Question 36 in the *Long Rules* of St. Basil] to leave the brotherhood when he is harmed spiritually by staying in it."[631]

Metropolitan Hierotheos Vlachos has a similar understanding of the meaning of the phrase "until death," for he wrote: "The priest, after hearing the confessions and vows of the postulant monk says: 'Truly, you have chosen a good and blessed work, but only if you complete it. Good things are acquired with toil and achieved with pain.' The beginning is good, but there must also be a continuation, since man must struggle against the powers of darkness until the end of his life. This is why the phrase 'until death' is used in the service [of the Great Schema]"[632] And St. John Cassian, commenting on Philippians 2:8, wrote: "'He [Jesus] humbled Himself, having become obedient'—not 'for a while,' as that other

---

[628] I. M. Kontzevich, *The Acquisition of the Holy Spirit in Ancient Russia* (Platina: St. Herman of Alaska Brotherhood, 1989), 72.

[629] This phrase is from the service of tonsure into the Great Schema: "Do you vow to preserve, even unto death, obedience to the Igumen, and to all the Brethren in Christ?" (*The Great Book of Needs*, vol. 1, 364). It is also from Phil. 2:8: "Although he was in the form of God, he humbled himself, having become obedient unto (μέχρι) death, even the death of the cross."

[630] Πετρακάκου, *Μοναχικοὶ Θεσμοί,* 121.

[631] Μουρατίδη, *Ἡ Ὑπακοὴ ἐν τῇ Ἀρχαίᾳ Ἐκκλησίᾳ,* 93–94.

[632] Ἱεροθέου, *Ὁ Ὀρθόδοξος Μοναχισμός,* 526; Hierotheos, *Orthodox Monasticism,* 471.

[monk] who was possessed by a diabolical spirit and by pride had said, but—'unto death.'"[633]

On the other hand, St. Basil the Great says that monastics should obey their elder's orders even if it should seem to involve death.[634] Likewise, St. John of Sinai taught: "A simple monk is like a dumb but rational and obedient animal ... who never answers back to the master who yokes him. The upright soul does not talk back to his superior. Instead, he follows where he is directed to go and will raise no protest even if sent to his death."[635]

Elder Aimilianos explained the consequences of following one's own logic instead of obeying one's elder:

> If you resort to logic, you will certainly come into conflict with the instructions you have received from the elder, and your mind will fall into such a weakened state that you will not be able to receive the truth. Not only will you sin, but also you will become isolated from the brotherhood. Logic isolates man and makes him earthly. It makes a son of God into a mere human, because when a man subjugates himself to the rationale of human logic, he ceases to be a son of God, and he becomes a son of earth, of mud. Then he falls into spiritual darkness; he loses discernment—the ability to know what is good and what is evil. Consequently, he falls into darkness of soul, into despair, into objecting, into evil. He does not know how to behave, and he is disturbed, troubled, tired; he loses his endurance of soul. He wants to eat strong food in order to be fortified. When he sleeps, he is stultified and falls into an unprecedented downward spiral. In this state, you can't understand the truth, because this is painful to feel that you are guilty. In this case you must have a basic power of humblemindedness to be able to admit your fault. But since this is painful, we put up a shield so that they don't strike us, and the shield is the thought that we are right.[636]

Consequently, a monk under obedience must bear in mind that his "right" to hold on to his own judgment is only in regards to the instances in which his elder would contradict the commandments of Christ, as explained by St. Basil above.[637] And since such instances are extremely rare, it follows that a monk in fact does renounce even his own rational judgment in all other matters when his opinion conflicts with that of his elder.

5) Obeying Harmful Orders

Notwithstanding the foregoing patristic admonitions towards disobedience under certain circumstances, several teachings of the holy Fathers show that this does not mean that a disciple may disobey whenever he disagrees with a decision of the abbot, ostensibly

---

[633] Ramsey, *John Cassian: The Institutes,* 271 (xii. 29).

[634] See footnote #623 on page 110.

[635] Luibhéid, *John Climacus: The Ladder of Divine Ascent,* 217.

[636] Γέροντος Αἰμιλιανοῦ, *Νηπτικὴ Ζωὴ καὶ Ἀσκητικοὶ Κανόνες,* 215–16.

[637] See footnote #617 on page 109.

claiming that he is being harmed spiritually and that the abbot is somehow breaking the commandments of God indirectly. On the contrary, the holy Fathers frequently preferred to err on the side of obeying even in instances of potential spiritual harm and when possibly breaking the commandments of God—even to the point of obeying orders to steal[638] and murder![639] St. John of the Ladder that this is the sign of true obedience:

> Let us trust with firm confidence those who have taken upon themselves the care of us in the Lord, even though they order something apparently contrary and opposed to our salvation. For it is then that our faith in them is tested as in a furnace of humiliation. For it is a sign of the truest faith if we obey our superiors without any hesitation, even when we see the opposite of what we had hoped for happening.[640]

Likewise, the *Rule of the Master* states: "Whether for good or for ill, what happens among the sheep is the responsibility of the shepherd, and he who gave orders is the one who will have to render an account when inquiry is made at the judgment, not he who carried out the orders, whether good or bad."[641] St. John the Prophet went as far as to advise Abba Dorotheos of Gaza to obey the abbot even if the order seems sinful. He told him:

> He who wants to be a monk should not hold onto his own will at all in anything. This is what Christ taught us when he said: "I have come into the world not to do My own will."[642] For he who wants to do one thing and declines to do something else is either trying to present himself as being more discerning than the one giving orders, or else is being mocked by the demons. So then you should obey in everything, even if it

---

[638] "It was said that Abba Saius and Abba Moue lived together. Abba Saius was very obedient, but he was very harsh. To test him, the old man said to him, 'Go and steal.' Through obedience Abba Saius went to steal from the brethren, giving thanks to the Lord in everything. Abba Moue took the things and returned them secretly" (Ward, *The Sayings of the Desert Fathers,* 229).

[639] "One of the Thebans once came to Abba Sisoes wanting to become a monk, and the elder asked him if he had anybody in the world. 'I have one son,' he said, and the elder said to him: 'Go and throw him into the river, then you will become a monk.' After he set out to throw his son into the river the elder sent a brother to prevent him. The brother said: 'Stop, what are you doing?' And he said: 'The abba told me to throw him in,' so the brother said to him: 'The elder also said: "Do *not* throw him in,"' and leaving his son he came to the elder and became a well-tried monk on account of his obedience" (Wortley, *The Alphabetical Sayings of the Desert Fathers,* 283 [Sisoes 10]). Similarly, the *Gerontikon* relates the incident of an abbot who ordered his disciple to throw his son into a burning furnace. After doing so, "the fire of the oven became dew and it did not burn the boy. His father won the same glory that the Patriarch Abraham had" (vid. Chrysostomos, *The Evergetinos, Book I,* 291).

[640] Holy Transfiguration Monastery, *The Ladder of Divine Ascent,* 47.

[641] Eberle, *The Rule of the Master,* 123.

[642] Jn. 6:38.

seems sinful to you. For your abbot who gives the orders will bear the judgment himself, since he is responsible for giving account on your behalf.[643] If the command seems too heavy for you, ask him about it and leave the matter to his discretion.[644]

St. Sophrony of Essex wrote to a monk: "If you accomplish any task out of obedience in all good conscience, you are dispensed from answering for it before God. The one who gave you the order answers, and thus your conscience remains always at peace."[645]

To resolve the apparent contradiction between these teachings *encouraging* obedience to sinful orders and the aforementioned teachings *prohibiting* such obedience, St. Ignatius Brianchaninov concludes:

> Obedience to elders in the form in which it was practised in ancient monasticism is not given to our time.... An indispensable condition of such submission is a Spirit-bearing Guide who by the will of the Spirit can mortify the fallen will of the person subject to him in the Lord, and can mortify all the passions as well....
>
> It is obvious that the mortification of a fallen will which is effected so sublimely and victoriously by the will of the Spirit of God cannot be accomplished by a director's fallen will when the director himself is still enslaved to the passions. "If you wish to renounce the world and learn the life of the Gospel," said St. Symeon the New Theologian to the monks of his time, "do not surrender [entrust] yourself to an inexperienced or passionate master, lest instead of the life of the Gospel you learn a diabolical life." ...
>
> According to the word of the Lord: *If a blind man leads a blind man, both will fall into a ditch* (Mt. 15:14).... Elders who take upon themselves the rôle of the ancient holy Elders without having their spiritual gifts should know that their very outlook or way of thinking, their reason or understanding, and their knowledge are self-deception and diabolic delusion which cannot fail to give birth to a corresponding fruit in the person guided by them....
>
> It will be useless to point out to us that St. Zachariah who was living in obedience to an inexperienced elder ... or St. Acacius found salvation while living with a cruel elder.... Both were in obedience to incompetent elders, but they were guided by the counsels of Spirit-bearing Fathers and the most edifying examples which were in abundance before their eyes. Therefore, they could only have remained in outward obedience to their elders. These cases are outside the general rule and order....
>
> Perhaps you retort: "A novice's faith can take the place of an incompetent elder." It is untrue. Faith in the truth saves. Faith in a lie and in diabolic delusion is ruinous according to the teaching of the Apostle: "They refused to love the truth that would save them [he says of those who are voluntarily perishing]. Therefore, God will send them [i.e., will permit them to suffer] a strong delusion, so that they will believe a lie, that all may be condemned who do not believe the truth but delight in falsehood."[646] ...

---

[643] Cf. Heb. 13:17.

[644] Νικοδήμου τοῦ Ἁγιορείτου, *Βαρσανουφίου καὶ Ἰωάννου: κείμενα διακριτικὰ καὶ ἡσυχαστικὰ (ἐρωταποκρίσεις)*, τόμος β´ (Καρέας: Ἰ.Μ. Τιμίου Προδρόμου, 1996), 147–48; see also Chryssavgis, *Barsanuphius and John, Letters*, vol. 1, 282–83 (letter 288).

[645] Sakharov, *Striving for Knowledge of God*, 290.

[646] 2 Thes. 2:10–12.

There have been instances (they are very, very rare) when faith, by the special providence of God, has operated through sinners and achieved the salvation of these sinners.... Instances of this kind are exceptions.... We shall act very wrongly if we take these instances as models for imitation....

Monastic obedience in the form and character in which it was practised by the monks of old is a lofty spiritual mystery. Its attainment and full imitation have become impossible for us. We can only examine it reverently and intelligently, and appropriate its spirit. We show right judgment and evince salutary intelligence when, in reading about the rules and experiences of the ancient Fathers and of their obedience ... we see at the present time a general decline of Christianity and recognize that we are unfit to inherit the legacy of the Fathers in its fullness and in all its abundance.[647]

Although some of St. Joseph the Hesychast's[648] and Elder Ephraim's[649] teachings give the impression that the grace of obedience will always magically protect a disciple from harm, this is not the whole story. For when I discussed this matter with Elder Ephraim and asked: "When does the grace of obedience protect a disciple from harmful orders?" his reply was: "The orders must be right." And then to illustrate his point, he told me about a pregnant woman who had suffered harm by obeying the medical advice of her spiritual father who was an abbot. Furthermore, St. Joseph the Hesychast once explained to St. Ephraim of Katounakia that the reason why he had lost some grace while obeying his elder was because the order was sinful.[650] When St. John of Sinai mentions the case of a disciple suffering

---

[647] Brianchaninov, *The Arena*, 43–47.

[648] For example, St. Joseph the Hesychast taught: "When a person is obeying an elder, it doesn't matter if the command is wrong; it will turn out well for him simply because he is being obedient" (Γέροντος Ἐφραίμ, Ὁ Γέροντάς μου Ἰωσήφ, 182; see also Elder Ephraim, *My Elder Joseph the Hesychast*, 255).

[649] Elder Ephraim wrote: "Even if the command that the disciple is given is wrong, God will bless it anyway for obedience's sake" (Γέροντος Ἐφραίμ, Πατρικαὶ Νουθεσίαι, 167; see also Elder Ephraim, *Counsels from the Holy Mountain*, 125). He also gave the example of the time he blindly obeyed the bad advice of Fr. Arsenios to plant onions upside-down. Elder Ephraim said: "Not only did they all sprout, but they even turned out wonderfully. It was due to exact obedience that they turned out all right" (Γέροντος Ἐφραίμ, Ὁ Γέροντάς μου Ἰωσήφ, 238; see also Elder Ephraim, *My Elder Joseph the Hesychast*, 329–30).

[650] During World War II, an international philanthropic organization sent tons of canned food to Greece in order to help those who were homeless and starving because of the war. It was decided (unjustly) that each brotherhood in Katounakia would also receive a large hamper with 75 pounds of canned foods. Elder Nikephoros sent his disciple, St. Ephraim of Katounakia, to take a hamper of canned foods for their brotherhood. But as soon as St. Ephraim picked it up, he perceived that all his spiritual strength was depleted, and he felt as if he were just a biological mass of flesh and blood with no soul, like a brute beast. Afterwards he asked St. Joseph the Hesychast why he had lost so much grace, and he replied: "My child, do you know that I didn't go and get a hamper? I had also heard about it, but I didn't send any of my disciples to get one. I want to be fed by the sweat of my brow, by carving wooden crosses, not by things I didn't earn. Didn't you realize that those alms were for people who had lost their homes and were suffering? How could you go and take them?" "But I'm under obedience!" objected St. Ephraim. "I agree; I'm not denouncing you. You had no choice. But your elder does not have such precise criteria. Nevertheless, God allowed *you* to suffer this loss of grace, so that tomorrow you could teach your spiritual children that such actions are sinful." (This unpublished anecdote was related to me on October 24, 2011, by Fr. Nectarios of Vigla, a disciple of St. Ephraim of Katounakia.)

damage while under obedience, he concludes: "Though he has fallen, he is not dead," thus acknowledging the damage but also showing that it is not too serious.[651]

Elder Ephraim also in his own life once found it beneficial to be intentionally disobedient to his holy elder St. Joseph the Hesychast and even to lie to him when his elder was sick and refused medical help.[652] The surprising thing about this incident is that when Elder Ephraim later admitted what he had done, St. Joseph commended him and told him with a smile and a hug: "This little head is full of brains!"

Even St. Ephraim of Katounakia (who attached extreme importance to obedience) concluded that an experienced disciple may disobey his elder. He once wrote to a beginner:

> Obedience with discernment [i.e., not blindly obeying everything] comes after years of struggle. You, at this young age, should have "blind obedience." Do you see what St. John of the Ladder says? Once an elder visited a novice and someone who had been a monk for fifteen years. He said to the novice, "Sing a worldly song."
> "May it be blessed," he replied and began to sing.
> Then the elder turned to the monk and said, "Sing a worldly song."
> "Forgive me," the monk replied and did not sing.
> Both of them acted well. The monk's reply to the elder is not considered disobedience. However, if the novice had acted in this way, he would have been disobedient since he was still a novice. You must first pass through the stage of blind obedience. You ought to say nothing else but, "May it be blessed." After ten or fifteen years comes obedience with discernment, which is the result of blind obedience.[653]

These incidents demonstrate one should not absolutize the virtue of obedience, since there are rare occasions in which exceptions can be made. Nevertheless, this requires great caution and discretion.

6) Obedience and Freedom

Typically, obedience is understood as doing something that one does not want to do. Curiously, however, St. Basil the Great and St. Pachomios mention that obedience to the abbot should be *voluntary*. St. Pachomios wrote in his monastic rule: "Let there be peace and harmony among them, and let them *willingly* [emphasis added] be subject to their

---

[651] The entire quotation of St. John of Sinai is as follows: "If, without constraint, anyone receives some task from his father, and in doing it suffers a stumble, he should not ascribe the blame to the giver but to the receiver of the weapon. For he took the weapon for battle against the enemy, but has turned it against his own heart. But if he forced himself for the Lord's sake to accept the task, though he previously explained his weakness to him who gave it, let him take courage; for though he has fallen, he is not dead" (Holy Transfiguration Monastery, *The Ladder of Divine Ascent*, 39).

[652] See Elder Ephraim, *My Elder Joseph the Hesychast*, 607–8.

[653] *Elder Ephraim of Katounakia*, trans. Tessy Vassiliadou-Christodoulou (Mount Athos: H. Hesychasterion "Saint Ephraim," 2003), 193.

superiors."[654] And St. Basil wrote: "This head should exercise such authority, the brethren *voluntarily obeying* [emphasis added] only in submissiveness and humility."[655] What this means for the disciple is that when he is asked to do something that he doesn't want to do, not only does he need to execute the request, but also he needs to refocus his attention so that he can voluntarily choose to obey the request.[656] In other words, he needs to remind himself of the value of obedience or reconnect with the love he has for his elder so that his obedience will be voluntary and thus joyful.

The question then arises: What happens when a disciple is unable to obey *voluntarily*? In other words, since St. Basil says that obedience should be done voluntarily, does this give a disciple the right to disobey whenever his own will prevents him from voluntarily obeying because he does not like the abbot's orders? The dozens of patristic quotes regarding obedience in the previous pages clearly indicate that this is not what St. Basil meant. Besides, immediately after that sentence, St. Basil continues:

> As, according to the Apostle, authority established by God should not be resisted (for they who resist the ordinance of God are condemned[657]), so it is appropriate also in this case for the rest of the community to be persuaded that such power is given to the superior not arbitrarily but by the divine will, so that progress as God would have it may be unhindered, while he commands what is useful and profitable to the soul, and the others receive his good counsels with docility. It is in every way fitting that the community be obedient and under subjection to a superior.[658]

St. Basil was calling obedience voluntary in the same spirit that Christ said, "if anyone *wants* to come after Me…,"[659] "if you *want* to be perfect…,"[660] etc. Christ showed us that genuine Christian service and love are not coercive. Thus, these words of St. Basil are also a reminder for the *abbot,* since he needs to bear in mind that when his disciples do not want to obey him, it is not his duty to become a dictator by forcing them with threats and punishments. As Elder Aimilianos expressed in the *Regulations of the Holy Cenobium of*

---

[654] *Regula Pachomii,* Praec. ac Leges 179; PL 23:83C; as translated in Barry, *Commentary on the Rule of Saint Benedict,* 435.

[655] Wagner, *Saint Basil: Ascetical Works,* vol. 9, 210; Βασιλείου τοῦ Μεγάλου, Ἀσκητικὰ Α΄, ΕΠΕ 8, 132.

[656] One method that helps to accomplish this is to reconnect with one's deeper values and principles. A way of doing this is presented in more detail in chapter 5, section 13) vii) on page 223.

[657] Vid. Rom. 13:1–2.

[658] Βασιλείου τοῦ Μεγάλου, Ἀσκητικὰ Α΄, ΕΠΕ 8, 132–35; see also Wagner, *Saint Basil: Ascetical Works,* vol. 9, 210.

[659] Mt. 16:24.

[660] Mt. 19:21.

the Annunciation: "The Abbess shall act and shall command the nuns with authority, but also with discernment and respect 'not by constraint but by consent' (1 Pet. 5:2)."[661]

The Church teaches that we are to imitate God in His respect for human freedom. According to a second-century Christian text: "God persuades, He does not compel; for force is no attribute of God."[662] St. Barsanuphius the Great had the same understanding, for he advised John of Beersheba: "Do not force the will, but only 'sow in hope.'[663] For our Lord, too, did not force anyone, but only preached the Gospel, and whoever wanted, listened.... You know that we have never placed a bond on anyone, let alone on ourselves."[664] Thus, the goal of a spiritual father is to love his disciples as God loves man: respecting his freedom.

This respect for man's freedom was taught by the Apostle Peter, who wrote: "Shepherd the flock of God among you, exercising oversight not under compulsion, but voluntarily."[665] Commenting on this, St. Nicodemos of the Holy Mountain explained:

> The chief of the Apostles is teaching spiritual pastors to shepherd their rational flocks through their voluntary free will and not use force or compulsion to lead them on the straight and royal road of virtue, since they have been honored by God with free will and freedom of choice. For this reason they should not be coerced like irrational beasts. Since irrational beasts lack rationality and free will, we domineeringly drag them where we want and do not let them go where they themselves irrationally rush. But since men have free will and the ability to discern rationally between good and evil, they must be freely and voluntarily guided by their rational shepherds and only through words should be taught, not only dogmatic truths but also virtuous deeds, so that what is good and virtuous will not lack a reward by being done through compulsion instead of voluntarily. This is why also the Lord did not force anyone to follow Him, but He encouraged those who were willing by saying: "If anyone wishes to come after Me" (Mk. 8:34).[666]

Metropolitan Kallistos Ware elaborated on the importance of voluntary obedience as follows:

> The obedience offered by the spiritual child to the abba is not forced but willing and voluntary. It is the task of the starets to take up our will into his will, but he can only do this if by our own free choice we place it in his hands. He does not break our will, but accepts it from us as a gift. A submission that is forced and involuntary is obviously devoid of moral value; the starets asks of each one that we offer to God our

---

[661] Elder Aimilianos, *The Authentic Seal,* 175. St. Iosif Volotsky also understood these words of the Apostle Peter as being applicable to an abbot (vid. Goldfrank, *The Monastic Rule of Iosif Volotsky,* 242).

[662] *Epistle to Diognetus,* vii, 4.

[663] 1 Cor. 9:10.

[664] Chryssavgis, *Barsanuphius and John: Letters,* vol. 1, 52, 66 (letters 35, 51).

[665] 1 Pet. 5:2.

[666] Νικοδήμου τοῦ Ἁγιορείτου, Ἑρμηνεία εἰς τὰς Ἑπτὰ Καθολικὰς Ἐπιστολὰς τῶν Ἁγίων καὶ πανευφήμων Ἀποστόλων Ἰακώβου, Πέτρου, Ἰωάννου καὶ Ἰούδα (Θεσσαλονίκη: Ὀρθόδοξος Κυψέλη, 1986), 317–18.

heart, not our external actions. Even in a monastic context the obedience is voluntary, as is vividly emphasized at the rite of monastic profession: only after the candidate has three times placed the scissors in the abbot's hand does the latter proceed to tonsure him. This voluntary offering of our freedom, however, even in a monastery, is obviously something that cannot be made once and for all, by a single gesture. We are called to take up our cross *daily* (Lk. 9:23).[667]

Likewise, St. Porphyrios of Kafsokalyvia explained:

If a monk is to make progress in a monastery, he needs to engage willingly in spiritual struggle without pressure from anyone else. He needs to do everything with joy and eagerness and not as a chore. A monk is not a person who is forced to do something mechanically and reluctantly. Whatever he does, he does solely out of love for the heavenly Bridegroom, out of divine eros. He doesn't bring thoughts of hell or death into his mind.[668] Monasticism mustn't be a negative flight from the world, but a flight of divine love and divine worship....

Whatever you do under compulsion and whatever causes your soul to kick instinctively and protest, causes you harm. This is something I've said many times. I have seen monks and lay people of every age leaving the Church and abandoning God entirely, because they are unable to bear the inner pressure and the pressure from other people. Pressure causes a person not only to react negatively against the Church, but not to want the Church at all. It does not have a positive effect. It bears no fruit. He does whatever it is, albeit reluctantly, because his elder or spiritual father told him to. He says to himself, for example, "Now I must go to Compline." Yes, he does the thing, but whatever is done in a mechanical way is harmful and not beneficial.

You are often forced to do what is good. But it mustn't be done under duress; it's not beneficial, it's not spiritually edifying. Take, for example, the Jesus Prayer. If you force yourself to say it, after a time you will weary of it and you will throw it away; and then what happens? If you do it as a chore, the pressure builds up inside you until it bursts out in some evil. Pressure of this kind can even make you not want to go to church at all. Go to church in a different spirit, not with pushing and shoving, but with pleasure and joy.[669]

For this same reason, St. Paisios of the Holy Mountain used to say:

---

[667] Metropolitan Kallistos Ware of Diokleia, "The Spiritual Guide in Orthodox Christianity," (http://churchmotherofgod.org/articleschurch/articles-about-the-orthodox-church/2348-the-spiritual-guide-in-orthodox-christianity.html).

[668] At first glance, this statement of St. Porphyrios may seem to contradict the many saints who recommend remembering death. (For some examples of this, see "remembrance of death" in the index of this book.) Upon deeper examination, however, it becomes clear that St. Porphyrios is simply teaching that love is superior to fear, which is the lowest of three ways to please God. As explained by Abba Dorotheos of Gaza: "There are three dispositions of the soul, as St. Basil the Great tells us [vid. PG 31:896B], by which we can be pleasing to God. That is, we can be pleasing to God either when we fear damnation (and therefore find ourself in the situation of a slave); or fulfill the commandments of God because we seek the gain that we will receive as a reward from God for our personal benefit (and at this point we resemble a hireling); or for goodness itself (thus finding ourselves in the position of a son)" (Metropolitan Chrysostomos, *Our Holy Father Dorotheos of Gaza*, 76–77).

[669] Chrysopigi, *Wounded by Love*, 158, 165–66.

> A person who is sick must eat whether or not he has an appetite, because he knows that the food will do him good. Likewise, when we are not in the mood for spiritual things, we should move ourselves to action through love, knowing that it will do us good, even if we don't feel like doing so. It takes forcefulness [βία], not forcing oneself [ζόρισμα] and pressure. Spiritual forcefulness is not forcing oneself, but it is something helpful.[670]

In other words, our ascetical struggles should not be done because we are telling ourselves that due to extrinsic reasons we "should" or "must" do them. This would be *forcing oneself* through involuntary pressure and coercion. On the contrary, we need to exert ourselves and make the effort (that is, use *forcefulness*) to reconnect with our deeper values and our love for God and neighbor. Once we have refocused in this manner, then out of love—and love entails sacrifice when it is genuine and selfless—we can voluntarily follow the commandments of God and of our elder because we are intrinsically motivated, which gives rise to joy and peace. St. Theophan the Recluse saw the importance of intrinsic motivation in the spiritual life and taught that the law of God should "imprint itself on the heart, and man, acting according to this law, will act as if from himself, unconstrained, so that this law will not lie on him, but will as it were proceed from him."[671]

Archimandrite Symeon Kragiopoulos explained the difference between a healthy forcefulness rooted in intrinsic motivation and an unhealthy coercion coming from extrinsic circumstances:

> When you, as a free being with volition and awareness decide to constrain yourself to do what you have determined what needs to be done as a rational person who knows the truth, this is not coercion....
>
> Although you are compelling yourself, this is not a form of coercion. No. When you notice yourself trying this way and that to get out of doing something—to be lazy, to be overcome with sloth and indifference, to pretend that you don't understand—you sit yourself down and tell yourself: 'You *shall* do it.' Of course, this has value in the spiritual struggle—not when circumstances oblige you to do something, but when you freely do it.[672]

In line with this approach, Metropolitan Hierotheos Vlachos observed:

> The desire for the monastic life must be free from all compulsion, that is, it must develop in a spirit of freedom, because "salvation belongs to those who choose it, not

---

[670] Ἱερομονάχου Ἰσαάκ, *Βίος Γέροντος Παϊσίου τοῦ Ἁγιορείτου* (Χαλκιδική: Ἱερὸν Ἡσυχαστήριον «Ἅγιος Ἰωάννης ὁ Πρόδρομος», Μεταμόρφωσις, 2004), 428; see also Hieromonk Isaac, *Elder Paisios of Mount Athos,* trans. Hieromonk Alexis (Trader) and Fr. Peter Heers (Chalkidiki: Holy Monastery "Saint Arsenios the Cappadocian," 2012), 403.

[671] St. Theophan the Recluse, *The Path to Salvation,* trans. Hieromonk Seraphim Rose, new edition (Safford: Holy Monastery of St. Paisius: 2016), 17.

[672] π. Συμεὼν Καραγιοπούλου, *Ψυχαναγκασμός* (Θεσσαλονίκη: Ἱερὸν Ἀνδρῷον Ἡσυχαστήριον «Ἡ Ἁγία Τριάς», 2019), 19, 20.

to those who are compelled by force."[673] Besides, free will is a characteristic of the divine image that man received from God, and not even God Himself violates it, since "this would be the same as destroying free will and the human being" (St. Nicholas Cabasilas). A person should choose the monastic life as a result of various influences, which may be psychological, material, and this-worldly.[674]

St. Sophrony of Essex also saw that compulsion is foreign to true Christian liberty:

> A spiritual director never tries to subject a novice's will to his own human will, but in the course of everyday life it might happen that he would find himself obliged to insist on having his directions obeyed—a situation in which no obedient novice would place his *staretz*. In virtue of his high responsibility before God, the ascetic effort required of a *staretz* is much more onerous than that required of the novice. But this responsibility occurs only when the novice gives unqualified obedience; where this is not the case the novice bears the full weight of responsibility for his actions and loses the benefits of obedience. It is no part of the *staretz's* purpose, however, to relieve his disciple of responsibility, but to teach him the true Christian life and true Christian liberty, for which it is necessary to overcome in oneself, through the spiritual feat of obedience, the passions of self-will and love of power. Anyone who seeks to dominate his fellow-man, or even to encroach on his liberty, thereby inevitably destroys his own liberty too, since the very fact of such an infringement of another person's freedom involves a breach with the divine life of love to which man is called.
>
> ...
>
> Monastic obedience is not a "discipline." Now the very existence of every human institution or society depends upon the co-ordination of the actions of its members; and this co-ordination is achieved through discipline, the essence of which lies in the subjection of the will of the youngest to that of the oldest or of the "majority." Such subjection is usually enforced by compulsion; but, even where there is a willing and reasoned acceptance of discipline as being an essential condition for the continued existence of the community, discipline does not cease to be discipline, since its underlying principle is the subordination of one man's will to that of another.
>
> Monastic obedience, on the other hand, is a religious act and, as such, must be freely consented to or it loses its religious significance. Such obedience can be spiritually fruitful only when it betokens the voluntary submission of will and judgment to one's *staretz* for the sake of arriving at *God's will*. It is in its relation to this search for the will of God that the essence of our obedience lies.
>
> The novice recognizes his own incapacity to discover for himself the will of God, and so he turns to his spiritual father, whom he believes is more worthy than he to know God's will. The *staretz* does not try to destroy the novice's will and does not subjugate it to his own arbitrary will, but assumes the heavy burden of responsibility, and thereby becomes a collaborator with God in the divine act of the creation of man.... If the abbot and other elders in the monastery are ever obliged to have recourse to "discipline" to constrain the brethren, this is a sure sign of the debasement of monasticism and, possibly, of a total forgetting of its purpose and essence.[675]

---

[673] St. Maximos the Confessor, "On the Lord's Prayer" in Palmer, Sherrard, Ware, *The Philokalia*, vol. 2, 289.

[674] Ἱεροθέου, Ὁ Ὀρθόδοξος Μοναχισμός, 523; Hierotheos, *Orthodox Monasticism,* 468–69.

[675] Sakharov, *Truth and Life,* 85, 88–89.

Discipline imposed by others does not help in repentance and does not help the soul to develop and become a person.[676]

Elaborating on this, St. Sophrony's disciple Archimandrite Zacharias added:

Obedience, like every other Christian virtue, must be a free and voluntary act in order to have eternal value before God.... The free will of man, together with his reason, are the most precious of his natural gifts; and when obedience is at work, it offers these two faculties, the will and the reason, as the most pleasing sacrifice to God.... From the above it is clear that obedience is radically different from discipline, and surpasses it as heaven surpasses earth. Discipline means submission to a superior human will for the sake of earthly benefit. Discipline subjects man in an impersonal way to a "rule," to the "Law," the "Typicon," the "Institution," the "Administration." Discipline favours the general over the particular, or the majority over the individual. In contrast, obedience is a free act of faith in God and is always accomplished in His name.... By cutting off his own will and denying his own reasonings the monk does not lose his personality, nor does he come to self-annihilation, as it seems to people in the world. On the contrary, he rises above the limits of his created nature and becomes manifestly a true person-hypostasis. He becomes the bearer of divine life, and a bearer of all humanity.[677]

Bishop Irenei (Steenberg) expressed a similar outlook:

In the monastic tradition we see obedience not as the oppressive avenue of mindless slavery, but as the life-creating context of authentic freedom. It is only the one who is willing—freely—to offer up his well-practiced regime of self-rule to the guidance and care of another, who begins to see just how enslaving his former "freedom" had truly been. Within the monastic culture the monk or nun begins to see how obedience to the self (which is the context from which every person comes into monasticism, whatever his background in particular terms) had in fact been a shackle; how the lack of obedience to another in fact meant an absolute and unlimited obedience to one's own desires, one's understandings, one's evaluations, all of which are profoundly deformed by the wound of sin.[678] Just as Adam's troubles began when he determined not to let God be his Lord, but instead to let his mind be lord over him—deciding for himself what was good and what was bad, and how to act—so the monastic comes to realize that he has fallen prey to the same self-enslavement, and that the only true freedom comes from wholly attaching the heart to the God who would set it free.

This emphasis upon freedom is another characteristic of the monastic life, given birth by these three vows [of chastity, poverty, and obedience]. While to outside eyes it may appear that the monk lives a quite constrained life—prescribed clothing,

---

[676] Metropolitan of Nafpaktos Hierotheos, *"I Know a Man in Christ": Elder Sophrony the Hesychast and Theologian,* trans. Sister Pelagia Selfe (Levadia: Birth of the Theotokos Monastery, 2015), 300.

[677] Archimandrite Zacharias, *The Enlargement of the Heart* (Dalton: Mount Thabor Publications, 2006), 224–29.

[678] Similarly, St. Joseph the Hesychast said: "When we are not obeying our elder, we will end up obeying many 'elders,' that is, many wills, many passions, many demons, and in the end we will be enslaved to them in hell" (Γέροντος Ἐφραίμ, *Ὁ Γέροντάς μου Ἰωσήφ,* 234; see also Elder Ephraim, *My Elder Joseph the Hesychast,* 326).

prescribed hours, prescribed prayers, proscribed activities—the irony of the monastic life, the "foolishness" it presents to the world (cf. 1 Cor. 1:18), is that the monk or the nun is often the person who feels the most free in all of God's creation. Yes, there are hard labors and long struggles; but through them tired and world-beaten hearts find a new communion in the "life-creating Spirit," Who bears them up to a life that soars as if in flight. This can only be done through a full respecting of each person's full freedom. There is, there can be, no coercion in monasticism. Everything undertaken is undertaken of free choice, knowingly, with assent.…

[A monk] is obedient to his elder, to the monastery abbot, but never out of obligation and never as a denial of his freedom. Genuine obedience is a shaping of freedom, not an elimination of it. Thus through dedication to his chastity, poverty, and obedience, the monastic finds himself set free to discover the authentic person God has called him to be, and will spend the remainder of his life growing into the maturity of that calling.[679]

Along the same lines, Metropolitan Jonah (Paffhausen) taught:

Authentic monastic obedience is profoundly personal, a communion of love, a willing self-offering by the disciple which is devoid of coercion or compulsion. It is through this profound personal relationship of love that the disciple is transformed and empowered to transcend his ego and passions and to control his thoughts. Through this relationship the disciple is enabled to work out his growth to maturity through purification by self-denial. Being loved, he can grow in love, and be illumined by the grace of God, which is love, forgiveness, acceptance, and healing. The spiritual father becomes God's co-worker in bringing a man up from the state of an isolated individual into an authentic person. The authentic relationship of elder and disciple in holy obedience can only work in the context of complete freedom, as the disciple's free offering to God of his obedience to his elder. The grace of self-denial in obedience breaks down the ego, self-centeredness, and self-will. Thus the father begets a son, who in turn becomes a father. The community becomes one in Christ in the bond of love.[680]

Igumen Chrysostomos Koutloumousianos expressed the same viewpoint:

In monasticism, obedience is the way to maturity in Christ. The final goal of obedience is not a submission of one's conscience to another person's will. The final goal is the attainment of humility and discernment through the willing suppression of one's self-centered will. In this route, both the elder and the spiritual child are struggling to see and follow God's will. The spiritual child does not merely learn how to practice blind obedience, he learns to see his own condition and discern and judge his own demeanor, and understand what is really blessed in his life. Thus, the spiritual father must try to stir up the gentleness of his child's soul to respond to God's love. To stimulate free obedience that heals and liberates the soul instead of the irresistible obedience that harms the soul and renders her coarse.

Spiritual paternity culminates in *kenotic* [i.e., self-emptying, sacrificial] love. It becomes the conduit through which the spiritual child is initiated into the spiritual

---

[679] Alexei Krindatch, *Atlas of American Orthodox Christian Monasteries,* Assembly of Canonical Orthodox Bishops of the United States of America (Boston: Holy Cross Orthodox Press, 2016), 6–7.

[680] *Divine Ascent: A Journal of Orthodox Faith,* no. 5, Holy Monastery of St. John of Shanghai and San Francisco, 13.

freedom of God's ineffable love. This means that the spiritual father is not expected to impose his will or assert himself in an authoritarian manner. If he applies methods of coercion that crush the [spiritual] child's conscience, no matter his best intentions, he engraves into the soul of his child the image of a transcendental tyrant obstructing his spiritual progress. The human being does not line up either by use of military discipline, austerities, or penances. Commenting on such and similar cases in pastoral work, St. Paisios the Athonite says: "If you try to correct someone by beating him, you succeed nothing. On the Day of Judgment, Christ will say to you: 'Were you another Diocletian?' And to the corrected man He will say: 'Whatever good you did, you did it under coercion.' Therefore, we shall not strangle the other with a view of sending him to Paradise."

...

As an icon and a servant of Christ, the spiritual father is a servant of his reasonable flock. In all his activities and conduct—in thought, word, and deed—he must not exercise dominion but rather service, *διακονία*. And since this word *διακονία* has become a sort of cliché, we must repeat that *διακονία* entails love, respect, truth, discretion, and active concern for the other's edification. The model for the spiritual father can be drawn from the beautiful metaphor given by St. Paul: "As a nurse cherisheth her children, willing to impart not only the word but also his own soul."[681] Such a portrayal displays the maternal aspect of spiritual paternity, which is, after all, shared also by the spiritual mothers.

A description of the spiritual father is rendered also in the life of St. Pachomios: "Abba was utterly tranquil. His conduct was such that nobody would hesitate in disclosing his own thoughts. The brothers revealed everything to him, receiving immediately their healing, for they saw him joyful and welcoming." The spiritual father cannot be but sober, joyful, and approachable. It goes without saying that he sends nobody away and that he knows how to listen. As a great American novelist Henry David Thoreau says: "It takes two to speak the truth: one to speak and another to hear."[682] So the spiritual father's empathy overwhelms even the justified urge to express severe criticism or condemnation.[683]

Elder Ephraim grasped and lived these concepts of authentic spiritual fatherhood. His genuine, heartfelt care for his disciples inspired us to love him and voluntarily obey him. In the thousands of interactions I had with him, not once did he use his authority as a means of forcing me to do something, nor did he stoop to the level of threats, punishments, or even rewards to sway my will. This is not to say, however, that he never gave me orders or never cut off my will. Whenever he did cut off my will, though, my submission sprang from the love and trust which he had earned.

---

[681] Cf. 1 Thes. 2:7–8.

[682] Henry David Thoreau, *A Week on the Concord and Merrimac Rivers,* (Boston: Houghton, Mifflin, 1893), 352.

[683] https://www.ancientfaith.com/specials/oca_diocese_of_the_south_2019_pastoral_conference/spiritual_paternity_therapeutic_relationship_or_manipulation

Chapter Four:
Virginity

1) Reason for Virginity

A CORE ATTRIBUTE of monastics is virginity, which is why it is included in the monastic vows for receiving the Great Schema.[684] St. Ambrose of Milan explained the benefit of virginity for those who want to be dedicated to God: "Virginity cannot be commanded, but must be wished for, for things which are above us are matters for prayer rather than under mastery. 'But I would have you,' he [St. Paul] says, 'without cares. He that is unmarried careth for the things that belong to the Lord, how he may please the Lord: But he that is married careth for the things that are of the world, how he may please his wife. There is a difference also between a wife and a virgin. The unmarried woman careth for the things of the Lord, that she may be holy both in body and in spirit: but she that is married careth for the things of the world, how she may please her husband.'[685] I am not indeed discouraging marriage, but am enlarging upon the benefits of virginity."[686] Thus, since virginity leaves a person more free to care for pleasing God, it is natural that people who want to dedicate themselves to God have embraced virginity ever since the beginning of Christianity.[687]

St. Ambrose elaborated further on the advantages of virginity:

---

[684] In the tonsuring service of the Great Schema, the postulant is asked by the abbot: "Will you keep yourself in virginity, chastity, and piety even unto death?" And the postulant replies: "Yes, God helping me, Reverend Father" (*The Great Book of Needs,* vol. 1, 333).

[685] 1 Cor. 7:32–34.

[686] *Nicene and Post-Nicene Fathers, Second Series,* vol. 10: *Ambrose: Select Works and Letters,* Philip Schaff, ed. (New York: Christian Literature Company, 1896), 367.

[687] For example, St. Athenagoras the Philosopher in the second century wrote: "You would find many among us, both men and women, growing old unmarried, in hope of living in closer communion with God" (*Fathers of the Second Century: Hermas, Tatian, Athenagoras, Theophilus, and Clement of Alexandria,* vol. 2, Ante-Nicene Fathers, Philip Schaff, ed. [New York: Christian Literature Company, 1887], 146; see also Justin Martyr, *First Apology* 15:6).

The days shall come when they shall say: "Blessed are the barren, and the wombs that never bare" (Lk. 23:29). For the daughters of this age are conceived, and conceive; but the daughter of the kingdom refrains from wedded pleasure, and the pleasure of the flesh, that she may be holy in body and in spirit. I do not then discourage marriage, but recapitulate the advantages of holy virginity. This is the gift of few only, that is of all.... I am comparing good things with good things, that it may be clear which is the more excellent. Nor do I allege any opinion of my own, but I repeat that which the Holy Spirit spake by the prophet: "Blessed is the barren that is undefiled" (Wis. 3:13). First of all, in that which those who purpose to marry desire above all things, that they may boast of the beauty of their husband, they must of necessity confess that they are inferior to virgins, to Whom alone it is suitable to say: "Thou art fairer than the children of men, grace is poured on Thy lips" (Ps. 44:2). Who is that Spouse? One not given to common indulgences, not proud of possessing riches, but He Whose throne is for ever and ever.[688]

Contemporary Orthodox authors have observed: "Marriage is an image of the union of Christ with the Church,"[689] whereas, "monastic life does not constitute an image, but it itself is the mystical marriage of the soul with the heavenly Bridegroom."[690]

2) Value of Virginity

In the first century, St. Clement of Rome pointed out that Christ and the greatest saints were virgins:

It was the Virgin's womb which bore the Son of God, our Lord Jesus Christ; and the body which our Lord put on, and in which He accomplished His combat in this world, He took from the Holy Virgin. Know in this the majesty and glory of virginity. Dost thou wish to be a Christian? Imitate Christ in all things. St. John [the Baptist] was an angel, sent before the face of the Lord, and among them that are born of women there hath not arisen a greater than he, and this holy angel of the Lord was a virgin.... Another John, who lay on the breast of the Lord, Who loved Him greatly, was also holy,[691] which was why the Lord so loved him. Then there were Paul, Barnabas, Timothy and others whose names are written in the Book of Life; they all loved this form of holiness and continued in purity to the end of their ascetic lives, thus proving themselves true imitators of Christ and sons of the living God ... for those who are like unto Christ are in perfect likeness of Him.[692]

---

[688] *Nicene and Post-Nicene Fathers, Second Series,* vol. 10*: Ambrose: Select Works and Letters,* 369.

[689] Παταπίου Μοναχοῦ Καυσοκαλυβίτου, «Ἡ Ἀκολουθία τοῦ Μεγάλου Σχήματος. Ἑρμηνεία καὶ θεολογία τῶν εὐχῶν τῆς μοναχικῆς καθιερώσεως», *Θεολογία,* 1/2011, 166.

[690] Ἀρχιμανδρίτη Νικοδήμου Μπαρούση, *Ἁγίου Νικηφόρου Καλλίστου, Βίος καὶ Πολιτεία τῆς Ὁσίας Εὐφροσύνης,* εἰσαγωγή (Ἀθῆναι, 1998), 13.

[691] A footnote in *Truth and Life* states: "From the context it is obvious that the words *holy* and *holiness* (three lines below) here mean *virgin* and the *state of virginity*" (Sakharov, *Truth and Life,* 93).

[692] As translated from the Greek and Latin text of PG 1 in: Sakharov, *Truth and Life,* 92–93.

St. Methodios of Olympus in the early fourth century wrote about the loftiness of virginity:

> Virginity is supernatural, amazing, and glorious ... the most fertile land of the Church and its flower.... Chastity is a very rare virtue and difficult to achieve. Just as it is so lofty and magnificent, likewise it encounters tremendous dangers. Therefore, it requires people with a mighty and a brave character who have completely redirected the urges for pleasure and have directed the chariot of their soul high above.... Some who desired this virginity ... because they lacked maturity and a desire to struggle, turned back after completing half the journey, since they had not embraced a frame of mind sufficient for the undertaking. For we must not only keep our bodies chaste ... but also our souls.... What did the Lord—the Truth and the Light—do when He came down to earth? He kept his flesh without corruption by adorning it with virginity. Therefore, we, too, if we are to become "in the likeness" of God, let us honor the virginity of Christ with a sense of honor.[693]

St. Methodios then quoted the passage in Revelation[694] about the redeemed 144,000 virgins singing a new song and following the Lamb and concluded: "This shows that the Lord leads the choir of virgins. Note also that the rank of virgins is great in God's eyes."[695]

St. Methodios added that virginity walks on earth but "her head touches the heavens,"[696] and is the "most brilliant and glorious star of all Christ's charisms."[697] He also said that nothing is superior to chastity in its power to return mankind to Paradise.[698] Virginity is the most precious offering and gift and the greatest vow that a man may make to God.[699] The embrace of virginity is the key way one moves from being God's image to being God's likeness, and quickly causes violent passions to wither away.[700]

St. Ambrose also taught that virgins are given a special reward in Heaven:

> And so they who have [merely] fulfilled the commandments are able to say: "We are unprofitable servants, we have done that which was our duty to do" (Lk. 17:10).

---

[693] Μεθοδίου Ὀλύμπου, Συμπόσιον, ΒΕΠΕΣ 18, 17–18, 20.

[694] "And I looked, and, lo, a Lamb stood on the mount Sion, and with him an hundred forty and four thousand, having His Father's name written in their foreheads. And I heard a voice from heaven, as the voice of many waters, and as the voice of a great thunder: and I heard the voice of harpers harping with their harps: And they sang as it were a new song before the throne, and before the four beasts, and the elders: and no man could learn that song but the hundred and forty and four thousand, which were redeemed from the earth. These are they which were not defiled with women; for they are virgins. These are they which follow the Lamb whithersoever He goeth. These were redeemed from among men, being the firstfruits unto God and to the Lamb. And in their mouth was found no guile: for they are without fault before the throne of God" (Rev. 14:1–5).

[695] Μεθοδίου Ὀλύμπου, Συμπόσιον, ΒΕΠΕΣ 18, 20.

[696] As translated in Archpriest Josiah B. Trenham, *Marriage and Virginity according to St. John Chrysostom* (Platina: St. Herman of Alaska Brotherhood, 2013), 63.

[697] Ibid.

[698] Ibid.

[699] Ibid.

[700] Ibid.

The virgin does not say this, nor he who sold all his goods, but they rather await the stored-up rewards like the holy Apostle who says: "Behold we have forsaken all and followed Thee, what shall we have therefore?" (Mt. 19:27). He says not, like the unprofitable servant, that he has [merely] done that which was his duty to do, but as being profitable to his Master, because he has multiplied the talents entrusted to him by the increase he has gained, having a good conscience, and without anxiety as to his merits he expects the reward of his faith and virtue. And so it is said to him and the others: "Ye which have followed Me, in the regeneration, when the Son of Man shall sit in the throne of His glory, shall also yourselves sit upon twelve thrones, judging the tribes of Israel" (Mt. 19:28).[701]

This great honor given to virgins is the just reward for their great struggle. As St. Theognostos wrote:

> There is no greater struggle than the struggle for self-restraint and virginity. He who honors celibacy is admired even by the angels and is crowned not less than athletes are. If, bound to flesh and blood, he always strives to imitate through chastity the immaterial nature of the angels, terrible is the battle he has to fight; and if he is successful, so truly great is his achievement that it appears virtually impossible and beyond our nature. Indeed, it would be impossible if God did not help us from above, supporting the weakness of our nature, mending what is rotten, and somehow raising us from the ground through divine eros and through hope for the gifts held in store for us.[702]

Likewise, St. Athanasios the Great said: "Ascetical life is burdensome and abstinence is difficult to bear, but nothing is sweeter than the heavenly Bridegroom. Here we toil a little, but there we shall receive eternal life as a reward."[703]

St. Sophrony of Essex explained that virginity is supernatural not contranatural:

> The Church's millennial experience has proved beyond all doubt that preclusion of the sexual function not only causes no psychological or physical harm but, on the contrary, when correctly interpreted, increases man's physical endurance, his longevity and his mental health, while at the same time conducing to his spiritual development. In recent years numerous scientific works have confirmed the spiritual fruitfulness of what contemporary psychology sometimes terms 'sublimation.' One can rejoice at this confirmation; throughout the ages the celibacy of the monk has never ceased to be distorted and even opposed as a pathological phenomenon, a "going against nature." However, contemporary scientific experience in this field is still too insignificant to be compared with the centuries-old experience of the Church, or to enrich it, so that it does not yet hold much interest for monks. Leaving aside any detailed examination of the dogmatic and anthropological aspects of the question, let me merely remark that for us the fundamental and incontestable justification of this vow (to which all the other arguments finally come round) lies in the "example" given us by the Lord Himself. "I

---

[701] *Ambrose: Select Works and Letters,* 403–4.

[702] Θεογνώστου, «Περὶ πράξεως καὶ θεωρίας καὶ περὶ ἱερωσύνης» ἐν *Φιλοκαλία τῶν Ἱερῶν Νηπτικῶν,* τόμος β´ (1991), 268 (κεφ.ξζ´); see also Palmer, Sherrard, Ware, *The Philokalia,* vol. 2, 375 (ch. 67).

[703] Μ. Ἀθανασίου, *Περὶ Παρθενίας,* ΒΕΠΕΣ 33, 72.

have given you an example."[704] Only a lunatic would venture to say that Christ's life "went against nature."[705]

3) Angelic Nature of Virginity

Numerous saints taught that virginity is an angelic way of life that provides a foretaste of the future life in heaven. For example, St. Ambrose wrote:

> And for you, holy virgins, there is a special guardianship, for you who with unspotted chastity keep the couch of the Lord holy. And no wonder if the angels fight for you who war with the mode of life of angels. Virginal chastity merits their guardianship whose life it attains to. Why should I continue the praise of chastity in more words? For chastity has made even angels. He who has preserved it is an angel; he who has lost it a devil. And hence has religion also gained its name. She is a virgin who is the bride of God, a harlot who makes gods for herself. What shall I say of the resurrection of which you already hold the rewards: "For in the resurrection they will neither be given in marriage, nor marry, but shall be," He says, "as the angels in heaven" (Mt. 22:30). That which is promised to us is already present with you, and the object of your prayers is with you; ye are of this world, and yet not in this world. This age has held you, but has not been able to retain you.[706]

St. John of Sinai also compared the virginal life with the angelic life: "Purity means that we put on the angelic nature. Purity is the longed-for house of Christ and the earthly heaven of the heart. Purity is a supernatural denial of nature, which means that a mortal and corruptible body is rivalling the celestial spirits in a truly marvellous way. He is pure who expels fleshly love with divine love, and who has extinguished the fire of passion by the fire of Heaven."[707]

St. Gregory of Nyssa wrote that virginity is "a kind of art and power of a more divine life that teaches those living in the flesh to imitate the nature of the bodiless angels."[708] St. Leander of Seville (in sixth-century Spain) wrote in his monastic rule: "A virgin may marry, but she who does not is numbered among the angels.... Do you see, dearly beloved sister, how virgins hold the chief place in the kingdom of God? And not undeservedly, for they had contempt for the world's vanity and thereby reached the heavenly kingdom."[709]

The early Desert Fathers shared this same understanding of the angelic nature of monasticism. Abba Anoub mentioned that he viewed "the lifestyle of monks as a most holy

---

[704] Jn. 13:15.

[705] Sakharov, *Truth and Life,* 90–91.

[706] *Ambrose: Select Works and Letters,* 371.

[707] Holy Transfiguration Monastery, *The Ladder of Divine Ascent,* 104.

[708] Περὶ Παρθενίας, 5; PG 46:348B.

[709] Barlow, *The Fathers of the Church: Iberian Fathers,* vol. 63, 193, 194.

way of life equal to the angels."[710] Abba Hyperechios wrote: "A dispassionate monk who has not been wounded by the arrows of pleasure is an earthly imitator of the angels."[711] St. Serapion said: "Know, O monastics most honorable to God, how many misfortunes Christ has freed you from; know how many disasters you have avoided; know what kind of life you are living, for your way of life is equal to the angels. For just as in the resurrection of the dead the righteous 'neither marry nor are given in marriage but are as angels in heaven,' in the same way you, by living together in this manner, eagerly anticipate what is to come. Who, then, would not call you blessed for having chosen a carefree way of life? Who would not embrace your mode of life in the deserts? Who would not desire your stillness?"[712]

Numerous other saints supported this view of angelic monasticism. St. Basil the Great wrote: "These [monks] have imitated the life of the angels, for they—like the angels—have kept a common life with exactitude. Among the angels there is no quarrelling or disputes or arguments. Everything belongs to each of them."[713]

St. John Chrysostom taught: "Tell me, how did Elias and Elisha and John [the Baptist]—these true lovers of virginity—differ from the angels? In no way, other than by being bound to mortal nature. In other ways, if one were to examine carefully, one would find them not at all inferior to the angels.... That it was virginity that made them great is evident from this: if they had a wife and children, they would not have easily dwelt in the desert, they would not have despised houses and other objects of this life. But as it was, they were free of these bonds and lived on earth as if they were beings in the heavens."[714] Elsewhere, St. John Chrysostom added: "They should put her [i.e., the virgin of Christ] in the marketplace as a statue of philosophy for all to see and be amazed as if beholding an angel who has just now descended from heaven."[715]

St. Athanasios the Great exclaimed: "O continence, the life of the angels and the crown of holy men!"[716] St. Isidore of Pelusium wrote: "We think that [merely having] a tattered cloak and a beard and a staff is sufficient for us to live the angelic way of life."[717] St. Ephraim the Syrian said: "Beloved brethren, since we wear the Angelic schema, let us not fight on the Devil's side, but let us aspire as far as possible to the life of the Angels. For the habit must be accompanied by a way of life and by deeds; without deeds, the schema

---

[710] Κατ' Αἴγυπτον τῶν Μοναχῶν Ἱστορία, Subsidia Hagiographica 53, ἐκδ. Festugière, Bruxelles 1971, παρ. 5–7, 7 καὶ 91–92.

[711] *Παραίνεσις Ἀσκητῶν τοῦ Μακαρίου Ὑπερεχίου,* Μ΄, PG 79:1480.

[712] PG 40:932D.

[713] Βασιλείου τοῦ Μεγάλου, *Ἀσκητικαὶ Διατάξεις,* κεφ. ιη΄, παρ. 3, PG 31:1384B.

[714] *Περὶ Παρθενίας* 69, PG 48:591

[715] *Περὶ τοῦ τὰς Κανονικὰς μὴ Συνοικεῖν Ἀνδράσιν,* PG 47:527.

[716] *Περὶ Παρθενίας,* 24.

[717] Ἰσιδώρου Πηλουσιώτου, *Ἐπιστολὴ 92,* Θωμᾷ Μοναχῷ, PG 78:245.

is of no value. Do the Angels perchance dwell in Heaven amidst quarreling and jealousy, as we see happening, nowadays, among monks?"[718] St. Isaac the Syrian wrote: "The angels continually visited these men [i.e., the anchorites] because their modes of life were so similar; and as being troops of a single Sovereign, at all times they kept company with their comrades-in-arms, that is to say, those who embraced the desert all the days of their life, and took up their abode in mountains and in dens and caves of the earth because of their love for God."[719]

St. Symeon of Thessalonica explained:

> The monastic schema is called angelic and is indeed so, since it promises to imitate the angels' chastity, non-possessiveness, hymns, prayers, obedience, and purity.[720] …
>
> How is the schema of repentance also called angelic? Someone might say that it is because angels do not fall and neither is it in their nature to fall. Let such a person hear that God alone is unchanging and unable to fall, as He ever is and remains unchangeable. As for those who are created, they are subject to change. This is evident, since some of the angels have fallen. But to be an angel means being careful, humbling oneself, obeying God, being a clean minister, and doing His will, as it is written [vid. Ps. 102:19]. Therefore, a monk likewise, although having fallen human nature, has the power and eagerness to trample upon all the might of the enemy, and nothing shall in no wise harm him. Thus he departs from the worldly life, and by leaving parents and wife and children and siblings, he imitates the life of the angels. He becomes detached from mundane things below and has no relatives in the flesh and is not accountable to them, but he takes up the cross of Christ on his shoulders, follows in His footsteps, is obedient, and denies all things, without doing his own will. This is the work of angels.[721]

4) Duration of Virginity

A person who becomes a monk is obliged to remain a monk for the rest of his life. According to St. Basil, "a virgin [i.e., a nun] is to be regarded as the bride of Christ, and a chosen vessel dedicated to the Lord,"[722] and therefore he says that if she breaks her vow she is to be punished as though convicted of adultery. St. Basil adds that this principle is

---

[718] Chrysostomos, *The Evergetinos, Book I,* 279.

[719] Holy Transfiguration Monastery, *The Ascetical Homilies of Saint Isaac the Syrian,* 158 (Homily 5).

[720] PG 155:197A.

[721] PG 155:489AB.

[722] *Nicene and Post-Nicene Fathers, Series II,* vol. 8, *Basil: Letters and Select Works,* 237 (Epistle 199:18). Calling virgins dedicated to God "brides of Christ" was already an established tradition by the time of St. Basil in the fourth century. For his contemporary, St. Athanasios the Great, wrote: "Such as have attained this virtue [of virginity], the Catholic Church has been accustomed to call the brides of Christ" (*A Select Library of Nicene and Post-Nicene Fathers of the Christian Church: Athanasius: Select Works and Letters,* Series II, Philip Schaff, ed., vol. 4 [New York: Christian Literature Company, 1892], 252).

extended to men also.[723] Similarly, St. John Chrysostom wrote to Monk Theodore who was considering marriage: "It is no longer possible for thee to observe the right conditions of marriage. For if he who has been attached to a heavenly bridegroom deserts him, and joins himself to a wife the act is adultery, even if you call it marriage ten thousand times over; or rather it is worse than adultery in proportion as God is greater than man."[724] A similar understanding was prevalent also in early Egyptian monasticism, as is evident from the incident of a monk whom St. Pachomios saved from "being estranged from God by leaving the schema."[725]

St. Benedict dictated that a monk should put his vow in writing:

> Let him who is received [into the brotherhood] promise in the oratory, in the presence of all, before God and His saints, stability, the conversion of morals, and obedience, in order that, if he should ever do otherwise, he may know that he will be condemned by God "Whom he mocketh." Let him make a written statement of his promise in the name of the saints whose relics are there, and of the Abbot there present. Let him write this document with his own hand … and with his own hand place it on the altar.…
>
> If on the devil's suasion he should ever consent to leave the monastery (which God forbid) he should be then stripped of his monastic habit and cast out. But let him not receive the document of his profession which the Abbot took from the altar, but let it be preserved in the monastery.[726]

Commenting on this, Evgenia Zhoukova wrote in a dissertation entitled "The Origin and Evolution of the Service of the Monastic Schema": "In this manner it is shown that the monk's vow is made to God Himself, so that even if he leaves the monastery his vow remains in force, since whatever is dedicated to God can no longer fall away from its current state to its former state."[727] The fathers in the early days of Egyptian monasticism had the same understanding. For when a monk was expelled after failing to comply to repeated admonitions, the fathers would remove his monastic clothing before expelling him. This, however, did not indicate that he had lost his monastic identity.[728]

The Fourth Ecumenical Council stated: "If any virgin has dedicated herself to the Lord God, or any men likewise have become monks, let them not be permitted to engage in marriage."[729] But since this was written in AD 451 (before the practice of making rasophore

---

[723] *Basil: Letters and Select Works,* 237 (Epistle 199:19); see also Question 14 in his *Long Rules.*

[724] *Chrysostom: On the Priesthood, Ascetic Treatises, Select Homilies and Letters, Homilies on the Statues,* 113 (Letter 2).

[725] Βίος τοῦ ἐν ἁγίοις πατρὸς ἡμῶν Παχωμίου, 37 ἐν: F. Halkin, *S. Pachomii Vitae graecae* (Brussels: Subsidia Hagiographica 19, 1932); ΒΕΠΕΣ, τ. 40, 206.

[726] *Rule of St. Benedict,* Chapter LVIII.

[727] Ζουκόβα, Γέννηση καὶ Ἐξέλιξη τῆς Ἀκολουθίας τοῦ Μοναχικοῦ Σχήματος: 233.

[728] See Veilleux, *Pachomian Koinonia,* vol. 2, 21–22, 88–94.

[729] Agapius and Nicodemus, *The Rudder,* 261 (Canon XVI).

monks was established in the twelfth century), some people have argued that this rule applies only to great-schema monks, since great-schema monks make explicit vows, whereas rasophore monks do not.

For example, in 1906 Bishop Nicodemos Milas (a professor of canon law) reasoned that a rasophore monk may marry in his influential book, *Ecclesiastical Law of the Eastern Orthodox Church*.[730] More recently, in 2005 Archimandrite Ieronymos Nikolopoulos reached the same conclusion in his study entitled Περὶ τῶν Ρασοφόρων Μοναχῶν ("Regarding Rasophore Monks").[731] Likewise, the doctoral thesis of Stephania Dyrou in 2008 entitled Τὸ Μέγα καὶ Ἀγγελικὸ Σχῆμα ὡς Δεύτερο Βάπτισμα ("The Great and Angelic Schema as a Second Baptism")[732] presents the historical background of the evolution of the rasophore and then, based on a comparison of the prayers read for a rasophore and for the small schema, concludes that a rasophore does not have a monastic identity.

Convincing rebuttals of these views, however, may be found in the article Περὶ τῆς Ἀξίας ἣν Κέκτηται ἐν τῇ Ἐκκλησίᾳ ἡ εἰς Ἀρχάριον Ρασοφοροῦντα Ἱερὰ Ἀκολουθία ("Regarding the Value Which the Holy Service for a Beginner Becoming a Rasophore Has in the Church")[733] written by Abbot Tikhon of Stavronikita Monastery. Another rebuttal may be found in the article by an Athonite monk entitled Ἀκολουθία εἰς ἀρχάριον ρασοφοροῦντα – ἢ κατὰ πόσον ὁ ἔχων ὑποστῇ τὴν ἀκολουθίαν εἰς ἀρχάριον ρασοφοροῦντα μετέχει τῆς μοναχικῆς ἰδιότητος ("The Service for a Beginner Becoming a Rasophore: or, to what degree a person who has undergone the service for a beginner becoming a rasophore partakes of monastic identity").[734] Generally speaking, most Athonites view a rasophore as having all the obligations of a monk, whereas a number of people in the Church of Greece view a rasophore as having only the obligations of a novice.

The first objections to the opinion that rasophores may leave monasticism were made the 12th century by Patriarch Theodore Balsamon[735] (a well-respected canonist) and St. Eustathios of Thessalonica, who wrote regarding rasophores:

> Do you not know, O beginner monk , that you, too, after your official—though subtle [λεπτή][736] and unspoken—tonsure were immediately dedicated to God? … At your enrollment to serve [in monasticism], witnesses were present whom I must

[730] Νικοδήμου Μίλας, Τὸ Ἐκκλησιαστικὸν Δίκαιον τῆς Ὀρθοδόξου Ἀνατολικῆς Ἐκκλησίας (Ἀθήνα: Τύποις Π. Δ. Σακελλαρίου, 1906), 935.

[731] Vid. www.myriobiblos.gr/texts/greek/nicolopoulos_rasoforoi.html

[732] Vid. https://www.scribd.com/doc/226545045/aggeliko-sxima-pdf

[733] «Γρηγόριος ὁ Παλαμᾶς», τεῦχος 831, Νοεμ.-Δεκεμ. 2009; vid. http://tinyurl.com/m2vhgug

[734] «Θεοδρομία», Ἰούλιος-Σεπτέμβριος, 2008; http://www.impantokratoros.gr/rasoforos-monachos.el.aspx

[735] Vid. Γ. Α. Ράλλη καὶ Μ. Ποτλῆ, Σύνταγμα τῶν Θείων καὶ Ἱερῶν Κανόνων, Τόμος Δ΄ (Ἀθήνησιν: Γ. Χαρτοφύλακος, 1854), 498, καὶ Τόμος Β΄, 664–67.

[736] In contrast to the "subtle" tonsure of a beginner monk, St. Eustathios called the tonsure of a great-schema monk "top" [κορυφαίαν] and "great" [μεγάλην] (vid. PG 135:792, 793).

mention. Angels are holding in their hands the contract of your servitude. Do not think that the divine mystery of your dedication is not known to God and His angels.... The rank you have is great, O beginner monk. You have already been enrolled to serve the King. Woe, then, to whoever tries to separate you from this service and lead you away. And who would do this other than Satan, the prince of darkness? But he will be unable to do so if you hold on tightly to God. But in order to understand that a person like you can no longer be a layman, try taking off your holy clothes. You will find out through experience that in the world you are unable to accomplish any of the things provided for by your monastic identity even if you make ten thousand attempts. For there is no one at all who would dare to detach from God someone like you who is dedicated to God without being anathematized.[737]

Likewise, St. Nicodemos of the Holy Mountain, in *The Rudder* in a footnote to Canon 43 of the Sixth Ecumenical Council, emphatically stated that rasophore monks may not marry because: 1) hair was cut from their head[738] which denotes their consecration to God; 2) they have worn the raso; 3) they wear a monastic hat; 4) they have changed their name; and 5) they have had two special prayers read over them that thank God for bringing them to the monastic life.[739]

Commenting on the Service of a Rasophore, Evgenia Zhoukova wrote:

This Service reminds us very much of the ancient forms of receiving a candidate we found in the lives of the saints. It is brief; the vow is silent, since the catechism and its acceptance preceded the service (which is evident from the rubrics of this service

---

[737] PG 135:869D–872C.

[738] Although St. Nicodemos includes the cutting of the hair as one of the reasons why a rasophore monk may not marry, the service for making rasophore monks does not explicitly state whether or not hair should be cut (i.e., tonsured). Because it is not explicitly mentioned in recent editions of the *Euchologion*, some abbots do not cut the hair when making rasophore monks while others do. In the late twentieth century, however, the Holy Community of the Holy Mountain decided that the hair of novices *should* be cut when they are made rasophore monks so that they become more fully aware that they are being tonsured and therefore cannot subsequently marry.

[739] To quote St. Nicodemos in full: "It is plain that all those who arrive at the point of being rasophores (i.e., of having donned the rason, or monk's habit, or the black garb affected by monks in general) can no longer throw aside their rason and marry. God forbid! For how could they possibly dare to do this at a time when they have already cut off the hair of their head, a fact which denotes that they have rejected from their head any and every worldly concern and have consecrated their life to God? How could that be possible when in point of fact they have even donned the rason with a blessing, and have put on the calymmauchion [i.e., monastic hat], and have changed their name; and two special prayers have been read to them by the priest in which he thanks God for having redeemed them from the vain and worldly life and having called them to the decent and modest profession of monks, and begs Him to accept and welcome them into His soterial yoke? Again we ask, if one who has merely promised to become a monk, without so much as having donned the rason (or monk's habit), ought not to break, but, on the contrary, ought to carry out his promise (and see the Footnote to Canon XXVIII of Basil), in accordance with the scriptural passage saying, 'Thou shalt perform thy vows to the Lord' (Mt. 5:33; Deut. 23:23), how much more is it not incumbent upon one to do so after he has actually put on the rason? That is the reason that Balsamon (in his interpretation of Canon V of the 1st-&-2nd) says that a person who has put on the rason is not permitted thereafter to become a layman, but, on the contrary, he will be for this compelled to carry out his earlier aim. If he is unwilling to do this, says Balsamon, he is to be punished severely" (Agapius and Nicodemus, *The Rudder,* 342).

[preserved in Slavonic versions]). We would even say that this Service which is done until today is the oldest form of the Service of the Great (in terms of its meaning) and Angelic Schema....

    In written sources regarding the saints until the seventh century we can see the singular nature of the monastic schema, which consists of different items depending on the location and era. The notion of a "great schema" or a "great-schema monk" did not exist. From the moment one has renounced the world and has worn the ascetical/monastic/canonical/holy/angelic schema (that is, any garments that indicate a renunciation of the world and render one a monk in the eyes of the world) regardless of the place (whether in a brotherhood, in the desert, or in a house) one is considered an ascetic and a monk. I believe that if we today are to be faithful to monastic tradition, no one would dare to consider a rasophore as not being a monk or as not being a complete monk who has the right to remove his schema (i.e., his garments) and return to the world.[740]

The canon law professor P. I. Panagiotakos concurred: "The contrary opinion formulated now and then—which leads to the unacceptable conclusion that a rasophore monk has the right to abandon ascesis whenever he wants and to return to the world and to marry without an impediment as if he has not vowed to keep the sacred promise of virginity—is not only unsound and mistaken but altogether unsupportable legally and canonically; it fatally wounds the canonical order of the Church, and it slights the prevailing *akriveia* [i.e., exactitude towards the canons] regarding this matter from the foundation. Besides, the ancient tradition in monastic life applied to this matter has firmly established and applied this *akriveia,* which it continues to apply unaltered until today."[741]

5) Superiority of Celibacy to Marriage

    Countless saints throughout the centuries have expressed the opinion that the path of celibacy is superior to the path of marriage. St. Athanasios the Great taught:

    There are two ways in life, as touching these matters. The one the more moderate and ordinary, I mean marriage; the other angelic and unsurpassed, namely virginity. Now if a man choose the way of the world, namely marriage, he is not indeed to blame; yet he will not receive such great gifts as the other. For he will receive, since he too brings forth fruit, namely thirtyfold (vid. Mk. 4:20). But if a man embrace the holy and unearthly way, even though, as compared with the former, it be rugged and hard to accomplish, yet it has the more wonderful gifts: for it grows the perfect fruit, namely an hundredfold.[742]

---

[740] Ζουκόβα, *Γέννηση καὶ Ἐξέλιξη τῆς Ἀκολουθίας τοῦ Μοναχικοῦ Σχήματος,* 314, 310.

[741] Π. Ἰ. Παναγιωτάκου, *Σύστημα τοῦ Ἐκκλησιαστικοῦ Δικαίου - Τὸ Δίκαιον τῶν Μοναχῶν,* Τόμος Δ΄ (Ἀθῆναι: Πουρναράς, 1957), 101–2.

[742] *Athanasius: Select Works and Letters,* 557 (Letter to Amun). Similarly, St. Jerome taught: "The yield thirtyfold signifies wedlock.... The yield sixtyfold refers to widows who are placed in a position of distress and tribulation.... Moreover, a hundred ... indicates the crown of virginity" (*A Select Library of Nicene and Post-Nicene Fathers of the Christian Church: Second Series,* vol. 6: *St. Jerome,* Henry Wace, ed. [New York:

St. Gregory the Theologian said: "It is better to be free of these bonds [of marriage], rendering everything to God and to the things above.... Marriage is concern about spouse and loved ones. Whereas for virginity, it is Christ."[743] "It so surpasses marriage and the fetters of the world even as the soul is apt to be more excellent than the flesh and the wide heaven than the earth; as the stable life of the blessed is more excellent than transitory life; as God is superior to man.... These [virgins] are the lights of the world, bright mirrors of the light: they see God, are seen by God and belong to God."[744]

St. John Chrysostom agreed: "Is virginity a good [thing]? Yes, I fully agree. But is it better than marriage? I agree with this, too.... Virginity is as much superior to marriage as heaven is to earth, as the angels are to men, and, to use far stronger language, it is more superior still. For the angels, though they do not marry and are not given in marriage, are not a mixture of flesh and blood. They do not pass time on earth and endure trouble from passions.... But mankind, inferior in its nature to blessed spirits, forces its own nature and, in so far as it can, vies eagerly to equal the angels.... Do you grasp the value of virginity? That it makes those who spend time on earth live like the angels dwelling in heaven? It does not allow those endowed with bodies to be inferior to the incorporeal powers and spurs all men to rival the angels.... What, then does Paul say under the inspiration of the Lord? 'Now for the matters you wrote about. A man is better off having no relations with woman' (1 Cor. 7:1)."[745]

In the same vein, St. Jerome wrote: "I praise wedlock, I praise marriage, but it is because they give me virgins. I gather the rose from the thorns, the gold from the earth, the pearl from the shell.... 'Concerning virgins,' says the apostle [Paul], 'I have no commandment of the Lord' (1 Cor. 7:25). Why was this? Because his own virginity was due, not to a command, but to his free choice.... What is freely offered is worth more than what is extorted by force.... When he is discussing continence and commending perpetual chastity,

---

Christian Literature Company, 1893], 67). These quotes suggest that the early Church fathers understood the words of Christ in Matthew 19:29 as referring to the reward for monastic virginity: "And every one that hath forsaken houses, or brethren, or sisters, or father, or mother, or wife, or children, or lands, for My name's sake, shall receive an hundredfold, and shall inherit everlasting life."

[743] Gregory the Theologian, Εἰς σωφροσύνην (*On Self-restraint*), PG 37:643A–644A.

[744] Gregory the Theologian, Παρθενίης ἔπαινος (*In Praise of Virginity*), PG 37:538A.

[745] *John Chrysostom: On Virginity, Against Remarriage,* trans. Sally Rieger Shore (New York: Edwin Meller Press, 1983), 14–17. Elsewhere St. John said: "So, do not prefer over virginity that which was admitted because of your weakness. Rather, do not even put them on the same level" (*On Virginity,* PG 48:545).

he uses the words, 'I would that all men were even as I myself.' And farther on, 'I say, therefore, to the unmarried and widows, it is good for them if they abide even as I.'[746],[747]

St. Ambrose also cited St. Paul to show the superiority of virginity: "Marriage, then, is honourable, but chastity is more honourable, for 'he that giveth his virgin in marriage doeth well, but he that giveth her not in marriage doeth better' (1 Cor. 8:28). That, then, which is good need not be avoided, but that which is better should be chosen."[748] St. Clement wrote: "He will give to virgins a notable place in the house of God … better than the place of those who have passed a wedded life in sanctity and whose 'bed has not been defiled' (Heb. 13:4)."[749]

St. John Chrysostom said: "Even though marriage be honorable (Heb. 13:4), yet it can only go so far as not to defile those who engage in it. But to produce Saints is not within the power of marriage but of virginity."[750] Developing this concept, St. John of the Ladder wrote: "Who amongst [laymen] has ever worked any miracles? Who has raised the dead? Who has driven out devils? no one. All these are the victorious rewards of monks, rewards which the world cannot receive; and if it could, then what is the need of asceticism or solitude?"[751] St. Barsanuphius of Optina added to this:

> True blessedness can only be acquired in a monastery. You can be saved in the world, but it is impossible to be completely purified… or to rise up and live like the angels and live a creative spiritual life in the world. All the ways of the world … destroy or at least slow down the development of the soul. And that's why people can attain the angelic life only in monasteries…. Monasticism is blessedness; the most blessed state that is possible for a person on this earth. There is nothing higher than this blessedness, because monasticism hands you the key to spiritual life.[752]

---

[746] 1 Cor. 7:8. Similarly, the second-century Shepherd of Hermas (considered canonical scripture by St. Irenaeus and other early Church fathers) wrote: "There is no sin in marrying again, but if they remain unmarried they gain greater honour and glory with the Lord" (*Shepherd of Hermas,* Mandates, iv. 4).

[747] *A Select Library of Nicene and Post-Nicene Fathers of the Christian Church: Second Series,* vol. 6: *St. Jerome,* 30 (*Letter XXII to Eustochium:* 20).

[748] *Ambrose: Select Works and Letters,* 403. Likewise, St. Methodios of Olympus in his *Banquet of the Ten Virgins,* after quoting everything that St. Paul had to say about virginity, concluded that virginity is given the "highest prize" (vid. *Ante-Nicene Christian Library: Translations of the Writings of the Fathers Down to A.D. 325, Volume 14: The Writings of Methodius* [New York: Christian Literature Company, 1880], 36 [Discourse 3, ch. 13–14]).

[749] *Ante-Nicene Christian Library: Translations of the Writings of the Fathers Down to A.D. 325,* vol. 8: *The Writings of Cyprian,* (New York: Christian Literature Company, 1868), "Two Epistles Concerning Virginity," i. 4, 56.

[750] St. John Chrysostom, *On Virginity* 30, PG 48:554.

[751] Holy Transfiguration Monastery, *The Ladder of Divine Ascent,* 13 (step 2:10).

[752] As quoted in "Monasticism in the 21st Century: A Viable Alternative or a Forgotten Ideal?" Mother Ephrosynia, Convent of Lesna, France (http://stpaisiusmonastery.org/about-the-monastery/about-monasticism/monasticism-in-21st-century/); see also Afanasiev, *Elder Barsanuphius of Optina,* 340, 631.

In the same spirit, Elder Ephraim observed: "The supernatural miracles of monastics and their spiritual state—the fruit of their ascetical struggles—show what monasticism is. Struggling to live the Christian life in the world is indeed a godly pursuit, but it does not even come close to the spiritual wealth and closeness to God produced by monasticism. 'A tree is known by its fruit' (Mt. 12:33). A whole army of monastics has filled heaven. How many Righteous saints [i.e., those who were not monastics, clergy, or martyrs] do we have? You can count them on your fingers."[753] And St. Symeon of Thessalonica stated: "There are many paths to salvation, but monasticism is the most perfect path."[754]

St. John the Damascene wrote: "Virginity is the angelic way of life and the characteristic of every bodiless nature.... As much as an angel is superior to man, by the same amount is virginity more honorable than marriage. What am I talking about angels for? Christ Himself, the boast of virginity not only was born from the Father without beginning, change, or [conjugal] union, but also He became man like us for our sake by taking on flesh from the Virgin without union, and He demonstrated the true and complete virginity in Himself.... Marriage is good for those who lack continence, but virginity is better because it increases the soul's fertility and offers prayer to God as a ripe fruit."[755]

Several saints in the fourth century viewed monastics as soldiers of Christ, including St. Serapion of Thmuis,[756] St. John Chrysostom,[757] and St. Basil the Great. St. Basil taught that monastics enjoy greater honor than laymen, just as soldiers of a king deserve more honor than civilians:

> A king's edicts addressed to his subjects are solemn enough, but greater and more regal are his orders to his soldiers. As if military orders are being proclaimed, therefore, let that man give ear who desires what is of great and celestial worth, who wishes to be ever Christ's comrade.... A soldier has rations from the king; he need not get rations for himself nor concern himself in this regard. Everywhere the houses of subjects are open to him, by the king's command. He need not trouble about a house. His tent is pitched in the streets, bare necessities are his food, water is his drink, and his sleep is what nature gives and no more. Many are his marches and vigils; he contends against heat, against cold. He fights the foe and faces extreme dangers and often, it may be, death. But a glorious death and honors and royal gifts are his lot. His life is laborious in war, splendid in peace. The prize of valor, and the crown awarded to one whose life is a successful record of good actions, is to be entrusted with rule, to be called the King's friend, to stand near the king, to be the foremost among his subjects, to plead on behalf of his friends outside, for whatever they desire.

---

[753] From a homily given at the Holy Monastery of Philotheou.

[754] As quoted in Ἀρχιμανδρίτου Γεωργίου, Ὀρθόδοξος Μοναχισμὸς καὶ Ἅγιον Ὄρος, 111.

[755] PG 94:1210–12 (St. John of Damascus, *On the Orthodox Faith*, IV, 24).

[756] St. Serapion of Thmuis wrote: "Blessed are you [monks] who serve as soldiers to the Trinity in one essence" (PG 4:936D–937A).

[757] See St. John Chrysostom, *A Comparison between a King and a Monk/Against the Opponents of the Monastic life*, 71.

Come, then, O soldier of Christ, take to heart these small lessons from human affairs and bear in mind the eternal blessings. Set before yourself a life without house, city, or possessions. Be free, released from all worldly cares, lest you be fettered by the desire for a woman or by cares for a child....

But you who love the heavenly way of living and practice the angelic life and desire to become a fellow soldier of Christ's holy disciples, brace yourself to endure afflictions and come manfully to the assembly of the monks.[758]

In his work *The Clothing of Virgins* St. Cyprian of Carthage, speaking of the dignity of the virginal state, says: "Virgins are the flowering buds of the Church; the glory and ornament of spiritual grace ... a work of praise and honour whole and uncorrupted; the image of God corresponding to the holiness of the Lord; the most illustrious members of Christ's flock ... and the more there aboundeth virginity the greater the increase of joy in the mother."[759]

St. Gregory Palamas taught that overcoming passions and attaining salvation is easier for those living in virginity:

This cleansing [from the passions] can also be accomplished by those who live in marriage, but with utmost difficulty. For this reason, everyone who from their youth has found favor in God's sight, perceives eternal life through the penetrating eye of the mind—and in fact falls in love with that eternal goodness—and duly flees marriage....

Paul addresses those who are married: "The appointed time is short, in that from now on let those who have wives live as though they had none, and those who deal with the world as though they had no dealings with it."[760] I personally consider married life to be more difficult than the labors of virginity. Experience testifies that fasting is easier than the moderation of eating and drinking. I will speak rightly and truly: to one who is not interested in being saved, I have nothing to say; but to one who is concerned with one's own salvation, let this one know—life in virginity is more beneficial and much easier than married life....

One fact is certain: when gold is mixed with copper, then it is called "fool's gold"; but when copper is gold-plated then it appears more exquisite than it is and is much more brilliant. And thus it is with you, O virgin! When one of the married women yearns for you and your virginal life, this offers her glory. However, when you begin to yearn for that which is theirs, you bring disgrace upon yourself, for this desire returns you back once again to the world.[761]

After enumerating the difficulties of married life, St. Serapion of Thmuis wrote enthusiastically about the delights of monastic virginity:

But you abide in the wilderness free from cares, attending only to your luminous life. Oh, how much superiority in honor your holy and sacred schema has! Oh, how

---

[758] Βασιλείου τοῦ Μεγάλου, *Ἀσκητικὰ Α΄*, ΕΠΕ 8, 82–85, 98–99; see also Wagner, *Saint Basil: Ascetical Works,* vol. 9, 9–10, 18, and Clarke, *The Ascetic Works of St. Basil,* 55–56, 62.

[759] Sakharov, *Truth and Life,* 93 (an English translation of *De Habitu Virginum,* iii, 3, 189. Corpus Scriptorum Ecclesiasticorum Latinorum [Vienna, 1868]).

[760] 1 Cor. 7:29, 31.

[761] *Saint Gregory Palamas: Treatise on the Spiritual Life,* trans. Daniel M. Rogich (Minneapolis: Light and Life Publishing Company, 1995), 43, 46–47.

much spiritual fragrance it emits! Oh, what a marvelous lifestyle you have chosen! No words can sing its praises! Oh, what a profession that touches heaven! Oh, what a profession that unites you with God! Oh, what a profession that portrays the angels! Oh, what a profession that preserves being in the image of God! Oh, what a profession that stands beside God! Oh, what a profession most honorable to God! Oh, what a profession by which the world is saved![762]

It would be a mistake to think that the holy Fathers viewed virginity as superior to marriage merely because they themselves were all celibate and therefore biased. For even St. Gregory of Nyssa (who was married[763]) wrote: "The more exactly we understand the riches of virginity, the more we must bewail the other [married] life; for we realize by this contrast with better things, how poor it is. I do not speak only of the future rewards in store for those who have lived thus excellently, but those rewards also which they have while alive here; for if any one would make up his mind to measure exactly the difference between the two courses, he would find it well-nigh as great as that between heaven and earth."[764]

Notwithstanding this patristic opinion that celibacy is superior to marriage, this does not mean that it is God's will for everyone to remain celibate. Many ostensibly "superior" monastics have lost their salvation while many supposedly "inferior" laymen have been saved. Celibacy is a particular calling that God has given only to few people. For when the Apostles concluded: "It is not good to marry," Christ replied: "Not everyone can receive this saying, but only those to whom it is given." Commenting on this passage, St. John Chrysostom said:

> What then saith Christ? He said not, "yea, it is easier [not to marry], and so do," lest they should suppose that the thing is a law; but He subjoined, "Not everyone can receive this saying, but only those to whom it is given," raising the thing, and showing that it is great, and in this way drawing them on, and urging them. But see herein a contradiction. For He indeed saith this is a great thing; but they, that it is easier. For it was meet that both these things should be done, and that it should be at once acknowledged a great thing by Him, that it might render them more forward, and by the things said by themselves it should be shown to be easier, that on this ground too they might the rather choose virginity and continence. For since to speak of virginity seemed to be grievous, by the constraint of this law He drove them to this desire.[765]

---

[762] Σεραπίωνος Θμούεως, Ἐπιστολὴ πρὸς μονάζοντας, PG 40:933C.

[763] He himself gives evidence of his married status when he wrote concerning virginity and its value: "Blessed are they who have the freedom to choose what is better and have not been blockaded by assuming the common way of life as we have; we are prevented from the boast of virginity as if by a chasm.... Therefore we are but spectators of others' goods, and witnesses of the blessedness of each" (Gregory of Nyssa, *On Virginity*, 3; PG 46:325A–C).

[764] *A Select Library of Nicene and Post-Nicene Fathers of the Christian Church: Second Series*, vol. 5, *Gregory of Nyssa*, ed. Philip Schaff (New York: Christian Literature Company, 1893), 345 (*On Virginity*, Chapter 3).

[765] *St. Chrysostom: Homilies on the Gospel of St. Matthew*, 365.

Likewise, St. Cyprian of Carthage made the following comments on that scriptural passage: "Nor does the Lord command this [i.e., virginity], but He exhorts it; nor does He impose the yoke of necessity, since the free choice of the will is left. But when He says that in His Father's house are many mansions, He points out the dwellings of a better habitation."[766]

Moreover, the whole point of comparing the two paths is not to enable those who are supposedly "superior" to gloat pridefully over those who are "inferior" (as St. John of Sinai warns[767]) but rather to encourage those who are free to choose between the two paths to follow the one that is likely to produce superior results for him or her personally. Since the manner in which a person lives his life is more important than which mode of life he has chosen, St. Symeon the New Theologian said: "Many regard the monastic way as the most blessed way. For my part, however, I would not set any way above the others; nor would I praise one and depreciate another. But in every situation, it is the life lived for God and according to God that is entirely blessed."[768]

6) Inferiority of Virginity

Another point worth pondering is that since married life *is* more difficult, perhaps it would not be unreasonable to deduce that it also has a greater reward when successfully lived in a God-pleasing manner. Metropolitan Kallistos Ware wrote in his introduction to the *Ladder*: "It is a great thing, says John, to achieve stillness in the isolation of a hermit's cell; 'but it is incomparably greater to have no fear of turmoil, and to remain steadfast under its assault with a fearless heart, living outwardly with men but inwardly with God.'"[769] Just as attaining hesychia is a greater feat for someone living in the world than for someone living in a hermitage, by extension one could also surmise that attaining chastity—which entails not merely continence but a transformation of carnal desire into eros for God[770]—

---

[766] *Ante-Nicene Christian Library:* vol. 8: *The Writings of Cyprian,* "On the Dress of Virgins," 349 (Chapter 23).

[767] "It is possible to belittle those living in the world out of conceit; and it is also possible to disparage them behind their backs in order to avoid despair and to obtain hope" (Holy Transfiguration Monastery, *The Ladder of Divine Ascent,* 12).

[768] As quoted in http://www.orthodoxa.org/GB/orthodoxy/society/love.htm

[769] Luibhéid, *John Climacus: The Ladder of Divine Ascent,* 52.

[770] According to Orthodox theology, the passible faculties (i.e., the faculties of the soul subject to passion, which are the incensive power "θυμικόν" and the appetitive aspect "ἐπιθυμητικόν") are God-given and therefore do not need to be suppressed but rather should be used as God intended. St. Basil the Great wrote: "By the way it is used each of the other faculties also becomes either evil or good for the one who possesses it. As for the soul's faculty of desire, one who uses it for the enjoyment of the flesh and the consumption of impure pleasure is disgusting and licentious, while one who turns it toward the love of God and the longing for eternal good things is enviable and blessed" ("Homily against Anger," *On the Human Condition: St Basil the Great* [New York: St. Vladimir's Seminary Press, 2005], 89). St. Maximos the Confessor said: "Even the passions become good if we wisely and diligently detach them from what is bodily and direct them towards

is a greater feat for someone married than for someone celibate (even though this does not mean that a person seeking chastity should choose marriage any more than a person seeking hesychia should remain in the world).

St. Cyprian of Carthage agreed with this reasoning. He wrote: "Assuredly to have guarded one's purity from the womb, and to have kept oneself an infant even to old age throughout the whole of life, is certainly the part of an admirable virtue; only that if never to have known the body's seductive capacities is the greater blessedness, to have overcome them when once known is the greater virtue."[771]

Clement of Alexandria wrote more boldly:

> True manhood is shown not in the choice of a celibate life; on the contrary the prize in the contest of men is won by him who has trained himself by the discharge of the duties of husband and father and by the supervision of a household, regardless of pleasure or pain,—by him, I say, who in the midst of his solicitude for his family shows himself inseparable from the love of God and rises superior to every temptation which assails him through children and wife and servants and possessions. On the other hand, he who has no family is in most respects untried. In any case, as he takes thought only for himself, he is surpassed by him who is inferior, as far as his own personal salvation is concerned, but who is superior in the conduct of life, inasmuch as he actually preserves a faint image of the true Providence.[772]

---

the acquisition of what is heavenly. This happens, for example, when we turn desire into a noetic yearning for heavenly blessings" (Palmer, Sherrard, Ware, *The Philokalia,* vol. 2, 179). He also taught: "When a man's intellect [nous] is constantly with God, his desire grows beyond all measure into an intense longing for God.... When it [i.e., the nous] has reintegrated its possible aspect, it redirects this aspect towards God, as we have said, filling it with an incomprehensible and intense longing for Him" (Palmer, Sherrard, Ware, *The Philokalia,* vol. 2, 73). Similarly, St. Gregory Palamas wrote to Barlaam: "We have not been taught that dispassion is the putting to death of the soul's passionate part; on the contrary, it is the conversion of the passionate part from the lower to the higher" (St. Gregory Palamas, *Triads,* II, 2, 19). Likewise, the Athonite Fathers wrote: "Once the soul's passible aspect is transformed and sanctified—but not reduced to a deathlike condition—through it the dispositions and activities of the body are also sanctified, since body and soul share a conjoint existence" ("Declaration of the Holy Mountain in Defence of Those Who Devoutly Practise a Life of Stillness," 6; Palmer, Sherrard, Ware, *The Philokalia,* vol. 4, 423). As for eros, St. Maximos the Confessor taught: "God is the producer and generator of love and eros.... In so far as the eros originates from Him, He can be said to be the moving force of it, since He generated it" (PG 4:265C). St. John Chrysostom said about eros in marriage: "This is not something human, but it is God Who sows these loves (ἔρωτας)" (PG 51:230). St. Gregory of Nyssa showed that eros can be either shamefully directed to the flesh or praiseworthily directed to the immaterial Bridegroom, for he wrote: "Intensified love is called eros, in which no one is put to shame when he does not aim it at the flesh, but rather he takes pride in the wound when he receives the point of immaterial desire in the depths of his heart" (PG 44:1048C). In the same vein, St. Gregory Palamas said: "When desire is redirected from the flesh to the spirit it raises us to such heights" (*The Homilies of Saint Gregory Palamas,* vol. 1, trans. Christopher Veniamin [South Canaan: St. Tikhon's Seminary Press, 2002], 58). And Archimandrite Zacharias taught that a monk living in virginity "transforms every energy into a spiritual force, so as to keep his spirit in constant association with the Spirit of God. A life of spiritual virginity is an exalted art and culture, whose fundamental value lies in the 'guarding of the intellect'" (Zacharias, *Christ, Our Way and Our Life,* 138).

[771] *Ante-Nicene Christian Library:* vol. 8: *The Writings of Cyprian,* 588.

[772] *Stromata* Book 7, Chapter 12, as translated in *Alexandrian Christianity: Selected Translations of Clement and Origen with Introduction and Notes,* vol. 2 of Library of Christian Classics, E. L. Oulton and H.

One could argue that even St. John of Sinai would also agree with this reasoning. For he warns monks: "Be on the lookout for this trick and wile of the thieves [i.e., the demons]. For they suggest to us that we need not separate ourselves from people in the world, and maintain that we shall receive a great reward if we can look upon women and still remain continent. We must not believe these suggestions, but rather do the opposite."[773] The fact that St. John does not try to disprove this suggestion of the demons but simply advises monks not to pay attention to it, seems to imply that he believes that it is indeed a greater feat to remain completely chaste in the presence of women than to do the same in their absence, but he discourages us from attempting this because there is a high probability of failure.

St. John Chrysostom, however, explained that the greater difficulty of the married life does *not* merit greater reward. He wrote that married Christians "must expend greater effort if they wish to be saved, because of the constraint imposed on them. For the person who is free of bonds will run more easily than the one who is enchained. Will the latter then receive a greater reward and more glorious crown? Not at all! For he placed this constraint upon himself when he was free not to."[774]

In conclusion, these patristic statements seem to imply that celibacy is not *ipso facto* superior to marriage, but its superiority lies in the practical reality that it is more likely to be conducive to spiritual growth, or "increase the fertility of the soul," as St. John the Damascene put it: "Marriage is good for those lacking in self control; but better is virginity, which increases the fertility of the soul."[775]

7) Virginity of Soul

Christ taught that true chastity is not just external but internal: "Whosoever looketh on a woman to lust after her hath committed adultery with her already in his heart."[776] Elaborating on this precept, the holy Fathers taught that virginity that is merely external is insufficient. For example, Blessed Augustine wrote in his monastic rule:

> Although your eyes may chance to rest upon some woman or other, you must not fix your gaze upon any woman. Seeing women when you go out is not forbidden, but it is sinful to desire them or to wish them to desire you, for it is not by tough or passionate feeling alone but by one's gaze also that lustful desires mutually arise. And do not

---

Chadwick, ed. (United Kingdom: Westminster Press, 1954), 138, and in *Fathers of the Second Century: Hermas, Tatian, Athenagoras, Theophilus, and Clement of Alexandria*, 543.

[773] Holy Transfiguration Monastery, *The Ladder of Divine Ascent*, 15–16.

[774] *Against the Opponents of the Monastic Life* 3, PG 47:376, as translated in Trenham, *Marriage and Virginity according to St. John Chrysostom*, 148.

[775] PG 94:1212 (St. John of Damascus, *On the Orthodox Faith* IV.24).

[776] Mt. 5:28.

say that your hearts are pure if there is immodesty of the eye, because the unchaste eye carries the message of an impure heart. And when such hearts disclose their unchaste desires in a mutual gaze, even without saying a word, then it is that chastity suddenly goes out of their life, even though their bodies remain unsullied by unchaste acts. And whoever fixes his gaze upon a woman and likes to have hers fixed upon him must not suppose that others do not see what he is doing. He is very much seen, even by those he thinks do not see him. But suppose all this escapes the notice of man—what will he do about God who sees from on high and from whom nothing is hidden? ... So when you are together in church and anywhere else where women are present, exercise a mutual care over purity of life.[777]

Likewise, St. Columbanus wrote in his monastic rule: "Of what value is it if he [a monk] is a virgin in body but not in mind? For God, being spirit, lives in that spirit and in that mind which seems to him undefiled, in which there is no adulterous thought, no stain of a polluted spirit, and no spot of sin."[778] St. Gregory Palamas said that virginity is "keeping thoughts from consenting to any evil."[779] And St. Isaac the Syrian taught: "A virgin is not merely one who keeps his body undefiled by intercourse, but one who feels shame before himself even when he is alone."[780] St. John Cassian wrote: "Some strong words of Saint Basil, the bishop of Caesarea, are apropos. He said: 'I do not know woman, but I am not a virgin.' Well indeed did he understand that the incorruption of the flesh consists not so much in abstaining from woman as it does in integrity of heart, which ever and truly preserves the incorrupt holiness of the body by both the fear of God and the love of chastity."[781]

Furthermore, St. Basil the Great taught that not only carnal thoughts sully a monk's virginity but all the passions do:

> Virginity is a help to such devotion, for those who pursue this gift [of being in the likeness of God] in a spiritual manner. For merely abstaining from the procreation of children does not constitute the gift of virginity. On the contrary, the whole of one's life and character must be virginal, illustrating in every action the integrity required of the virgin. For it is possible to commit fornication in speech and adultery with the eye, to be polluted through the hearing, to receive defilement in the heart, and to transgress the bounds of temperance by lacking control in partaking of food and drink.[782] ...

> Anger, jealousy, bearing a grudge, falsehood, insolence, arrogance, unseasonable talking, slackness in prayer, desire for goods one does not possess, negligence in observing the commandments, ostentation in dress, vain regard for one's appearance,

---

[777] *The Rule of St. Augustine,* iv, 4–6.

[778] Oliver Davies and Thomas O'Loughlin, *Celtic Spirituality,* 249.

[779] Ἁγίου Γρηγορίου Παλαμᾶ, «Ὁμιλία ΜΔ΄. Εἰς τὸν Ἅγιον Ἀπόστολον καὶ Εὐαγγελιστὴν καὶ τῷ Χριστῷ ἐξόχως ἠγαπημένον Ἰωάννην τὸν Θεολόγον», τόμος 11 (Θεσσαλονίκη: ΕΠΕ, 1986), 48, παρ. 3.

[780] Holy Transfiguration Monastery, *The Ascetical Homilies of Saint Isaac the Syrian,* 171 (Homily 6).

[781] Ramsey, *John Cassian: The Institutes,* 161 (vi. 19).

[782] Βασιλείου τοῦ Μεγάλου, *Ἀσκητικὰ Α΄,* ΕΠΕ 8, 128–29; see also Wagner, *Saint Basil: Ascetical Works,* vol. 9, 207–8.

meetings and conversations beyond what is necessary and fitting—all these must be most carefully avoided by one who has dedicated himself to God by virginity, because yielding to one of them is almost as perilous as committing an expressly forbidden sin.[783]

St. Joseph the Hesychast taught that chastity makes a person fragrant:

When a person fights to keep his body pure and his mind chaste from dirty thoughts, his life and his prayer ascend like fragrant incense to the heavens. I have seen in practice what I am telling you. No sacrifice to God is more fragrant than chastity of the body which is obtained with a bloody and dreadful struggle. I have much to say about this blessed chastity, the fruit of which I have tasted and eaten. But you are not able to bear right now what I would say. Only one thing will I tell you now: when such people change their underclothes—which they might do only once every three or six months—they give off a fragrance that fills the entire house as if a refreshing vial of myrrh had been opened. This is a sign from God of their blessed chastity and most holy virginity.[784]

St. Sophrony of Essex wrote: "Chastity—σωφροσύνη—as the word itself shows, signifies integrity or fulness of wisdom. In the Church the concept embodies not only mastery over sexual impulses or the complex of the flesh in general, and, in this sense, 'victory over nature,' but the acquisition of the combination of perfections proper to wisdom, which will be expressed by a constant dwelling in God 'with all one's mind, with all one's heart.'[785] In its most complete realization the ascetic feat of chastity may restore man in the spirit to his virginal state."[786]

St. John of Sinai warned that some dangerous behaviors can seem deceptively innocent because they do not give rise to a temptation immediately:

I have seen some give way to luxury and not at once feel the attacks of the enemy. I have seen others eat with women and converse with them, and at the time have no bad thoughts whatsoever in their mind. They were thus deceived and encouraged to grow careless and to think that they were in peace and safety, and they suddenly suffered destruction in their cells. But what bodily and spiritual destruction comes to us when we are alone? He who is tempted knows. And he who is not tempted does not need to know.[787]

Elaborating on this, St. Sophrony of Essex wrote:

As well as the sexual act, there are not a few other forms of depravity and self-abuse of which the Orthodox Church bans description, in order not to encourage any image of sin in the mind of writer or reader. The Church conceives of three spiritual

---

[783] Βασιλείου τοῦ Μεγάλου, Ἀσκητικὰ Α΄, ΕΠΕ 8, 130–31; see also Wagner, *Saint Basil: Ascetical Works,* vol. 9, 209.

[784] Γέροντος Ἰωσήφ, Ἔκφρασις Μοναχικῆς Ἐμπειρίας, 192; see also Elder Joseph, *Monastic Wisdom,* 173.

[785] Cf. Mk. 12:30.

[786] Sakharov, *Truth and Life,* 94.

[787] Holy Transfiguration Monastery, *The Ladder of Divine Ascent,* 112–13.

states of mankind: the supra-natural, the natural and the infra- or un-natural. Virginity and monastic chastity, understood as the gifts of grace, belong to the first; to the second, the marriage which has been blessed; to the third, any other form of sexual life, which will be spiritually either infra-natural or against nature. The Fathers said: "Attempt not the supra-natural lest you fall into the un-natural." Hence the rule never to admit anyone to monasticism without a preliminary period of trial. The monk who does not preserve his chastity ranks far lower than the man bound in a virtuous marriage, which the Church recognizes as a way of salvation. Since the monk who has pronounced vows of chastity is deprived of the right to a marriage blessed by the Church, any transgression on his part against chastity is considered a fall; a fall, moreover, into an un-natural state. A normal sober marriage preserves a man's physical and moral health whereas any other mode of sexual life, even if it only takes the form of reverie, has a disintegrating effect on the whole man, mentally and physically. This disintegrating action is particularly powerful in the monk who sins thus and so breaks vows made before God: the inner conflict engendered in him consequent on loss of grace assumes an incomparably more profound character, and the torments of remorse may reach the point of black despair. The imagining of sexual relations, in the absence of the normal physical act, has in many cases led to serious mental illness and even to total madness. Psychiatrists can testify to the frequency of such instances."[788]

8) Acquiring Chastity

St. John of Sinai dedicated Step 15 of *The Ladder* to chastity, in which he explains the practices that help us acquire it. He taught that although ascetic efforts and avoidance are helpful, what really helps is humility, obedience, prayer, remembrance of death, and confession:

He who fights this adversary [of sensuality] by bodily hardship and sweat is like one who has tied his foe with a string. But he who opposes him by temperance, sleeplessness and vigil is like one who puts a yoke on him. He who opposes him by humility, freedom from irritability and thirst is like one who has killed his enemy and hidden him in the sand[789] … Offer to the Lord the weakness of your nature, fully acknowledging your own powerlessness, and imperceptibly you will receive the gift of chastity.[790] … He who attempts to stop this [carnal] war by temperance, and by that alone, is like a man who has the idea of escaping the sea by swimming with one hand. Join humility to temperance, because without the former the latter is useless.[791]

Who has conquered his body? He who has crushed his heart. And who has crushed his heart? He who has denied himself. For how can he not be crushed who has died to his own will?[792] … If you clearly know the profound weakness which is in both you and me ["me" refers to a personification of the flesh], you have bound my hands. If

---

[788] Sakharov, *Truth and Life,* 95–96.

[789] Holy Transfiguration Monastery, *The Ladder of Divine Ascent,* 105.

[790] Ibid., 106.

[791] Ibid., 109.

[792] Ibid., 119.

you starve your appetite, you have bound my feet from going further. If you take the yoke of obedience, you have thrown off my yoke. If you obtain humility, you have cut off my head.[793]

On these occasions [of carnal temptation], the best aids for us are sackcloth, ashes, all-night standing, hunger, moistening the tongue in moderation when parched with thirst, dwelling amongst the tombs, and above all, humility of heart; and if possible, a spiritual father or zealous brother, one spiritually mature, to help us.[794]

Let us, by every means in our power, avoid either seeing or hearing of that fruit which we have vowed not to taste. For it is absurd to think ourselves stronger than the Prophet David;[795] that is impossible.[796]

Always let the remembrance of death and the Prayer of Jesus, being of single phrase, go to sleep with you and get up with you; for you will find nothing to equal these aids [against carnal warfare] during sleep.[797] ... For those who have not yet obtained true prayer of the heart, violence in bodily prayer is a great help [against carnal warfare]—I mean stretching out the hands, beating the breast, sincere raising of the eyes to Heaven, deep sighing, frequent prostrations.... Raise on high the eyes of your soul, if you can; but if not, your bodily eyes. Hold your arms motionless in the form of a cross, in order to shame and conquer your Amalek[798] by this sign. Cry to Him Who is able to save, not with cleverly spun phrases but in humble words, preferably making this your prelude: "Have mercy on me, for I am weak" (Ps. 6:2). Then you will know by experience the power of the Most High, and with invisible help you will invisibly drive away the invisible ones.[799]

As an aid against carnal warfare, St. Nicodemos of the Holy Mountain emphasized the importance of guarding our eyes. He wrote:

We must cut off seeing those beautiful bodies which incite the soul to shameful and inappropriate desires.... Listen to Solomon crying out: "Let your eyes look directly forward, and your gaze be straight before you."[800] Listen also to Job who said: "I have made a covenant with mine eyes; how then shall I look upon a virgin?"[801] ... Solomon orders us not to be ensnared by our eyes: "Let not the desire of beauty overcome you,

---

[793] Ibid., 120.

[794] Ibid., 113. Similarly, St. Isidore of Seville wrote in his monastic rule: "He who burns with temptations of fornication should pray without ceasing and abstain and not be ashamed to confess the heat of the lust by which he burns, because once defeated, the vice is quickly cured, but if it lurks it will be hidden more and more as it creeps down more deeply. In fact, he who neglects to make it known does not at all desire to cure it" (*Monastic Studies,* no. 18, 20–21).

[795] Vid. 2 Kings 11.

[796] Holy Transfiguration Monastery, *The Ladder of Divine Ascent,* 114.

[797] Ibid., 112.

[798] Vid. Ex. 17:8–16.

[799] Holy Transfiguration Monastery, *The Ladder of Divine Ascent,* 118.

[800] Prov. 4:25.

[801] Job 31:1.

neither be enmeshed through your eyes."[802] St. Gregory the Theologian, going still further, would have us avoid even a careless glance. He added this to the saying in Proverbs: "Be not captivated by your eyes, and if at all possible, not even by a careless glance."[803] Interpreting this, the commentator Nicetas Stethatos wrote the following: "'Do not be captivated by your eyes' implies not only a curious and lingering look, but, if possible, not even a cursory look that comes upon you by chance, thereby protecting yourselves even from a careless glance that may mislead your eyes. Because this is extremely difficult, he added the phrase 'if possible.'" ...

What must one do when captivated by the eyes? If this thief ever comes and captivates you, fight against him and do not allow an idol of Aphrodite—that is, of any shameful desire—to be impressed upon your soul. How? Either by taking refuge in God through prayer, which is the most secure way (as the psalm says, "deliverance comes only from the Lord"[804]), or by turning your imagination to another spiritual thought so that one imagination wipes out another and one idol destroys another. According to the popular maxim, "One peg drives out the other." This seems to be the activity that St. Gregory the Theologian did when he wrote: "A face caught my attention but was checked; I set up no image of sin. Was an image set up? Yet, the experience of sin was avoided."[805] Do you hear what he is saying? The image of sin stood before him but was not impressed upon his imagination. Thus he was directly freed from the experience, namely from the consent or the act of sin.

If then the devil does not cease to tempt you with the idol of that person that has been impressed upon your imagination, St. John Chrysostom[806] and St. Synkletike[807] advise you to use this method in order to be delivered from his wiles: With your mind gouge out the eyes of that idol; tear the flesh off its cheeks and cut off its lips. Remove the beautiful skin that is visible, and meditate on how what is hidden underneath is so disgusting that no man can bear to look upon it without hatred and disgust. It is after all no more than a skull covered with skin and an odious bone filled with blood and fearful to behold.[808]

St. Isaac the Syrian taught that reading and prayer are what assist chastity: "If you love chastity, banish shameful thoughts by exercising yourself in reading and prolonged prayer; then you will be inwardly armed against their natural causes. But without reading and prayer, purity cannot be present in the soul."[809]

---

[802] Prov. 6:25.

[803] Gregory the Theologian, "Homily on the New Lord's Day" (Λόγος ΜΔ΄, 6).

[804] Cf. Ps. 3:8.

[805] From the tetrastich iambic poetry of St. Gregory the Theologian.

[806] Vid. *A Select Library of Nicene and Post-Nicene Fathers of the Christian Church: First Series,* vol. 12, *Saint Chrysostom: Homilies on the Epistles of Paul to the Corinthians,* ed. Philip Schaff (New York: Christian Literature Company, 1889), 316 (Homily 7).

[807] Vid. Holy Apostles Convent, *The Great Synaxaristes of the Orthodox Church, January,* 163.

[808] Νικοδήμου τοῦ Ἁγιορείτου, Συμβουλευτικὸν Ἐγχειρίδιον (Βιέννη: Schrämbl, 1801), 49–51; see also *Nicodemos of the Holy Mountain: A Handbook of Spiritual Counsel,* trans. Peter A. Chamberas (New York: Paulist Press, 1989), 87–88.

[809] Holy Transfiguration Monastery, *The Ascetical Homilies of Saint Isaac the Syrian,* 171 (Homily 6).

Chapter Five:
Monastic Behavior

1) Schedule

AS SAINT JOSEPH TAUGHT,[810] it is of prime importance to have a regular daily schedule with appointed times for personal prayer, liturgical worship, work, and rest. The general order of Athonite monasteries is as follows: In the middle of the night the monks keep vigil in their cells for a few hours. In that time they say the Jesus prayer noetically and/or orally, do prostrations, *stavrota*,[811] and perhaps some spiritual reading. After this, they gather together in the church for the Midnight Office, Orthros, First Hour and Divine Liturgy.[812] After an optional light breakfast (without talking unless absolutely necessary) we had a brief rest.[813] After waking,

---

[810] "St. Joseph the Hesychast would never change his schedule "because he knew that changing it would adversely affect his prayer. He emphasized in his teachings: 'If you work less or more during the daytime, your body will be affected analogously. This will scatter your nous, which will reduce your eagerness for prayer.' This is why he kept his schedule with great precision, even at times in his life when it was difficult to do so" (Γέροντος Ἐφραίμ, Ὁ Γέροντάς μου Ἰωσήφ, 190; see also Elder Ephraim, *My Elder Joseph the Hesychast,* 267).

[811] *Stavrota* (σταυρωτά) denotes the practice of making the sign of the cross each time the Jesus prayer or some other brief prayer is repeated.

[812] In his monastic rules, St. Athanasios of Meteora "ordained that all the brothers in his charge should assemble in the church not only for the night offices on Sunday and the other great feasts, but that without fail they should also perform the service each day according to the correct tradition of the *typikon*. For often enough they can become careless either because of the malice of the enemy or sluggishness of the body, at times too because of distraction or too much to eat" (Thomas and Hero, *Byzantine Monastic Foundation Documents,* 1460–61).

[813] The practice of breaking up sleep into two separate times is an ancient tradition originating in the Mediterranean where most people take a siesta, especially in the summer. The fifth-century "Canons of Marūtā" advise monks: "In the summer, when the days are hot, they shall work early as long as it is cool; and when the day becomes hot they shall sit for reading until the time of mid-day-service; after the service they shall take food and rest until the turn of the day (i.e., early evening): and when the day becomes cool they shall go out for work until the time of evening meal, and they shall take food after the service" (Vööbus, *Syriac and Arabic Documents,* 143). Likewise, *The Rule of the Master* says: "Immediately after Sext [i.e., the Sixth Hour, which is at noon] has been said, whether it is after dinner or during a fast, let everyone take a moderately long nap on his bed. Thus they will sleep through the midday period and the burning heat, and for their bodies

each of us began whatever tasks he had been assigned. Abba Isaiah recommended: "When you wake up each morning, first study the word of God before resuming your manual labor."[814] At midday we had lunch together while one of the fathers read. Afterwards, we resumed our assigned tasks until about half an hour before the evening services, which consisted of the Ninth Hour, Vespers, Dinner, and Small Compline. After this, we retired to our cells for a little bit of private time, and then went to sleep early so that we would be able to wake up for our vigil well rested.

An ancient monastic tradition is to seek forgiveness from each other at the end of every day, which is why in Athonite monasteries the monks do a full prostration to the others at the end of Compline. For example, the *Rule for the Monastery of Compludo* states:

> As they say farewell to each other [before bedtime] and stand by one another in reconciliation and absolution, they shall make mutual forgiveness of their sins; and by humble piety those who have been separated from the company of the brothers because of slight faults shall earn forgiveness.... Then, going to their cells in deep silence and with composed countenance and quiet step, no one walking closer to another than the space of a cubit or even daring to look at another, each shall go to his bed.[815]

Abba Dorotheos taught: "A person should examine himself every evening as to how he spent the day, and again every morning as to how he spent the night."[816] Likewise, Abba Nistherus said: "A monk is obliged to make account each evening and morning. 'What have we done that God wants, and what have we not done of that which He does not want?' He should thus examine himself throughout his whole life."[817] St. Basil the Great taught in the same vein: "When the day is over and all work, both bodily and spiritual, has come to an end, before going to rest it is fitting that each man's conscience be examined by his own heart. And if anything improper has occurred—a forbidden thought or speaking beyond what is fitting, negligence in prayer or inattention in psalmody or desire of the ordinary life of the world—the sin should not be concealed, but confessed publicly, so that through the prayers of the community the malady of the one who has fallen into such an evil may be

---

fatigued by fasting and labor the supplement of sleep at noontime will compensate for the shortness of the nights in this season [of summer], and the brother will then be alert when he rises during the night in summertime since he has had some sleep during the day" (Eberle, *The Rule of the Master*, 212). St. Symeon the New Theologian also suggested taking a nap only in the summer: "After you have risen from the meal [at mid-day] ... run off to your cell ... and pick up your book. When you have read for a short time, if it is summer, lie down on your mat and take a short nap.... If it is winter, after reading a little take hold of your manual work" (C. J. de Catanzaro, *Symeon the New Theologian: Discourses*, 281). Research suggests that most cultures practiced some kind of segmented sleep until the late 17th century (vid. Roger Ekirch, *At Day's Close: Night in Times Past* [New York: Norton, 2005], 303–4).

[814] Chryssavgis and Penkett, *Abba Isaiah of Scetis*, 50.

[815] Barlow, *The Fathers of the Church: Iberian Fathers*, vol. 63, 157.

[816] Wheeler, *Abba Dorotheos: Discourses and Sayings*, 182.

[817] Abba Nistherus, PG 65:308C; see also Ward, *The Sayings of the Desert Fathers*, 155.

cured."[818] Elder Ephraim described how his holy elder implemented this: "A monk should examine his conduct every evening to see where he made progress and where he stumbled so that he can make a new beginning of repentance and correction. When St. Joseph the Hesychast did this, he would scrutinize how his day had passed, where he had made mistakes, which passions were active, which weaknesses were still an issue, and what thoughts had passed through his mind."[819]

Elder Ephraim taught that when we lie down it is important to continue saying the Jesus prayer until we fall asleep, because this helps protect us from the carnal temptations that typically assault us at such times. Likewise, St. Isidore of Seville wrote:

> The couch of the monk should not be involved in any shameful thought but only in the contemplation of God. While he is reclining, let him have rest of body and quiet of heart and by embracing good thoughts drive evil thoughts away. Let him reject evil and shameful thoughts, for the movement of the mind is disturbed by its own imagination and the thought of the waking person will be such as the image that occurs in sleep. He who is polluted by a nocturnal emission should not delay to make this known to the father of the monastery and deservedly attribute this as his own fault. He secretly should do penance knowing that unless a disgraceful thought of his mind had gone before it, the flow of unclean pollution would not follow disgracefully. An illicit thought comes before it and unclean temptation swiftly makes him foul.
>
> He who has been deceived by a nocturnal dream will stand in the sacristy at the time of office and will not dare to enter the church the same day before he is washed with water and tears. Indeed in the law, those who are polluted by a nocturnal dream are ordered to go out of the camp and not to return before they wash at evening.[820] And if carnal people did this, what should a spiritual servant of Christ do? He ought to consider his defilement greater and be kept far from the altar, and to fear greatly in body and mind, and with the symbolism of water produce tears of penitence so that not only should he be eager to wash with water but also with tears because he is polluted by an unclean defilement.[821]

2) Prayer

In his monastic rule, St. Christodoulos of Patmos wrote on the central place of prayer for a monk:

---

[818] Βασιλείου τοῦ Μεγάλου, *Ἀσκητικὰ Α΄*, ΕΠΕ 8, 142–43; see also Wagner, *Saint Basil: Ascetical Works*, vol. 9, 215.

[819] Γέροντος Ἐφραίμ, *Ὁ Γέροντάς μου Ἰωσήφ*, 274; see also Elder Ephraim, *My Elder Joseph the Hesychast*, 383.

[820] Deut. 23.

[821] *Monastic Studies*, no. 18, 20.

Before all else it is assuredly fitting to speak of our true employment, that which has priority over all others, I mean the doxology of praise to God. For it is in view of this one thing that, from very "not being" (of this I am convinced) "we have been brought into being"[822] and adorned with reason, in order to honor the Creator with uninterrupted hymn-singing. Besides everything else, the fact that the character and pursuit of the monastic life is called angelic leads to this conclusion. Hence it is that God's creature, man, is shown to be, in the words of [Gregory] the Theologian, "the angels' descant (ἀντίφωνον)," repeating what they do as closely as his nature will allow.[823]

Then let this hymn be uninterrupted and unlimited. Whence our blessed and inspired fathers, having broken off every kind of human relationship and earthly care, clinging spiritually with all their might to their supreme desire, spent the whole "time of their exile"[824] in prayers and spiritual hymns, seeking, not carelessly but steadfastly, "the kingdom of heaven within them"[825] according to the Lord's saying in the Gospels. Because of their constant prayer and their unwavering hope, they found it, having traded prudently and most profitably, and, like the merchant who is deemed happy, bought for all the visible world the pearl that may well be called precious.[826] They had heard and understood the holy psalmist David shouting: "Let my mouth be filled with praise that I may hymn thy glory, and thy majesty all the day,"[827] and again: "I will bless the Lord at all times, his praise shall be continually in my mouth,"[828] and the Apostle exhorting: "Pray without ceasing,"[829] but also our Lord and Savior himself, on one occasion weaving into a parable the obligation to pray and not lose heart,[830] on another giving an explicit order and saying: "Watch and pray, that ye enter not into temptation."[831] ... [The holy Fathers] obeyed eagerly and observed the [command] strictly."[832]

---

[822] Cf. *Liturgies Eastern and Western,* vol. 1, F. E. Brightman, ed. (Oxford: Clarendon Press, 1896), 369, lines 27–29, and 384, lines 27–28.

[823] Cf. Gregory Nazianzen, *Carmina,* I, PG 37:513A, and Pseudo-Basil, *Constitutiones asceticae,* PG 31:1384B.

[824] 1 Pet. 1:17.

[825] Lk. 17:21.

[826] Mt. 13:46.

[827] Ps. 70:8.

[828] Ps. 33:1.

[829] 1 Thes. 5:17.

[830] Vid. Lk. 18:1.

[831] Mt. 26:41.

[832] Thomas and Hero, *Byzantine Monastic Foundation Documents,* 586–87.

Abba Isaac (in fourth-century Egypt) also saw prayer as the highest work of monks: "Monastic perfection and the purity of heart consist in the acquisition of unceasing prayer."[833]

St. Basil the Great emphasized the central role that prayer and labor have in monasteries:

> I wish you to know that we rejoice to have assemblies of both men and women, whose conversation is in heaven and who have crucified the flesh with the affections and lusts thereof; they take no thought for food and raiment, but remain undisturbed beside their Lord, continuing night and day in prayer. Their lips speak not of the deeds of men: they sing hymns to God continually, working with their own hands that they may have to distribute to them that need.[834]

Regarding the role of prayer in the monastic life, St. Porphyrios of Kafsokalyvia taught: "The whole secret is prayer, self-giving, and love directed towards Christ. Monastic life is carefree and joyous. A monk must taste the sweetness of prayer and be attracted by divine love. He will not be able to endure the monastic life if he does not know the sweetness of prayer. Without this he will not be able to stay in the monastery."[835] Likewise, St. Joseph the Hesychast believed that prayer is so central to monasticism that he said: "A monk who has not learned to say the Jesus prayer does not know why he became a monk."[836]

Not only do we set time aside for saying the Jesus prayer during our private vigil, but also during the day we say it out loud as much as we can while doing our daily tasks. According to our spiritual forefathers, saying the Jesus prayer orally has numerous benefits: it keeps us connected with God; it burns the demons; it discourages idle talk; it benefits those who hear us; it sanctifies our work, and it even leads to dispassion.[837] Elder Ephraim taught: "A beginner who is taught the prayer must begin by saying with his mouth, 'Lord Jesus Christ, have mercy on me,' and must make an effort to pull his nous away from worldly things. The sound produced by his voice will attract his nous to pay attention to the prayer, and thus, little by little it will get used to being collected instead of scattered."[838]

In his *Testament,* St. John of Rila also encouraged saying the Jesus prayer orally: "Manual labor must not be neglected by you, however, but work must be in your hands,

---

[833] As quoted by St. John Cassian in *Ἀββᾶ Κασσιανοῦ: Συνομιλίες μὲ τοὺς Πατέρες τῆς Ἐρήμου,* Ἱερὰ Μονὴ Τιμίου Προδρόμου, Τόμος Α΄ (Καρέα: Ἐκδόσεις «Ἑτοιμασία», 2004), 327; see also Ramsey, *John Cassian: The Conferences,* 329.

[834] *Basil: Letters and Select Works,* 247.

[835] Chrysopigi, *Wounded by Love,* 158.

[836] Γέροντος Ἰωσήφ, *Ἔκφρασις Μοναχικῆς Ἐμπειρίας,* 363; see also *Monastic Wisdom,* 311.

[837] These teachings of St. Joseph the Hesychast and Elder Ephraim are explained in Elder Ephraim, *My Elder Joseph the Hesychast,* 392–404, and Elder Ephraim, *Counsels from the Holy Mountain,* 291–366.

[838] Γέροντος Ἐφραίμ, *Πατρικαὶ Νουθεσίαι,* 426; see also Elder Ephraim, *Counsels from the Holy Mountain,* 341.

and the prayer 'Lord Jesus Christ, Son of God, have mercy on me, a sinner' must be permanently on your lips, as well as the memory of death in your mind. This was the practice of the ancient desert fathers."[839]

St. Gregory of Sinai taught that we should alternate oral and silent prayer:

> Some fathers teach that the prayer should be said aloud; others, that it should be said with the nous. I recommend both ways. For at times the nous becomes listless and cannot say the prayer, while at other times the same thing happens to the mouth. Thus we should pray both vocally and with the nous. But when we pray vocally we should cry out quietly and calmly and not loudly, so that the voice does not disturb and hinder the nous's perception and concentration.[840]

Elder Ephraim recommended (citing the example of what St. Joseph the Hesychast had told his nuns from Pontus whose native language was not Greek) that each person should say the Jesus prayer in the language with which he feels most comfortable. Elder Ephraim also commented sadly on some monks who did not have the good habit of holding a prayer-rope during the day at least when their hands were free. St. Theodore of Sanaxar also viewed this as an important habit, for he wrote in his monastic rule: "The prayer-rope, which is always to be carried by the monk, is a weapon, constantly reminding him of noetic prayer borne in the heart. Not only the monastic brethren but every new novice in the Sanaxar Monastery goes to every service with his prayer-rope for a constant reminder of inner prayer."[841] St. Paisios of the Holy Mountain similarly taught: "The prayer-rope must never leave your hand, for it is the rope we pull one, two, five, or ten times so that our spiritual oil is finally liquified and our spiritual engine of unceasing prayer ignites. Even after your engine has started, do not set aside your prayer-rope so that the others are not encouraged to put theirs aside as well before they have even begun."[842]

St. John of Sinai described the value of prayer as follows: "Prayer is the mother and also the daughter of tears, the propitiation for sins, a bridge over temptations, a wall against afflictions ... a source of virtues ... food for the soul ... the wealth of monks ... the reduction of anger, the mirror of progress ... the queen of virtues."[843]

St. Sophrony of Essex taught: "The aim is not to pray without ceasing (when it is done mechanically and formally); the aim is our communion with God, which is also achieved through prayer."[844] Thus, he wrote to a hieromonk:

---

[839] Thomas and Hero, *Byzantine Monastic Foundation Documents,* 133.

[840] Γρηγορίου τοῦ Σιναΐτου, «Περὶ τοῦ πῶς δεῖ καθέζεσθαι τὸν ἡσυχάζοντα», ἐν *Φιλοκαλία τῶν Ἱερῶν Νηπτικῶν,* τόμος δ΄ (1991), 80; see also Palmer, Sherrard, Ware, *The Philokalia,* vol. 4, 276.

[841] *Little Russian Philokalia, Volume V: Saint Theodore of Sanaxar* (Platina: St. Herman of Alaska Brotherhood, 2000), 163.

[842] Elder Paisios, *Epistles,* 70.

[843] Holy Transfiguration Monastery, *The Ladder of Divine Ascent,* 212.

[844] Hierotheos, *"I Know a Man in Christ,"* 382.

Remember that the commandment about love for God with all our heart, with all our thought, with all our mind, also tells us that when we stray from God with our mind, this means we are sinning against the first commandment. For this reason we, who are incapable of remaining in prayer—let alone pure prayer—must try to arrange things, to organize our life and allocate our time in such a way that if possible we can be perpetually immersed in a spiritual atmosphere: in prayer, reading, services, reflecting on the things of God, etc., alternating between these various activities.[845]

Likewise, Elder Ephraim taught us that a monk should be doing two things constantly: prayer and contemplation. By "contemplation" (*θεωρία*) he meant contemplating divine things: the glory of heaven, the darkness of hell, our departure from this life, things written in the Bible and by the holy Fathers, etc.[846] One benefit of this kind of contemplation is that it will keep us in a spiritual mode of thinking, which enables us to face temptations and address problems more effectively. Elder Ephraim explained:

We should never stop contemplating death and other such meditations. All these contemplations bring watchfulness to the soul and purify and cleanse the mind so that it may feel the contemplation better. This contemplation is a barrier for evil thoughts. When we have this spiritual contemplation within us, we shut out evil thoughts; there is no room for them in us because that contemplation has occupied the space of the mind. When we do not have godly contemplations, then we are indeed overcome by passionate contemplations instead.[847]

The remembrance of death is also a powerful aid in keeping the commandments. The Wisdom of Sirach teaches: "Remember thy last, and thou shalt never sin unto eternity."[848] St. Anthony the Great explained this principle to his disciples as follows: "In order not to be negligent or to retreat before ascetic labors, it is good to remember always the words of the Apostle, who says, 'Each day I die to myself' [1 Cor. 15:31]. For if we too lived our lives as though we were dying each day, we certainly would not sin."[849] St. Gregory the Theologian added: "Always bear in mind that frigid death awaits you, and you will encounter a less fearsome death."[850] The *Enchiridion* attributed to St. Neilos of Ancyra says: "Above all keep death before your eyes every day, and you will neither think of trivialities nor have

---

[845] Sakharov, *Striving for Knowledge of God,* 158–59.

[846] Although the Greek word *theoria (θεωρία)* is also used in reference to a lofty state bestowed by God on man during noetic prayer, Elder Ephraim is refering here to man's voluntary mental contemplation of divine things, as is evident from his description of *theoria* in Elder Ephraim, *My Elder Joseph the Hesychast* on page 83.

[847] Γέροντος Ἐφραίμ, *Πατρικαὶ Νουθεσίαι,* 199; see also Elder Ephraim, *Counsels from the Holy Mountain,* 152–53.

[848] Sir. 7:36.

[849] Chrysostomos, *The Evergetinos, Book I,* 37.

[850] Γρηγορίου Ναζιανζοῦ, *Ἔπη Ἠθικά· Γνῶμαι Δίστιχοι λα´*; PG 37:911A.

excessive desires."[851] St. Theodore the Studite wrote: "How should one struggle? By having the fear of God in one's heart. Where there is fear, there is keeping of commandments from meditating on death. Where there is meditation on death, there is deliverance from passions."[852] And St. John of Sinai devoted an entire step of *The Ladder* (Step 6) to this fundamental virtue.[853]

Another benefit of contemplation is that it will fortify our prayer. St. John Cassian taught:

> Before the time of prayer we must put ourselves in the state of mind we would wish to have in us when we actually pray. It is an inexorable fact that the condition of the soul at the time of prayer depends upon what shaped it beforehand. The soul will rise to the heights of heaven or plunge into the things of earth, depending upon where it lingered before the time of prayer.[854]

St. John of Sinai also observed how the remembrance of God throughout the day clears the path for progress in prayer:

> Prepare yourself for your set times of prayer by unceasing prayer in your soul, and you will soon make progress. I have seen those who shone in obedience and who tried, as far as they could, to keep in mind the remembrance of God, and the moment they stood in prayer they were at once masters of their minds, and shed streams of tears, because they were prepared for this beforehand by holy obedience.... The time and discipline of prayer show the monk's love for God.[855]

Our prayer should continue even when we are not in church. As St. Silouan the Athonite said:

> The soul that loves the Lord cannot help praying, for she is drawn to Him by the grace she has come to know in prayer. We are given churches to pray in, and in church the holy offices are performed according to books. But we cannot take a church away with us, and books are not always at hand, but interior prayer is always and everywhere possible. The Divine Office is celebrated in church, and the Spirit of God dwells therein, but the soul is the finest of God's churches, and the man who prays in his heart has the whole world for a church. However, this is not for everyone.[856]

Likewise, St. Basil the Great taught: "Prayer time should cover the whole of life, but since there is absolute need at certain intervals to interrupt the bending of the knee and the chanting of psalms, the hours appointed for prayer by the saints should be observed."[857]

---

[851] Νείλου Ἀσκητοῦ, *Ἐγχειρίδιον (Ἐπικτήτου)*, κεφ. κη´; PG 79:1296A.

[852] Θεοδώρου Στουδίτου, *Ἐπιστολὴ ρλδ´*; PG 99:1429.

[853] Vid. Holy Transfiguration Monastery, *The Ladder of Divine Ascent*, 66–70.

[854] Luibhéid, *John Cassian: Conferences*, 139–40.

[855] Holy Transfiguration Monastery, *The Ladder of Divine Ascent*, 216–17.

[856] Sakharov, *Saint Silouan the Athonite*, 294.

[857] Wagner, *Saint Basil: Ascetical Works*, vol. 9, 212.

The traditional way to achieve unceasing prayer is through the Jesus prayer. According to the text that Sts. Callistus and Ignatius Xanthopoulos attributed to St. John Chrysostom:

> A monk when he eats, drinks, serves, travels or does any other thing must continually cry: "Lord, Jesus Christ, Son of God, have mercy upon me!" so that the name of Jesus, descending into the depths of the heart, should subdue the serpent ruling over the inner pastures and bring life and salvation to the soul. He should always live with the name of Lord Jesus, so that the heart absorbs the Lord and the Lord the heart, and the two become one.[858]

It is crucial that monastics pray not only for themselves but also for the whole world. St. Silouan the Athonite said:

> A monk is someone who prays for the whole world, who weeps for the whole world; and in this lies his main work.... It is not for the monk to serve the world with the work of his hands. That is the layman's business. The man who lives in the world prays little, whereas the monk prays constantly. Thanks to monks, prayer continues unceasing on earth, and the whole world profits, for through prayer the world continues to exist; but when prayer fails, the world will perish.... But if a monk be lukewarm and indifferent, and has not arrived at a state wherein his soul continually contemplates the Lord, then let him wait upon pilgrim travellers and assist with his labours those who live in the world. This, too, is pleasing to God. But rest assured that it is not the monastic life by a long way.[859]

St. Paisios of the Holy Mountain warned of the danger monastics face if they fail to pray for the world:

> When the monk forgets his family and doesn't think of others either, that is, doesn't pray for the world, this is very bad. We come to the monastery, we abandon our family, and we end up forgetting not only our family but even more so the others. We see things spiritually, but we don't share in others' pain spiritually. We don't make spiritual progress, to be able to feel their problems, and there is a danger of becoming insensitive. Indifference creeps in and the heart becomes like stone.[860]
>
> A monk in order to progress spiritually must soften his hard heart, and try to make it like a mother's heart.[861]
>
> If monks and nuns aren't careful, their hearts can become very hard. Lay people see accidents, the suffering of others, and are pained. We don't see this suffering and may pray only for ourselves. That is, if we don't work on ourselves to learn to feel the misfortunes of others, so that we will be able to pray for them from the heart, we may become hard-hearted. We may reach the point of wanting to make ourselves comfortable and having a heart stony from indifference, a condition that is contrary to the Gospel. The monk must care for, be pained over, and in general pray for the people.

---

[858] E. Kadloubovsky and G. E.H. Palmer, *Writings from the Philokalia: On Prayer of the Heart,* 193–94.

[859] Sakharov, *Saint Silouan the Athonite,* 409–10.

[860] Elder Paisios, *Spiritual Awakening,* 349.

[861] Ibid., 362.

This is not a distraction, but, on the contrary, he himself is helped by the prayer, and so are the others.[862]

St. Theophan the Recluse taught: "One of the means of renewing the Jesus Prayer and bringing it to life is by reading, but it is best to read mainly about prayer."[863] Therefore, to facilitate this, we have included the following list of books on prayer in chronological order of publication. We have placed an asterisk beside the ones we have found especially helpful or inspiring:

On Prayer in General:

    The Philokalia, trans. G.E.H. Palmer, Philip Sherrard, and Kallistos Ware

  * *The Ladder of Divine Ascent* (Step 28), St. John of Sinai

    The Ascetical Homilies of Saint Isaac the Syrian, Holy Transfiguration Monastery

    Isaac of Nineveh (Isaac the Syrian) "The Second Part," trans. Sebastian Brock

  * *The Evergetinos* (Book Two: Hypotheses X, XI; Book Four: Hypotheses VIII–XIV)

    The Arena: An Offering to Contemporary Monasticism (Chapters 17–26), Bishop [St.] Ignatius Brianchaninov

    The Path of Prayer, Saint Theophan the Recluse

  * *Saint Silouan the Athonite* (Part I, Chapter 6; Part II, Chapter 2), Saint Sophrony

    On Prayer, Archimandrite [Saint] Sophrony (Sakharov)

    Living Prayer, Beginning to Pray, and *Courage to Pray,* Metropolitan Anthony Bloom

    Wounded by Love (Part Two, On Prayer), Saint Porphyrios

  * *Fire from the Holy Mountain,* Elder Ephraim[864]

    Elder Ephraim of Katounakia, (Part Two: Prayer)

    Spiritual Awakening (Part Five, Chapter One), Saint Paisios of the Holy Mountain

    On Prayer: Problems and Temptations, Archimandrite Aimilianos of Simonopetra

    The Beginnings of a Life of Prayer, Archimandrite Irenei Steenberg

    On Prayer (Spiritual Counsels, Volume VI), Saint Paisios the Athonite

On the Jesus Prayer:

  * *Writings from the Philokalia on Prayer of the Heart,* trans. Kadloubovsky and Palmer

    The Philokalia: Volume 5, Anna Skoubourdis

    Gregory Palamas: The Triads, ed. John Meyendorff

---

[862] Ibid., 349–50.

[863] Igumen Chariton of Valamo, *The Art of Prayer: An Orthodox Anthology,* trans. E. Kadloubovsky and E.M. Palmer (London: Faber and Faber, 1966), 92.

[864] This is Elder Ephraim's private prayer diary— Μέθεξις Θεοῦ in Greek—which I translated into English with the title: *Fire from the Holy Mountain.* Although it has not been published in English yet, my preliminary English translation may be downloaded from: www.stnilus.org/fire.pdf

Holy Hesychia: In Defence of the Holy Hesychasts, Book One, Saint Gregory Palamas

Elder Basil of Poiana Marului: Spiritual Father of St. Paisy Velichkovsky

* *Nicodemos of the Holy Mountain: A Handbook of Spiritual Counsel* (Chapter 10)

Unseen Warfare (Chapters XLVI–LIII), Saints Nicodemus of the Holy Mountain and Theophan the Recluse

The Watchful Mind: Teachings on the Prayer of the Heart, by a Monk of Mount Athos

* *The Way of a Pilgrim* and *The Pilgrim Continues His Way*

On the Prayer of Jesus, Bishop [Saint] Ignatius Brianchaninov

* *The Art of Prayer,* compiled by Igumen Chariton of Valamo

On the Invocation of the Name of Jesus, by a Monk of the Eastern Church (Lev Gillet)

The Jesus Prayer, by a Monk of the Eastern Church (Lev Gillet)

The Name of Jesus, Irénée Hausherr

The Power of the Name: The Jesus Prayer in Orthodox Spirituality, Kallistos Ware

His Life is Mine (pp. 99–128), Archimandrite [Saint] Sophrony (Sakharov)

* *Counsels from the Holy Mountain* (Chapter 15), Elder Ephraim

* *The Art of Salvation* (Vol. I: Homilies 11, 33; Vol. II: 2, 28, 30), Elder Ephraim

* *A Night in the Desert of the Holy Mountain,* Archimandrite Hierotheos Vlachos

Obedience is Life: Elder Ephraim of Katounakia (Chap. 4c), Elder Joseph of Vatopedi

Abbot Haralambos Dionysiatis: The teacher of noetic prayer (Part 2, Chapter A)

The Enlargement of the Heart (pp. 114–163), Archimandrite Zacharias

Two Elders on the Jesus Prayer, Igor V. Ksenzov

* *Treasure in Earthen Vessels,* Fr. Stephen Muse

Saint John Chrysostom and the Jesus Prayer: A Contribution to the Study of the Philokalia, Frs. Maximos Constas and Peter Chamberas

Hesychasm, Archimandrite Zacharias

When reading about prayer—or undertaking any spiritual endeavor, for that matter—humility must be a fundamental ingredient. St. Paisios of the Holy Mountain taught that books that discuss prayer "help those who have humility. They do not, however, help those who have pride and aim to attain spiritual heights within a certain period of time so as to become Neptic Fathers [i.e., like the Church Fathers who wrote about watchfulness]."[865]

3) Prayer Technique

Several Fathers of the Church described techniques that assist prayer. St. Symeon the New Theologian taught: "Sitting in a quiet cell, alone in a corner, do what I tell you: Close

---

[865] Saint Paisios the Athonite, *Spiritual Counsels, Volume VI: On Prayer,* trans. Fr. Peter Chamberas (Thessaloniki: Holy Hesychasterion "Evangelist John the Theologian," 2022), 192.

the door and lift up your mind from all that is vain and passing. Then rest your beard on your chest and direct your physical eyes with all your mind toward yourself. And hold your breath a little, in order to keep your mind there and to find the place of the heart, where all the powers of the soul are used to being found."[866]

St. Nicephoros described the practical method of saying the Jesus prayer as follows:

> Seat yourself, then, gather your nous, and lead it through your nose into the respiratory passage through which your breath passes into your heart. Put pressure on your nous and compel it to descend with your inhaled breath into your heart....
>
> Moreover, when your nous is firmly established in your heart, it must not remain there silent and idle, but it should have as its ceaseless work and meditation the prayer, "Lord Jesus Christ, Son of God, have mercy on me," and should never stop doing this. For this prayer keeps the nous from distraction, renders it impregnable to assaults of the enemy, and every day increases its love and desire for God.
>
> If, however, in spite of all your efforts you are unable to enter the realms of the heart in the way I have enjoined, do what I now tell you and with God's help you will find what you seek. You know that everyone's discursive faculty is in his breast; for when our lips are silent we speak and deliberate and formulate prayers, psalms and other things in our breast. Banish, then, all thoughts from this faculty—and you can do this if you want to—and give to it the prayer, "Lord Jesus Christ, Son of God, have mercy on me," and compel it to cry out this prayer always instead of other thoughts. If you continue to do this for some time, the entrance to your heart will undoubtedly open to you through this method in the way we have explained, and as we ourselves know from experience.[867]

St. Nicodemos of the Holy Mountain elaborated on this technique:

> Since the nous—the activity of the nous—from a very early age is accustomed to being scattered toward the perceptible things of the world, when you say this sacred prayer do not breathe continually as is natural to our nature, but restrain your breath until your inner voice says the prayer once. Then continue breathing, as the holy Fathers also teach. First of all, by slightly restraining your breathing, the heart is pressed and troubled and feels pain for not receiving its natural amount of oxygen. Through this method, the nous is much more easily collected and returns to the heart, not only because of the pain and suffering of the heart but also because of the pleasure that is created from this warm and vivid remembrance of God. For when God is remembered, one experiences pleasure and gladness, as the psalmist said: "I remembered God and was made glad."[868] The nous naturally returns and is collected to any member feeling pain or pleasure, according to the philosopher Aristotle. Secondly, by slightly restraining one's breathing, one's hard and thick heart is refined, and the liquids within the heart are warmed through this moderate suffering. Consequently it becomes soft, sensitive, humble, and more capable of contrition and of pouring out tears. Likewise, the brain becomes more refined, as the activity of the nous also becomes more refined, more unified, more clear, and more capable of uniting with

---

[866] As quoted in Staniloae, *Orthodox Spirituality*, 264.

[867] Νικηφόρου Μονάζοντος, «Λόγος περὶ νήψεως καὶ φυλακῆς καρδίας» ἐν Φιλοκαλία τῶν Ἱερῶν Νηπτικῶν, τόμος δ´ (1991), 27–28; see also Palmer, Sherrard, Ware, *The Philokalia*, vol. 4, 205–6.

[868] Ps. 77:3.

God's supernatural illumination.... This restraining of the breathing also unites all the powers of the soul to return to the nous and through the nous to God, which is a marvelous thing.[869] ...

Once you have brought your nous into the heart, it should not just stay there, looking and doing nothing, but should find reason (λόγον), that is, the inner voice (ἐνδιάθετον λόγον) of the heart through which we think, compose essays, make judgments, analyze, and read whole books silently, without saying a single word with the mouth. After the nous has found this inner voice, do not let it say anything else except this short, single-phrased prayer: "Lord Jesus Christ, Son of God, have mercy on me." But this is not enough. It is also necessary to activate the soul's will so that you say this prayer with all your will and power and love. To put it more clearly, let your inner voice say only the prayer, let your nous pay attention through its spiritual vision and hearing to the words of the prayer alone and especially to the meaning of the words, without imagining any forms, shapes, or any other perceptible or intelligible thing, internal or external, even if it is something good.... Let all your will cleave to the same words of the prayer with love, so that the nous, the inner voice, and the will—these three parts of your soul—will be one, and the one three, for in this way man, who is an image of the Holy Trinity, is united with the Prototype.[870]

Elder Ephraim taught: "As you inhale, say the prayer once, following it to the heart, and as you exhale, repeat the prayer once again. Establish your nous where the breath stops, in the place of the heart, and without distraction follow, by inhaling and exhaling, the prayer being inhaled and exhaled: 'Lord Jesus Christ, have mercy on me!'"[871] He also taught that we can say the prayer faster (i.e., more than one time while inhaling or exhaling) or slower (i.e., half the prayer while inhaling and the other half while exhaling).

He also recommended restraining the breathing slightly: "The nous is accustomed to run around and only remains where we feel pain. Therefore, pause momentarily after you inhale; do not exhale immediately. This will cause a slight, harmless pain in the heart, which is the place where we want to establish our nous. This small pain greatly assists by attracting the intellect like a magnet and holding it there to serve the nous somewhat like a servant.[872] Elder Ephraim told us: "When we were on the Holy Mountain ... we said the prayer for two, three, four, five hours with inhaling and exhaling. Of course, when sleep fought us, we would get up and go outside to say the prayer out loud for more 'relaxation,' so to speak. But when sleep was not an issue, we would stay inside all night."[873]

---

[869] Νικοδήμου τοῦ Ἁγιορείτου, *Συμβουλευτικὸν Ἐγχειρίδιον*, 161–63; see also Chamberas, *Nicodemos of the Holy Mountain: A Handbook of Spiritual Counsel*, 160–61.

[870] Νικοδήμου τοῦ Ἁγιορείτου, *Συμβουλευτικὸν Ἐγχειρίδιον*, 161; see also Chamberas, *Nicodemos of the Holy Mountain: A Handbook of Spiritual Counsel*, 159–60.

[871] Γέροντος Ἐφραίμ, *Πατρικαὶ Νουθεσίαι*, 417; see also Elder Ephraim, *Counsels from the Holy Mountain*, 338.

[872] Ibid.

[873] Γέροντος Ἐφραίμ, *Πατρικαὶ Νουθεσίαι*, 441; see also Elder Ephraim, *Counsels from the Holy Mountain*, 350.

St. Ephraim of Katounakia attached less importance to breathing techniques. For when he was asked if we should control our breathing when we practice noetic prayer, he replied: "No, this is the beginning of mental [noetic] prayer. Mental prayer itself is an act of the holy grace. When the soul is ready, then God promotes it to the perfection of mental prayer. Until then, we ought to pray by repeating the Jesus prayer, always having obedience as our firm foundation. One's breathing does not necessarily have to be connected to prayer. This is a secondary element. More importantly, prayer should not be related to the heartbeat, but rather with the place of the heart; not with the heartbeat, no."[874]

Similarly, St. Paisios of the Holy Mountain taught that repentance is much more important than methods when praying:

> ⁍   In order to gather our mind in our heart at the hour of prayer, it is very helpful to hold our breath slightly, but not constantly, for the heart is harmed by this bodily contraction. The heart, of course, is not cleansed by this bodily contraction, but rather through a humble, *philotimo* sigh of repentance, originating from the depth of our heart. This sigh brings divine consolation, while physical contraction, when one pressures himself egotistically and without discernment, brings despair and anxiety.[875]

A disciple of St. Paisios, noted that he

> considered the external elements [of prayer] spoken of by the fathers of the *Philo-kalia*, such as a small stool, darkness ... the inclination of the head, one's breathing, and so on, to be nothing more than aids. If these aspects of prayer are overemphasized, they can cause psychosomatic harm or lead a person into delusion. He accepted the use of breathing methods associated with the Jesus prayer when they were joined to it in a natural rather than an artificial manner.[876]

St. Gregory Palamas explained the role of breathing techniques for beginners in prayer:

> To teach beginners especially to look at themselves and to bring their mind within through respiration isn't something reproachable. Because it wouldn't be right for any sensible man to prevent him who hasn't yet the mind capable of contemplating itself, to concentrate by just any method. The mind of those who are at the beginning of this struggle, even when it concentrates, jumps around continually and therefore must be brought back continually because they are inexperienced. Their mind, being very unstable, gets away from them all the time and contemplates itself with difficulty. For this reason there are some that counsel them to watch their respiration and to hold their inhaling and exhaling a little and to thus succeed in concentrating the mind by it. This continues until, making progress with the help of God toward the good and making their mind inaccessible to what is around it and making it pure, they will be able with precision to bring it back to a "unified recollection."[877]

---

[874] Vassiliadou-Christodoulou, *Elder Ephraim of Katounakia,* 121–24.

[875] Elder Paisios, *Epistles,* 123.

[876] Hieromonk Isaac, *Elder Paisios of Mount Athos,* 471–72.

[877] «Ὑπὲρ τῶν Ἱερῶς Ἡσυχαζόντων», Λόγος 1.2.7 (ΕΠΕ 54, 132), as translated in Staniloae, *Orthodox Spirituality,* 272–73.

St. Nicodemos of the Holy Mountain taught that prayer is a shortcut to purification. He wrote: "This method [of noetic prayer] purifies our nature faster [than ascesis], because the very work and subject matter with which it is occupied is the first, catholic, and most comprehensive commandment of all: for man to love God with all his soul, all his heart, all his power, and all his mind."[878]

Elder Ephraim also viewed prayer and watchfulness as a shortcut to purity of heart:

Our Fathers have left us a tremendous inheritance of limitless value, which cannot be measured, weighed, or calculated. This inheritance is called watchfulness. Watchfulness means attention to thoughts, fantasies, and the movements of the senses....

Before the holy Fathers—those teachers of watchfulness—systematized noetic prayer, monks would occupy themselves primarily with virtues belonging to praxis. Ascesis done with the body is called praxis, whether it is fasting, abstinence, prostrations, vigil, the church services, obedience, humility, etc. They called this praxis "somewhat beneficial," while they called watchfulness "greatly beneficial." ...

But when the work of watchfulness came to light as a systematic method, then the amount of ascesis was reduced—not as something unnecessary, but because the Fathers dedicated themselves more to spiritual work than to praxis. Through the work of watchfulness they were liberated from thoughts, and the passions were reduced. The work of watchfulness granted them purity of heart. This is why they did not have such an absolute need for bodily ascesis in order to attain purity of soul....

For when the work of watchfulness purifies the nous and heart, while giving prudent care to the exterior senses of the body as well as to the interior senses of the soul, then a monk does not need much ascesis to reach the same goal.[879]

Dumitru Stăniloae summarized the patristic writings on the method of prayer as follows:

1. These methods are not considered absolutely necessary, but only auxiliary means for those who haven't been able to gather their minds within and to recite without interruption the words of the Jesus Prayer....

2. Until we attempt to use these methods, it is necessary for us to get used to saying it in a more simple way, and less systematically, but ever more frequently and with our thought concentrated, either on the whole of the Jesus Prayer, or at least on two or three words of it: "Jesus! Lord Jesus! Lord Jesus Christ, have mercy on me!" At the same time we must be advanced in freedom from the passions and from care.

3. When we begin to apply the recommendation of these methods we are not on the highest steps of the spiritual life....

4. Prayer during these phases isn't yet mental prayer, but the Jesus prayer. It becomes mental prayer when there is no longer the need for either words or methods, and the mind is occupied with it unceasingly, along with the heart.[880]

---

[878] Νικοδήμου τοῦ Ἁγιορείτου, *Συμβουλευτικὸν Ἐγχειρίδιον*, 168; see also Chamberas, *Nicodemos of the Holy Mountain: A Handbook of Spiritual Counsel*, 163–64.

[879] Γέροντος Ἐφραίμ, *Πατρικαὶ Νουθεσίαι*, 391–93; see also Elder Ephraim, *Counsels from the Holy Mountain*, 315–16.

[880] Stanilaoe, *Orthodox Spirituality*, 282.

Repentance is a key ingredient in prayer. According to Elder Sergei of Vanves: "In prayer, the most important thing is our spiritual attitude. A spirit of contrition must accompany our prayers. Christ did not come to bring us a technique but to teach us to repent."[881] St. Nikolai Velimirovich said: "Prayer without repentance is of no use, but as soon as prayer is linked with repentance, God hearkens to it."[882] The anonymous hesychast quoted by Metropolitan Hierotheos Vlachos in *A Night in the Desert of the Holy Mountain* taught: "I must emphasize that the awareness of our unworthiness is absolutely necessary for the Jesus prayer to act within us."[883] Likewise, St. Sophrony of Essex said: "True prayer comes exclusively through faith and repentance accepted as the only foundation. The danger of psychotechnics is that not a few of us attribute too great significance to method *qua* method. In order to avoid such deformation the beginner should follow another practice, which, though considerably slower is incomparably better and more wholesome—to fix attention on the Name of Jesus Christ and on the words of the prayer. When contrition for sin reaches a certain level, the mind naturally heeds the heart."[884]

St. Sophrony of Essex also emphasized the importance of repentance in prayer. He wrote to a hieromonk:

> As far as the Jesus prayer is concerned, though I have already spoken to you about the union of the mind with the heart while one is practising the prayer, it will be better, however, if you simply accustom yourself to the words of the prayer, enclosing your mind in the words. And it is good if the heart all the while is sharing with feeling in the prayer, which includes repentance. "Have mercy upon me, a sinner." And when the heart, by feeling the words of the prayer, delights in the name of Jesus Christ, the mind is then attracted of its own accord towards the heart. Only one thing is necessary: sweet repentance before our Lord Jesus Christ, with full concentration….
>
> We should not direct our efforts towards achieving the highest spiritual dispositions or states, as you are. I told you that man is led into contemplation by divine grace after repentance, after great and deep humility, and that contemplation comes utterly unexpectedly to man; that the path to adoption as a son of God is repentance.[885]

Continuing these teachings of his elder, Archimandrite Zacharias added:

> What we seek as we practise this prayer is the union of the intellect with the heart. It is impossible to achieve this union through techniques. Some procedures can help the attention of the intellect to find entry to the heart, but not to establish its abode in

---

[881] Jean-Claude Larchet, *Elder Sergei of Vanves: Life & Teachings,* trans. Monastery of St. John of San Francisco (Manton: Divine Ascent Press, 2012), 124.

[882] Nikolai Velimirović, *Homilies: A Commentary on the Gospel Readings for Great Feasts and Sundays throughout the Year,* Volume Two: Sundays after Pentecost, trans. Mother Maria (Birmingham: Lazarica Press, 1998), 111 (Homily on the 11th Sunday after Pentecost).

[883] Hierotheos Vlachos, *A Night in the Desert of the Holy Mountain,* Second Edition, trans. Effie Mavromichali (Levadia: Birth of the Theotokos Monastery, 1995), 65.

[884] Sakharov, *His Life is Mine,* 112–13.

[885] Sakharov, *Striving for Knowledge of God,* 191–92, 305.

the heart. There is a great danger that beginners and inexperienced ascetics may over-value such physical methods, and this can lead to a distortion in spiritual life. Authentic prayer is born out of faith and repentance. These are its solid basis. In continuity with the ancient tradition of the holy Fathers, Fr. Sophrony recommends, as the most correct and sure way of praying, the concentration of the mind's attention on the name of Jesus Christ and the words of the prayer. Even though this is a slower means of joining the action of heart and mind, it is more natural physiologically and more beneficial than any exterior technique. When brokenheartedness over one's sin is intensified, and conformity to the commandments of Christ reaches a certain fulness, the intellect then unites with the heart in an organic, natural way.[886]

Dr. Jean-Claude Larchet also pointed out the secondary role played by psychosomatic techniques in prayer: "As the Jesus Prayer in its full perfection is permanent pure prayer, presupposing the whole of the ascetic life as a prerequisite, it requires that all the stages of praxis be successfully completed. In light of these spiritual requirements, the psychosomatic method appears to be secondary and would be useless apart from this combination of conditions.... The description of the former [i.e., the psychosomatic method] only takes up several pages in the *Philokalia,* while the presentation of the latter [i.e., the ascetic life] takes up hundreds of pages."[887]

4) Vigil

The night has always been viewed as the best time for prayer. The monastic canons attributed to St. Anthony the Great advise: "Perform your prayer at night before going to church."[888] St. Chrodegang explained the reason why prayer should be done at night:

> That the zeal for holy vigil was chosen as singularly desirable for the saints of God goes back to ancient origins. Sanctus [Prophet] Isaiah said the following about vigils, "In the night my soul awakens to You, God." And David said, "In the middle of the night I arose to praise You, Lord, for the rightfulness of Your justice." ...
>
> Also in His gospel the Saviour announced His future coming at the same time as He taught His followers how to keep vigils, and He said this: "Blessed are the servants whom their lord finds watching when he comes. Whether he will come in the evening," He said, "at midnight, or at cock-crow, blessed are those whom he finds awake." ...
>
> And our Lord did indeed not only teach through words how to keep vigils, but also confirmed it through His own example. Truly the gospel says that the Saviour was persevering in divine prayers all through the night. Likewise Paul and Silas, when they were in public jail, prayed to God at midnight....

---

[886] Zacharias, *Christ, Our Way and Our Life,* 162; see also Sakharov, *On Prayer,* 142.

[887] Jean-Claude Larchet, *Therapy of Spiritual Illnesses: An Introduction to the Ascetic Tradition of the Orthodox Church,* vol. 2, trans. Fr. Kilian Sprecher (Montréal: Alexander Press, 2012), 110–11.

[888] Rule #13, PG 40:1067C. Cited also in Γέροντος Αἰμιλιανοῦ, *Νηπτικὴ Ζωὴ καὶ Ἀσκητικοὶ Κανόνες,* 40, 516.

Therefore then it befits us to chant during these hours and to have the zeal for our prayers during the Divine Office, and to strengthen and arm ourselves securely for our last day in such expectation. There is a kind of heretics who believe that holy vigils are worthless, and they say, "Night was created for rest, just as day for work." These heretics are called "Nyctates" in Greek, and we in our language may call them slumberers, or sleepyheads, and they may also be called dozers.[889]

This is why ever since the beginning of monasticism, monks have placed special emphasis on rising at night for prayer. St. Chariton in the early fourth century required that monks stay awake six hours[890] during the night, which was the accepted quota.[891] Likewise, St. Basil the Great advised: "Divide the time of night between sleep and prayer."[892]

St. Isaac the Syrian boldly wrote: "Prayer offered up at night possesses a great power, more so than the prayer of the day-time. Therefore all the righteous prayed during the night.... There is nothing which even Satan fears so much as prayer that is offered during vigilance at night.... Let every prayer that you offer in the night be more precious in your eyes than all your activities of the day."[893] Similarly, St. Paisios of the Holy Mountain observed: "Prayer during the night is much more beneficial than prayer during the day, just as nighttime rain is more favourable to plants than rain during the day."[894] St. Joseph the Hesychast taught from his experience: "Keeping vigil with awareness of its true nature and with watchfulness and prayer bestows great spiritual gifts upon a Christian who works at it."[895]

In the same spirit, Elder Aimilianos taught his monks:

One hour of prayer at night has more power than ten hours of prayer in the daytime. Whoever fails to use these nighttime hours usually passes his hours and days very unproductively. Are you sleeping at midnight? Your life will always be a weak life. Your being is paralyzed when you don't have the night your own because you cannot receive the Spirit. God knows and recognizes the night, but "the night" means keeping vigil at night continually. Whether you are in your cell or out of the monastery, you should be before God at night. Know that this time belongs to God. This time is the

---

[889] Langefeld, *The Old English Version of the Enlarged Rule of Chrodegang,* 367.

[890] In the Near East and Europe until about the 14th century, night and day were each divided into twelve "hours," regardless of the season. ("Are there not twelve hours in the day?" –Jn. 11:9) Thus, the duration of six such "hours" at night at St. Chariton's latitude of 32° lasted 5 modern hours on the summer solstice and 7 modern hours on the winter solstice, as is evident from an astrolabe.

[891] Vid. Patrich, *Sabas, Leader of Palestinian Monasticism,* 225.

[892] PG 31:244CD (*Homily on the Martyrdom of Julitta,* 4).

[893] Holy Transfiguration Monastery, *The Ascetical Homilies of Saint Isaac the Syrian,* 523 (Homily 75), 450 (Homily 64).

[894] Elder Paisios, *Epistles,* 121.

[895] Γέροντος Ἐφραίμ, *Ὁ Γέροντάς μου Ἰωσήφ,* 276; see also Elder Ephraim, *My Elder Joseph the Hesychast,* 386.

time when you will wrestle and will face God. And God must become *your* God. It is the time of your own ladder.[896]

St. Isaac the Syrian warned that carelessness during the daytime can ruin our prayer in the nighttime:

> I deem it impossible that a man who has chosen for himself this great and divine labor [of keeping vigil] ... should not guard himself by day from the disturbance of encounters and the cares of occupations, lest he be found destitute of the wondrous fruit and the great delight which he looks to enjoy from his vigil. And I dare say that whosoever neglects this does not know why he toils and refrains from sleep, suffers hardship in his prolonged psalmody, in the weariness of his tongue, and in night-long standing, since his mind is not in psalmody nor in his prayer....
>
> Why do you wear yourself out, when at night you sow, but during the day you dissipate your toil which is thus rendered unfruitful, when you scatter the wakefulness, sobriety, and fervor which you have gained through night vigil, and without a reasonable excuse you vainly undo your labor by your disturbing intercourse with men and with things?[897]

Elder Aimilianos also taught his monks about the struggle of keeping vigil at night:

> The night is the realm into which a monk immerses himself and truly lives. The night has great importance because it is the hour and place of mystical encounters, the experience of our pain and struggle. It is also the darkness of our souls and our hope of light. The night is a direct confrontation of our self, which is nothing but nakedness and poverty. At night there is no one for you to speak with; there is no friend or the consolation of having someone else; there is no praise, nor is there even a response, which itself is a form of love. It is like a place bare of trees, and when you see this boundless dimension you are overcome with despair. This is why many lack the strength and endurance, the martyric perseverance and patience to proceed in this struggle of the night.... The monks who keep vigil are the voice of the Church.[898]

St. Joseph the Hesychast explained why it is beneficial to begin saying the Jesus prayer as soon as we wake up: "After sleep the nous of man is fresh and clear. It is in an ideal state for us to give it, as its first spiritual food, the name of our Lord and God and Savior Jesus Christ."[899] Elder Ephraim said: "Be careful with your first thoughts after sleep. Dreams, fantasies—whether good or bad—whatever sleep bequeathed to us, we must obliterate immediately. And right away we must immediately take the name of Christ as the breath of our soul. Meanwhile, after we throw a little water on our face to wake up, and after we have a cup of coffee or something else [such as a piece of bread or some fruit] to invigorate

---

[896] Γέροντος Αἰμιλιανοῦ, *Νηπτικὴ Ζωὴ καὶ Ἀσκητικοὶ Κανόνες*, 455–56.

[897] Holy Transfiguration Monastery, *The Ascetical Homilies of Saint Isaac the Syrian*, 222–23 (Homily 20).

[898] Ἀρχιμ. Ἐλισαίου, «Ἡ Μοναχικὴ Κλῖμαξ τοῦ Γέροντος Αἰμιλιανοῦ», ἐν *Σύναξις Εὐχαριστίας· Χαριστήρια εἰς Τιμὴν τοῦ Γέροντος Αἰμιλιανοῦ*, 23.

[899] Γέροντος Ἐφραίμ, *Πατρικαὶ Νουθεσίαι*, 414; see also Elder Ephraim, *Counsels from the Holy Mountain*, 335.

us—as long as our vigil begins long before midnight—we say the Trisagion [preceded by 'Heavenly King'[900]], recite the Creed, and 'It is truly meet' to the most holy Theotokos, and then we sit in our place of prayer with the weapon against the devil—the prayer-rope—in hand."[901]

The reason why Elder Ephraim advised having coffee and/or a snack only if it is before midnight is because ancient tradition dictates that one should partake of Holy Communion or antidoron only on an empty stomach. St. Nicodemos wrote in his comments of Canon XXIX of the Sixth Ecumenical Council:

> If anyone is in danger of dying, he must commune even after having eaten, according to Canon IX of Nicephoros. When St. Chrysostom was blamed for having administered the Communion to some persons after they had eaten, he wrote in his letter to Bishop Kyriakos: "If it is true that I did this, may my name be stricken from the book of bishops. But if they say this to me once, and start quarreling, let them consider St. Paul, who baptized a whole household right after supper. Let them also consider Christ Himself, who gave the Communion to the Apostles right after supper." Hence it is evident that those who are about to commune have permission up to midnight to drink water, and thereafter they must not put anything in their mouth until they have communed.[902]

In the event, however, that the Divine Liturgy is served only a few hours after midnight (as is commonly done on the Holy Mountain), Elder Ephraim taught that ideally at least five or six hours should have passed from the last time we ate or drank something. Similarly, St. Paisios of the Holy Mountain said that prior to receiving Holy Communion a person should not have eaten anything for at least six hours and not drunk water for at least four hours.

Regarding our bodily stance during vigil, Elder Aimilianos taught:

> But where should I sit? Do I prefer to sit in an armchair? I may. Does sitting in an armchair make me sleepy? I will sit in another chair or on a bench or on my low, wooden bed. Also, I may sit on a stool with three legs so that if I fall asleep, I will fall over and wake up. I may do whatever I want, as long as I am peaceful. For when I am peaceful, I am in control of my breathing, the beating of my heart, my spirit, everything. Then I can say: "Come, my God," and I will notice it. But when my heart is beating irregularly, when my breathing is irregular, when within me I am strong-willed, how will I notice God? ... So I need to be at peace, to be rested—not so much physically as spiritually. Subordinating sleep and being at peace are a preparation.[903]

Elder Ephraim said that his elders "began their vigil by reciting the Trisagion, the Creed, and Psalm 50. Then they sat down for a while and meditated on death, hell, the joy of the

---

[900] Vid. Elder Ephraim, *Counsels from the Holy Mountain*, 346.

[901] Γέροντος Ἐφραίμ, *Πατρικαὶ Νουθεσίαι*, 415–16; see also Elder Ephraim, *Counsels from the Holy Mountain*, 336.

[902] Agapius and Nicodemus, *The Rudder*, 325.

[903] Γέροντος Αἰμιλιανοῦ, *Νηπτικὴ Ζωὴ καὶ Ἀσκητικοὶ Κανόνες*, 461.

righteous in heaven, and other such thoughts that would benefit their souls. They concluded this stage of contemplation by pondering that everyone else would be saved, while only they would go to hell. In this manner, they acquired compunction, mourning, and repentance. However, they would not spend too much time in that stage of contemplation. As soon as their nous was collected and their heart felt contrition, they began saying the prayer. Francis [i.e., St. Joseph] said it noetically, whereas Fr. Arsenios whispered it quietly."[904]

Elder Aimilianos taught his monks what inner stance we need during prayer:

How should we stand before God? First of all, we stand as His simple children. Our vigil is the time of our love with God. Just as people in the world have the hours when they want to love and be loved, likewise we have the hours when we live with our dear Christ, the hours when we await Him, and He awaits us; when we try to show our love in a way that He appreciates. If you bring to me a candy, you win my heart. You win the heart of someone else by bringing him a book. If you bring him a candy, you fail. It is the same with God. He wants you to bring him His kind of gifts and presents—the ones that He appreciates.[905]

Only "a heart contrite and humbled will God not despise."[906] When, however, I have an awareness of my virtue, my gifts, my holiness, when I seek from God divine illumination, when I seek from Him that I, too, become great, I cannot have contrition of heart.[907]

Contrition of heart may be attained also through my stance and with certain thoughts that I will have about God or with anything else. All these things are of course merely introductory exercises. I may also kneel before God and beseech Him to forgive my sin, of which I am probably unaware. I don't imagine it, but I know that I am a sinner.[908]

In order to help our heart and mind to repent, we try to create an atmosphere that is serious, dignified, contrite. At that time, and especially at the most lofty and beautiful moments, if something comes to mind, don't write it down; let it go.[909]

I seek contrition of heart and prostrations not as a magical means but as something I need. God doesn't need contrition. God does not even need my virtues or my vices or even the contrition of my heart. I am the one who needs contrition in order to be able to stand before Him.[910]

Elder Aimilianos also emphasized the importance of purity in prayer:

After contrition of heart and repentance comes the purity of life by which we see God.... With the term "purity" we mean the purity from sin, and above all the purity of the mind. Especially at this stage [during vigil] we must not let our mind occupy

---

[904] Γέροντος Ἐφραίμ, *Ὁ Γέροντάς μου Ἰωσήφ,* 67; see also Elder Ephraim, *My Elder Joseph the Hesychast,* 83.

[905] Γέροντος Αἰμιλιανοῦ, *Νηπτικὴ Ζωὴ καὶ Ἀσκητικοὶ Κανόνες,* 458–59.

[906] Ps. 50:19.

[907] Γέροντος Αἰμιλιανοῦ, *Νηπτικὴ Ζωὴ καὶ Ἀσκητικοὶ Κανόνες,* 461.

[908] Ibid., 462.

[909] Ibid., 463.

[910] Ibid., 465–66.

itself with something else besides prayer. When you are doing your vigil, a very beautiful thought might come. Drive it away. You might have a remembrance of God's love, Who was crucified for you. Keep thoughts about the Cross away from you at that time. You don't need anything. The only thing you need is purity, that is, the emptying of the mind of everything good or bad. You might have the desire to say: "My dear God, may I be dead and empty for Thy sake." No; nothing of the sort. At that time the mind must remain without colors, empty; it must be freed from everything so that you can fill it with the Jesus prayer or with other short prayers of the saints. If we are unable to do noetic prayer continuously, it is possible to fill our time with many prayers. Certainly noetic prayer is the prayer that is the most positive, the most concise, the most decisive, the most fruitful, and the most pleasing to Christ. Purity of the mind is a basic prerequisite for us to obtain thereafter the purity of the depth of our soul from the passions.[911]

So we strive to empty our mind and fill it with the words we are saying to God. Our mind goes only to the words and the meaning of the words. [912]

Elder Aimilianos taught that a further ingredient to prayer is joy:

Likewise, in our prayer we will seek joy of our heart from God; we seek this joy as evidence of His presence and love. We have the right to seek this. When we do not know God and live without Him, our life is so heavy and harsh that we need something that will make our life lighter and our prayer ethereal so that it may ascend more easily. We can achieve this through joy. Joy is a celebration of the heart, an excursion, a relaxation and enjoyment of the mind, an experience of the soul, something that remains with us in life. Joy gives us great boldness and eagerness and happiness to begin our vigil, to desire it, to increase it. But what if our vigil is as hard as dying, as dark as the blackness of the night, and as heavy as the heaviest cloud that can fall upon us? Then what do we do? Then, let us weep, let us labor, let us beg God and threaten Him to give us joy. We shall not stop our vigil; we will make it an offering of our heart, as a struggle, as a sacrifice.[913]

The final ingredient needed in prayer is fire. Elder Aimilianos said:

In our vigil, we need something else in addition: a flaming fire. This is not something we can obtain on our own; only God can give it to us. God is He Who "maketh His ministers a flame of fire."[914] The flame is the fire that ignites within us, the desire to keep vigil, the uplifting of ourselves, our flight, which makes us not only bear to keep vigil but even makes us not want to stop. Two, three, seven, fifteen hours may pass, and we will think that only five minutes have passed. The time comes for us to stop, since our responsibilities require it, and it hurts to stop our vigil. But when God makes us into a fire at the time of vigil, gradually our entire life becomes fire. Just as the fingers of the saints would become lit torches,[915] and their light would ascend to

---

[911] Ibid., 466–67.

[912] Ibid., 467.

[913] Ibid., 468.

[914] Ps. 103:4.

[915] "Abba Lot visited Abba Joseph [of Panepho] and said to him: 'Abba, to the best of my ability I do my little *synaxis,* my little fasting; praying, meditating, and maintaining *hesychia*; and I purge my logismoi [thoughts] to the best of my ability. What else then can I do?' The elder stood up and stretched out his hands

heaven, our own existence can become like that. Without fire, the spaceship doesn't ascend to the moon, so how will I ascend to heaven without fire? So let us entreat God to make fiery our prayer, our ascents, our vigil, the cries of our hearts, our prostrations, our labors, our asceticism, everything. Through contrition of heart, prostrations, the purity of mind by which we see God, with the joy, and the flaming fire (which is necessary for us to be transported to the other life), our vigil, our prayer, our cell, our soul become a fruitful place where one can find God and embrace Him. And the Farmer—God—can cultivate our being.[916]

Interspersing different kinds of prayer enables us to remain spiritually alert. St. Paisios of the Holy Mountain wrote: "Variety in vigil is very helpful. When one is alone, he may first do full prostrations, then small ones, and then say the Jesus Prayer sitting down or kneeling and repeat this sequence depending on the time he has to offer. This method is very helpful, for it creates spiritual liveliness and drives away the weariness of inaction through interspersed spiritual movements, prostrations. Moreover, it drives away sleepiness and brings spiritual lucidity during prayer."[917]

Elder Aimilianos taught that the most important time for a monk is his vigil:

> The prayer rule is the marrow of our existence, the most refined and serious part of the monastic life. It shows if we have God or if we don't have Him, if we have the desire to acquire Him or not. Whoever does not do a prayer rule is certainly fooling himself if he thinks he has the Holy Spirit. The Holy Spirit does not operate and speak in us if we have no night life. And if we lack the appropriate conditions for the night life, let there be at least the desire and yearning to create such conditions, so that someday we may have this night life. God will see our desire and will accomplish it.… This vigil brings illumination to the soul and unites it with God. During vigil, man is illumined, his intellect is purified, thoughts depart, and the mind remains alone so that it may fly and ascend to God, and enjoy Him and love Him and become acquainted with Him. For henceforth God becomes *his* God and not some unknown God. Of course, no matter how unknown our God is, we will not abandon our vigil. We shall become tired and shall suffer in order to live with Him.[918]

---

to heaven; his fingers became like ten lamps of fire. He said to him: 'If you are willing, become altogether like fire.'" (Wortley, *The Alphabetical Sayings of the Desert Fathers,* 152; PG 65:229D).

[916] Γέροντος Αἰμιλιανοῦ, *Νηπτικὴ Ζωὴ καὶ Ἀσκητικοὶ Κανόνες,* 469–70.

[917] Elder Paisios, *Epistles,* 123–24. Once when I sat beside Elder Ephraim in an airplane, I expected that he would be praying with his prayer-rope throughout the entire flight, since he had told us the importance of saying the Jesus prayer continuously. But to my surprise, soon after takeoff he put away his prayer-rope and began reading Vespers silently from his prayer book. Puzzled, I asked him: "Geronda, what's going on? I thought we're supposed to say the Jesus prayer all the time." He replied, "No, my child; we need variety in prayer. Just as you get tired of eating the same food all the time, likewise you get tired of praying if you don't have variety in prayer."

[918] Γέροντος Αἰμιλιανοῦ, *Νηπτικὴ Ζωὴ καὶ Ἀσκητικοὶ Κανόνες,* 451–52.

The central role of the night life for a monk led Elder Aimilianos to this bold conclusion: "Monastic life is completely immersed in the night, with only a part of it extending its branches into the daytime."[919]

The daily prayer rule that Elder Ephraim gave his monks (in addition to attending all the services) is to do three 300-knot prayer-ropes *stavrota*, i.e., at each knot making the sign of the cross and saying, "Lord Jesus Christ, have mercy on me," as well as one 300-knot prayer-rope *stavrota* saying "Most Holy Theotokos, save me." Health permitting, a monk will also do 100 prostrations daily as a novice or rasophore, or 300 as a great-schema monk.[920] St. Theoliptos of Philadelphia advised: "Do not neglect prostration. It provides an image of man's fall into sin and expresses the confession of our sinfulness. Getting up, on the other hand, signifies repentance and the promise to lead a life of virtue. Let each prostration be accompanied by a noetic invocation of Christ [e.g., the Jesus prayer], so that by falling before the Lord in soul and body you may gain the grace of the God of souls and bodies."[921]

The duration of each monk's private vigil will depend on numerous variables, especially on his need for sleep and if his *diakonema* [i.e., assigned task] requires him to go to bed late. Elder Aimilianos recommended: "The vigil should last as long as possible, but we begin with one hour, and then we proceed to two, to four, to five hours. This comes naturally; your constitution grows accustomed to it.... Likewise, the time at which we do our vigil differs. Some of the holy Fathers preferred to continue their day with their vigil and to rest in the morning hours. Others (who were the majority) did the opposite. They would rest and then get up fresh to do their vigil. Others slept a little, kept vigil, and then again rested a little. Each person may have his own way. Be that as it may, what is more suitable to our context is to prefer the hours at or after midnight for keeping vigil."[922]

Vigil is generally kept in one's own cell, but it may also be kept outdoors (weather permitting) or in a chapel. Since noetic prayer is the most profitable method of prayer (when done with attention), we endeavor to spend most of our time occupying ourselves with it. When, however, we are unable to focus on noetic prayer, we say the prayer in a whisper or out loud. We also read prayers (such as the Prayers for Preparation Before Holy Communion and the Salutations to the Theotokos).

---

[919] Ibid., 511.

[920] St. Nicodemos of the Holy Mountain wrote: "The prayer rule of great schema and perfect monks, according to the Holy Fathers, is that every twenty-four hours they do 300 genuflections—full prostrations, that is [vid. Skoubourdis, *The Philokalia, Vol. 5,* 64]. According to the authorities in Mount Athos, however, they should do 120 genuflections and twelve full prayer-ropes of lesser (i.e., bowing) prostrations. As for small-schema and stavrophore monks: 100 genuflections and six prayer-ropes with bows; and rasophores: 100 genuflections and three prayer-ropes with bows" (Agapius and Nicodemus, *The Rudder,* 457–58).

[921] Palmer, Sherrard, Ware, *The Philokalia,* vol. 4, 185.

[922] Γέροντος Αἰμιλιανοῦ, *Νηπτικὴ Ζωὴ καὶ Ἀσκητικοὶ Κανόνες,* 454–45.

A monk may also read spiritual books during his vigil. St. Joseph the Hesychast recommended: "Read the lives of saints [during your vigil] and other compunctious and beneficial books."[923] Since, however, reading brings less profit than praying, only a small fraction of time during vigil is allotted to reading. As St. John of Sinai instructed: "Devote the greater part of the night to prayer and only what is left to recital of the psalter."[924] Elder Aimilianos explained this approach in more detail:

> When we are unable to pray much during our prayer rule [at night], we read the Old and New Testament, the Fathers of the Church, or the Psalter in order to assist our human weakness. In reality however, these hours are for prayer, as St. Anthony says.[925] Nevertheless, our reading then is not just any reading but that which cultivates more our heart, our nous, and peace, so that we can make our prayer livelier. It is not just a matter of praying, but our prayer should be God-bearing, a piercing cry that will reach heaven and shake it. Consequently, we incorporate reading into our prayer time because it promotes prayer. However, the more a soul progresses, reading diminishes and prayer increases.[926]

Elder Aimilianos was once asked: "When reading fails to inspire us but we are in the mood for work, can we use the time of vigil for working?" He replied: "In only one situation can this be done: when a person is unable to do a long prayer rule and wants to do some handicraft so that he can pray and be at peace. Then this is in line with tradition. He can do this as long as he needs to. In the old days, the Desert Fathers did their handicraft also at night. In this manner, their minds did not wander, their prayer ascended to God, and their eyes filled with tears. This can be done, but the elder's blessing is necessary."[927] This is in line with what St. John of Sinai wrote: "I wanted to forbid those who were still children [i.e., spiritually immature] all bodily work at the time of vigil, but he who carried sand all night in his cloak restrained me"[928]—referring to St. Pachomios who did this in order to resist sleep and remain in vigil. Likewise, St. Theoliptos of Philadelphia advised: "To dispel sleep and indolence while practicing mental prayer you may occupy your hands with some quiet task, for this, too, contributes to the ascetic struggle. All such tasks when accompanied by prayer quicken the intellect, banish listlessness, give youthful vigor to the soul, and render the intellect more prompt and eager to devote itself to mental work."[929] Elder Aimilianos added that work during vigil must be done with a sense of God's presence:

---

[923] Γέροντος Ἰωσήφ, Ἔκφρασις Μοναχικῆς Ἐμπειρίας, 399; see also Elder Joseph, *Monastic Wisdom*, 339.

[924] Holy Transfiguration Monastery, *The Ladder of Divine Ascent*, 210 (Step 27:77).

[925] See footnote #888 on page 166.

[926] Γέροντος Αἰμιλιανοῦ, Νηπτικὴ Ζωὴ καὶ Ἀσκητικοὶ Κανόνες, 41.

[927] Ibid., 43.

[928] Holy Transfiguration Monastery, *The Ladder of Divine Ascent*, 211 (Step 27:84).

[929] Palmer, Sherrard, Ware, *The Philokalia*, vol. 4, 185.

When the hours of vigil are endless, a monk may even decorate the time with written work that does not distract him but is a break, with the realization that he is setting God before him, and he is writing or doing some particular work. Am I a pastor? I may do my pastoral work or study the canons of the Church. Am I a disciple? I may do something connected to my tasks of obedience, or I may read a theological book…. I may also read some Church services…. So I may read, pray, work with my hands, and enrich my time, as long as I do not stop being before God.[930]

5) Reading

The holy Fathers taught that reading helps us in three ways: it teaches us how to fulfil our spiritual duties, it concentrates the mind to pray better, and it inspires us to live with greater zeal. St. Isaac the Syrian taught: "Combine spiritual reading with prayer, for this destroys the confusion that comes from without, provides material for mental prayer, and concentrates the mind."[931] Likewise, St. Basil the Great wrote: "The study of inspired Scripture is the chief way of finding our duty…. Prayers, too, after reading, find the soul fresher and more vigorously stirred by love towards God."[932] Similarly, St. John of Sinai said: "Reading enlightens the mind considerably, and helps it concentrate."[933] St. Ignatius Brianchaninov said: "The chief occupation of a novice in his cell should be the reading and study of the Gospel and of the whole New Testament."[934] He even advised monks: "Never cease studying the Gospel till the end of your life. Do not think you know it enough, even if you know it by heart."[935] St. John Chrysostom said: "It is not possible for anyone to be saved without continually taking advantage of spiritual reading…. The ignorance of Scripture is a great cliff and a deep abyss; to know nothing of the divine laws is a great betrayal of salvation."[936]

To encourage his monks to read, St. Theodore the Studite had a lending library and a librarian, and he set aside a time in the middle of the day for them to read or take a nap.[937] Likewise, most of the early monastic rules of Western Europe allotted a specific time for daily reading. For example, *The Rule of Tarn* orders: "From the sixth hour until the ninth,

---

[930] Γέροντος Αἰμιλιανοῦ, *Νηπτικὴ Ζωὴ καὶ Ἀσκητικοὶ Κανόνες,* 477–78.

[931] Chrysostomos, *The Evergetinos, Book IV,* 158.

[932] *Basil: Letters and Select Works,* 111 (Letter 2).

[933] Holy Transfiguration Monastery, *The Ladder of Divine Ascent,* 210.

[934] Brianchaninov, *The Arena,* 21.

[935] Ibid., 15. St. Ignatius explained that with the word "Gospel" he means the whole New Testament (vid. ibid., 21).

[936] St. John Chrysostom, *On Wealth and Poverty,* trans. Catharine Roth (New York: St. Vladimir's Seminary Press, 1984), 60.

[937] Νικολάου, «Ἡ Θεολογία τῆς Κοινοβιακῆς Ζωῆς», 49.

let them have time for quiet and also for reading…. But in the wintertime once Matins and Prime [i.e., the First Hour] have been finished, all will be allowed to have time for reading until Terce [i.e., the Third Hour].… Those who are in charge of the cultivation of the fields cannot be bound by this regulation on account of the harshness of their work; as their time or work demands, the labor itself will manifest the tasks to be imposed. Let them be governed by the judgment of the prior in such a way that they nonetheless have leisure for two hours of reading."[938]

St. Pachomios encouraged his monks to memorize Scripture: "There shall be no one whatever in the monastery who does not learn to read and does not memorize something of the Scriptures. One should learn by heart at least [!] the New Testament and the Psalter."[939] And his second successor, Horsiesios, wrote: "Let us be wealthy in texts learned by heart. Let him who does not memorize much memorize at least ten sections along with a section of the Psalter."[940] Likewise, St. Gennadius the Patriarch of Constantinople in the 5th century attached such great importance to memorizing Scripture that he would not ordain anyone who did not know the Psalter by heart.[941]

When the successor of St. Paisius Velichkovsky asked a general of the demons, "What is your greatest weapon against the monastics in these our times?" the demon was constrained by the might of God to confess: "Our whole concern at present is to keep monks and nuns away from spiritual occupations, especially prayer and the reading of those smoky books. Why don't you spend more time taking care of your gardens and vineyards, of your fishing and schools for the young, of your hospitality for all those good people who come here during the summer for the fresh air and pure water? The monastics who busy themselves in such pursuits are caught in our nets like flies in a spider's web."[942]

Elder Aimilianos recommended in the *Regulations of the Holy Cenobium of the Annunciation:* "Another important occupation of the sisters, apart from poring over and delighting in the Scriptures, shall be the fruitful study of Patristic and theological writings, since they provide the knowledge and conditions necessary for cenobitic behavior and spiritual duties."[943] One reason why reading improves cenobitic behavior is because it helps us maintain a philosophical outlook towards life without getting bogged down in trivialities. As St. Nectarios of Aegina wrote to his nuns: "Your life is Christian philosophy.

---

[938] *Monastic Studies,* no. 17, 227–28.

[939] Veilleux, *Pachomian Koinonia,* vol. 2, 166.

[940] Ibid., 202.

[941] See the prolegomena of the Canonical Epistle of St. Gennadius in *The Rudder.* To be sure, part of the reason why these early saints emphasized the memorization of Scripture was because few people in those days possessed their own manuscripts of the Bible.

[942] Metrophanes, *Blessed Paisius Velichkovsky,* 261.

[943] Elder Aimilianos, *The Authentic Seal,* 161–62.

A philosopher is never distressed.... Philosophical thought is the chief characteristic of your [monastic] way of life."[944] Likewise, St. Sophrony of Essex advised his monastics: "You need to be serious in the daily life of our monastery and always keep your spirit in the depths of spiritual matters. With this stance you will avoid all the petty conflicts that make our life—how can I put it—petty, measly."[945]

The amount of time a monk should read depends on several factors, such as how much free time he has, how much he benefits from reading (as opposed to praying or working or helping someone else), how much he already knows, how much he needs to know, etc. This is why when St. Sophrony of Essex was a young monk (and had already studied theology) his spiritual father advised him: "Read only a few pages—a quarter or half an hour a day—but with attentiveness, and apply them in your life."[946] In the same spirit, St. John of Sinai wrote: "Let what you read lead you to action, for you a doer. Putting these words into practice makes further reading superfluous."[947]

St. Nicodemos of the Holy Mountain also emphasized the importance of applying what one reads:

> Be eager to read ... not merely for the love of learning but also for the sake of ascetic endeavors and discipline, as St. Mark [the Ascetic] wrote: "Understand the words of Holy Scripture by putting them into practice, and do not fill yourself with conceit by speaking at length on theoretical ideas."[948] Another Father said: "He who loves knowledge must also love discipline, for mere knowledge does not light a lamp."[949] You will acquire this light if you contemplate on the ordinances found in Scripture and ponder that they were written to correct you and not the others, as again St. Mark said: "The humble person who has a spiritual life reads the Holy Scripture and understands everything to refer to him and not to others."[950,951]

Elder Aimilianos taught that the amount of time spent reading depends on the intensity of one's prayer:

> The more time passes, the more prayer increases and reading decreases. We read as much as is necessary to have excellent and perfect prayer. But there is another reason for reading. One might be able to say that he can pray all night and doesn't need to read. This is not right because he can become isolated in his prayer, grow callous

---

[944] Strongylis, *St. Nectarios of Pentapolis and the Island of Aegina,* vol. 2, 57–58 (Letter #8).

[945] Σωφρονίου, *Οἰκοδομῶντας τὸν Ναὸ τοῦ Θεοῦ, Τόμος Α΄,* 320–21.

[946] Σωφρονίου, *Οἰκοδομῶντας τὸν Ναὸ τοῦ Θεοῦ, Τόμος Β΄,* 24.

[947] Holy Transfiguration Monastery, *The Ladder of Divine Ascent,* 210.

[948] cf. Palmer, Sherrard, Ware, *The Philokalia,* vol. 1, 116.

[949] Hesychios the Presbyter, *On Watchfulness and Holiness* 80; see also Palmer, Sherrard, Ware, *The Philokalia,* vol. 1, 176.

[950] Ibid., 110.

[951] Νικοδήμου τοῦ Ἁγιορείτου, *Συμβουλευτικὸν Ἐγχειρίδιον,* 215–16; see also Chamberas, *Nicodemos of the Holy Mountain: A Handbook of Spiritual Counsel,* 190.

within himself, fall into haughtiness, and slip away from the path of the Fathers. He must continually be fed with the word of God, either through the mouth of the prophets and Apostles, or through the mouth of the great preachers—the great Church Fathers. If he is not being fed, his prayer runs the risk of becoming barren. This is why the saint [i.e., the Gallic author of *The Rule of Macarius*] especially emphasized reading.

The saint wanted monks to be a complete man, not just someone who prays. When you are on fire and illumined by the Holy Spirit, and your nous and heart penetrate the heavenly world, and you enter Paradise while still in this life, and mysteries are revealed to you; when you see the cherubim and the seraphim and perceive what the All-holy Trinity means and how the saints and the angels are, then you can stop reading. You no longer need the light of books.[952]

The following is a list of some of the most beneficial books (in our opinion) that should be read by monastics in addition to the Bible:

Monastic Classics:
> *The Life of Saint Anthony*
> *The Ladder*
> *Abba Dorotheos of Gaza*
> *The Sayings of the Desert Fathers* (i.e., the *Gerontikon*)
> *The Evergetinos*
> *The Ascetical Homilies of Saint Isaac the Syrian*

Writings of the Holy Fathers:
> Saint Basil the Great (especially his *Long* and *Shorter Rules*)
> Saint John Chrysostom
> Saint John Cassian
> *The Philokalia*

Lives of Monastic Saints:
> *Saint Seraphim of Sarov*
> *Saint Paisius Velichkovsky*
> Elders of Optina

Books about Recent Saints:
> *Saint Nectarios of Aegina*
> *Saint Silouan the Athonite*
> *Saint John Maximovitch*

Teachings of our Elders:
> *Monastic Wisdom*
> *My Elder Joseph the Hesychast*
> *Counsels from the Holy Mountain*
> *The Art of Prayer* and the unpublished homilies of Elder Ephraim at Philotheou

Books by or about Contemporary Elders:
> Saint Paisios the Athonite
> Saint Porphyrios of Kafsokalyvia
> Saint Ephraim of Katounakia, etc.

---

[952] Γέροντος Αἰμιλιανοῦ, *Νηπτικὴ Ζωὴ καὶ Ἀσκητικοὶ Κανόνες*, 378–79.

Other Books:
> *The Life of the Virgin Mary, the Theotokos*
> *The Synaxaristes* (Lives of the Saints for every day of the year)
> *The Way of a Pilgrim*
> *The Explanation of the New Testament* by Blessed Theophylact

Since many monastics find reading a book more pleasant than doing work, a common temptation for them is to let others work while they read. St. Isidore of Seville warns such monks: "If anyone wants time for reading so as not to work, they are in opposition to the same reading because they do not do what they read there. For it is written, 'Let those who work eat their own bread' (2 Thes. 3:12)."[953]

St. Eustathios of Thessalonica believed that reading also secular books helps monks:

> The monastic life is the art of arts and science of sciences and is the standard of philosophy, since he who lives alone, trusting in God and looking to Him, is a true philosopher. But how can one philosophize if he neither has the "salt"[954] of an education nor has experienced the illumination of spiritual praxis? The most important thing of all for a monk is to be close to God, as this is his calling, and this is why he must be a learned man (σχολαστικός). If he is close to Him, then he beholds Him, as it is written: "Study (σχολάσατε) and know God."[955] But how can someone know God if both his eyes are incapacitated? It is understood that one eye symbolizes practice and the other theory, and the distance separating them is as small as the width of a hair. This is because perfect theory goes hand in hand with the practical application of virtue, and practice without theory is blind. A theoretical understanding of many things is acquired through books, in which there are sacred doctrines and analyses of difficult scriptural passages and sacred narratives. These books are instructive representations of divine facts, and they are lights that lead to good deeds, exemplify good behavior, and exhort to do what is correct.

> As for me, I would prefer that monks make anthologies also of secular writings, opinions, and sayings. The most holy Fathers in the old days selected these things and made honey, storing them up in those sweet books of theirs, in which they put words sweeter than honey and honeycomb, and pleased God by working in this manner. I myself would love to have such monks here. But instead, the monks here scorn non-Christian books as well as Christian books, especially the books that delve deeper into God and divine matters. I hope they acquire some prudence and stop behaving foolishly like this.[956] …

> You peasant monk, what will you do if some serious controversial ecclesiastical matter arises, and the people of the Church need to fight for the truth? You and those around you are members of the Church and not just ordinary members. What will you do then? How will you speak, since you have in a sense pulled out your tongue and cut it off along with your lips? In other words, you lack the suitable theological education

---

[953] *Monastic Studies,* no. 18, 12–13.

[954] Vid. Col. 4:6: "Let your speech always be with grace, as though seasoned with salt."

[955] Cf. Ps. 45:10. Most saints have understood this psalm verse to mean: "**Be still** (σχολάσατε) and know that I am God." But the verb σχολάζω can mean either "to study" or "to be still," depending on the context.

[956] PG 135:848C–849A.

by which complex issues are primarily solved and corrected. What use will your knowledge of material matters be then? You squander countless hours on them and have abandoned studying books and reading things that lead you to lofty matters that help us approach God. Not only do you not strive for such a good thing, but you even attack those who do. The only three things you boast doing are venerating in church, going to your cell, and going to the refectory. You don't understand that these things are insufficient to bring a true monk to perfection. What he needs more than anything else is knowledge. And I am speaking not only of theological knowledge but also of knowledge which proceeds from various and different fields of learning (as I have already said), by which one becomes useful to whomever one meets.

Besides, how did those great saints become wise? Was it perhaps by roaming through villages and cities, examining the roads and alleys, wasting their time with sockets and blocks? Or was it by isolating themselves and occupying themselves with all kinds of reading?[957]

Likewise, St. Basil the Great also perceived the benefit of being proficient in worldly knowledge. He wrote: "Since many people in their zeal for these [worldly studies] have neglected knowledge about God and have grown old in their vain search, an understanding of learning is necessary to enable one not only to choose learning that is beneficial but also to avoid the learning that is foolish and harmful."[958]

St. Nectarios of Aegina explained that although St. Basil objected to monks abandoning their monastic life in order to pursue worldly studies, St. Nectarios felt that it is not improper for monks to study something practical in their spare time. He wrote:

The spirit of what I wrote [to Sister Akakia] was in accordance with what St. Basil the Great had expressed. He said that after joining monasticism it is satanic to turn away from it in order to pursue a worldly education, since such a person leaves the divine wisdom from heaven, abandons the knowledge coming from revelation, and seeks to know human wisdom. In my opinion, he is speaking about those who lose the desire for heavenly wisdom and abandon their philosophical life in the monastery in order to be taught human wisdom, which distances them from God and cools their love for the Lord. However, I do not believe that learning a little grammar [of Koine Greek] in a practical manner for correctly reading and writing and understanding the texts of Scripture is contrary to the spirit of monasticism, since it does not require leaving the monastery, nor does it make a person abandon monastic life and divine eros, but during one's spare time one merely learns in a practical and methodical way the forms and rules of grammar."[959]

St. Nicodemos of the Holy Mountain also perceived the benefit of much learning. He wrote:

The wise Isocrates said: "If you love to learn you will become very knowledgeable; what you have learned keep by constant study, and whatever you have not yet learned, seek to do so through the sciences. In this manner, you will learn quickly what others

---

[957] PG 135:849D–852B.

[958] PG 31:397BC (Homily 12 on Proverbs 1:6).

[959] Strongylis, *St. Nectarios of Pentapolis and the Island of Aegina,* vol. 2, 157 (Letter #79); Ἅγιος Νεκτάριος Πενταπόλεως, *Κατηχητικαὶ Ἐπιστολαί,* Ἐπιστολὴ 79.

have discovered with difficulty."[960] Another wise man said: "The award of victory is given to those who run the race, whereas primacy in understanding is given to those who are disciplined. Ignorance, as a harsh illness, is followed by many sins, while education, as a pleasant field, produces all good things."[961] Indeed, "there is no substitute for a cultivated soul."[962] "A multitude of wise men is the salvation of the world, and a sensible king (and a bishop) is the stability of his people."[963] It is indisputable that the love of learning and constant reading produces well-educated people even out of those who were unlearned.[964]

At first glance, one might think that St. Gregory Palamas completely disagreed with what St. Eustathios wrote on the previous page, since St. Gregory wrote: "We do not forbid anyone to initiate himself in worldly education if he wishes, at least if he has not adopted the monastic life. But we would not advise anyone to devote himself to this unendingly, and we absolutely forbid them to expect any accurate knowledge of divine things from it, since it is not possible to extract any teaching about God from such an education."[965]

However, a closer look at St. Gregory's stance reveals that his primary objection was regarding those who, because of their failure to differentiate between worldly and divine wisdom, presumed that a worldly education by itself could lead to salvation and the knowledge of God.[966] He perceived a potential benefit from secular writings, for he wrote: "Worldly education serves natural knowledge. It can never become spiritual unless it is allied to faith and love of God, and it can never become spiritual unless it has been regenerated not only by love, but also by the grace which comes from love."[967] In other words, he is saying that a worldly education *can* be spiritually beneficial by God's grace if the person has faith and love of God. And St. Gregory also taught: "There is something of benefit to be had even from the profane philosophers."[968]

---

[960] Ἰσοκράτους, *Πρὸς Δημόνικον* 18.

[961] From the *Life* of St. Cyril Phileotes.

[962] Sir. 21:17.

[963] Wis. 6:24.

[964] Νικοδήμου τοῦ Ἁγιορείτου, *Συμβουλευτικὸν Ἐγχειρίδιον,* 223; see also Chamberas, *Nicodemos of the Holy Mountain: A Handbook of Spiritual Counsel,* 194.

[965] Saint Gregory Palamas, *The Triads in Defence of the Holy Hesychasts: Book 1,* trans. Robin Amis (Hermitage: Praxis Press, 2002), 44.

[966] St. Gregory Palamas "pointed out that knowledge by itself has not benefitted anyone, because it is incapable of securing man's purification, spiritual perfection, or knowledge of God. Therefore, St. Gregory emphasized that secular wisdom is not only unnecessary for man's salvation and perfection, but it can even become destructive if it is changed from a preparatory occupation to an end in itself" (Γεωργίου Π. Θεοδωρούδη, *Θεία καὶ Ἀνθρωπίνη Σοφία κατὰ τὴν Πατερικὴν Παράδοσιν τῆς Ὀρθοδόξου Ἐκκλησίας* [Θεσσαλονίκη: Κυρομάνος, 1998], 170).

[967] Palamas, *The Triads in Defence of the Holy Hesychasts: Book 1,* 41.

[968] For the entire quotation, see the text referenced in footnote #2433 on page 458.

This is why, according to St. Athanasios Parios: "In his youth, St. Gregory Palamas devoted himself to the study and acquisition of external (secular) philosophy. For it was proper for his noble nature to be equipped with the instruments provided by philosophy.... Then he became proficient in physics and logic, and in other subjects on which Aristotle had written."[969]

6) Behavior in Church

St. Symeon the New Theologian taught how one should behave in church:

> Let it be noted that he who has already outwardly laid aside the earthly man with his attitude of mind, and by assuming the monastic habit clothed himself with the heavenly man, must rise at midnight before Orthros and recite the prescribed prayer. After so doing he must rise with all to go to the service of praise, and with attention and vigilance go through the whole service. He must pay particular attention to the beginning of the hymnody, that is, the six psalms, the psalm verses, and the lections [from the *Synaxarion*], with great concentration, without relaxation of body or putting one foot in front of another or leaning on walls or pillars, but holding his hands securely together, the feet equally being on the ground, and the head immobile without nodding here and there. The mind must not wander off, nor the thoughts be occupied with curiosity or interest in the more careless brethren as they talk or whisper to each other. On the contrary, the eye and the soul must be kept free from distraction and pay attention to nothing else but the psalmody and the reading and, as far as possible, to the meaning of the words of the divine Scripture that are being sung or read, so that not one of these words may pass in vain, but rather that his soul may derive nourishment from all of them and attain to compunction and humility and the divine illumination of the Holy Ghost.[970]
>
> Go off with all the rest to the Office and stand in the temple as though you were in the company of angels in heaven, with trembling because you regard yourself unworthy even to stand there with your brethren. As you stand pay heed to yourself so that you do not look around you with curiosity at the brethren, how each of them stands or how he sings, but pay attention to yourself alone, to the psalmody, and to your sins. Remember also the prayer that you offered in your cell; do not at all carry on any conversation or speak any idle word to anyone during Office, nor depart from thence before the final prayer. If you are able, do not sit down even for the reading, but withdraw to a hidden spot and listen standing. Listen as though it were God Himself speaking to you through the reader, God Who "is above all" (Rom. 9:5). But if you yourself are told to read the lessons, do so with the attitude that you are unworthy that your mouth should read the divinely inspired Scriptures to the brethren.[971]

---

[969] Constantine Cavarnos, *Saint Athanasios Parios* (Boston: Institute for Byzantine and Modern Greek Studies, 2006), 82.

[970] C. J. de Catanzaro, *Symeon the New Theologian: Discourses,* 274–75.

[971] Ibid., 323.

Many other Church Fathers also emphasized the importance of paying attention to the meaning of liturgical texts. For example, St. John Cassian wrote about the monks of fourth-century Egypt: "For it is not a multitude of verses but rather the understanding of the mind that pleases them, and this they pursue with all their strength: 'I shall sing with the spirit and I shall sing with the understanding as well' (1 Cor. 14:15). Hence they consider it better to sing ten verses with a modicum of comprehension than to pour out the whole psalm with a distracted mind."[972] Blessed Augustine said (and was quoted by St. Caesarius of Arles): "When you pray to God in psalms and hymns let the heart ponder what the mouth utters."[973] Similarly, St. Peter of Damascus wrote: "The troparia to be found in the liturgical books are intended to assist us in understanding these books as well as other texts.... We should pay attention to the meaning of the psalms and troparia, becoming in this way totally aware of our ignorance."[974] St. Barsanuphius the Great wrote: "As far as reading and psalmody go, one must keep one's intellect alert to the words of the text and assume within one's soul the meaning concealed in them."[975] Likewise, St. Joseph the Hesychast wrote: "The nous should hunt out the meaning of the hymn. The intellect should be sweetened by the thoughts of the nous and should be led up to contemplating them."[976] A novice once wrote about St. Seraphim of Sarov: "Then he began to rebuke me gently, saying: 'Some people apparently read well [in church], but they don't understand the meaning of what they are reading.'"[977]

St. Ambrose of Milan also attributed importance to the comprehension of liturgical texts: "The virtue of silence, especially in Church, is very great. Let no sentence of the divine lesson escape you.... Is anything more unbecoming than the divine words should be so drowned by talking, as not to be heard, believed, or made known, that the sacraments should be indistinctly heard through the sound of voices, that prayer should be hindered when offered for the salvation of all?"[978]

St. Gregory Palamas taught that understanding what is sung transforms us: "It is impossible for anyone who stands in God's holy Church collecting his thoughts, lifting his mind to God, occupying his understanding with the sacred singing from the beginning until the end and waiting patiently, not to undergo a divine change, in accordance with his attention to God and His teachings."[979]

---

[972] Ramsey, *John Cassian: The Institutes,* 44 (ii. 11.1).

[973] Hugh of St. Victor, *Explanation of the Rule of St. Augustine,* 28.

[974] Palmer, Sherrard, Ware, *The Philokalia,* vol. 3, 194.

[975] Chryssavgis, *Barsanuphius and John: Letters,* vol. 2, 55 (letter 428).

[976] Γέροντος Ἰωσήφ, Ἔκφρασις Μοναχικῆς Ἐμπειρίας, 58; see also Elder Joseph, *Monastic Wisdom,* 58.

[977] Moore, *St. Seraphim of Sarov: A Spiritual Biography,* 231.

[978] *Ambrose: Select Works and Letters,* 382–83.

[979] Veniamin, *The Homilies of Saint Gregory Palamas,* vol. 1, 262.

St. John Cassian described how quiet the monastic church services were in fourth-century Egypt: "When they come together, then, to celebrate the aforementioned services (which they call *synaxes*), everyone is so silent that, even though such a large number of brothers has gathered, one would easily believe that no one was present apart from the person who stands to sing the psalm in their midst. This is especially the case when the prayer is concluded. Then there is no spitting, no annoying clearing of throats, no noisy coughing, no sleepy yawning emitted from gaping and wide-open mouths, no groans and not even any sighs to disturb those in attendance."[980] Likewise, St. Ambrose advised: "Abstain from groans, cries, coughing, and laughter at the Mystery."[981]

Ever since the beginning of monasticism, the importance of not talking during church has been emphasized. The monastic rule attributed to St. Anthony the Great states: "Take care not to speak at all in church."[982] Likewise, St. Efthymios the Great "gave instructions that no one was to talk in church during the time of office, nor in the refectory while the brethren were eating."[983] St. Symeon the New Theologian also advised: "Do not at all carry on any conversation or speak any idle word to anyone during Office."[984] St. John Chrysostom explained the reason for not speaking in church:

> When someone is talking with the earthly king, he contrives every possible way to display great reverence for him. For this reason, by the position of the head, with the tone of voice, clasped hands, joined legs, and control over the whole body, he chooses his words from among those the latter desires.... You are standing before the heavenly King before Whom the angels tremble as they stand. You have abandoned your conversation with Him and are talking about dung and dust and spider webs.[985]

Similarly, St. Seraphim of Sarov said: "Never, God forbid, not for anything, not for anyone should one speak in the sanctuary [i.e., the altar], even if one were to have to suffer for it, for the Lord Himself is present there! And in fear and trembling all the Cherubim and Seraphim and all the Powers of God stand before Him. Who then will speak before His face!"[986] St. John the Almsgiver "made sure to correct as much as he could those who talked heedlessly in Church. If he saw that someone remained uncorrected after the first and second counsel, he immediately threw him out of the Church and repeated to him the words of the Master Christ: 'The house of God must be a house of prayer.'"[987]

---

[980] Ramsey, *John Cassian: The Institutes*, 43 (ii. 10).

[981] *Ambrose: Select Works and Letters*, 383.

[982] Rule #25, PG 40:1069A. Cited also in Γέροντος Αἰμιλιανοῦ, *Νηπτικὴ Ζωὴ καὶ Ἀσκητικοὶ Κανόνες*, 517.

[983] Cyril of Scythopolis, *Lives of the Monks of Palestine*, 13.

[984] C. J. de Catanzaro, *Symeon the New Theologian: The Discourses*, 323.

[985] PG 56:101–2 (as translated in: Goldfrank, *The Monastic Rule of Iosif Volotsky*, 126–27).

[986] Moore, *St. Seraphim of Sarov: A Spiritual Biography*, 64.

[987] Chrysostomos, *The Evergetinos, Book II*, 104.

There are differing opinions regarding whether or not something necessary may be discussed during church. St. John Chrysostom taught against this: "Someone may say [attempting to justify discussions during the church service] that there is evil in unsettled affairs and concerning the real needs of our lives, but we shall not say this at all. This pretext is demonic and the enticement of the Devil, and this word is vain. Indeed God, when scorned, scatters the assembly. Although we have a great deal to arrange in our lives, there are other times to hold meetings about them."[988]

St. Basil the Great, however, allowed for some exceptions. He taught: "Conversation may not take place at the hour when the Office is being held within the house, except by those who are responsible for the care and maintenance of good order and the arranging of work, and then only in cases of urgent need; and not even then without deliberation but with careful consideration both of place and discipline and reverence and the avoidance of offence."[989] Similarly, St. Seraphim of Sarov said: "One should never speak in church about anything else except strictly necessary church matters and about the church."[990] Elder Ephraim also taught that discussions during church are to be avoided, but he permitted brief things to be said only as a concession for the sake of convenience, because at St. Anthony's Monastery and at Philotheou Monastery the only place where many of us would see each other was during church.

Nevertheless, we must bear in mind that even if we say something very brief to someone else during church, our few words have the potential not only to terminate his prayer but even to throw him into a state of inner turmoil. Even if our words do not trouble him, they could create a distraction for him that could trigger a train of thoughts that might not stop until the end of the service, thus preventing him from praying. Likewise, his verbal or even nonverbal response can have the same distracting effect on us.

Elder Aimilianos pointed out another danger of speaking in church: "If someone in church speaks to you, and you answer him, he will realize that you are bored in church, and this is why you are so eager to start a conversation. In this manner, the wall that preserves God's boundaries will fall, and the other person will continually come to talk with you."[991]

In the event that we do say something during church, a way to be considerate of other people's prayerfulness is to take care to speak not merely in a quiet voice but in a whisper.

---

[988] PG 56:103 (as translated in: Goldfrank, *The Monastic Rule of Iosif Volotsky,* 128).

[989] Clarke, *The Ascetic Works of St. Basil,* 293 (Rule 173 in the *Shorter Rules*).

[990] Moore, *St. Seraphim of Sarov: A Spiritual Biography,* 64.

[991] Γέροντος Αἰμιλιανοῦ, *Νηπτικὴ Ζωὴ καὶ Ἀσκητικοὶ Κανόνες,* 64.

As St. Iosif Volotsky wrote: "During the chant in the church and the refectory, when brothers come to the superior with spiritual or physical matters, he shall converse with them briefly and calmly, in a whisper."[992]

Gerondissa Makrina of blessed memory[993] gave the following rules to her nuns: "Inside the church we should walk very quietly with our head down, with great reverence and the fear of God. With the same reverence we should stand during the services. Laughter and talking are forbidden at the chanter's stand (punishment: abstention from Holy Communion)."[994] Elder Ephraim considered every movement from one place to another during the service to be a kind of disorderliness. That is why he frequently expressed his sad displeasure with some who were constantly leaving their stall.

The Second Rule of the Fathers (written in Gaul in the fifth century) states: "They will see to it that all of the brothers not falter nor go out of doors unnecessarily at the time of office."[995] St. Athanasios of Athos attached so much importance to remaining in church that he wrote in his rule: "There is also a doorkeeper who guards the entrance to the church, whose first task is to demand of those who come late a reason for their tardiness, and then, after one exit, he forbids those who want to leave at an inopportune moment from going out again."[996] St. Symeon the New Theologian explained: "So make this a law for yourself, that you never leave before the last prayer of the Office, unless there is urgent necessity or physical need. As we have said, remain standing in your place, for, as it is written, 'He who endures to the end will be saved.'[997] Not only will he be saved, but he will receive help, at first without perceiving it in the illumination that comes from Almighty God."[998]

Elder Aimilianos taught his monks the importance of standing:

> During the church service it is natural to be standing. If others are sitting, that doesn't mean that I should also sit. It is likely that they are sick—or more likely that they are indolent souls, especially if the service is brief. When Vespers lasts forty-five minutes and the morning service lasts two and a half hours, can't we remain standing? If not, either our brain isn't working properly, or we are exhausted due to the scattering

---

[992] Goldfrank, *The Monastic Rule of Iosif Volotsky,* 275.

[993] Gerondissa Makrina Vassopoulou was a holy disciple of St. Joseph the Hesychast and then of Elder Ephraim. Her biography and homilies have been published in the book *Words of the Heart: Gerondissa Makrina Vassopoulou,* (Goldendale: St. John the Forerunner Greek Orthodox Monastery, 2018).

[994] Rules #23–24. Similarly, St. Columbanus wrote in his communal rule: "Him who is smiling at the synaxis, that is, at the office of prayers, [is to be punished] with six blows; if his laughter has broken out aloud, with an imposition, unless it has happened pardonably" *Sancti Columbani Opera,* 149: http://www.ucc.ie/celt /online/T201052.html

[995] Franklin, *Early Monastic Rules,* 37. Likewise, Gerondissa Makrina wrote: "During the services, it is forbidden to go in and out of the church without great necessity" (Rule #22).

[996] Thomas and Hero, *Byzantine Monastic Foundation Documents,* 25.

[997] Mt. 10:22.

[998] C. J. de Catanzaro, *Symeon the New Theologian: Discourses,* 276.

of our personality. For the most part, exhaustion is not a matter of labor but a matter of feebleness of soul. Whenever someone is sitting, it is usually because his soul is ill. Few are the bodily reasons for which someone needs to remain seated....

So I will not also sit during the service, merely because my brethren are unbalanced. On the contrary, by standing I should remind the others that we are angels and are praying together as angels. When all the saints and angels stand with fear and trembling in the altar, it is incomprehensible for us to be sitting. Of course, in the monastery we implement tolerance, kindness, and leniency so that we do not offend the other person. Does he want to sit? Let him sit.... But if someone is sitting [during the service] merely because the others are sitting, he is sinning before God, even if unawares.[999]

The holy Fathers attached great importance to the manner of singing in church. They stated in Canon LXXV of the Sixth Ecumenical Synod: "We wish those who attend church for the purpose of chanting neither to employ disorderly cries and to force nature to cry out aloud, nor to foist in anything that is not becoming and proper to a church; but, on the contrary, to offer such psalmodies with much attentiveness and contriteness to God."[1000] Commenting on this, St. Nicodemos of the Holy Mountain wrote:

The chanting, or psalmody, that is done in churches is in the nature of begging God to be appeased for our sins. Whoever begs and prayerfully supplicates must have a humble and contrite manner; but to cry out manifests a manner that is audacious and irreverent. On this account the present Canon commands that those who chant in the churches refrain from forcing their nature to yell, but also from saying anything else that is unsuitable for the church.... [They] shall offer their psalmodies with great care to God, who looks into the hidden recesses of the heart; i.e., into the psalmody and prayer that are framed mentally in the heart rather than uttered in external cries.[1001]

Similarly, St. Gregory of Sinai instructed: "Our psalmody should be angelic, not unspiritual and secular. For to psalmodize with clamour and a loud voice is a sign of inner turbulence."[1002] Likewise, St. John Chrysostom said: "We should offer up doxologies to God with fear and a contrite heart, in order that they may be accepted like fragrant incense."[1003] Abba Pambo taught: "It behooves us to offer our prayers to God with fear and trembling, tears and sighs, and for our voices to be sober, contrite, measured, and humble."[1004] St. Silouan the Athonite added: "Sing to God in love and humility of spirit, for the Lord rejoiceth therein."[1005]

---

[999] Γέροντος Αἰμιλιανοῦ, *Νηπτικὴ Ζωὴ καὶ Ἀσκητικοὶ Κανόνες,* 93–94.

[1000] Agapius and Nicodemus, *The Rudder,* 379.

[1001] Ibid., 380.

[1002] Palmer, Sherrard, Ware, *The Philokalia,* Vol. 4, 278–79.

[1003] St. John Chrysostom, "I Saw the Lord Sitting on a Throne," as quoted in Agapius and Nicodemus, *The Rudder,* 380.

[1004] Chrysostomos, *The Evergetinos, Book II,* 94–95.

[1005] Sakharov, *Saint Silouan the Athonite,* 455.

As with any pleasure, caution is needed with the pleasure of singing that it lead us towards God instead of away from Him. St. Basil the Great warned: "When pleasure predominates during psalmody, then through this pleasure we are brought down to passions of the flesh." St. Jerome recommended: "Let the servant of God sing in such a manner that the words of the text rather than the voice of the singer cause delight."[1006] In the same spirit, Blessed Augustine declared: "When it happens to me that the song moves me more than the thing which is sung, I confess that I have sinned blamefully and then prefer not to hear the singer."[1007] St. John of Sinai, counselled: "Let us examine during psalmody what kind of sweetness comes to us from the demon of fornication and, on the other hand, what kind of sweetness come to us from the words of the Spirit and from the grace and power contained in them."[1008]

St. Chrodegang advised that those who cannot sing well should remain silent: "For those who are not expert in this skill [of singing] it is more fitting that they be silent until they have learned it better, rather than wanting to sing what they cannot sing, and, therefore causing the others to be out of tune."[1009] St. Nicetas of Remesiana, however, recommended that such people should just sing more quietly: "If one cannot sing in tune with the others, it is better to sing in a low voice rather than drown the others. In this way he will take his part in the service without interfering with the community singing."[1010]

7) Behavior in one's Cell

St. Paisius Velichkovsky summarized the teachings of the holy Fathers on behavior in one's cell in the regulations for his monastery as follows:

> The brethren must live in their cells with the fear of God. According to the tradition of the holy Fathers they must prefer mental prayer over any other ascetical labor, as God's love, the source of virtue, is fulfilled in the heart by the mind. This is the teaching of many God-bearing Fathers. Besides prayer, they have psalmody and guided reading of the Old and New Testaments and of instructive patristic writings. Not only in their cells but in all places, and during any activity, the brethren must remember death and their sins, the dread Judgment of Christ, eternal torments, the Kingdom of Heaven and self-reproach. The brethren must exercise themselves in the arts or handicrafts designated to them by their superior. Idleness is not permitted, for it is the source

---

[1006] As quoted in *St. Meinrad Historical Essays,* vol. 2 (Indiana: St. Meinrad Seminary, 1931), 13.

[1007] Augustine, *Confessions,* PL 32:800.

[1008] Holy Transfiguration Monastery, *The Ladder of Divine Ascent,* 111.

[1009] Langefeld, *The Old English Version of the Enlarged Rule of Chrodegang,* 376.

[1010] *Nicetas of Remesiana, Sulpicius Severus, Vincent of Lerins, Prosper of Aquitaine,* Fathers of the Church, vol. 7 (Washington, D.C.: Catholic University of America Press, 1949), 75.

of every evil. Premature departure from one's cell and useless conversation must be avoided and fled from as one flees from poison.[1011]

St. Paisios of the Holy Mountain also taught the primary place of prayer is in one's cell: "It befits a monk to be alone and, when alone in his cell, to find rest most of all in his prayer. After all, this is why he is called a monk[1012]—to live alone with God and, instead of talking with people, to converse unceasingly with God. The more he avoids conversations with men, the more he is helped in his prayer and, consequently, by his prayer helps others."[1013]

8) Behavior at Meals

The angel who appeared to St. Pachomios instructed him to tell his monks: "While eating they shall cover their heads with their hoods, so that a brother may not see his brother chewing. Nor shall one talk while eating or cast his eyes anywhere besides his own plate or table."[1014] It is evident from the writings of St. John Cassian that the monks of fourth-century Egypt heeded this instruction from the angel. For he wrote: "While they are eating with their hoods drawn lower than their eyebrows lest a free view facilitate a roving curiosity, they can see nothing more than the table and the food that is put on it or taken off of it. The result of this is that no one notices how or how much another person is eating."[1015]

Elder Aimilianos explained why this was done: "The Fathers were embarrassed to eat in the presence of others, so they would cover their face. Because of this, also in the monasteries monks would lower their cowls, not only so that they would not see each other, but also so that they would not speak and fall into temptation. A third reason was so that others would not see them eating. In this way, no one knew if they were eating or how much they were eating.[1016]

St. Pachomios added: "If anything is needed at table no one shall dare to speak, but he shall make a sign to the ministers by a sound. When you come out of the meal you shall not speak while going back to your own place."[1017] Nikon of the Black Mountain explained: "It is proper that there be great precision, so that at the refectory table no one speaks any word whatever other than the verse and the lection. For the divine Fathers say concerning

---

[1011] Chetverikov, *Starets Paisii Velichkovskii,* 135.

[1012] In Greek the word for "monk" is μοναχός, which means "alone."

[1013] Elder Paisios, *Epistles,* 122.

[1014] Veilleux, *Pachomian Koinonia,* vol. 2, 127.

[1015] Ramsey, *John Cassian: The Institutes,* 87 (iv. 17). As for us, however, since the contemporary shape of the cowls of male monastics prevents us from using them as blinds, we can at least preserve the spirit of this rule by making a deliberate effort to keep our eyes from wandering.

[1016] Γέροντος Αἰμιλιανοῦ, *Νηπτικὴ Ζωὴ καὶ Ἀσκητικοὶ Κανόνες,* 214.

[1017] Veilleux, *Pachomian Koinonia,* vol. 2, 150.

this: 'The holy sacrificial altar and the brotherhood's table at dinner time are equivalent.'"[1018]

St. John Cassian mentioned that the original Egyptian practice was to keep silence at meals without a reading.[1019] But the practice advocated by St. Basil the Great of having one monk read to the others during meals[1020] prevailed as monasticism developed.

St. Symeon the New Theologian advised how to behave at meals as follows:

> When you have begun to eat together with your fathers and brethren, take heed to yourself. Sit in total recollection and silence without talking to anyone at all, but pay attention to the reading and so be nourished in soul, no less than in body, from the inspired utterances of the Spirit. Since you have a twofold being, that is, composed of soul and body, you must likewise have twofold nourishment....
>
> Do not be curious about the portions that are set before you on the table, which happens to be larger or smaller, but accept with all thankfulness the amount that is given to you. But eat it with restraint; in all respects avoid satiety, considering yourself to be unworthy of the common table of the brethren.[1021]

St. Benedict taught: "Let the deepest silence be maintained [during meals] that no whispering or voice be heard except that of the reader alone. But let the brethren so help each other to what is needed for eating and drinking, that no one need ask for anything. If, however, anything should be wanted, let it be asked for by means of a sign of any kind rather than a sound. And let no one presume to ask any questions there, either about the book or anything else, in order that no cause to speak be given [to the devil] (Eph. 4:27; 1 Tim. 5:14), unless, perchance, the Superior wisheth to say a few words for edification."[1022]

St. Sophrony of Essex did just this, for he "used to interrupt the reading [during meals] and comment on what was read. At times of particular inspiration, he would continue speaking for hours, until the next meal."[1023] *The Rule of the Master* suggested that during the meal the abbot should ask the fathers questions about what was just read in order to make sure that they are paying attention.[1024] *The Rule of Tallaght* (written in eighth-century

---

[1018] As quoted in Goldfrank, *The Monastic Rule of Iosif Volotsky,* 180 (referring to Nikon, *Taktikon* 1:6).

[1019] Vid. Ramsey, *John Cassian: The Institutes,* 87 (iv. 17).

[1020] Vid. Clarke, *The Ascetic Works of St. Basil,* 296 (Rule 180 in the *Shorter Rules*).

[1021] C. J. de Catanzaro, *Symeon the New Theologian: Discourses,* 278–79.

[1022] *Rule of St. Benedict,* Chapter XXXVIII. Complete silence during meals was also required by *The Rule for Nuns of St. Caesarius of Arles:* "If there be some need, she ... shall seek what is necessary by nod rather than by speech" (McCarthy, *The Rule for Nuns of St. Caesarius of Arles,* 175).

[1023] Σωφρονίου, *Οἰκοδομώντας τὸν Ναὸ τοῦ Θεοῦ, Τόμος Α´,* 22.

[1024] "While the Rule is being read during the meal, let the abbot, in order to stimulate careful listening by all the brothers, ask any of the brothers at any of the tables, as he pleases, what was read. When one of the brethren repeats what he heard, therefore, it will be evident that he was at that time paying closer attention to the reading than to his stomach, and when one deaf through negligence does not tell what he heard, the presumption will be that he loved the flesh more than the spirit. He must be scolded by his abbot then and there, and rightly so, for his inattention. So each and every brother, afraid of being embarrassed should he be

Ireland) however, recommends that they should be questioned the following day.[1025] The *Rule of the Master* advises: "The reader shall read in an orderly way, taking his time, so that the hearers, though occupied, may clearly recognize what it is they have to fulfill in their deeds."[1026]

St. Athanasios I, the Patriarch of Constantinople, wrote in his monastic rules: "Let neither the superior nor any brother leave the table except for a compelling reason. Let both the superior himself and all [others] have the same bread and wine and cooked food. No one should talk at table, but [all] should pay attention to the readings and delight in the enlightenment from this reading. They should also gratefully glorify [God] the provider of the food."[1027]

St. Ephraim the Syrian said: "Are you sitting at the table to eat? Be attentive to yourself and do not look right and left like an ill-mannered person. A monk who eats the whole pieces of food [instead of the leftovers] is lacking in manners. Do not disdain leftovers, for the Lord told His disciples to gather up the fragments that were left over, lest anything should be lost (Mt. 14:20).... He who does not talk during mealtimes is like one who eats his bread with honey."[1028] Similarly, Abba Isaiah taught: "When you sit at the table with brothers ... stretch out your hand only [to the area immediately] before you, but if something lies in front of another person, do not reach out to it.... Your knees should be held firmly together.... When you are eating, do not raise your head toward your neighbor, nor look here or there, and do not speak unnecessarily."[1029]

A mistake sometimes made by monastics is to complain about the food. St. Ephraim the Syrian advises us: "Do not be thankful just today for the food on your table; indeed, if tomorrow the food is not to your liking, do not murmur against the cook or the one responsible for the refectory."[1030] The *Rule of Paul and Stephen* says: "Let us accept God's gift

---

questioned, will not let his mind wander elsewhere but will pay attention to what is being read" (Eberle, *The Rule of the Master,* 180).

[1025] "He whose duty it was to read ate his own meal earlier at the hour of None [i.e., the ninth hour]. The next day each monk was questioned on the subject of the reading to ensure that they were attentive to what was being read" (Maidín, *The Celtic Monk,* 122).

[1026] *Regula Magistri* 24:18 (as translated in Barry, *Commentary on the Rule of Saint Benedict,* 406).

[1027] Thomas and Hero, *Byzantine Monastic Foundation Documents,* 1501.

[1028] Chrysostomos, *The Evergetinos, Book II,* 169.

[1029] Chryssavgis and Penkett, *Abba Isaiah of Scetis,* 48. Gerondissa Makrina wrote almost the same advice for her nuns: "We should go to the refectory immediately when the semantron strikes. During the meal, there must be absolute silence, our feet should be together, and we should not look at other people's plates. As soon as we have finished eating, we should not look around with curiosity but should lower our heads with reverence and the fear of God" (Rule #17).

[1030] Chrysostomos, *The Evergetinos, Book IV,* 470.

[of food] with no quarreling, no murmuring or resentment."[1031] Likewise, Abba Isaac said: "He who at table chatters, laughs, or reviles the food has withdrawn from God and God has withdrawn from him."[1032] And Abba Isaiah taught: "If a brother cooks something and it does not turn out well, do not say to him, 'You have cooked badly'—as this will mean death for your soul—but examine yourself, thinking that, had you heard this from someone else, you would feel very sad, and then you will find rest."[1033]

Since "the tongue is strengthened by an abundance of food,"[1034] according to St. John of Sinai, the holy Fathers warned against excessive talking after a meal. Abba Isaiah said: "When the office concludes, or when you rise from the meal table, do not delay one another by speaking either about God or about the world, but let each one of you enter his own cell and weep for his sins. If it is necessary to speak to each other, converse only a very little with humility and respect, as if God was listening to you."[1035] Likewise, St. Lazaros of Mt. Galesion said that after church or the meal we should

> go straight to our cell, not clustering together to spend time in idle talk, not sitting drinking and eating together, not leaving our cells out of *akedia* [i.e., listlessness] and going to the cells of others—unless it should be necessary—but rather remaining steadfastly in our own cell. Lest, he [St. Lazaros] would say, leaving our own cells and going off to those of others, we should see or hear or say things we would rather not. For this is what leads to words, in this way we come to judge our brothers and abuse them, till the blinded soul loses her way and strays from the right goal. We give up looking at ourselves to gossip about the faults of others, unable to stop ourselves or recognize our own weakness, we begin bandying insults and quarreling and daily provoking scandals with the brothers.[1036]

St. Nectarios of Aegina wrote to the abbess of his monastery: "The female body was made to have greater needs because it was intended to tire more quickly. For this reason, women who want to emulate the diet of men tire quickly. A woman has a natural need for more food and more sleep. Remember that you are women, and do not try to rival men."[1037]

Monastics keep all the appointed fasts of the Church. In addition to fasting on Wednesdays and Fridays (as laymen do), monastics fast on Mondays as well, in honor of the angels, whom they strive to imitate. On fasting days, fish, eggs, dairy products, oil, and wine are not consumed.

[1031] Barry Hagan, "The Rule of Paul and Stephen," ch. 18.

[1032] As quoted in Goldfrank, *The Monastic Rule of Iosif Volotsky,* 134.

[1033] Chryssavgis and Penkett, *Abba Isaiah of Scetis,* 70.

[1034] Holy Transfiguration Monastery, *The Ladder of Divine Ascent,* 100 (Step 14:24).

[1035] Chryssavgis and Penkett, *Abba Isaiah of Scetis,* 40.

[1036] Thomas and Hero, *Byzantine Monastic Foundation Documents,* 159.

[1037] Strongylis, *St. Nectarios of Pentapolis and the Island of Aegina,* vol. 2, 182 (Letter #99); Ἅγιος Νεκτάριος Πενταπόλεως, *Κατηχητικαὶ Ἐπιστολαί,* 193 (Ἐπιστολὴ 99).

The canons of the Church prohibit olive oil on fasting days, but they do not mention whether or not other oils are allowed.[1038] Elder Ephraim held the opinion that other vegetable oils are generally to be avoided on fasting days, although he would frequently make exceptions and allow them. He also taught that it is not necessary to check the ingredients of a food that is usually allowed during a fast (such as bread) before eating it. If, however, we are aware that a food that is usually allowed during a fast does contain non-fasting ingredients (such as dairy products), then he said we should not eat it during a fast. As for dietary supplements (such as fish oil capsules or protein powder containing egg), he believed that such things may be consumed even during a fast if taken for health reasons.

St. Symeon the New Theologian emphasized how beneficial fasting is:

> Let each one of us keep in mind the benefit of fasting and what gifts from God he has enjoyed in these few [fasting] days and so become more eager for the days to come. For this healer of our souls is effective, in the case of one to quieten the fevers and impulses of the flesh, in another to assuage bad temper, in yet another to drive away sleep, in another to stir up zeal, and in yet another to restore purity of mind and to set him free from evil thoughts. In one it will control his unbridled tongue and, as it were by a bit,[1039] restrain it by the fear of God and prevent it from uttering idle or corrupt words.[1040] In another it will invisibly guard his eyes and fix them on high instead of allowing them to roam hither and thither, and thus cause him to look on himself and teach him to be mindful of his own faults and shortcomings. Fasting gradually disperses and drives away spiritual darkness and the veil of sin that lies on the soul, just as the sun dispels the mist. Fasting enables us spiritually to see that spiritual air in which Christ, the Sun who knows no setting, does not rise, but shines without ceasing. Fasting, aided by vigil, penetrates and softens hardness of heart. Where once were the vapors of drunkenness it causes fountains of compunction to spring forth. I beseech you, brethren, let each of us strive that this may happen in us![1041]

Many other saints also praised the value of fasting. St. Photios the Great wrote: "Fasting is a medicine that cleanses the passions."[1042] Abba Hyperechios said: "Fasting is a check against sin for the monk. He who discards it is like a 'rampaging stallion' (cf. Jer. 5.8)."[1043] St. Neilos the Ascetic wrote: "The bread of fasting is good because it is free of the leaven

---

[1038] For example, St. Nicodemos of the Holy Mountain wrote in his interpretation of the 69th Apostolic Canon: "Fasting on every Wednesday and Friday ought to be done by 'eating dry bread' [ξηροφαγία] in a similar manner as in the case of Lent. 'Eating dry bread' is the eating of bread once a day, at the ninth hour, without eating olive oil [ἔλαιον] or drinking wine" (Agapius and Nicodemus, *The Rudder,* 125).

[1039] Vid. Jas. 3:3, 8.

[1040] Eph. 4:29; Mt. 12:36.

[1041] C. J. de Catanzaro, *Symeon the New Theologian: The Discourses,* 168–69.

[1042] PG 88:1041.

[1043] Ward, *The Sayings of the Desert Fathers,* 238.

of pleasures."[1044] St. Isaac the Syrian said: "A mourner [in Syriac this word is also used to denote a monk] is he who passes all the days of his life in hunger and thirst for the sake of his hope in good things to come."[1045]

St. Joseph the Hesychast loved fasting so much that he would do extra "lents" in addition to Great Lent by eating only food without oil for forty consecutive days.[1046] St. Paisios of the Holy Mountain commented: "In the old days, our holy Fathers greatly preferred food without oil and lengthy fasts, and this is why they had sanctity and physical health and strength. On the contrary, nowadays with the hyperconsumerism in foods in their variety and quantity, the sanctity of monks has decreased and their physical and spiritual illnesses have increased."[1047]

Many monasteries have the custom of receiving Communion only following a fasting day. For example, at Philotheou Monastery on Mount Athos, even though the Divine Liturgy was served daily, we received Communion only every Tuesday, Thursday, and Saturday, as well as every other Sunday, but daily during fasting periods. The reason for this custom is that experience has shown that eating only dry foods the day or days prior to receiving Communion helps a person be more prepared. The liturgical historian Ioannis Fountoulis explained the origin of this custom:

> [In Apostolic times] fasting was not considered a prerequisite for approaching Holy Communion. The Divine Liturgy was performed in the evening at common meals, the "love-feasts" (ἀγάπη), after everyone had already eaten at the common table. That is, they repeated with precision the practice of the Lord, Who established the Mystery "after dinner" (Lk. 22:20) in the upper chamber of holy Sion. Later, out of reverence, the Divine Liturgy was separated from meals and took place in the morning. Then the custom of abstaining from all food from midnight until the time of Communion gradually began to appear. This was—and continues to be until today—the official and required preparatory fast for Holy Communion.... This "eucharistic fast" is required by many canons.[1048]
>
> Fasting for many days (eating dry food, that is, and not the complete abstention from food) as preparation for Holy Communion was unknown to the ancient Church. The most distinctive proof of this is the Sunday liturgy. Serving the liturgy presupposes that the faithful will commune. But how could they commune if fasting the previous

---

[1044] PG 79:1244.

[1045] Holy Transfiguration Monastery, *The Ascetical Homilies of Saint Isaac the Syrian,* 170 (Homily 59).

[1046] Vid. Elder Ephraim, *My Elder Joseph the Hesychast,* 156.

[1047] As quoted in Χριστοδούλου, *Ὁ Ὀρθόδοξος Μοναχισμός,* 87–88.

[1048] Ἰωάννου Μ. Φουντούλη, *Ἀπαντήσεις εἰς Λειτουργικὰς Ἀπορίας,* Τόμος Α΄, ἔκδοση στ΄ (Ἀθήνα: Ἀποστολικὴ Διακονία τῆς Ἐκκλησίας τῆς Ἑλλάδος, 2006), 120–21. The canons requiring a eucharistic fast are Canon XLVIII in Carthage, Canon XXIX of the Sixth Ecumenical Council, and Canon IX of St. Nicephoros the Confessor.

day were obligatory, considering that fasting on Saturday (except for only Holy Saturday) is forbidden by the canons with strict penances?[1049]

This practice [of eating dry food the previous day or days] probably began during the Turkish Occupation [of Greece], and is due to an attempt to make the faithful as perfectly prepared as possible, as well as to make them approach the Mystery at less frequent intervals.[1050]

Since the custom of eating dry food on the day or days prior to Holy Communion is only a historically recent practice in the Church, it follows that this cannot be an inherent prerequisite for receiving Holy Communion, despite its great benefit. St. Nicodemos of the Holy Mountain had a similar understanding, for he wrote: "In spite of the fact that fasting before partaking of Communion is not decreed by the divine canons, nevertheless, those who are able to fast even a whole week before it, do well."[1051]

9) Punctuality

It is important that monks come on time to church and meals—not only for the sake of order and for not scandalizing laymen, but even for the inherent spiritual benefit. Abba Dorotheos related an incident about an elder who saw an angel setting a holy seal on the brethren in church:

> The man in bright raiments said to him: "I am an Angel of the Lord, and I have been given a command to seal with the sign of the Cross all those who are in Church from the beginning of the service, on account of their eagerness, diligence, and good intentions."
>
> The Elder replied, saying, "Why, then, do you make the sign of the Cross over the place of some of those who are missing?"
>
> The holy Angel answered him: "Those brothers who are diligent and of good intention, but out of some need or illness are missing with the blessing of their spiritual Father, or who, in obedience to some command are busy somewhere else and not in attendance for that reason—these, despite their absence, I seal with the sign of the Cross, since in spirit they are with those who are chanting the service. Only those who would otherwise be able to be present, but because of their laziness are absent, am I commanded not to seal with the sign of the Cross, for they are made unworthy thereof by their own actions."[1052]

St. Barsanuphius of Optina once told his closest disciple about a similar incident in Kiev:

[1049] Ibid., 121. For the canons forbidding fasting on Saturday, see Apostolic Canon LXIV and Canon LV of the Sixth Ecumenical Council.

[1050] Ἰωάννου Μ. Φουντούλη, *Ἀπαντήσεις εἰς Λειτουργικὰς Ἀπορίας*, Τόμος Β΄, ἔκδοση δ΄ (Ἀθήνα: Ἀποστολικὴ Διακονία τῆς Ἐκκλησίας τῆς Ἑλλάδος, 1994), 65.

[1051] Νικοδήμου τοῦ Ἁγιορείτου, *Πηδάλιον*, 336 (commentary on Canon XII of the Sixth Ecumenical Council); see also Agapius and Nicodemus, *The Rudder*, 307.

[1052] Metropolitan Chrysostomos, *Our Holy Father Dorotheos of Gaza*, 186.

You need to go to services before the bell rings, so that the bell finds you already in church. Why is that? Because at that time the Mother of God enters the church.... Once he [St. Paisius of Kiev] was coming to Vespers; the bells had already rung. There was no one in the church. The altar-attendant put everything in order and walked out of the church. He was left alone. Suddenly he heard a rustling, as if someone were walking. He looked and saw a tall, majestic Woman accompanied by the holy Apostle Peter and someone else. She glanced into the church and uttered the following words: "They have rung for Vespers and there are no monks." Then, turning to St. Paisius, she blessed him, signing him with a broad sign of the Cross, and left the church, rising up from the earth at the same time. St. Paisius went out of the church after her to watch her. She rose up higher and higher, until she disappeared entirely from his sight."[1053]

Some monastic canons assigned punishments to those who come late to the services. For example, St. Lazaros of Mt. Galesion "ordered that to those who did not arrive for the service at the beginning of the matins, the cellarer should not supply the portion of wine allotted to them, or even, sometimes, food."[1054] And St. Caesarius of Arles wrote: "She who comes late, after the signal has been given to Office or to work, will be subject to rebuke as is fitting. If, after a second or a third admonition she does not correct the fault, she should be withdrawn from community life and from the common meal."[1055]

10) Silence

Antiochos (the author of the *Pandects*) concisely declared the reason for monastic silence: "A monk should say many things to God, but few to men; for immoderate loquacity, which distracts the mind, not only makes him idle with regard to spiritual work, but also surrenders him to the demon of listlessness."[1056] St. Ephraim the Syrian observed: "He who speaks much among brothers will be hated, whereas he who keeps a watch over his mouth will be loved."[1057] St. Diadochos taught: "Just as, when the doors of the baths are left continually open, the heat inside is quickly driven out, so also the soul, when it wishes to say many things, even though everything that it says may be good, disperses its concentration through the door of the voice."[1058] Moreover, Christ Himself warns us of the danger of idle talk: "Every idle word that men shall speak they shall give account thereof in the day of judgment;"[1059]

[1053] Afanasiev, *St. Barsanuphius of Optina*, 786.

[1054] Thomas and Hero, *Byzantine Monastic Foundation Documents*, 159.

[1055] McCarthy, *The Rule for Nuns of St. Caesarius of Arles*, 174.

[1056] Chrysostomos, *The Evergetinos, Book II*, 356.

[1057] Ibid., 355.

[1058] Ibid., 357

[1059] Mt. 12:36.

Abba Arsenios remarked: "I have often repented of having spoken, but never of having been silent."[1060] St. Benedict wrote: "The eleventh degree of humility is, that, when a monk speaketh, he speak gently and without laughter, humbly and with gravity, with few and sensible words, and that he be not loud of voice, as it is written: 'The wise man is known by the fewness of his words' (Sir. 21:27)."[1061] The "Rule of St. Ailbe" states: "Two-thirds of piety consists in being silent."[1062] St. Sophrony of Essex observed: "When someone talks a lot, he becomes spiritually weak."[1063] Elder Aimilianos taught his monks: "Silence characterizes a man of God, for within silence is God and prayer. Speaking and discussions are a departure from our true state."[1064]

St. Basil the Great saw silence as especially beneficial for novices. He wrote:

> The practice of silence is beneficial for novices. For, if they control the tongue, they will both give sufficient proof of continence and will learn in quiet, eagerly, and attentively, from those that are skilled in instruction, how they must ask questions and answer each individual question. For there is a tone of voice, a moderateness in length, a propriety of time, and a specific appropriateness in the use of words which are especially characteristic of those leading the devout life, and these qualities cannot be taught to one who has not acquired them by constant practice. By reason of its restful quiet, silence induces forgetfulness of the past and affords leisure to learn good habits. Consequently, silence should be kept, except, of course, for the chanting of the psalms, unless some private need pertaining to the care of one's soul or an emergency in the task at hand should arise or some similar question require an answer.[1065]

There are numerous examples from the lives of the saints who took the matter of silence after church services very seriously. For example, "Abba Macarius the Great said to the brothers at Scetis, when he dismissed the assembly, 'Flee, my brothers.' One of the old men asked him: 'Where could we flee beyond this desert?' He placed his finger on his lips and said: 'Flee that!' And he went into his cell, shut the door, and sat down."[1066] The fourth-century *Regulations of Horsiesios* command: "When the synaxis is dismissed, let us recite [prayers] until we reach our houses. Let no one speak to his neighbor as he leaves the synaxis. Even for matters that relate to the community."[1067] Likewise, St. John Cassian

---

[1060] Ward, *The Sayings of the Desert Fathers*, 18.

[1061] *Rule of St. Benedict*, Chapter VII.

[1062] Maidín, *The Celtic Monk*, 25. This intriguing claim makes one wonder what the other third consists of!

[1063] Hierotheos, *"I Know a Man in Christ,"* 382.

[1064] Γέροντος Αἰμιλιανοῦ, *Νηπτικὴ Ζωὴ καὶ Ἀσκητικοὶ Κανόνες*, 101.

[1065] Βασιλείου τοῦ Μεγάλου, *Ἀσκητικὰ Α΄*, ΕΠΕ 8, 250–51; see also Wagner, *Saint Basil: Ascetical Works*, vol. 9, 263 (Question 13 in the *Long Rules*).

[1066] PG 65:270B; see also Ward, *The Sayings of the Desert Fathers*, 131 (Macarius 16).

[1067] Veilleux, *Pachomian Koinonia*, vol. 2, 201.

wrote: "When the psalms are finished, then, and the daily gathering … has broken up, none of them dares to linger or to chat for a while with anyone else."[1068]

St. Symeon the New Theologian taught:

> Once the morning Office of praise is finished, do not, as soon as you have left the church, start talking to one man and the other and so be distracted in idle talk…. If on your way [back to your cell] you see a brother by himself, or sitting down with others and chatting outside the time, make a reverence and pass in silence. Do not go to sit with them, but be mindful of the psalmist's saying, "Blessed is the man that hath not walked in the counsel of the ungodly, nor stood in the way of sinners, and hath not sat in the seat of the scornful."[1069] For such people are a plague, as Paul says, "Bad company ruins good morals."[1070] If a plague is anything, so is also corruption. Do not then, beloved, sit with those who talk idly, and do not say, "I too want to hear what you are saying," but as I have said, make a reverence and pass by. Observe silence and solitude: silence by saying to yourself, "What good have I to say, who am altogether mud and a fool? Besides, I am a stranger and unworthy to speak and listen and to be numbered among men."[1071]

With the same understanding, St. Gregory Palamas said:

> When you come out after the dismissal on the Lord's Day and are at leisure from earthly work for the sake of Him whose day it is, carefully search to see if there is an imitator of the apostles [immediately after the Resurrection] who mostly stays indoors, longing for God with silent prayer, psalmody and other suitable practices. Approach such a person and enter his small room with faith as though you were entering a heavenly place containing the Spirit's sanctifying power.[1072]

It is particularly harmful to have discussions following the Divine Liturgy, especially if one has just received Holy Communion. When Abba Isaac of Thebes was asked why he would flee from the brethren at the end of the Divine Liturgy, he replied: "I am not running away from the brothers but from the evil craftiness of the demons. For if a person has a lighted lamp and hangs around, standing out in the wind, it is extinguished by it. So we who are enlightened by the Holy Spirit in the holy Eucharist, if we hang around outside the cell, our mind is darkened."[1073] This is why Elder Athanasios of Gregoriou taught: "Be careful. After Liturgy, withdraw somewhere, and in silence experience whatever you have been given. Avoid speaking—and never laugh—after Divine Liturgy."[1074]

[1068] Ramsey, *John Cassian: The Institutes,* 47 (ii. 15.1).

[1069] Ps. 1:1.

[1070] 1 Cor. 15:33.

[1071] C. J. de Catanzaro, *Symeon the New Theologian: Discourses,* 276–77.

[1072] Veniamin, *Saint Gregory Palamas: The Homilies,* 143.

[1073] Wortley, *The Alphabetical Sayings of the Desert Fathers,* 162.

[1074] Archimandrite Cherubim (Karambelas), *Contemporary Ascetics of Mount Athos,* vol. 1 (Platina: St. Herman of Alaska Brotherhood, 2000), 110.

The holy Fathers found great benefit in keeping silence also in the evening before going to bed. St. Benedict taught: "Monks should always be given to silence, especially, however, during the hours of the night.... After going out from Compline, let there be no more permission from that time on for anyone to say anything."[1075] Likewise, *The Rule of the Master* orders:

> Then [after Compline] the abbot says to all: "Now, brothers, bestir yourselves, so that, everything having been taken care of, there be no occasion requiring us to talk. For it is now time to commend ourselves to the Lord, and now that we have finished all the duties of the day and are entering upon the night, let our mouth be closed to rest from speech as also our eyes for sleep." So when all this has been done, though permission to speak and give some order may still be granted, when Compline is at an end let them say this verse: "Set a watch, O Lord, before my mouth and a gate around my lips" (Ps. 140:3). Then let them begin the silence and go to bed, and let them keep so strict a silence that one would think not a single one of the brothers were there at all.[1076]

The rule of St. Waldebert also says: "From the hour of compline, when prayer is given over to capturing sleep, none should presume to say anything at all unless some great need of the monastery demands it."[1077] Likewise, the 8th-century rule of St. Chrodegang declared: "After the singing of Compline they shall keep the utmost silence and perform secret prayers with anxiety for their sins, and afterwards thank God for His merciful heart and His guardianship."[1078] The 14th-century typikon of the Monastery of St. John the Forerunner in Serres had a similar understanding:

> No one shall have permission to sit in the courtyard of the monastery and carry on a conversation after the dismissal of compline and after bowing to the superior and receiving his absolution. This was the rule legislated by the holy fathers themselves. In fact, such activity was totally forbidden. Just as they forbid such a practice as evil and conducive to spiritual harm, so I, too, forbid it. Therefore, those who wish to make progress as God [wishes], should each withdraw to his own cell after greeting the superior; each one should turn his attention quietly and peacefully to himself, and to God, and he should look to nothing else but to propitiating our universal judge and God for the sins, both conscious and unconscious, which he committed during the entire day.[1079]

In the 15th century St. Iosif Volotsky had the same rule for silence but exempted the abbot: "After Compline, as the God-bearing Fathers discerned, it is not proper to stand and converse in the monastery or to assemble in the cells. Only the *hegumen* may speak out

---

[1075] *Rule of St. Benedict,* Chapter XLII.

[1076] Eberle, *The Rule of the Master,* 191.

[1077] J. A. McNamara and J. Halborg, *The Rule of a Certain Father to the Virgins,* chapter 9.

[1078] Saint Chrodegang, *The Old English Version of the Enlarged Rule of Chrodegang,* Brigitte Langefeld, ed. (Frankfurt am Main: P. Lang, 2003), 369.

[1079] Thomas and Hero, *Byzantine Monastic Foundation Documents,* 1606–7.

about the needs of the cloister, but for the sake of good order he shall speak in a cell."[1080] Gerondissa Makrina wrote in her rules to nuns: "Discussions are forbidden after Compline (punishment: 100 prostrations)."[1081]

Elder Ephraim also taught that speaking is absolutely forbidden during vigil, and is only permitted after Compline for something extremely urgent. He explained that the reason why speaking is prohibited after Compline is because it usually harms a monastic's subsequent vigil, either because those discussions keep him up late or simply because their content will still be on his mind when he is trying to pray in his vigil. A further practical reason for silence after Compline and after the Divine Liturgy is that these are times when most of the fathers rest, and their sleep could be disturbed if others are talking nearby.

In his commentary on James 1:19 ("let every man be swift to hear, slow to speak"), St. Nicodemos of the Holy Mountain included the following Patristic teachings:

> Abba Nistheros said to Abba Joseph: "Be silent, and when a conversation takes place, it is better to listen than to speak."[1082] And a wise man once said: "We have two ears but one tongue so that we would listen more than we speak."[1083] Likewise St. Basil the Great in his book *On Virginity*[1084] said: "Since nature took into account the necessary ratio of listening to speaking, it provided for us two ears and one tongue, since we should listen to instruction twice as much as we speak."[1085] ... The author of Ecclesiastes said: "A fool multiplies words."[1086] St. John of Karpathos also mentions this verse of James as follows: "A single unbecoming word prevented Moses from entering the Promised Land.[1087] We should not suppose, then, that talkativeness is only a minor disease. Lovers of slander and gossip shut themselves out from the kingdom of heaven.... A wise man said well: 'Better to slip from a height to the ground than to slip with your tongue.'[1088]"[1089,1090]

[1080] Goldfrank, *The Monastic Rule of Iosif Volotsky,* 142.

[1081] Rule #15.

[1082] Ward, *The Sayings of the Desert Fathers,* 130 (Nistheros 3).

[1083] Zeno of Citium (as quoted by Diogenes Laërtius, *Lives and Opinions of Eminent Philosophers,* Book 7, trans. R. D. Hicks [United Kingdom: Harvard University Press, 1972], 23).

[1084] According to Alban Butler: "The book *On Virginity,* under the name of St. Basil, cannot be his work, and is absolutely unworthy to bear so great a name, ... [since] it is addressed to Letoius, bishop of Melitene.... [who] was only made a bishop in 381, two years after the death of St. Basil." Vid. Alban Butler, *The Lives Of The Fathers, Martyrs, And Other Principal Saints,* vol. 4 (New York: Benziger Bros., 1902), 573.

[1085] PG 30:712.

[1086] Eccl. 10:14.

[1087] Vid. Num. 20:12.

[1088] Eccl. 20:18.

[1089] Ἰωάννου τοῦ Καρπαθίου, «Πρὸς τοὺς ἐν τῇ Ἰνδίᾳ μοναχοὺς γράψαντας αὐτῷ παραμυθητικὰ κεφάλαια ρ΄» ἐν *Φιλοκαλία,* τόμος α΄ (1893), 177, κεφ. ϟ΄; see also Palmer, Sherrard, Ware, *The Philokalia,* vol. 1, 319 (St. John of Karpathos 90).

[1090] Νικοδήμου τοῦ Ἁγιορείτου, *Ἑρμηνεία εἰς τὰς Ἑπτὰ Καθολικὰς Ἐπιστολάς,* 62–63.

One method used by the holy Fathers to facilitate more silence was to avoid close proximity with others when walking. For example, "they used to say about Abba Ammōes that when he was on his way to church he would not allow his disciple to walk very close to him, but at a distance. And if he came to ask him about *logismoi* [thoughts], no sooner did he speak to him than he would immediately chase him away, saying: 'I do not let you be very close to me in case some alien discourse should raise its head while we are speaking of spiritual benefit.'"[1091] Similarly, St. Joseph the Hesychast would not allow Fr. Arsenios to walk near him when travelling, but they intentionally remained apart in order to avoid talking.[1092]

St. Caesarius of Arles wrote in his rules for nuns how to work with silence: "They shall do their work, and they should not busy themselves with idle talk according to that saying of the Apostle, 'that they work quietly'[1093] and another saying: 'In much speaking you will not avoid sin.'[1094] And therefore you must speak entirely of that which pertains to the edification and usefulness of the soul. When however the necessity of the work requires it, then they may speak. While the rest are working together, one of the sisters shall read until Terce [i.e., three hours after dawn]; moreover let not meditation on the word of God and the prayer of the heart cease."[1095] Likewise, St. Fructuosus of Braga wrote in his *Rule for the Monastery of Compludo:* "While they work they are not to exchange stories or pleasantries or jokes, but as they work they shall quietly meditate each to himself."[1096]

St. John of Sinai taught in the *Ladder:* "Let us practise extreme silence and ignorance in the presence of the superior. For a silent man is a son of philosophy, always acquiring much knowledge. I have seen a monastic who used to snatch the words from his superior's lips [i.e., he interrupted him], but I despaired of his living in submission when I saw this led to pride and not to humility."[1097]

Elder Aimilianos described the true spirit of silence in the *Regulations of the Holy Cenobium of the Annunciation:*

> In all places within the cenobium quietude shall naturally be sought, since it is proper to monastics "to live for God alone and to occupy their minds with the most divine matters in quietude."[1098] In appropriate places, the nuns may converse for company and edification or may sing hymns in seemly freedom under the eye of the Lord

---

[1091] Wortley, *The Alphabetical Sayings of the Desert Fathers,* 66.

[1092] Vid. Elder Ephraim, *My Elder Joseph the Hesychast,* 176–77.

[1093] 2 Thes. 3:12.

[1094] Prov. 10:19.

[1095] McCarthy, *The Rule for Nuns of St. Caesarius of Arles,* 176.

[1096] Barlow, *The Fathers of the Church: Iberian Fathers,* vol. 63, 162.

[1097] Holy Transfiguration Monastery, *The Ladder of Divine Ascent,* 43 and Ἰωάννου τοῦ Σιναΐτου, *Κλῖμαξ* (Ὠρωπὸς Ἀττικῆς: Ἱερὰ Μονὴ Παρακλήτου, 2002), 98.

[1098] *Χρυσόβουλλον αὐτοκράτορος Μιχαὴλ Η΄ Παλαιολόγου,* vid. Franz Miklosich, Josef Müller, *Acta Et Diplomata Graca Medii Aevi Sacra Et Profana,* vol. 4 (Cambridge: Cambridge University Press, 1871), 333.

Who is everywhere present. A stultifying and timorous atmosphere shall not prevail, but rather one of seemly and legitimate freedom. The conversation shall not, however, turn to worldly things. It shall be "seasoned with salt,"[1099] conducted in all refinement and courtesy, turning to things "of good report and pure"[1100] and befitting [monastics]. During the hours of the night, however, all encounters shall be avoided, and at all times any discussion shall be avoided which is pointless, chatty, or gossipy. It shall be a profound inner conviction that the whole of our life together, in its everyday reality, beyond its visible aspect, shall be called holy, a convocation and assembly together with the choirs of angels.[1101]

Elder Aimilianos elaborated more on the value of silence to his monks:

During times of work, the holy Fathers would keep silent. Thus, we keep silent in trapeza and at work. We say only things we have read in the Gospel, what God has told us to say, and what our work requires us to say. Perhaps someone will object: "Won't we suffer boredom with silence?" On the contrary, it is with words that we suffer boredom because they are always the same and because we wound people, and we as a body fall apart....

Another illness is talking a lot while working. Undoubtedly, when something is done with a discussion, perhaps something good will happen but never something perfect, because it is not an acceptable sacrifice to God. It is a work and labor that does not bear divine fruit, so we do not obtain a treasure in heaven. Only with silence does work become an acceptable sacrifice to God. Our words are an indication of our individualism, our thoughts, our ideas, our knowledge. They reveal that we are just a number in the world and not a member of the body of Christ. If we examine our discussions, we will see that we do not say anything that results from tears in prayer and in our vigil, nothing that is a revelation of the Lord. We say whatever our own individualism hides. But even if we say something spiritual, even then one can find the seeds of our individualism.[1102]

Keeping silence is of no use if inwardly one is judging. As Abba Poemen said: "Someone may seem to be silent, but if in the heart one is condemning others, then one is babbling ceaselessly. And there may be another who talks from morning till evening, and yet in the heart that person is truly silent. That person says nothing that is not profitable."[1103] Elder Ephraim once observed sadly: "Nowadays, [the sin of] judging is as common as bread and cheese [i.e., very prevalent]."

[1099] Col. 4:6.

[1100] Cf. Phil. 4:8.

[1101] Elder Aimilianos, *The Authentic Seal,* 179.

[1102] Γέροντος Αἰμιλιανοῦ, *Νηπτικὴ Ζωὴ καὶ Ἀσκητικοὶ Κανόνες,* 221.

[1103] Ward, *The Sayings of the Desert Fathers,* 171 (Poemen 27).

11) Mutual Respect

Evagrios the Solitary expressed the ideals of monastic brotherly love as follows: "Blessed is the monk who regards every man as God after God. Blessed is the monk who sees everyone's salvation and progress with great joy as if they were his own.... A monk is he who is separated from all and united with all. A monk is he who regards himself as linked with every man, through always seeing himself in each person."[1104]

One way to show respect is to address others with their appropriate title. Gerondissa Makrina wrote to her nuns: "When we address one another, the word 'sister' must precede their name: for example, 'Sister Eleni.'"[1105] This is essentially the same as what St. Benedict wrote: "In naming each other let no one be allowed to address another by his simple name; but let the older style the younger brethren, 'brothers'; let the younger, however, call their elders, 'fathers,' by which is implied the reverence due to a father."[1106] Similarly, St. Chrodegang wrote in his rule: "In addressing each other it is not permitted for any of them to address another by his name only but, according to Roman custom, he shall call him by name first and then add the distinction of his rank. Thus one says: 'Leofwine prior, Wulfstan precentor, Byrhthelm deacon, Cyneweard sexton, Ælfnoð oblate,' and so with everybody."[1107] The reason for these rules was to encourage mutual respect when dealing with the other members of the monastery.

In Athonite monasteries, novices are not addressed with the title "brother" but are simply called by their name because they have no tonsure and are therefore still laymen for all practical purposes. The tonsured monks, however, are called "*Father* so-and-so" by their fellow monks. In one of his homilies at Philotheou Monastery, Elder Ephraim sharply denounced the practice of some monks who were using nicknames for other monks. St. Donatus of Besançon would have agreed with avoiding this kind of familiarity, since he wrote in his rules for nuns: "Any who is called 'little sister' or who call one another 'little sister' [is to be punished with] forty blows if they so transgress."[1108]

St. Sophrony of Essex told his monastics: "Respect every member of this [monastic] family as a gift from our heavenly Father, and pray for each one every day: in the morning and in the evening before you go to sleep at night.... If God grants us love for everyone within our monastic community, this way will be able to inspire also those who come to us. If we lack love amongst us, how will we be able to preach love to others? The gift of

---

[1104] Νείλου τοῦ Ἀσκητοῦ, «Λόγος περὶ προσευχῆς» ἐν *Φιλοκαλία,* τόμος α΄ (1893), 109, κεφ. ρκα΄–ρκε΄; see also Palmer, Sherrard, Ware, *The Philokalia,* vol. 1, 68–69 (Evagrios the Solitary 121–25).

[1105] Rule #4.

[1106] *Rule of St. Benedict,* Chapter LXIII.

[1107] Langefeld, *The Old English Version of the Enlarged Rule of Chrodegang,* 362.

[1108] Donatus of Besançon, "Regula ad Virgines: a Working Translation," ch. 32.

loving in a manner that is heavenly, godly, and eternal does not come easily; it comes through the lamentations of the evening, of the night, when we are alone."[1109]

St. Nicodemos of the Holy Mountain also highlighted how critical it is not to lack love. He wrote: "Monasticism requires that monks have meekness and tranquillity of heart.... If you do not eradicate hatred from your heart and plant love instead, and if you do not stop speaking evil of your brethren, know that (and excuse me for my boldness) in vain you are dwelling in the mountains and hills. In vain are all your ascetical struggles and labors and sweat. Should we say what is even greater? Even if you were to undergo martyrdom for the sake of Christ, your martyrdom would be in vain if you have hatred."[1110]

An important way of showing respect is to listen sincerely to what the other person is trying to tell us. As Stephen Covey observed: "If I were to summarize in one sentence the single most important principle I have learned in the field of interpersonal relations, it would be this: *Seek first to understand, then to be understood....* [This] involves a very deep shift in paradigm. We typically seek first to be understood. Most people do not listen with the intent to understand; they listen with the intent to reply. They're either speaking or preparing to speak."[1111]

It is worth noting that Covey found this maxim of "seeking first to understand" to be the most difficult principle to live. He admitted: "When I am really tired and already convinced I'm right, I really don't want to listen. I may even pretend to listen."[1112] The essence of this pitfall consists in a shift of one's intent from wanting to connect with the other person to wanting to prove who is right. "And I," most of us think, "am certainly the one who is right!" Therefore, if we want people to listen to us, no matter how right we believe we are, we should bear in mind Theodore Roosevelt's astute insight: "Nobody cares how much you know, until they know how much you care."[1113] For even if we are in fact right, human nature makes the other person much more willing to accept our words and change if he knows that we care enough to listen to him.

[1109] Σωφρονίου, *Οἰκοδομῶντας τὸν Ναὸ τοῦ Θεοῦ, Τόμος Α΄*, 307.

[1110] As quoted in the lecture delivered by Archimandrite George Kapsanis "Orthodox Monasticism according to St. Nicodemos of the Holy Mountain" during the First Conference "St. Nicodemos of the Holy Mountain: His Life and Teaching," September 21–23, 1999 (http://www.pigizois.net/pneumatikoi_logoi/orthodojos_monaxismos.htm).

[1111] Stephen R. Covey, *The Seven Habits of Highly Effective People: Powerful Lessons in Personal Change* (New York: Free Press, 2004), 237, 239. This principle of "seeking first to understand" is essentially the same as the principle behind the "talking stick" (mentioned in footnote #439 on page 74 herein) but is implemented with only one other person rather than with a group.

[1112] Ibid., 325.

[1113] Doris E. Curtis, Bryan C. Curtis, *Inspirational Thoughts to Warm the Soul: Quotations, Stories, and More* (Bloomington: iUniverse, 2011), 52. This is the same thing as Marshall Rosenberg's emphasis: "The number one rule of our training [in Nonviolent Communication] is: *empathy before education.*"

Another challenging form of respect is to maintain brotherly love even towards someone who is not present at a conversation that is critical of him. As Stephen Covey put it: "One of the most important ways to manifest integrity is to *be loyal to those who are not present.* In doing so, we build the trust of those who are present. When you defend those who are absent, you retain the trust of those present."[1114] As a way to implement this, he suggested: "Assume everything you say about another they can overhear; now speak accordingly."[1115] Covey elaborated on this point by giving the following examples:

> Suppose you and I were talking alone, and we were criticizing our supervisor in a way that we would not dare to do if he were present. Now what will happen when you and I have a falling out? You know I'm going to be discussing your weaknesses with someone else. That's what you and I did behind our supervisor's back. You know my nature. I'll sweet-talk you to your face and bad-mouth you behind your back. You've seen me do it.
>
> That's the essence of duplicity. Does that build a reserve of trust in my account with you?[1116]
>
> On the other hand, suppose you were to start criticizing our supervisor and I basically told you I agree with the content of some of the criticism and suggest that the two of us go directly to him and make an effective presentation on how things might be improved. Then what would you know I would do if someone were to criticize you to me behind your back?
>
> For another example, suppose in my effort to build a relationship with you, I told you something someone else had shared with me in confidence. "I really shouldn't tell you this," I might say, "but since you're my friend...." Would my betraying another person build my trust account with you? Or would you wonder if the things you had told me in confidence were being shared with others?
>
> Such duplicity might appear to be making a deposit with the person you're with, but it is actually a withdrawal because you communicate your own lack of integrity.[1117]

Rather than criticizing someone or complaining to him, the loftiest path would be to refrain from expressing one's displeasure while forgiving him with love and blaming oneself with humility. When, however, we lack the love and humility to do so wholeheartedly, then

---

[1114] Covey, *The Seven Habits of Highly Effective People,* 196.

[1115] Covey, *The 8th Habit,* 58. From the following words of St. Sophrony of Essex, it is evident that he managed to follow this difficult principle in his life: "Even if, for example, the abbot were in the same place [where I was hearing the confession of his monks] behind a curtain and heard what I was saying when someone complained about him, he would not find anything inappropriate in my words" (Σωφρονίου, *Οἰκοδομώντας τὸν Ναὸ τοῦ Θεοῦ, Τόμος Α´,* 42).

[1116] Covey is referring to his concept of an "emotional bank account" which he explains as follows: "It is like a financial bank account into which you make deposits and take out withdrawals—only in this case you make emotional deposits and withdrawals in your relationships that either build or destroy them" (Covey, *The 8th Habit,* 165).

[1117] Covey, *The Seven Habits of Highly Effective People,* 196.

trying to suppress one's displeasure often leads to coldness and resentment. An effective way of avoiding this pitfall is to implement "Nonviolent Communication."[1118]

In our attempts to show brotherly love to one another, caution is necessary that we not show preferential love to those who have a more likeable character. St. Basil said:

> Since they [the monks] are clearly obliged to love one another with an equal measure of affection, exclusive groups and factions are detrimental to the community; for he who loves one more than the others betrays his lack of perfect love for the others. Likewise, both unseemly strife and particular affection should be banished from the monastery, for enmity is engendered by strife, and from particular friendship and factions arise suspicions and jealousies. In every instance, the loss of equality is the origin and foundation of envy and hatred on the part of those who are slighted thereby. Therefore, we have received a commandment from the Lord to imitate the goodness of Him Who "maketh the sun to rise upon the just and the unjust."[1119] As then God grants a share of light impartially to all, so let those who imitate God send forth a ray of love equally brilliant for all alike. For wherever love falls short, hatred entirely supplants it.... The love of all toward all, therefore, should be equal and impartial.[1120] ...
>
> What can compare with this [monastic] way of life? What is more blessed? What is more genuine than connection and unity? People from various races and countries have come and united themselves with such precision that one soul is seen in many bodies, and the many bodies appear as the members of one opinion.... They are each others' equal servants and each others' masters ... because love makes them subject themselves to each other, and it assures freedom through their personal volition.[1121] ...
>
> The brethren should betray no sign of anger, of unforgivingness, or envy, or contentiousness, whether in bearing, gesture, word, glance of the eye, expression of countenance, or by anything calculated to arouse a companion's ire.[1122]

St. Nectarios of Aegina also wrote about the danger of partial friendship, which he understood as an expression of love that is not divine (i.e., rooted in Christ) but human. He warned his nuns in a letter to them:

> Your love towards me should not come about as the result of thought or because of my love for you, but it should be an overflowing of the love of the Lord. That is, it should flow from our common bond of love. This love is the pure kind of love in spirit, which the evil one is unable to exploit or deviously try to change little by little into commonplace, human love. When this latter sort of love builds up in only one of the persons, it produces hate in the other person—the one being loved. When it builds up in both persons, it produces romantic love. For this reason, when we show love toward others—whether they be of the same gender or the opposite gender, but especially those whom we might be capable of loving romantically—we ought to examine our

---

[1118] See chapter 5) section 13) of this book on page 211.

[1119] Mt. 5:45.

[1120] Βασιλείου τοῦ Μεγάλου, *Ἀσκητικὰ Α΄*, ΕΠΕ 8, 148–49; see also Wagner, *Saint Basil: Ascetical Works*, vol. 9, 219–20.

[1121] PG 31:1381D–1384A (*Ἀσκητικαὶ Διατάξεις, κεφ. ιη΄*).

[1122] Wagner, *Saint Basil: Ascetical Works*, vol. 9, 214.

relationships daily, lest our love does not proceed from Christ's bond of love and does not overflow from the fullness of love.

He who is vigilant with his love and preserves it pure and unadulterated by human things is also protected from the traps of the evil one, who endeavors to inspire human love towards those whom we love and then to change it into romantic love, and he deceives in their sleep people who love each other with a human love. And when a person connected to the love of the Lord loathes a person who loves him humanly, the evil one makes him seem to have a heart wounded by romantic love. Therefore, you must have great caution with the love you have for one another and for me as well and for everyone else so that you are not ensnared by the evil one.[1123]

Contemporary sociologists have observed that what is most detrimental to a long-term relationship is not arguing in itself but the way two people argue. Their observations were made in the context of married couples, and therefore we monastics ought to question to what degree these findings can be applied to the relationship a monk has with his elder or his fellow monks. In our opinion, most of their findings do apply to all relationships due to the commonality of human nature, and therefore we monastics can glean insights from their studies.

One group of researchers explained as follows the behaviors that are the most detrimental to relationships:

[The relationship scholar Howard Markman] learned that by focusing on only a few behaviors, he could predict with startling accuracy whether a given married couple is headed for divorce. More importantly, he found that if he could help couples practice a few similarly critical behaviors, he could reduce their chances of divorce or unhappiness by over one-third. You don't have to study what interests the couples share in common or how they were raised or any of a thousand different ways they treat each other. Merely watch how they argue. If Markman and his colleagues can watch a couple for just 15 minutes, they can predict with 90 percent accuracy who will and who won't be together and happy five years later! During those 15 minutes, Markman will invite a couple to discuss some topic about which they disagree. If the argument involves a significant amount of blaming, escalation, invalidation, or withdrawal, the future is bleak. If, on the other hand, the same couple opens tough conversations with statements that communicate respect and shared purpose, and halts emotional escalation in a respectful way to take a time out, the future will be entirely different.[1124]

The same group of researchers found that the four most damaging behaviors in an argument are: criticism, defensiveness, contempt, and stonewalling. Commenting on this, they wrote:

[Criticism, defensiveness, and contempt] … could be considered forms of psychological violence and, quite frankly, seem to be rather obvious predictors of dissatisfaction. It's hard to attack one another and remain satisfied with a relationship. In

---

[1123] Strongylis, *St. Nectarios of Pentapolis and the Island of Aegina*, vol. 2, 216–17 (Letter #121); see also Ἀρχιμ. Νεκταρίου Ζιόμπολα, *Ὁ Ἅγιος Νεκτάριος, ὁ κορυφαῖος καὶ λαοφιλὴς τῶν καιρῶν μας*, β´ ἔκδοση, (Ἀθήνα: 2009), 106 (Ἐπιστολὴ 5, Δεκεμβρίου, 1907).

[1124] Kerry Patterson, Joseph Grenny, David Maxfield, Ron McMillan, Al Switzler, *Influencer: The Power to Change Anything* (New York: McGraw-Hill, 2008), 28.

contrast, stonewalling is a form of silence and could easily be seen as less important. But that would be wrong. Silence is actually a powerful predictor of dissatisfaction. Related research shows that only 40 percent of divorces are caused by frequent and ferocious fights. Instead of going at it vociferously, couples learn to avoid skirmishes by avoiding each other. Over time, their friendship fades and the relationship withers.[1125]

Furthermore, the same group of researchers also found what words and actions help a relationship:

> Small actions can have a large *positive* impact. For example, University of Utah psychology professor Timothy Smith recruited 150 couples with an average marriage tenure of thirty-six years. He asked these seasoned couples to discuss a topic they had a difficult time resolving. Many launched into stressful exchanges about chores or spending.... But some couples did little things the others didn't. Even as the talking heated up, there would be occasional expressions of warmth. At times it could just be a tiny term of endearment tacked onto the beginning of an expression of frustration: "Sweetheart, I can't understand a word you're saying!" ... Smith discovered not only that these little gestures profoundly related to happiness with the relationship, but also that their presence related to substantial decreases in heart disease as well.[1126]

Thus, if the married couple is able to express themselves to each other lovingly *even* during a disagreement, the likelihood of divorce is very low. Even without explicitly using terms of endearment, an inner disposition of brotherly love will naturally reveal itself through one's tone of voice and body language, which constitute 93 percent of communication.[1127] As the colorful Greek saying goes: "Love and a cough cannot be hidden."

Showing respect to others is not merely a matter of words and deeds but even of thoughts. As St. Sophrony of Essex warned his monastics:

> Every time you are in your cell or wherever and are thinking in a disparaging way towards your brothers or sisters, you are destroying life, and the brothers or sisters whom you are criticizing feel it and are wounded. How does this happen? Even between those who do not pray there is a psychological sensitivity, and they perceive the psychic waves, the psychic energy that others are emitting. No one notices anything; he doesn't hear any words; he doesn't see any gestures. That which happens, happens in secret—yet life is destroyed.[1128]

[1125] Patterson, Grenny, Maxfield, McMillan, Switzler, *Change Anything,* 216–17.

[1126] Ibid., 217–18.

[1127] Studies have shown that spoken words account for only seven percent of the meaning people derive from conversations pertaining to feelings or attitudes. Paralinguistic information (i.e., prosody, pitch, volume, intonation, speed, etc.) accounts for thirty-eight percent. The majority of meaning, fifty-five percent, comes from unspoken information. When this nonverbal information (also known as "body language") conflicts with words, listeners will typically pay more attention to the speaker's body language (vid. Albert Mehrabian, *Nonverbal Communication* [Chicago: Aldine-Atherton, 1972]).

[1128] Σωφρονίου, *Οἰκοδομώντας τὸν Ναὸ τοῦ Θεοῦ, Τόμος Α΄,* 70–71.

If someone—I won't stop repeating this—allows himself to have bad thoughts about someone else, this destroys life because everyone has in his heart an innate perception that enables him to feel what others have within themselves.[1129]

Every thought, positive or negative—even when we are alone in our cell—is an energy and a power that is reflected in the life of the whole monastery. When thoughts are positive, when prayer is fervent of one for another and of one for all and of all for one, then the walls of the monastery are strengthened. On the contrary, however, when our thoughts take a turn for the worse and instead of loving we criticize our brother, then this makes cracks in the walls of the monastery and everything falls apart.[1130]

A crucial factor for the health of a community is its unity. St. Basil the Great observed: "Whenever a group of men aiming at the same goal of salvation adopt the life in common, this principle above all must prevail among them—that there be in all one heart, one will, one desire, and that the entire community be, as the Apostle enjoins, 'one body consisting of divers members'(1 Cor. 12:12)."[1131] This is why St. Theodore the Studite exclaimed: "What a good thing peace and oneness of mind are for a community!"[1132] In the same spirit, St. Athanasios of Athos wrote: "Although the entire fullness of the community is joined together from diverse links, they form one heart in their common life, one will, one desire, and one body, as the apostle prescribes."[1133] Unity within a monastery is so important that St. Benedict Biscop urged his disciples on his deathbed to preserve "peace, unity, and concord of the society."[1134] Venerable Bede added to this:

> In proof [of the importance] of this, he [St. Benedict] would repeatedly instance the kingdom of Israel ever uninvaded and invincible to foreign nations, whilst united under the banners of one of its native generals; but no sooner disunited, in punishment of the sins of its inhabitants, by domestic broils and rival contests, then it was shaken to its foundation, and speedily fell down in ruins. To this also he would often add the known warning given in the text of the Gospel: 'Every kingdom divided against itself shall be made desolate' (Mt. 12:25).[1135]

In order to preserve peace and order in the monastery, monastics need to accept corrections humbly. St. Caesarius of Arles instructed his nuns: "She who is admonished, chastised,

---

[1129] Ibid., 298.

[1130] Ibid., 313.

[1131] Βασιλείου τοῦ Μεγάλου, *Ἀσκητικὰ Α΄*, ΕΠΕ 8, 144–45; see also Wagner, *Saint Basil: Ascetical Works,* vol. 9, 217.

[1132] Θεοδώρου Ἡγουμένου τῶν Στουδίου, *Μικρὰ Κατήχησις*, Emmanuel Auvray, ed. (Paris: Apud V. Lecoffre, 1891), 207 (κατήχησις νη΄).

[1133] Thomas and Hero, *Byzantine Monastic Foundation Documents,* 260.

[1134] Venerable Bede, *The Lives of the Abbots of Wearmouth: Benedict, Ceolfrid, Easterwine, Sigfrid, and Huetbert,* trans. Rev. Peter Wilcock (London: George Garbutt, 1818), 25.

[1135] Ibid., 30.

corrected for any fault whatever shall not answer in any way to the one accusing."[1136] Similarly, *The Rule of Tarn* states: "Let it be judged wrong to answer back when blamed even with a sharp rebuke for any fault, but by humbling himself let him be taught to continue correcting the fault, because God has promised in return that he will give grace to the humble (vid. Prov. 3:34)."[1137] In the same spirit, St. Joseph the Hesychast taught that proper speech for a monk is to say only "Evlogison" and "May it be blessed."[1138] In other words, when he makes a mistake and is corrected, he should not make thousands of excuses but simply say, "Evlogison," that is, "Forgive me." And when someone tells him to do something that cuts off his will, he should humbly give in and say, "May it be blessed." As St. Columbanus put it: "No matter how distasteful the command imposed on him may be, he shall always say to his superior: 'Not as I will, but as thou wilt' (Mt. 26:39), after the example of our Savior, who says elsewhere: 'I came down from heaven, not to do My will, but the will of Him that sent Me' (Jn. 6:38)."[1139]

Another aspect of traditional monastic speech that Elder Ephraim taught us is when one's name is called to answer with "Evlogison" (which roughly corresponds in English to "Bless" or "Pardon?") rather than saying "What?" or "Yes?" The following incident shows that the Desert Fathers also emphasized courtesy in speech: "One day Abba Theodore was entertaining himself with the brethren. While they were eating, they drank their cups with respect, but in silence, without even saying 'pardon.' So Abba Theodore said, 'The monks have lost their manners and do not say, "pardon."'"[1140]

12) Communication

St. Basil attached great importance to the way we speak. He wrote:

> Most importantly, one should endeavor not to be ignorant how to converse but should know how to ask questions in a non-argumentative manner; to answer without desire of display; not to interrupt someone when he is saying something profitable, or to desire to put in a word of one's own in order to show off; to be balanced in speaking and hearing; not to be ashamed of learning, or to be grudging in giving information, nor to pass another's knowledge for one's own ... but to refer it candidly to the true parent. The middle tone of voice is best, neither so quiet as to be inaudible, nor to be tiresome from its loud volume. One should reflect first what one is going to say, and then give it utterance: be courteous when addressed; amiable in social intercourse; not

---

[1136] McCarthy, *The Rule for Nuns of St. Caesarius of Arles,* 174.

[1137] *Monastic Studies,* no. 17, 225.

[1138] Vid. Elder Ephraim, *My Elder Joseph the Hesychast,* 332.

[1139] Oliver Davies and Thomas O'Loughlin, *Celtic Spirituality,* 256.

[1140] Ward, *The Sayings of the Desert Fathers,* 74.

aiming to be pleasant through joking, but cultivating gentleness in kind admonitions.[1141]

St. Columbanus presented the following ideal of humble communication in a monastery:

> He who has replied to a brother on his pointing something out, "It is not as you say," except for seniors speaking honestly to juniors, [shall be punished] with an imposition of silence or fifty blows; unless this only be allowed, that he should reply to his brother of equal standing, if there is something nearer the truth than what the other says and he remembers it, "If you recollect rightly, my brother," and the other on hearing this does not repeat his assertion, but humbly says, "I trust that you remember better; I have erred in speech by forgetfulness, and am sorry that I said ill." These are the words of the sons of God, if "nothing be in contention nor in vainglory, but in lowliness of spirit each reckoning the other better than himself" (Phil. 2:3). But let him who has justified himself be considered not a spiritual son of God but a carnal son of Adam.[1142]

13) Nonviolent Communication

"Nonviolent Communication" refers to a method of communicating developed by Marshall Rosenberg and presented in his book *Nonviolent Communication: A Language of Life*.[1143] In this section, we shall attempt to summarize his most helpful insights. We believe that his method is worth including in a book on monastic life because our experience has shown that the vast majority of interpersonal conflicts in a monastery (or anywhere, for that matter) can be averted or resolved through this method. Moreover, it provides tools for acquiring greater self-awareness.

A core principle of Nonviolent Communication—originally named "Compassionate Communication"[1144]—is that all human behavior stems from attempts to meet needs which are universally shared by all human beings, regardless of their background, gender, upbringing, or culture.[1145] Understanding and acknowledging these fundamental human

---

[1141] *Basil: Letters and Select Works,* 111 (Letter 2).

[1142] *Sancti Columbani Opera,* 151: http://www.ucc.ie/celt/online/T201052.html

[1143] Marshall Rosenberg, *Nonviolent Communication: A Language of Life,* Third Edition (Encinitas: Puddle-Dancer Press, 2015).

[1144] Rosenberg has said that he regrets the choice of the term "nonviolent" because it is often misunderstood in Western culture. He said that he had chosen this term "to refer to our natural state of compassion when violence has subsided from the heart. While we may not consider the way we talk to be 'violent,' our words often lead to hurt and pain, whether for others or ourselves" (Richard D. Bowers and Nelle Moffett, *Empathy in Conflict Resolution: The Key to Successful NVC Mediation* [Scotts Valley: CreateSpace Independent Publishing Platform, 2012], 12).

[1145] Research by Louis Tay and Ed Diener in 2011, which analyzed the data of 60,865 participants from 123 countries, supported this theory that the same universal human needs exist worldwide regardless of cultural differences. Vid. www.ncbi.nlm.nih.gov/pubmed/21688922

needs creates a shared basis for empathic connection, cooperation, and harmonious relationships. Fundamental needs are never in conflict, but conflict arises when someone has adopted a specific strategy for meeting some of his needs which does not meet the needs of others, and when he has not considered other strategies that would meet everyone's needs. Nonviolent Communication (NVC) proposes that if people can identify their needs, the needs of others, and the feelings that surround these needs, harmony can be achieved.

Rosenberg found that the most effective way of meeting everyone's needs while maintaining love, peace, and honesty in a dialogue is to express oneself using the following four components of *observation, feeling, need,* and *request*:

1) Make a factual, specific, and neutral *observation* devoid of evaluation and judgment.
2) Honestly reveal what inner *feelings* I have in connection with that observation. (Or if the focus is on the other person, guess what the other person is feeling, and ask to verify your guess.)
3) Identify the universal *need* triggering that feeling of mine. (Or if the focus is on the other person, guess which need triggered a feeling in the other person, and verify your guess.)
4) Make a specific and doable *request* as a possible strategy for meeting the unmet need.

This four-component process can be used in two ways: to honestly express ourselves or to empathically hear others. For example, we could say: "When I see your unwashed dishes in the kitchen sink for more than twenty-four hours [observation], I feel sad and worried [feelings] because I value orderliness in the monastery [need]. So would you be willing from now on to leave your dishes in the sink for no more than one hour before washing them? [request]" Alternatively, the focus can be on the *other person's* feelings and needs instead of our own. For example, we could say: "I heard you speaking so loudly that I could hear from outside what you said about Father N. [observation]. Are you frustrated [feeling] because you want fair treatment? [need]" In this example, the request is the question asking if we understood him correctly. Our first guess at what the other person's feelings and needs are doesn't have to be correct; if it isn't he will probably correct us immediately. What is important is that the focus of our dialogue is on his feelings and needs rather than on his opinions. In this manner it is easy to connect with him because we are seeing the humanity in him without any judgments or viewing him as an enemy.

An important point to be made is that this approach of dealing with undesirable behavior is completely different from the typical approach. The typical way (whether in society, in a family, or even in a monastery) that we deal with the undesirable behavior of others is to try to correct it by pointing out to them what rules, laws, or norms they are transgressing. The problem with this typical approach is that it allows us to be disconnected with the deeper reasons why those rules were made in the first place. From this disconnected state, it is all too easy to coldly show the other person how wrong he is (and often with an air of superiority and judgmentalism), without any vulnerability or human emotion (except perhaps anger) on our part. On the contrary, the approach of NVC protects us from falling into this legalistic approach by helping us to uncover the underlying principles and by helping us to reveal to the other person how we feel.

This approach of transcending laws—which is what St. Sophrony of Essex implemented in his monastery[1146]—is certainly more difficult because it requires courage, honesty, and humility on our part. Yet these are virtues that keep us fully alive and transmit to others that same aliveness. The words of St. Paul would be appropriate here: "The letter of the law killeth, but the spirit of the law giveth life."[1147] This is not to say that rules should be abolished or are not helpful for "doing all things with orderliness,"[1148] but we must bear in mind the three inherent dangers of following rules instead of values:

1) They frequently lead to a resentful submission or even rebellion rather than the voluntary obedience envisioned by St. Pachomios[1149] and St. Basil the Great;[1150]
2) they rarely inspire intrinsic motivation; and
3) they tend to produce Pharisees.

The Lord has said about people like the Pharisees: "This people draw nigh to Me with their mouth, and they honour Me with their lips, but their heart is far from Me; but in vain do they worship Me, teaching the commandments and doctrines of men."[1151] After Christ's repeated attempts to teach the Jews to grasp the *spirit* of the law, it is a great tragedy when we Christians once again revert to legalism, merely replacing the Jewish laws with Christian laws. And it is an even greater tragedy when we monastics behave pharisaically, as St. Maximos the Confessor observed happening in his day.[1152]

The following true story illustrates how an NVC approach can be used as a more effective option than resorting to laws, even when an appropriate law does exist:

As I was driving one day through a small village, I was stopped by a policeman just after a bend in the road where I had absentmindedly driven slightly across the

---

[1146] See the paragraph associated with footnote #1811 on page 337.

[1147] Cf. 2 Cor. 3:6.

[1148] Cf. 1 Cor. 14:40.

[1149] See quotation associated with footnote #654 on page 118.

[1150] See quotation associated with footnote #655 on page 118.

[1151] Mk. 7:6–7 and Is. 29:13.

[1152] "I hear the things that our Lord was saying to denounce the Pharisees to be referring to us [monastics], the present-day hypocrites, who have been counted worthy of so much grace yet persist in things worse than them" (Μαξίμου Ὁμολογητοῦ, *Λόγος Ἀσκητικός*, κεφ. λζ΄, PG 90:941D).

center line. In a flash, seeing the policeman made me aware that I had been distracted and reactivated in me a longstanding rebelliousness against the stereotype of the blankety-blank, cocky small-town cop. And, clinging to this preconceived idea, I was expecting to be given the usual lecture ("You've just broken rule number XYZ of the traffic code. The fine is fifteen hundred francs. That's the way it is; you have no choice") or some similar moralizing discourse ("Are you out of your mind, driving like that in a village? Have you no sense?!"). I parked my car at the side of the road and waited with a rising sense of dread about what I knew would soon ensue. The policeman came up to me and greeted me... very courteously: "Sir, I'm worried [feeling] because I'm in charge of safety [need] in this village when the children come out of school. When I see you driving across the center line, I'm not sure [feeling] that you're aware of the risks [need] for the children who might be walking along this road or crossing it. How do you respond when I say that to you? [request]"

I almost asked him to repeat what he had said because I simply couldn't believe what I had just heard. This officer had observed a scenario without judging me. He was conveying to me his feeling, indicating to me his need, and requesting me to tell him how I felt! I marveled at the awareness of this man; he wasn't there to punish, reprimand, or constrain but to point out and remind me of a value and a need: safety. He wasn't acting threateningly or punitively; he was inviting me to be responsible. Though I wanted to jump out of the car and give him a hug, I quietly answered him that I was embarrassed at my absentmindedness, that the safety of people and particularly the safety of children was very close to my heart, and that his conscientious and responsible attitude was an invitation to me to be more aware and more responsible at the wheel. He wished me a good journey, and I drove off quite contented.

I can assure you that this story still keeps me alert when I'm driving, much more so than if I had been required to pay a fine to buy judiciary peace. This policeman, who might well have adopted a "breakwater" attitude (saying, for example, "You are in the wrong; you must pay"), still comes to my mind like a compassionate beacon—a marker I reflect on with respect and warm feelings—and that continues to urge me to greater watchfulness on the road"[1153]

In the rest of this section on Nonviolent Communication, we shall elaborate on some important aspects of its four components and other issues.[1154]

i) Component 1: Observations

If we add an evaluation or a judgment to our factual observation, others are likely to hear it as criticism and become defensive and argumentative. Whereas when we translate judgments and interpretations into factual observations, it is easier to take responsibility for our reactions by directing our attention to our own needs as the source of our feelings, rather than to the faults of the other person. Thus, such factual observations pave the way

---

[1153] Thomas d'Ansembourg, *Being Genuine,* trans. Godfrey Spencer (Encinitas: PuddleDancer Press, 2007), 209–10.

[1154] Several sentences in the remainder of this section on NVC are quoted or paraphrased from articles by Inbal Kashtan and Miki Kashtan at baynvc.org/basics-of-nonviolent-communication/ and www.wanttoknow.info/inspiration/nonviolent_communication_summary_nvc

towards greater connection with ourselves and with others. Adding even a positive evaluation to our factual observation (saying, for example, "When you did that good thing…") can detract from the connection, since our opinions about what is good depends on our own subjective preferences, background, and experiences, which may differ from that of the other person, opening the door to misunderstandings.

Rosenberg explained: "NVC does not mandate that we remain completely objective and refrain from evaluating. It only requires that we maintain a separation between our observations and our evaluations."[1155]

In an ongoing process of dialogue, there is often no need to mention either the observation (it is usually clear in the context of communication) or the request (since we may be already acting on an assumed request for empathy).

ii) Component 2: Feelings

In order to express a feeling in NVC, we usually use the phrase "I feel" followed by an adjective (such as "afraid," "satisfied," "anxious," etc.). A common mistake made in trying to implement this method is to substitute thoughts for feelings by using the phrase "I feel" followed by the words "that," "like," or a noun or pronoun. Since the phrase "I feel that…" is synonymous with "I think that…," it is evident that this phrase introduces a thought and not a feeling. For example, the statement: "I feel [that] the abbot should give more homilies" is not an expression of what the heart is feeling but what the mind is thinking. Since understanding someone's opinions can only produce a shallow connection, whereas understanding someone's feelings and needs engenders a deep connection, NVC suggests that we focus on feelings and needs.

The key to identifying and expressing feelings is to focus on words that describe our inner experience rather than words that describe our interpretations of people's actions. For example, "I feel lonely" describes an inner experience, whereas "I feel unloved [by you]" describes a mental interpretation of someone else's behavior. Many words ending in "-ed" refer to an outside person or entity rather than the speaker: "abandoned," "betrayed," or "cheated" suggest blame for what someone else did, whereas the actual feelings of the speaker might be "lonely," "distraught," or "resentful." Our feelings may be *triggered* by the actions and words of others but not *caused* by them. Our feelings arise directly out of our experience of whether our needs seem to us to be met or unmet in a given circumstance. Our assessment of whether or not our needs are met almost invariably involves an interpretation or belief. When our needs are met, we may feel happy, satisfied, peaceful, etc. When our needs are not met, we may feel sad, scared, frustrated, etc. When we express our feelings, we continue the process of taking responsibility for our experience with less likelihood of others hearing criticism or blame of themselves. Thus, by expressing our unique

---

[1155] Marshall Rosenberg, *The Nonviolent Communication Training Course Workbook* (Encinitas: Puddle-Dancer Press, 2006), 7.

experience in the moment of a shared human reality of needs, we create the most likely opportunity for another person to see our humanity and to experience empathy and understanding for us, and respond in a way that meets both of our needs.

A teacher of NVC made this important observation: "Feelings are always related to your body and never involve others."[1156] All genuine feelings (such as fear, happiness, anxiety, surprise, etc.) have been shown to have a direct effect resulting in specific sensations in particular places of our body[1157] (although being aware of these sensations requires that we have enough "presence" to sense our body). On the other hand, pseudo-feelings are cerebral and contain hidden interpretations and judgments of others. For example, when we say: "I feel abused/misunderstood/insulted/ignored, etc.," what we are really saying is "I feel that (i.e., I think that) someone else has abused/misunderstood/insulted/ignored me." These words show what we are *thinking* about other people's actions and how we interpret them rather than what we are directly *feeling*. That this is true can be demonstrated by the fact that someone who is ignored might feel relief rather than sorrow, depending on the situation and depending on his or her ability to view the situation from a different perspective.

When discussing past events, focusing on one's feelings that are alive within oneself at the present moment about those past events is more helpful than bringing up feelings experienced in the past. St. Sophrony of Essex had the same approach, as his niece related: "He always wanted us to tell him the current state of our lives. He did not want to hear about the past. He wanted to know about the present; what we were feeling!"[1158]

iii) Component 3: Needs

It is important not to confuse strategies with needs. A need is always about oneself, not about another. In the context of NVC, a need is a basic human quality, such as a need for food, safety, meaning, understanding, love, etc.[1159] A strategy, on the other hand, typically involves specific people taking specific actions in order to fulfill one's needs. Referring to a specific person, location, action, time, or object is characteristic of a strategy rather than a fundamental human need. The key to identifying, expressing, and connecting with needs is to focus on words that describe shared human experience rather than words that

---

[1156] http://www.drlwilson.com/articles/nonviolent_communication.htm

[1157] Vid. Lauri Nummenmaa et al., "Bodily Maps of Emotions," November 27, 2013, PNAS Early Edition, http://m.pnas.org/content/early/2013/12/26/1321664111.full.pdf

[1158] Dimitra B. Daviti, *Memories of Elder Sophrony of Essex,* trans. Anthony John Smith (Thessalonica: Holy Convent of the Transfiguration of the Savior, 2013), 50–51.

[1159] According to Fr. Stephen Muse (an Orthodox pastoral counselor), our fundamental human needs may be subdivided into four realms: physical needs, emotional needs, intellectual needs, and spiritual needs. For his expanded list of fundamental human needs, see Stephen Muse, *When Hearts Become Flame,* Second Edition (South Canaan: St. Tikhon's Seminary Press, 2015), 295. Based on his list of needs, we have created our own list and posted it at: www.stnilus.org/needs.pdf

describe the particular strategies to meet those needs. The internal shift from focusing on a specific strategy to connecting with underlying needs often results in a sense of liberation; we are encouraged to free ourselves from being attached to one particular strategy by identifying the underlying needs and exploring alternative strategies.

Another liberating realization is that if all human behavior is merely an expression of needs, the only two things a person can ever really be saying (whether in words or actions) are "please" and "thank you." A person says "please" with his words or actions when he wants a need of his to be met, and he says "thank you" with his words or actions when a need of his has been met. This paradigm for viewing human behavior is a powerful tool for engendering compassion, because it transforms the way we view someone who is behaving selfishly, rudely, or even violently.

Although it can be challenging to identify needs accurately, it is more transformative than merely identifying feelings, because it is when needs are identified that a deeper connection can take place, since all people share the same fundamental human needs. Our capacity for being at peace is not dependent on having our needs met. Even when many needs are unmet, meeting our need for self-connection can be sufficient for inner peace, especially when we have a deep relationship with Christ. Understanding, naming, and connecting with our needs helps us improve our relationship with ourselves, as well as fostering understanding with others, so we are all the more likely to take actions that meet everyone's needs.

Being aware of our needs empowers us to separate stimulus from cause. That is, this approach gives us the clarity to see how another person's behavior may be a *stimulus* for my anger, but the actual *cause* of my anger lies within me. Separating stimulus from cause also frees us from "guilt trips" (i.e., motivating others through guilt). For example, instead of saying: "It disappoints me when you come late to church," we could say: "When I see you miss church several times a week [observation], I feel concerned [feeling] because I care for your spiritual well-being [need]. Do you share this concern of mine? [request]"

Honestly revealing our true feelings and admitting our needs sometimes requires great courage and humility because this makes us vulnerable. Yet it is precisely this vulnerability that moves others to view us compassionately and motivates them to want to help us by finding a way for our needs to be met. They will be much more receptive to hearing a suggestion of ours regarding their behavior if we can express it in terms of how we personally feel about it and which needs of ours are not met because of their behavior, rather than in terms of how wrong we think their behavior is. Even if their behavior directly violates a biblical commandment or a patristic teaching, experience has shown that pointing this out to someone before establishing a compassionate connection with them often leads to undesirable results: they may either become obstinate and seek to justify their actions, or they may resentfully submit while increasing their bitterness towards us and perhaps also even towards the author whose commandment we cited.

iv) Component 4: Requests

In making a request, our aim is to identify and suggest a specific strategy or action that we believe will meet our needs and others' needs, and then check with others involved about their willingness to participate in meeting our needs in this way. In a given moment, it is our connection with another that determines the quality of their response to our request. Therefore, in the beginning stages of a dialogue using NVC, our first requests might be "connection requests" intended to foster connection and understanding and to determine whether we have sufficiently connected before moving to a "solution request." An example of a "connection request" might be: "Could you tell me what feelings this triggers in you?" An example of a "solution request" might be: "Would you be willing to take off your shoes when you come in the house?"

One of the "connection requests" most necessary for achieving good communication is the request for feedback in order to ensure that we have been understood. This can take the form of the question: "Would you be willing to tell me what you heard me say?"[1160] Another level of getting feedback would be to ask the other person how he thinks the conversation is going, by saying something like: "How are we doing with this conversation?" or "Time out—how are we doing resolving this issue?"

When making a "solution request," it is most helpful to phrase it positively rather than negatively. For example, "Would you be willing to clean up your cell?" is more effective than "Would you be willing to stop making a mess?" Furthermore, the more specific a request is, the more likely we will get what we want and the more likely the other person will be willing to comply. For example, "Would you be willing to hang up your clothes and throw away the plastic wrappers on the floor?" is more effective than just "Would you be willing to clean up your cell?"

When our request is specific and doable, there is a greater likelihood for achieving what we want. For example, if we request: "I would like you to be more thoughtful," even if the other person agrees to this, he might not know exactly what he should do differently. A much more specific and doable request would be: "I would like you to ask me before taking tools from where I'm working."

The most important thing to remember when making a request in NVC is not to demand compliance. A *request* is asking the other person to do something voluntarily, whereas a *demand* forces him either to submit or rebel, and this approach can hinder connection. In other words, a request that is not a demand leaves the other person free to say yes or no. If we react to a refusal of our request by blaming, insulting, laying a guilt trip,

---

[1160] Since we may hesitate to phrase this question in these words because it sounds unnatural, another way to verify that we have been understood is to ask: "Do you know what I mean?" And if they reply affirmatively, then we can say something like: "Just so that I can be sure that you get what I'm saying, can you please tell me what you think I mean?" Or: "I'm not sure if I expressed myself clearly. Can you please tell me what you understood me saying?"

threatening, or punishing the person who refused to comply with it, it is clear that our request was actually a demand. This is where it is paramount to bear in mind that the goal of NVC is not compliance but to achieve an honest, empathy-based relationship. Shifting from demands to requests entails a paradigm shift: we shift from trying to meet our own needs to trying to create a quality connection with the other person. Once this connection has been made, the result of this connection will be that both our needs and the other person's needs will matter to both of us, and then it will be easy to find a way for both people's needs to be met.

When the other person sees that he has the freedom to respond negatively, we may not gain immediate assent to our wishes, but we are more likely to get our needs met over time because we are building the trust that everyone's needs matter. Within an atmosphere of such trust, goodwill increases, altruism flourishes, and with it a willingness to support each other in getting our needs met.

There are times in life (especially in hierarchical organizations) when a person with authority will choose to make a demand that is not merely a request. In such instances, the authority may still exhibit care for the feelings and needs of his subordinates. To avoid misunderstandings, the authority should make it clear to the subordinate that he is making a demand. But in the event that this is not done, it is beneficial if the subordinate asks for this clarification.

When someone declines to comply to our request, this does not have to be the end of the dialogue. On the contrary, we can empathize with that negative response by guessing what needs of his are preventing him from complying. After he has received sufficient empathy, he will be able to hear our own feelings and needs, which we could express by saying for example: "I am disappointed because I was hoping that you would want to contribute to the orderliness of the monastery," and adding the request: "Would you be willing to clean your cell as soon as you finish the section of the book you are reading?" or even: "Can you think of a solution that would meet both of our needs?" Experience has shown repeatedly that once both parties have succeeded in fully understanding each other's needs, then from that point it is easy to find a mutually satisfactory solution.

Through NVC we are seeking a "win-win"[1161] resolution in which everyone is intrinsically motivated by the joy inherent in compassionate giving rather than by extrinsic motivators such as punishments and rewards. If a person is doing something merely because of a punishment or reward, he will probably stop doing it as soon as we are not present to give the punishment or reward. Moreover, if someone agrees to our request merely out of fear, guilt, shame, obligation, or the desire for a reward, this compromises the quality of connection and trust between him and us. Since people do not always express all their feelings

---

[1161] A "win-win" resolution is one in which all parties involved believe that the resolution is to their advantage. This concept is elaborated on by Stephen R. Covey in "Habit 4" of *The 7 Habits of Highly Effective Families.*

verbally, it is important for us to pay attention to non-verbal cues that can reveal that their agreement is not wholehearted.

v) Empathy in NVC

Empathy is central in NVC, and the key ingredient for empathy is presence, according to Rosenberg. This involves being in the present moment and aware of one's body (since feelings have a bodily manifestation). It is a non-judgmental state in which one observes oneself and notes as well what the other person is observing, feeling, needing and requesting. This kind of "watchfulness" and "presence" is the opposite of our habitual state of "waking sleep" in which we float through our day like automatons, mindlessly reacting to whatever circumstances and people come our way as if on auto-pilot. Moreover, Rosenberg emphasized that people need not just our empathy but empathy in conjunction with our honesty.

The principles of NVC are also useful for silently "communicating" with ourselves—that is, for dealing internally with a situation. This means listening through any interpretations and judgments of ourselves that we are making in order to clarify how we are feeling and what we are needing. For example, when we are angry, NVC can be used to identify our unmet needs. Once they have been identified, the anger invariably transforms into another feeling (such as sorrow or fear) that will help us deal with the situation productively rather than destructively. This is why Rosenberg defines anger as "a tragic expression of an unmet need." Since anger is a result of thoughts of blame and judgment, it is caused by being "in the head," whereas when we are connected with our feelings and needs, we are "in the heart," which is what transforms the anger into a different feeling. This is much more beneficial (and more psychologically and spiritually healthy) than reacting violently out of anger or repressing it (which invariably leads to physical and psychological symptoms).[1162]

The process of NVC enables us to hear others empathically by perceiving the feelings and needs behind their expressions and actions, regardless of how they express themselves, even if their expression or actions include judgments, demands, and physical violence. This entails "translating" their violent words or actions into an expression of their unmet needs and their corresponding feelings. Empathic connection can happen silently, but in times of conflict, verbally communicating to another person that we understand their feelings and that their needs matter to us can be a powerful turning point in difficult situations. Demonstrating our understanding of their needs does not mean that we are sacrificing our own needs or pretending that we are not in pain because of their violent words or actions; it is merely a temporary shift of our focus from our needs to theirs.

[1162] As a clinical psychologist observed: "Where there is repressed anger, not only will there be a symptom, there *must* be a symptom" (Henry Kellerman, *Psychoanalysis of Evil: Perspectives on Destructive Behavior* [London: Springer Science, 2014], 61).

Implementing the process of NVC during a dialogue typically consists of switching between three modes of expression:

1) Giving empathy to the other person by guessing their feelings and needs, usually followed by a connection request ("Did I understand you?"),

2) Honestly expressing one's own feelings and needs to the other person, often followed by a connection request ("Do you understand me?"), and

3) Giving oneself empathy by silently reconnecting with one's own feelings and needs. (This is especially necessary when anger, guilt, or shame is triggered in us by something the other person said.)

NVC can be used successfully even when the other person is ignorant of its principles and methods. This is because if we have the inner strength and presence of mind to remain in an empathic state by reflecting back to the other person what his feelings and needs are while respecting his autonomy, the other person will invariably be touched by this. This increases his own capacity for compassion for himself and for us, thus greatly increasing the likelihood that both his and our needs will be met peacefully. Granted, this might not happen during the first few exchanges of words. The more empathy the other person needs, the longer it will take in the conversation before his need for being understood will be met, rendering him ready to listen to our own feelings and needs.

Rosenberg warned that this four-component method is not meant to be implemented robotically. He explained: "The essence of NVC is to be found in our consciousness of these four components, not in the actual words that are exchanged."[1163] He emphasized that the most important aspect of this method is that we put ourselves into the frame of mind of wanting to connect with the other person—not on the level of mental agreement regarding particular strategies for fulfilling needs but on the level of the heart by empathizing with each other's feelings and being aware of each other's needs. This method will fail if we try to take advantage of it merely as a trick to get our way. We need to be aware that its purpose is not to make the other person conform to our will. On the contrary, Rosenberg taught that it is a tool to facilitate an empathic connection with the other person "in a way that enables compassionate giving to take place. It's giving that comes from the heart willingly, where we are giving service to ourselves and others, not out of duty, obligation, nor out of fear of punishment, hope for a reward, not out of guilt or shame, but for what I consider is our nature, our nature to enjoy giving to one another."[1164] "Through its emphasis on deep listening—to ourselves as well as others—NVC fosters respect, attentiveness, and empathy, and engenders a mutual desire to give from the heart."[1165]

[1163] Rosenberg, *The Nonviolent Communication Training Course Workbook*, 3.

[1164] Marshall Rosenberg, *Practical Spirituality: Reflections on the Spiritual Basis of Nonviolent Communication* (Encinitas: PuddleDancer Press, 2004), 7.

[1165] Rosenberg, *The Nonviolent Communication Training Course Workbook*, 2.

Experience has shown over and over again that once an empathic connection has been made at the level of feelings and needs, a transformation happens in which one or both people experience a shift in attention. This can lead to a shift of needs or generate new reserves of kindness and generosity. As a result, both people will naturally work together to find a solution that meets everyone's needs. Not only that, but the solution that arises will typically be found in only a few minutes—not in a few minutes from the time the dialogue began but from the time both sides have fully grasped each other's needs. This happens naturally because we human beings inherently enjoy contributing to the well-being of others, once we have connected with our own and others' needs and can experience our giving as coming from choice.

The four-component method of NVC often helps us relate to others, but the crux of its success lies in our ability to connect compassionately with our own and with others' humanity. Since the inner intent is the most important aspect of this method, its four-component process is not even necessary when our heart is in the right place. Besides, if we always were to express ourselves using the four-component process, others could interpret this artificial way of speaking as a *lack* of sincerity and honesty, which is the exact opposite of what is intended. While the formal format of NVC is designed to help us focus our consciousness at the level of the heart, an informal approach with more casual words (or even wordlessly through the look on our face or through our body language) can achieve that same connection.

vi) Apologies and Gratitude

NVC enables us to do something much deeper than just apologize, but rather to share our mourning with someone whom we have offended. Rosenberg explained:

> Apology is based on moralistic judgment, that what I did was wrong and I should suffer for it.... That's radically different from mourning ... which is based on life-serving judgments. Did I meet my own needs? No. Then what need didn't I meet? When we are in touch with our unmet need, we never feel shame, guilt, self-anger, or the depression that we feel when we think that what we did was wrong. We feel sadness, deep sadness, sometimes frustration, but never depression, guilt, anger, or shame. Those four feelings tell us we are making moralistic judgments at the moment we are feeling those feelings.[1166]

Thus, instead of apologizing, we could express our mourning in this manner: "Father, when I see how my actions have contributed to your pain [observation], I feel very sad [feeling]. I care for you and it is important to me that I support you [need]. Please forgive me [request]." It goes without saying that this kind of message will touch someone much more deeply than even a heartfelt "I'm sorry."

[1166] Marshall Rosenberg, *Living Nonviolent Commuication: Practical Tools to Connect and Communicate* (Boulder: Sounds True, 2012), 74.

The NVC process also enables us to express gratitude to others in a way that they will appreciate much more than by praising them or by simply saying, "Thank you." It consists of the same four components of NVC (observation, feeling, need, request) but without the request, since we have no requests when we are grateful and our needs have been met. In other words, we first mention precisely what the other person did, then we honestly say how this made us feel, and finally we express what need of ours was met. For example, we could say: "When you sacrificed your time in order to listen to me [observation], I was relieved and touched [feelings] because I really needed some understanding [need] for what I've been going through."

One point that Rosenberg failed to make is that this method of expressing apologies and gratitude can be used even in the way we speak to God as a way of repenting and glorifying Him. For example, we could say, "Lord, when I consider how often I neglect to pray to Thee [observation], I feel deep regret and sorrow [feelings], because I desperately need connection and communion with Thee Who art the source of life and joy and peace [needs]. Have mercy on me, and forgive me [request]." It is worth asking ourselves how this kind of repentance would affect our souls differently from repentance in which we might callously state: "Forgive me, Lord; I skipped my prayer rule several times."

As for expressing gratitude to God, one could say for example: "As I witness the beauty of creation out in the forest [observation], I am overcome with awe and amazement [feelings] at the magnificence of Thy works, and it brings me great peace to appreciate such exquisite beauty [needs]." A nun once confessed to me that when she tried expressing her gratitude to God using the method of NVC, she was moved to the point of tears.

vii) Other Applications of NVC

Rosenberg taught: "Nonviolent communication is designed to help us remain conscious of choice at every moment."[1167] By viewing situations through the prism of NVC, we become more aware of our needs and deeper values. Having connected with these needs, we can then consciously choose to meet them, regardless of how unpleasant the circumstances may be. For example, when we are doing a task we dislike, rather than doing it out of a sense of forced obligation, we can be at peace with the situation by telling ourselves: "I *choose* to do this unpleasant thing because I want such-and-such benefit (or because I value such-and-such a principle—such as the principle of cooperation, or of cutting off my will out of love for Christ or love for my brother)" instead of saying: "Like it or not, I *have to* (or "should") do this unpleasant thing. Period." Hearing the word "should" from within or from someone else takes all the joy out of doing a task. As Elder Aimilianos said: "The word 'must' [or 'should'] has never moved anyone to do anything. On the contrary, it makes you feel like a slave and discourages you from moving forward. The force of 'must'

[1167] Rosenberg, *The Nonviolent Communication Training Course* (Boulder, CO: Sounds True, 2006), Disc 1.

moves neither God, nor the heart ... [and] is something that unravels and comes apart very easily."[1168]

Expressing ourselves through NVC helps us to avoid labeling people, which depersonalizes them and breaks the commandment of Christ: "Judge not."[1169] For example, instead of muttering to ourselves: "That person is lazy," we could say: "I am feeling frustrated [feeling] because I value cooperation [need], and he has been sitting in the garden for three hours [observation]." Furthermore, labeling is dangerous because it not only places a person within a limiting box, but it can also serve to perpetuate a harmful behavior. For example, if I tell myself: "I'm just a glutton," I may come to believe that this passion is an integral part of my being, and therefore abandon trying to resist it.

When receiving criticism, rather than retaliating (with a counter-attack that can be verbal, physical, or only in our thoughts) we can instead use the principles of NVC, either to sense our own feelings and needs, or to sense the other person's feelings and needs that produced his criticism. Rosenberg said: "No matter what words people use to express themselves, we listen for their observations, feelings, and needs, and what they are requesting to enrich life."[1170] When this is done out of a sincere attempt to connect with the other person, it inevitably leads to constructive results. Likewise, when someone orders us to do something unpleasant, instead of rebelling or resentfully submitting, we can choose to connect with the other person's needs empathically and then voluntarily obey.

Viewing other people's criticism, insults, and judgments through the lens of NVC enables us receive their otherwise hurtful words without being wounded or viewing them as enemies, because we are able to see that they are simply fellow human beings with unmet needs. Their strong words can even give us joy, because we can now see those words as an opportunity to show them compassion and find a way to satisfy their unmet needs.

Although all communications could be expressed using the four-component process of NVC, this is not necessary. It is primarily our emotionally charged messages that are worth phrasing in such language, not only for the benefit of others but even for our own benefit. It is in times of conflict or reactivity to others that NVC is most needed, in order to transform our disconnected state of being and return us to our compassionate intention and our attention to the present. With practice, many people have found that using NVC to

---

[1168] Archimandrite Aimilianos of Simonopetra, *The Way of the Spirit: Reflections on Life in God,* trans. m. Maximos Simonopetrites [Nicholas Constas] (Athens: Indiktos, 2009), 5.

[1169] Mt. 7:1.

[1170] Rosenberg, *Nonviolent Communication: A Language of Life,* 74. This is reminiscent of what Blessed Augustine taught: "In whatever a man says, we should consider only his meaning" (M. F. Toal, *Sunday Sermons of the Great Fathers,* vol. 4 [San Francisco: Ignatius Press, 2000], 308).

empathize silently with themselves is sufficient by itself to resolve inner conflicts and conflicts with others, as it transforms our experience of life.

viii)   Drawbacks and Limitations of NVC

A serious block to communication can be a lack of time. If the two (or more) people have not allotted enough time to communicate, they are likely to fail to connect at a satisfactorily deep level. Context is also important: trying to communicate with someone on a serious matter while simultaneously doing some other task is likely to be less effective than trying to do so when both people have little to distract them.

One seeming drawback of NVC is that it appears to require more time to communicate with this method than with our habitual manner of communication. It is only a seeming drawback, however, because the extra time spent for using NVC is far outweighed by all the time typically wasted when poor communication results in conflicts, many of which can last for years—not to mention all the stress and disturbing thoughts that accompany serious conflicts.

A real drawback of NVC—or rather, a real challenge of NVC—is that despite the method's simplicity, it is very challenging to implement. Not only can it require a great deal of presence to fathom what we or others are feeling and needing when emotions are complex, but it can also require a great deal of humility to admit our feelings and needs, especially if our culture teaches us that we shouldn't have certain needs. Another challenge is that it is precisely the times when we need NVC the most (when we are feeling intense negative emotions) that it is also the most difficult to think clearly and calmly enough to implement the principles of NVC.

Since the success of NVC depends on the ability to empathize, it may be ineffective when used with people whose defense mechanisms have drastically diminished their capacity for empathy. People suffering from personality disorders, such as Borderline Personality Disorder and Narcissistic Personality Disorder may maintain a psychological structure that challenges them in the area of empathy. Furthermore, those known as psychopaths and sociopaths may even be biologically incapable of empathy.[1171]

ix) NVC and Orthodoxy

While the *psychology* advocated by NVC is in line with Christian ethics (e.g., NVC emphasizes virtues such as love, patience, honesty, peacefulness, etc.), a few *ontological* implications of NVC ought to be clarified before they could be considered Christian. For example, Rosenberg suggests that we avoid referring to moral absolutes such as "right," "wrong," "good," and "bad," because they enable us to express ourselves impersonally

---

[1171] Vid. www. systemsthinker.com/interests/communicationtechniques/nonviolentcommunication.shtml

without revealing what is going on inside ourselves, which inhibits other people from connecting with us. Perhaps Rosenberg's personal belief was that such moral absolutes do not even exist. We as Orthodox Christians, however, can still maintain our belief in the existence of good and evil and sin while implementing NVC, simply by not using this framework to appoint ourselves as the judges of how right or wrong or sinful we think someone or his actions are. Instead, we may focus on fundamental human needs and leave the judgment to God. Besides, in the original Judeo-Christian understanding, "sin" (ἁμαρτία in Greek[1172] and חֵטְא in Hebrew[1173]) is not a moral infraction but "missing the mark" of God's will and love.

Another example of Rosenberg's teachings that at first glance may appear to conflict with Orthodoxy is his critical stance towards self-reproach. On the one hand, the prayers of the holy Fathers and the Church's hymnography are full of belittling expressions of self-reproach. Rosenberg, however, discourages self-admonishment because it leads to destructive shame or guilt.[1174] Nevertheless, upon examining more carefully what Rosenberg and the holy Fathers are really saying, it becomes clear that their approaches do not conflict because they are talking about two different kinds of self-reproach. On the one hand, Rosenberg is pointing out the harm of *unhealthy* self-reproach that leads to what St. Paul called "worldly sorrow," whereas the holy Fathers promoted *healthy* self-reproach, which leads to "godly sorrow." As St. Paul wrote: "Godly sorrow produceth a repentance without regret, leading to salvation, but worldly sorrow produceth death."[1175] The holy Fathers also used the term χαρμολύπη ("joy-making sorrow")[1176] to describe godly sorrow. St. John Cassian explained the important difference between these two kinds of sorrow as follows:

> Godly sorrow, nourishing the soul with the hope given by repentance, is mixed with joy. Therefore it renders man eager and obedient with reference to every good work: accessible, humble, gentle, forbearing, and patient in enduring all the suffering or tribulation God may send us. From this are known the fruits of the Holy Spirit in man, namely, joy, love, peace, long-suffering, goodness, faith, self-restraint (Gal. 5:22). But from the opposite kind of sorrow we come to know the fruits of the evil spirit, which are: despondency, impatience, anger, hatred, objection, despair, and laziness with regard to prayer. We should avoid this kind of sorrow.[1177]

[1172] Vid. Henry George Liddell and Robert Scott, *A Greek-English Lexicon,* Ninth Edition (Oxford: Oxford University Press, 1996), 77.

[1173] Vid. James Strong, *The Strongest Strong's Exhaustive Concordance of the Bible* (Grand Rapids: Zondervan, 2001), 1498–99.

[1174] Vid. Rosenberg, *Nonviolent Communication: A Language of Life,* 130–31.

[1175] 2 Cor. 7:10.

[1176] Vid. *The Ladder,* step 7.

[1177] Κασσιανοῦ τοῦ Ῥωμαίου, «Πρὸς Κάστορα Ἐπίσκοπον» ἐν *Φιλοκαλία τῶν Ἱερῶν Νηπτικῶν, τόμος α´* (1991), 75–76; see also Palmer, Sherrard, Ware, *The Philokalia,* vol. 1, 88.

Thus, *healthy* self-reproach springs from a tender awareness that we have grieved God and/or our neighbor, both of whom we want to love. (To express this in NVC terminology, we would say that connecting with our need to love God and our neighbor while recalling our actions that failed to meet this need of ours elicits feelings not of shame and guilt but of some kind of grief that mobilizes us to repent.[1178]) Healthy self-reproach does not lead to despair because we have faith that God loves and forgives us. This is the kind of self-reproach that the Lord taught St. Silouan the Athonite: "Keep thy mind in hell and despair not."[1179] *Unhealthy* self-reproach, however, springs from an egocentric, "worldly sorrow," when we see that the idol of our self-image has been shattered. Unhealthy self-reproach is often fostered by a legalistic, non-Orthodox understanding of sin as a mere breaking of a rule, rather than by the Orthodox understanding of sin as missing the mark. Because unhealthy self-reproach is rooted in pride and *philautia* (self-love) and is steeped in worldly sorrow, it "produceth death,"[1180] namely, depression and despair. It is only this unhealthy self-reproach that Rosenberg rightly denounces as joyless and ineffective. Yet, by not explaining thoroughly enough in his book that there is also a healthy kind of self-reproach (as promoted by the holy Fathers), some readers may assume that NVC discourages all kinds of self-reproach. Thus, although there is nothing unacceptable in the NVC approach to self-reproach, it lacks the spiritual depth found in the holy Fathers' understanding of self-reproach. This is to be expected, since NVC presents merely a helpful *psychology,* without attempting to present a correct *ontology* of the Uncreated, as is found only in the Orthodox faith.

Orthodoxy begins with a distinct ontology preserved by the holy Fathers and the Councils of the Church, which is different than that which undergirds heterodox literature. As long as this is recognized and appropriate discernment is made, science and psychology and NVC are able to contribute in a variety of ways.[1181]

Bearing in mind what limitations NVC has in regards to our spiritual life will help us keep NVC (and psychology in general) in perspective. The primary spiritual limitations of

---

[1178] Vid. Rosenberg, *Nonviolent Communication: A Language of Life,* 132–33.

[1179] Sakharov, *Saint Silouan the Athonite,* 183.

[1180] 2 Cor. 7:10.

[1181] The role that contemporary psychological methods (such as NVC) can play in the spiritual life of an Orthodox Christian is a complex and controversial topic that we shall not attempt to address here. Suffice it to say, however, that we agree with the following stance of Elder Antonios Romaios of Gregoriou Monastery on the Holy Mountain: "I accept any anthropological science that aids human self-knowledge because essentially this greatly assists the work of pastoral theology, since it creates the most correct dynamic for receiving ... the grace of God. I never believed that there should be a predisposition such as the kind which some of our beloved fellow clergymen have, who, as a matter of principle and of the faith, reject the considerable contribution of psychology or psychiatry. Of course, I do not accept or adopt or am unaware of the theoretical, clinical, and practical mistakes that these sciences can make" («Συνέντευξη μὲ τὸν ἱερομόναχο Ἀντώνιο Ρωμαῖο, 1° μέρος», Ψυχῆς Δρόμοι, τεῦχος 1 [Ἰούνιος 2011], 143–44).

NVC are as follows: it presents a humanistic approach to living virtuously that fails to include crucial aspects of the Christian life, such as the need for divine grace, prayer, and faith. NVC also overlooks the influence of God's grace and the reality of demonic influences. Furthermore, in Christianity we often choose to sacrifice our own needs out of love for God or for our neighbor, thus transcending NVC's approach of trying to meet everyone's needs. Moreover, NVC by itself does not lead to salvation and theosis.

These shortcomings of NVC are not problematic for us Orthodox Christians, as long as we bear in mind that its role is not to replace Orthodox spirituality but to complement it. That is, NVC certainly can be used in conjunction with the ascetical approach of living the spiritual life in an Orthodox manner, because it is essentially a tool that enables people to express the compassion that they otherwise might have failed to access without NVC's method. A living saint would probably have little need for learning the method of NVC, since "Christ [Who is Love] lives in him,"[1182] and thus a saint would already be at a level at which he constantly expresses himself compassionately. As for the rest of us who have not yet attained that level, we can undoubtedly benefit from methods such as NVC until by God's grace and our spiritual struggle we become "a perfect man, unto the measure of the stature of the fulness of Christ."[1183]

14) Helping Others

The holy Fathers attached utmost importance to brotherly love. Abba John the Dwarf said: "'It is not possible to build a house from the top down; one must build it from the foundation to the top.' 'What does this saying mean?' his disciples asked him. The elder replied: 'The foundation is your neighbor, whom you must win over to Christ by your love—and this must be done first; for on him depend all the commandments of Christ.'"[1184] As St. Anthony put it: "Life and death depend on our neighbor: for if we win over our brother, we win over God, but if we offend our brother, we sin against Christ."[1185] Elder Aimilianos wrote for his nuns: "The touchstone of authenticity for the sisters shall be the love they bear towards the others, which is what the Lord requires above all else. The heart of each shall be open, full of simplicity, sincerity and affection, admitting all the others, with love that is deep, strong, manly, and spiritual."[1186]

[1182] Cf. Gal. 2:20.

[1183] Eph. 4:13.

[1184] Chrysostomos, *The Evergetinos, Book III,* 290.

[1185] Wortley, *The Alphabetical Sayings of the Desert Fathers,* 32 (Anthony 9).

[1186] Elder Aimilianos, *The Authentic Seal,* 147.

St. Euthymios taught: "If your brother calls you while you are occupied with your manual work, make haste to see what he wants and work with him, leaving aside your own work."[1187] Elder Ephraim also taught us the same thing but added that we should refuse to help only if, in doing so, we would have to neglect what we are under obedience to complete. In such a case, we should explain to him which responsibilities of ours are preventing us from helping him. And if we truly love our brother as ourself and want to "do unto others as we would have them do unto us,"[1188] the way in which we refuse to help will be full of commiseration and sorrowful apology for being unable to help, rather than an attitude of: "That's your problem, not mine," which, needless to say, should never be said by a Christian and especially not by a monk—and even more so not by a monk in a cenobium where all things are shared in common.

St. Sophrony of Essex instilled this sense of commonality in his brotherhood. He told them:

> Monasticism, with the principle of obedience, makes man capable of embracing everyone with his love. So this is what we ought to preserve in our monastery. I pray continually that each one of us will acquire the consciousness that this small [monastic] family is my life. And the sufferings or illness of any one of us at all are really the common illness of us all.[1189]
>
> I was amazed that John the Theologian in his description of the Mystical Supper of Christ says that the Lord gave a new commandment to the Apostles: "love one another."[1190] So each one of us in monasticism should set as a primary goal to experience our brotherhood as a single human being.[1191]

It is easy to forget this elementary principle of demonstrating brotherly love. As we see in *The Sayings of the Desert Fathers:* "A brother asked an elder: 'How is it that some struggle in their way of life and yet do not receive the grace that the Fathers of old received?' The elder replied: 'Back then there was love, and each one drew his neighbor upwards; but now that love has grown cold, each one drags his neighbor downwards. This is why we do not receive grace.'"[1192]

Another aspect of brotherly love entails caring for the sick. St. Waldebert wrote in his rule for nuns:

> Those who are bound by infirmity should be cared for following the model the Author declares when He says "Whatsoever ye would that men should do to you, do

---

[1187] Chrysostomos, *The Evergetinos, Book III*, 290.

[1188] Lk. 6:31.

[1189] Σωφρονίου, *Οἰκοδομῶντας τὸν Ναὸ τοῦ Θεοῦ, Τόμος Α´*, 160–61.

[1190] Jn. 13:34.

[1191] Σωφρονίου, *Οἰκοδομῶντας τὸν Ναὸ τοῦ Θεοῦ, Τόμος Γ´*, 139.

[1192] Chrysostomos, *The Evergetinos, Book III*, 291.

ye even so to them."[1193] Though this might be applied to all, it is shown particularly in the infirmary because the Lord said, "I was sick and ye visited Me."[1194] Therefore, the sick should be cared for as though Christ were receiving the same ministrations in person. Therefore revere anyone who devotes care to the sick for Christ, for she ministers to Christ in the sick. And let it be the care of the abbess that they have a separate cell with every convenience; that she spare no external labour which might save pain to those who are sick in body. And if the time, as the Lenten season, demands that the others change their lives, exception is always made for the sick; that they shall be served food as well as drink generously. The use of the baths or the best medical care is introduced. This is conceded reluctantly to the healthy, particularly the young. The abbess should take such care of the sick as she hopes to receive from the Lord.[1195]

The *Rule of St. Ailbe* explains the spirit of self-sacrifice that should prevail in a monastery: "When, through obedience, they go to carry out their duties, let their spirit be: 'This is a heavy task, brother; let me do it.'"[1196] With this mindset, monks in the old days would argue in order to bear the burden of doing extra work themselves. For example, among the Desert Fathers

> there was a certain solitary who had another solitary as his disciple. The latter lived in a cell ten miles away from him. One day, his thoughts said to him: "Summon the brother to come here and receive his bread." But then he reflected: "Am I going to make my brother trek ten miles for the sake of bread? No, I will take the bread to him myself." So he took the bread and set off to visit his disciple.
>
> While on his way ... an angel appeared before him ... saying: "The very steps that you take for the sake of the Lord are counted and are reckoned worthy of great reward in the sight of God." Then, giving thanks to God for the words of the angel, the ascetic went on his way, rejoicing. He arrived at the brother's cell, bearing the loaves of bread, and recounted to him the love for mankind that God had shown to him. After giving him the bread, he returned to his own cell.
>
> On the following day, he again took some loaves of bread and went to visit another monk. It so happened that the latter was coming towards him at the same time for the same purpose, and they met each other on the way. The one who was going said to the one who was coming: "I had a treasure, and you sought to rob me of it?" The other monk replied to him: "Does the narrow gate have room only for you? Allow me to enter it together with you." And at once, as they were speaking, an angel of the Lord appeared to them and said: "This 'quarrel' of yours has ascended to God as an odor of sweet savor."[1197]

St. Silouan showed by example that we ought to do what people ask of us, even if there is no particular personal benefit in doing so:

[1193] Mt. 7:12.

[1194] Mt 25:36.

[1195] J. A. McNamara and J. Halborg, *The Rule of a Certain Father to the Virgins,* chapter 15.

[1196] Maidín, *The Celtic Monk,* 23.

[1197] Chrysostomos, *The Evergetinos, Book III,* 297–98.

One feast-day when Father Benjamin of Kaliagra and Father Silouan were walking through the monastery woods Father Benjamin suggested that they should go and see Father Ambrosios, a remarkable and well-known *staretz*, who was then confessor to the Bulgarian monastery of Zographou. Silouan agreed at once, and they set off. Father Benjamin was curious to know what Silouan would ask of the *staretz*.

"I am not thinking of asking him anything," replied Silouan. "I have no problems at the moment."

"Then why are you coming?"

"Because you wanted me to."

"Yes, but people go to see a *staretz* for the sake of edification."

"I am subduing my will to yours, and that is of greater benefit to me than any advice from the Staretz."[1198]

A complication in implementing this kind of brotherly love, though, occurs when a "Martha" habitually tries to get a "Mary" to help her out. On the one hand, since the Lord clearly said that Mary has chosen the better portion,[1199] it seems that it would be a mistake for Mary to leave the "one thing needful" in order to help out Martha with the work. On the other hand, however, St. John Cassian praised the monks of Egypt for putting obedience to others above all other virtues:

> When they are seated in their rooms and devoting their energies to both work and meditation and they hear the sound of someone knocking at the door and striking at the cells of different ones, calling them to prayer or to some kind of work, they immediately rush out of their rooms.... [The one in his room] is striving with all his energy and zeal to pursue the virtue of obedience. It is this that they prefer not only to manual labor or to reading or to the peace and quiet of their cells but even to all other virtues, such that they judge everything else as negligible in comparison with it and are content to undergo any loss whatsoever as long as they do not violate this good in any respect.[1200]

Similarly, St. Ephraim of Katounakia found out the hard way that one can lose grace even by justifiably refusing to help a brother—the justification being that one is in a good state of prayer and does not want to lose it. As he himself related:

> I remember one time I went to my cell to pray a bit. In fact, I found myself in a grace-filled state of prayer. Suddenly, my brother monk Procopios came and knocked on the door, saying, "Papa, the fire for the food has gone out."
>
> I thought to myself, "Now that I'm in the midst of the activity of grace, let's savor the joy, and when the sensation of grace has finished, then I'll go tend to the work."
>
> "I'll go in just a little while to take care of it," I told him.
>
> I didn't have time to finish my words before grace had left me. Wasn't that disobedience? I was disobedient and set forth my own opinion, even though Fr. Procopios wasn't the elder but my brother. Then I reprimanded myself: "Wretch! You were disobedient and lost grace as well."

[1198] Sakharov, *Saint Silouan the Athonite,* 59.

[1199] Lk. 10:38–42.

[1200] Ramsey, *John Cassian: The Institutes,* 83–84.

That's why I say, be obedient and you will find prayer. Don't look at prayer because prayer itself depends upon obedience.[1201]

Thus, St. Symeon the New Theologian taught his monks: "Do not make your longing for prayer a pretext for turning away from anyone who asks for your help; for love is greater than prayer."[1202]

Although we should be eager to help others, we ourselves should avoid burdening others by asking them for help unnecessarily. As Thomas Jefferson put it: "Never trouble another for what you can do yourself."[1203]

15) Noise

St. Paisios of the Holy Mountain vehemently opposed the noise that prevails everywhere nowadays. He said:

> The restless secular spirit of our times, with its supposed civilization, has unfortunately destroyed even the sacred sites of the desert that bring so much peace and sanctification to souls.[1204]
>
> Secularization is the greatest enemy of the monk—even greater than the devil.[1205]
>
> Even there [on the Holy Mountain] you cannot find a quiet spot; everywhere you go they are opening up forest roads! Cars are everywhere! Even the most remote and quiet places can now be reached by car! I wonder what these people are seeking in the wilderness! When a gentle wind from the desert stirred the reeds, Arsenios the Great would say, "What sound is this? Is it an earthquake?" I wonder what the holy Fathers would have said if they had seen and heard what is happening today! ...
>
> I remember in our monastery, we used to carry water in containers from a spring and would slowly lift it to the third floor with a windlass. Now they bring the water up with an engine and you hear its constant noise.
>
> "But, Geronda [a nun objected], these machines make our lives easier."
>
> Oh, there are too many of these devices around! ... This constant buzzing removes us from the real monastic way of life. Why then do you have a sign outside that says *Hesychasterion*?[1206] Why do you not write "buzzing place" or "a place of unrest"? What is the use of the monastery if there is no peace and tranquillity? When the monk makes use of all these noisy devices, he does away with the preconditions for prayer

---

[1201] Elder Joseph of Vatopaidi, *Obedience Is Life: Elder Ephraim of Katounakia,* 118.

[1202] Palmer, Sherrard, Ware, *The Philokalia,* vol. 4, 58 (ch. 143).

[1203] Paul Leicester Ford, *The Works of Thomas Jefferson,* vol. 12 (New York: G. P. Putnam's Sons, 1905), 75.

[1204] Elder Paisios of the Holy Mountain, *With Pain and Love for Contemporary Man,* trans. Cornelia A. Tsakiridou, Maria Spanou (Thessalonica: Holy Monastery "Evangelist John the Theologian," 2006), 190.

[1205] Holy Hesychasterion "Evangelist John the Theologian," *Saint Paisios the Athonite,* trans. Peter Chamberas (Thessaloniki, 2018), 460.

[1206] Many small monasteries in Greece are called a "hesychasterion" (ἡσυχαστήριον), which literally means "a place of quiet (ἡσυχία)."

and the monastic way of life. For this reason, we should avoid using noisy devices as much as possible. That which people today consider to be conveniences do not actually help the monk achieve his goal. A monk cannot find in such a noisy environment what he set out to find by becoming a monk. To be tranquil is very important. Even if one is not actually praying, tranquillity will put him in a state of prayer....

This is why it is good for monasteries to be located in isolated areas, away from the rest of the world, away from archaeological sites, worldly noises, and great numbers of people....

External tranquillity, living away from the world, along with discerning asceticism and unceasing prayer, will soon bring about the inner tranquillity, the peace of the soul, which is an essential precondition for the more refined and more profound prayer of the heart.[1207]

Similarly, whenever Elder Ephraim heard the fathers using a gas-powered blower, he wanted them to stop because such tools ruin the monastery's peace and quiet. He frequently added that such noisy tools are inappropriate for use in a monastery. Likewise, he was so disturbed by the noise made by the air-conditioning units outside the buildings and by the refrigeration unit outside the refrigeration building, that he asked us if we could turn them off before he had to walk by them. He even expressed his displeasure with the relatively quiet, low rumbling sound of the air handler that ventilated the ground level story of his house where we lived. And like St. Silouan the Athonite, he was bothered even by the ticking of a clock in his cell.[1208]

Despite the drawbacks of noise, St. Paisios added that we can counteract the negative effect of noise through a proper inner stance:

Since unfortunately modern man uses noisy devices even for small things, it is important, if we ever find ourselves in a noisy place, to cultivate good thoughts to counter the noise....

It's not so much the external noise that is disturbing, but one's internal concerns and anxieties. You can always avoid hearing noises, but you cannot avoid worries. At the root of it all is the mind. Our eyes could be looking at something without really seeing it. When I am praying, I may have my eyes open, but I don't really see anything....

A person must attain a kind of divine absence of mind, in order to experience inner tranquillity and not be distracted by noise while praying. One can actually attain such a state of divine absent-mindedness where he no longer hears the noise, or he hears it only when he wants or, actually, when his mind comes back from Heaven.[1209]

Shouting was completely unacceptable in the monasteries of St. Pachomios. He declared: "Chatting, not only with strangers but with our own brothers, or shouting when speaking, we must hold as an abomination. For this is the way with the idle and with those who are

---

[1207] Elder Paisios, *With Pain and Love for Contemporary Man,* 190–94.

[1208] Archimandrite Sophrony Sakharov, *Saint Silouan the Athonite* [New York: St. Vladimir's Seminary Press, 2020], 161.

[1209] Ibid., 195.

heedless of their souls' fervour.... If someone needs to ask his neighbor a question, he must do so quietly, without shouting."[1210] St. Basil the Great said that people who shout should not even be in the monastery: "Whoever in giving advice or an order uses a very loud, piercing tone gives an impression of arrogance thereby and should not be in a religious community."[1211] In his rules for nuns, St. Caesarius of Arles wrote: "They should never speak in a loud voice, according to that saying of the Apostle: 'Let all clamor be removed from you'[1212] because this is not at all becoming or proper."[1213] St. Fructuosus of Braga wrote in his *Rule for the Monastery of Compludo:* "It is unbefitting for a monk to be noisy in speech, or wrathful, jesting, or mocking."[1214] Likewise, Elder Aimilianos told his monks: "Anyone who raises his voice in the cells or hallways deserves many penances. Such people reveal the boorishness of their soul and disgrace their parents and themselves. There is no greater debasement for a person than to be heard shouting.... In order to be heard, don't shout from far away; make the effort to go near to the other person. This is what courtesy dictates."[1215]

Gerondissa Makrina also taught her nuns to avoid unnecessary noises: "We should not knock loudly on the doors, but very carefully. With one hand we will open them, and with the other hand we will close them.... After lunch it is forbidden to gather and talk or shout, which would bother the other sisters.... We should not shout (punishment: 50 prostrations)."[1216] Likewise, St. Columbanus wrote in his monastic rule: "Him who has spoken with a shout, that is, has talked in a louder tone than the usual, [is to be punished] with six blows."[1217] St. Donatus of Besançon also wrote: "None who are there [in the monastery's infirmary] should speak in a loud voice that can be heard outside.... If they do, let them suffer a supposition of silence or fifty blows."[1218]

16) Laughter

Many of the holy Fathers criticized all kinds of laughter quite harshly. St. Basil the Great wrote:

[1210] Veilleux, *Pachomian Koinonia,* vol. 2, 202, 210.

[1211] Wagner, *Saint Basil: Ascetical Works,* vol. 9, 221.

[1212] Cf. Eph. 4:31.

[1213] McCarthy, *The Rule for Nuns of St. Caesarius of Arles,* 174.

[1214] Barlow, *The Fathers of the Church: Iberian Fathers,* vol. 63, 167.

[1215] Γέροντος Αἰμιλιανοῦ, *Νηπτικὴ Ζωὴ καὶ Ἀσκητικοὶ Κανόνες,* 101.

[1216] Rules #6, #8, and #18.

[1217] Stephen Spencer, *SCM Studyguide to Church History* (London: SCM Press, 2013), 81.

[1218] Donatus of Besançon, "Regula ad Virgines: a Working Translation," ch. 11.

Being overcome with unrestrained and immoderate laughter is a sign of intemperance and shows that one cannot control his emotions and suppress his soul's laxity by a stern use of reason. It is not unbecoming, however, to show merriment of soul by a cheerful smile, though only so far as Scripture says: "A glad heart maketh a cheerful countenance" (Prov. 15:13); but raucous laughter and uncontrollable shaking of the body are not indicative of a well-regulated soul, or of personal dignity, or self-mastery. This kind of laughter Ecclesiastes also reprehends as especially subversive of firmness of soul in the words: "Laughter I counted error" (Eccl. 2:2), and again: "As the crackling of thorns burning under a pot, so is the laughter of fools" (Eccl. 7:7). Moreover, the Lord appears to have experienced those emotions which are of necessity associated with the body, as well as those that betoken virtue, as, for example, weariness and compassion for the afflicted; but, so far as we know from the story of the Gospel, He never laughed. On the contrary, He even bemoaned those who are controlled by laughter (Lk. 6:25).[1219]

St. Gregory the Theologian taught: "Laughter deserves the laughter [i.e., contempt] of those who reason well—and especially crude laughter which is worse than all."[1220] St. John Chrysostom taught that laughter is unbecoming to monastic mourning and asceticism:

> Do ye not hear Paul saying, "Let filthiness and foolish talking and jesting be put away from you" (cf. Eph. 5:4)? He places "jesting" along with "filthiness," and dost thou laugh? … And dost thou, a solitary, laugh at all and relax thy countenance? Thou that art crucified? Thou that art a mourner? Tell me, dost thou laugh? Where dost thou hear of Christ doing this? Nowhere…. This is the season of grief and tribulation, of discipline and subjection [of the body], of conflicts and sweating, and dost thou laugh?[1221]

St. Pachomios decreed: "Let absolutely no one laugh, so that there will not apply to us the reproach of the Scriptures, *They make bread for laughter* (Eccl. 10:19)."[1222] Abba John the Dwarf related: "Once when the brothers were eating at an *agapē* [meal], one of the brothers laughed at table, and Abba John wept when he saw him, saying: 'What on earth can that brother have in his heart that he laughed when he should rather have wept, since he is eating at an *agapē*?'"[1223] St. John of Sinai instructed monks: "If nothing goes so well with humility as mourning, certainly nothing is so opposed to it as laughter…. He who sometimes mourns and sometimes indulges in luxury and laughter is like one who pelts the dog of

---

[1219] Βασιλείου τοῦ Μεγάλου, *Ἀσκητικὰ Α´*, ΕΠΕ 8, 266–67; see also Wagner, *Saint Basil: Ascetical Works,* vol. 9, 271 (Question 17 in the *Long Rules*).

[1220] PG 91:997.

[1221] *Saint Chrysostom: Homilies on the Gospel of St. John and Epistle to the Hebrews,* Nicene and Post-Nicene Fathers of the Christian Church, vol. 14 (New York: Christian Literature Company, 1889), 442.

[1222] Veilleux, *Pachomian Koinonia,* vol. 2, 210.

[1223] Wortley, *The Alphabetical Sayings of the Desert Fathers,* 133 (John Colobos 9).

sensuality with bread. In appearance he is driving it away, but in fact he is encouraging it to be constantly with him"[1224]

St. Theodore the Studite reminded his monks that laughter is contrary to their lofty calling:

> Why, my children, have we come here, having departed from the world and having separated ourselves from our parents and relatives and friends and cities and home-lands? ... Was it not to save our souls? Was it not to please the Lord? Was it not to acquire the eternal blessings? Was it not to have our sins forgiven that we had com-mitted in our lives? Was it not to live angelically, imitating the bodiless spirits and especially our holy and thrice-blessed fathers? So how is it that we do the opposite? Instead of weeping we laugh; instead of purifying ourselves we dirty ourselves; instead of being restrained we behave boldly; instead of fasting we lack self-control; instead of obeying we are insolent; and instead of being humble we exalt ourselves.[1225]

Antiochos of the Lavra of St. Savas wrote: "It is not permitted that Christians laugh at all—and especially monks, who have crucified themselves to the world.... We have not been called to levity and laughter, only to hear, 'Woe unto thee,' but to be within [Paradise] through the consolation of mourning. For our entire struggle is for our soul, and there is great danger of eternal torment."[1226]

St. James the Brother of the Lord wrote: "Be afflicted and mourn and weep; let your laughter be turned into mourning, and your joy to gloom."[1227] Commenting on this, St. Nicodemos of the Holy Mountain, wrote: "The outpouring and joy of Christians' hearts should only reach the point of calmly smiling, as Sirach has said: 'A wise man will scarcely smile a little' (Sir. 21:20)."[1228]

The Rule of Paul and Stephen, took a more moderate stance and cautioned only against immoderate laughter: "All of us should beware of indulging without moderation in jesting and laughing ... for who does not know that laughter beyond measure is the gate to disorder and folly?"[1229] The biographer of St. Lazaros of Mt. Galesion "mentions him smiling on a number of occasions and even joking at the folly of his monks or visitors, often as a means of gentle reproach."[1230] Elder Ephraim also was more lenient (perhaps as a practical accom-modation to our contemporary culture, or perhaps as a concession because we are not at a

---

[1224] Holy Transfiguration Monastery, *The Ladder of Divine Ascent,* 71, 72.

[1225] Θεοδώρου τοῦ Στουδίτου, *Κατήχησις ιζ΄,* τ. 18, ΕΠΕ, 392.

[1226] PG 89:1721CD.

[1227] Jas. 4:9.

[1228] Νικοδήμου τοῦ Ἁγιορείτου, *Ἑρμηνεία εἰς τὰς Ἑπτὰ Καθολικὰς Ἐπιστολάς,* 134. Although a complete translation of this commentary by St. Nicodemos has not been published in English yet, the first draft of my translation of his commentary on James and Jude may be downloaded from: www.stnilus.org/James.pdf

[1229] Barry Hagan, "The Rule of Paul and Stephen," ch. 38.

[1230] Richard P. H. Greenfield, *The Life of Lazaros of Mt. Galesion: An Eleventh-century Pillar Saint* (Washington, D.C.: Dumbarton Oaks, 2000), 22.

high enough spiritual state such that laughter causes more harm than good). He expressed the opinion that laughter (even for monastics) is not only acceptable but it is a sign of normality. He not only appreciated jokes but even told a few innocent ones himself.[1231] Nevertheless, he did agree with St. Basil that *loud* laughter is unbecoming, and he also warned us that if we are so overcome by laughter that we reach the point of tears, we can expect a punishment to come from God for our lack of control.

St. Eustathios of Thessalonica also had a moderate stance towards monastic laughter:

> [A great-schema monk] should be cheerful and at times smile decorously. In fact, if the humor is greater he should even laugh. I do not like those who have permanently ostracized laughter from their life, since I have heard [in Scripture] that those who weep now are blessed because they will laugh.[1232] Therefore, this kind of servant of God [i.e., a monk] should do likewise when something funny happens. He should have a sweet look, and with this sweetness he will attract the attention of his listeners. He should display a genuine friendliness like our Lord Who is "comely in beauty" (cf. Ps. 44:2).[1233]

Commenting on the canon attributed to St. Anthony the Great: "May your face always be downcast,"[1234] Elder Aimilianos explained to his monks:

> The saint did not mean that we should be gloomy. Man must be serious, not a joker or frivolous. A frivolous person is always laughing. When someone laughs when he is speaking to you or when you are giving him advice or correcting him, such a person is immature. With this canon, St. Anthony is trying to prevent relationships of familiarity that waste time, which are the result of talking too much. When you are serious, other people respect you and acknowledge you.... So you should need to guard yourself from your surroundings, so that people don't approach you too easily. They should love you but simultaneously respect you. No one respects the person who is bubbly, idle, a complainer.[1235]

Further excerpts from the holy Fathers condemning familiarity and laughter may be found in Book II of *The Evergetinos*. The monastic editors of this in English added this reasonable conclusion: "Here, the Fathers put forth a high standard of sobriety, as a warning against frivolity and witless guffawing, cackling, and undignified displays of jocularity. Humor and subdued laughter are not inimical [i.e., hostile] to proper Christian or—within limits—

[1231] For example, one day as he left his house he saw a cat eating from the dish of cat food outside the house. When he came back three hours later and saw the same cat eating there again, he said with a knowing smile: "That cat has been eating for three hours!" But he also avoided excess humor. For example, when he was given an extremely playful poodle that behaved hilariously at times, he kept it only for a month before deciding to give it away because it was ruining our monastic seriousness.

[1232] Cf. Lk. 6:21.

[1233] PG 135:752C.

[1234] PG 40:1073A, Rule #74, as cited in Γέροντος Αἰμιλιανοῦ, *Νηπτικὴ Ζωὴ καὶ Ἀσκητικοὶ Κανόνες*, 161.

[1235] Γέροντος Αἰμιλιανοῦ, *Νηπτικὴ Ζωὴ καὶ Ἀσκητικοὶ Κανόνες*, 161–62.

monastic life. But the strict observance of the desert Fathers should serve as a guideline for controlling such behavior."[1236]

17) Frugality

The holy Fathers and contemporary elders were always careful not to be wasteful even in minor things. For example, when Elder Ephraim saw a small night light in an outlet on the wall that remained on during the daytime, he told us to unplug it so that it would not waste electricity. Likewise, Gerondissa Makrina considered frugality important enough to mention in her rules for her nuns that they should not leave lights on.[1237] When there were holes in the heels of Elder Ephraim's socks, instead of replacing them he merely rotated them (so that the hole would be on the top and thus not visible) and continued wearing them.[1238] (But we, of course, gave him new socks as soon as he took off those socks with holes.) From the following quote of his, it seems that he learned this frugality from St. Joseph the Hesychast: "He [St. Joseph] was also very cautious to be frugal with our belongings. With quotes from the Bible and patristic writings, he taught us the values of living frugally and treasuring the smallest morsel of food so as not to lose God's blessing. This is why whenever he dropped a grain of wheat or a little piece of rusk, he would always bend down and pick it up, even later in his life when he had difficulty moving."[1239]

Elder Ephraim was also cautious not to let any food spoil and was grieved when we carelessly did so. The *Regulations of Horsiesios* spoke of this: "Let no one let anything spoil through his negligence, knowing that it is the fruit of others' labor or of his own.... For nothing escapes God, not even a widow's two mites, or a glass of fresh water.... In truth we will be questioned [by the Judge] about every deed."[1240] Likewise, the communal rule of St. Columbanus commands: "Whoever of the brethren, to whom the care of cooking or serving has been entrusted, has spilt any drop, it is ordained to correct him by prayer in church after the end of the office, so that the brethren pray for him.... In the same manner let him who has lost the crumbs be corrected by prayer in church.... But if through negligence or forgetfulness or failure of care he has lost more than usual either of fluids or of

---

[1236] Chrysostomos, *The Evergetinos, Book II,* 268.

[1237] Rule #10.

[1238] This kind of frugality is what Abba Dorotheos would call "acting according to conscience in material things" (vid. Scouteris, *Abba Dorotheos: Practical Teaching on the Christian Life,* 104).

[1239] Γέροντος Ἐφραίμ, Ὁ Γέροντάς μου Ἰωσήφ, 325; see also Elder Ephraim, *My Elder Joseph the Hesychast,* 468.

[1240] Veilleux, *Pachomian Koinonia,* vol. 2, 208.

solids, let him do penance with a long pardon in church by prostrating himself without moving any limb while they sing twelve psalms at the twelfth hour."[1241]

St. John Cassian wrote: "During the week of a certain brother, as the bursar was going about he noticed 3 lentils lying on the ground. They had slipped out of the hands of the weekly server, along with the water in which they were soaking, as he was hastening to prepare them for cooking. He at once consulted the abba on this matter, and he judged him a pilferer and a waster of sacred goods and suspended him from prayer. This crime of negligence was not forgiven him until he had absorbed it by an act of public repentance. For they believe that not only they themselves are not their own but that everything that is theirs has been consecrated to the Lord. Hence whatever has once been brought into the monastery must, in their judgment, be treated with all respect as sacrosanct."[1242] Likewise, when a monk at the monastery of St. Savas cooked too many lima beans and threw out the extra, St. Savas gathered up the beans, made a delicious meal out of them, and reproached the cook.[1243]

Therefore, we should be careful also not to waste or break anything out of carelessness. St. Basil the Great wrote:

> "How should the working monks care for the tools entrusted to them?"
> "First of all as things consecrated and offered to God; secondly remembering that without them they cannot render the diligent service that is due from them."
> "What if a man loses a tool through carelessness or spoils it contemptuously?"
> "Let him that spoils it be judged sacrilegious, and he that loses it guilty of sacrilege, since they are all dedicated to the Lord and offered to God."[1244]

Similarly, the fifth-century *Rule of the Four Fathers* taught:

> The brothers must also know that everything whatever that is handled in the monastery, be it utensils or iron tools or anything else, has been consecrated. Should any of the brothers treat anything negligently, let him know that he has his portion with that king who drank with his concubines from the consecrated vessels of God's house, and what sort of punishment he deserved.[1245]

St. Benedict agreed with this and wrote: "Let him regard all the vessels of the monastery and all its substance, as if they were sacred vessels of the altar."[1246] *The Rule of the Master* states: "If any of the monastery's utensils are broken by anyone through carelessness, the

---

[1241] *Sancti Columbani Opera,* 147, 161. http://www.ucc.ie/celt/online/T201052.html

[1242] Ramsey, *John Cassian: The Institutes,* 88.

[1243] Vid. *The Great Synaxaristes of the Orthodox Church: December* (Buena Vista: Holy Apostles Convent, 2003), 242–43.

[1244] Clarke, *The Ascetic Works of St. Basil,* 282 (Rules 143–44 in the *Shorter Rules*).

[1245] *Regula Quattuor Patrum* [12]:27–30 (as translated in Barry, *Commentary on the Rule of Saint Benedict,* 380).

[1246] *Rule of St. Benedict,* Chapter XXXI.

one who broke them is not to go to table until he has penitently made satisfaction to the abbot, going down on his knees in humility."[1247] St. Porphyrios of Kafsokalyvia was so careful not to break things that he was able to say: "Never in my life have I broken a dish or glass."

18) Visitors

St. John Chrysostom urged laymen to visit monasteries with the following words:

> Inquire diligently for holy men, men that are truly such, who, in the retirement of the desert, cannot beg, but are wholly devoted to God. Take a long journey to visit them, and give with thine own hand. For thou mayest profit much in thine own person, if thou givest. Dost thou see their tents, their lodging? Dost thou see the desert? Dost thou see the solitude? Often when thou hast gone to bestow money, thou givest thine whole soul. Thou art detained, and hast become his fellow-captive, and hast been alike estranged from the world....
>
> Go then to their tabernacles. To go to the monastery of a holy man is to pass, as it were, from earth to heaven. Thou seest not there what is seen in a private house. That company is free from all impurity. There is silence and profound quiet. The words "mine and thine" are not in use among them. And if thou remainest there a whole day or even two, the more pleasure thou wilt enjoy.[1248]

St. Paul taught: "Render honour to whom honour is due."[1249] Therefore, special guests are treated with greater honor. As St. Isidore of Seville wrote: "And although the good of hospitality ought to be shown graciously to all, still, to monks and clerics a more abundant display of honor and hospitality must be shown."[1250] Likewise, the Rule of St. Pachomios states: "When people come to the door of the monastery, they shall be received with greater honor if they are clerics or monks.... If they wish to join the assembly of the brothers at the time of prayer and *synaxis,* and they are of the same faith ... they shall be brought in to pray."[1251]

In accordance with that rule and the numerous canons in *The Rudder* forbidding praying with heretics,[1252] the non-Orthodox do not participate in prayers in church and in the

---

[1247] Eberle, *The Rule of the Master,* 164.

[1248] *St. Chrysostom: Homilies on Galatians, Ephesians, Philippians, Colossians, Thessalonians, Timothy, Titus, and Philemon,* 455–56 (Homily 14 on 1 Tim. 5:8).

[1249] Cf. Rom. 13:7.

[1250] *Regula Monachorum* 21, as translated in Barry, *Commentary on the Rule of Saint Benedict,* 451.

[1251] Veilleux, *Pachomian Koinonia,* vol. 2, 153–54.

[1252] See Apostolic Canons 10, 45, and 64; and canons 6, 9, 32, 33, and 34 of the Synod in Laodicaea. These canons were ratified by the 1st canon of the 4th Ecumenical Council, the 2nd canon of the 6th Ecumenical Council, and the 1st canon of the 7th Ecumenical Council.

refectory. However, the holy Fathers have made some exceptions to this rule for the sake of *economia* (i.e., leniency). As Fr. Anastasios Gotsopoulos explains:

> For reasons of *economia* it has been permitted in the past for heretics or non-Christians to attend Orthodox worship—even the Divine Liturgy—when they are disposed to acquainting themselves with the worshipping life of our Church. One of the most characteristic examples is the attendance of the Divine Liturgy in the Holy Temple of Hagia Sophia in Constantinople by a delegation of Russian idolaters and the subsequent Christianization of the entire Russian people.
>
> Furthermore, the blessed Chrysostom would invite heretics to the temple where he preached, in the hope that they would return to the truth of the Church: "Here I invite the heretic. He either attends or does not attend. If he does attend, let him be taught by my voice. If he does not attend, let him learn through whatever you have heard."[1253]
>
> On broadening the aforementioned suggestion of St. Nicephoros the Confessor regarding the entry into heretics' temples for the purpose of venerating the holy relics in there, we can accept that the entry of heterodox in Orthodox Temples is likewise permitted, if they desire to venerate holy relics that we safeguard in our temples and that they too respect. Any prohibition of entry and veneration of the holy relics would naturally be a far cry from the genuine ecclesiastic spirit. And of course in cases where the heterodox "return" holy relics to our Church, reasons of hospitality and gratitude will dictate their presence (for the sake of *economia*) in the related ecclesiastic functions, naturally without any active liturgical participation in our Orthodox worship.
>
> The Patriarchs of Constantinople Gennadios Scholarios,[1254] Dositheos of Jerusalem,[1255] and the Archbishop of Ochrid (Bulgaria) Demetrios Chomatianos when referring to those heretics who come respectfully to attend our Orthodox worship and ask for our blessing, all recommend that we do not send them away, but on the contrary even offer them antidoron and our holy water. (We would remind the reader of the visitation of God's grace on the holy New-martyr Ahmet through antidoron.)[1256] It is characteristic that while Gennadios allows the Orthodox to bless the heretics, he discourages them from asking for the blessing and holy water of the heretics! "It is therefore enough, that you do not ask for their blessing, for they are heterodox, and separate." Demetrios of Ochrid feels the need to justify this suggestion of his, saying that "this custom has the power to gradually attract them fully towards our holy ethos and dogmas."[1257]
>
> Another case where heretics are permitted to participate in an Orthodox Service by *economia* is during the funeral service and burial that is performed by *economia* for a heterodox person by an Orthodox Priest, when there are no pastors of the dogma of

---

[1253] "Homily on the Priest-Martyr Phokas," PG 50:702.

[1254] X. A. Siderides, Martin Jugie, L. Petit, *Γενναδίου Σχολαρίου, Ἅπαντα*, τ. 5, 201–2. Πρβλ. Μητρ. Προῑλάβου Καλλινίκου, «Πῶς δεῖ δέχεσθαι τοὺς ἐξ αἱρέσεων προσερχομένους», *Θεολογία*, τ. 9 (1931), 242–43.

[1255] «Δοσιθέου Ἱεροσολύμων πρὸς Μιχαὴλ Βελιγραδίου», ἐν Κ. Δελικάνη, *Τὰ ἐν τοῖς κώδιξι τοῦ Πατριαρχικοῦ Ἀρχειοφυλακείου σωζόμενα ἐπίσημα ἐκκλησιαστικά ἔγγραφα*, τόμος Γ΄, ἐν Κωνσταντινουπόλει, (φωτοαναστατική ἐπανέκδοση, 1999), 684.

[1256] See *Συναξαριστής Νεομαρτύρων* (Θεσσαλονίκη: Ὀρθόδοξος Κυψέλη, 1989), 509.

[1257] Ράλλη καὶ Ποτλῆ, *Σύνταγμα τῶν Θείων καὶ Ἱερῶν Κανόνων*, Τόμος Ε΄, 435.

the deceased,[1258] as well as during the performance of the Sacrament of Matrimony,[1259] when the one member happens to be a heterodox (mixed Marriage).[1260]

St. Benedict wrote in his monastic rule: "On no account let anyone who is not ordered to do so, associate or speak with guests; but if he meet or see them, having saluted them humbly, as we have said, and asked a blessing, let him pass on saying that he is not allowed to speak with a guest."[1261] Likewise, Gerondissa Makrina gave the following rules to her nuns: "It is forbidden to pay attention to and look curiously at the visitors. Likewise we may not speak with visitors without a blessing. If they ask us something, we will refer them to the appropriate sister. When people who know us visit, we will speak with them after obtaining a blessing from the Abbess, who will decide how long we will be with them."[1262] Similarly, Elder Ephraim forbade his monks to speak with visitors unless they had a blessing to do so.

Elder Aimilianos explained how the virtue of watchfulness transforms a monk's approach towards others, including visitors:

> Watchfulness is a jump from the present, fake, deceptive, worldly life to the true life. Without watchfulness, no matter how determined a monk may be, he is only fooling himself. Watchfulness (basically of the mind but also of the heart) raises man above the ground. Someone who is walking on a muddy path becomes full of mud and becomes one with the clay, whereas someone on horseback is untouched by it and suffers no change. The same thing happens to him who has watchfulness: he is up high and has a lofty path. Watchfulness is being carefree of everything. I am not interested in this and that; I am not interested when one person leaves, when another whines, why someone else didn't smile, etc. It takes a complete indifference and ignorance and unconcern of everything. A small interest immediately makes me a fleshly person, walking in the mud. It takes an indifference not only in thought but also in works and deeds. For example, you see two visitors enter the monastery, and you wonder: "Who are these two people who came in?" What does it matter to you? What are you, the gatekeeper? And this thought alone is sufficient to bring you down to the muddy path, to a mundane life.[1263]

[1258] Βλ. ὑπ' ἀριθμ. 1621/343/15. 3. 1891 Ἐγκύκλιος τῆς Ἱ. Συνόδου, ἐν Σ. Γιαννοπούλου, *Συλλογὴ Ἐγκυκλίων τῆς Ἱερᾶς Συνόδου τῆς Ἐκκλησίας τῆς Ἑλλάδος ἀπὸ τοῦ 1833 μέχρι σήμερον* (Ἀθῆναι, 1901), 574–75. For the service [for such a funeral] see: *Μικρόν Εὐχολόγιον ἢ Ἁγιασματάριον* (Ἀθῆναι: Ἀποστολικὴ Διακονία, 1999), 276. For more analysis on the development of the ecclesiastical praxis regarding the burial of heterodox, see. Ἱ. Κοτσώνη, *Ἡ κανονικὴ ἄποψις περὶ τῆς ἐπικοινωνίας μετὰ τῶν ἑτεροδόξων (intercommunio)* (Ἀθῆναι, 1957), 242–47.

[1259] Ἱ. Καρμίρη, *Τὰ Δογματικὰ καὶ Συμβολικὰ Μνημεῖα τῆς Ὀρθοδόξου Καθολικῆς Ἐκκλησίας*, τ. Β΄ (Ἀθῆναι: 1953), 1003. «Β΄ Προσυνοδικὴ Πανορθόδοξος Διάσκεψις», ἐν Δ. Παπανδρέου, *Πρὸς τὴν Ἁγίαν καὶ Μεγάλην Σύνοδον* (Ἀθῆναι, 1990), 37.

[1260] http://oodegr.co/english/oikoumenismos/ou_dei.htm

[1261] *Rule of St. Benedict*, Chapter LIII.

[1262] Rules #25 and #26.

[1263] Γέροντος Αἰμιλιανοῦ, *Νηπτικὴ Ζωὴ καὶ Ἀσκητικοὶ Κανόνες*, 447–48.

19) Relatives

The holy Fathers have traditionally applied the following words of the Lord to monastics: "If any man come to me and hate not his father and mother and wife and children and brethren and sisters, yea, and his own life also, he cannot be my disciple."[1264] Of course, the sense of the word "hate" here is to become emotionally detached from one's relatives. Thus, the *Rule of St. Comghall* states: "If you have a son or family and have decided to leave them [to become a monk], you are then to regard yourself as dead; you must not seek out your relations, or even think about them."[1265] Likewise, *The Rule of the Master* says: "Let him [who has joined the monastery] know that henceforth his parental home is foreign to him. Let him make up his mind that now he no longer has access to its threshold, for unless one leaves father or mother or brothers or home he cannot be a disciple of Christ."[1266] For this same reason the fifth-century Syriac *Rules of Rabbūlā for the Monks* state: "The *rešai-dairātā* shall not allow the brothers to meet with their relatives nor that they go out and go to them, in order that they do not relax in their zeal."[1267] *The Rule of Tarn* was less strict and recommended merely that "parents should not be allowed to come and go with frequency"[1268] and "let no one attend the wedding banquet of his brothers."[1269]

St. John of Sinai elaborated on the stance of monastics towards their relatives:

> It is not from hatred that we separate ourselves from our own people or places (God forbid!), but to avoid the harm which might come to us from them. In this, as in everything else, it is Christ who teaches us what is good for us. For it is clear that He often left His parents according to the flesh. And when He was told, "Thy Mother and Thy brethren are seeking for Thee," our good Lord and Master at once showed us an example of dispassionate hatred when He said: "My mother and My brethren are they who do the will of My Father who is in Heaven" [cf. Mt. 12:50]....
>
> Longing for God extinguishes longing for our parents. And so anyone who says he has both is deceiving himself. He should listen to Him who says, "No one can serve two lords" [Mt. 6:24]. "I have not come," says the Lord, "to bring peace on earth (that is, love of parents for sons, and love of brothers for brothers who have resolved to serve Me), but war and a sword" [cf. Mt. 10:34] in order to separate lovers of God from lovers of the world, the lovers of material things from lovers of spiritual things, the lovers of fame from the humble-minded. For strife and separation delight the Lord when they spring from love for Himself.[1270]

[1264] Lk. 14:26.

[1265] Maidín, *The Celtic Monk,* 35.

[1266] Eberle, *The Rule of the Master,* 264.

[1267] Vööbus, *Syriac and Arabic Documents,* 30.

[1268] *Monastic Studies,* no. 17, 229.

[1269] Ibid., 230.

[1270] Holy Transfiguration Monastery, *The Ladder of Divine Ascent,* 16–17.

In the same spirit, St. Basil the Great also said:

> Even in the beginning of your renunciation of the world show yourself a man, and, that you may not be dragged down by attachments to your blood relatives, strengthen yourself by exchanging mortal for immortal aspirations.[1271] …
>
> Above all, we [monastics] renounce the devil and carnal passions, in having given up secret, shameful things, ties of physical relationship, human friendships, and any mode of life that conflicts with the strictness of the Gospel of salvation. And what is still more necessary: he that has stripped off the old man with his deeds,[1272] "who is corrupted in accordance with the lusts of deceit,"[1273] denies himself. Also, he repudiates all worldly affections which could hinder him from reaching the goal of piety. Such a one, moreover, regards as his true parents those who in Christ Jesus have brought him forth by the Gospel and looks upon as his brethren those who have received the same spirit of adoption.[1274] …
>
> A man who is strongly seized with the desire of following Christ can no longer be concerned with anything pertaining to this life, not even with the love of his parents or relatives when this is in opposition to the precepts of the Lord (for in this case these words apply: "If any man come to me and hate not his father and mother" and so on).[1275]

Elder Aimilianos explained this in more detail in the *Regulations of the Holy Cenobium of the Annunciation*:

> In their contacts with people from outside the community, the nuns shall not forget that monastic experience follows the severance of bonds with the world and estrangement to all things temporal, and liberation from social ties and duties. It is acquired through labours by day and by night and indefatigable struggles. As a result, remembrance "of one's former life"[1276] or involvement in the life of the outside world constitutes a breach in the wall cloistering the monastic state.
>
> Parents and siblings of any nun shall be considered parents and siblings of the whole community and "provided they live according to God"[1277] shall enjoy all honor and support. It should be clear, however, that members of the cenobium shall be cut off from their own family.[1278] Visits by relatives or friends to their cells shall be avoided. Nuns shall converse with visitors, known to them or not, only after being

---

[1271] Wagner, *Saint Basil: Ascetical Works,* vol. 9, 18.

[1272] Col. 3:9.

[1273] Eph. 4:22.

[1274] Βασιλείου τοῦ Μεγάλου, *Ἀσκητικὰ Α΄,* ΕΠΕ 8, 226–29; see also Wagner, *Saint Basil: Ascetical Works,* vol. 9, 253.

[1275] Βασιλείου τοῦ Μεγάλου, *Ἀσκητικὰ Α΄,* ΕΠΕ 8, 230–31; see also Wagner, *Saint Basil: Ascetical Works,* vol. 9, 254.

[1276] Wagner, *Saint Basil: Ascetical Works,* vol. 9, 296 (Question 32 in the *Long Rules*).

[1277] Ibid., 295 (PG 31:996A).

[1278] Although cutting oneself off entirely from one's relatives has often been implemented in Orthodox monasticism, it is not something that Elder Ephraim and many other contemporary elders have implemented in their monasteries. Instead, we endeavor to maintain the most beneficial balance between too much and too little communication with relatives.

given the obedience. They shall reveal nothing to people who do not belong to the community, nor shall they introduce into it any ideas or events from the outside, unless they have a blessing to do so.[1279]

20) Correspondence

According to ancient monastic traditions, the abbot has the authority to open the mail of his monks and to withhold any letters or gifts that he deems could be spiritually harmful for them to have. For example, St. John Cassian said: "When all the brothers have come together for the synaxis he shall beg for pardon, prostrate on the earth, until the service of prayers is concluded ... if he tries to receive someone's letter or to reply to one without [the permission of] his abba."[1280] St. Christodoulos of Patmos wrote: "Do not, any of you, receive a letter without the superior's knowledge, or send one clandestinely."[1281] The thirteenth-century typikon of the Monastery of Machairas says: "If anyone is found writing to anyone or receiving a letter without the permission of the superior, let him eat dry food for three days."[1282] In the same spirit, the typikon of the Monastery of St. John the Forerunner of Phoberos wrote: "Those who acquire some possessions contrary to the rule of the monastery ... without the knowledge of the superior will be liable to punishment. Similar to them is ... the person who receives messages from friends and relatives, and replies to them."[1283]

Likewise, St. Benedict taught: "Let it not be allowed at all for a monk to give or to receive letters, tokens, or gifts of any kind, either from parents or any other person, nor from each other, without the permission of the Abbot. But even if anything is sent him by his parents, let him not presume to accept it before it hath been made known to the Abbot. And if he order it to be accepted, let it be in the Abbot's power to give it to whom he pleaseth."[1284] St. Caesarius of Arles agreed: "Letters should be received secretly from no one, not even from relatives, nor should letters of any kind whatever be sent without the permission of the abbess."[1285]

St. Fructuosus of Braga also wrote in his *Rule for the Monastery of Compludo:* "No monk is to accept any presents or to receive letters."[1286] The Syriac *Rules for the Nuns*

[1279] Elder Aimilianos, *The Authentic Seal,* 181.

[1280] Ramsey, *John Cassian: The Institutes,* 85–86 (iv. 16).

[1281] Thomas and Hero, *Byzantine Monastic Foundation Documents,* 594.

[1282] Ibid., 1157.

[1283] Ibid., 923.

[1284] *Rule of St. Benedict,* Chapter LIV.

[1285] McCarthy, *The Rule for Nuns of St. Caesarius of Arles,* 189.

[1286] Barlow, *The Fathers of the Church: Iberian Fathers,* vol. 63, 164.

(written sometime between the fifth and eighth centuries) state: "It is not lawful for any of the sisters ... to write a letter nor to receive from anybody without the knowledge of the *rīšat dairā*."[1287] The *Rule of Tarn* likewise states: "Anyone who presumes to receive anyone's letters and gifts, if he does not at once make public what he received and from whom, shall undergo a very severe punishment."[1288] Elder Aimilianos explained in the *Regulations of the Holy Cenobium of the Annunciation*: "Exchange of letters, all information from the outside or communication from within, as well as visits outside the cenobium, plainly constitute communion with the world, which the nun has renounced."[1289]

21) Entering Someone Else's Cell

Abba Isaiah said: "Let no one at all enter another brother's cell,"[1290] and St. Pachomios taught: "Without the order of the superior, nobody will be permitted to enter in the cell of another brother."[1291] Likewise, St. Symeon the New Theologian advised: "Do not enter into the cell of anyone without the permission of him who is your father according to God."[1292] The typikon of the Monastery of Machairas (early 13th century) also gave a punishment for doing this: "If anyone, without permission or absolute necessity, enters into the cell of another or sleeps [in it] or starts doing handiwork, let him be banished from the church and the refectory for three days and eat dry food."[1293] In the same spirit, Gerondissa Makrina gave a punishment of fifty prostrations for doing this.[1294]

Gerondissa Makrina also wrote: "When we are about to enter the cell of the Abbess or of another sister, we should knock on the door and say, 'Through the prayers of our holy Fathers.' Only when we hear the answer, 'Amen,' will we open the door."[1295] Elder Ephraim agreed with this teaching and was displeased with some monastics who instead of saying, "Through the prayers of our holy fathers," merely said, "Through the prayers." In other traditions, the Jesus prayer is said instead whenever entering a room. St. Herman of Alaska explained how this rule helped protect him from temptations:

[1287] Vööbus, *Syriac and Arabic Documents*, 67.

[1288] *Regula Tarnatensis* 19:1–4 (as translated in Barry, *Commentary on the Rule of Saint Benedict*, 455).

[1289] Elder Aimilianos, *The Authentic Seal*, 181.

[1290] Chryssavgis and Penkett, *Abba Isaiah of Scetis*, 40.

[1291] Πετρακάκου, *Μοναχικοὶ θεσμοί*, 112 (Μ. Παχωμίου «Κανόνες»); see also Veilleux, *Pachomian Koinonia*, vol. 2, 161.

[1292] C. J. de Catanzaro, *Symeon the New Theologian: Discourses*, 276.

[1293] Thomas and Hero, *Byzantine Monastic Foundation Documents*, 1157.

[1294] Rule #11.

[1295] Rule #5.

His disciple Gerasim once entered the elder's cell without saying the typical prayer; he did not receive an answer to any of his questions to Father Herman. The next day, he asked the elder the reason for his silence the previous day. Father Herman answered, "When I arrived on this island and settled in this deserted place, demons came to me many times in human and animal form as if for some necessity. I often endured various offenses and temptations from them, so now I do not speak to those who enter my cell without a prayer."[1296]

Traditionally, a monastic does not lock the door to his cell. St. Pachomios decreed: "No one shall sleep in a locked cell; nor shall anyone get a locked room except by order."[1297] Likewise, St. Caesarius of Arles wrote in his rules for nuns (and was paraphrased by Donatus of Besançon in his own rules[1298]): "No one may be permitted to choose a separate room, nor to have a cell or a chest, or anything of this nature, which can be locked for private use."[1299] The typikon of the Monastery of St. John the Forerunner of Phoberos (written in the twelfth century) explains the reason for this: "Things that are locked up are all secret and their owner does not wish them to be revealed. But all your possessions are in common and are open, and therefore there will be no need among you for the use of keys. It should be recognized by everyone that the person who does this is a thief and does not wish what is hidden by him to be revealed and for this reason he uses a lock."[1300] St. Gerasimus of the Jordan made the rule for his lavra that "the cells should always be left open, and any brother in need should be at liberty to take what was found in a cell if its occupier was absent."[1301]

Even though St. Pachomios taught that the *monks* are not allowed to enter each other's cells, St. Benedict taught that the *abbot* has the duty of entering their cells. The cells should be "frequently examined by the abbot to prevent personal goods from being found. And if anyone should be found with anything that he did not receive from the Abbot, let him fall under the severest discipline."[1302] Although we do not know precisely how often St. Benedict wanted the abbot to examine their cells, Abba Shenoute the Great (in the 4th

---

[1296] Sergei Korsun with Lydia Black, *Herman: A Wilderness Saint,* trans. Priest Daniel Marshall (Jordanville: Holy Trinity Publications, 2012), 135.

[1297] Veilleux, *Pachomian Koinonia,* vol. 2, 162.

[1298] "No one is allowed to choose a separate establishment or have a bedroom or cupboard or anything private which can be closed with a key" (Donatus of Besançon, "Regula ad Virgines: a Working Translation," ch. 11).

[1299] McCarthy, *The Rule for Nuns of St. Caesarius of Arles,* 174.

[1300] Thomas and Hero, *Byzantine Monastic Foundation Documents,* 924.

[1301] Chitty, *The Desert a City,* 90.

[1302] *Rule of St. Benedict,* Chapter LV.

century)[1303] and the typikon of the Monastery of Evergetis (in the 11th century)[1304] decreed that this should be done once a month, whereas St. Fructuosus of Braga (in the 7th century) recommended twice a week.[1305]

22) Exiting the Monastery

A part of monastic renunciation of the world is to remain within one's monastery as much as possible. St. Anthony the Great taught: "Just as fish perish when they lie exposed for a while on the dry land, so also the monks relax their discipline when they linger and pass time with you [laymen in the world]. Therefore, we must rush back to the mountain, like the fish to the sea—so that we might not, by remaining among you, forget the things within us."[1306] Likewise "[Saint] Chariton laid down the precept [in the early fourth century] that monks must not emerge frequently from their cells, but rather stay inside as much as possible."[1307] St. Basil the Great wrote: "Departure from the monastery … is not permitted except for a duty or an emergency…. To avoid dissipation of the heart, refrain as much as you can from going abroad [i.e., outside your monastery] at all. Have you deserted your cell? Then you have left continency behind you; you have lowered your gaze toward the world."[1308]

In the era of St. Pachomios "the monastery wall was intended to isolate the monks and protect them from the outside world and its temptations. In the 'White Monastery' of Shenoute, it was possible to leave the monastery only through a tunnel[!]"[1309]

St. Neilos the Ascetic wrote: "Let us avoid staying in cities and villages; so that their inhabitants run to us. Let us seek the wilderness and so draw after us the people who now shun us. For Scripture praises those who 'leave the cities and dwell in the rocks, and are

---

[1303] "Twelve times per year—once a month—the father superior shall enter all the houses of the congregation and inspect all cells that are within them and all alcoves and all vessels that are holding their portion that they have put there, so that he might know whether they have an excess beyond the ordinance that is laid down, or whether someone has committed impiety by taking anything into his cell against the edifying rule that is laid down" (Layton, *The Canons of Our Fathers: Monastic Rules of Shenoute*, 167).

[1304] "The superior must do this also, that is he should enter your cells once a month whenever he wishes, and if any have extra items, he should take them away and deposit them in the storehouse or give them to those in need" (Thomas and Hero, *Byzantine Monastic Foundation Documents*, 491).

[1305] "Twice a week the abbot and prior should turn over and examine carefully each one's bed, to see that no one has anything superfluous concealed there" (*Regula Complutensis* 4 (1101A) as translated in Barry, *Commentary on the Rule of Saint Benedict*, 462).

[1306] *Athanasius: The Life of Antony and the Letter to Marcellinus,* Classics of Western Spirituality, trans. Robert C. Gregg (New York: Paulist Press, 1979), 93.

[1307] Patrich, *Sabas, Leader of Palestinian Monasticism*, 225.

[1308] Wagner, *Saint Basil: Ascetical Works,* vol. 9, 221, 21.

[1309] Patrich, *Sabas, Leader of Palestinian Monasticism*, 20.

like the dove' (cf. Jer. 48:28). John the Baptist also lived in the wilderness and the population of entire towns came out to him."[1310]

The holy Fathers of the Fourth Ecumenical Council ratified this approach by teaching that "monks in every city and country be subject to the Bishop, and embrace quietude, and pay heed only to fasting and prayer, while continuing in the places patiently whereunto they have been assigned, without intruding upon or meddling in ecclesiastical affairs, nor leaving their own monasteries, unless at any time they be permitted to do so by the Bishop of the city on account of some exigency."[1311] Bearing this in mind, St. Symeon the New Theologian wrote to his disciple Arsenios: "Do not go out from the monastery frequently. Once a month for serious matters is sufficient for you."[1312]

St. Gregory Palamas explained why monks should stay in their monastery:

> What good does it do us to take flight from the world once and for all and find refuge in houses of prayer consecrated to God, but then to leave them daily and become involved in the world again? Tell me how, if you love frequenting the town squares, you will avoid the incentives to passions which bring about the death of the soul, separating a man from God? This death comes upon us through our senses, as if through windows within us.[1313]
>
> Do you think we, who have been born and brought up in the world, can avoid being harmed, or suffering wounds and a change for the worse in our inner selves, when we are faced with the passions in their various guises, and with hearing and joining in prolonged and unseemly conversations? That would be absolutely impossible. For these reasons the Fathers imitated the Forerunner of grace [i.e., St. John the Baptist], bade farewell to the world, and fled the company of those devoted to it.[1314]

When St. Máel Ruain was asked by a monk how to conduct himself, he replied: "I advise you to remain always in the place where you normally dwell. Have nothing to do with the affairs of the world. Never go to a law court with anyone, or to any gathering to intercede for anyone. Instead stay at home in prayer, meditating on your reading, and giving instruction, should there be anyone who desires such of you."[1315]

St. Nectarios of Aegina urged his nuns not to leave their convent even in order to attend a vigil service. He explained: "A vigil outside of the convent allows the nuns' minds to wander, and they lose everything they sought to gain by attending the vigil. I ardently

---

[1310] Νείλου τοῦ Ἀσκητοῦ, «Λόγος ἀσκητικός», ἐν Φιλοκαλία, τόμος α΄ (1893), 119; see also Palmer, Sherrard, Ware, *The Philokalia,* vol. 1, 214.

[1311] Agapius and Nicodemus, *The Rudder,* 248 (Canon IV).

[1312] Ὁ Ἅγιος τοῦ Φωτὸς καὶ τοῦ Θείου Ἔρωτος, Ὅσιος Συμεὼν ὁ Νέος Θεολόγος (Κάλαμος: Ἱ. Μονῆς Ἁγ. Συμεὼν τοῦ Νέου Θεολόγου, 2000), 49.

[1313] *Saint Gregory Palamas: The Homilies,* Christopher Veniamin, ed. (Essex: Monastery of St. John the Baptist, 2009), 397.

[1314] Ibid., 321–22.

[1315] Maidín, *The Celtic Monk,* 103.

advise that you remain in the convent. Seek solitude, and in it you will find what you desire. You may go out to take a walk for a little while, walking around the convent all together. Let no one go anywhere by herself."[1316]

Elder Aimilianos explained why a monk should not go out of his monastery as follows:

When we go out of our monastery, we are no longer with our brethren but with worldly people. This is dangerous and serious, apart from the moral dangers this entails. A true monk passes through a fearsome trial. A monk has learned to follow an early morning schedule, to be in a vigilant state, in a quiet atmosphere, and in general to have a humble stance. When he goes out into the world, the conditions change, and then he does not know how to behave. If one could live the Gospel in the world, there would be no need to become a monk. So when a monk leaves his monastery, his powers are weakened. This is why St. Augustine says [in his monastic rule][1317] that another monk should accompany him. In this manner he will be strengthened and will pass through this exceptional situation and will return to his monastery as soon as possible—if possible even the same day, as the holy Fathers say. Furthermore, it is good that two monks go out in order to avoid criticism. When you are by yourself, people can say many things about you. But when there is someone else with you, whatever evil they say about you will not be believable.... Besides, a single day outside the monastery means that at least two months will pass without true prayer.[1318]

The holy Fathers would also pay great attention to whom they would send out of the monastery. For the most part, they would send a competent monk along with an older monk. The competent monk would be a specialist in the matter at hand, whereas the older monk has another spirit; he lives in another world. The older monk does not conform to the younger monk; they have two different worldviews. In other words, the holy Fathers took care that tradition would be secured with the specialist, so that experience would be joined to power in order that they would do something correctly.[1319]

When a monk goes into the world to take care of a particular need for which he has obtained the blessing, he may not take advantage of being in town to take care of other matters for which he has not obtained the blessing. As stated in *The Rule of Tarn:* "If any of the brothers is directed by a senior to go to the city, castle, or locality on some business, let him not dare approach any place except that to which he was assigned."[1320]

The holy Fathers teach that a monk may not exit the monastery without the abbot's permission. For example, St. Pachomios wrote: "No one should have leave to go out into the field or go walking in the monastery or proceed outside the monastery's wall, unless

---

[1316] Strongylis, *St. Nectarios of Pentapolis and the Island of Aegina,* vol. 2, 60 (Letter #9).

[1317] "If it is necessary for us to go out [of the monastery] for some matter, two of us shall go together" (Rule #8, as cited in Γέροντος Αἰμιλιανοῦ, *Νηπτικὴ Ζωὴ καὶ Ἀσκητικοὶ Κανόνες,* 208.

[1318] Γέροντος Αἰμιλιανοῦ, *Νηπτικὴ Ζωὴ καὶ Ἀσκητικοὶ Κανόνες,* 208–9, 214.

[1319] Ibid., 212.

[1320] *Monastic Studies,* no. 17, 224. With the same understanding, St. John the Prophet told a monk who had been sent to Jerusalem but also went to pray at the Jordan without a blessing: "You should go nowhere without an explicit blessing; for whatever takes place according to one's own thought, even it if appears to be good, is in fact not pleasing to God" (Chryssavgis, *Barsanuphius and John,* vol. 2, 4 [letter 356]).

he has asked the superior of the house, and he has granted permission."[1321] In response to the question if a monk may go away anywhere without mentioning it to the superior, St. Basil replied: "Since the Lord says: 'I am not come of Myself but He sent Me' (Jn. 7:28), how much rather should one of us not allow himself anything?"[1322] St. Benedict wrote in his rule: "Let him be punished who shall presume to go beyond the enclosure of the monastery, or anywhere else, or to do anything, however little, without the order of the Abbot."[1323] And St. Columbanus taught: "The mortification of the monk is threefold: he must never think what he pleases, never speak what he pleases, never go where he pleases."[1324]

The Rule of the Master states: "Let him [who wants to join the monastery] know that he may not go outside the monastery without orders from the superior."[1325] Likewise, the holy Fathers of the Sixth Ecumenical Council stated: "Men who are leading the solitary life (of monasticism) may themselves step out, when there is urgent need of their doing so, only with the blessing of the one in charge of the monastery."[1326] The anonymous Syriac *Rules for the Nuns* order: "It is not lawful for any of the sisters to go on a journey that is farther than one mile without the permission of the *sā'ūrā*."[1327] St. Iosif Volotsky made the following exception: "No one [may] go outside the monastery without a blessing. Monasteries which are in desolate places, situated far from cities and from villages, do not have so much need to be concerned over this."[1328]

St. Benedict taught: "Let the brethren who are to be sent on a journey recommend themselves to the prayers of all the brotherhood and of the Abbot. And after the last prayer at the Work of God, let a commemoration always be made for the absent brethren."[1329] At Philotheou Monastery we implemented this advice by commemorating the names of the absent fathers during the Paraklesis. St. Sophrony of Essex viewed this approach as a natural expression of the awareness that a monastic community is like a single organism. He told his monastics: "Please, when one of you is away, pray intensely for the person away and for every sick [member of our community]. You should live as a single body."[1330]

[1321] *Regula Pachomii*, Praec. 84 (74B) as translated in Barry, *Commentary on the Rule of Saint Benedict*, 523. This translator added the following remark: "Walking in a pachomian monastery might well take one quite a distance from one's own house and work!" (ibid.).

[1322] Clarke, *The Ascetic Works of St. Basil*, 274 (Rule 120 in the *Shorter Rules*).

[1323] *Rule of St. Benedict*, Chapter LXVII.

[1324] Oliver Davies and Thomas O'Loughlin, *Celtic Spirituality*, 255.

[1325] Eberle, *The Rule of the Master*, 264.

[1326] Agapius and Nicodemus, *The Rudder*, 346 (Canon XLVI).

[1327] Vööbus, *Syriac and Arabic Documents*, 68.

[1328] Goldfrank, *The Monastic Rule of Iosif Volotsky*, 285.

[1329] *Rule of St. Benedict*, Chapter LXVII.

[1330] Σωφρονίου, *Οἰκοδομώντας τὸν Ναὸ τοῦ Θεοῦ, Τόμος Β΄*, 419.

St. Benedict added: "On the day that the brethren return from the journey, let them lie prostrate on the floor of the oratory at all the Canonical Hours, when the Work of God is finished, and ask the prayers of all on account of failings, for fear that the sight of evil or the sound of frivolous speech should have surprised them on the way. Let no one presume to relate to another what he hath seen or heard outside of the monastery, because it is most hurtful."[1331] Likewise, *The Rule of Tallaght* says that St. Máel Ruain ordered his monks "not to seek news of those who came to visit them, or even to carry on a conversation with them. Such news, he felt, was the cause of much harm and disturbance in the mind of the one to whom it was told."[1332] Elder Ephraim recollected about his elder, St. Joseph the Hesychast:

> Geronda would not let anyone talk about outside news: to speak about so-and-so, what he did, how he was doing. We did not know what was happening outside our hut. He ensured that there would be no idle talk. Criticism of others was nonexistent. When someone tried to say something like that, Geronda would strictly correct him and say: "You'll lose the grace of God, you wretch, and then you'll be kicking yourself. Why are you sitting around criticizing? What does it matter to you? There's no room in here for news—only onwards! Silence and the prayer! Nothing else.... What other people are doing out there is none of our business. It is forbidden to talk about what other people are doing. We have to pay attention to what *we* are doing."[1333]

Other Athonite saints of the twentieth century were opposed to learning news from the media. St. Silouan the Athonite once told a hieromonk who believed that newspapers helped him to pray by seeing people's sufferings: "I don't care for newspapers with their news ... because reading newspapers clouds the mind and hinders pure prayer.... Newspapers don't write about people but about events, and then not the truth. They confuse the mind and, whatever you do, you won't get at the truth by reading them."[1334] St. Paisios of the Holy Mountain often remarked: "Only once in my life did I read a newspaper—to find out when I would be recruited to serve my military tour of duty [i.e., before becoming a monk]. If something happens, either it will become known and I, too, will hear of it, or I will learn of it through prayer."[1335]

Special caution with our eyes is needed whenever we are away from our monastery. Abba Isaiah taught: "If you travel to a city or town, let your eyes look downward so that no inner warfare is aroused once you return to your cell."[1336] Because of this potential

---

[1331] *Rule of St. Benedict,* Chapter LXVII.

[1332] Maidín, *The Celtic Monk,* 109.

[1333] Γέροντος Ἐφραίμ, Ὁ Γέροντάς μου Ἰωσήφ, 339, 62; see also Elder Ephraim, *My Elder Joseph the Hesychast,* 439–40, 81.

[1334] Sakharov, *Saint Silouan the Athonite,* 73.

[1335] Chamberas, *Saint Paisios the Athonite,* 454.

[1336] Chryssavgis and Penkett, *Abba Isaiah of Scetis,* 52.

danger, Elder Ephraim wanted his monks to avoid going into town as much as possible. The seventh-century Persian *Rules of Bābai* advise: "If a necessity compels a monk to go out from his monastery, this shall be in the fear of God and piety, and he shall not go out except because of an emergency; he shall not be seen in the town and village, and if it must be, he shall keep head and eyes down in order that he might not harm himself and become the cause of perdition for others."[1337] St. Savas was so strict with applying this principle that he drove a monk out of his monastery who had immodestly looked at a woman walking by:

> One day, the godly one [St. Savas] was walking to the Jordan from Jericho with a young disciple, and they passed a large group of lay folk, among whom was an exquisite maiden. After the crowd had gone by, the elder, wishing to test the disciple, commented, "I noticed that the maiden who just walked by is blind in one eye."
> "No, Father," answered the disciple. "She can see with both."
> "You are mistaken, child," said the elder, but the disciple insisted that the girl could see perfectly well. Then the elder asked, "How can you be certain?"
> "Father," replied the disciple, "I studied her face carefully and can assure you that she has two beautiful, healthy eyes."
> To this the elder said, "When you were looking so closely at her face, did you not remember the words of the Holy Scriptures which declare, *My son, let not the desire of beauty overcome thee, neither be thou caught by thine eyes, neither be captivated with her eyelids* (Prov. 6:25)? Because you do not guard your eyes, I will no longer permit you to live in my cell!"[1338]

The Sayings of the Desert Fathers recorded for posterity the following example of a monk who had great caution with his eyes:

> Abba Isidore once went to visit Abba Theophilus, the archbishop of Alexandria. When he returned to Scete the brothers asked him: "How was the city?" and he said: "To tell you the truth, brothers, I did not see anybody's face other than the archbishop's." They were troubled when they heard this and they said: "Were they utterly destroyed, abba?" "Not so," he said, "but my *logismos* [thought] did not overcome me to look at anybody." They were astonished when they heard this and strengthened in their resolve to keep their eyes from wandering.[1339]

St. Cosmas Aitolos said: "Just as it is difficult for a lamb to associate with a wolf without being eaten and for twigs to be among coals without igniting, it is likewise difficult for a monk to associate with women (and a nun with men) without being defiled and scandalized. The only way a monk can be saved is by fleeing far from the world."[1340] With the same understanding, St. Joseph the Hesychast wrote:

[1337] Vööbus, *Syriac and Arabic Documents,* 180.

[1338] Saint Demetrius of Rostov, *The Great Collection of the Lives of the Saints, Volume IV: December,* Thomas Maretta, ed. (Manchester, MO: Chrysostom Press, 2000), 109–10.

[1339] Wortley, *The Alphabetical Sayings of the Desert Fathers,* 145 (Isidore of Scete 8).

[1340] Ἐπισκόπου Αὐγουστίνου, *Κοσμᾶς ὁ Αἰτωλός* (Ἀθῆναι: «Ὁ Σταυρός», 1971), 246.

If a monk needs to go out into the world, let him go. However, he must be all eyes and all light: he must see very clearly, so that he won't suffer any harm while trying to help others. Young monks and nuns, who are still in the prime of life, are especially in danger when they go out into the world, since they are walking among many snares. As for those who have somewhat matured in age and have become withered through ascesis, the danger is not so great. They are not harmed so much as they benefit others, as long as they have experience and knowledge. But in general, a monk does not acquire any benefit from the world—he only gets praises and glory, which clean him out and leave him bare. And woe to him if God's grace does not protect him according to the need and purpose for which he went out.[1341]

St. Basil the Great wrote to his disciple Chilo: "Do not then for your kinsfolk's sake abandon your place: if you abandon your place, perhaps you will abandon your mode of life. Love not the crowd, nor the country, nor the town; love the desert, ever abiding by yourself with no wandering mind, regarding prayer and praise as your life's work."[1342] Likewise, St. Isaac the Syrian said: "A bird, wherever it may be, hastens back to its nest, there to hatch its young; and a monk possessing discernment hastens to his cell, there to produce the fruit of life."[1343]

Despite the drawbacks of leaving one's monastery, St. Basil perceived also the benefit of not remaining constantly cloistered:

> Each [monk] should remain for the most part in peace in his own dwelling and live there patiently, so that this [behavior] will bear witness to his stability. He should not be completely cloistered, but with confidence he should go out when necessary (as long as his conscience does not bother him) and visit the brethren who are great and beneficial because of their strictness of life. He should go out—as we said—with moderation and in an irreproachable manner. Going out will often dispel the negligence that has come to the soul. It gives him some strength and refreshment; it inspires him to resume pious struggles with eagerness.[1344]

When St. Basil the Great was asked what trades are suitable for monastics, he emphasized selecting trades that minimize the need for exiting one's monastery:

> Trades should be chosen which allow our life to be tranquil and undisturbed, involving no difficulty in the procuring of the materials proper to them, nor requiring much exertion in selling the articles produced, nor leading to unsuitable or harmful association with men or women. In all things we must keep in mind that our special aim is simplicity and frugality.... As for the arts of building, carpentry, the smith's trade, and farming—these are all in themselves necessary for carrying on life, and they provide much that is useful. They should not, therefore, be repudiated by us for any reason inherent in themselves, but, as soon as they cause us anxiety or sever our union with the brethren, we must turn away from them, choosing in preference the trades

---

[1341] Γέροντος Ἰωσήφ, Ἔκφρασις Μοναχικῆς Ἐμπειρίας, 55; see also Elder Joseph, *Monastic Wisdom*, 56.

[1342] *Basil: Letters and Select Works,* 440 (Letter 42).

[1343] Holy Transfiguration Monastery, *The Ascetical Homilies of Saint Isaac the Syrian,* 366 (Homily 59).

[1344] Ἀσκητικαὶ Διατάξεις, κεφ. ζ´, ΕΠΕ, Τόμος 9, 456. (PG 31:1365–68).

which allow us to lead recollected lives in constant attendance on the Lord and do not cause those who follow the practices of the devout life to be absent from psalmody and prayer or draw away from their schedule those who are devoted to pious deeds. Those trades, then, which involve no detriment to the life we have undertaken are to be given a decided preference—agriculture especially, since its proper function is the procuring of necessities and farmers are not obliged to do much traveling or running about hither and thither.[1345]

St. Basil even felt that monks who went about in public to secure the necessities of life were sullying their reputation.[1346]

St. Benedict also emphasized the importance of monastic self-sufficiency: "If it can be done, the monastery should be so situated that all the necessaries, such as water, the mill, the garden, are enclosed, and the various arts may be plied inside of the monastery, so that there may be no need for the monks to go about outside, because it is not good for their souls."[1347] Similarly, *The Rule of the Master* says:

> Everything necessary should be within, inside the gates, which means, oven, machines, lavatory, garden, and all that is required, so there may not be frequent occasion for the brothers to go outside repeatedly and mingle with people of the world. Were we to appear before the eyes of the devout and be venerated as angels by them, it would more be to our damnation, and it would be improper [for them] to say *Benedicte* [εὐλογεῖτε] to us unworthy of it, since we might be considered saints which we are not. Or, on the other hand, the holy habit would be cheapened by the ridicule of some unbelievers as it went about in public and on the streets. Therefore, since all these things are located inside, let the gate of the monastery be always shut so that the brothers, enclosed within with the Lord, may so to say be already in heaven, separated from the world for the sake of God.[1348]

Likewise, St. Paul of Mount Latros wrote: "Above all, you must not step easily out of the monastery without need, since it is both unsuitable to the [monastic] profession and dangerous."[1349] Abba Paul the Great, the Galatian, said: "A monk who has the bare necessities in his cell but goes out to care for more is being fooled by the demons, for I myself have suffered this."[1350]

St. Basil delineated how a monk should exit his monastery:

> Permission to travel should be granted to him who is able to make the journey without harm to his soul and with profit to his companions. If there is no suitable

---

[1345] PG 31:1017; see also Wagner, *Saint Basil: Ascetical Works,* vol. 9, 311–12 (Question 38).

[1346] "The reputation of the rest of the brethren [except for him who has been assigned the task of procuring necessities] should be kept unsullied and blameless by their not being required to go about in public to secure the necessities of life" (Wagner, *Saint Basil: Ascetical Works,* vol. 9, 211).

[1347] *Rule of St. Benedict,* Chapter LXVI.

[1348] Eberle, *The Rule of the Master,* 284.

[1349] Thomas and Hero, *Byzantine Monastic Foundation Documents,* 141.

[1350] PG 65:381B; see also Ward, *The Sayings of the Desert Fathers,* 204.

person, it is better to endure every inconvenience and trouble, even to the point of death, in the lack of necessary supplies, rather than to allow certain harm to the soul for the sake of physical comfort.... After returning, he who went should be examined [by the superior] as to the incidents which occurred, the sort of persons he met along the way, the words he spoke with them, the thoughts of his soul, and as to whether he passed every day and night in the fear of God or went astray and violated any of the rules, either by yielding to external circumstances or by giving in to his own indolence.[1351]

St. Columbanus assigned the following punishment for this: "He who dares to make a journey without the permission of the superior, by going out free and unrestrained without any need, let him be chastised with fifty strokes."[1352]

Father Epiphanios Theodoropoulos of blessed memory explained why it is unnecessary for a monk to leave his monastery in order to help others:

I dare to claim that *every* monk (every true monk, that is) is a missionary! I say "*every* monk" because my intent is not to limit the identity of the missionary only to those monks who have the grace of the priesthood and leave their holy monastery and (with the permission of their bishop) tour the cities and villages, teaching and hearing confessions. Nor do I limit the identity of the missionary to those who have literary talent (and are sometimes exceptionally skilled) and publish wonderful books which edify thousands of souls even for generations (such as St. Nicodemos). I, my brothers, believe—and don't think I'm crazy, for I shall justify this belief of mine—that even those monks who never step out of the enclosure of their monastery and never wrote a single page are missionaries.

"You must be referring to their prayer," some of you might say. I certainly do refer to their prayer but not only to prayer. The power of prayer—and especially of prayer by people whose life in God is purified or being purified—has great boldness before God; it is mighty. One heartfelt tear shed by a holy person is able to accomplish what would have taken many sermons and books. But prayer is just one of the means (but the foremost) by which a monk does missionary work, that is, by which he helps to save souls. There are two other ways, my brothers.

The second way is this: Has a monastery ever been established without becoming a magnet that attracts people? Has there ever been a hermit "in dens and mountains and caves"[1353] without entire armies of pilgrims seeking from him either a word of consolation or merely to see his face, which teaches much and greatly edifies them? This happens not only in the old days but even nowadays. How many who "labor and are heavy laden"[1354] with the journey of this life have taken refuge in holy monasteries to find a little peace of soul? How many people have benefited by the evocative atmosphere that prevails in the sacred services there? How many unbelievers and spiritually indifferent people have visited holy monastic dwellings for the sake of tourism and have felt twinges in their hearts because of what they saw there? Often a single visit sufficed to put their disbelief or indifference to the test. Let monks not go out into the

---

[1351] Βασιλείου τοῦ Μεγάλου, *Ἀσκητικὰ Α΄*, ΕΠΕ 8, 372–75; see also Wagner, *Saint Basil: Ascetical Works,* vol. 9, 320–21 (Question 44 in the *Long Rules*).

[1352] *Sancti Columbani Opera,* 165. http://www.ucc.ie/celt/online/T201052.html

[1353] Heb. 11:38.

[1354] Mt. 11:28.

world; let the world go to them. Let them remain hidden within their cloistered enclosure. Their light shines and illuminates the surrounding areas; sometimes it even illuminates places far away. Let them not say much; they have "the quiet eloquence of a holy life."

The third way is this: A monk, whether he is silent or preaches, is the loudest sermon—a sermon not with words but deeds—a powerful, stirring sermon. What do missionaries, the workers of our Church, preach in their sermons, my brothers? What do they write about in their books? Which subjects? What do they urge us to do? To love God, to pray, to fight against our evil habits, to partake of the holy Mysteries, to repent for our sins, to be humble, not to be attached to material goods, to have "our way of life in heaven,"[1355] etc. But isn't this exactly what a monk preaches, not with his words but with his example?[1356]

23) Expulsion

Knowing when to expel a monk is a delicate matter requiring much discernment. On the one hand, St. Isidore of Seville taught: "Although someone is immersed in the abyss of repeated and most serious vices, still he must not be cast out of the monastery but restrained in keeping with the type of sin, in case he who could have been amended by a penance of long duration, should on being cast out be devoured by the devil's mouth."[1357] On the other hand, however, most of the holy Fathers taught that when someone in the monastery is harming the rest of the brotherhood, he should be permanently expelled "lest one diseased sheep infect the whole flock," as St. Benedict said.[1358]

For example, the Elders of Scetis said: "If a brother is found to have a shortcoming that does not harm the brotherhood, they should put up with him. But if he troubles the rest of the brothers, they should expel him so that others are not lost along with him."[1359] With the same understanding, St. Basil the Great wrote:

> If he [i.e., the disobedient monk] is neither converted after much admonition nor cures himself by his own actions with tears and lamentations, being, as the proverb has it, "his own destroyer," we should, as physicians do, cut him off from the body of the brethren as a corrupt and wholly useless member. Physicians, indeed, are wont to remove by cutting or burning any member of the body they find infected with an incurable disease, so that the infection may not spread further and destroy adjacent areas one after the other.[1360]

[1355] Phil. 3:20.

[1356] Ἀρχιμ. Ἐπιφανίου Ἰ. Θεοδωροπούλου, «Μοναχὸς καὶ ἱεραποστολή», Ἄρθρα-Μελέται-Ἐπιστολαί, τόμος Α΄ (Ἀθῆναι: Ἰ. Ἡσυχαστήριον Κεχαριτωμένης, 1981), 664–67.

[1357] Isidore of Seville, *Regula monachorum* (*Rule for Monks*), rule 15 (PL 103:568BC).

[1358] *Rule of St. Benedict,* Chapter XXVIII.

[1359] Παύλου Μοναχοῦ, Εὐεργετινός, τόμος Δ΄, 667; Chrysostomos, *The Evergetinos, Book IV,* 478.

[1360] Wagner, *Saint Basil: Ascetical Works,* vol. 9, 290 (Rule 28).

The 11th-century typikon of the Monastery of Petritzonitissa also called for expelling incorrigible monks:

> But if any of the brothers is proved to be unwilling to live according to the terms of the rule but opposes it and considers the reproof of the superior harsh and unhelpful and does not consider his rebuke to be for his own help and benefit, fighting against his shepherd and doctor and not accepting his reproof … such a person will be possessed by the devil…. If such a person remains without improvement, then it is better that after the first and second and third piece of advice and rebuke he be cut off like a rotten limb and be far away from the divine flock.[1361]

The *Regula Orientalis* likewise expelled those who could not amend their behavior: "If there is anyone so hard and such a stranger to the fear of the Lord that he is not amended by so many chastisements and so many pardons, he should be cast out of the monastery and regarded as an outsider, in case others should be endangered by his vice."[1362] Similarly, St. Athanasios of Athos declared: "Those, however, who do not improve their attitudes even by these means, but persist in the same behavior even after lengthy punishment, as diseased limbs should be cut off from the rest of the body of the community, so that their own contagion may not spread to their neighbors"[1363] St. John of Rila had the same approach: "If somebody is found among you who sows weeds, discords and other temptations, you have to eliminate at once such a man from your assembly, so that this will not be transfigured into a devouring canker, according to the apostle, and not to spread the evil among the good ones, and 'lest any root of bitterness spring up and cause trouble by it, and the many be defiled' (Heb. 12:15); and the wicked wolf not trouble the peaceful flock of Christ, because this sort [of men] will appear."[1364]

In addition to incorrigible monks, monks who slandered others were also expelled from some monasteries. St. John of Sinai wrote of the monks in an exemplary monastery: "Above all, they strove never to injure a brother's conscience. And if ever someone showed hatred of another, the shepherd banished him like a convict to the isolation monastery. Once when a brother spoke ill of a neighbor, the holy man, on hearing him, had him expelled immediately. 'I'm not having a visible devil here along with the invisible one,' he said."[1365] In the same spirit the Syrian *Anonymous Rules for the Communities* decreed: "A monk who is a slanderer of his brothers and throws quarrel, shall cease or go from the

---

[1361] Thomas and Hero, *Byzantine Monastic Foundation Documents*, 539.

[1362] *Regula Orientalis* 35, as translated in Barry, *Commentary on the Rule of Saint Benedict*, 370.

[1363] Ibid., 225.

[1364] Thomas and Hero, *Byzantine Monastic Foundation Documents*, 132.

[1365] Luibhéid, *John Climacus: The Ladder of Divine Ascent*, 95. The literal meaning of the word διάβολος ("devil") in Greek is "slanderer."

monastery as an enemy of the peace since he has become a companion to that one—the slanderer of God in the Paradise."[1366]

24) Clothing

The holy Fathers taught that a monk's clothes should be ascetical. St. Basil the Great wrote:

> An ascetic must not seek fine clothes or shoes but should prefer the more base in order to show humility in this as well.[1367]
>
> The humble and abject spirit [of monks] is attended by a gloomy and downcast eye, neglected appearance, unkempt hair, and dirty clothes; consequently the characteristics which mourners effect designedly are found in us as a matter of course. The tunic should be drawn close to the body by a girdle; but let the belt not be above the flank, for that is effeminate, nor loose, so as to let the tunic slip through, for that is slovenly; and the stride should be neither sluggish, which would argue a laxity of mind, nor, on the other hand, brisk and swaggering, which would indicate that its impulses were rash. As for dress, its sole object is to be a covering for the flesh adequate for winter and summer. And let neither brilliancy of colour be sought, nor delicacy and softness of material.[1368]

In the same vein, the holy Fathers of the Seventh Ecumenical Council said (as paraphrased by St. Nicodemos): "The iconoclasts, besides rejecting holy icons, rejected also everything making for decency in the matter of clothing, and were wont to laugh at those wearing cheap or paltry garments (that is why they were wont to call monks 'darkics,' that is to say, wearers of dark-colored clothes, making fun of the decency of the monkish habit).... Ever since the beginning men in holy orders have been wearing humble clothes."[1369]

St. Gregory the Dialogist observed: "If there were not virtue in humble dress, the evangelist [Matthew] would not have noted so minutely of John the Baptist that 'he had his garment of camels' hair' [1370]" [1371] Likewise, in the 11th century St. Lazaros of Mt. Galesion said: "As far as clothing goes, he [a monk] should always make use of more humble garments. In short, the person who truly wishes to be saved must seek everything

---

[1366] Vööbus, *Syriac and Arabic Documents,* 76.

[1367] Μεγάλου Βασιλείου, *Ἀσκητικαὶ Διατάξεις,* PG 31:1420C.

[1368] *Basil: The Letters, Volume 1, Letters 1–58,* Loeb Classical Library, no. 190 (Boston: Harvard University Press, 1926), 21 (Letter 2).

[1369] Νικοδήμου τοῦ Ἁγιορείτου, *Πηδάλιον,* 336 (Canon XVI of the Seventh Ecumenical Council).

[1370] Mt. 3:4.

[1371] Pope Saint Gregory the Great, *Parables of the Gospel,* trans. Nora Burke (Chicago:Scepter Press, 1960), 150.

that tends toward humility and simplicity and innocence, and avoid things which are grand and have only vain repute."[1372]

Abba Isaac the Priest criticized some other monks who lacked this kind of simplicity: "Our fathers and Abba Pambo wore old, patched up clothes made of palm-fiber; now you are wearing expensive clothing. Go away from here."[1373] St. Theodore the Studite told his monks:

> The adornment of a monk is when he seeks to be unadorned. The beauty of a monk is not to strut arrogantly … preening—allow me to say it— like a whoremonger with nice belts and garments and shoes, but to keep the soul's ethos modest, to stand firm without yielding to the passions, to have inner peace from improper desires; additionally, to be rough, unwashed for the most part, poorly dressed with a patched raso, a patched cowl and other clothes. Whereas seeking new changes of clothes that are very thin and well dyed is lustful covetousness.[1374]

St. Theodore the Studite also taught (and St. Athanasios of Athos[1375] quoted him nearly verbatim in his own rule): "You shall not possess very distinctive or expensive clothing besides the priestly vestments. Rather, you shall put on humble clothes and shoes in imitation of the fathers. You shall not spend lavishly either for your own lifestyle or for the reception of guests. This will distract you since it belongs to a life devoted to pleasure."[1376]

The reason why a monk should have humble clothes, according to Abba Dorotheos, is because they give rise to a humble disposition: "The dispositions of a man riding a horse differ from those of a man riding a donkey; those of the man seated on a throne from those of a man sitting on the floor. The dispositions of one beautifully clothed differ from one clad in rags."[1377]

Abba Pambo taught that our monastic clothing should not be better than that of other monks: "The monk should wear a garment of such a kind that he could throw it out of his cell and no-one would steal it from him for three days."[1378] Likewise, St. John Cassian taught that monastic clothes "should be commonplace, so as to be indistinguishable in terms of novelty of color and cut from what is worn by other men of this chosen orientation [i.e., of monastics].… Finally, it should be different from the apparel of this world in that it is kept completely in common for the use of the servants of God."[1379] He also added:

[1372] Greenfield, *The Life of Lazaros of Mt. Galesion,* 288–89.

[1373] Wortley, *The Alphabetical Sayings of the Desert Fathers,* 148 (Isaac of the Cells 7).

[1374] Θεοδώρου τοῦ Στουδίτου, *Μεγάλη Κατήχησις,* 428.

[1375] Vid. Thomas and Hero, *Byzantine Monastic Foundation Documents,* 259.

[1376] Ibid., 79.

[1377] Wheeler, *Dorotheos of Gaza, Discourses and Sayings,* 102.

[1378] Ward, *The Sayings of the Desert Fathers,* 197.

[1379] Ramsey, *John Cassian: The Institutes,* 22 (i. 2.1).

But we ourselves [i.e., the monks of Gaul as opposed to those in Egypt] should keep only those things that the situation of the place and the custom of the region permit. For the harshness of the winter does not allow us to be satisfied with sandals or *colobia* [i.e., short-sleeved cassocks] or a single tunic, and wearing a little hood and having a *melotis* would evoke derision rather than edification in the beholder. Hence we are of the opinion that, of the things we have mentioned above, we should wear only what is in keeping with the humility of our profession and the character of the climate, so that the whole point of our clothing may not consist in strangeness of apparel, which might be offensive to persons of the world, but in decent simplicity.[1380]

While most early monastic saints quoted above encouraged "dirty clothes" that are "unwashed for the most part," St. John Cassian taught: "In no respect should [clothing] be self-consciously meticulous, but neither, on the other hand, should it be grimy with filth accumulated by neglect."[1381] Likewise, Elder Aimilianos taught that monks should have moderation in their cleanliness, avoiding the extremes of being slovenly and excessively tidy. He said:

The washing of clothes reveals a person's soul, his virtue, his ego, his illnesses, his passions—everything. How much more so when the cleanliness of his clothes becomes a need, and he takes care that there be not the slightest spot on them, when he wants to keep ironing them with perfect folds. Then he is not only not a monk, but he is not even a rational human being, because these things show that he squanders his efforts on things of no value. Washing clothes expresses the cleanliness of your soul, and you do it for the sake of the brotherhood, since uncleanliness creates problems for others. When Elder Amphilochios of Patmos saw someone [who wanted to join his monastery] who lacked cleanliness, he would tell him: 'You are a great ascetic; you aren't suitable for our monastery.' In this way, he was forced either to leave or to conform to the demands of the brotherhood. One who is unclean amidst the clean shows his egotism and what a failure he is in his inner world.[1382]

In the same spirit, Elder Ephraim taught us that we must be careful not to wear raggedy clothes in order to avoid scandalizing contemporary Americans who equate dingy clothes with disreputability.

Elder Aimilianos also warned against desiring nice clothes, since this springs from self-love:

When someone carefully selects his own cowl, his own shoes, his own clothes, this reveals that he is not just a disorderly person but someone whom Satan is leading astray. This applies especially to nuns; people should not be able to tell her that her clothes are beautiful and nicely tailored to fit her. It is better that people call a nun immoral than to tell her that her clothes fit her perfectly. There is no worse criticism than this. When someone is immoral, he can repent and perhaps correct himself. But as for the tremendous evil of self-love, of egotism, who can correct it? Christ is

---

[1380] Ibid., 26.

[1381] Ibid., 22 (i. 2.1).

[1382] Γέροντος Αἰμιλιανοῦ, *Νηπτικὴ Ζωὴ καὶ Ἀσκητικοὶ Κανόνες*, 312–13.

obtained by having clean, simply sewn or patched-up clothes that would fit everyone—not by having that which fits the shape of our body perfectly. Such clothes are for a girl in the world who wants to get married. But how can a nun be decked up in clothes with a collar, nicely sewn and ironed?[1383]

St. Iosif Volotsky wrote: "Just as we have said concerning foods and beverages, that it is good to select the simple and unexcessive and to do everything with the counsel of the spiritual superior; by the same model, have clothing that is necessary, simple, very mean, and appropriate for the place and climate, and do not by means of demonic cunning seek out the very expensive and excessive."[1384] In the same spirit, Gerondissa Makrina taught her nuns: "We must be economical with our clothing and with our shoes and socks as well. We should have only what is absolutely necessary and not fill our cells with various things.... We will patch our old clothes."[1385] St. Sebastian of Optina said: "Why did they disperse the monasteries? Because monks began to ride around on troikas and wear soft cotton fabric. But in the past monastics wore canvas podrasniks and cotton-wool blend riassas, and labored conscientiously. Those were true monks."[1386] These patristic exhortations for simplicity and equality in clothing may also be applied to other material items that monastics have.

25) Shoes

Several early Christian writers viewed shoes as something to be worn only when absolutely necessary. In the second century, Clement of Alexandria wrote:

> [Women] ought for the most part to wear shoes; for it is not suitable for the foot to be shown naked: besides, woman is a tender thing, easily hurt. But for a man bare feet are quite in keeping, except when he is on military service. "For being shod is near neighbor to being bound." To go with bare feet is most suitable for exercise, and best adapted for health and ease, unless where necessity prevents. But if we are not on a journey, and cannot endure bare feet, we may use slippers or white shoes; dusty-foots the Attics called them on account of their bringing the feet near the dust, as I think.[1387]

[1383] Ibid., 264–65.

[1384] Goldfrank, *The Monastic Rule of Iosif Volotsky,* 135.

[1385] Panagia Odigitria Monastery, *Words of the Heart,* 524.

Γερόντισσα Μακρίνα Βασσοπούλου, *Λόγοι Καρδίας,* (Βόλος: Ἱερᾶς Μονῆς Παναγίας Ὁδηγητρίας, 2012), 595.

[1386] Tatiana V. Torstensen, *Elder Sebastian of Optina,* trans. David Koubek (Platina: St. Herman of Alaska Brotherhood, 1999), 368.

[1387] *Fathers of the Second Century: Hermas, Tatian, Athenagoras, Theophilus, and Clement of Alexandria,* 267.

In the fourth century, St. Pachomios ordered: "No one shall go to the *synaxis* or to the refectory with shoes on his feet."[1388] Commenting on the fourth-century monks of Egypt, St. John Cassian wrote:

> They refuse shoes as being forbidden by gospel precept,[1389] even when bodily infirmity or a winter morning's chill or the intense midday heat demands them, and they only put sandals on their feet. They understand that this use of them, with the Lord's permission, means that if, once having been placed in this world, we cannot be utterly removed from the care and worry of this flesh and are unable to be completely rid of it, we should at least provide for the necessities of the body with a minimum of preoccupation and involvement.[1390]
>
> But although they legitimately use sandals, since they were conceded by the Lord's decree,[1391] they nonetheless do not allow them on their feet when they approach to celebrate or to receive the most holy mysteries, considering that they must keep literally what was said to Moses and to Joshua the son of Nun: "Undo the strap of your sandal, for the place on which you stand is holy ground" (Ex. 3:5; Jos. 5:15).[1392]

Perhaps St. John Maximovitch had this principle in mind, for he "always celebrated [the Divine Liturgy] barefoot to the great displeasure of some people."[1393]

Abba Isaiah taught: "If there is any need to go outside, he [i.e., a monk] should put on his sandals, but while he is in his cell, he should try not to wear sandals."[1394] Evidently, monks in fourth-century Byzantium were also barefoot, since this is how St. Gregory the Theologian described them,[1395] and since St. John Chrysostom commented on the grief of a rich father seeing his son dressed in shabby monastic garments and barefoot.[1396] The *Rule*

[1388] Veilleux, *Pachomian Koinonia,* vol. 2, 162 (Rule #102).

[1389] "Nor leathern pouch for your journey, neither two coats, neither sandals, nor yet staves; for the workman is worthy of his food" (Mt. 10:10).

[1390] Ramsey, *John Cassian: The Institutes,* 26.

[1391] "But be shod with sandals; and not put on two coats" (Mk. 6:9).

[1392] Ramsey, *John Cassian: The Institutes,* 26. The editor of the English edition of *The Institutes* remarked: "The practice of wearing shoes or sandals when celebrating or receiving the eucharist seems to have varied in Christian antiquity. For example, the Riha Paten and the Stuma Paten, both Byzantine works and both dating from the late sixth century, show the apostles barefoot as they receive Communion from the hands of Christ. On the other hand, the illuminated Rossano Gospels, another Byzantine production from roughly the same period, depicts a similar scene in which the apostles are shod" (Ibid., 32).

[1393] Hieromonk Makarios of Simonos Petra, *The Synaxarion: The Lives of the Saints of the Orthodox Church, Volume Five: May, June,* trans. Mother Maria (Rule) and Mother Joanna (Burton) (Ormylia: Holy Convent of the Annunciation of Our Lady, 2005), 557.

[1394] Chryssavgis and Penkett, *Abba Isaiah of Scetis,* 48.

[1395] Vid. "To Those Who Slander Monks and to False Monks" (Εἰς ἑαυτὸν 1, 44, PG 36:1351).

[1396] Vid. "Homily to an Unbelieving Father" (Λόγος Β΄, PG 47:340).

for the Monastery of Compludo forbade wearing shoes except in winter,[1397] and the "Canons of Marūtā" allowed only sandals.[1398]

Numerous saints from the earliest centuries until modern times chose to go barefoot. St. Joseph the Hesychast sometimes went barefoot out of poverty[1399] or for asceticism in the snow[1400] or just out of an apparent preference to do so.[1401]

Other monastic rules, however, do allow footwear. For example, sandals are mentioned by St. Maximos the Confessor[1402] and St. Germanos of Constantinople.[1403] Shoes are mentioned by St. Basil the Great,[1404] and both shoes and boots are recommended by St. Theodore the Studite[1405] and St. Athanasios of Athos.[1406]

When St. Paisios of the Holy Mountain lived in Sinai, due to walking barefoot "the soles of his feet had hardened and become like the soles of shoes."[1407] When he was asked why he walked barefoot, he replied: "The shoes we were born with never wear out; the more you use them the stronger they become."[1408] The way the body is strengthened by walking barefoot has been explained by one researcher as follows:

> By feeling the ground, the vestibular system (the balance system) is triggered, stimulating new neural connections and remapping their minds for greater balance. Walking barefoot results in greater muscle strength for both balance and support. As the feet strengthen, plantar fasciitis diminishes, foot neuromas go away, bunions begin to dissipate, and other conditions such as hammertoes go away. Even the arthritic foot begins to slowly heal itself as it develops greater strength, flexibility, and blood flow. The increased circulation means less aches and pains, less varicose veins, and warmer feet and legs in the winter.
>
> Furthermore, since the sole of most shoes is much thicker at the heel than at the toe, the resulting unnatural tilt ruins our posture and strains our hamstrings, lower back, upper back, shoulders, and neck. It also affects our gait, putting force on our hips,

---

[1397] "In the case of shoes, the custom to be followed is that those who wish may wear shoes in the winter from November 1 to May 1; but, in the summer months, they may be protected only with sandals" (Barlow, *The Fathers of the Church: Iberian Fathers,* vol. 63, 159).

[1398] "They shall not wear shoes upon their feet but sandals, shank-bands, and leather strap-shoes" (Vööbus, *Syriac and Arabic Documents,* 148).

[1399] Elder Ephraim, *My Elder Joseph the Hesychast,* 133.

[1400] Vid. ibid., 84.

[1401] Vid., ibid., 313.

[1402] Vid. PG 90:841BC.

[1403] Vid. PG 98:396B.

[1404] Vid. Clarke, *The Ascetic Works of St. Basil,* 291 (Rule 168 in the *Shorter Rules*).

[1405] Vid. Thomas and Hero, *Byzantine Monastic Foundation Documents,* 79, 115.

[1406] Ibid., 228.

[1407] Chamberas, *Saint Paisios the Athonite,* 231.

[1408] Ibid.

knees, and feet when we walk. Studies have even shown that walking barefoot decreases blood pressure, cortisol, stress, and inflammation throughout the body by stimulating the many nerve endings on the bottom of the feet.[1409]

Another benefit of being barefoot is that it electrically grounds the body. Studies have shown that this boosts immunity, improves brain activity, moderates heart rate variability, improves glucose regulation, decreases blood viscosity, helps regulate both the endocrine and nervous systems, and reduces chronic pain, cortisol and stress.[1410] All this contributes to the pleasant feeling people have when they are barefoot.

Other studies have shown that where barefoot and shod populations co-exist, as in Haiti, injury rates of the lower extremity are substantially higher in the shod population, and that wearing shoes increases the likelihood of ankle sprains because it either decreases one's awareness of foot position or increases the twisting torque on one's ankle during a stumble.[1411] Daniel Howell explained the mechanism for this is as follows:

> When the [shod] foot lands on a rock or root, the hard sole rotates and the ankle takes the brunt of the force, causing injury. By contrast, the bare foot is excellent at deforming around such objects and conforming to the terrain, sparing the ankles from excessive twisting. Studies have demonstrated that shod runners suffer more injuries per mile than barefoot runners and that expensive running shoes cause twice the injuries as cheap running shoes.[1412]

Since odor-causing bacteria (such as *Staphylococcus* and *Pseudomonas*) and fungi (such as *Tinea pedis,* or "athlete's foot") require a dark, moist environment to survive, being barefoot eliminates foot odor, according to the American Academy of Dermatology.[1413] More seriously, the blisters and contact dermatitis caused by shoes enable those bacteria to penetrate the skin and cause infections.[1414] Howell adds: "Shoes not only favor the growth of pathogenic microbes, but they also prevent our exposure to beneficial 'good' bacteria. Recent studies indicate that exposure to certain harmless soil bacteria actually elevates our mood, reduces depression, and boosts the immune system."[1415] Specifically, "exposure to the soil bacterium *Mycobacterium vaccae* ... induces the release of serotonin in the brain.

[1409] www.runbare.com/barefoot-benefits

[1410] See www.mindbodygreen.com/0-9099/the-surprising-health-benefits-of-going-barefoot.html and www.grounded.com/earthing-grounding-studies

[1411] www.oandp.com/articles/2010-04_06.asp

[1412] Daniel Howell, *The Barefoot Book: 50 Great Reasons to Kick Off Your Shoes,* (Alameda: Hunter House Publications, 2010), 96.

[1413] Ibid., 14.

[1414] Ibid.

[1415] Ibid., 15.

Elevated serotonin levels are well-known for elevating your mood and warding off depression."[1416]

Howell elaborates on several other physiological detrimental effects of wearing shoes:

Most shoes also deform the foot's natural shape and act as a cast that immobilizes joints and causes muscles to atrophy.[1417]

Shoes reduce the gripping and push-off functions of the toes ... dramatically reduce the spring action of the arch [and] reduce considerably the shock-absorption function of the arch.[1418]

Since a finished shoe contains literally hundreds of chemicals remaining from the manufacturing process, ... these chemicals can produce severe allergic reactions.... The leading known allergens are potassium dichromate from chrome-tanning leather, ethyl butyl thiourea found in rubber, and mercaptobenzothiazole and p-tertiary butyl-phenol formaldehyde resin found in glues. As if the mere presence of these chemicals is not bad enough, the heat and moisture inside the shoe facilitates leaching of these chemicals from the shoe materials while simultaneously increasing the absorption properties of the skin.[1419]

Bare feet are of course more vulnerable to puncture wounds, but the experience of numerous barefoot runners is that such injuries are actually rare.[1420]

Naturally [i.e., when barefoot], the body's weight is supported primarily by the head of the first metatarsal, and push-off is achieved by the great toe during walking. Constant shoe wearing physically moves the toes together, and body weight is transferred to the [weaker] second and third metatarsals; push-off is achieved by the [weak] second and third toes by habitually shod feet.[1421]

One of the immediate benefits of walking barefoot is that it puts no restrictions on the dorsalis pedis artery or other vessels and allows unrestricted blood flow. In addition, because the feet are not immobilized in a rigid shoe when walking barefoot, they experience considerable freedom of movement. The extra flexing, twisting, and muscle movements that occur when walking in feet unbound by shoes stimulates blood circulation throughout the lower extremities. Not only does all this flexing and twisting encourage blood flow, it also improves the flow of interstitial fluids (i.e., lymph) through the lymphatic vessels.... Thus, increased mobility in the foot helps to cleanse the tissues of toxins, dead-cell debris, and microbial invaders, in addition to reducing swelling (i.e., edema) in the ankles. Finally, barefoot walking restores a natural gait and allows for the full range of motion in the foot and ankle joints. These changes

---

[1416] Ibid., 133.

[1417] Ibid., 16.

[1418] Ibid., 44–45.

[1419] Ibid., 49, 67.

[1420] Ibid., 97. The reason why puncture wounds are rare is because exposing the feet to rough surfaces makes the skin on the soles of the feet much thicker and harder without forming callouses, since callouses are the result of *shear* forces on the skin's surface. In my own experience, I have found that after only a couple months of walking barefoot on slightly rough surfaces, my feet could then painlessly handle extremely rough surfaces (such as gravel with jagged edges and dirt roads strewn with pointy little rocks). Attempts to walk on such surfaces initially caused intense discomfort and occasional bleeding, but after my soles thickened, the feeling elicited by walking on such surfaces was more akin to a pleasant massage.

[1421] Ibid., 59.

improve joint mobility and reduce pressure on the bones and soft structures of the forefoot and knee. Indeed, since shoe-induced changes in gait are often responsible for lower-back pain and are now considered to be a major cause of knee arthritis—a condition that afflicts millions of older Americans—it stands to reason that walking barefoot should delay the onset and/or reduce the severity of these conditions.... Three out of four Americans will visit a podiatrist during their lifetimes, most of them because of shoe-related problems to their feet.[1422]

Greater flexion at the knee and plantar flexion at the ankle are observed in barefoot runners, which also reduce the impact forces on the knee and ankle. These adjustments presumably happen to reduce plantar discomfort; it is the body's successful reading of the tactile information from the foot leading to stress-reducing modifications in gait. The cushioned outer sole, midsole, and insole of shoes severely limit the tactile information the brain receives about impact, leading to *greater* impact on joints from the foot to the spine.[1423]

According to Dr. Marty Hughes, "The incidence of foot problems in barefoot and minimally shod populations is somewhere around 3 percent, whereas the incidence of foot problems in our [American] society is somewhere between 70 and 80 percent, and the problems they [the barefoot] encounter are mostly of a traumatic nature, such as dropping something on an uncovered foot."[1424]

Likewise, a "Survey in China and India of Feet That Have Never Worn Shoes" observed: "No instances among the barefoot feet were found of: Onychrocryptosis, Hyperidrosis, Bromidrosis, Hallux Valgus, Hallux Varus, Bursitis at the first or fifth metatarsophalangeal articulations.... These figures prove that restrictive footgear ... causes most of the ailments of the human foot.... Footgear is the greatest enemy of the human foot."[1425] Another study wrote: "All writers who have reported their observations of barefooted people agree that the untrammeled feet of natural men are free from the disabilities commonly noted among shod people—hallux valgus, bunions, hammer toes, and painful feet.... Millions of Indians, both American and Asian, and Congoids wander their native savannas and rain forests without protection, inconvenience, or complaint. Footgear, therefore, would appear to be unnecessary."[1426]

All these health benefits of being barefoot should be no surprise, for if God "made all things in wisdom,"[1427] it follows that He would also design the feet of man—who is the

---

[1422] Ibid., 88–89, 121.

[1423] Ibid., 92.

[1424] www.youtube.com/watch?v=xWAlBzSeuxo

[1425] Samuel B. Shulman, "Survey in China and India of Feet That Have Never Worn Soles," *The Journal of the National Association of Chiropodists,* vol. 49, (1949): 26–30.

[1426] Steele F. Stewart, "Footgear—Its History, Uses and Abuses," *Clinical Orthopaedics and Related Research,* vol. 88, (1972): 119–30.

[1427] Cf. Ps. 103:26.

crown of His creation—to function most efficiently in their natural state. Leonardo da Vinci, marvelling at the wisdom of the foot's design, drew detailed anatomical diagrams of the bones in the human foot and declared: "The human foot is a masterpiece of engineering and a work of art."[1428] One could even argue that God would not have created the soles of our feet with such a high density of nerve endings (more than 100,000 per sole) if He wanted us to deaden that sensitivity by covering them with a thick slab of leather or rubber.

Although people in extreme climates have been wearing shoes for insulation for at least 5,000 years,[1429] it was not until the Dark Ages in Europe that wearing shoes began being viewed as a status symbol and being barefoot was associated with being poor.[1430] After the Industrial Revolution, when the mass-production of shoes began in the late 19th century, shoes became affordable to everyone in Western society, and everyone began wearing them to avoid being stigmatized as poor.[1431] As a result, wearing shoes became a cultural norm in Western society, and being barefoot became socially unacceptable. Since this cultural prejudice still prevails today, to avoid scandalizing people we monastics living in Western society should take care to wear shoes or sandals when we are in public (following the example of St. John Maximovitch, who put on his shoes when people ridiculed him for being barefoot).[1432] Selecting minimalist footwear can reduce the harm caused by rigid shoes with thick soles, raised heels, chemicals, etc.

26) Other Rules of Conduct

St. Pachomios taught: "It will not be allowed to exchange [among the brothers] the things that are received from the prior."[1433] The *Regula Orientalis* quoted this rule of St. Pachomios and then added: "No one may accept anything from another unless the prior has given permission."[1434] Likewise, Gerondissa Makrina wrote to her nuns: "It is forbidden to

---

[1428] Winston Collins and Jack Alexander McIver, *All About Shoes: Footwear Through the Ages* (Toronto, Bata Limited, 1994), 60.

[1429] Vid. Kate Ravilious, "World's Oldest Leather Shoe Found—Stunningly Preserved," *National Geographic* (June 9, 2010). http://news.nationalgeographic.com/news/2010/06/100609-worlds-oldest-leather-shoe-armenia-science/

[1430] Richard Keith Frazine, *The Barefoot Hiker* (Berkeley: Ten Speed Press, 1993), 98.

[1431] Vid. http://staffscc.net/shoes1/?p=126

[1432] Vid. Fr. Seraphim Rose and Abbot Herman, *Blessed John the Wonderworker,* Third, Revised Edition (Platina: St. Herman of Alaska Brotherhood, 1987), 48–49.

[1433] Veilleux, *Pachomian Koinonia,* vol. 2, 162 (Rule #106).

[1434] Franklin, *Early Monastic Rules,* 65.

eat something or to give something to another sister without a blessing."[1435] These rules do not apply to trivial items, of course, such as pens, paper, batteries, etc.

Gerondissa Makrina wrote the following rule for her nuns: "We should walk around the monastery humbly and decorously, with our hands crossed, without rushing."[1436] This rule is remarkably similar to what St. Paisius Velichkovsky told his monks: "A monk must be in everything a monk … they should have a meek manner of walking, with the hands folded on the chest, the head bent down, the eyes cast down toward the ground, the heart directed upwards to God, and the mind in the ceaseless prayer of Jesus, and that in everyone there should be unhypocritical love."[1437] Abba Isaiah had a slightly different approach and taught: "When [a monk is] walking, his hands should be held firmly against his side, so that they do not move to and fro as in the case of secular people."[1438] Similarly, whenever St. Sebastian of Optina "saw someone walking through the church quickly and without the fear of God, or swung his arms, or shoved others, or even behaved that way outside in the courtyard [of the monastery], he would reprimand him in front of everyone, for the edification of all.… [He taught:] 'One should walk quietly and calmly, not taking big steps or stamping one's feet, especially in church, even when in a hurry. After all, the world watches us and takes an example from us.'"[1439] In the same spirit, the nuns of St. Paisios of the Holy Mountain told of him:

> Upon seeing a sister animatedly swinging her arms while she walked in the church, he reproached her, "Why are you moving about like that? In church, one must walk like the angels during the Great Entrance. Have you seen how the angels walk in the icon, 'The Heavenly Divine Liturgy'?" That icon represented how Father Paisios wanted the sisterhood to present itself—not only in the church, but everywhere. Attire, walk, gaze, speech—everything—he wanted everything to be properly suited to the monastic, the nun.[1440]

Athonite monasteries do not have mirrors, and monastics do not look at their reflection in a window, since this encourages vainglory and self-love. St. Nicodemos wrote the following advice to laymen:

> [There is] an irrational passion and vain preoccupation which certain sensual people have in decorating their homes with large and luxurious mirrors.… I beseech you to avoid this kind of vain and condemnable pleasure.… If you do have mirrors, please remove them as things altogether improper for the Christian way of life.… Plato

---

[1435] Rule #27.

[1436] Rule #3.

[1437] Metrophanes, *Blessed Paisius Velichkovsky,* 177.

[1438] Chryssavgis and Penkett, *Abba Isaiah of Scetis,* 52. Once when Elder Ephraim noticed a monk swinging his arms while walking, he didn't think it was a serious enough flaw to correct, but he did point out to me how inappropriate it looked.

[1439] Torstensen, *Elder Sebastian of Optina,* 355.

[1440] Chamberas, *Saint Paisios the Athonite,* 285–86.

used to say that one should look into a mirror only when he happens to be angry, so that by seeing the harshness in his face, the disorderly movements of his hands, and the unnatural shaking of his body, he may be ashamed of himself and despise this passion that is so irrational and wild.[1441]

If this is how he advised *laymen* to avoid using mirrors, one can imagine how he would have urged monastics to avoid using mirrors even more so.

Abba Daniel said: "Our Holy Fathers Anthony, Pachomios, Ammoun, Serapion, and other God-bearing Fathers have decreed that no monk should strip bare without great necessity, or unless he is seriously ill. For, when they wanted to cross rivers for particular needs and no ferry was available, unable to endure being naked because of the shame that they felt before the Holy Angels accompanying them and the sun that shed its light on them, although there was no one to see them, they nonetheless entreated God to help them."[1442] Therefore, we monastics should be careful never to be naked when changing or washing, and should be careful with our eyes as Abba Isaiah taught: "Do not look at yourself with disrespect [i.e., immodestly] while putting on your clothes."[1443]

Some of the holy Fathers were opposed not only to monks bathing but even to washing their face with water. However, not all ancient monasteries followed this strictness. For example, the typikon of the influential eleventh-century Monastery of Evergetis stated:

> There should be a bath for the sick and it should be heated ... [but] you should live completely without bathing. For although we have built a bath in the monastery, yet it was not that you should live in an effeminate way, bathing and being in good physical condition, but that the sick could be comforted, if necessary. However we give permission for those who are healthy to have a bath three times during the year ... but extra bathing, if necessary, should be permitted at the discretion of the superior.[1444]

Leo, Bishop of Nauplia, in the twelfth century encouraged more frequent bathing in the typikon for the monastery he founded in Areia: "You should bathe on [every] Saturday, except during Lent."[1445]

St. Eustathios of Thessalonica taught that monks need to be careful that their appearance does not scandalize laymen:

> [These unspiritual monks] are starting to wear luxurious clothes that have nothing to do with the monastic garment, while their bellies bulge so much that they can no longer carry their own weight, and they delegate their transportation to powerful mules. They who never used to refuse to travel by foot now refuse to walk on the earth.... But when a great distance must be travelled, then it is necessary to ride some animal.

[1441] Νικοδήμου τοῦ Ἁγιορείτου, Συμβουλευτικὸν Ἐγχειρίδιον, 58–59; see also Chamberas, *Nicodemos of the Holy Mountain: A Handbook of Spiritual Counsel*, 92, 96.

[1442] Chrysostomos, *The Evergetinos, Book III*, 125.

[1443] Chryssavgis and Penkett, *Abba Isaiah of Scetis*, 95.

[1444] Thomas and Hero, *Byzantine Monastic Foundation Documents*, 491.

[1445] Ibid., 965.

Riding an animal can also be necessary for the sake of propriety, when someone must make a good appearance and not be disparaged as someone boorish. These kinds of things must often be observed for the sake of foolish people who are unable to see the inner man but judge externals. Therefore, a great-schema monk should not be repulsive in his appearance so that he is not ridiculed by simpletons....

So, just as special food and baths for cleanliness and new clothes are good at times, likewise a great-schema monk should use a means for transportation without overdoing it. He will do so in a reverent manner, bearing in mind Him Who, as it is written, rode on a colt without a saddle (vid. Mk. 11:7).[1446]

In the same spirit, Elder Ephraim told us that nowadays laymen would be scandalized if we monastics smelled bad due to lack of cleanliness, and therefore we should wash regularly. He also said that we should wash ourselves carefully beforehand every time we need to see a doctor. Moreover, whenever we needed to go into town, he wanted our clothes to have a neat and clean appearance. Also, he told the fathers in the bookstore (who come into direct contact with the visitors) that they need to make a good impression on the visitors not only by their behavior but also by their neat appearance.

Several ancient monastic typika prohibit monastics from being the sponsor for weddings and baptisms, so that they will not be involved in worldly cares.[1447] Likewise, St. Nicodemos of the Holy Mountain wrote the following in his interpretation of Canon IV of the Fourth Ecumenical Council: "Peter the Chartophylax says that monks must not become godfathers to children being baptized except in cases of urgent necessity.... Nicephorus the Chartophylax also says that the Church mandatorily prescribes it as a law to abbots and exarchs of monasteries that the monks are not to be allowed to form relations as godfathers with the parents of children." The reason for this, according to *The Rule for Nuns of St. Caesarius of Arles,* is: "She who for the love of God has disdained the freedom to have children of her own ought not wish for nor possess this freedom belonging to others, so that without any hindrance she may give her time unceasingly to God."[1448] The compiler of *Byzantine Monastic Foundation Documents* points out, however, that although the associations of monastics with laymen by serving as their godparents "were regarded as improper for monks and nuns, the number of prohibitions suggests that they were not uncommon."[1449] Elder Ephraim agreed with this prohibition, although he did make an exception for nuns and allows them to become godmothers, to accommodate for their motherly instincts.

Abba Isaiah advised: "Do not stretch your body when others are looking. If you must yawn, do not open your mouth and this will be avoided. Do not open your mouth widely

---

[1446] PG 135:749BC,752B–D.

[1447] For example, see Thomas and Hero, *Byzantine Monastic Foundation Documents,* 78, 238, 644, 1621.

[1448] McCarthy, *The Rule for Nuns of St. Caesarius of Arles,* 174.

[1449] Thomas and Hero, *Byzantine Monastic Foundation Documents,* xx.

when you laugh; it is rude to do so."[1450] An alternative to this recommended by Elder Ephraim is to make the sign of the cross over our mouth when yawning or laughing.

The way monks should sleep was described in the following rule written on the bronze tablet given by an angel to St. Pachomios: "Let them sleep not lying down, but let them make reclining chairs of masonry and sleep sitting on these chairs after covering them with their blankets. At night let them wear linen tunics and be belted."[1451] St. John Chrysostom mentioned about monks in the fourth century: "There are none sleeping naked."[1452] St. Benedict taught his monks: "Let them sleep clothed and girded with cinctures or cords, that they may be always ready."[1453] The *Rule of the Master* added to this: "The brothers must sleep clothed and girded, because a brother is not allowed to touch his naked members, for from this, impure desires are introduced into the mind. When he touches his naked members he is straightway titillated by the heart's desire for women, and as a result his members are defiled during sleep."[1454] Likewise, St. Donatus of Besançon wrote in his rule for nuns: "They should sleep clothed, their girdles bound with all gravity and modesty and always ready for divine service."[1455]

The ancient Syriac "Rules Attributed to Ephrēm" state: "When you are walking on the street, dignify your steps and discipline your look; and control your countenance; and do not eat anything on the street in order that the discipleship of monasticism will not be despised."[1456] Similarly, in the *Ordo Monasterii* (the first monastic rule in Latin, written in the fourth century) it says: "No one must eat or drink outside the monastery without permission, for this is contrary to the monastery's discipline."[1457] Likewise, Elder Ephraim did not want his monks stopping at restaurants while doing errands in town, although he did allow us to bring food and drink with us when necessary.

St. Pachomios wrote in his monastic precepts: "No one may clasp the hand or anything else of his companion; but whether you are sitting or standing or walking, you shall leave a forearm's space between you and him."[1458] Likewise, St. Donatus of Besançon wrote in his rules for nuns: "It is forbidden that any take the hand of another for affection whether

---

[1450] Chryssavgis and Penkett, *Abba Isaiah of Scetis*, 48.

[1451] Veilleux, *Pachomian Koinonia*, vol. 2, 126.

[1452] *St. Chrysostom: Homilies on Galatians, Ephesians, Philippians, Colossians, Thessalonians, Timothy, Titus, and Philemon*, 456 (Homily XIV on 1 Tim. 5:8).

[1453] *Rule of St. Benedict*, Chapter XXII.

[1454] *Regula Magistri*, 11:114 (as translated in Barry, *Commentary on the Rule of Saint Benedict*, 344).

[1455] Donatus of Besançon, "Regula ad Virgines: a Working Translation," ch. 65.

[1456] Vööbus, *Syriac and Arabic Documents*, 19.

[1457] *Ordo Monasterii*, 8 (vid. www.mostly-medieval.com/explore/ordo.htm).

[1458] Veilleux, *Pachomian Koinonia*, vol. 2, 161.

they stand or walk around or sit together. She who does so, will be reproved with twelve blows.[1459]

The typikon for the Holy Mountain known as the "Tragos" written by Emperor John Tzimiskes states: "During the period of Holy Lent, all the solitary ascetics and those living in community should spend the time in silence, and they should not visit one another except for a good reason, an emergency, or to seek treatment for evil and shameful thoughts."[1460] In the same spirit, Elder Ephraim also taught us that Great Lent is a time for more prayer and silence.

The "Tragos" also states: "Regarding unknown priests coming here, we must insist that they do not have authority, either privately or publicly, to presume to celebrate the Divine Liturgy, unless they have an official letter from their bishops or some solid testimony in their favor."[1461]

The Rule of Paul and Stephen recommended having a "lost-and-found" so that the monks could find their missing items more easily: "If anyone finds anything whatever which another brother has lost whether in a cell or outside, he should not keep it in his possession for even one day and if possible not even one hour. Rather he should put whatever he has found in the designated place. Then the one who has lost it may look for it in that place and will not need to endure the uncertainty and the work of going from person to person to look for it."[1462] St. Athanasios of Athos had a bronze hook on the door of the nave of the church where lost items would be hung.[1463]

[1459] Donatus of Besançon, "Regula ad Virgines: a Working Translation," ch. 32.

[1460] "Typikon of Emperor John Tzimiskes, 'Tragos,'" ch. 16, Thomas and Hero, *Byzantine Monastic Foundation Documents*, 238.

[1461] Ibid.

[1462] Barry Hagan, "The Rule of Paul and Stephen," ch. 30.

[1463] Vid. Richard P. H. Greenfield and Alice-Mary Talbot, *Holy Men of Mount Athos*, 215.

Chapter Six:
General Monastery Issues

1) Orthodoxy

AINT BASIL THE GREAT WROTE in his *Discourse on Ascetical Discipline:* "It befits him [i.e., a monk] not to dispute about Father and Son and Holy Spirit, but he should freely confess in thought and word the uncreated and consubstantial Trinity and say to them who put this matter to question that we ought to be baptized according to the tradition we have received, and hold the belief in which we have been baptized, and worship according as we have believed."[1464]

In the same spirit, Elder Aimilianos stated in the *Regulations of the Holy Cenobium of the Annunciation:*

> Following the Orthodox monastic tradition, the holy Cenobium shall confess its faith in One, Holy, Catholic,[1465] and Apostolic Church, in the sacred and holy Canons, in the holy Creed, and in the holy Fathers, in whose spirit and tradition it lives, not opposing them at any point. The nuns shall study, learn, experience, and love matters concerning the faith and dogma, though a contentious spirit shall not be cultivated, since this would disrupt and disturb the sanctity and dignity of the Cenobium, shattering and fracturing any possibility of a spiritual life.... The abbess shall not tolerate any divergence of interference with the faith, but shall direct the community wisely in the Orthodox spirit.[1466]

[1464] Wagner, *Saint Basil: Ascetical Works,* vol. 9, 33.

[1465] The meaning of the word "catholic" (καθολική) here is of course "universal" and has nothing to do with the papacy (commonly known as the "Roman Catholic Church"), which has been condemned unequivocally as a heresy by the Constantinopolitan Councils of 1170, 1341, 1450, 1722, 1838, and 1895, as well as by Saints Germanos of Constantinople, Gregory Palamas, Mark of Ephesus, Symeon of Thessalonica, Paisius Velichkovsky, Nicodemos of the Holy Mountain, Cosmas Aitolos, Nectarios of Pentapolis, Justin Popović, and many contemporary elders.

[1466] Elder Aimilianos, *The Authentic Seal,* 173–74.

2) Work

Countless monastic fathers of the Church emphasized the value of manual labor because it leads to humility and salvation, and it enables a monk to support himself and even give alms.

St. Athanasios the Great wrote about the monks of Egypt: "Each one of them procures so much profit for the monastery every day from their own work and sweat that it is sufficient not only for their own needs but also for serving the guests and providing for the poor."[1467] St. Basil the Great saw the same benefit in work: "We must toil with diligence and not think that our goal of piety offers an escape from work or a pretext for idleness, but occasion for struggle, for every greater endeavor.… Not only is such exertion beneficial for bringing the body into subjection, but also for showing charity to our neighbor in order that through us God may grant sufficiency to those of the brethren who are in want."[1468] It was this understanding of work that led Abba Achillas to say: "Since yesterday evening up to this time, I have been plaiting rope at full pace, though, in fact, I do not need to do so much work. However, I am working thus, lest God find it necessary to chastise me, saying, 'Why, despite the fact that you are able, do you not work?' Therefore, I labor with all my strength."[1469]

St. Efthymios the Great also saw the importance of working productively:

> In addition to keeping watch on the thoughts within, monks, especially young ones, ought to practise bodily labor, remembering the words of the Apostle, "We labor day and night so as not to be a burden on anyone" (1 Thes. 2:9), and "These hands ministered to me and to those with me" (Acts 20:34). While those in the world endure labor and hardship in order to support wives and children from their work, pay the first-fruits to God, do good according to their power and in addition be charged taxes, it is absurd if we are not even to meet the needs of the body from manual labor but to stay idle and immobile, reaping the fruit of the toil of others, especially when the Apostle orders the idle not even to eat (vid. 2 Thes. 3:10).[1470]

The Rule of Paul and Stephen understood work as a way to avoid passionate thoughts while also helping the needy:

> [The Apostle Paul] said of himself that he labored with his own hands in hunger and thirst, in cold and nakedness, by day and by night so that neither he nor those with him might lack anything necessary. On the other hand, since we have a second set of clothes and shoes for our own use and a provision of food daily from the gifts of God that is more than enough, we exhort you not to love idleness. Rather each of you should work together and, as you are able, with sincerity and single-heartedness.…

[1467] "Letter to Castor," PG 28:856D.

[1468] Wagner, *Saint Basil: Ascetical Works,* vol. 9, 306 (Question 37 in the *Long Rules*).

[1469] Chrysostomos, *The Evergetinos, Book II,* 48.

[1470] Cyril of Scythopolis, *The Lives of the Monks of Palestine,* 13.

The monk who does not keep his body busy can never keep his mind free from sordid thoughts, as Solomon says: "The lazy are beset by their passions" (cf. Prov. 13:4), and "idleness contrives many wicked things" (Sir. 33:29). Let those who have been lazy up to now shed this vice, and let them promptly take up every work, for it is written: "Do not hate hard work or farm work which was created by the Most High" (Sir. 7:15). Then, by the Lord's gift and our own work, we can find for ourselves an abundance of goods that we need each day, and we can respond in reasonable and moderate ways to those whom spiritual love invites us to visit. Through our due service, we can help those in grave need by our own labor, for it is certain that the Lord our Redeemer has commanded that "it is more blessed to give than to receive" (Acts 20:35).[1471]

The holy Fathers believed that toil is inherent to monasticism. "One of the Fathers asked Abba John the Dwarf, 'What is a monk?' He said, 'He is toil. The monk toils at all he does. That is what a monk is.'"[1472] In the same spirit, Abba Isidore the Priest said: "Brethren, haven't we come here to find toil? But now there is no more toil here. So I am going to take my sack and go where there is toil, and there I will be at rest."[1473]

With the same understanding of toil being characteristic of true monks, St. Benedict wrote in his rule: "If, however, the needs of the place, or poverty should require that they do the work of gathering the harvest themselves, let them not be downcast, for then are they monks in truth, if they live by the work of their hands, as did also our forefathers and the Apostles. However, on account of the faint-hearted let all things be done with moderation."[1474] He also said: "No person is ever more usefully employed than when working with his hands or following the plough, providing food for the use of man."[1475] As written in the Wisdom of Sirach: "Life will be sweet for the self-reliant and the hardworking."[1476]

Several saints taught that we will receive a future reward from God for our work. For example, St. Pachomios taught his monks: "About him who watches over the grinding or the milling. Let them apply themselves to the work they are doing, in the fear of God and without any relaxation, knowing that no good deed that man does for God shall be lost. On the contrary, our good deeds will be a relief to us all on the day of the great judgement."[1477] Likewise, St. Ephraim the Syrian wrote: "This is no shame for you if you are in obedience in the Lord, and do with your own hands what is good; for this distress and this affliction,

---

[1471] Barry Hagan, "The Rule of Paul and Stephen," ch. 33–34.

[1472] Ward, *The Sayings of the Desert Fathers,* 93.

[1473] As quoted in Χριστοδούλου, Ὁ Ὀρθόδοξος Μοναχισμός, 102.

[1474] *Rule of St. Benedict,* Chapter XLVIII.

[1475] Alfred Wesley Wishart, *A Short History of Monks and Monasteries* (New Jersey: Albert Brandt, 1902), 403.

[1476] Sir. 40:18.

[1477] Veilleux, *Pachomian Koinonia,* vol. 2, 212.

which you endure for the Lord's sake, will become for you a cause of eternal life."[1478] St. Basil the Great said: "An ascetic should undertake even the most menial tasks with great zeal and eagerness, knowing that everything done for God is not small but great and spiritual and worthy of heaven, yielding heavenly rewards."[1479] Aware of these rewards, St. Joseph the Hesychast "worked very much and would only stop at the times allowed by our schedule. He told me [i.e., Elder Ephraim], 'When a monk comes to realize that he is working for God, he becomes very eager.'"[1480]

Some of the early Desert Fathers worked not for the sake of producing something but purely for spiritual benefit. For example:

> Abba Paul, one of the most upright of the fathers ... lived in the vast desert ... and could not do any other work to support himself because his dwelling was separated from towns and from habitable land by a seven days' journey.... He used to collect palm fronds and always exact a day's labor from himself just as if this were his means of support. And when his cave was filled with a whole year's work, he would burn up what he had so carefully toiled over each year, to that extent proving that without manual labor a monk can neither stay in one spot nor ever mount to the summit of perfection. And so, although the obligation of earning a livelihood did not demand this course of action, he did it just for the sake of purging his heart, firming his thoughts, persevering in his cell, and conquering and driving out *acedia* [i.e., listlessness].[1481]

St. Anthony the Great was taught by an angel to alternate work and prayer in order to avoid listlessness:

> Once when the holy Abba Antony was residing in the desert, overcome by *accidie* [i.e., listlessness] and a great darkening of *logismoi* [thoughts], he was saying to God, "Lord, I want to be saved and my *logismoi* do not leave me alone. What am I to do in my affliction? How am I to be saved?" Going outside his cell a little way, Antony saw somebody like himself, sitting working—then standing up from his work and praying; sitting down again, working at rope-braiding, then standing to pray once more. It was an angel of the Lord sent to correct Antony and to assure him. And he heard the angel saying: "Act like this and you shall be saved." He experienced much joy and courage on hearing this and, acting in that way, he went on being saved.[1482]

St. John Cassian also understood how work safeguards monks from temptations. He wrote: "There is a saying among the ancient Fathers of Egypt that a monk who is working is tempted by one demon, while an idle one is attacked by a numberless multitude of

---

[1478] Chrysostomos, *The Evergetinos, Book I,* 223.

[1479] *Ἀσκητικαὶ Διατάξεις,* κεφ. κγ΄, ΕΠΕ, Τόμος 9, 518–20.

[1480] Γέροντος Ἐφραίμ, *Ὁ Γέροντάς μου Ἰωσήφ,* 355; see also Elder Ephraim, *My Elder Joseph the Hesychast,* 435.

[1481] Ramsey, *John Cassian: The Institutes,* 233 (x. 24).

[1482] Wortley, *The Alphabetical Sayings of the Desert Fathers,* 31 (Antony 1).

demons."[1483] He also said: "It is hardly possible to determine what depends on what here—that is, whether they practice manual labor ceaselessly thanks to their spiritual meditation or whether they acquire such remarkable progress in the Spirit and such luminous knowledge thanks to their constant labor."[1484]

The Desert Fathers viewed labor as a means to an end. For example, Abba Isaac (in fourth-century Egypt) taught: "Since man is weak and instable and prone to evil, his entire spiritual struggle is focused on the acquisition of purity and dispassion. And this is precisely why we persistently pursue bodily labor. For bodily labor leads to contrition of heart."[1485] Likewise, another Desert Father stated: "The path that leads to humility is that of bodily labors that beget understanding."[1486] Commenting on this, Abba Dorotheos asked:

> What relationship does bodily labor have with the disposition of the soul? I will explain this to you: When the soul fell away from the keeping of the commandments of God to disobedience, it gave itself over ... to love of pleasure ... having come to love the things of the body.... From then on, therefore, this wretched soul has suffered together with the body and conforms with all that it does. This is why the Elder said that bodily labor leads to lowliness of mind.... Labor, therefore, humbles the soul. And when the body is humbled, the soul is humbled with it.[1487]

Likewise, Elder Aimilianos explained in the *Regulations of the Holy Cenobium of the Annunciation* that manual labor "is a commandment of God, an instrument of humility and of bonding between the sisters and a way of contributing to society itself.... [But] work aimed exclusively at increasing wealth or at expending the strength of a nun is a deviation from the monastic way."[1488]

In the tradition of cenobitic monasteries, each monk is assigned his own *diakonema*.[1489] In some monasteries, the monks rotated *diakonemata* on a regular basis, while in others a monk would keep the same *diakonema* for years. For example, St. John Cassian described how monasteries in the Holy Land had a different monk to cook each week, whereas in Egypt a monk was appointed to be the cook permanently:

[1483] Ramsey, *John Cassian: The Institutes,* 233 (x. 23).

[1484] Ibid., 46 (ii. 14).

[1485] As quoted by St. John Cassian in Ἀββᾶ Κασσιανοῦ: Συνομιλίες μὲ τοὺς Πατέρες τῆς Ἐρήμου, Τόμος Α΄, 327–28; see also Ramsey, *John Cassian: The Conferences,* 329.

[1486] Metropolitan Chrysostomos, *Our Holy Father Dorotheos of Gaza,* 64.

[1487] Ibid., 65–66.

[1488] "Regulations of the Holy Cenobium of the Annunciation, Ormylia, Halkidiki," in Elder Aimilianos, *The Authentic Seal,* 161, 177.

[1489] A *diakonema* (διακόνημα in Greek, plural *diakonemata,* which means "ministry") is the task assigned to a monk. The Russian word for this is послушание, which is the same word used in Russian for "obedience," i.e., the act of obeying. Because of this, many monastic texts translated from Russian into English call the task assigned to a monk his "obedience." But since which of the two meanings of the word "obedience" is not always clear from the context, we prefer to use the transliterated word *diakonema.*

But among the Egyptians ... there is no weekly taking of turns, lest as a result of this activity anyone be hindered from obligatory work. Instead, the responsibility for provisions and for cooking is committed to a very trustworthy brother, who continues to carry out this task with regularity so long as his strength and his age permit. For he is not worn out with any great bodily labor inasmuch as they do not devote much care to preparing and cooking their food, since they mostly make use of dry and uncooked food, and the leaves of leeks that are cut every month, charlock, granulated salt, olives, and tiny salted fish, which they call maenomenia, are their highest pleasure.[1490]

St. Sophrony of Essex pointed out the danger of a *diakonema* being monopolized by only one monk: "For every task, for every *diakonema*, we must have two people completely capable of doing them, so that one may replace the other in the event that some difficulty arises. Otherwise, the monastery's entire life will depend on the 'eccentricities' of whomever, and everything will be stuck."[1491]

St. Sophrony of Essex reminded his monastics to incorporate love into their work:

Begin with a desire to serve others with love, as [Saint] Silouan did, who, when they asked him, served hundreds and thousands of monks in the refectory. He was very happy that Christ loves these people who are God's children, and he served them with great love. This person was simple, but his thought was grand and very pleasant. If you maintain this attitude, then all the necessary tasks of daily life—even those that aim to serve those who come to our monastery—can become like a delicious food for you. And at night, due to this attitude in serving, your heart will be very tender, and you will weep before God because of your failings and because of your love.[1492]

When we work, it is important to maintain our inner peace. As Abba Dorotheos taught:

Whatever should happen, whether of small or great importance, let us not show undue concern about it and let us not give it great regard. Of course, indifference is a bad thing. But neither is it, once more, a good thing for one to become so preoccupied with something that happens that he loses his irenic [i.e., peaceful] disposition, such that the soul is harmed.... Be convinced that every task that you fulfill, great or small, as I earlier said, is but an eighth of what is asked of us. Indeed, to maintain your peace, even if thereby you should fail at your obedience, is four eighths, or half, of what has been asked of you. Do you see the difference?

Therefore, if you undertake some task, and you wish to do it perfectly and fully, take care to do it perfectly, which is, as I said, an eighth of the task; but also take care to keep your internal state unharmed, which is four eighths of the task. If, however, for some reason you drift away from or violate this command, and you or another suffers harm, you have gained nothing, since, in fulfilling your obedience, you are losing four eighths, i.e., your irenic disposition, for the sole purpose of protecting the one eighth, i.e., the completion of your task.... If I should happen to send anyone among you to do any obedience whatever, and you should see any disturbance or harmful thing at all arise, cease immediately....

[1490] Ramsey, *John Cassian: The Institutes,* 89–90.

[1491] Σωφρονίου, *Οἰκοδομῶντας τὸν Ναὸ τοῦ Θεοῦ, Τόμος Α΄,* 295.

[1492] Ibid., 220.

Should one yet see, at some moment, his neighbor or himself aggrieved, stop, back down, and do not persist to the point that there ensues spiritual harm. For it is better, and I say this a thousand times over, for some work not to come about as you wish and as circumstances demand, than contumaciously [i.e., stubbornly] or according to one's prerogative, since it is obvious that the latter course will upset you and grieve others. You will thus lose the four eighths. And there is a great difference in the harm done.[1493]

St. Paisios of the Holy Mountain was asked if we should take our time and work slowly in order to maintain our calm, and he replied: "Yes, because when we work calmly, we maintain our serenity, and then our whole day is sanctified…. Our goal should not be to do many things and be in constant anxiety."[1494] Furthermore, when he was teaching some boys to learn carpentry, "they worked diligently, but also took frequent breaks to read from the Lives of Saints. 'If we work constantly,' he explained, 'we will forget God.'"[1495]

St. Paisios also taught that one's inner disposition while working is transmitted to the work:

When monastic handicrafts are made with peace of mind and prayer, they are sanctified and they also sanctify the people who use them. Then it makes sense for lay people to seek these handiworks from us as a blessing. On the contrary, any work made with haste and nervousness transmits this demonic condition to others. Work done with haste and anxiety is the mark of a very secular person. Instead of giving people a blessing, what these troubled souls impart on others with their handiwork is their troubled state. A person's state affects not only the work that he does, but also the materials, the wood that he is using! The final product of a man's work reflects his spiritual state. If he is upset and angry and swears, his work will not bring a blessing to others. But if he chants, if he says the Jesus Prayer, his work is sanctified. The first condition is demonic, the other is divine.[1496]

Likewise, Elder Ephraim said that because his elder St. Joseph while cooking "said the prayer constantly out loud, God's grace sanctified the food and made it delicious."[1497]

Tasks that require little mental concentration are more suitable for monks because they do not hinder prayer. St. Sophrony of Essex wrote to a monk: "If the task is done out of obedience and not out of passion, it will not destroy spiritual peace, but actually build it up. And if, in addition, it is a very simple task (for example, digging soil, cutting wood, cooking

---

[1493] Metropolitan Chrysostomos, *Our Holy Father Dorotheos of Gaza,* 92–94.

[1494] Elder Paisios, *With Pain and Love for Contemporary Man,* 206–7.

[1495] Chamberas, *Saint Paisios the Athonite,* 196.

[1496] Elder Paisios, *With Pain and Love for Contemporary Man,* 207; see also Γέροντος Παϊσίου Ἁγιορείτου *Λόγοι Α΄: Μὲ Πόνο καὶ Ἀγάπη γιὰ τὸν Σύγχρονο Ἄνθρωπο,* Β΄ ἔκδοσις (Σουρωτή, Ἱερὸν Ἡσυχαστήριον «Εὐαγγελιστὴς Ἰωάννης ὁ Θεολόγος», 1999), 192.

[1497] Γέροντος Ἐφραίμ, *Ὁ Γέροντάς μου Ἰωσήφ,* 260; see also Elder Ephraim, *My Elder Joseph the Hesychast,* 370.

food and suchlike), it doesn't prevent one from praying the Jesus prayer while one is actually doing the job. That is why true monks prefer simple work."[1498] For this same reason St. Joseph the Hesychast "did not like making wood carvings with great variety or fancy designs with fine details because the mental concentration needed for such work would captivate the mind and hinder it from turning to God."[1499]

A nun once asked St. Paisios of the Holy Mountain: "When a task is mental, such as translation, how can one possibly say the Jesus prayer to sanctify the work one is doing?" He replied: "When the task requires mental concentration, your work will be sanctified when your mind is focused on God. Then you will be living in the atmosphere of God, even if you are not able to say the prayer.... Make sure that you take a short break every one or two hours and say the Jesus prayer."[1500]

Another beneficial occupation while working is to chant ecclesiastical music (assuming this would not disturb someone else nearby). *The Rule of Tarn* advised: "Let the plowman holding his plow handle sing 'alleluia,' the sweating reaper refresh himself with psalms, and while the vinedresser cuts the curved vine branch, let him sing something from the Psalms of David. Let these be your poems; these, so to speak, your love songs; these, the whistling of the shepherd; these, the tools of agriculture."[1501] St. Athanasios of Athos wanted his monks to sing psalms in order to avoid idle chitchat: "He did not permit the brethren who were in engaged in manual labor ... to accompany their labors with idle chitchat, but he made it an unbreakable rule that they were to sing psalms and not engage in idle conversation, so that their work would be blessed and their souls hallowed."[1502] Since, however, the Jesus prayer is much more beneficial than chanting,[1503] we endeavor to spend more time praying than chanting.

St. Paisios of the Holy Mountain believed that a monk is helped to mature spiritually when he has the freedom to regulate his own work schedule. When he served at the woodworking shop at the Monastery of Esphigmenou, he

> moved about with spiritual freedom in regard to his scheduled work. For example, on a day [prior to] when a vigil was scheduled, he worked many hours without rest. On the day after, however, and for as many days as the spiritual condition that had been generated in him by the vigil lasted, he did not go to the woodworking shop, but instead, did spiritual work in his cell: study, praying using his *komboschoini* [prayer-rope] and prostrations. Thus, there were times that he worked in the woodworking shop

---

[1498] Sakharov, *Striving for Knowledge of God,* 292.

[1499] Γέροντος Ἐφραίμ, *Ὁ Γέροντάς μου Ἰωσήφ,* 357; see also Elder Ephraim, *My Elder Joseph the Hesychast,* 436.

[1500] Elder Paisios, *With Pain and Love for Contemporary Man,* 208.

[1501] *Monastic Studies,* no. 17, 227.

[1502] Richard P. H. Greenfield and Alice-Mary Talbot, *Holy Men of Mount Athos,* 255.

[1503] See footnote #1797 on page 334.

for fifteen hours a day and times that he worked spiritually in his cell for three consecutive days.

That was the type of spiritual freedom that pervaded the Monastery of Esphigmenou. Each Brother loved the monastery as his home, and also loved his work and his spiritual duties, and in accordance with his spiritual condition, was also able to fully utilise his time in a *philotimo-filled* way....

Having experienced for himself the benefit of that spiritual freedom, he recommended that that same spirit be present in coenobitic monasteries, because, as he used to say, it helps the monk to mature spiritually. "The monk," he said, "must move about with a type of freedom that does not mean that he will have his own will, but that he will utilise his time such that he completely gives himself over, both to chores and to spiritual duties. For this to happen, however, one must cultivate obedience, *philotimo,* and spiritual nobility. The heart of the monk must be aflame with the spirit of sacrifice; he must love the monastery even more than his home—otherwise, he may fall into the habit of loafing about. In other words, freedom is very good, but if there is no *philotimo,* it can be dangerous.[1504]

St. Paisios warned of the danger of becoming attached to one's work:

> Give your legs and your hands to work but not your heart. [In other words,] you should not give your heart to material things. Some people give their whole self to material things. They spend the entire day trying to do a job well and don't think of God at all.... When a task is simple, it helps if the mind is not absorbed by it. But when the task is complex, then it makes sense to become somewhat absorbed mentally, but don't let that take over the heart.... When you work, you should not forget Christ. Do your work joyfully, but keep your mind and your heart focused on Christ. If you do this, not only you will not get tired, but you will also be able to do your spiritual work.[1505]

St. Paisios also warned of the dangers of working excessively:

> Those who work too hard and are full of worries forget God.... It is advisable for people who wish to live spiritually, especially monastics, to avoid certain pursuits, which obstruct them from their spiritual goal. They should not get involved in endless tasks, for there is never an end to work. If monks or nuns do not learn to do the internal, spiritual work, they will seek to escape in external activities. People who attempt to complete endless tasks will end their lives with all kinds of spiritual imperfections....
>
> Many times, unfortunately, even a monk will be deceived and draw a worldly form of pleasure from his work. It is in man's nature to do good because his Creator is good. But the monk is striving to transform himself from a human being into an angelic being. This is why when it comes to material things, his work must be limited to the bare necessities, so that he will have time for spiritual work. Then, the joy that he feels will come from the fruit of his spiritual labor; it will be a spiritual joy, abundant nourishment for himself and for everybody else.[1506]
>
> Much care is needed so as not to expend all our bodily strength on handwork. If we are careless, we won't be able to carry out our spiritual duties, or, we will do them,

---

[1504] Chamberas, *Saint Paisios the Athonite,* 134–35.

[1505] Elder Paisios, *With Pain and Love for Contemporary Man,* 205–6.

[1506] Ibid., 210–11.

but without motivation, waiting impatiently for ... [our prayer rule] to come to an end."[1507]

One holy tradition that helps us not to be too caught up in endless tasks is to rest from work on Sunday. The holy canons state: "Christians must not Judaize and rest on Saturday but must work on this day preferring to rest as Christians on Sunday if able to do so."[1508] Therefore, on Sundays and great feast days of the Church we only do work that is absolutely necessary (e.g., cooking, washing dishes, caring for any plants and animals that require daily attention, etc.). Other tasks that are not time-sensitive (such as construction) are not done on such days, even though it could be justified by the reasoning that it is for the Lord and therefore permissible on the Lord's day.[1509] Such a justification is following the letter of the law rather than the spirit of the law.

Sundays should not merely be a day of minimal work but should also be a day devoted to spiritual tasks, and thus truly be the Lord's day. St. Ignatius the God-bearer wrote (to laymen): "Let each one of us take his Sabbath spiritually, by rejoicing in meditation of the law, not in comfort of the body, not in dancing and noises, in which there is no sense."[1510] In the same vein St. Athanasios of Athos wrote to his monks: "It should be noted that we must not spend the days on which we are free from manual labor in idleness and laughter, but rather in prayer and reading, so that on feasts such as these we may receive enlightenment of soul and spiritual grace, and not condemnation."[1511]

3) Hardship

Enduring hardships is such an essential aspect of monasticism that it has been included in the catechism of receiving the monastic schema as follows:

> If, therefore, you have chosen to follow Him in truth, and if you ardently desire to be called, not falsely, His disciple, be prepared from this present time, not for comfort, nor for freedom from care, nor for physical nourishment, nor for any of the pleasing and sweet things upon earth, but for spiritual struggles, for abstinence of flesh, for purity of soul, for spiritual and bodily poverty, for sincere mourning, for all the sorrowful and painful things of the joy-giving life in God. For you must be hungry, and thirst,

---

[1507] Elder Paisios, *Epistles*, 125.

[1508] Agapius and Nicodemus, *The Rudder*, 564 (Canon XXIX of the Synod in Laodicea).

[1509] The word for Sunday in Greek is Κυριακή, which literally means "the Lord's [day]."

[1510] Pseudo-Ignatius, *Epistle to the Magnesians 9, Ante-Nicene Fathers,* Vol. 1: *The Apostolic Fathers with Justin Martyr and Irenaeus,* Alexander Roberts and James Donaldson, ed. (Edinburgh: Eerdmans Publishing Company, 1867), 62–63.

[1511] Thomas and Hero, *Byzantine Monastic Foundation Documents*, 228.

and endure nakedness, and accept reproach and ridicule, insult and persecution, and lay up many other grievous things, by which life in God is distinguished.[1512]

St. Basil the Great warned against living a soft life:

> "I chastise my body and bring it into subjection"[1513] lest at any time, because my blood is in good condition and overheated, my corpulence may become an occasion of sin. Do not flatter your flesh with sleep and baths and soft coverings, but say always these words: "What profit is there in my blood, whilst I go down to corruption?"[1514] Why do you treat with honor that which a little later shall perish? Why do you fatten and cover yourself with flesh? Or, do you not know that the more massive you make your flesh, the deeper is the prison you are preparing for your soul?[1515]

In the same spirit, St. Eustathios of Thessalonica wrote to a monk: "You have selected the rough life. Why are you now following the easy way which is dangerous and will likely lead to defeat? You have already chosen the harsh life. Therefore you should avoid delicate living."[1516] St. Isaac the Syrian explained: "The path of God is a daily cross. No one has ascended into Heaven by means of ease."[1517] He also said: "Afflictions suffered for the Lord's sake are more precious to Him than every vow and sacrifice; and the odor of their sweat surpasses every fragrance and choice incense. Regard every virtue performed without bodily toil as premature, stillborn fruit of the womb."[1518] Elsewhere he wrote: "Ease and idleness are the destruction of the soul, and they can injure her more than the demons. The demons are unable to act where the soul resides in light, that is, in the laudable labors of virtue."[1519]

St. Paisios of the Holy Mountain agreed:

> The easy life does not help. Comfort is not appropriate for a monk; it's a disgrace for those living in the wilderness. Perhaps you were raised spoiled, but now, if you are in good health, you must get used to hardship. Otherwise you are not a true monk.... Deprivation helps a lot. When people are deprived of something, they come to appreciate it more. When we deprive ourselves voluntarily, with discernment and humility for Christ's love, we feel spiritual joy.... Today most people are not deprived of anything

---

[1512] *The Great Book of Needs,* vol. 1, 365. The full text of the catechism is found below on page 399.

[1513] 1 Cor. 9:27.

[1514] Ps. 29:8.

[1515] *Saint Basil: Exegetic Homilies,* vol. 46 (Washington, D.C.: Catholic University of America Press, 1963), 223 (Homily 14 on Psalm 29).

[1516] PG 135:904A.

[1517] Holy Transfiguration Monastery, *The Ascetical Homilies of Saint Isaac the Syrian,* 430 (Homily 59).

[1518] Ibid., 177 (Homily 6).

[1519] Ibid., 371 (Homily 48).

and for this reason they lack *philotimo*. If one has not worked hard, he cannot appreciate the hard work of others.[1520]

Elder Aimilianos also noted the spiritual value of deprivation: "Only a person in deprivation while being content with what he has can love God and have a spiritual life…. [St. Paul said:] 'I have learned to be content in whatever circumstances I am … and to be in want.'[1521] He who has learned how to be in want is happy. He who desires to have everything—just in case he catches a cold or is in pain or gets a little wet or tired—is incompetent for survival. But the more you learn to bear suffering, the more you become a suitable instrument of God's grace."[1522]

St. Gregory of Sinai explained in more detail the importance of toil:

Here we should set forth the toils and hardships of the ascetic life and explain clearly how we should embark on each task, lest someone who coasts along without exerting himself, merely relying on what he has heard, and who consequently remains barren, should blame us or others, alleging that things are not as we have said. For it is through travail of heart and bodily toil that the work can properly be carried out. Through them the grace of the Holy Spirit is revealed. This is the grace that we and all the faithful are given at baptism but which through neglect of the commandments has been stifled by the passions…. No activity, whether bodily or spiritual, unaccompanied by toil and hardship bears fruit; "for the kingdom of heaven is entered forcibly," says the Lord, "and those who force themselves take possession of it" (Mt. 11: 12), where "forcibly" and "force" relate to the body's awareness of exertion in all things.

Many people for many years may have been working spiritually without exerting themselves, or may still be working in this way; but because they do not assiduously embrace hardships with heartfelt fervor and have repudiated the severity of bodily toil, they remain devoid of purity, without a share in the Holy Spirit. Those who work spiritually, but do so carelessly and lazily, may think that they are making considerable efforts, but they will never reap any harvest because they have not exerted themselves and basically have never experienced any real tribulation. A witness to this is he who says, "However exalted our way of life may be, it is worthless and bogus if our heart does not suffer."[1523] Sometimes when we fail to exert ourselves we are in our listlessness carried away by spurious forms of distraction and plunged into darkness, thinking we can find rest in them when that is impossible. The truth is that we are then bound invisibly by unloosable cords and become inert and ineffective in everything we do, for we grow increasingly sluggish, especially if we are beginners. For those who have reached the stage of perfection everything is profitable in moderation. The great Ephraim also testifies to this when he says, "Persistently suffer hardships in order to avoid the hardship of vain sufferings." For unless, to use the prophet's phrase, our loins are exhausted by the weakness induced through the exertions of fasting, and unless

---

[1520] Elder Paisios, *With Pain and Love for Contemporary Man,* 166, 161, 162; see also Γέροντος Παϊσίου, Μὲ Πόνο καὶ Ἀγάπη γιὰ τὸν Σύγχρονο Ἄνθρωπο, 156.

[1521] Phil. 4:11–12.

[1522] Γέροντος Αἰμιλιανοῦ, Νηπτικὴ Ζωὴ καὶ Ἀσκητικοὶ Κανόνες, 329, 260.

[1523] Ἰωάννου τοῦ Σιναΐτου, Κλῖμαξ PG 88:816A; see also Holy Transfiguration Monastery, *The Ladder of Divine Ascent,* 79 (step 7:64).

like a woman in childbirth we are afflicted with pains arising from the constriction of our heart, we will not conceive the Spirit of salvation in the earth of our heart.[1524] Instead, all we will have to boast about is the many profitless years we have spent in the wilderness, lazily cultivating stillness and imagining that we are somebody. At the moment of our death we will all know for certain what its fruit was.[1525]

A text attributed to St. Athanasios the Great emphasized the need for tremendous labors: "The saints despised this world, knowing what good things they were about to inherit. Thus, he who has rest in this world should not hope to receive the eternal rest, for the kingdom of heaven does not belong to those who rest here but to those who seek that life in great affliction and anguish. For they who have received the kingdom have not received it free but with tremendous labors and copious sweat."[1526]

Archimandrite Zacharias of Essex explained why monastics need hardship: "The Lord said that we enter the kingdom through the 'strait gate,' through the 'narrow way.'[1527] Monasticism tries to create this 'narrow way' for us to go through, and to leave behind the 'old skin,' like the snake. The snake goes through a narrow hole in order to leave behind its old skin, and it comes out with a new one. Monasticism tries to organize life in a way that will give the monk opportunities to endure certain hardships, so that he may thereby leave behind the 'old skin.'"[1528]

Even the non-Orthodox have observed that hardships and suffering in general are what forge character. As Edwin Chapin put it: "Out of suffering have emerged the strongest souls; the most massive characters are seared with scars."[1529] Aeschylus wrote: "Wisdom comes alone through suffering."[1530] Henry Ward Beecher said: "We are never ripe till we have been made so by suffering."[1531] And Louis E. Bisch observed: "Suffering is a cleansing fire that chars away triviality and restlessness."[1532]

[1524] Cf. Is. 21:3; 26:18.

[1525] Γρηγορίου τοῦ Σιναΐτου, «Περὶ ἡσυχίας καὶ περὶ τῶν δύο τρόπων τῆς προσευχῆς» ἐν *Φιλοκαλία τῶν Ἱερῶν Νηπτικῶν*, τόμος δ΄ (1991), 78–79 (κεφ. ιδ΄); see also Palmer, Sherrard, Ware, *The Philokalia*, vol. 4, 272–74 (ch. 14).

[1526] *Pseudo-Athanasius on Virginity*, Corpus Scriptorum Christianorum Orientalium, vol. 593, trans. David Brakke (Louvain: Peeters, 2002).

[1527] Mt. 7:14.

[1528] Zacharias, *The Enlargement of the Heart*, 243.

[1529] Josiah Hotchkiss Gilbert, *Dictionary of Burning Words of Brilliant Writers* (New York: Wilbur B. Ketcham, 1895), 567.

[1530] David R. Slavitt, *Aeschylus,* vol. 2 (Philadelphia: University of Pennsylvania Press, 1998), x.

[1531] Stanley Irving Stuber, Thomas Curtis, *Treasury of the Christian Faith: An Encyclopedic Handbook of the Range and Witness of Christianity* (New York: Clark Association Press, 1949), 707.

[1532] Andy Zubko, *Treasury of Spiritual Wisdom: A Collection of 10,000 Powerful Quotations for Transforming Your Life* (San Diego: Blue Dove Press, 2003), 456.

The underlying principle is that moderate challenges are what strengthen us. In the realm of physical strength, bodybuilders select weights that are neither trivially light nor impossibly heavy to lift. Likewise, in the realm of mental strength, educators present to pupils concepts and problems that are neither obviously self-evident nor completely unfathomable. So, too, in the spiritual realm, we who want to increase our spiritual strength will benefit by facing challenges and temptations that are neither trivial nor overpowering in magnitude. In the words of the Prophet Isaiah: "With a small affliction Thou didst instruct us."[1533]

St. Paisios of the Holy Mountain pointed out that toil strengthens both our body and soul, whereas modern conveniences do the opposite:

> In the past, people worked with tools that made them stronger. Nowadays, the tools that we use at work make us need physiotherapy and massages.... When conveniences become excessive, man is rendered useless and lazy. Even though we can turn something by hand, we think to ourselves, "No, I'll just press a button and it will turn by itself." When someone gets used to doing things the easy way, he wants to have it easy all the time.... Modern comforts have stupefied people, and the sloth we see in so many today has brought on many diseases.[1534] In the past, it would take so much work just to thresh the wheat! The labour was hard but then the bread was so sweet![1535]
>
> Because modern conveniences have exceeded all bounds, they have become inconveniences. Machines have multiplied and so have distractions; man has been turned into a machine.... All of these modern comforts make the cultivation of conscience in people difficult. In the old days, people used to work with animals and were more compassionate. If you overloaded an animal and the poor thing kneeled down from the weight, you felt bad for it.... Today people own lots of devices made of steel, but, unfortunately, even their own hearts have turned into steel.[1536]
>
> Make sure that you advance in spiritual matters and not in equipment and comfort. Do not delight in these things. If monasticism abandons the ascetic life, it will not be monasticism anymore. If you put convenience above monasticism, above ascesis, you

---

[1533] Is. 26:16 (LXX).

[1534] Dr. Jean-Claude Larchet made a similar observation: "The development of domestic appliances ... reduces physical activity in a way that harms health.... [This] reduces or eliminates for the habitually inactive even the light activity of household chores that might have improved their body tone" (Jean-Claude Larchet, *The New Media Epidemic: The Undermining of Society, Family and Our Own Soul,* trans. Archibald Andrew Torrance [Jordanville: Holy Trinity Publications, 2019], 77). Specifically, numerous studies have shown that physical exertion of the body improves: sleep quality, stress levels, mood, self-esteem, mental focus, bone density, muscle mass, cardiovascular health, gene expression, skin quality, blood pressure, cholesterol, metabolic rate, the immune system, insulin sensitivity, lung function, strength, endurance, coordination, balance, flexibility, life expectancy, and overall fitness. It also decreases the risk of coronary disease, diabetes, strokes, dementia, migraines, cancer, glaucoma, and injuries. Exercise has also been shown to reduce the intensity of the following chronic health conditions: osteoporosis, depression, Parkinson's disease, arthritis, and fibromyalgia. Furthermore, a physically strong body mitigates the effects of aging.

[1535] Elder Paisios, *With Pain and Love for Contemporary Man,* 163, 161. Hard-earned bread is sweet because accomplishments requiring exertion (whether spiritual, mental, or physical) naturally give rise to a wholesome satisfaction. Labor-saving devices deprive us of this.

[1536] Ibid., 152–53.

will not prosper. The monk avoids conveniences because they do not help him spiritually.... In doing our chores, we sometimes may [try to] justify the use of machines or other conveniences to do our work faster and have more time for our spiritual life. As a result our life becomes stressful and full of concerns and anxieties, and we come to resemble lay people rather than monks.[1537]

Technology can offer some help for daily needs. However, where do the needs end? One thing leads to another, and we become unable to stop at any given point. Simplify your needs and cast the daily cares out of your life.[1538]

One day, Elder Theophylactos of New Skete saw Satan going past the huts of the skete with his tongue out, mocking the monks and saying: "Ha, ha, ha! The monks have abandoned the Jesus prayer and have worldly distractions. They have got lots of work to do." When some monks had installed the telephone link in the skete, Elder Theophylactos had seen Saint John the Baptist looking very sad.[1539]

St. Sebastian of Optina also understood the value of physical labor and avoiding ease, for when he "was somewhat younger and stronger in health, he refused to use transportation, saying, 'I'm a monk; I should go on foot and not ride.' And he would walk long distances."[1540]

4) Poverty

St. Sophrony of Essex explained what is meant by monastic poverty:

The third basic [monastic] vow, that of *non-acquisition* (ἀκτημοσύνη), known in the West as the vow of poverty, naturally completes the first two [vows (of obedience and chastity)], and with them forms an indissoluble unity for the attainment of pure prayer and, at the same time, a more perfect identification with God through likeness to Christ, Who has so little concern to possess the things of this world that He "had not where to lay His head."[1541] Experience shows every man that in order to arrive at pure prayer it is essential to free the mind from burdensome preoccupation with material possessions.

The monastic vow to renounce the spirit of acquisitiveness stresses the struggle against the passion for acquiring (πλεονεξία) and the love of money (φιλαργυρία) and things. The monk promises not so much to live in poverty as to free his spirit from the desire to possess. The sign of success here is the appearance of a powerful desire not to possess, so that the true ascetic does not even spare his own body. Only thus is it possible to live a really royal life of the spirit....

The love of possessing banishes love for God and one's fellow-man. People do not see this, and do not want to understand that their unrighteous aspirations are the source of the sufferings of the whole world. St. John Climacus says: "Love of money (that is,

---

[1537] Ibid., 159.

[1538] Chamberas, *Saint Paisios the Athonite,* 462.

[1539] Elder Paisios, *Athonite Fathers and Athonite Matters,* 155.

[1540] Torstensen, *Elder Sebastian of Optina,* 368.

[1541] Mt. 8:20.

cupidity) is 'called the root of all evil'[1542]; and this is indeed so, for covetousness gives rise to theft, envy, separations, enmities ... cruelty, hatred, murder and wars."[1543]

Therefore, to break free from the bondage of petty cares, in order to purify our minds and allow our spirits to delight in a truly imperial liberty—or, more exactly, in a God-like liberty—renunciation of this sphere, too, is essential.[1544]

St. Basil the Great began his *Discourse on Ascetical Discipline* by stating: "First and foremost, the monk should own nothing in this world."[1545] And St. Synkletike taught:

> Poverty, for those who can endure deprivation, is the greatest good. Those who endure it suffer in the body, on the one hand, yet, on the other hand, grant comfort and delight to their souls. Just as well-made clothing is washed and made clean the more that one beats it and wrings it out, so the more one beats and wrings out the strong soul with willful monastic poverty, the more it is strengthened.
>
> On the contrary, those souls that are ill in thought and show love for ruinous material goods come to suffer. These souls, as soon as they are beset even slightly by material deprivations, are lost; just as worn and torn clothing cannot withstand washing, so, in the same manner, these souls are lost, since they cannot withstand the harsh cleansing of virtue....
>
> The Lord addressed these same people [who seek the virtues], saying: "Take no thought for the morrow" (Mt. 6:34). "Behold the fowls of the air: for they sow not, neither do they reap, nor gather unto barns; yet your Heavenly Father feedeth them" (Mt. 6:26). And these poor people, having nothing, the Devil has few ways to harm, since the majority of sorrows and gains follow on the heels of incursions for the purpose of looting money.
>
> Hence, where there is poverty, the nemesis of our souls can do no evil. Do they have holdings to burn? Indeed, they have none. Beasts of burden to kill? Where to find such things? An opportunity to harm their beloved relatives? They too have been left behind. From all of this, we can conclude that monastic poverty constitutes the greatest victory over the Enemy and is the most valuable treasure of life.[1546]

St. Ephraim the Syrian said: "A monk who loves material things is like unto a barren palm tree; contrarily, a poor monk is like a palm tree rich with leaves and which rises up to Heaven."[1547] Antiochos of Pandects added:

> Poverty indicates that the monk who applies it in his life is sincere. The monk who has no possessions resembles an eagle, who flies high above the earth. The monk who has not a single possession shows himself to be only temporarily on earth. Since he has acquired none of the temporary goods of this world, by this indifference to them it is obvious that he desires things eternal. A poor man mimics, by his poverty, Elias, John (the Baptist), and the Disciples of the Lord. Like them, he can say: "Behold, we

---

[1542] 1 Tim. 6:10.

[1543] PG 88:929A.

[1544] Sakharov, *Truth and Life,* 101, 102–3.

[1545] Wagner, *Saint Basil: Ascetical Works,* vol. 9, 33.

[1546] Chrysostomos, *The Evergetinos, Book IV,* 6–7.

[1547] Ibid., 21.

have forsaken all, and followed Thee; what shall we have therefore?" (Mt. 19:27). And he, like them, will hear that which the Savior said: "You, having abandoned all and having followed Me, shall receive a hundredfold and shall inherit everlasting life (cf. Mt. 19:29)."[1548]

In the same spirit, St. Gregory Palamas said:

> Let us cleanse the eye of our understanding by reaching up with our deeds, words and thoughts towards God. There would be nothing to drag us down if we were only to look, as far as we can, at John [the Baptist]'s way of life. He went around without a roof over his head, so let us be content with a small shelter, and may each one of us gladly accept the modest room which the superior gives us, remembering him who was homeless all his life long. He was satisfied with "locusts," the name of a type of fruit, and "wild honey,"[1549] a plant which grows wild in the desert, the roots of which were used as food by the Fathers who dwelt there after him. So he lived on fruit and plant roots, or honey from the mountains, had only one garment, and wore a girdle of skin about his loins, thus showing ... that he possessed the virtue of poverty.[1550]

An ascetic Elder in the *Gerontikon* explained: "Greatly love poverty; do not desire to have valuable objects and various other material goods in your cell. When your soul seeks something and does not attain it, it sighs and is humbled. Indeed, in this condition, God intervenes and comforts your soul, granting it compunction."[1551]

St. Isaac the Syrian had much to say about the benefits of poverty and non-possessiveness:

> Love poverty with patience, that your mind may be collected and secured from wandering. Detest superfluity, that you may preserve your thoughts untroubled.[1552]
>
> Nothing brings such serenity to the mind as voluntary poverty.[1553]
>
> Without non-possessiveness the soul cannot be freed from the turmoil of thoughts; and without stillness of the senses she will not perceive peace of mind.[1554]
>
> No one can achieve true non-possessiveness unless he resolves within himself to endure tribulations with gladness. And no man can endure tribulations unless he believes that there is something more excellent than bodily comfort, the which he will receive in recompense for the afflictions that he has prepared himself to undergo. The love of afflictions must first have stirred in the man who has prepared to deprive himself of possessions, for only thereafter does the thought come to him to possess

---

[1548] Ibid., 11.

[1549] Vid. Mt. 3:4; Mk. 1:6.

[1550] *The Homilies of Saint Gregory Palamas,* vol. 2, trans. Christopher Veniamin (South Canaan: St. Tikhon's Seminary Press, 2002), 220–21 (Homily 40).

[1551] Chrysostomos, *The Evergetinos, Book IV,* 21.

[1552] Holy Transfiguration Monastery, *The Ascetical Homilies of Saint Isaac the Syrian,* 143 (Homily 4).

[1553] Ibid., 150 (Homily 4).

[1554] Ibid., 159–60 (Homily 5).

none of the things of this world. And every man who draws nigh to affliction is first made steadfast by faith, and then he approaches afflictions.[1555]

The beginning of the path of life is continually to exercise the mind in the words of God, and to live in poverty. For when a man waters himself with one, it aids in the perfection of the other. That is to say, to water yourself with the study of the words of God helps you in achieving poverty, while achieving freedom from possessions affords you the time to attain to constant study of the words of God; and the help provided by them both speedily erects the entire edifice of the virtues.[1556]

The more the mind takes leave of care for these visible things, my beloved brethren, and is concerned with the hope of future things (according to the measure of its elevation above care), the more it is refined and becomes translucent in prayer. And the more the body is freed from the bonds of worldly affairs, the more the mind is also made free.... Therefore the Lord gave as a commandment that before all else a man should hold fast to non-possessiveness, and withdraw from the turmoil of the world, and release himself from the cares common to all men. He said, "Whosoever forsaketh not his entire human state and all that belongeth to him, and renounceth not himself, he cannot be My disciple (cf. Lk. 14:26)."[1557]

As long as a man chooses to be free of possessions, departure from life always arises in his mind. He makes the life after the resurrection his continual study, and at all times he contrives to make preparation that will be useful yonder. He acquires disdain for every suggestion of honor and bodily ease that is sown in his thoughts, and the thought of scorning the world is lively in his mind at every moment. His mind becomes bold, and he acquires a heart that is always strong and courageous in every fear and danger of impending death; and he does not even fear death itself, because his attention is always upon it, as something that approaches him, and he awaits it.[1558]

The love of God, therefore, comes by converse with Him; the converse of prayer comes through stillness; stillness comes through non-possessiveness; non-possessiveness through patience; patience through the hatred of passionate desires; the hatred of passionate desires is born of the fear of Gehenna and the earnest expectation of blessings. The passionate desires are hated by the man who knows their fruits, and what they prepare for him, and of what good things they deprive him. Thus every discipline is connected with that which is higher. But if one of these middle ones should fail, those following will be unable to stand, and it will appear that all are undone and lost. What is more than this lies beyond explanation.[1559]

Furthermore, St. Isaac the Syrian believed that afflictions stemming from poverty have a beneficial effect on the soul. He wrote:

How much benefit, thanksgiving, and humility is produced by the incursion of these spurs [of afflictions] is an easy matter for all to learn for themselves.... God has made these instructors plentiful for you, lest being free from them, and immune to and having no part in tribulations, and feeling yourself superior to every fear, you should

---

[1555] Ibid., 340 (Homily 42).

[1556] Ibid., 113 (Homily 1).

[1557] Ibid., 444–45 (Homily 63).

[1558] Ibid., 509 (Homily 74).

[1559] Ibid., 446 (Homily 63).

forget the Lord your God and turn away from Him, and fall into believing in many gods, just as many have done. For although these men had a passible nature like your own, were subject to want, and were scourged with these very griefs, yet in a brief space of time, because of paltry riches, fleeting power, and ephemeral health, they not only fell into polytheism, but in their madness they had the audacity to declare themselves god by nature.

… For this reason, then, He has made His remembrance abound in your heart by means of sufferings and griefs, and He has spurred you toward the gate of His mercy with the fear of hostile forces. And by means of deliverance from these things, He has implanted in you seeds of love for Him…. Then He will cause you to perceive both the holiness of His glory and the secret mysteries of His nature's goodness. Whence could you have known these things, if adversities had never befallen you?[1560]

Despite the many spiritual advantages of lacking possessions, the primary danger of possessions is becoming attached to them. Abba Zosimas always liked to say: "It is not possessing something that is harmful, but being attached to it."[1561] Although Abba Gelasios demonstrated that it is possible to maintain an inner non-possessiveness while living in a monastery with many possessions,[1562] Elder Ephraim commented that this feat of Abba Gelasios is extremely difficult.

Monks have taken a vow of poverty[1563] and ideally have forsaken all things in order to follow Christ and attain perfection. As Christ said: "If thou wilt be perfect, go and sell that thou hast, and give to the poor, and thou shalt have treasure in heaven; and come follow Me."[1564] If this ideal is implemented by living simply, a significant result will be that people who see monks without fancy conveniences will be inspired by their genuine dedication to the Gospel rather than scandalized by their luxuries. This is crucial, for as St. Isaac the Syrian taught: "The monk ought to be in his appearance and all his actions an

---

[1560] Ibid., 162–63 (Homily 5).

[1561] John Chryssavgis, *In the Heart of the Desert: The Spirituality of the Desert Fathers and Mothers* (Bloomington: World Wisdom: 2008), 69.

[1562] "They used to say of him [i.e., Abba Gelasius] that he undertook a life of poverty and withdrawal in youth. There were many others who, at that time, embraced the same way of life as he in the same parts. Among them there was an elder of supreme simplicity and poverty, living alone in one cell until he died, even though he had disciples in his old age. He disciplined himself until death to observe the commandment not to possess two tunics nor (together with his companions) to take thought for the morrow. When (at the instigation of God) Abba Gelasius came to set up the coenobion, much land was offered to him. He also acquired beasts of burden and oxen for the needs of the coenobion. He [i.e., an angel] who at first revealed to the godly Pachomius that he should set up a coenobion was working with this father too in all that concerned the setting up of the monastery. The above-mentioned elder, seeing him immersed in these things and maintaining a sincere affection for him, said to him: 'Abba Gelasius, I am afraid that your *logismos* [thinking] is attached to the lands and the rest of the property of the coenobion,' to which he replied: 'Your *logismos* is more attached to the needle with which you work than is the *logismos* of Gelasius to the property'" (Wortley, *The Alphabetical Sayings of the Desert Fathers,* 87 [Gelasius 5]).

[1563] For the details of this vow, see footnote #2109 on page 398.

[1564] Mt. 19:21.

exemplar of profit to those who see him,"[1565] and he warned: "He who creates temptations for laymen will not behold the light."[1566] Likewise, St. John of Sinai wrote that "the monastic life is a light for all men ... and they should give no scandal in anything they say or do. For if the light becomes dark, then all the deeper will be the darkness of those living in the world."[1567] If our calling as monastics is to be a light to laymen and to inspire them by our good example, we may fall short of living up to this calling if they see us living with just as many (if not more) worldly comforts as they have.

Elder Ephraim was very concerned about people being scandalized when seeing monks owning something fancy. For example, when someone wanted to buy him a brand new luxury car, he was appalled at the extravagance and was strongly opposed to having something so fancy. He refused to accept that car also because he was concerned about what people would say when they saw a monastery having something so luxurious. He wanted to get a good used car instead, for one-third the price, or a less luxurious new one for half the price.

St. John Chrysostom was also concerned about the impression made on laymen by what monks possessed:

> And their [monks'] dress is suitable to their manliness. For not indeed, like those with trailing garments, the enervated and mincing, are they dressed, but like those blessed angels, Elijah, Elisha, John, like the apostles; their garments being made for them, for some of goat's hair, for some of camel's hair, and there are some for whom skins suffice alone, and these long worn.... [When a poor man] shall see [monks who are the] children of rich men and descendants of illustrious ancestors clothed in such garments as not even the lowest of the poor, and rejoicing in this, consider how great a consolation against poverty he will receive as he goes away.[1568]

St. Palladios also pointed out the benefit of merely seeing a monk with humble attire: "The appearance of their faces abloom with grey hairs, and the arrangement of their dress, together with their conversation so free from arrogance, and the piety of their language—all this and the grace of their thoughts will increase your strength, even should you be afflicted with spiritual dryness. 'The attire of the man and the gait of his feet and the laughter of his teeth show him for what he is' (Sir. 19:30) as Wisdom says."[1569]

Moreover, we should embrace poverty not merely for the sake of what other people might think of us but also for its inherent spiritual benefit. Christ warned us: "How hardly

---

[1565] Holy Transfiguration Monastery, *The Ascetical Homilies of Saint Isaac the Syrian*, 196 (Homily 11).

[1566] As quoted in Goldfrank, *The Monastic Rule of Iosif Volotsky*, 178 (referring to Nikon of the Black Mountain, *Pandektes* 33:248).

[1567] Luibhéid, *John Climacus: The Ladder of Divine Ascent*, 234.

[1568] *St. Chrysostom: Homilies on the Gospel of St. Matthew*, 400.

[1569] Palladius, *The Lausiac History*, 29.

shall they that have riches enter into the kingdom of God!"[1570] "And He said to them all, 'If any man will come after Me, let him deny himself, and take up his cross daily, and follow Me. For whosoever will save his life shall lose it: but whosoever will lose his life for My sake, the same shall save it.'"[1571] This is why the fifth-century Syriac *Rules of Rabbūlā for the Qeiāmā* declare: "All those who have become disciples of the Messiah shall not be covetous to possess more than their needs, but they shall distribute it to the poor."[1572] In the same spirit St. Nilus Sorsky wrote: "We must not have in our own possession in our cells any dishes or any objects of great value and beauty. So also the structure of the hermitage and other buildings of the skete monastery should be built of cheap and unadorned materials, as Basil the Great says, namely, that the building materials should be easily found everywhere and purchased at low cost.... Nor should these be the cause for any cares and preoccupations and worries so that we do not fall into contact with the spirit of the world."[1573]

Chariton the Superior wrote on the importance of poverty for monastics in his testament for Koutloumousiou Monastery on the Holy Mountain:

> I beg them [i.e., the monks], call upon them, and as a father I advise them that they preserve poverty as the paternal inheritance we have received from those old monks whose memory is eternal. The monks are well aware of the benefits which derive from poverty.... Is there any way in which monks who have made promises to deny the world and what is in the world, can then justify betraying their promises? ... They have to face the wrath of God because not only have they not denied themselves, according to the commandments, and taken up their cross and followed (Mt. 10:38; Lk. 14:27), but on the pretext of fulfilling the Savior's command which forbids [giving] to God ... they strive for something.[1574]

Elder Arsenios Boca said: "Whoever for God's sake lives in poverty acquires a treasure that is never lost. The more a person renounces worldly comforts, the more he is counted worthy of enjoying the delights and blessings of God through the Holy Spirit. The further away from the world you are, the nearer you are to God."[1575]

St. Ignatius Brianchaninov explained why poor and simple buildings help monastics achieve their goal:

> It was not without reason that the holy fathers observed extreme simplicity in their clothing, in the furniture and appurtenances of their room or cell, in their monastic buildings, and even in the construction and adornment of their churches. The thought and heart of a weak person correspond with his or her outward circumstances. This is

---

[1570] Lk. 18:24.

[1571] Lk. 9:23–24.

[1572] Vööbus, *Syriac and Arabic Documents,* 42.

[1573] Maloney, *Nil Sorsky: The Complete Writings,* 45, 78.

[1574] Thomas and Hero, *Byzantine Monastic Foundation Documents,* 1426–27.

[1575] Γεροντικὸ Ρουμάνων Πατέρων, 189.

something quite incomprehensible for inexperienced and inattentive people. If a monk wears elegant clothes, if his cell is carefully furnished with an air of taste and luxury, if even the churches of a monastery are magnificent buildings, shining with gold and silver, and provided with rich vestries, then the monk's soul will certainly be vainglorious, full of conceit and self-satisfaction, and he will be a stranger to compunction and the realization of his sinfulness. Filled with vainglorious pleasure and gratification which is taken for spiritual joy, such a soul remains in darkness, self-delusion, hardness and deadness, as if in the midst of a triumphant festival. On the other hand, when a monk's clothing is simple, when he lives like a pilgrim in his cell as if he were in a tent or hut and has only what is essential in it, when the church serves as a place of prayer and thanksgiving, confession and weeping, without distracting and enrapturing him by its splendour, then his soul borrows humility from his outward surroundings, is detached from everything material, and is transported in thought and feeling to that unescapable eternity that confronts all men. Such a soul endeavours by repentance and the fulfilment of the Gospel commandments to prepare himself in good time for a blessed reception in eternity.[1576]

St. Paisios of the Holy Mountain also saw great inherent benefit in monastic poverty and simplicity:

> I know monks who cannot really enjoy the spiritual spirit; they rejoice in the worldly spirit. They have never felt this thrill of joy, the joy that comes from simplicity. Austerity is a great help to the spiritual life. A monk should only own what he needs and what befits him. He should limit himself to what will ease his life a bit and not aspire to worldly possessions. For example, a military blanket will take care of his needs; he does not need a colourful or embroidered blanket. This is how simplicity and spiritual valour set in! Give things to a monk and you will destroy him. It's when he rids himself of what he owns that he finds rest. Collecting things will destroy a monk.[1577]
>
> Monks should love the poverty that they promised God they would observe. Unfortunately, however, they do not limit themselves to bare necessities, to simple things, so much for themselves as for the monastery in general.[1578]
>
> All those things that lay people use to make their lives easier will enslave the monk instead of helping him. The monk must try to minimize his needs and simplify his life. Otherwise he will not be set free. There is a difference between being clean and enjoying luxury. Using the same tool for different jobs will make the monk less demanding. At Sinai Monastery, I used a can for making both tea and porridge.[1579]
>
> In general, it helps a lot to keep things simple. You should own simple and sturdy things. What is humble and simple is appreciated even by laypeople and it will certainly help the monk. It will remind him of poverty, of pain, and of the monastic life. Once King George [in the early 20th century] visited the Monastery of Great Lavra on Mount Athos and the fathers served him on a silver tray. When he saw it he said, "I

[1576] Brianchaninov, *The Arena,* 157–58.

[1577] Elder Paisios, *With Pain and Love for Contemporary Man,* 175.

[1578] Elder Paisios, *Epistles,* 55.

[1579] Elder Paisios, *With Pain and Love for Contemporary Man,* 176.

was expecting something simpler from you, perhaps a wooden tray. I am tired of silver trays."[1580]

When St. Paisios was asked how a monk should use modern conveniences, he replied:

He should always have fewer and simpler things than the rest of the people. I feel much better when I use wood for heating, cooking, and handiwork....

If a monk or a nun does not think in a monastic way, then everything becomes a necessity and he becomes worse than those who live in the world. Monks must live in humbler circumstances than they did when they lived in the world, never better. We should not have better things here than we did at home. In general, the monastery must be poorer than the homes in which we were raised. This will help the monk with his interior life and will also be of help to lay people. God has provided that we do not find peace in possessions and comforts. If laymen are troubled by all these modern comforts, you can imagine how much more they trouble the monk.[1581]

Secular people say, "How lucky are the wealthy people who live in palaces and have all kinds of conveniences!" On the contrary, blessed are those who have succeeded in simplifying their lives and freeing themselves from the yoke of worldly progress, of the many conveniences that have become inconveniences, and have consequently rid themselves of the dreadful anxiety that plagues so many people today.... The more people distance themselves from a natural, simple life and embrace luxury, the more they suffer from anxiety.... Worldly stress is the result of worldly happiness, worldly pleasures, and self-indulgence.[1582]

I could ask others to help me take care of my hut, but I can make do with the way things are. Why should I spend money on a wall when there is so much need elsewhere? ... If I have a 500-drachma bill, I prefer to buy small crosses and icons and give them to someone in need, to help him. It gives me great joy to give to others. Even if I need something, I will not spend the money on myself.... You must pray and only do those chores that are absolutely necessary. All these things that usually take our time are really so short-lived. Is it worth wasting our time when so many are suffering and people are dying from starvation? The simple buildings and the humble belongings transport the monastics mentally to the caves and the austere dwellings of our holy Fathers, and are of great spiritual benefit. Worldly belongings remind monks of the world and turn them into secular souls.

Christ was born in a manger. If we find comfort in worldly things, Christ will turn His back to us, something He never did to anyone. He will say, "I had nothing; why did you need so much? Is that what is written in the Gospels? Did you see Me do as you are doing? You do not live in the world, you are monks. What should I do with you? Where should I put you?[1583]

We should be worried about the right things. Christ will ask us what spiritual work we have accomplished, how we helped the world in spiritual matters. He will not ask what buildings we made. He will not even mention them. We will be held accountable for our spiritual progress. I want you to grasp what I am trying to say. I am not saying

---

[1580] Ibid., 176–77.

[1581] Ibid., 157.

[1582] Ibid., 182, 167; see also Γέροντος Παϊσίου, *Μὲ Πόνο καὶ Ἀγάπη γιὰ τὸν Σύγχρονο Ἄνθρωπο,* 171.

[1583] Elder Paisios, *With Pain and Love for Contemporary Man,* 180–81; see also Γέροντος Παϊσίου, *Μὲ Πόνο καὶ Ἀγάπη γιὰ τὸν Σύγχρονο Ἄνθρωπο,* 170–71.

that one must not construct buildings and not construct them well, but one must take care of the spiritual life first and then mind the rest, and do all that with spiritual discernment.[1584]

Nevertheless, St. Paisios did acknowledge that monasteries involved in philanthropic work could have wealth and some modern conveniences. He said of St. Athanasios of Athos: "The monastery had eight hundred to one thousand monks during his time and many people sought help there. There were numerous poor and hungry people who gathered at the Lavra Monastery to find food and shelter.... He had to create a modern kind of oven so that he would have bread to give to people. The Byzantine emperors had endowed the monasteries with a lot of property because they served as charitable institutions. The monasteries were established to help people spiritually and materially, which is why the emperors endowed them so well."[1585]

According to the 13th-century *Typikon for the Monastery of the Archangel Michael*, "the accumulation of wealth by monasteries is morally indefensible while others live in poverty."[1586] Specifically, it stated:

> The superior should not be eager to store up money in the monastery.... To those then who have renounced the world and those in the world and for this reason also the bitter ruler of this world, and who have promised to live on a higher plane and to partake of the angelic manner of life to the best of their strength, how much pardon would this practice deserve? Or what defense will those who, after their holy monastic promise, have engaged in such practices make to the implacable, fearsome Judge? How can they enrich themselves while others in the world are poor and worn out by the deprivation of necessities?[1587]

The Emperor Nicephoros Phokas (who nearly became a monk) declared in a novel (i.e., a law) which he ordained in the tenth century:

> The Word of God the Father taught us that wealth and many possessions prevent our salvation and that it is difficult for the rich to enter the Kingdom. He wanted us to live so simply that He not only wanted us to have no staff, bag, or second tunic,[1588] but He even prohibited worrying about tomorrow's food.[1589]
>
> But now I see in monasteries and sacred convents a conspicuous illness (and I call this greed an illness), and I know not what cure to contrive or how to correct the excess. What caused this? Which fathers taught them such extravagance and led them to "false

---

[1584] Elder Paisios, *With Pain and Love for Contemporary Man*, 181; see also Γέροντος Παϊσίου, *Μὲ Πόνο καὶ Ἀγάπη γιὰ τὸν Σύγχρονο Ἄνθρωπο*, 170.

[1585] Elder Paisios, *With Pain and Love for Contemporary Man*, 160.

[1586] Thomas and Hero, *Byzantine Monastic Foundation Documents*, 1208.

[1587] Ibid., 1226.

[1588] Vid. Lk. 9:3.

[1589] Vid. Mt. 6:34.

frenzies"[1590] (to quote the divine David)? They endeavor to acquire endless stretches of land, luxurious buildings, herds of horses, oxen, camels, and countless other animals. By directing all their soul's attention to these things, they have made the monastic life no different than the worldly life, even though God on the contrary has ordered us to be free of such things. For He said, "Do not worry about what to eat or drink,"[1591] and gave us the example of the birds to reproach us.[1592] What did the divine Apostle say? "These hands ministered to my own needs and to the men who were with me,"[1593] and: "If we have food and covering, with these we shall be content."[1594]

Look at the lives of the holy Fathers who shone forth in Egypt, Palestine, Alexandria, and everywhere else, and you will find them living so frugally and simply that it was as if they lived only for their soul and approached the incorporeality of the angels. After all, Christ said that the Kingdom belongs to the forceful, and the forceful seize it[1595] and that through many tribulations we must enter it.[1596]

So when I see those who have vowed to follow this kind of life and are marked for this lifestyle by the pledge of the schema completely breaking their vows and contradicting the schema, I know not how to avoid calling this thing a farce. I would say that it blasphemes the name of Christ.[1597]

This emperor's attempts to fight the illness of greed in some monasteries were apparently unsuccessful, considering that two centuries later St. Eustathios of Thessalonica addressed the same problem:

Monastic life means a rejection of the world—not a desire for it. It means withdrawing from it—not approaching it. It is a life free of worldly cares—not a life full of them. But for you, renouncing the world has meant becoming more worldly.... You are led away from your goal by working too much, which makes you worry about many things. You have abandoned your primary work while occupying yourselves with secondary matters. You are ignorant of the refined things that bring you in contact with angels, while you strive for coarse and heavy things by which the nous which God gave you is dragged down to earth, paralyzed and unable to ascend.... It is this kind of discordant, unharmonious, sloppy, and completely inappropriate behavior of these superficially great monks that the memorable emperors of old decided to prohibit in the monasteries they themselves established, as if they had foreseen what would happen if they would not take certain wise measures. This counterfeit practice, which

---

[1590] Ps. 39:6.

[1591] Cf. Mt. 6:25.

[1592] Vid. Mt. 6:26.

[1593] Acts 20:34.

[1594] 1 Tim. 6:8.

[1595] Cf. Mt. 11:12.

[1596] Cf. Acts 14:22.

[1597] Νικηφόρου Φωκᾶ, «Ἡ Νεαρά» ἐν Ράλλη καὶ Ποτλῆ, *Σύνταγμα τῶν Θείων καὶ Ἱερῶν Κανόνων*, Τόμος Ε΄, 261–62.

destroys monastic life, does not benefit the monks themselves and harms those who would imitate them.[1598]

In the same spirit, St. Paisios of the Holy Mountain warned his nuns:

Unfortunately, the secular spirit has entered many monasteries, because, nowadays, some fathers promote the monastic life through a secular channel and do not lead souls to the Patristic spirit of Grace. I discern an anti-patristic spirit prevailing in the monasteries today. They do not accept what is truly good, the tradition of the Fathers of the Church. They do not live in a patristic manner; instead, they level the spiritual heights in the name of obedience and the breaking of the will, and then go on to serve their own secular desires....

We should not aim to surpass the secular people in secular achievements. This secular progress harms even those who live in the world, let alone the monk. We should run so fast spiritually that lay people will be forced to do something. If we just behave like a very spiritual lay person, we will not help them, because they already have an example of lay people who are highly spiritual. We must surpass them....

Why don't we give some thought about the holy Fathers whom we study continually, where and how they lived? The Lord said: "The foxes have holes, and the birds of the air have nests; but the Son of Man hath nowhere to lay His head."[1599] What a tremendous thing! And you see how they were trying to imitate Christ in those caves! They experienced Christ's joy, because they emulated Christ in everything. Their full attention was focused on that one thing. The holy Fathers had transformed the desert into a spiritual state, and we today are turning it into a secular state. While the Church of Christ is departing to the desert in order to be saved, we are converting the desert into a secular state, and we scandalize people who will not only remain helpless but will also have nothing to hold on to....

Today, there are monks who live the monastic life on the outside. They do not smoke, they live a chaste life, they read the *Philokalia,* and they constantly talk about the Fathers of the Church. They are not different from lay people who are pleased with themselves because as children they did not tell any lies and always made the sign of the cross, went to Church and later as adults were careful with moral matters. Well, that's what is happening in some monasteries today, and many lay people find that attractive. But, as they get acquainted with the monks or nuns, they realize that they maintain a secular spirit and are not really different from people who live in the world.

How can a monk move the heart of a layperson, when he is spiritually drained? Alcohol will lose its pungency if we leave the bottle open. It can no longer kill germs and neither will it ignite if you light it. And if you put it in the gas stove or lamp, it will also destroy the wick. Likewise, if the monk is not careful, he drives divine Grace away and, in the end, is left only with his Monastic Habit. He too will be like the alcohol that has lost its spark. He won't be able to cauterize the devil. "Angels are a light for monks, and monks are a light for men."[1600] He will not even be a light to others. Do you realize how destructive this secular spirit is? If this true spirituality leaves monasticism, nothing is left.... The greatest contribution to society will be made by monasteries that do not have the secular mindset and have reached a spiritual state. They will

---

[1598] PG 135:820CD, 824BC, 832A.

[1599] Mt. 8:20; Lk. 9:58.

[1600] Luibhéid, *John Climacus: The Ladder of Divine Ascent,* 234.

not need to say much or do anything else, because they will be able to speak through their way of life. This is what the world needs today....

If we are to enjoy spiritual health and angelic delights, we must detach ourselves from the spirit of secular progress.[1601]

Let us lay our cell bare of wealth and our soul of passions so that our life and mission as monks acquire meaning, for where there is material wealth there is spiritual poverty.[1602]

Likewise, a contemporary Athonite monk who became a metropolitan (Nikolaos Hatzi-nikolaou of Mesogea and Lavreotiki) wrote:

Monasteries are traditionally known for their voluntary poverty, frugality, and simplicity in living. The truth is that this tradition has been somewhat shaken in our days. But wherever it does exist, it gives the best answer to the deceit of hyper-consumerism and to the dead end of pleasure-seeking materialism. This constitutes the priceless treasure of monastic life, and it must in no way be lost. The narrow and low doors; the dimmed lighting; the lack of worldly comforts; the profound connection with nature and natural ways ... make the outline of a very gentle life with an exceptionally frugal use of the senses that is certainly rare and especially brings rest. All these things are missing from contemporary life, but as a rule are endemic to monasteries. This is why every visit to a monastery—in addition to the blessing of the pilgrimage and the stillness—rewards people with a rare relaxation of their soul's deepest parts. "Stillness mortifies the outward senses and resurrects the inward movements, whereas an outward manner of life does the opposite, that is, it resurrects the outward senses and deadens the inward movements."[1603] The atmosphere of life in a monastery wakes up our inner world and gives rest to the natural man....

The classic pastoral approach is usually based on knowing the customs of the contemporary world and era, and consequently on being completely informed and up-to-date. On the contrary, the monastic pastoral approach could draw its strength and base its outreach not on being up-to-date but by relying on well-tested timelessness and by being qualitatively different. In other words, the more removed one becomes from the things of the world, the more one can help the world.[1604]

A counterintuitive benefit of poverty is that it actually makes one *more* eager to share instead of less eager. As Simon Sinek observed: "When we have less, we tend to be more open to sharing what we have. A Bedouin tribe or nomadic Mongolian family doesn't have much, yet they are happy to share because it is in their interest to do so ... because their survival depends on sharing, for they know that they may be the travelers in need of food

---

[1601] Elder Paisios, *With Pain and Love for Contemporary Man*, 80–86.

[1602] Ibid., 189.

[1603] Holy Transfiguration Monastery, *The Ascetical Homilies of Saint Isaac the Syrian*, 303 (Homily 37).

[1604] "The Contribution of Women's Monasticism in the Pastoral Life of the Church," http://www.imml.gr/index.php?option=com_content&view=article&id=289:gynaikios-monaxismos&catid=19:2012-01-29-11-12-07

and shelter another day. Ironically, the more we have, the bigger our fences, the more sophisticated our security to keep people away and the less we want to share."[1605]

One pitfall for successful monasteries is that their success can lead to a material wealth that distracts them from their spiritual goals. As one historian observed in regards to monasteries in Western Europe:

> Ascetic work ethics and rational design of work roles made the medieval monasteries the most efficient production organizations of that time. They accumulated immeasurable wealth which trapped those monks who strove for the monastic ideal of an ascetic life led in poverty, and brought about severe conflicts. Thus the medieval monastery became the first bureaucratic "iron cage."[1606]

Due to this phenomenon, "by the seventh century, monasticism [in Western Europe], which had originally arisen from the desire for self-mastery, self-transcendence, and union with God, embracing the ideal of the voluntary removal of the individual from society, had become closely identified with land-owning and the interests of royalty and aristocracy."[1607] Although St. Eustathios of Thessalonica in the 12th century sharply criticized monks who made *deliberate* efforts to acquire wealth, he believed that it is not reprehensible but even praiseworthy for them to become rich when someone bestows wealth on them out of reverence for their virtuous lifestyle.[1608] However, this opinion of his conflicts with the stance of the many monastic saints quoted earlier in this chapter.

5) Luxury

Luxurious living is diametrically opposed to a life devoted to God. The Apostle Paul wrote that a celibate woman ostensibly dedicated to God "that liveth in pleasure is dead while she liveth."[1609] St. Cyril of Jerusalem warned: "Every worldly luxury is sweet at the time it is used, but it greatly darkens and terribly inebriates him who accepts it."[1610] St. Isaac the Syrian emphasized the importance of avoiding comforts and embracing hardships:

> A man can never learn what divine power is while he abides in comfort and spacious living.... You wish to ascend to Heaven, and to receive that Kingdom, communion with God, the consolation of the spiritual goods of yonder blessedness, the

---

[1605] Simon Sinek, *Leaders Eat Last,* 117.

[1606] A. Kieser, "From Asceticism to Administration of Wealth. Medieval Monasteries and the Pitfalls of Rationalization," *Organization Studies* 8, 1987, 104.

[1607] Dunn, *The Emergence of Monasticism,* 207.

[1608] Vid. PG 135:784D–788A.

[1609] 1 Tim. 5:6.

[1610] Κύριλλος Ἀλεξανδρείας, τόμος β΄ τῆς ὀκτατ., 918.

fellowship of the angels, and immortal life, and you ask if this path requires toil? Great is this marvel![1611]

It is the spirit of the devil, not the Spirit of God, that dwells in those who pass their life in ease. The Spirit of God is not pleased with bodily comforts, nor does He find a life of ease acceptable but one of hardship.[1612]

One of those who love God [i.e., St. Paul] said, "I have given oath that I die daily" [cf. 1 Cor. 15:31]. By this the sons of God are set apart from the rest of mankind: they live in afflictions, but the world rejoices in luxury and ease. For it is not God's good pleasure that those whom He loves should live in ease while they are in the flesh. He wishes them rather, so long as they are in this life, to abide in affliction, in oppression, in weariness, in poverty, in nakedness, isolation, want, sickness, degradation, buffetings, contrition of heart, bodily hardship, renunciation of relatives, and sorrowful thought. He wishes them to possess an aspect differing from all creation, a habitation unlike that of the rest of men, and to live in a solitary and quiet dwelling, unknown to the sight of men and bereft of any sign of the gladdening things of this life; mourning is found within [their dwelling], and cheerfulness far from it; distresses press frequently upon it; nor do they fully have the body's needs as do the rest of men; their bedding is the ground.... they are sombre, but the world is joyous; they fast, but the world lives in pleasure.[1613]

The seventh-century Celtic *Rule of Carthage* includes "restraint in the use of comforts" as one of the basic characteristics of monastics.[1614] St. Gregory Palamas said that wealth and luxury "prevent the ripening of the [spiritual] fruits worthy of the divine harvest."[1615]

According to St. Joseph the Hesychast, "one does not become a monk through luxury and comforts."[1616] The following incident from his life reveals that he even believed that luxuries hinder a monk's prayer and deprive him of the right to ask God for mercy:

Using all the money he had earned through iconography, Father John had bought the most luxurious items: sofas, fancy chandeliers, and even a gas-powered refrigerator! Such things were unheard-of on the Holy Mountain in those days. When St. Joseph the Hesychast saw all this, he sadly commented: "Can a monk living in a place like this say, 'Lord Jesus Christ, have *mercy* on me'? He has already received mercy! I doubt a person can say the prayer in here."[1617]

[1611] Holy Transfiguration Monastery, *The Ascetical Homilies of Saint Isaac the Syrian,* 504, 505–6 (Homily 72).

[1612] Ibid., 433 (Homily 60).

[1613] Ibid., 434 (Homily 60).

[1614] Vid. Maidín, *The Celtic Monk,* 78.

[1615] *Saint Gregory Palamas: Treatise on the Spiritual Life,* 41.

[1616] Γέροντος Ἰωσήφ, Ἔκφρασις Μοναχικῆς Ἐμπειρίας, 53; see also Elder Joseph, *Monastic Wisdom,* 54.

[1617] Γέροντος Ἐφραίμ, Ὁ Γέροντάς μου, 672; see also Elder Ephraim, *My Elder Joseph the Hesychast,* 583.

In the same spirit, St. Sophrony of Essex said: "When we are truly broken [i.e., humble], God hears our prayers; when we are comfortable, He does not answer."[1618]

St. John Chrysostom preached that luxuries harm the body and blind the soul:

> Now then that unbelievers should have these feelings [of sadness due to the fleeting nature of pleasures], is no marvel; but when they who have partaken of so great mysteries and learned such high rules of self-denial concerning things to come, delight to dwell in things present, what indulgence do they deserve? [None.] Whence then arises their loving to dwell in present things? From giving their mind to luxury, and fattening their flesh, and making their soul delicate, and rendering their burden heavy, and their darkness great, and their veil thick. For in luxury the better part is enslaved, but the worse prevails; and the former is blinded on every side and dragged on in its maimed condition; while the other draws and leads men about every where, though it ought to be in the rank of things that are led.... It is not the body which blinds the soul; far from it, O man; but the luxury.[1619]

If this is how he warned *laymen* of the harm of luxuries, one could only imagine how he would have censured *monastics* living in luxury. For the following teaching of his shows that he associated voluntary virginity with voluntary poverty:

> In truth there is a great difference between virtue and evil, and a great difference. One is wide and easy, but the other is narrow and full of tribulation. Luxury is wide and easy, but poverty and need are narrow and full of tribulation. So just as in this life the ways are opposed—the person who chooses virginity travels the narrow road of tribulation, and so does the person who pursues chastity, embraces voluntary poverty, and scorns vain glory ... —so also in the time of punishment and recompense, there is a great distance to be found between their requitals.[1620]

St. Lazaros of Mt. Galesion taught that comforts destroy monasticism:

> The fathers of old always sought out the deserts and the most uncomfortable places, not those which had springs and leafy trees and other physical comforts. For this reason they were well able to subordinate their irrational carnal impulses because they did not easily find the materials that beget the passions. For in the Skete [of Egypt], just as the holy fathers themselves predicted, as long as the place was uncomfortable it abounded in the lodgings and dwellings of the monks but, from the moment when, one after another, they began to transport fertile soil from elsewhere for growing vegetables and set up trees and cisterns in front of their doors, the Skete went into decline and was delivered to destruction.[1621]

St. Maximos the Confessor likewise observed that comforts destroy a monk:

> The achievements of worldly people constitute the failings of monks, and the achievements of monks constitute the failings of worldly people. For example, the

---

[1618] Σωφρονίου, *Οἰκοδομώντας τὸν Ναὸ τοῦ Θεοῦ, Τόμος Α΄*, 191.

[1619] Schaff, *Saint Chrysostom: Homilies on the Epistles of Paul to the Corinthians*, 242 (Homily 39 on 1st Corinthians).

[1620] Roth, *On Wealth and Poverty*, 139.

[1621] Greenfield, *The Life of Lazaros of Mt. Galesion*, 310.

achievements of worldly people are wealth, fame, power, luxury, comfort, children, and what is consequent upon all these things. But the monk is destroyed if he obtains any of them. His achievements are the total shedding of possessions, the lack of fame and power, self-control, hardship, and all that is consequent upon them.[1622]

St. Paisios of the Holy Mountain ridiculed the monastic pursuit of conveniences:

Who could doubt that with all of the modern conveniences the monastery can function more easily? If every monk could have his mother by his side to take care of him, no doubt, that would also be convenient. And, if there were a tape player in the church playing the prayers, that would also be very relaxing. But still more soothing would it be if the stalls [the wooden seats in church] were converted into beds. It would also certainly be relaxing for an ascetic if he had a small machine made just for the turning of his prayer-rope and a phony straw ascetic to do his prostrations and the prayer-ropes, while he could get a soft mattress to lie down and rest his worn-out flesh. Without a doubt, all of these things comfort the flesh but leave the soul empty and miserable, besides generating feminine sentimentality and worldly anxiety....

All monks should avoid, as much as possible, modern means in the operation of the monastery, and should respect the desert by adapting to it. Then, the desert will grant us its divine stillness and we shall be assisted in the desertion of our souls from the passions. It is not right to want to adapt the desert to our worldly self, for it is a sin to abuse the desert. Any of the modernistic monks may build a monastery on top of an apartment building so that he may have all the conveniences of the world he wants and so that he may enjoy the city lights and ascend to the third heaven via the elevator, and let him leave the desert in peace.[1623]

The greatest enemy of our soul's salvation—even greater than the devil—is the worldly spirit, for it sweetly misleads us and in the end eternally embitters us. Yet, if we saw the devil himself, we would be terrified and forced to run to God, and then we would secure Paradise. Monks who compete with worldly people in all fields of worldly development reveal that they have taken a wrong turn. Besides, they themselves are able to perceive this in the worldly anxiety they suffer.[1624]

Metropolitan Nikolaos Hatzinikolaou also lamented the modernization of Mount Athos and wrote:

You meet God more easily walking along a path than on the road in a car, with its exhaust fumes, the clouds of dust, and the noise, speed and convenience. "For the gate is small and the way is narrow that leads to life (Mt. 7:14)." ... The feet are replaced by wheels ... exhaust fumes take the place of exertion ... instead of the scents of nature there is the stench of petrol or diesel fumes ... instead of an animal we see an engine ... instead of feeling the heat of the sun on one's face, the dust of the road covers one's

---

[1622] Μαξίμου τοῦ Ὁμολογητοῦ, «Ἑκαντοντὰς τρίτη περὶ ἀγάπης» ἐν *Φιλοκαλία τῶν Ἱερῶν Νηπτικῶν*, τόμος β΄ (1991), 38 (κεφ. πδ΄); see also Palmer, Sherrard, Ware, *The Philokalia*, vol. 2, 96–97 (ch. 85).

[1623] Elder Paisios, *Epistles,* 56–58.

[1624] Ibid., 97.

hair and clothes … we replace what is natural and divine with the arrogance of human achievement.[1625]

Henry David Thoreau's experiment of living a simple life in the wilderness for two years led him to discover that simplicity fosters a deeper understanding of life, which makes one more "awake" and able to "live deliberately," whereas luxuries do the opposite. He wrote:

> Only one in a million is awake enough for effective intellectual exertion, only one in a hundred million to a poetic or divine life. To be awake is to be alive. I have never yet met a man who was quite awake…. I went to the woods because I wished to live deliberately, to front only the essential facts of life, and see if I could not learn what it had to teach, and not, when I came to die, discover that I had not lived…. I wanted to live deep and suck out all the marrow of life, to live so sturdily and Spartan-like as to put to rout all that was not life.[1626]
>
> Most of the luxuries, and many of the so-called comforts of life, are not only not indispensable, but positive hindrances to the elevation of mankind.[1627]… In proportion as he simplifies his life, the laws of the universe will appear less complex, and solitude will not be solitude, nor poverty poverty, nor weakness weakness.[1628]

St. Sophrony of Essex believed that seeking comfort and less menial tasks in a monastery are petty desires stemming from lack of faith that ruin monasticism. He said:

> If we have firm faith we can make our life in the monastery truly suitable for eternal salvation. This is a heavenly mystery. But if in the monastery we seek petty things, such as comfort and tasks not so menial, then everything surely will go to waste…. Remember the noteworthy maxim that a monk on the Holy Mountain once told me: "There is no task that in itself debases the grandeur of man's being; only sin debases the divine life within us." And I will add that the most suitable tasks for monastic life are those from which we do not run the risk of acquiring passions.[1629]

One ascetic elder in the *Gerontikon* was asked: "Why, Father, is it not possible for those of our generation to maintain the ascetic life of the Fathers before us?" "Because," the elder answered, "it neither loves God, nor does it flee away from people, nor does it disdain the material goods of this world; for in the soul of a man who flees from other men and from materialism, there begins to be born a spontaneous contrition and desire for the ascetic life…. A man, if he does not flee to a place where he earns his bread only with great labor, cannot succeed in the ascetic life."[1630] An abbot of a monastery asked Abba Poemen, "How

---

[1625] Metropolitan Nikolaos of Mesogaia, *Mount Athos: The Highest Place on Earth* (Athens: En Plo Editions, 2007), 136–38.

[1626] Henry David Thoreau, *Walden,* vol. 1 (Boston: Houghton, Mifflin, 1854), 142–43.

[1627] Henry David Thoreau, "Walden" in Carl Bode, ed., *The Portable Thoreau* (Harmondsworth: Penguin Books, 1982), 269.

[1628] Henry David Thoreau, *Walden,* vol. 2 (Boston: Houghton, Mifflin, 1854), 499.

[1629] Σωφρονίου, *Οἰκοδομώντας τὸν Ναὸ τοῦ Θεοῦ, Τόμος Β΄,* 17, 386.

[1630] Chrysostomos, *The Evergetinos, Book I,* 106.

can I acquire the fear of God?" Abba Poemen replied: "How can we acquire the fear of God when our belly is full of cheese and preserved foods?"[1631]

Nevertheless, St. Basil the Great recommended moderation between abstinence and luxury: "The best rule and standard for abstinence is this: to seek neither luxury nor mortification of the flesh but to avoid the immoderation of both, so that the body may neither be disordered by obesity nor yet rendered sickly and so unable to perform the commandments."[1632] Although St. Joseph the Hesychast lived most of his life with tremendous deprivation and ascesis, he would have agreed with this moderate approach. For he said: "The conclusion I have drawn now after so many years and so much ascesis is that the ideal monastic path is to find a spiritual guide, to have light physical labor, and to have a schedule for prayer and fasting."[1633]

Yet in churches and chapels of a monastery, many saints of the Church wanted to use the absolutely best materials. For example, St. Neophytos, the founder of Docheiariou Monastery on Mount Athos wrote: "I added [to the existing buildings] the most precious cloths, and holy silver vessels, and all-venerable icons and holy books ... and I erected this most sacred and holy church ... and I adorned it with every beauty within my power, and as such I presented it for all to see. Nevertheless, all these things are for the glory and praise of God, and not for my own vain satisfaction."[1634] Likewise, St. Caesarius of Arles and St. Donatus of Besançon wrote in their monastic rules: "You will not use silver except in the services of the oratory."[1635]

Elder Ephraim, also believed that monastery churches should be richly adorned. One day during a meal in trapeza when the reading was the life of a Byzantine monastic saint that described how he adorned the church he built, Elder Ephraim leaned towards me and whispered with a smile, "Do you see how lavishly he adorned his church?"

Some saints, however, had a different approach and believed that even a church should be unadorned. For example, St. Nilus Sorsky wrote:

> Concerning the adornments of churches, St. John Chrysostom writes: "If anyone should wish to donate sacred utensils or any other adornment for the church, tell him to distribute his money to the poor, for no one has ever been judged for not decorating the church." And other saints say the same thing. St. Eugenia the Martyr also, when sacred silver vessels were offered to her, said: "It is not fitting for a religious in a monastery to have silver possessions." For this reason it is not fitting that we also

---

[1631] Ward, *The Sayings of the Desert Fathers*, 192. This quote has not been included to denounce eating cheese and preserved foods but merely as a reminder of how important deprivation was to the holy Fathers.

[1632] Wagner, *Saint Basil: Ascetical Works*, vol. 9, 211.

[1633] Γέροντος Ἐφραίμ, *Ὁ Γέροντάς μου Ἰωσήφ*, 406–7; see also Elder Ephraim, *My Elder Joseph the Hesychast*, 587.

[1634] Thomas and Hero, *Byzantine Monastic Foundation Documents*, 1307.

[1635] Donatus of Besançon, "Regula ad Virgines: a Working Translation," ch. 63; see also McCarthy, *The Rule for Nuns of St. Caesarius of Arles*, 185.

should possess gold and silver objects, not even for sacred vessels and other unnecessary adornments except to have only the bare necessities for the church.[1636]

Similarly, when St. Paisios of the Holy Mountain was asked how much decoration is appropriate in a church, he replied: "Considering the era in which we live, which is not Byzantium, the simpler the decoration is, even in a church, the better, for simplicity always helps."[1637]

6) Health

Just as the soul is more noble and important than the body,[1638] so the primary emphasis of a monastery should be on facilitating health of soul. But since the body is also God's special creation and since health of body is conducive to health of soul, physical health should be cared for as well. As St. Nectarios of Aegina explained:

> On account of this mutual influence [of soul and body], then, if man is to be happy, if he is to act in a way worthy of his calling, he needs to be healthy on both fronts, since without both being in good condition, he is unable to be happy and cannot be fit to perform the work of his calling. Since there are many things which undercut the health and well-being of the soul and body, man therefore ought to take great care to fortify both so as to keep them strong and robust. Thus they will be able to repel the innumerable assaults of enemies and be ready and prepared to enjoy that happiness which comes from the well-being of the two parts of the self, and at the same time be able to fulfill the work of his calling. Wherefore, as all know well, the training and exercise of both body and soul are inborn duties set upon man by both his very nature and his calling since a healthy body serves the soul willingly and readily, while a soul which has cultivated its faculties is sound, healthy, and governs the body prudently.[1639]

Likewise, St. Joseph the Hesychast observed that when the body is sick, "the soul suffers along with the body, even though the former is spiritual and bodiless.... [Then] the nous is unable to produce its noetic movements because it is hobbling together with the body....

[1636] Maloney, *Nil Sorsky: The Complete Writings,* 44.

[1637] Elder Paisios, *With Pain and Love for Contemporary Man,* 179. Both St. Nilus and St. Paisios supported their stance by citing the story of St. Pachomios, who intentionally made the pillars of his church crooked (vid. Veilleux, *Pachomian Koinonia,* vol. 2, 55–56), although Derwas Chitty questioned the veracity of this story (vid. Chitty, *The Desert a City,* 119).

[1638] As St. Gregory the Theologian said: "Just as the soul is more honorable than the body, it is more honorable to purify the soul than the body. If then the purity of the body is praiseworthy, see, I pray you, how much greater and higher is that of the soul" (Schaff, *Cyril of Jerusalem, Gregory Nazianzen,* "Oration 37," 344. PG 36:308A).

[1639] Saint Nektarios, *For Mind and Heart: St. Nektarios as Teacher,* trans. Rev. Dr. John Palmer (Columbia: New Rome Press, 2020) 46–47.

The demons excite carnal passions more than other passions when the body is exhausted and has collapsed."[1640]

Since contemporary medical experts agree that physical health depends primarily on proper diet, sufficient physical activity, medical attention, and the avoidance of toxic substances, a monastery should provide for these four fundamentals. Moreover, since "an ounce of prevention is worth a pound of cure,"[1641] the painless and inexpensive task of caring for physical health in this manner will save one from the painful and expensive task of trying to remedy health problems that arise due to neglecting one's health.

Although some of the holy Fathers felt that resorting to physicians evinced a lack of faith in God, St. Basil the Great taught: "The medical art has been vouchsafed us by God."[1642] In the same spirit, St. Barsanuphius the Great wrote to a monk: "We should not, however, place all our hope in these [medicines], but only in the God Who grants death and life, Who says: 'I shall wound, and I shall heal' (Deut. 32:39). When you read these [medical] books and ask others about these matters, do not forget that without God there can be no healing."[1643] St. Joseph the Hesychast at first wanted to heal others only through faith, prayer, and fasting, but later he changed his approach and wrote: "I am beginning to learn that both medicines and grace are necessary."[1644]

Eating unhealthy foods (e.g., junk food, sweets, sodas, highly processed foods, etc.) would be contrary to the principles of caring for bodily health and of not spending money on luxuries. In the words of St. Basil the Great:

> Whatever [food] is calculated to relieve our need [for nourishment] with the least trouble, this is to be employed.... Nothing, in fact, that is known to be harmful should be partaken of, for it is not reasonable to take food for nourishment which from within us would make war upon the body and hinder it in the accomplishment of the precept.... Furthermore, we should prefer by all means whatever is most easily procurable and not concern ourselves with costly fare and seek to obtain extravagant foods with expensive sauces on the pretext of continency. On the contrary, we should choose whatever is easy to obtain in each region, cheap, and available for general consumption, and use only those imported foods that are necessary to sustain life, like olive oil and similar products.[1645]

In the same spirit, Abba Dorotheos told his monks: "A man is perfectly able to satisfy the needs of his body with bread, vegetables, and a few olives, but he gives up doing so and

---

[1640] Γέροντος Ἰωσήφ, Ἔκφρασις Μοναχικῆς Ἐμπειρίας, 78, 79, 444; see also Elder Joseph, *Monastic Wisdom,* 76, 377.

[1641] Jared Sparks, *The Works of Benjamin Franklin,* vol. 1 (Boston: Whittemore, Niles, and Hall, 1856), 134.

[1642] Wagner, *Saint Basil: Ascetical Works,* vol. 9, 331 (Question 55 in the *Long Rules*).

[1643] Chryssavgis, *Barsanuphius and John,* vol. 1, 302 (letter 327).

[1644] Γέροντος Ἰωσήφ, Ἔκφρασις Μοναχικῆς Ἐμπειρίας, 284; see also Elder Joseph, *Monastic Wisdom,* 244.

[1645] *Saint Basil the Great: Ascetical Works,* vol. 9, 276 (Rule 19).

seeks something more tasty and more expensive—all this is against the conscience."[1646] St. Joseph the Hesychast wrote to a layman: "Take control of your appetite, and don't eat things you know will harm your health: fried foods, salty foods, sauces, pork, meats, salted fish, alcoholic drinks in general."[1647] Elder Ephraim preferred organic foods, and he frequently avoided produce when he found out that it was not organic.

St. Basil the Great was concerned that laymen would be scandalized if they saw monastics preoccupied with gratifying their appetites with tasty foods. He wrote in his monastic rules: "That we should run about searching for anything [edible] not demanded by real necessity, but calculated to provide a wretched delight and ruinous vainglory, is not only shameful and out of keeping with our avowed purpose, but it also causes harm of no mean gravity when they who spend their lives in sensual gratification and measure happiness in terms of pleasure for the appetite see us also taken up with the same preoccupations which keep them enthralled."[1648]

Several of the holy Fathers recommended avoiding all delicious food. For example, St. Basil the Great wrote that we should "satisfy our need with the plainer foods and those necessary to sustain life, avoiding the evil of taking our fill of them and abstaining absolutely from those foods whose sole purpose is to give delight."[1649] He also wrote: "Continency has only one rule: complete abstinence from all that tends to harmful pleasure."[1650] The reason for this, according to St. Isidore of Seville, is that a monk should "curb the cravings of his palate" because by growing accustomed to renouncing pleasures, he will be more able to control his lust.[1651]

Nevertheless, many contemporary Athonite elders (including Elders Ephraim and Aimilianos) would offer sweets to their disciples because they could see that the pleasure of tasting something delicious from time to time would lead them to glorify God rather than increase their passions. They also instructed the monastery's cook to serve foods that are both nourishing and tasty.

7) Aesthetics

A monastery belongs to God and therefore should be a place of beauty. Granted, a few monastic saints turned away from the beauty of nature because it distracted them from their

---

[1646] Wheeler, *Dorotheos of Gaza: Discourses and Sayings,* 107.

[1647] Γέροντος Ἰωσήφ, *Ἔκφρασις Μοναχικῆς Ἐμπειρίας,* 284; see also Elder Joseph, *Monastic Wisdom,* 244.

[1648] *Saint Basil the Great: Ascetical Works,* vol. 9, 277 (Rule 20 in the *Long Rules*).

[1649] Ibid., 274 (Rule 18).

[1650] Ibid., 275 (Rule 19).

[1651] Vid. *Monastic Studies,* no. 18, 10.

intense prayer. For example, in the early days of monasticism, "Mother Sara, who dwelt above the river and was sixty years old, had never looked out [from her abode] and seen the river."[1652] Commenting on this, St. Anatoly (Zertsalov) of Optina said: "I identify more with those saints who loved nature, like St. Sergius, St. Savva of Zvenigorod, Sts. Anthony and Theodosy. They chose the most beautiful locations for their monasteries because nature raises man up to God."[1653]

In order to make a monastery beautiful, it should be aesthetically pleasing to all five senses:

1) It should be pleasing to the eyes by consisting of beautiful, clean,[1654] and well-kept buildings, gardens, and landscaping. Every item should be kept in its place, so that it can be easily found and so that things are not scattered around in a disorderly manner. Studies have shown that people living in a disorganized place have a higher risk for heart disease,[1655] are less active,[1656] are more depressed and fatigued,[1657] have higher levels of the stress hormone cortisol,[1658] have greater difficulty working efficiently and focusing on a particular task,[1659] sleep less well,[1660] and waste more time.[1661] Only the absolutely most necessary items should be kept, since 80%

[1652] *The Paradise of the Holy Fathers,* trans. E. A. Wallis Budge, vol. 2 (London: Chatto & Windus, 1907), 46.

[1653] Saint Anatoly (Zertsalov) of Optina, *A Collection of Letters to Nuns,* 263–64.

[1654] Elder Ephraim emphasized keeping the monastery clean. Once he was upset with me when he saw me pass by a small piece of paper outside without picking it up and throwing it away. Gerondissa Makrina also believed that a monastery should look tidy: "It is forbidden to hang blankets and other clothes on the balconies where all the visitors can see them" (Rule #29).

[1655] Vid. http://newsinfo.iu.edu/web/page/normal/14627.html

[1656] Ibid.

[1657] One study found that women who described their living spaces as "cluttered" or full of "unfinished projects" were more likely to be depressed and fatigued than women who described their homes as "restful" and "restorative." Vid. http://www.ncbi.nlm.nih.gov/pubmed/19934011

[1658] Ibid. Structure makes life predictable and orderliness enables one to speed through routine tasks.

[1659] Specifically, researchers found that the visual cortex can be overwhelmed by task-irrelevant objects, making it harder to allocate attention and complete tasks efficiently. Vid. http://www.ncbi.nlm.nih.gov/pubmed/21228167

[1660] A survey conducted by the National Sleep Foundation found that people who make their beds every morning are 19 percent more likely to report regularly getting a good night's sleep. Vid. https://sleepfoundation.org/sites/default/files/bedroompoll/NSF_Bedroom_Poll_Report.pdf

[1661] Finding items in a disorganized place takes more time, and studies have estimated that people waste a total of more than 8,000 hours in their life searching for misplaced items.

of things kept are never used,[1662] and since getting rid of clutter eliminates 40% of the housework.[1663]

2) It should be pleasing to the ears by having traditional Orthodox chanting in the services, by not using loud machinery, by discouraging people from shouting, and by disallowing conversations during rest times.

3) It should be pleasing to the nose by minimizing the use of machines that pollute the atmosphere and by having plenty of flowers and trees, as St. Nectarios of Aegina[1664] and Elder Ephraim wanted for their monasteries. But we should avoid using perfumes for our rooms, clothes, or bodies, since this is condemned by the Prophet Amos,[1665] the Prophet Isaiah,[1666] St. Gregory the Theologian,[1667] Clement of Alexandria,[1668] the Seventh Ecumenical Council,[1669] and St. Nicodemos of the Holy

---

[1662] According to the National Association of Professional Organizers as quoted in http://simplyorderly.com/surprising-statistics/

[1663] According to the National Soap & Detergent Association as quoted in http://simplyorderly.com/surprising-statistics/

[1664] St. Nectarios "saw that trees were planted in his convent and throughout the entire island of Aegina.... Specifically, he sent 2,018 mulberry and fruit trees" (Strongylis, *St. Nectarios of Pentapolis and the Island of Aegina*, vol. 2, 35).

[1665] "Woe to those ... who drink wine in bowls and anoint themselves with the finest oils" (Amos 6:6).

[1666] "The Lord will smite ... the heads of the daughters of Zion.... Instead of perfumes there will be rottenness ... and instead of a rich robe, a girding of sack cloth" (Is. 3:17–24).

[1667] St. Gregory taught: "Let us be healed also in the smell, that we be not effeminate; and be sprinkled with dust instead of sweet perfumes" (Oration XL "On Holy Baptism"), and "Angels walking upon earth are they who practise chastity.... Let all vain ornament be banished ... and perfume enticing to pleasure" (Lecture XII "On the Words *Incarnate,* and *Made Man*").

[1668] "The use of crowns and ointments is not necessary for us; for it impels to pleasures and indulgences, especially on the approach of night. I know that the woman brought to the sacred supper 'an alabaster box of ointment' (Mt. 26:7), and anointed the feet of the Lord, and refreshed Him.... But the woman not having yet received the Word (for she was still a sinner), honoured the Lord with what she thought the most precious thing in her possession—the ointment.... I know, too, the words of Aristippus the Cyrenian. Aristippus was a luxurious man. He asked an answer to a sophistical proposition in the following terms: 'A horse anointed with ointment is not injured in his excellence as a horse, nor is a dog which has been anointed, in his excellence as a dog; no more is a man,' he added, and so finished. But the dog and horse take no account of the ointment, whilst in the case of those whose perceptions are more rational, applying girlish scents to their persons, its use is more censurable.... Day by day their thoughts are directed to the gratification of insatiable desire, to the exhaustless variety of fragrance. Wherefore also they are redolent of an excessive luxuriousness. And they fumigate and sprinkle their clothes, their bed-clothes, and their houses. Luxury all but compels vessels for the meanest uses to smell of perfume.... It is highly requisite for the men who belong to us to give forth the odour not of ointments, but of nobleness and goodness. And let woman breathe the odour of the true royal ointment, that of Christ, not of unguents and scented powders; and let her always be anointed with the ambrosial chrism of modesty, and find delight in the holy unguent, the Spirit" (*Fathers of the Second Century: Hermas, Tatian, Athenagoras, Theophilus, and Clement of Alexandria*, 253–54).

[1669] "Every luxury and adornment of the body is alien to the priestly order. Bishops or clergymen, therefore, who adorn themselves with splendid and conspicuous clothes need to be corrected; but if they insist upon it,

Mountain.[1670] Besides, 95% of scented items nowadays derive their fragrance from artificial chemicals (many of which have been proven to be toxic)[1671] rather than from fragrances naturally found in God's creation.

4) It should be pleasing to the sense of touch by keeping buildings at a moderate temperature.

5) It should be pleasing to the sense of taste by serving wholesome and healthy food.

Caution is needed to avoid excessive decoration. St. Theodore of Sanaxar wrote in a rule for nuns: "Every luxury, worldly entertainment, or excessive decoration of the cell is strictly forbidden, just as is the use of anything silk or colored, other than cotton or wool

---

they must be condemned to a penance. Likewise as regards those who anoint themselves with perfumes" (Agapius and Nicodemus, *The Rudder,* 444 [Canon XVI]).

[1670] "One must guard the sense of smell pure from the fragrances of myrrhs and perfumes, for they not only weaken the manly character of the soul and make it effeminate, but they (more than any other thing) also incite the soul toward fornication and other moral licentiousness. As external assaults upon the senses bring about a corresponding tendency and change in the body, likewise the changes in the body effect corresponding changes in the soul.... Marcus Aurelius had the habit of using expensive and sweet-smelling myrrh in his lamps so that as it burned he would be pleased by its fragrance. Behold, what level of foolishness the hedonistic desire to please the sense of smell can reach! Not far from this foolishness is also the habit of those who attempt to please all their senses through the use of fragrances in general. They like to add fragrant substances to everything—their foods, their drinks, their clothes, their mattresses, and so forth.... If you really want your body to be fragrant and to exude a pleasant odor, do not remain idle. Move it, work it, and force yourself. Do fifty or even one hundred prostrations every day and as many reverences as you can. [Note: this advice of St. Nicodemos was not addressed to monks.] Bodily activity naturally generates heat, which makes the body thin and evaporates or digests its superfluous liquids.... This is why the bodies of virtually all the craftsmen and laborers and especially of ascetic monks do not exude any heavy odor, but rather exude a pleasant and fragrant odor" (Νικοδήμου τοῦ Ἁγιορείτου, Συμβουλευτικὸν Ἐγχειρίδιον, 69–72; see also Chamberas, *Nicodemos of the Holy Mountain: A Handbook of Spiritual Counsel,* 101–3).

[1671] "Until the 20th century, perfumes were made from natural ingredients derived directly from plants and animals. As fragrances became more widespread, they also became more synthetic. The National Academy of Sciences reports that 95% of the chemicals used in fragrances today are synthetic compounds derived from petroleum, including known toxins capable of causing cancer, birth defects, central nervous system disorders and allergic reactions.... Fragrance chemicals do not end with a bottle of perfume or cologne. They can be found in common items such as hair care products, hairsprays, deodorants, body lotions, sunscreens, after-shaves, shaving gels, as well as laundry detergents, fabric softeners, dryer sheets, scented plug-ins, scented candles, potpourri, alleged air *fresheners,* most cleaning products, antibacterial creams, disinfectants, magazines, and even in trash bags and pesticides—and the list goes on.... Many chemicals used to make perfumes and other scented products are listed on the Environmental Protection Agency's (EPA) **Hazardous Waste List** [emphasis in original].... Medical conditions generally aggravated by exposure: kidney disorders, liver disorders, heart disorders, skin disorders, ... headache, giddiness, stupor, irritability, fatigue, tingling in the limbs.... [When] absorbed and stored in body fat, it metabolizes to carbon monoxide, reducing oxygen-carrying capacity of the blood.... [This ingredient] formerly used in **chemical warfare** [emphasis in original] ... can cause loss of memory and muscle control, **brain damage** [emphasis in original], problems with speech, hearing, and vision" (Connie Pitts, *Get a Whiff of This,* [Bloomington: 1stBooks, 2003], xix, xviii, 49, 48, 56–57).

material of exclusively black color."[1672] St. Paisios of the Holy Mountain warned that these worldly decorations can captivate our heart:

> We must avoid worldly things and not let them occupy our heart; we must use only the simplest means to accommodate our needs. We must make sure, however, that the few things we use are solid. If I use a beautiful thing, I give all my heart to that beauty and I leave nothing for God. You pass by somewhere and you see a house with pretty marble work, designs, engravings.... You admire the stones, the bricks, and you leave your heart there....
>
> Women are especially vulnerable to this kind of deception. Few of them do not waste their hearts on vanities. What I am trying to say is that the devil robs them of their rich heart through all these ephemeral, colorful, and shiny trinkets. Let's say, one of them needs a plate. She will search for the one with a flowery pattern, as if the food would turn sour if the plate had no flowers! Some spiritual women may, instead, be moved by serious patterns such as a double-headed eagle and so on. And they wonder, "Why don't spiritual things touch me?" How can the heart be moved by spiritual things, when it is scattered in cabinets and plates?[1673]

8) Cenobitic Life

The cenobium is a microcosm of the Church: a body in which different members have different abilities. They all work together for the common benefit, and all are harmed when one member is harmed. This concept is based on the words of St. Paul: "Ye are the body of Christ and members in particular ... when one member suffers, all the members suffer with it."[1674]

St. Basil the Great described this principle as follows:

> The one to whom general supervision [of the monastery] is entrusted, who appraises what has already been accomplished and plans and provides for what is to be done, exercises the function of the eye, so to speak. Another does the work of the ear or the hand in listening to orders and executing them, and so on for each member of the body. It is important to bear in mind, therefore, the analogy of the parts of the body, where neglect or failure to use the members for the end for which they were made by God, the Creator, brings each individual member into danger. If the hand and the foot, for example, would not follow the guidance of the eye, the former would bring inevitable and fatal ruin upon the whole body and the latter would stumble or even fall from a height.[1675]

Theodore the Studite taught his monks the same outlook:

[1672] St. Herman of Alaska Brotherhood, *Little Russian Philokalia, Volume V: Saint Theodore of Sanaxar,* 116.

[1673] Elder Paisios, *With Pain and Love for Contemporary Man,* 74.

[1674] 1 Cor. 12:27,26.

[1675] Βασιλείου τοῦ Μεγάλου, *Ἀσκητικὰ Α΄,* ΕΠΕ 8, 298–99; see also Wagner, *Saint Basil: Ascetical Works,* vol. 9, 286 (Question 24 in The *Long Rules*).

Since we are all members of one another, let us distribute the particular activities to each and utilize the gifts of each for each other.... If I am a hand, I am not honored less than my eye; nor if I am a foot am I bereft of the honor that my lips have. For in all parts I am one and the same, in both honor and dishonor.[1676]

St. Macarius explained how this concept should be internalized by the monks:

The brethren, therefore, regardless of what work they are doing, ought to conduct themselves toward each other in love and cheerfulness. And the one who works should say of him who is praying: "I also possess the treasure which my brother possesses since it is common." And let him who prays say of him who reads: "What he gains from reading redounds also to my advantage." And he who works let him thus say: "The work which I am doing is for the common good." For as the members of the body, being many, are one body (1 Cor. 12:12) and help each other while each still performs its own function—as the eye sees for the whole body and the hand labors for all the members and the foot walks, sustaining all the members, and another member suffers with all the others—so also the brethren should be among themselves. Thus he who prays should not judge the one working because he is not praying. Neither should he who works condemn the one praying because he is resting while he himself is at work. Neither should he who is serving condemn another. But let each one do whatever he is doing for the glory of God. He who reads should regard the one praying with love and joy with the thought: "For me he is praying." And let him who prays consider that what the one working is doing is done for the common good. And thus the highest concord and peace and oneness of souls "in the bond of peace" (Eph. 4:3) will bind them together so that they can live together in sincerity, simplicity, and the blessing of God. It is evident that the most important element among these is the perseverance in prayer. Above all, one thing is required: that one should have treasure in his soul and the life which is the Lord in his mind, so that, whether he works or prays or reads, he should have that possession which cannot be lost, which is the Holy Spirit.[1677]

In his monastic rule, St. Christodoulos of Patmos emphasized the importance of holding everything in common:

Among our good things, I will start with the one that most makes us what we are, the most comprehensive. What could this be other than our life together as a community, our spiritual unity and companionship? "What other way of life is brighter or more exalted or more full of grace for man?" to quote Basil the Great; absolutely none, if indeed this incomparable achievement is properly to be called human and not angelic. For certainly those true ascetics who observed cenobitic discipline rigorously, truly emulated the angels, presenting, in their virtues, their sharing of everything, their way of living, a perfect copy of the angelic condition. "Communion of life may be called perfect where private property is banished, whence conflict of wills is expelled, where everything is held in common, souls, wills, bodies and those things that nurture the body and procure its well-being; common the struggles, common the merchandise of hope, common the crowns, so that in several bodies a single soul is seen, and several

---

[1676] Θεοδώρου Στουδίτου, *Μεγάλη Κατήχησις,* 463–64 (ὁμιλία 81, 121).

[1677] Maloney, *Pseudo-Macarius: The Fifty Spiritual Homilies and the Great Letter,* 47–48.

bodies are revealed as the instruments of one soul."[1678] The life that is worthy to be praised according to the *Ascetic Rules* of Basil the Great is the one you and those who come after you will pursue living here.[1679]

The holy Fathers of the Church condemned the practice of monks having their own possessions because they perceived that this exhibits a lack of brotherly love. For example, St. Anthony the Great said: "Those who renounce the world but want to keep something for themselves are torn in this way [as dogs tearing after meat] by the demons who make war on them."[1680]

A striking ramification of this principle of owning nothing is that even the casual use of the word "my" was condemned. St. John Cassian taught: "Not even orally may anyone dare to call something his own, and that it is a great crime for a monk to say with his own mouth, 'my book,' 'my writing tablets,' 'my pen,' 'my tunic,' or 'my sandals.' If ever an expression of this sort slips out, through inadvertence or ignorance, he is to make appropriate reparation for it."[1681] Likewise, St. Basil the Great wrote: "The Scripture absolutely forbids the words 'mine' and 'thine' to be uttered among the brethren, saying: 'And the multitude of believers had but one heart and one soul; neither did anyone say that aught of the things which he possessed was his own' (Acts 4:32)."[1682] St. John Chrysostom, describing monasteries of his day, said: "There is not mine and thine, but this expression is exterminated, that is a cause of countless wars."[1683] St. Athanasios of Athos also made sure that among his monks "the chilling phrase that separates us from charity, 'this is mine, that is yours,' never became part of their lives."[1684]

Blessed Augustine gave the reason for having nothing of one's own in his monastic typikon: "No one will claim anything as his own—neither garment nor anything else—for we have chosen the apostolic way of life."[1685] Monasticism is apostolic in the sense that monastics live together, holding all things in common, just as in the days of the apostles "all those who had believed were together and had all things in common."[1686]

Many other saints prohibited personal ownership. St. Athanasios of Meteora wrote: "By no means should anyone living among them [at the monastery] possess his own private

---

[1678] PG 31:1381C (Ἀσκητικαὶ Διατάξεις, κεφ. ιη΄).

[1679] Thomas and Hero, *Byzantine Monastic Foundation Documents*, 585–86.

[1680] Ward, *The Sayings of the Desert Fathers*, 5.

[1681] Ramsey, *John Cassian: The Institutes*, 84. St. Fructuosus of Braga also agreed with this and included it in his *Rule for the Monastery of Compludo* (vid. Barlow, *The Fathers of the Church*, vol. 63, 159).

[1682] Wagner, *Saint Basil: Ascetical Works*, vol. 9, 295 (Rule 32 in the *Long Rules*).

[1683] *St. Chrysostom: Homilies on the Gospel of St. Matthew*, 420 (Homily 72:3).

[1684] Richard P. H. Greenfield and Alice-Mary Talbot, *Holy Men of Mount Athos*, 215

[1685] As quoted in Γέροντος Αἰμιλιανοῦ, *Νηπτικὴ Ζωὴ καὶ Ἀσκητικοὶ Κανόνες*, 191.

[1686] Acts 2:44.

property. This is why it is called a community. For wherever this kind of equality does not exist, we must not speak of a community, but of an assembly of thieves and a dwelling for the sacrilegious."[1687] St. Benedict wrote: "The vice of personal ownership must by all means be cut out in the monastery by the very root."[1688] St. Columbanus wrote: "Whatsoever little or much thou possessest of anything, whether clothing, or food, or drink, let it be at the command of the senior and at his disposal, for it is not befitting a religious [i.e., a monastic] to have any distinction of property with his own free brother."[1689] St. Waldebert explained in his rule for nuns: "She must have nothing of her own in the monastery but rather have given up all in the Lord's name. What faithful soul to whom the world is crucified and she to the world would claim anything of her own from the things of this world? Indeed being dead to the world, why should she somehow begin to live in the world through any desire for temporal things or greed for wealth, who through contempt of the world has begun to live for God?"[1690]

The First-and-Second Council ratified these patristic views and decreed: "Monks ought not to have anything of their own. Everything of theirs ought to be assigned to the monastery."[1691] In the days of early Egyptian monasticism, when it was discovered that a monk had laid up one hundred coins from the proceeds of his labor, they buried the money with him, repeating over his grave: "Thy money perish with thee"[1692] (just as Peter said to Simon the Sorcerer in Acts 8:20).

Since a monk no longer owns whatever things he brought to the monastery, he has no right to reclaim them if he decides to leave. This is what St. Nicodemos of the Holy Mountain wrote in his interpretation of Canon XIX of the Seventh Ecumenical Council: "As for those things (whether they are chattels, that is to say, or real estate of any kind) which a person may possess either as dowry from his parents or as belongings of his own and which he may consecrate to the monastery in which he has decided to take up his abode as a monk, the present Canon decrees that these things are to remain inalienable from the monastery in accordance with the promise or vow of the one who consecrated them, no matter whether he stays in the monastery or departs from it for reasons of his own and of his own free will. But if he should depart from the monastery in consequence of any occasion (such as we

---

[1687] Thomas and Hero, *Byzantine Monastic Foundation Documents,* 1460.

[1688] *Rule of St. Benedict,* Chapter XXXIII.

[1689] A. W. Haddan and W. Stubbs, *Councils and Ecclesiastical Documents Relating to Great Britain and Ireland II, i* (Oxford: Oxford University Press, 1873), 119.

[1690] J. A. McNamara and J. Halborg, *The Rule of a Certain Father to the Virgins,* chapter 17.

[1691] Agapius and Nicodemus, *The Rudder,* 461 (Canon VI).

[1692] Lydia Maria Francis Child, *The Progress of Religious Ideas: Through Successive Ages,* vol. 3 (New York: James Miller, 1855), 235–36.

shall mention in the Interpretation of the following c. XXI of this same 7th) due to the abbot, he can take them back."[1693]

Thus, in a traditional cenobitic monastery, all possessions, money, food, tools, etc., are held in common and belong only to the monastery. As St. Theodore the Studite wrote: "You shall always be vigilant that all things in the community be held in common and be indivisible and that nothing be owned on the part of any individual, not even a needle."[1694] Therefore, it is strictly forbidden for one of the monks (or even the abbot) to have his own things that other monks cannot have. For according to "The Third Rule of the Fathers": "Let it not be allowed for any abbot to claim anything as his own, although through God's favor all things remain in his power."[1695]

Yet this does not necessarily mean that all monks have the blessing to use something merely because another monk does. For example, a monk might not have permission to use a computer if the abbot judges that it would not be advantageous for him or the monastery. Likewise, a complicated piece of equipment that is fragile or dangerous or requires training to use properly (such as a chainsaw) might "belong" to the only monk who knows how to use it. And for the sake of practicality, there will be several personal items that the monks claim as their own (such as clothes, living quarters, etc.). The monks will need to be careful, however, that they are not using this claim of practicality merely as a false pretext to cover their possessiveness or attachment to something.

Paradoxically, monks are encouraged to attempt to give special treatment to their elder as an expression of their love and respect for him, but an abbot is not allowed to have things that the rest of the monks do not have. Thus, in a spiritually healthy monastery, the monks should continually be trying to give special treatment to their abbot, while he should constantly be refusing it!

Elder Aimilianos taught that the principle of having no possessions of one's own in a cenobium applies even to one's mindset. He said: "When you join the monastery and have brought something from the world, you will hand it over to the abbot. If you hold on to the smallest thing—whether it has to do with your body, your soul, or your mindset—this will separate you from the brotherhood and will not allow you to cleave spiritually to it; you will be a stranger to the brotherhood."[1696]

Even though all in a cenobium have a common goal and struggle, and the holy Fathers unanimously condemn idiorrhythmic behavior, this does not mean that the abbot should treat all monks in the same manner with a "one-size-fits-all" approach that disregards the

---

[1693] Agapius and Nicodemus, *The Rudder,* 448.

[1694] Thomas and Hero, *Byzantine Monastic Foundation Documents,* 78.

[1695] Franklin, *Early Monastic Rules,* 53.

[1696] Γέροντος Αἰμιλιανοῦ, *Νηπτικὴ Ζωὴ καὶ Ἀσκητικοὶ Κανόνες,* 234.

individuality, personhood, and uniqueness of each monk. Elder Aimilianos wrote in the *Regulations of the Holy Cenobium of the Annunciation*:

> For all members of the cenobium, God shall be common; common, too, the enterprise of salvation; all things shall be common. However, without infringement of the cenobitic tradition, consideration shall be taken in regard to all things, of the circumstances, things conducive to unity, the needs of each nun, her age, place of birth, number of years in the monastic life, health, physical constitution, education, powers of comprehension and former and present spiritual condition. The Abbess shall arrange the programme of each nun with justice and in all wisdom, in a spirit of understanding and freedom, in order to encourage the development of a personal spiritual life, for the renewal of the inner self. Special care and attention shall be shown to nuns who are advanced in age or are sick. The Abbess shall order all things: nourishment, sleep, blankets, dress and the degree of abstemiousness and asceticism "measuring what is needful to each."[1697] This freedom, however, should not disturb the smooth operation of the cenobium, nor the essential equality between all the sisters.[1698]

9) Food

Just as monks in a cenobitic monastery cannot have their own possessions, likewise they cannot have their own foods that others do not have. As stated in *The Rule of Paul and Stephen*: "No brother should be allowed to be so bold as to bring to table for himself anything to eat that has been specially prepared for him—whether fruit or any kind of vegetable or spice or anything else, lest some small occasion of injustice give rise to rancor among the brothers or open the dreadful door leading to one's own peculiar concerns."[1699]

Several of the holy Fathers forbid the abbot of a monastery from having his own special foods. For example, St. Symeon the New Theologian wrote to an abbot: "Do not prepare expensive meals for yourself, and leave your [spiritual] children neglected with poor, fasting, and despicable foods. Rather, let the meal be common for both you and your children, unless there is someone ill."[1700] The same equality applies to the cooks as well. St. Pachomios ordered that the cooks "shall eat nothing but what has been prepared for the brothers in common, nor shall they dare to prepare special foods for themselves."[1701]

Nevertheless, this does not necessarily mean that all monks will follow the same diet; a monk whose body reacts adversely to certain foods served to the brotherhood should have something else to eat. Moreover, when a monk is ill he should be allowed to eat special

---

[1697] Dmitrievskij, "Τυπικὸν Ἀρχιστρατήγου Μιχαήλ," *Opisanie*, vol. 1, 777.

[1698] Elder Aimilianos, *The Authentic Seal*, 174–75.

[1699] Barry Hagan, "The Rule of Paul and Stephen," ch. 28.

[1700] Συμεὼν Ν. Θεολόγου, *Κατηχητικὸς Λόγος ΙΗ΄*, Sources Chrétiennes 104, 304; ΕΠΕ Φ 19Δ, 198; C. J. de Catanzaro, *Symeon the New Theologian*, 222.

[1701] Veilleux, *Pachomian Koinonia*, vol. 2, 151.

foods that will strengthen him, as well as non-fasting foods on fasting days. As St. Anthony the Great taught: "Do not break the fast on Wednesdays and Fridays except because of a serious illness."[1702] Elder Aimilianos, however, commenting on this rule reminded his monks: "There are moving incidents of monastics and laymen who, whether at their homes or in the hospital, did not break the fast even though they were gravely ill. They kept the fast, not whining or complaining, but maintaining their joy, their peace. For although they were sick, God was *present* with them on their bed and on their headrest."[1703]

This approach of making accommodations for the ill was applied consistently throughout the history of monasticism. For example, St. Basil the Great wrote:

> As regards nourishment to be given the sick for their relief or to one who is exceptionally weary from strenuous work or who is preparing to undertake a laborious task, such as a journey or some other work, superiors will prescribe according to the need, in conformity with the words: "Distribution was made to each according as every one had need" (Acts 2:45).[1704]

St. Athanasios of Meteora wrote: "As far as food, drink, and clothing are concerned, what the last of the monks has let the first have, making allowance for illness."[1705] Similarly, St. Paisius Velichkovsky said: "The type of food prepared must be the same for all the brethren. Only the sick, according to the Fathers, may have special foods that are good for them and, even then, according to the discretion of the superior."[1706]

An ancient monastic tradition is to abstain from eating meat for the sake of self-mortification. Origen attested to this in the 3rd century by comparing the abstinence of meat by Christian monks with that of the Pythagoreans and explaining that their motivation is completely different: "We abstain from meat because we want to 'put to death whatever belongs to our earthly nature: sexual immorality, impurity, lust, evil desires' (cf. Col. 3:5), whereas the Pythagoreans do it 'for the sake of the myth of reincarnation.'"[1707] St. Anthony the Great advised in his monastic canons: "Do not eat meat at all."[1708] The following accounts in the *Sayings of the Desert Fathers* show that the most pious monks of 4th-century Egypt abstained from meat:

[1702] PG 40:1067D (Rule #21), as cited in Γέροντος Αἰμιλιανοῦ, *Νηπτικὴ Ζωὴ καὶ Ἀσκητικοὶ Κανόνες*, 517.

[1703] Γέροντος Αἰμιλιανοῦ, *Νηπτικὴ Ζωὴ καὶ Ἀσκητικοὶ Κανόνες*, 55.

[1704] Wagner, *Saint Basil: Ascetical Works,* vol. 9, 275 (Question 19 in the *Long Rules*).

[1705] Thomas and Hero, *Byzantine Monastic Foundation Documents,* 1460.

[1706] Chetverikov, *Starets Paisii Velichkovskii,* 135.

[1707] Ὀριγένης, *Κατὰ Κέλσου,* Ε΄ 49, ΒΕΠ 10, 47.

[1708] PG 40:1067D, Rule #20, as cited in Γέροντος Αἰμιλιανοῦ, *Νηπτικὴ Ζωὴ καὶ Ἀσκητικοὶ Κανόνες*, 516.

... While they were eating, a fowl was brought to them; the bishop took it and gave it to Hilarion, but the elder said to him: "Forgive me, but I have not eaten flesh since I took the habit."[1709]

... As they [the monks] were eating with him [the bishop in Alexandria], veal was set on the table and they began eating indiscriminately. Taking a slice, the bishop gave it to the elder nearest to him saying: "Here, this is a good slice; eat, abba." They however replied: "We [thought we] were eating vegetables until now; if it is flesh, we are not biting on it," and not one of them went on tasting it.[1710]

Some of the fathers happened to visit the villa of a person who loved Christ, and Abba Poemen was of their number. While they were eating, some meat was put out and they all ate except for Abba Poemen. Aware of his discretion, the elders were amazed that he was not eating. When they got up they said to him: "You are Poemen and you acted like that?" In reply the elder said to them: "Forgive me, fathers; you ate and nobody was offended. But if I had eaten, since many brothers come to be with me, they would have been hurt, saying: 'Poemen ate meat and we do not eat it?'"—and they were amazed at this discretion.[1711]

[Isidore the Priest] said: "If you are practicing *askēsis* according to the rules, do not be conceited when you fast. For if you become arrogant on this account, it is better to eat meat; because it is better for a person to eat meat than to become puffed up and boastful."[1712]

Also in the 4th century, St. John Chrysostom mentioned that in monasteries meat is not eaten: "[In] monasteries, ... there is no impure savor of rich food, no blood shed,"[1713] and St. Basil the Great taught that monastics should not "be eager for flesh meat."[1714] St. Fructuosus of Braga in the 7th century explained in his *Rule for the Monastery of Compludo*: "No one is permitted to eat or even to taste meat, not that we consider the creature of God unworthy, but that abstinence from meat is deemed useful and proper to monks."[1715] In the 9th century, St. Theodore the Studite wrote: "God did not give two gospels: one for married people and another for monks. The Gospel is the same for everyone.... The only differences in lifestyle between the faithful married man and the monk are marital relations and eating meat. All the other commandments—love for God and one's neighbor, faith and trust in God, patience in afflictions, humility, almsgiving, prayer, forbearance, repentance, fasting, chastity—are commandments of God for all without exception, both laymen and

---

[1709] Wortley, *The Alphabetical Sayings of the Desert Fathers,* 96 (Epiphanius 4).

[1710] Ibid., 126 (Theophilus 3).

[1711] Ibid., 255 (Poemen 169).

[1712] Ibid., 157 (Isidore the Priest 4).

[1713] *St. Chrysostom: Homilies on Galatians, Ephesians, Philippians, Colossians, Thessalonians, Timothy, Titus, and Philemon,* 456 (Homily 14 on 1 Timothy).

[1714] *Basil: Letters and Select Works,* "On the Perfection of the Life of Solitaries," 128 (Letter 22).

[1715] Barlow, *The Fathers of the Church: Iberian Fathers,* vol. 63, 160.

monks, who desire their salvation."[1716] In the 11th century, Nikon of the Black Mountain wrote: "But when he [Kyr Peter of Antioch] most wickedly expounds, through his own passionate mentality, that in the monastic life it is permitted to eat meat, here he has been caught up in the fall of the Franks."[1717] Likewise, in the 12th century Blessed Theophylact wrote many criticisms of the Roman Catholics, including the practice of their monks who drank meat broth.[1718]

In the 18th century, Elder Basil of Poiana Mărului pointed out in his essay *On Monastic Abstinence from Meat:*

> There is a great multitude of divine fathers, both anchorites and those living in communities, who received food sent to them by God—but never meat.[1719]
>
> … Likewise, the all-hymned Virgin Theotokos herself, out of love for monastic abstinence from meat, in a personal visitation gave these three commandments to that blessed Dositheos: "Fast, do not eat meat, and pray frequently."[1720]

In his Interpretation of Canon LI of the Holy Apostles in *The Rudder*, St. Nicodemos of the Holy Mountain explained the reason why monks avoid meat:

> [Monks] ought to abstain from eating meat because of three good reasons. First, because the aim and end of the monastic profession is sobriety, virginity, and the restraint and suppression of the body. But the eating of meat, which is the richest of all foods in fat and grease, is in consequence unfavorable to sobriety and virginity, which is the same as saying that it is unfavorable to the aim and end of monastic life, owing to its tendency to tickle the flesh and to raise a war of wanton appetites and desires against the soul. Accordingly, if, as St. Basil contends, monks ought to restrict themselves to a diet that is not rich, but, on the contrary, of little nutritiousness; and if they ought neither to eat the more savory and flavory foods, since these conduce to the development of a love of pleasure, according to the same saint (see "Against Plato," the 71st of his discourses); how, then, can it be said that it is all right for them to eat meat, which is the richest of all foods, and the most nourishing, and most savory and flavory? Secondly, monks ought not to eat meat, because in doing so they are violating this most ancient custom among monks.… [St. Nicodemos cites examples of St. John Chrysostom, St. Theophano, Emperor John Glycys, St. Greogry Palamas, Emperor Nicephorus III Botaniates, St. Nicephorus the Confessor, St. Theophylact of Bulgaria, St. Meletios the Confessor, and St. Dositheos.] Thirdly, and lastly, monks ought not to eat meat … even more so because of the common scandal which it causes to the hearts of the multitude. "The monks eat meat." This is a proposition which even when merely heard becomes a stumbling block to many men.[1721]

[1716] *Κατηχήσεις Ἁγίου Θεοδώρου τοῦ Στουδίτου,* as cited in: https://psigmataorthodoxias1.wordpress.com/2010/09/22/

[1717] As cited in *Elder Basil of Poiana Marului: Spiritual Father of St. Paisy Velichkovsky,* trans. a Monk of the Brotherhood of Prophet Elias Skete, Mount Athos (Liberty: St. John of Kronstadt Press, 1996), 153.

[1718] As cited in http://dipnosofistis.blogspot.com/2010/07/blog-post_03.html

[1719] *Elder Basil of Poiana Marului,* 140.

[1720] Ibid., 144.

[1721] Agapius and Nicodemus, *The Rudder,* 92–93.

Elder Aimilianos taught: "The ancient [monastic] custom of not eating meat does not mean that it is a sin, but this custom exists because meat (cooked in various ways) becomes enticingly delicious. Furthermore, it is a food that greatly fortifies, whereas a monk should live in abstention. That is to say, he should weaken his body instead of feeding it. First of all, meat fattens the body, and second, it weakens the personality of man because he learns to take pleasure. A man who takes pleasure—whether in sleep or in any other enticing activity—is unsuitable for spiritual struggles."[1722] It was this ascetical mindset that led St. John of Sinai to recommend: "Let us deny ourselves fattening foods first, then foods that warm us, and then what makes our food pleasant."[1723]

Gravely ill monastics, however, may eat meat according to the Interpretation of Canon LI of the Holy Apostles in *The Rudder.* Likewise, St. Benedict wrote: "Let the use of meat be granted to the sick and to the very weak for their recovery. But when they have been restored let them all abstain from meat in the usual manner."[1724] Similarly, St. Pachomios allowed the sick and old monks to eat pigs' feet (but not their meat). For St. Palladios wrote that the monasteries of St. Pachomios "even raise swine. When I criticized this practice, they told me, 'It is a custom we have received in the tradition, to raise them with the win-nowings and the vegetable left-overs and all that is left over and thrown out, that it not be wasted. The swine are to be killed and the meat sold, but their feet must be given to the sick and the old, because the country is small and heavily populated.' For the Blemmyes people live near them."[1725]

St. Caesarius wrote in his rule for nuns: "Fowls are to be brought forth only for the sick; they are never to be served in community. No flesh meat is ever to be taken at all for nourishment; if, by chance, someone should be gravely ill, she may take it by the order and permission of the abbess."[1726] According to the eighth-century Irish *Rule of Tallaght,* St. Máel Ruain "did not permit venison, liver, or fat in the refectory, even at Easter, for a period of over twenty years, though eventually he did allow these because of the famine by which the land was stricken."[1727] Elder Cleopa Ilie also believed that there are exceptions to the rule prohibiting monks from eating meat, for he said: "According to the order of monastic life and the holy canons, monks are not allowed to eat meat, unless they are being

---

[1722] Γέροντος Αἰμιλιανοῦ, *Νηπτικὴ Ζωὴ καὶ Ἀσκητικοὶ Κανόνες,* 54.

[1723] Ἰωάννου τοῦ Σιναΐτου, *Κλῖμαξ* PG 88:865B; see also Holy Transfiguration Monastery, *The Ladder of Divine Ascent,* 99.

[1724] *Rule of St. Benedict,* Chapter XXXVI.

[1725] Veilleux, *Pachomian Koinonia,* vol. 2, 128.

[1726] McCarthy, *The Rule for Nuns of St. Caesarius of Arles,* 203–4.

[1727] Maidín, *The Celtic Monk,* 102.

given hospitality by laymen who are unaware that monks don't eat meat or they don't have any other food to give them to eat."[1728]

Due to the different physical needs of different people, monastics should be free to eat whatever is necessary, even if this entails eating at times different than usual (but always with the blessing of the abbot). For St. Basil the Great wrote: "It is also impossible to lay down a rule that the time for taking food as well as the manner of taking it and its quantity be the same for all. The objective, however—satisfying need—must be common to all alike."[1729] Similarly, St. John Cassian wrote that we should "use only the food that is needful for strengthening our infirmity, and not that which desire demands.... Fasting and continence consist in moderation.... Each must fast as much as necessary for the taming of fleshly warfare."[1730] As Abba Poemen put it: "We have not been taught to kill our bodies, but to kill our passions."[1731]

St. Nilus Sorsky suggested that monks use trial and error in order to determine the optimal amount of food to eat:

> In regard to the daily measure and quantity of food to be eaten, the Fathers have taught that each person should freely determine for himself in the following way: If a monk seems to feel an excessive fullness after a meal, let him decrease the amount during the next meal. But when he sees that the amount of food he had taken was inadequate to sustain his bodily energy, let him then increase the amount a bit more. And in this way after he has learned what is necessary through experience, he should settle upon such a quantity of food that can support his bodily strength. Thus he will not be a slave to the pleasure of the palate, but be guided by what is truly necessary.... In general a novice can be guided by the best rule, namely to stop eating food when he feels still a bit hungry. But if he feels full, he does not sin in this. But having allowed himself to eat to satiety, let him reproach himself. In this manner he will transform the attack of his enemy and put himself on the path to victory over the enemy.[1732]

As an extension of the principles of cenobitic life, not only should possessions and food be held in common but also tasks. As St. Caesarius of Arles wrote to his nuns: "All works shall be done in common."[1733]

[1728] Γέροντος Κλεόπα Ἠλίε, *Πνευματικοὶ Διάλογοι (Ἐρωταπαντήσεις)* (Θεσσαλονίκη: Ὀρθόδοξος Κυψέλη, 1990), 149 (ἀπόκρισις 211).

[1729] *Saint Basil the Great: Ascetical Works,* vol. 9, 275 (Question 19 in the *Long Rules*).

[1730] Ramsey, *John Cassian: The Institutes* V, 7, 8, 9.

[1731] Ward, *The Sayings of the Desert Fathers,* 193.

[1732] Maloney, *Nil Sorsky: The Complete Writings,* 72.

[1733] McCarthy, *The Rule for Nuns of St. Caesarius of Arles,* 189.

10) Money

Almsgiving is a natural expression of love for neighbor encouraged in the New Testament. Christ taught: "Give to him that asketh thee,"[1734] St. John the Baptist said: "He that hath two coats, let him impart to him that hath none, and he that hath food, let him do likewise,"[1735] and St. Paul wrote: "They asked only one thing, that we remember the poor, which was actually what I was eager to do."[1736]

Therefore, a monastery should always make a point of giving to the needy, following the example of the great monastic saints. For example, St. Basil the Great wanted one of the monks in a monastery to be "entrusted with the task of distribution [of alms]."[1737] St. Theodore the Studite wrote: "You shall not store up gold in your monastery, but you should share your abundance of whatever sort with those in need at the portal of your court as the holy fathers did."[1738] Elder Ephraim wrote about St. Joseph the Hesychast: "Geronda's boundless love towards others was evident in his two-fold almsgiving: material and spiritual. Materially, he took care to give whatever he could to other people, in terms of food, clothing, and shelter. Spiritually, he cared for their salvation primarily with his continuous prayers and his many letters. Geronda never hesitated to give away so much that nothing would remain for himself and his brotherhood."[1739] St. Joseph showed the importance of giving alms specifically to poor nuns in his teachings[1740] as well as in his deeds.[1741]

Nevertheless, St. Basil advised: "Experience is needed in order to distinguish between cases of genuine need and of mere greedy begging."[1742] St. Christodoulos of Patmos wrote in his rule that the monastery should give alms even when it itself lacks sufficient resources:

> I had wished to lay down here express rules for charity loved-of-God, and feeding the poor or hospitality, through which, to quote Scripture, "They entertained angels unawares,"[1743] besides care for men shipwrecked or otherwise in straits, finding themselves, whether intentionally or through some accident, on this island and begging for help. For I am exceedingly concerned about all such, the truth is, in anguish. I am burned up. So far, however, the monastery has not enjoyed sufficient resources, and I

[1734] Mt. 5:42.

[1735] Lk. 3:11.

[1736] Gal. 2:10.

[1737] Clarke, *The Ascetic Works of St. Basil,* 268 (Rule 100 in the *Shorter Rules*).

[1738] Thomas and Hero, *Byzantine Monastic Foundation Documents,* 79.

[1739] Γέροντος Ἐφραίμ, *Ὁ Γέροντάς μου Ἰωσήφ,* 325–26; see also Elder Ephraim, *My Elder Joseph the Hesychast,* 467).

[1740] Vid. Elder Joseph, *Monastic Wisdom,* 303.

[1741] Vid. Elder Ephraim, *My Elder Joseph the Hesychast,* 34.

[1742] *Basil: Letters and Select Works,* 208 (Letter 150).

[1743] Heb. 13:2.

did not think that I should lay down a rule on the quantities to be given. Nevertheless I exhort and enjoin in a brotherly fashion in Christ all those my spiritual fathers and brothers who will successively govern our monastery to give all possible thoughts to what I am saying, to provide for the poor and always attach great importance to caring for them, never neglecting the needy, but giving to them in proportion to the means of the monastery.[1744]

The *Rule of St. Comghall* orders: "You may not buy, sell, or conceal the mercy of God. Whatever you acquire over and above your needs is to be given to the poor."[1745] St. Athanasios of Meteora wrote in his monastic rule: "If there should be a surplus of grain, wine, or oil, they [the monks] should not go around selling it"[1746] but should hand it out free of charge. Likewise, St. Lazaros of Mt. Galesion decreed that "once a year, at the end of the month of August, the superior is to carry out a check, and if he finds any surplus from the produce of the estates, it shall be collected and carried to Bessai [the local peasants], but if he finds no surplus he shall not harry [the steward] nor demand anything of him so that this should not be the cause of his reducing those settled here to hardship."[1747]

For items produced and sold by the monastery St. Benedict suggested: "As regards the prices of these things, let not the vice of avarice creep in, but let it always be given a little cheaper than it can be given by seculars, 'that God may be glorified in all things' (1 Pet. 4:11)."[1748] Likewise, *The Rule of the Master* explains: "Let inquiry be made about the price for which seculars could sell it, then let it always be sold at a lower evaluation and for sufficiently less money to make it evident that in this regard spiritual men are distinguished from seculars by the difference in what they do, since they are not, out of commercialism which is the enemy of the soul, seeking profit beyond what is just but are even benevolently agreeing to accept a price lower than what is just."[1749]

St. Paisios of the Holy Mountain also warned against this spirit of commercialism: "Do you know how a monastery living a thoroughly spiritual life can positively affect people in the world? When there is devotion, fear of God, and neither worldly rationalism nor a commercial spirit, this is what moves and inspires lay people. But unfortunately the commercial spirit is gradually entering into the very marrow of monasticism."[1750]

St. Basil the Great taught that a wealthy monastery should give alms also to poorer monasteries:

[1744] Thomas and Hero, *Byzantine Monastic Foundation Documents,* 592 (Rule #25).

[1745] Maidín, *The Celtic Monk,* 34.

[1746] Thomas and Hero, *Byzantine Monastic Foundation Documents,* 1460.

[1747] Ibid., 164.

[1748] *Rule of St. Benedict,* Chapter LVII.

[1749] Eberle, *The Rule of the Master,* 250.

[1750] Elder Paisios, *Spiritual Awakening,* 367–68.

[Question:] "If there are brotherhoods near one another and one is poor while the other makes difficulties about sharing with its neighbour, how ought the poor one to feel towards the one that will not impart its goods?"

[Answer:] "How can they who have been taught in the love of Christ to lay down even life itself for one another be stingy as regards the things of the body? They seem to forget His words: 'I was an hungred and ye gave Me no meat, etc.' (Mt. 25:42). But if this should happen, the poor brethren ought to be long-suffering, fully convinced that they will receive consolation in the world to come, following the example of Lazarus (vid. Lk. 16:19–22)."[1751]

Most important, however, is not the amount of the alms we give but the disposition with which we give them. As St. Paul said, "God loveth a cheerful giver,"[1752] and as Kahlil Gibran said poetically: "There are those who have little and give it all. These are the believers in life and the bounty of life, and their coffer is never empty. There are those who give with joy, and that joy is their reward.... You give but little when you give of your possessions. It is when you give of yourself that you truly give."[1753] In the same vein, Elder Ephraim also taught that the greatest form of almsgiving is not by giving money or possessions but by giving consoling words and offering prayer for one's neighbor. Similarly, Elder Paisius of Sihla said: "The highest almsgiving of monks is to be always poor in all material things and to pray for everyone."[1754]

St. Isaac the Syrian taught: "If you have something above your daily needs, give it to the poor, and then go with boldness to offer your prayers, that is, to converse with God as a son with his Father. Nothing can bring the heart so near to God as almsgiving."[1755] But St. Isaac also added that monastics living in stillness do not need to abandon it for the sake of almsgiving:

> If because of our way of life we are far from the habitation and intercourse of men and from the sight of them, there is no need for us to leave our cell, our solitary and secluded dwelling, and to give ourselves over to roaming throughout the world to visit the sick and busy ourselves with ministrations of such matters. For it is obvious that such a thing brings a man from a higher state to a lower one. Howbeit if a man lives in the society of men and his dwelling is near to them and he is comforted by the labors of other men, whether at a time of sickness or of health, then he must render the same service.... And if he should see ... [someone] in straitness, yea rather Christ Himself outcast and worn with weariness, and he should flee and hide himself from him, falsely imagining that he is practising stillness, then he, and those like him, are without mercy.[1756]

[1751] Clarke, *The Ascetic Works of St. Basil,* 297 (Rule 181 in the *Shorter Rules*).

[1752] 2 Cor. 9:7.

[1753] Kahlil Gibran, *The Prophet* (London: Alfred A. Knopf, 1926), 29.

[1754] Bălan, *A Little Corner of Paradise,* 203.

[1755] Holy Transfiguration Monastery, *The Ascetical Homilies of Saint Isaac the Syrian,* 150 (Homily 4).

[1756] Ibid., 529 (Homily 76).

Canon IV of the Fourth Ecumenical Council states: "The Bishop of the city is required to make proper provision for monasteries." St. Nicodemos of the Holy Mountain explains what this "provision" entails:

> Just as monks ought to confine their activities to the works that belong to monks, so ought also bishops to have diligence and foresight in providing for their monasteries, by protecting the monks and bestowing alms in exigencies either out of their own pocket or out of the poor money of the church, in accordance with Apostolic Canon XLI and Canon XXV of Antioch, for two reasons: 1) in order that the monks may remain quiet and free from temptation; and 2) in order that he may himself derive therefrom something in the way of benefit to his soul.

11) Martha versus Mary

In the conflict between Martha and Mary in the Gospel of St. Luke,[1757] the holy Fathers interpreted the "one thing needful" as clinging to God. According to Abba Moses and St. John Cassian:

> To cling always to God and to things of God—this must be our major effort, this must be the road that the heart follows unswervingly. Any diversion, however impressive, must be regarded as secondary, low-grade, and certainly dangerous. Martha and Mary provide a most beautiful scriptural paradigm of this outlook and of this mode of activity.[1758]

This is why St. Eustathios of Thessalonica warned: "It is reprehensible for a monastery to become only a 'Martha.'"[1759] Elder Gabriel of Dionysiou wrote: "From the beginning, Eastern Orthodox monasticism has sat by the feet of Jesus, like Mary, whom the Lord called blessed, and in silence and humility has listened to His words. By contrast, Western Monasticism follows the work of Martha, 'troubling itself about many things' in the midst of the world and of noisy society."[1760] Likewise, Elder Paisius of Sihla said:

> Today there is a great argument between the two sisters of Lazarus, Martha and Mary, as to who chose the good part. In the monasteries everywhere, Martha suppresses Mary and does not let her pray much, and Mary weeps inconsolably. If we put the church services and the praise of God first—that is, Mary—and then obedience and handiwork second—that is, Martha—then all of our monasteries and churches would flourish, and the devil would be cast out from among men.[1761]

St. Paisios of the Holy Mountain elaborated on this principle and said:

[1757] Vid. Lk. 10:38–42.

[1758] Luibhéid, *John Cassian: Conferences,* 42–43.

[1759] PG 135:854C.

[1760] Constantine Cavarnos, *Modern Orthodox Saints: Blessed Elder Gabriel Dionysiatis* (Boston: Institute for Byzantine and Modern Greek Studies, 1999), 129.

[1761] Bălan, *A Little Corner of Paradise,* 203.

When we reduce the number of our chores, there will come, naturally, a bodily rest and a thirst for inner spiritual work, which comforts and never tires us....

When physical fatigue lacks a spiritual sense, or rather, when it is not the result of a spiritual need and therefore justified, it rouses anger in man and makes him rough....

There are some things that can always be left out, so that spiritual matters may take precedence. Too much work and too many worries will make a monk secular and give him a secular sensibility. His life will then be full of stress and secular anxiety, and he will experience in this life a portion of hell, endless cares, worries, and disasters. But when the monk has no concern for material things and is instead mindful only of his salvation and the salvation of all human beings, then he has God as his Steward and men as his helpers.[1762]

People today do not live simply and for this reason they suffer from too many distractions. They open too many fronts of activity and lose themselves with many cares. As for me, I just try to take care of one or two things, and then I start thinking about something else. I never try to do too many things at the same time.... for if I do not finish what I have started, I cannot find peace.[1763]

The monks in sixth-century Nisibis apparently worked excessively and left no time for prayer and reading, because Abraham of Kaškar began his monastic rules with the following observation and admonition:

Since the time when we settled down in this place, we brothers who dwell here have labored and wearied ourselves to excavate the caves and to build the cells for ourselves in order to dwell in them and wherefore we have approached this manner of life only recently, we have neglected to lay on ourselves anything that is commensurate with this manner of life. But now since we have rested a little from the bodily toil and labor and since we have come to ourselves, we have consulted together to choose something for us from the divine books and from the sayings of the holy Fathers, something which is fitting for the healing of our abscesses and for the remedy of our sores....

Above all there is tranquillity according to the command of the fathers and according to the Apostle to the Thessalonians as he says: "We beseech from you, brothers, that you would superabound and be diligent to become quiet and assiduous in your affairs."[1764] And again he says: "But this we command to you and ask from you in our Lord Jesus the Messiah that in quietness they may work and eat their bread."[1765] And again says Isaiah: "The work of righteousness shall be peace, and the service of righteousness quietness."[1766] ... And from Marcus the Monk: "If the body be not quiet, the mind cannot be quiet."[1767] Quietness, however, is preserved by two means: through constant reading and prayer, or by the service of hands and through meditation. As Abba Isaiah says, and as also the Wise one says: "Idleness generates a multitude of evils." And again: "A man who does not do work is cast into desires all the time." So

---

[1762] Elder Paisios, *With Pain and Love for Contemporary Man,* 210–12.

[1763] Ibid., 203; see also Γέροντος Παϊσίου, *Μὲ Πόνο καὶ Ἀγάπη γιὰ τὸν Σύγχρονο Ἄνθρωπο,* 189.

[1764] 1 Thes. 4:10–11.

[1765] 2 Thes. 3:12.

[1766] Is. 32:17.

[1767] cf. Palmer, Sherrard, Ware, *The Philokalia,* vol. 1, 128 (#31).

then let us persevere in our cell in quietness, and let us flee from idleness that brings blame.[1768]

In order to avoid the trap of excessive labor, monastics must learn to be content with "temporary incompleteness." An example of such incompleteness is if something minor is not complete or in order when it is time for prayer or resting. Monastics need to have the discernment to recognize that it is minor and to have the sense of balance to leave it for tomorrow so that their monastic schedule and inner peace will not be disrupted. For such cases, the *Second Rule of the Fathers* states: "Nothing ought to come before prayers."[1769] St. John of Sinai warns monastics: "He who is busy with something and continues it when the hour of prayer comes is deceived by the demons. Those thieves aim at stealing from us one hour after another."[1770] Likewise, St. Sophrony of Essex said: "Don't let your work absorb you so much that you lose the prayer! If one of your jobs takes a very long time and it is not very important, leave it, if it keeps you from prayer. Don't get lost in details and lose communication with God."[1771]

If however, something *major* is not complete when it is time for prayer, the holy Fathers teach that we should not leave it undone, but instead we should miss the church service in order to finish it. For example, when St. Basil the Great was asked: "If he who is engaged in the cellar or kitchen or similar work fails to appear at the regular time of psalmody and prayer, does his soul escape harm?" he replied:

> Each man keeps his own rule by doing his own work, like a member in the body, and he suffers harm if he neglects the task assigned him.... If he cannot join the rest with his bodily presence, let him not be disturbed.... But we must beware lest anyone, able to fulfil his allotted task in good time and set an example to others, urge as an excuse that he is busy with work.[1772]

St. John of Sinai urged monks to discern when work is more important than prayer: "Let us keep wide awake with all vigilance, take care with all carefulness, watch with all watchfulness as to when and how service should be preferred to prayer; for this is certainly not always the case."[1773] Likewise, St. Mark the Ascetic taught that monks must discern when work is more necessary than prayer:

> [A monk] ought not to prefer every kind of ministry over prayer or be drawn to them when the need arises, except out of necessity. Nor, when confronted with some necessity and the need to do God's work, should he avoid and reject them under the

---

[1768] Vööbus, *Syriac and Arabic Documents,* 153–55.

[1769] Franklin, *Early Monastic Rules,* 37.

[1770] Holy Transfiguration Monastery, *The Ladder of Divine Ascent,* 217.

[1771] Daviti, *Memories of Elder Sophrony of Essex,* 132.

[1772] Clarke, *The Ascetic Works of St. Basil,* 283 (Rule 147 in the *Shorter Rules*).

[1773] Holy Transfiguration Monastery, *The Ladder of Divine Ascent,* 43.

pretext of prayer; he should, rather, understand the difference between them and devote himself of his own accord to doing God's work.... Prayer without ceasing ... is the service ordained for us [1 Thes. 5:17]. Because of this, we must prefer it over occupations that are not indispensable. This distinction all the apostles teach when they instruct the multitude who want to turn their attention to service. They said, "It is not right for us to neglect the word of God in order to serve tables.... We for our part will devote ourselves to prayer and to serving the word."[1774] ... What do we learn from these words? That it is good for those of us not yet able to devote ourselves to prayer to give ourselves to service, lest we fail in both; but for those who are able, it is better not to neglect what is superior.[1775]

St. Lazaros of Mt. Galesion taught what monks should do if they must miss the church services: "But if they have not a break [from work to attend church], they should ever have the *trisagion* on their tongue and in their mouth, and if the beginning of any psalm comes into their mind, let them hum it softly with their lips. If they cannot manage even this, at least let them not dispense with mental prayer."[1776]

A common pitfall is to treat minor matters as if they are major. This usually happens when we become passionately attached to doing a task—or just too excited about it—either because it is pleasant or because we have focused all our attention on the benefits of having it completed. As a result, we lose focus on the role it plays in the bigger picture, and then we become impatient and begin sacrificing more important things to complete it as soon as we can. It requires continual discernment—which St. Anthony the Great[1777] and St. John Cassian[1778] praised as the most excellent virtue—to remain on the "royal path,"[1779] without deviating either to the right through excessive zeal or to the left through slothfulness, as St. Basil taught: "He is upright in heart who does not have his mind inclined to excess nor to deficiency, but directs his endeavors toward the midpoint of virtue."[1780]

According to the holy Fathers, this virtue of discernment is not a matter of mental cleverness but the fruit of humility and obedience. As St. John of Sinai wrote: "Obedience is an abandonment of discernment in a wealth of discernment. ... From obedience comes

---

[1774] Acts 6:2–5.

[1775] Mark the Monk, *Counsels on the Spiritual Life,* trans. Tim Vivian (New York: St. Vladimir's Seminary Press, 2009), 228–29.

[1776] Thomas and Hero, *Byzantine Monastic Foundation Documents,* 160.

[1777] Vid. Luibhéid, *John Cassian, Conferences,* 61–62.

[1778] St. John Cassian said: "Discretion is a kind of acropolis and queen among the other virtues" (Chrysostomos, *The Evergetinos, Book III,* 234).

[1779] Num. 20:17.

[1780] *Saint Basil: Exegetic Homilies,* 176 (Commentary on Ps. 7:11; PG 29:244D).

humility, as we have said earlier. From humility comes discernment as the great Cassian has said with beautiful and sublime philosophy in his chapter on discernment."[1781]

There can also be a conflict between "Martha" and "Mary" on an institutional level of monasticism. In 15th-century Russia, two monastic saints had different approaches to the role of monasticism in society. On the one hand, St. Nilus Sorsky emphasized hesychasm, poverty, and patristic literature, while on the other hand St. Joseph Volokolamsk (also known as St. Iosif Volotsky) emphasized social work. In those days, the many donations that monasteries in Russia were receiving had made them quite wealthy, enabling the monks to live in opulence.[1782] St. Nilus lamented this situation and wrote: "Nowadays one does not see in the monasteries an observance of the laws of God according to the Holy Writings and the traditions of the Holy Fathers, but rather we act according to our own wills and human ways of thinking."[1783] Therefore, he went into the wilderness, where he was soon joined by many other monks who were inspired by his ideals. To govern them, he wrote a typikon which "reads more as a compendium of patristic quotations than a work of originality, with the reason being that his purpose was not to provide original conceptions, 'but rather to be faithful to the teachings of the Fathers.'[1784]"[1785]

The approach of St. Nilus was to live in such utter poverty and simplicity that they were unable to give alms. He wrote:

> It is not proper for us to possess any superfluities. In regard to giving alms to those who beg of us and lending, do not be disturbed, for, as Basil the Great says, this is not demanded of a monk, since he has nothing beyond his own needs and is not obliged to give such alms. And if one should say, "I have nothing," he is not lying, as St. Barsanuphius the Great says. "For a monk is exempt from giving alms. He can sincerely say: 'We have given up everything to follow you, the Lord.'" St. Isaac wrote: "Not to possess anything is higher than giving alms." The alms of a monk are to help a brother by a saving word given in time of need and to offer spiritual discernment, to comfort another in time of sorrow or any other need.[1786]

One historian noted that this approach

> greatly disturbed St. Joseph Volokolamsk, a monk who stressed that monastic possessions allowed for needed philanthropic work outside the monastery. Georges

---

[1781] Holy Transfiguration Monastery, *The Ladder of Divine Ascent,* 21, 47.

[1782] George A. Maloney, *Russian Hesychasm: The Spirituality of Nil Sorskij* (Netherlands: Mouton, 1973) 30.

[1783] Ibid., 254.

[1784] Ibid., 80.

[1785] Gregory K. Hillis, "To Be Transformed by a Vision of Uncreated Light: A Survey on the Influence of the Existential Spirituality of Hesychasm on Eastern Orthodox History" (http://library.byzantine-antiquities.org/axismundi05/2001/to_be_transformed_part2.html). This method of writing a monastic typikon was also employed by St. Philibert of Jumièges [in seventh-century Gaul], who "drew nectar from the flowers of earlier monastic writers, especially Basil, Macarius, Benedict, and Columbanus" (Dunn, *The Emergence of Monasticism,* 185).

[1786] Maloney, *Nil Sorsky: The Complete Writings,* 42–43.

Florovsky succinctly sums up the key disagreement between the Josephites and the Trans-Volga hermits (as Nilus's movement was called): "The former sought to conquer the world by means of social labor within it; the latter attempted to overcome the world through transfiguration and through the formation of a new man, by creating a human personality."[1787] Whereas the Trans-Volga hermits were very much entrenched in patristic heritage, the Josephites "hardly valued Byzantine tradition."[1788] However, the 1503 Synod of Moscow decided in favour of the Josephites; a decision which essentially created two very different monastic schools of thought. Josephite monasteries stressed formalism and ritualism over the inner life, and in the process broke any connection with the contemplative emphasis found in contemporary hesychasm.[1789] Thus, the weight of carrying Byzantine mystical tradition fell to the shoulders of the Trans-Volga hermits after Nilus's death in 1508. Interestingly, many intellectuals could be numbered among the Trans-Volga hermits, in contrast to the Josephites who exhibited a remarkable lack of intellectual life.[1790] …

It is also important to note that the Trans-Volga hermits produced the greatest proportion of canonised saints in Russia in the fifteenth and sixteenth centuries; a fact which demonstrates the depth of spirituality of these ascetics in comparison to the monks of the Josephite monasteries.[1791] In other words, despite the fact that the Josephite position on monastic possession became the official position of the Church, the Trans-Volga hermits acted as guardians of hesychastic mystical theology in Russia.[1792]

[1787] *A Source Book for Russian History from Early Times to 1917 - Vol. 1: Early Times to the Late Seventeenth Century,* George Vernadsky, ed. (New Haven: Yale University Press, 1972), 154.

[1788] *Ways of Russian Theology: Part One, Vol. V of The Collected Works of Georges Florovsky,* Richard S. Haugh, ed., Robert L. Nichols, trans. (Belmont: Nordland, 1979), 24. It is worth noting that some modern scholars challenge this traditional understanding of Sts. Nilus and Joseph. For example, David Goldfrank wrote: "The analysis since the 1950s of the genuine paper trail [i.e., the original historical sources] has led to a different historical picture…. Nil's and Iosif's different life styles, reflected in their respective monastic teachings and rules, did not lead in Nil's lifetime even to a literary debate, much less to a public politicized struggle between them over the propriety and fate of monastic estates and wealth or anything else" (*Nil Sorsky: The Authentic Writings,* David M. Goldfrank [Kalamazoo: Cistercian Publications, 2008], xii).

[1789] Ibid., 22.

[1790] Sergius Bolshakoff, *Russian Mystics* (Kalamazoo: Cistercian Publications, 1977), 45. It is interesting to note that in 12th-century Byzantium, a similar disdain of learning prevailed among the monks who were living in wealthy monasteries, which was described by St. Eustathios of Thessalonica as follows: "Furthermore, these kinds of monks despise learning…. They chase far away those who are divinely educated who are (to put it biblically) 'scribes trained for the kingdom of heaven, who bring out things new and old' (cf. Mt. 13:52)…. Only when both spiritual and earthly matters are philosophically understood with divine wisdom can these monks be united with God by striving towards Him correctly and wholeheartedly. But instead they prefer to be illiterate and utter ignoramuses" (PG 135:832D, 833B).

[1791] Maloney, *Russian Hesychasm,* 159.

[1792] Gregory K. Hillis, "To Be Transformed by a Vision of Uncreated Light."

The canonization of both St. Nilus and St. Joseph indicates that both of their approaches are God-pleasing. Yet it is clear that St. Nilus—like Mary in the Gospel—"chose the good part."[1793]

12) Typikon

Orthodox monasteries follow a schedule, known as its "typikon." The Athonite typikon calls for a full cycle of daily prayers: Midnight Office, Orthros, the First, Third, Sixth, and Ninth Hours, Vespers, and Compline, as well as celebrating the Divine Liturgy daily in its monasteries and daily or frequently in its sketes. In sketes on the Holy Mountain, some of the services are replaced by saying them privately on the prayer-rope. In the 18th century, St. Nicodemos of the Holy Mountain wrote how monks who are illiterate (or not attending the services) may replace the services: "In the case of Matins they must pass thirty prayer-ropes standing up and saying at every knot, 'Lord Jesus Christ, Son of God, have mercy on me.' In the case of Hours, ten prayer-ropes; in the case of Vespers, ten prayer-ropes; and in the case of the Compline, ten prayer-ropes, as prescribed by the rules in the Holy Mountain."[1794] Comparing these numbers with contemporary Athonite rules, it seems that St. Nicodemos must have been referring to prayer-ropes having 100 knots.

St. Sophrony of Essex once advised a hieromonk living alone to fulfill his prayer rule by saying the Jesus prayer not a specific *number* of times but for a specific *duration* of time. He wrote:

> I would dare in your case (though not in general) to replace the reading of Canons, Troparia, and Stichera, by prayer of a specific duration with the prayer-rope ... (as the soul desires: with a prayer book, or with the prayer-rope using your own words). Instead of Vespers 45 minutes, for Compline 45 minutes, for Matins two hours; in total, 3½ hours. Partly with books (Psalter, Horologion, Canons), partly with prayer-ropes, partly in your own way. In the latter case, you need to watch that this freedom not become an occasion for your mind to wander all over the world, and ensure that freedom simply gives the soul greater liberty to pray with more concentration, from the heart....
>
> You will spend time at prayer, either using the same books, reading more slowly and more attentively—without the fear of prolonging the Rule by several hours, and stopping when the time fixed has gone by, wherever you have come to in your reading—or else with prayer-ropes, still without haste, applying yourself to the prayer without paying attention to the number of prayer-ropes. Or, when the soul has a desire for prayer, let it pray calmly, without fearing that the prayer will not count towards the Rule, which would mean that in the end you have nonetheless to read the Canons, and this would become onerous. In a word, the soul must be free in relationship to the books, but free to pray, and not to let the mind daydream. If the mind is too lazy to

---

[1793] Lk. 10:42.

[1794] Agapius and Nicodemus, *The Rudder,* 458.

pray attentively, it is obligatory to make use of the books and the liturgical rule of the Church.[1795]

St. John of Sinai taught that private prayer procures greater benefit than chanting, unless despondency is an issue:

> He who is not alone but is with others cannot derive so much profit from psalmody as from prayer; for the confusion of voices renders the psalms indistinct.... Psalmody in a crowded congregation is accompanied by captivity and wandering of the thoughts; but in solitude, this does not happen. However, those in solitude are liable to be assailed by despondency, whereas in congregation the brethren help each other by their zeal.[1796]

Likewise, Elder Ephraim said that a monk who prays noetically will naturally declare:

> "Who needs chanting, or anything else for that matter?" Since the Desert Fathers possessed noetic prayer, they did not need such things. Of course, those prayers and services are sanctioned by the Church. But people who have found this method of noetic prayer, which is much higher than the conventional prayers, abandoned the conventionalities and laid hold of the essence.[1797]

St. Sophrony of Essex also viewed noetic prayer as the most lofty spiritual work: "Noetic practice is the kernel of true monastic life.... There is no higher or more perfect spiritual practice, and consequently neither is there a more difficult struggle."[1798] Since private prayer and noetic prayer are much more fruitful than conventional prayers, some monasteries allot more time for noetic prayer in one's cell and less time for the services.

Despite the superiority of noetic prayer, St. Isaac the Syrian explained why reading conventional prayers ("the Office") is still necessary:

> The heart acquires greater freedom of speech (with God) during [noetic] prayer than it does during the Office. But complete neglect of the Office causes pride, and it is out of pride that one falls away from God. You see, the very fact that someone forces himself to be subjected to a rule—when he is quite free in his way of life—keeps the soul humble.... This is why the holy Fathers—even though they possessed continual prayer, being filled with the Spirit and never ceasing for a moment from prayer—used to observe, not only in the matter of the Office, but also in that of prayer as well, all that was ordained in the matter of times set apart, and the specifically fixed numbers (of prayers), involving the visible participation of the body, and performed with kneelings.[1799]

[1795] Sakharov, *Striving for Knowledge of God*, 172–74.

[1796] Holy Transfiguration Monastery, *The Ladder of Divine Ascent*, 45, 217.

[1797] Γέροντος Ἐφραίμ, *Πατρικαὶ Νουθεσίαι*, 429; see also Elder Ephraim, *Counsels from the Holy Mountain*, 345.

[1798] Sakharov, *Striving for Knowledge of God*, 122.

[1799] Isaac of Nineveh (Isaac the Syrian), *"The Second Part," Chapters IV–XLI*, Corpus Scriptorum Christianorum Orientalium, trans. Sebastian Brock (Lovanii: Universitatis Catholicae Americae, 1995), 72.

St. Joseph the Hesychast attached great importance to staying on schedule. He said: "Without prayer, without watchfulness, without orderliness, without effort, without keeping to our schedule, we will be unable to acquire any of the treasures about which the Watchful Fathers speak."[1800] Likewise, Archimandrite George Kapsanis of Gregoriou Monastery taught: "Following the typika serves other spiritual goals as well. It expresses and cultivates in monks obedience to the traditions and institutions of the Church. In this manner it helps them to put themselves under the Church and in the Church instead of above the Church. It also ensures orderliness, concord, and unity of the brotherhood worshipping in the temple."[1801] This is a practical application of what St. Paul wrote, "Let all things be done decently and in order."[1802]

Nevertheless, it is important that to maintain a certain flexibility as regards the typikon, since rigidly insisting on orderliness gives rise to disorder by encouraging the letter of the law to the detriment of the spirit of the law. For example, if some minor deviation from the typikon is made during one of the church services, making a fuss over it could ruin everyone's peace and prayerfulness. When necessary, the deviation can be corrected afterwards. This approach is in line with the following teaching of Abba Isaiah: "Brethren, do not talk at all, except out of great necessity, in the refectory, or in the services, and do not correct anyone who chants, unless he asks you. For if he makes a mistake in one word and passes over it, he has passed over a simple word. Do not immediately tell him his mistake and agitate him."[1803]

Sometimes during church, disagreements arise regarding what should be chanted that lead to arguments and even bitterness and anger. Such incidents reveal that we have forgotten that the whole purpose of having a typikon is to avoid temptations rather than create them. If our aim in performing the church services is to pray, but then we ruin prayer in our attempt to perform the services "correctly," it is evident that we have lost the essence of why we are performing them in the first place. Therefore, since experience has shown us time and time again that we are unable (primarily because of our passions and egotistical desire to be "right") to follow the typikon with exactitude without being disturbed or disturbing others, it behooves us to sacrifice what is less essential. That is, it is preferable to take a forbearing attitude towards errors in following the typikon without a passionate attachment to its details so that we can pray in peace, rather than to enforce it with pharisaical perfection while destroying our peacefulness and prayer.[1804]

[1800] Γέροντος Ἐφραίμ, *Ὁ Γέροντάς μου Ἰωσήφ*, 282; see also Elder Ephraim, *My Elder Joseph the Hesychast*, 394–95.

[1801] Ἀρχιμανδρίτου Γεωργίου, *Ὀρθόδοξος Μοναχισμὸς καὶ Ἅγιον Ὄρος*, 80.

[1802] 1 Cor. 14:40.

[1803] Chrysostomos, *The Evergetinos, Book II*, 106.

[1804] For example, once I was chanting as second choir while a novice on the opposite side of the church was first choir. He began chanting "More honourable than the Cherubim" in the third mode because he mistakenly

Elder Ephraim had an exemplary stance toward the typikon: he rarely involved himself with its minute details, and only for serious deviations and omissions would he make corrections. St. Joseph the Hesychast was more concerned about brotherly love than about the proper order in church, for he wrote: "The thought comes and bothers you in church, 'Why should your brother chant again instead of you, since this is not the proper order?' You should tell it, 'It's better for my brother to be happy than for me.'"[1805]

St. Nectarios of Aegina emphasized to his nuns the importance of quality in prayer: "I want the words [of the services] to speak to your heart. I don't want you to execute the formality of prayer but to worship, because the heart is satisfied through worship and not through formalities—not with the quantity but with the quality of prayer."[1806] Likewise, Elder Justin Pîrvu the Confessor of blessed memory urged monastics to keep the formalities of prayer in their proper perspective:

> The Orthodox typikon is a secondary element in comparison to what our true essence, calling and mission really are. The typikon is a human, material thing. It is not dogma, a doctrine. Sure, it's important when and how to read Vespers or troparia, or to celebrate a Divine Liturgy in the right, proper order. But the really important thing for us to do is to crystallize the spirit of sacrifice that stands behind, and at the very core of, these exterior manifestations. I speak about the capacity of understanding the age we live in now and about where exactly we stand in the witness of the Christian Orthodox Truth. Does the monastic understand his mission in this very age we are confronted with? Because it is the monastic, in my opinion, that moves the world. He is the one that keeps up the flame of life and truth in the world. The monastic is the genius of Christianity. I'm not too sure that our reading troparia, Vespers and vigils, and our waking up at midnight and reading an akathist make our Lord that happy. I would like to see the man with the genius to renew monastic life in the sense of infusing it with its original creative force. That's what I want. But for the time being I can't see any such thing. We don't see that Orthodoxy—that is, the Truth—is being attacked from all sides by atheism, neo-Protestantism, indifference, and what not.... Monasticism is the greatest calling at this very hour. Monastic life—its light, its energy of sacrifice—is the only thing able to solve the present crisis.[1807]

---

thought that the canon of the ninth ode of the *Triodion* should precede the canon of the *Menaion*. I could have changed the mode to the right one when it was my turn to chant the following verse and sent someone across the church to correct him, but this seemed unnecessarily disruptive to me. Therefore, I chose to let him chant it in the wrong mode and the canons in the wrong order. Afterwards, I explained to him that the canon of the *Menaion* always precedes that of the *Triodion*—not because I believe that this convention has great spiritual importance (since the historical reason for this may have been purely practical) but because I know that by agreeing on such conventions we will be able to conduct the services in a more orderly fashion. Moreover, I honor the traditional order of liturgical worship as one of the treasures of the Orthodox Church, and therefore I do not want to begin picking and choosing which aspects of Orthodox tradition to follow.

[1805] Γέροντος Ἰωσήφ, Ἔκφρασις Μοναχικῆς Ἐμπειρίας, 143; see also Elder Joseph, *Monastic Wisdom,* 130.

[1806] As quoted in Καββαδία, Γέροντας καὶ Γυναικεῖος Μοναχισμός, 144.

[1807] *The Orthodox Word,* no. 174 (January–February 1994), 23–24.

On a deeper level, it is not only the *liturgical* typikon that threatens to kill the spirit of the law with the letter of the law, but even a *monastic* typikon runs the same risk. For this very reason, St. Sophrony of Essex did not compose a typikon for his monastery in Essex. He explained this danger to his disciples as follows:

> Monasteries are established (as we have said)[1808] when some people gather around an ascetic. After his death they keep the testament of the founder, but even so, this paternal character would gradually become less and less apparent, and the monastery would take the form of an institution structured around rules. For me, the presence of rules is an "obstacle" for spiritual life. In what way are they an "obstacle"? In the beginning of the organization of a life in common, the typikon has an important place for all who begin their [spiritual] life at the monastery. Since they do not yet have a deep spiritual experience, they follow the directives of the typikon. The spiritual father or the one responsible for the novices teaches them the typikon, and after one or two years they are able not to transgress it externally. Later, though, for some people this turns out to be a tremendous limitation[1809] of being, of the human person. Our goal of being formed as persons meets an unsurpassable obstacle there, since we certainly can't change the typikon every ten years. I am telling you that it is up to you to keep what I have implemented ever since the beginning: We do not have an appointed typikon, but we believe that each one of you must have a proper stance and approach in order to develop....
>
> This "form" that I have suggested to you is the most difficult, but it is also always the best, in my opinion. You must understand that we are taking a risk by living in this manner, taking into consideration the weakness of human passions. Remain in this "form" without an appointed typikon. But this requires us to be above the rules, as the Apostle Paul says: "For the righteous there is no law;"[1810] they transcend the law. Forgive me for asking you to transcend the laws. Carefully examine the words of the Apostle Paul that say that the laws were given after the transgressions, after the crimes. Naturally, sometimes we might have small problems, but this [way] is more perfect.[1811]
>
> Christ liberated us from all rules. Why enslave ourselves to rules that we make ourselves?[1812]

Commenting on this approach of St. Sophrony, his disciple Fr. Zacharias added that in their monastery "we follow one rule that the Fathers of the Golden Age of monasticism gave: we do our best, what we can, and we leave the rest to God. And therein lies humility. As long as we put ourselves in the Way of the Lord, He will meet us."[1813]

This was the same approach of St. Barsanuphius the Great, who wrote to a monk:

[1808] St. Sophrony is referring to what he had told them earlier, which is quoted herein on page 378.

[1809] The editor of St. Sophrony's book inserted the following comment here: "The typikon, like every other law, is a limitation for those who are led by the Spirit of grace and have installed in their heart 'the law of faith' (Rom. 3:27)."

[1810] Cf. 1 Tim. 1:9.

[1811] Σωφρονίου, *Οἰκοδομῶντας τὸν Ναὸ τοῦ Θεοῦ, Τόμος Α΄*, 43–45.

[1812] Zacharias, *The Enlargement of the Heart*, 220.

[1813] Ibid.

But as for the rule about which you inquired, you are going around in expanding circles in order to "enter through the narrow gate that leads to life" eternal (Mt. 7:14). Behold, Christ tells you quite concisely how you must enter.

Leave aside human rules and listen to Him Who says: "The one who endures to the end will be saved" (Mt. 10:22). Therefore, the one who does not endure will not enter in to life [eternal]. So do not look for a command. I do not want you to be "under law, but under grace" (Rom. 6:14). For it is said: "The law is laid down not for the righteous" (1 Tim. 1:9). We desire that you be among the righteous.[1814]

Similarly, the angel who gave a monastic rule to St. Pachomios told him: "As for the perfect, they have no need of legislation, for they have dedicated all their life to the contemplation of God by themselves in their cells. I have laid down rules for all those whose mind has not attained knowledge, so that at least fulfilling like servants the duties of monastic life, they may be established in confidence."[1815] St. Paisios of the Holy Mountain observed: "In some monasteries today … they fuss unnecessarily over details, but can't find time for the spiritual things that should be their first concern. If young people entering the monasteries merely exchange worldly anxiety for legalism in the monastery, they won't find peace."[1816] Similarly, St. Porphyrios of Kafsokalyvia warned: "It's possible for everything in a monastery to be well ordered, but for there to be no monastic life."[1817]

St. Sophrony later added these clarifications to his avoidance of having a typikon:

> Living in a cenobium, we will have many external limitations, such as the daily "program," a certain "typikon," some "rules," and the like. The Spirit, however, Who proceeds from God the Father, transcends all these forms and rules. We all ought to keep these externals—I mean obedience and all the other methods of monastic formation—because this will make us firm. They are necessary for initiating us step-by-step into the spiritual state that Christ Himself lived. Then we will see that there is nothing common, base, or trivial in our life.[1818]

> Glory to God, we are here [in this monastery] thirty-two years now, and we still don't have any typikon. But this cannot happen unless the members of the community understand their spiritual responsibility before the brethren and all the other people who come here [as visitors]. They ought to have a sense of responsibility, a personal awareness, which is something worth infinitely more than simply keeping an "appointed" rule. Why? Because an appointed rule cannot be easily tailored [to individual needs]. Let's take for example a classic rule: the Rule of Saint Benedict. For centuries, the Benedictine fathers have been following the same rule daily. But the Apostle Paul—that great figure whom the Providence of God gave us—says that no law led men to perfection,[1819] not even the law of Moses. This is a great problem, and it is very

---

[1814] Chryssavgis, *Barsanuphius and John: Letters,* vol. 1, 43 (letter 23).

[1815] Veilleux, *Pachomian Koinonia,* vol. 2, 127.

[1816] Elder Paisios, *Spiritual Awakening,* 375–76; see also Γέροντος Παϊσίου, *Πνευματικὴ Ἀφύπνηση,* 338.

[1817] Chrysopigi, *Wounded by Love,* 161.

[1818] Σωφρονίου, *Οἰκοδομώντας τὸν Ναὸ τοῦ Θεοῦ, Τόμος Β΄,* 61.

[1819] "Knowing that a man is not justified by the works of the law, but by the faith of Jesus Christ, even we have believed in Jesus Christ, that we might be justified by the faith of Christ, and not by the works of the

difficult for everyone to grasp it. The rules in a monastery can help primarily in the beginning [of one's monastic life], because if in the beginning we let someone free to decide on his own, he feels lost. Novices need very precise and strict counsels to operate. But later, then what? ... Do you understand why it is important that we not have a rule but that we rather be always responsible for every movement of our heart, of our mind?[1820]

My basic goal is for you to acquire the inspiration that never wanes. We might be crushed until the end by the difficulties of life, but we ought to preserve the inspiration that Christ brought to us which He described as "fire."[1821] Then our monastic life will be genuine. If, however, we keep only the external practices and typika, this will be very little—extremely little.[1822]

Of course, St. Sophrony was not recommending the kind of idiorrhythmic anarchy condemned by the holy Fathers. For St. Iosif Volotsky warned:

Now where are those who say: "It is better to live where there is no burden, constraint, or penances; one should instead live as he wishes"? What shall we say to them? They themselves have already demonstrated that they are more wretched than malicious worldlings, for worldlings will be called to account regarding the Lord's commandments, and monks even more so.... Why then did Saint Ephraim say: "There is a great calamity where laws and canons do not dwell"? ... Basil the Great says: "If we do not observe the divine commandments and the patristic traditions, demons enter us and create whatever they want."[1823]

Likewise, St. Paisios of the Holy Mountain observed that those who are spiritually immature need restrictions and commandments. For when someone criticized religion because it confines and restricts us, St. Paisios replied with the following examples:

Before he is born, the infant is protected within the womb of the mother; he is under confinement. After the child is born, the parents place their baby in a crib with a railing all around it. The crib is like a little prison; but the parents do this out of love, for the child's own good. When the child is learning to walk, they hold him by the hand, to protect him from falling. And when he grows up, there are the laws of the State, which he must observe. In other words, there is a need to have some restrictions, otherwise impunity and rebelliousness lead to destruction. In the same way, the commandments of God protect people so that they won't fall.[1824]

Thus, having a monastic typikon safeguards a monastic community. A compiler of ancient Celtic monastic rules observed: "To maintain a strict discipline while the founder and his

---

law: for by the works of the law shall no flesh be justified" (Gal. 2:16). "Therefore by the deeds of the law there shall no flesh be justified in His sight" (Rom. 3:20).

[1820] Σωφρονίου, *Οἰκοδομῶντας τὸν Ναὸ τοῦ Θεοῦ, Τόμος Β´*, 206–7, 209.

[1821] "I came to send fire on the earth, and how I wish it were already kindled!" (Lk. 12:49).

[1822] Σωφρονίου, *Οἰκοδομῶντας τὸν Ναὸ τοῦ Θεοῦ, Τόμος Β´*, 443–44.

[1823] Goldfrank, *The Monastic Rule of Iosif Volotsky*, 239–40.

[1824] Chamberas, *Saint Paisios the Athonite*, 450.

immediate successors lived was possible, but the absence of a written rule inevitably led to a certain decline in monastic observance in subsequent generations."[1825]

13) Hospitality

Orthodox monasteries traditionally offer hospitality as an expression of their love for neighbor. St. Theodoros the Great Ascetic wrote: "We too [like Abraham], then, should actively and eagerly cultivate hospitality, so that we may receive not only angels, but also God Himself."[1826] The *Rule of St. Ailbe* recommends: "Let there be a spotlessly clean house, with a good fire therein, for the guests. Let foot-washing and bathing facilities be provided for them, together with a comfortable bed."[1827]

According to St. Basil the Great, the abbot decides which visitors may or may not stay overnight, and he also decides how long they can stay. He wrote:

> The gates of the monasteries should be closed to women, and not even all men should enter, but only those whom the superior permits. Often, a lack of discrimination regarding visitors introduces into the heart a succession of untimely conversations and fruitless tales, and from idle talk comes the further descent to idle and useless thought.[1828]

Visitors are expected to attend all the services and to help with whatever work the monks are doing. It is important that the visitors understand that the monastery is not a place of vacation or entertainment but primarily a place of pilgrimage, prayer, and focusing on one's spiritual life. Therefore, they should come with a spiritual disposition and not make noise or laugh inappropriately, listen to worldly music, watch movies, play games, etc. Smoking, drinking, and drugs are strictly forbidden on the monastery grounds. As a concession to the weakness of visitors addicted to nicotine, however, some monasteries permit smoking in a designated location outside the monastery. In the event of misbehavior or any disorderliness, visitors are corrected by the guest master or the abbot. If they fail to conform, they are expelled from the monastery.

Even though small children and especially infants tend to "misbehave" by screeching, running, etc., they are more than welcome in a monastery, since Christ Himself said: "Allow little children, and forbid them not, to come unto me, for of such is the kingdom of

---

[1825] Maidín, *The Celtic Monk*, 9.

[1826] Palmer, Sherrard, Ware, *The Philokalia*, vol. 2, 32.

[1827] Maidín, *The Celtic Monk*, 25.

[1828] Βασιλείου τοῦ Μεγάλου, *Ἀσκητικὰ Α΄*, ΕΠΕ 8, 138–39; see also Wagner, *Saint Basil: Ascetical Works*, vol. 9, 213.

heaven."[1829] Besides, there is much truth in these observations of Fyodor Dostoyevsky: "The soul is healed by being with children."[1830] "They are sinless like little angels, and they are there to arouse our tenderness, to purify our hearts, and in a sense to guide us."[1831]

St. Sophrony of Essex told his monastics:

> St. Symeon the New Theologian had a particular stance toward small children: he bowed to them whenever he greeted them. You should have a similar stance toward the children that come to us. You should have towards them the same regard as towards other visitors. Know that in the Lord's sight all are very important, very beloved. You should be even more polite with the women and the children. When they come, meet them with respect and give them the freedom to live in this place as if it were their home, their homeland.[1832]

A spiritual daughter of St. Sophrony observed how he behaved around children:

> There were many times when he played with the children like a child himself. As you watched him you wondered where he found so much joy. How he played with them! Children would be so engrossed in his company that they gave you the impression that they were oblivious to everything else. He took them into his arms, squeezed them, kissed them, he became one with them. In turn they embraced him, kissed him, pulled his hair; what a spectacle it was![1833]

Elder Ephraim also behaved with great love, playfulness, and tenderness towards children, and they in turn were delighted to be in his presence.

Elder Ephraim taught the importance of dressing modestly in a monastery. For this reason he instituted a dress code that men wear long pants and long-sleeved shirts, and that women wear skirts and head coverings. One day when he stepped out of his confession room, he noticed a female tourist in the narthex wearing pants and no head covering. So he took one of the extra skirts and scarves and gave them to her with so much joy on his face and almost playfully that she was not at all embarrassed to be corrected in front of so many other people. Unfortunately, I have also witnessed the opposite: when a layman would indignantly correct a visitor for failing to follow our dress code, making the visitor feel embarrassed and unwelcome.

As with all rules, one must be careful not to enforce them with unbending austerity but with discernment. For example, if a woman is wearing a skirt that doesn't quite reach her ankles (as required by our dress code), it may be wiser to overlook this minor infraction rather than make a fuss over it, especially if she is coming for the first time. We could wait

---

[1829] Mt. 19:14. St. Basil the Great cited this scripture to justify the presence of children in a monastery not just as visitors but even as postulants (vid. Wagner, *Saint Basil: Ascetical Works,* vol. 9, 264).

[1830] Fyodor Dostoyevsky, *The Idiot,* (Hertfordshire: Wordsworth Editions, 1996), 61.

[1831] Fyodor Dostoevsky, *The Brothers Karamazov,* 427.

[1832] Σωφρονίου, *Οἰκοδομῶντας τὸν Ναὸ τοῦ Θεοῦ, Τόμος Α΄,* 293.

[1833] Daviti, *Memories of Elder Sophrony of Essex,* 79–80.

until she is on her way out or even until she comes again before instructing her about appropriate attire for a monastery. If the first thing visitors hear when coming to our monastery is that they have broken Rule #476, they might never return and may justifiably conclude that we have failed to follow in the footsteps of Jesus, Who dealt with "sinners" in a very different way. Woe to us if our behavior leads them to say these cutting words of Mahatma Gandhi: "I like your Christ. I do not like your Christians. Your Christians are so unlike your Christ."[1834]

Regarding this issue, Monk C. in Greece explained: "We have to be tolerant. If a woman comes to the monastery wearing pants or a man comes in sport pants and the monks scold them, what will be their impression of the Church? We have to be tolerant in order to bring them into the Church, and then we tell them about this and that.... [We] welcome the people without judging them in order to bring them to God."[1835] Commenting on this, a contemporary Orthodox writer concluded: "The visitor is Christ in their midst, an opportunity to serve rather than condemn. They are to be embraced in fraternal love, not sent out in the cold. A monastery without love has no hope for the cultivation of holiness in any form."[1836] Nevertheless, this matter requires some discernment, since love and permissiveness are not equivalent.

14) Internet

Using the internet provides many advantages which are already evident to most people: it quickly provides information on almost any subject matter for free; it facilitates communication and collaboration (via email, Zoom, etc.) with people who might otherwise be nearly inaccessible; it enables one to conduct business online and to locate and purchase useful items quickly that would otherwise be more expensive or even impossible to find. For monastics this is especially helpful, since it allows them to remain longer in their monasteries without needing to go out into the world. Furthermore, when going outside is dangerous (because of a deadly pandemic, a violent neighborhood, etc.), doing tasks online could even save one's life. In a nutshell, the internet can increase the number of things we are able to do, and it can decrease the time, money, effort, and potential danger needed to do them.

Notwithstanding these many benefits, a prudent person will adopt a tool or approach only when its benefits outweigh its drawbacks. Sadly, the vast majority of internet users

---

[1834] Ramnarine Sahadeo, *Mohandas K. Gandhi - Thoughts, Words, Deeds* (Mississauga: Xlibris, 2011), 22.

[1835] Stephen R. Lloyd-Moffett, *Beauty for Ashes: The Spiritual Transformation of a Modern Greek Community* (New York: St. Vladimir's Seminary Press, 2009), 174.

[1836] Ibid., 175.

(including myself at first)[1837] have adopted the "any-benefit" approach: if there is any benefit at all to a tool, it will be used regardless of how many and how serious its drawbacks are. This approach leads to a "digital maximalism," supported by the unchallenged underlying assumption that the more we use the internet the better off we are. Commenting on this approach, William Powers wrote

> This is a simple idea but one with enormous implications ... [making it] very clear how to organize your screen time and, indeed, every waking hour.... You can't be too connected, they say, so we should seek at all times to maximize our time with screens and minimize our time away.... When a crowd adopts a point of view en masse, all critical thinking effectively stops. The maximalist dogma is particularly difficult to challenge because it's all about joining the crowd, so it's self-reinforcing.[1838]

This chapter will attempt to challenge this point of view by exploring the numerous drawbacks of using the internet, categorizing them into *spiritual, physical, psychological,* and *cognitive* harm. My hope is that this chapter will help us make a more informed choice in deciding how much to use the internet.

i) Spiritual Harm

Internet access harms monastics spiritually because it exposes them to many worldly influences. Also, by having email, a monastic can be overwhelmed by dozens of emails and notifications every single day. All this is the opposite of the "solitude" and the "renunciation of the world" which the holy Fathers traditionally viewed as fundamental conditions for monastic life to flourish.[1839] For example, St. Basil the Great wrote:

> Quiet ... is the first step in our sanctification; the tongue purified from the gossip of the world; the eyes unexcited by fair color or comely shape; the ear not relaxing the tone or mind by voluptuous songs, nor by that especial mischief, the talk of light men and jesters. Thus the mind, saved from dissipation from without, and not through the senses thrown upon the world, falls back upon itself, and thereby ascends to the contemplation of God. ... We must strive after a quiet mind.... The wilderness is of the greatest use for this purpose, inasmuch as it stills our passions.[1840]

[1837] In fact, it was precisely because of my access to the internet that I was able to gather so much information for this book. Prior to completing my research on the adverse effects of the internet, I assumed the harm was negligible, and therefore I used it whenever I wanted to acquire more information about a topic or locate a quote. But now that I am fully aware of its many dangers, I have limited my internet usage to a bare minimum by not having access to it most of the time. To anyone else who would like practical advice how to regain a healthy balance in their use of the internet, I highly recommend reading *Digital Minimalism* by Cal Newport, as well as the chapter "Prevention and Treatment" in *The New Media Epidemic* by Jean-Claude Larchet and *Hamlet's Blackberry* by William Powers.

[1838] William Powers, *Hamlet's Blackberry* (New York: Harper Collins Publishers, 2010), 35, 49.

[1839] See chapter 1) section 3) on page 19 for more about solitude and renunciation of the world.

[1840] *Basil: Letters and Select Works,* 111, 110 (Letter 2); PG 32:225BC.

It seems unlikely that St. Basil would say that the passions of a monk even in the deepest wilderness are being stilled if he has a satellite connection to the internet.

Since St. Paisios of the Holy Mountain asked: "What will I get from [external] stillness ... if I have a radio with me?"[1841] one can only imagine what he would have said about having internet access in the wilderness. The advice of Abba Moses: "Go, sit in your cell, and your cell will teach you everything,"[1842] is certainly not applicable in the way he intended if a monk sitting in his cell can google anything that piques his curiosity! On the contrary, what Abba Moses meant was that minimizing external distractions leads to introspection, which leads to watchfulness and finding the Kingdom of God, which is within us. The internet takes us in the opposite direction.

Another problem is that it is nearly impossible to visit web pages without sometimes being exposed to provocative pictures. To avoid this kind of exposure is one of the reasons why several men's and women's monasteries are completely off-limits to visitors of the opposite gender. For "seeing begets desire," according to the maxim of the Hellenic philosophers quoted by St. Nicodemos of the Holy Mountain.[1843] Thus, monastics in such monasteries who use the internet will be negating the benefit they would have had from their isolation. As Patriarch Kirill of Moscow pointed out: "Many monks act, in my view, quite unreasonably. On the one hand, they leave the world in order to create favorable conditions for salvation, and on the other hand, they take their mobile telephone and start to enter the Internet where, as we know, there is a large number of sinful and tempting things."[1844]

St. Gregory Palamas expressed a similar sentiment to his fellow monks, centuries before it was possible to leave one's monastery by going online: "What good does it do us to take flight from the world once and for all and find refuge in houses of prayer consecrated to God, but then to leave them daily and become involved in the world again? Tell me how, if you love frequenting the town squares, you will avoid the incentives to passions which bring about the death of the soul, separating a man from God? The death comes upon us through our senses, as if through windows within us."[1845] When we are online, our senses of seeing and hearing are windows wide open to deadly spiritual influences.

Dr. Jean-Claude Larchet elaborates on what these deadly spiritual influences are that tempt us:

[1841] Hieromonk Isaac, *Elder Paisios of Mount Athos,* 455.

[1842] Ward, *The Sayings of the Desert Fathers,* 139.

[1843] Νικοδήμου τοῦ Ἁγιορείτου, *Συμβουλευτικὸν Ἐγχειρίδιον,* 40; see also St. Nicodemos's comments on guarding one's eyes quoted in the text referenced in footnote #808 on page 149 herein.

[1844] http://blogs.reuters.com/faithworld/2013/06/10russian-orthodox-patriarch-kirill-urges-monks-to-shun-internet-temptations/.

[1845] Veniamin, *St. Gregory Palamas: The Homilies,* 397.

The new media are always a temptation to turn from the task in hand, and also from our neighbor, our own spiritual benefit, and from God Himself.... The companies that manage the Internet organize it so that the user sees as much as possible of everything to which he is easily tempted. If we review the basic list of all the passions, compiled by Eastern Christian Tradition to guide man in his spiritual progress, we can see that there is not one to which the new media cannot tempt us, and that they cannot arouse, feed, maintain, or develop. They are as follows: love of the belly, or gluttony; avarice, or the love of money and the desire to acquire more money and goods; lust, or attachment to sexual pleasure; anger, which includes all forms of aggression; fearfulness, which includes disquiet and anxiety; sadness; *acedia,* the state of dissatisfaction, disgust, laziness, and instability; self-love, vanity or vain glory; and pride.[1846]

Pride and vanity are reinforced by counting the "likes" received, and by showing that one can collect more followers on Twitter, or "likes" from the so-called friends of Facebook than the next man. Those who use Facebook tend to show a flattering image of themselves, which surpasses reality. Their faults are erased and their qualities exaggerated. They even claim qualities that they never had. This has a bad effect not just on themselves, but on others who may feel put down by the outrageous exaggeration they see in the images that they take to be true. Psychologists have even found that it is a cause of depression, which concords with the teaching of the holy ascetics who saw pride and vanity as sources of sadness and acedia, two states that resemble what we now call depression.[1847]

The new media, especially the television, the Internet, and the social media, have created a world in parallel to the real world, a virtual world where the most important thing is to speak about what one does or intends to do, or to get others to speak of it. This has become more important than actually doing it. One's image is more important than one's identity.... [Thus] the Internet and Facebook have become fields where narcissism can easily develop.[1848]

Fr. Stephen Muse has observed that using the internet puts us in a disembodied state that renders us more susceptible to temptations. He wrote:

I have determined that for myself, extended internet use is monological and depletes the soul's vitality, leaving me empty inside. This is masked by the false sense of presence connected to the immediacy and interactive engagement with images coming from it. Attachment to mental images through the digital screen is contrary to the embodied state advocated by the Fathers who call for the *nous* to be gathered within the body in order to pray,[1849] rather than pouring out through the senses and imagination. As St. Theophan the Recluse noted, "Thoughts in the head are the place of deception." I think we can say the same for the power of internet as being a kind of proxy for "images in the mind" functioning as hypnotic suggestions that more easily by-pass critical faculties and disrupt the collected watchfulness and inner silence

---

[1846] Larchet, *The New Media Epidemic*, 147–48. All quotations herein from this publication are used by permission.

[1847] Ibid., 149.

[1848] Ibid., 39, 81, 97, 102, 146.

[1849] Fr. Stephen Muse elaborates on the importance of embodied prayer in his profound book: *Treasure in Earthen Vessels: Prayer and the Embodied Life* (South Canaan: St. Tikhon's Monastery Press, 2018).

needed for monastic life. After extended periods of use of digital media required for work, spending further time on the internet, as a distraction from tiredness, leaves a person more susceptible to craving stimulation and sensual excitement as a kind of compensation for being too long in a disembodied state. In actual fact, what is needed to replenish the devitalized inner state is deeply embodied presence with intentional collectedness in silence. Manual labor can also be restorative and reorient us to more natural rhythms of life disrupted by prolonged mental identification with digital media.[1850]

Likewise, Dr. Larchet describes how the internet divides and conquers the inner unity of our faculties, rendering us vulnerable to passions:

> The new media encourage strongly two elements of ancestral sin: (1) the loss of the inner unity of the faculties, which once were united in knowledge of God and doing His will, dispersing them among physical objects and their representations (thoughts, memories, and images), or the objects and passions that they arouse; (2) the resulting division, chopping up, and inner dispersion, which according to St. Maximus the Confessor, "breaks human nature into a thousand fragments."[1851] As other holy ascetics have said, the intelligence is then constantly distracted, floating, erring, and wandering here and there[1852] in a state of permanent agitation,[1853] quite the opposite of the deep peace it experienced in its former contemplation. The thoughts that once were united and concentrated become manifold and multifarious, spreading out in a ceaseless flow.[1854] They divide and disperse,[1855] leaking out in every direction,[1856] dragging and dividing the whole being of man in their wake. This leads St. Maximus the Confessor to speak of: "the scattering of the soul amongst outer forms according to the appearance of sensory things,"[1857] for the soul becomes multiple in the image of this sensory multiplicity that, paradoxically, she has created for herself, and which is simply an illusion arising from her incapacity to perceive the objective unity of beings through her ignorance of their relation to the One God in their origins and their end. Once the intelligence becomes dispersed and divided among the swarm of thoughts and sensations that it has engendered, all the faculties follow. Stirred up and excited by a multitude of passions, they pull in many directions, often opposed, at once, and make of man a being divided at every level. This process of the fall of man, described by the Church Fathers of Late Antiquity, continues today faster than ever, driven on by the new media.[1858]

[1850] Excerpt from a personal correspondence, 5/23/21.

[1851] *Questions to Thalassios,* 137.

[1852] Cf. Macaire d'Égypte, *Homélies (coll. II),* IV, 4; Isaac le Syrien, *Discours ascétiques,* 68.

[1853] Cf. Callisto et Ignacio Xanthopouloi, *Centuries,* 19, 23, 24, 25.

[1854] Macaire d'Égypte, *Homélies (coll. II),* XXXI, 6.

[1855] Cf. Nicétas Stéthatos, *Centuries,* III, 2; 6; 19.

[1856] Macaire d'Égypte, *Homélies (coll. II),* VI, 3.

[1857] *Mystagogie,* XXIII, PG 91:697C.

[1858] Larchet, *The New Media Epidemic,* 151–52.

A further problem with internet access is that it intensifies the temptation for us to waste time. As Dr. Larchet points out:

> The new media are a source of distraction and entertainment, far beyond anything known in the past, since they can be permanent and limitless. Formerly, someone who sought entertainment had to make a physical and psychological effort to move to the right place and pay the price demanded. The television and Internet bring it all into the home, offering a huge choice that requires no effort of any kind to be accessed.[1859]

> The new media … bring into the home a host of amusements that allow the real world to be forgotten with all its difficulties. They facilitate diversions in the sense Pascal gave to this word: they turn one's attention from one's own existential poverty and the anguish that it arouses.[1860]

The value of this painful awareness of one's own existential poverty is that it can lead one to repentance, prayer, and a search for deeper existential meaning.

Thus, the internet fosters escapism, which the Oxford English Dictionary defines as "the tendency to seek, or the practice of seeking, distraction from what normally has to be endured."[1861] If a person repeatedly copes with difficulties in life by distracting himself instead of by enduring them, his capacity for bearing hardship will erode. Such a person will lack the fortitude to deal with unpleasant things in life, making him impatient.

Surprisingly, a study published in the *Journal of the Association for Consumer Research* found that our working memory and problem-solving skills are reduced by the mere presence of a cell phone in the same room, even when it is turned off and out of sight, if we know it is there.[1862] More seriously, its presence degrades the quality of connection between people. As Sherry Turkle wrote:

> Studies show that the mere presence of a phone on the table (even if a phone is turned off) changes what people talk about. If we think we might be interrupted, we keep conversations light, on topics of little controversy or consequence. And conversations with phones on the landscape block empathic connection. If two people are speaking and there is a phone on a nearby desk, each feels less connected to the other than when there is no phone present. *Even a silent phone disconnects us.*[1863]

Something analogous happens also in the spiritual plane. In the experience of us monks and nuns on remote islands in Alaska, we have observed a tangible difference in the spiritual "feeling" or "atmosphere" of our monasteries when no devices are present that can connect to the internet. One of the monastics here described this feeling as a "sense of inner freedom" and "as if a hazy cloud over my soul has lifted."

[1859] Ibid., 150.

[1860] Ibid., 95.

[1861] As quoted in https://en.wikipedia.org/wiki/Escapism.

[1862] www.journals.uchicago.edu/doi/abs/10.1086/691462.

[1863] Turkle, *Reclaiming Conversation,* 21.

It should be no surprise that the internet creates a "hazy cloud," considering that it puts us repeatedly into an excited and distracted state that is the opposite of the quiet and focused state that is conducive to prayer. Dr. Larchet elaborates on this concept:

> The hyper-relational nature of the new media is to some extent dangerous for the personality. If it is too much with others, it has no time to be with itself. To develop and blossom, the person needs solitude as much as, if not more than, relationships. This is borne out by the experience of hesychast spirituality, which grew up in the Christian East as the ultimate means of self-development. The term "hesychia" means calm, isolation, and solitude. Psychiatrists are aware of many cases of emotional collapse, which are often marked by symptoms of depression and are caused by self-forgetfulness in people who are totally immersed in social activities. They also know the importance of solitude for self-construction through facing up to oneself. This is what Pascal emphasized long ago when he said, "All the troubles of men come from one thing only, which is that they do not know how to dwell at rest in a room."[1864]

> The new media destroy what the Eastern Spiritual Tradition refers to as hesychia. In truth, this state can only be lived to the full by monastics. Yet all who would lead a serious spiritual life need it in some measure. Hesychia is a way of life that requires solitude, outer silence, and inner calm. These three things are indispensable for spiritual life, especially in one of its essential activities: concentrated, attentive, and vigilant prayer. In contrast, the continual prompts from the new media are incompatible with the creation and maintenance of hesychia, not only in its fullness but also for even the briefest periods. It has no chance against the visual and audible signals to which most connected people respond immediately.[1865]

> Those who use the new media lose the initiative in their inner life and can no longer manage it. They are always on the watch for external stimuli.... There is no space left for those times of solitude that contribute to the construction and stability of psychological and spiritual life. There are no more times for the silence that is required for deep thought and the contemplation that nourishes spiritual life. The flow of inner life is constantly interrupted by phone calls that distract the attention with their ring tones, by emails, or by tweets with their sonorous alerts. The habit of immediately reacting and replying further fragments inner life and turns the life of the soul into a chain of inarticulate events.[1866]

> Spiritual life requires and cultivates stability in life, and to this end gives great importance to regularity, which comes from discipline and contributes to the mastery of all the faculties. The effects of the new media are quite the opposite of this state. As we have seen, using them often gives rise to disquiet that increases with use, or to dissatisfaction that the user seeks to assuage by always seeking something new. They drag all the powers of the soul into a continuous fast-flowing stream of disordered and disconnected impressions.[1867]

[1864] Larchet, *The New Media Epidemic,* 98.

[1865] Ibid., 150.

[1866] Ibid., 99.

[1867] Ibid., 151.

Dr. Larchet observes that the internet has even become a replacement for God. He wrote:

> Many users give the new media a central place in their lives: the place that God should occupy in the normal religious life of the faithful. They give them much time; they sacrifice their strength to them; they give up many things for them in what resembles a kind of detachment. Like ascetics, they give up food, and especially sleep, in their service and begin and end the day with them, just like religious folk with their morning and evening prayers.[1868]

> The new media have a power of attraction that consumes people's time and distracts them from traditional activities and from the world around them; and in this way they [i.e., the media] have undoubtedly contributed to this disenchantment with Christianity.[1869]

> Alain Finkielkraut observes correctly that with the new technologies: "we abandon a world of contemplation and reaching upwards and enter a world of openness and reaching sideways." As we use the Internet, we see how its web spreads horizontally, and how the movement of the spirit that moves within it is one of permanent alienation.[1870]

> Father Constantine Coman, a professor of the Theological Faculty of Bucharest, wrote recently that the new media ... are fertile ground for those worldly attitudes that a spiritual man flees as he seeks "the one thing needful" in depth. For they bring forth distraction, pleasure seeking, levity, curiosity, talkativeness, and empty gossip.[1871]

> The facts show that connection to the new media competes with connection to God, which is made through participation in liturgical services and through personal prayer.... The new media eat up time. The television does so and even more so the Internet. Through its links it entices the user to navigate further and further, capturing his attention and making him forget the passage of time. Anyone who has used the Internet has often found that a search that should have been quick took far longer than intended.

> In this competition between connections, the new media win hands down. In spite of all the love we may have for Him, to connect with God we must make an effort to withdraw from our environment and from our own thoughts in the widest sense (reasoning, imagination, memories, desires, etc.) and be vigilant and attentive; navigating the Internet is easy. It is enough to let oneself go to plunge into a pleasant world that always assuages our desires and passions. Moreover, there is a sense of total freedom, whereas to relate to God within the framework of serious and sincere religious practice implies permanent regularity and discipline.

> The monasteries themselves have managed to escape the invasion of the television, but find it harder to resist the new media. More and more monks, for various more or less valid reasons, now have access to a computer. More and more of them have a portable phone, which nowadays is a device that includes all the other media. In a coenobitic monastery, the rule may forbid or limit the use of portable media; but solitaries escape such control. Many hermits pass time on the Internet that could better

---

[1868] Ibid., 141.

[1869] Ibid., 142.

[1870] Ibid., 144.

[1871] Ibid.

have been given to prayer, and many monks spy through that small window every day on the world that they left through the front door.[1872]

The new media, especially the Internet, tend to take up time that should be used for prayer, even the time of monks. Those hermits who have become dependent often abbreviate drastically the divine services. Often smartphones remain switched on during the time of prayer, which they disturb with their ring tones. It is not uncommon to see the faithful, monks, or even the celebrants themselves look at their smartphones during divine services. They believe that they are justified by the need to be ready to serve their neighbor and the potential urgency of a call. It is vital to have a strict rule in these matters and to stick to it. The time for prayer must be preserved absolutely inviolable. All those potentially disturbing connections must be switched off.... Prayer can only be fruitful in silence, and so in solitude, in attention without outer or inner distraction, and in continuity for sufficient time without interruption.[1873]

The distractions caused by internet access are a serious spiritual problem. Abba Poemen, even though living long before the intense and constant distractions of our modern world, observed: "Distraction is the beginning of evils."[1874] One could only imagine what he might say today. Elder Aimilianos also observed how pernicious the temptation for distraction is. He wrote: "The most dreadful enemy created by post-industrial culture, the culture of information technology and the image, is cunning distraction. Swamped by millions of images and a host of different situations on television and in the media in general, people lose their peace of mind, their self-control, their powers of contemplation and reflection, and turn outwards, becoming strangers to themselves—in a word, mindless, impervious to the dictates of their intelligence."[1875]

All this outwardness caused by the internet reduces our capacity for watchfulness (νῆψις), which is a fundamental part of the spiritual life. Deuteronomy teaches: "Take heed to yourself and diligently guard your soul."[1876] Christ frequently instructed His disciples to keep vigilance,[1877] and they in turn taught this to others.[1878] The holy Fathers also emphasized the great importance of this virtue. For example, St. Peter of Damascus wrote: "Without attention and vigilance of spirit we cannot be saved and delivered from the devil, who, as a roaring lion, walketh about us, seeking whom he may devour."[1879] Likewise, St. Hesychios the Priest taught: "Just as it is impossible to live this present life without eating

---

[1872] Ibid., 146–47.

[1873] Ibid., 170.

[1874] PG 65:332C.

[1875] Elder Aimilianos, *The Authentic Seal,* 350.

[1876] Deut. 4:9.

[1877] Vid. Mt. 24:42; 25:13; 26:41; Mk. 13:33, 37; 14:38; Lk. 21:36.

[1878] Vid. Acts 20:28; 1 Cor. 16:13; 1 Pet. 5:8.

[1879] As quoted in Larchet, *The New Media Epidemic,* 152–53.

or drinking, so it is impossible for the soul to achieve anything spiritual and in accordance with God's will, or to be free from mental sin, without that guarding of the intellect and purity of heart, which is called watchfulness, even if one forces oneself not to sin through the fear of punishment."[1880]

An indirect spiritual danger is that using the internet provides governments and private companies with a tremendous amount of information about our lives. In 2013, the whistle-blower Edward Snowden revealed that the U.S. National Security Agency (NSA) is recording almost all phone calls, text messages, and emails of people around the world. Furthermore, the NSA knows where we have been and where we are now (whenever carrying a phone or a tablet); it tracks every online search, every website we visit, as well as every online purchase; and it can even clandestinely access the cameras and microphones of our electronic devices in real time.[1881] Snowden also revealed that many other governments and corporations around the world are spying on people in a similar fashion.

Snowden said that these institutions can "monitor and record private activities of people on a scale that's broad enough that we can say it's close to all-powerful.... They do this through new platforms and algorithms through which they're able to shift our behavior. In some cases they're able to predict our decisions—and also nudge them—to different outcomes.... And now [in 2019] these institutions, which are both commercial and governmental, have built upon that and ... have structuralized and entrenched it to where it has become now the most effective means of social control in the history of our species."[1882]

Even if the governments and corporations with all this information were not exploiting it at the present time, this does not mean that they never will. Judging from chapter 13 of the Book of Revelation and from the prophecies of several saints, it will only be a matter of time before governments do persecute Christians. The more information that governments have about people, the more easily they can decide whom they consider potential threats, and the more easily they can locate, manipulate, and persecute them. One can imagine how the anti-Christian regimes of the past could have intensified their persecution if they had access to all the information that current governments have of people who use the internet.

To summarize the foregoing paragraphs, we can say the internet harms us spiritually by: ruining our solitude and hesychia, exposing us to provocative pictures, feeding our pride and all the passions, distracting us, wasting our time, fostering escapism, sacrificing

---

[1880] Ἡσυχίου Πρεσβυτέρου, «Πρὸς Θεόδουλον», ἐν *Φιλοκαλία*, τόμος α΄ (1893), 92 (κεφ. ρθ΄); see also Palmer, Sherrard, Ware, *The Philokalia,* vol. 1, 181 (St. Hesychios the Priest 109).

[1881] https://www.expressvpn.com/blog/8-ways-the-nsa-spies-on-you/ See also: Edward Snowden, *Permanent Record* (New York: Pan Macmillan, 2020).

[1882] www.commondreams.org/news/2019/05/31/edward-snowden-technology-institutions-have-made-most-effective-means-social-control

our privacy, and replacing God. Aware of these spiritual dangers, Archimandrite Maximos Constas concluded that the internet is inherently detrimental to monasticism:

> Monks are called to live an apostolic life, and the Apostles did not transform the world because they were up on the latest news, or made use of the latest technologies, or because they had flashy web sites, or promoted themselves with the tricks and gimmicks of modern advertising, but because they were transformed by Christ; they were on fire for Christ; and they set the whole world on fire for Him. But a "monk" whose soul is filled with secular ideas and images from the computer, whose soul is informed by and conformed to the form of the world, will never be able to say even one Jesus Prayer without distraction, and will be useless to both God and man. Such a monk is neither crucified to the world, nor the world to him, because he loves the world more than God.[1883]

ii) Physical Harm

Using the internet is also *physically* detrimental to one's health in several ways. In a nutshell, it harms our eyesight, leads to sleep deprivation, compromises our posture, exposes us to radiation, compromises our breathing, and leads to an array of bodily ailments associated with a sedentary lifestyle. This section will substantiate each of these statements.

The internet harms our eyesight because almost all people access it by staring at a digital screen. Studies have shown that close computer work can cause light sensitivity, dry eye, blurred vision, double vision, fatigue, and headaches.[1884] In fact, about 40% of optometrists' patients suffer from eye strain due to computer vision syndrome.[1885]

The internet is also responsible for an increasing number of people suffering from sleep deprivation. As Dr. Jean-Claude Larchet wrote:

> The clinical sleep problems related to the new media are associated with a reduction of the time asleep below what is normal for a particular age group. This is not necessarily due to addiction, but may simply be caused by the need to view a late-night program to the end, the need to consult the Internet late at night, or the need to finish off email and SMS correspondence…. The result is tiredness upon waking in the morning, which continues throughout the day.[1886]

Most people using the internet are doing so in a position that compromises their posture. Especially when they are using a small device (such as a tablet or a smartphone) instead of a monitor mounted at an ergonomically ideal position, the device is typically held or placed far below eye level. This encourages the head to protrude and tilt downward, which increas-

---

[1883] Excerpt from a personal correspondence, 3/14/18.

[1884] "The Real Effects of Technology on Your Health," www.everydayhealth.com/emotional-health/internet-addiction/real-effects-technology-on-your-health/

[1885] Ibid.

[1886] Larchet, *The New Media Epidemic*, 79.

es the pressure on the neck's muscles, tendons, and ligaments as much as five-fold, depending on how bent the neck is.[1887] Since the neck is not able to withstand this amount of pressure over a prolonged period, it causes "text neck" (or "tech neck")—so called because this is the position in which most people send texts and use the internet. According to Dr. David DeWitt:

> Text neck typically begins as a relatively mild ache in the neck or upper back.... If not addressed, the continued forward head posture and hunched shoulders may worsen over time, which could lead to even more pain and reduced mobility in the neck, upper back, and shoulders. In some cases the excessive forward head posture may exacerbate or accelerate degenerative conditions in the cervical spine, such as cervical degenerative disc disease and/or cervical osteoarthritis.... Touchscreen element may bring shoulders and head further forward.[1888]

If the internet is accessed while seated, many physiological problems can ensue. Studies have shown that remaining relatively motionless for a long period of time (whether sitting at a desk or driving a car) damages one's physical health in many ways. In particular, doing this:

1) increases risk of heart disease by up to 64%.[1889]
2) impairs the body's ability to handle blood sugar, causing a reduced sensitivity to the hormone insulin, which helps carry glucose from the blood into cells where it can be used for energy, leading to diabetes,[1890]
3) increases likelihood of cancer,[1891]
4) leads to metabolic syndrome,[1892]
5) reduces one's non-exercise activity thermogenesis,[1893]

[1887] www.spine-health.com/conditions/neck-pain/how-does-text-neck-cause-pain

[1888] Ibid.

[1889] T. Y. Warren, V. Barry, S. P. Hooker, X. Sui, T. S. Church, S. N. Blair, "Sedentary Behaviors Increase Risk of Cardiovascular Disease Mortality in Men," *Medicine & Science in Sports & Exercise,* May 2010, 42(5): 879–85. http://www.ncbi.nlm.nih.gov/pubmed/19996993

[1890] E. Grandjean, W. Hünting, "Ergonomics of posture—Review of Various Problems of Standing and Sitting Posture," *Applied Ergonomics*, vol. 8, issue 3 (September 1977): 135–40. http://www.sciencedirect.com/science/article/pii/0003687077900023

[1891] Wei Zheng, Xiao Ou Shu, Yu Tang Gao, Joseph K. McLaughlin, Wong-Ho Chow, and William J. Blot, "Occupational Physical Activity and the Incidence of Cancer of the Breast, Corpus Uteri, and Ovary in Shanghai," *Cancer,* vol. 71, Issue 11, (1 June 1993): 3620–24. http://onlinelibrary.wiley.com/doi/10.1002/1097-0142%2819930601%2971:11%3C3620::AID-CNCR2820711125%3E3.0.CO;2-S/abstract

[1892] Marc T. Hamilton, Deborah G. Hamilton, and Theodore W. Zderic, "Role of Low Energy Expenditure and Sitting in Obesity, Metabolic Syndrome, Type 2 Diabetes, and Cardiovascular Disease," (September 2007): http://diabetes.diabetesjournals.org/content/56/11/2655.short

[1893] Ibid.

6) slows the clearance of fat from the blood stream and decreases the effect of insulin,[1894]

7) increases all-cause mortality by seven percent,[1895]

8) can lead to obesity due to lowered energy expenditure,[1896]

9) compromises posture by causing the pelvis to rotate backward which puts pressure on the lumbar discs and forces the head forward, causing the shoulders to curve,[1897]

10) creates a prolonged, static loading of tissues, which over time puts undue pressure on the lower back and stresses the surrounding muscles and joints,[1898] which can become the symptoms of chronic diseases,[1899]

11) can lead to rheumatic diseases such as osteoarthritis due to the "wear and tear" to the joints from excessive sitting,[1900] and

12) increases the risk of anxiety.[1901]

What is even more alarming is that most of these harmful results still apply to people who are physically active during the rest of the day.[1902]

A further concern with using the internet is the neurological damage caused by prolonged exposure to the non-ionizing electromagnetic radiation emitted by the devices that are used to access the internet. Such devices harm us not only through their extremely low frequency electromagnetic fields (which all electronic appliances and power lines create) but also through their radio-frequency radiation (which all cell phones and wireless devices emit). While some controversy exists regarding whether these forms of radiation actually harm us, the overwhelming majority of studies have found that they do. Specifically, as of August 2019, adverse biological effects were detected in 72% of the 305 studies

---

[1894] Hidde P. van der Ploeg, Tien Chey, Rosemary J. Korda, Emily Banks, Adrian Bauman, "Sitting Time and All-Cause Mortality Risk in 222,497 Australian Adults," *Archives of Internal Medicine* (2012): 172(6):494–500. http://archinte.jamanetwork.com/article.aspx?articleid=1108810

[1895] Ibid.

[1896] Ibid.

[1897] Donald D. Harrison, Sanghak O. Harrison, Arthur C. Croft, Deed E. Harrison, Stephan J. Troyanovich, "Sitting Bio-mechanics Part I: Review of the Literature," *Journal of Manipulative and Physiological Therapeutics* 22, no. 9 (November 1999), 594–609. http://www.sciencedirect.com/science/article/pii /S0161475499700205

[1898] Stuart M. McGill, "The Biomechanics of Low Back Injury: Implications on Current Practice in Industry and the Clinic," *Journal of Biomechanics* 30, no. 5 (May 1997): 465–75. http://www.sciencedirect .com/science/article/pii/S0021929096001728

[1899] E. Grandjean, W. Hünting, "Ergonomics of posture," 135–40. http://www.sciencedirect.com/science/article/pii/0003687077900023

[1900] Ibid.

[1901] Megan Teychenne, et al., "The Association between Sedentary Behaviour and Risk of Anxiety: a Systematic Review," *BMC Public Health* 15 (June 19, 2015): 513.

[1902] *American Journal of Epidemiology*, 2010, as cited in "The Real Effects of Technology on Your Health," www.everydayhealth.com/emotional-health/internet-addiction/real-effects-technology-on-your-health/

on radio-frequency radiation and in 91% of the 229 studies on static fields and extremely low frequency electromagnetic fields.[1903] The adverse effects found in these studies include: "cancer, Alzheimer's, ALS (Lou Gehrig's Disease), autism, male infertility, miscarriage, insomnia, allergic and inflammatory responses, heart palpitations and arrhythmias, memory loss, concentration/attention issues, and more."[1904] Furthermore, some studies suggest that the radiation from Wi-Fi can cause interruption of the brain glucose metabolism, increased permeability of the blood-brain barrier, interruption of cell metabolism, and breaks in DNA chains.[1905]

One final way the internet can harm our physical health is through a phenomenon called "email apnea" or "screen apnea." Linda Stone, a researcher and former executive at Apple and Microsoft, found that most people (about eighty percent) unconsciously hold their breath or breathe shallowly when responding to email or texting. This is serious because, according to research by Dr. Margaret Chesney and Dr. David Anderson:

> Holding one's breath contributes to stress-related diseases and disturbs the body's balance of oxygen, carbon dioxide, and nitric oxide, which help keep the immune system strong, fight infection, and mediate inflammation. It can affect our well-being and our ability to work effectively. Shallow breathing can also trigger a sympathetic nervous system "fight or flight" response. If we stay in this state of emergency breathing and hyperarousal for extended periods of time, it can not only impact sleep, memory, and learning, but also exacerbate anxiety and depression.[1906]

Fortunately, there are some ways to mitigate the physiological harm caused by the internet. To protect your eyes from strain when working with screens, the American Academy of Ophthalmology recommends:

> Sit about 25 inches (arm's length from the computer screen). Reduce screen glare by using a matte screen filter if needed. Take regular breaks using the "20-20-20" rule; every 20 minutes shift your eyes to look at an object at least 20 feet away for at least 20 seconds. When your eyes feel dry, use artificial tears to refresh them. Adjust your room lighting and try increasing the contrast on your screen to reduce eye strain.[1907]

[1903] See www.bioinitiative.org/wp-content/uploads/2019/08/Lai-Neuro-Percent

[1904] See www.greenwavefilters.com/electropollution-and-health

[1905] https://emfacademy.com/wifi-radiation-everything-need-know/

[1906] www.psychologytoday.com/us/blog/the-art-now/201411/email-apnea

[1907] www.aao.org/eye-health/tips-prevention/are-computer-glasses-worth-it

To help keep a healthy posture, it is best to mount the digital screen at or slightly below eye level.[1908] It is also helpful to shift periodically between standing and sitting, but standing most of the time.[1909] Adjustable-height desks allow one to work while standing or sitting, and anti-fatigue standing mats enable one to stand for long periods of time while also improving blood circulation and reducing muscle strain.[1910]

Screen apnea can be avoided by being conscious of your breathing and by acquiring the habit of breathing deeply with your diaphragm. The effects of exposure to electromagnetic radiation can be somewhat reduced by keeping electronic devices as far away from your body as possible and by keeping your body electrically grounded when using them.[1911]

iii)   Psychological Harm

The third category of harm ensuing from internet usage is *psychological.* Specifically, the internet harms our mental health by leading to depression, reducing our ability to empathize, increasing stress, impoverishing the quality of human connections, reducing productivity, and encouraging addictions. This section will address each of these issues.

While it is true that the internet does enable people to communicate more, studies have shown that this form of communication is too shallow to satisfy our need for human connection. One such study by the University of Michigan found that "frequent phone calls, emails, and other types of communication had no effect on [reducing] a person's risk for depression,"[1912] whereas having face-to-face interactions regularly does reduce the likelihood for depression. Since these healthy face-to-face interactions are increasingly being replaced by shallower digital communications, the result is increasing levels of depression in modern society.

Sherry Turkle pointed out several advantages of face-to-face conversations as opposed to digital ones:

> Humans require authentic, face-to-face connections to understand and relate to each other. Digital communication does not provide the vulnerability and real-time responsiveness required for key social abilities to manifest.... [Many studies] demonstrate that cell phones diminish conversations' topical depth, length, and corresponding feelings of closeness, empathy, and trust.[1913]
>
> Face-to-face conversation unfolds slowly. It teaches patience. We attend to tone and nuance. When we communicate on our digital devices, we learn different habits. As we ramp up the volume and velocity of our online connections, we want immediate

---

[1908] See www.healthycomputing.com/office/setup/monitor

[1909] See www.ehstoday.com/health/article/21915080/standing-at-work-the-good-the-bad-and-the-ugly

[1910] See www.ehstoday.com/health/article/21915379/new-study-confirms-benefits-of-antifatigue-mats and www.flexispot.com/spine-care-center/yes-you-should-use-a-standing-mat-heres-why/

[1911] See www.ncbi.nlm.nih.gov/pmc/articles/PMC3265077/ and www.pubmed.ncbi.nlm.nih.gov/27454187/

[1912] www.huffpost.com/entry/depression-in-person-email-phone_n_56127e6be4b0dd85030c8586

[1913] http://www.supersummary.com/reclaiming-conversation/summary/

answers. In order to get them, we ask simpler questions; we dumb down our communications, even on the most important matters.[1914]

Atsushi Senju, a cognitive neuroscientist … [showed] that the parts of the brain that allow us to process another person's feelings and intentions are activated by eye contact. Emoticons on texts and emails, Senju found, don't have the same effect. He says, "A richer mode of communication is possible right after making eye contact. It amplifies your ability to compute all the signals so you are able to read the other person's brain."[1915]

When you speak to people in person, you're forced to recognize their full human reality, which is where empathy begins.[1916]

Not only does internet communication encourage superficial relationships, but it also easily leads to misunderstandings. Researchers asked participants in a study to send either serious or sarcastic email to others. While 80% of email senders thought their tone could be readily identified, recipients correctly identified the tone only half the time. Even worse, the recipients believed they could accurately interpret the sender's tone 90% of the time. Overconfidence in our own ability to communicate and interpret emotional tone via email can lead us to take serious offense when none is intended. Furthermore, because email is rapid and we cannot see the immediate reaction of the recipient, misinterpretations can lead to hasty, tactless responses.[1917] Yet if we don't respond quickly enough to an email, we run the risk of offending the sender. A 2006 Cisco research paper concluded that failing to respond to a sender can lead to a swift breakdown in trust.[1918]

Although using the internet enables tasks to be done faster, there are invisible costs for this speed. Dr. Larchet observes:

It is by no means sure that the media [e.g., the internet] make us gain time. Shortening time makes it pass more quickly, so we have less of it, as each activity is lived less intensely. Moreover, the new media multiply the tasks we may perform, leaving us too little time for all of them…. By not having to wait, we gain time; but we lose the psychological and spiritual benefits of waiting: patience, the increase of desire and joy, and the feelings that come from delayed satisfaction. We feel more joy when we arrive at a mountaintop on foot than when we are just left there by a helicopter.[1919]

[1914] Turkle, *Reclaiming Conversation,* 35.

[1915] Ibid., 170–71.

[1916] http://www.nytimes.com/2015/10/04/books/review/jonathan-franzen-reviews-sherry-turkle-reclaiming-conversation.html

[1917] Justin, Kruger; Nicholas Epley, Jason Parker, and Zhi-Wen Ng, "Egocentrism over Email: Can We Communicate as Well as We Think?" *Journal of Personality and Social Psychology* 89, no. 6 (December 2005): 925–36.

[1918] As cited in John Freeman, *The Tyranny of Email: The Four-Thousand Year Journey to Your Inbox* (New York: Scribner, 2009), 7.

[1919] Larchet, *The New Media Epidemic,* 24.

Not only are we losing the joy of deeper satisfaction, but we are also being poisoned and spoiled by the instant gratification of having immediate access to almost anything. Elder Aimilianos observed: "Anyone who is able to satisfy his needs—and especially if he can do so immediately—becomes very callous towards God and his fellow man."[1920] Dr. Larchet explained the mechanism behind this phenomenon:

> In human life, there is no pleasure without pain, no joy without sadness, no happiness without suffering, no enjoyment without frustration, and no satisfaction without expectation. These things are well known to psychologists, and to writers and mystics. The intensity of joy depends on the intensity of desire, which in turn depends on its distance in space or time from its object. A world where, in reality or virtually, the magic of the Internet provides everything at once becomes a world bereft of true desire, a world without pleasure or joy, without happiness or enjoyment.[1921]

A further drawback of the internet's speed is increased stress. Dr. Larchet explained:

> Any request that reaches its destination quickly requires an equally rapid reply. This insistence on an instant reaction, implicit in modern communications, clearly stresses the person at the receiving end; but it also stresses the sender, for he no longer has the leisure to reflect, which flowed from the latency of old-fashioned communication. The stress rises with the number of requests coming in from the new means of communication, sometimes all at once. Letters sent by the postal service could be considered at leisure, and answered calmly at a favorable moment. The time needed to write, and the time and expense needed to post the letter limited messages to the essential, not so with emails, text messages, and tweets. Their minimalist style allows their proliferation, swamping those who receive them. Replying to all of them correctly is so hard as to be often impossible, and true communication is paralyzed.[1922]

> [In the days before email] once a letter was written, there was always a delay before it was posted, until the evening or the next morning. This allowed the writer time to re-read it, to reflect and repent, and to correct and improve it where necessary. The ease and speed with which emails can be sent encourages sending the first draft without any pause for reflection.... In the 1960s it was said that these machines would enable a civilization of leisure. But we now see that this was an illusion.[1923]

> The idea that IT [information technology] and modern communication technology would free up our time has also been shown up as a mirage. Everything is faster, but the amount of information to be handled has grown just as much, so, in the end, there is no benefit.[1924]

> [The internet] encourages the habit of speed, which becomes second nature in psychological life. It creates dependency, impatience, and boredom and disquiet and anxiety when things are slower and do not happen immediately.[1925]

1920 Γέροντος Αἰμιλιανοῦ, *Νηπτικὴ Ζωὴ καὶ Ἀσκητικοὶ Κανόνες,* 329.

1921 Larchet, *The New Media Epidemic,* 29.

1922 Ibid., 30.

1923 Ibid., 31–32.

1924 Ibid., 32.

1925 Ibid., 28.

Speed, instant access, and just-in-time are the touchstones of the new media and connected man; and speeding up each task along with multitasking creates a way of life with no dead time. But paradoxically, eliminating dead time removes time for living. Man cannot live to the full when he stifles his consciousness with unceasing activity. No more can he live fully in the giddiness of speed, or by surfing the web where he forgets himself, cut off from reality.... Man absolutely needs silence, solitude, and calm to maintain his equilibrium and to be fulfilled. Dead time is where man can take care of himself, can reflect freely, meditate, contemplate, and pray. This is the time he can devote to those dear to him and nourish a true relationship with them.[1926]

Scientific studies have reached the same conclusion that we have a fundamental need for quiet. Nicholas Carr wrote:

A series of psychological studies over the past twenty years has revealed that after spending time in a quiet rural setting, close to nature, people exhibit greater attentiveness, stronger memory, and generally improved cognition. Their brains become both calmer and sharper.... The reason ... is that when people aren't being bombarded by external stimuli, their brains can, in effect, relax. They no longer have to tax their working memories by processing a stream of bottom-up distractions. The resulting state of contemplativeness strengthens their ability to control their mind.... On the internet [there is] no peaceful spot where contemplativeness can work its restorative magic. There is only the endless, mesmerizing buzz of the urban street. The stimulations of the Net ... overwhelm all quieter modes of thought. One of the greatest dangers we face as we automate the work of our minds, as we cede control over the flow of our thoughts and memories to a powerful electronic system, is ... a slow erosion of our humanness and our humanity.[1927]

Solitude is a key ingredient for psychological health. The decades-long research of Sherry Turkle on the social effects of digital communication led her to conclude: "The capacity for solitude is a cornerstone for the capacity for relationship. Only when we can gather ourselves can we turn to others and really hear what they have to say, really hear who they are.... If you don't teach your children to be alone, they'll only know how to be lonely."[1928]

In order to achieve greater solitude, we must distance ourselves from distractions. Commenting on one of Plato's writings, William Powers points out:

In *Phaedrus*, Plato establishes a basic principle on which to build a new way of thinking about digital connectedness: In a busy world, the path to depth and fulfillment begins with distance ... [because] when we're alone, our thoughts and feelings are oriented inward, and experience tends to be relatively quiet and slow. In contrast, in a crowd—whether physical or virtual—our orientation is more external, simply because there's more happening, more demands on our attention.[1929]

[1926] Ibid., 34.

[1927] Nicholas Carr, *The Shallows* (New York: W. W. Norton, 2010), 219–20.

[1928] "The Empathy Gap: Digital Culture Needs What Talk Therapy Offers," www.psychotherapynetworker .org/magazine/article/1051/the-empathy-gap

[1929] William Powers, *Hamlet's Blackberry,* 97–98.

The more we connect [online], the more our thoughts lean outward. There's a pre-occupation with what's going on "out there" in the bustling otherworld, rather than "in here" with yourself and those right around you. What was once exterior and far away is now easily accessible, and this carries a sense of obligation or duty.... In addition, outwardness offers something more potent than mere duty: self-affirmation, demonstrable evidence of one's existence and impact on the world. In less-connected times, human beings were forced to shape their own interior sense of identity and worth—to become self-sufficient. By virtue of its interactivity, the digital medium is a source of constant confirmation that, yes, you do indeed exist and matter. However, the external validation provided by incoming messages and the number of times one's name appears in search results is not as trustworthy or stable as the kind that comes from inside.[1930]

The twentieth-century philosopher and theologian Paul Tillich pointed out that our language "has created the word 'loneliness' to express the pain of being alone. And it has created the word 'solitude' to express the glory of being alone."[1931] Commenting on this, William Powers added:

The best kind of aloneness is expansive and generous. To enjoy your own company is to be at ease not just with yourself but with everyone and everything in the universe. When you're inwardly content, you don't need others to prop you up, so you can think about them more freely and generously. Paradoxically enough, separation is the way to empathy. In solitude we meet not just ourselves but all other selves, and it turns out we hardly knew them.[1932]

The state of distraction fostered by the internet harms even our ability to show compassion. Sherry Turkle wrote: "In 2010, a team at the University of Michigan ... put together the findings of 72 studies conducted over a 30-year period and found a 40 percent decline in the markers for empathy (measured as the ability to recognize and identify the feelings of others) among college students. Most of the decline took place after 2000, which led the researchers to link it to the new presence of digital communications."[1933] Likewise, a study done in 2009 found a connection between distractions from digital technology and a loss of empathy. It concluded:

The more distracted we become, the less able we are to experience the subtlest, most distinctively human forms of empathy, compassion, and other emotions.... It would not be rash to suggest that as the Net reroutes our vital paths and diminishes our capacity for contemplation, it is altering the depth of our emotions as well as our thoughts.[1934]

[1930] Ibid., 47.

[1931] Paul Tillich, *The Eternal Now,* Lyceum Editions, vol. 114 (New York: Scribner Library, 1963), 11.

[1932] William Powers, *Hamlet's Blackberry,* 42.

[1933] www.psychotherapynetworker.org/magazine/article/1051/the-empathy-gap See also Turkle, *Reclaiming Conversation,* 171.

[1934] As cited in Nicholas Carr, *The Shallows,* 221.

Dr. Larchet explained how this happens:

> Certain analysts have found that the emotions of those who use the new media are enhanced, but their affections, especially their powers of empathy and compassion, are diminished.... This is due to their [i.e., the new media's] speed, and the rapid reactions required of their users, and to the near endemic state of distraction that they provoke.... [Studies] show that normally, from his own experience of physical pain, a person is able to feel compassion immediately for another who suffers in the same way. But if he is engaged in rapid activity, he is unable to feel such emotions, since they need time to develop. According to one of these researchers, even personal morality is compromised by most activities with the new media.[1935]

Another mechanism makes online communication a breeding ground for negative emotions. The techno-philosopher Jaron Lanier explained that "the primacy of anger and outrage online is ... an unavoidable feature of the medium: In an open marketplace for attention, darker emotions attract more eyeballs than positive and constructive thoughts. For heavy internet users, repeated interaction with this darkness can become a source of draining negativity."[1936]

Using the internet even leads to depression. The "Monitoring the Future" survey found in teenagers a direct and strong correlation between screen time and unhappiness.[1937] Other studies on college students[1938] and adults[1939] found a similar correlation between internet use and unhappiness. Several longitudinal studies indicate that it is the internet which is causing the unhappiness rather than vice versa.[1940]

Many people have personally experienced how the internet strengthens addictions and is in itself addicting. Dr. Larchet elaborates on these two aspects:

> Among the worst problems caused by the new media are addictions and dependencies. In extreme cases, which are in fact quite common, the media act as a drug: many people today are driven to use them in the same way as others are driven to use traditional narcotics and are dependent in the same way.[1941]
>
> When speaking of addiction, "cyber-addiction" must be distinguished from "cyber-assisted addiction." *Cyber-addiction* is an addiction to certain means of communication, especially the Internet and social media. Those who suffer from *cyber-assisted addiction* are not addicted to the new media themselves, but to the realities to

---

[1935] Larchet, *The New Media Epidemic,* 101–2.

[1936] As paraphrased in Cal Newport, *Digital Minimalism,* xii.

[1937] www.theatlantic.com/magazine/archive/2017/09/has-the-smartphone-destroyed-a-generation/534198/

[1938] M. G. Hunt, C. Lipson, & J. Young, "No More FOMO: Limiting Social Media Decreases Loneliness and Depression," *Journal of Social and Clinical Psychology* 37 (2018): 751–68.

[1939] Sherman, L. E., Mina, M., & Greenfield, P. M., "The Facebook Experiment: Quitting Facebook Leads to Higher Levels of Well-being," *Cyberpsychology, Bahavior, and Social Networking* 19 (2016): 661–66.

[1940] https://worldhappiness.report/ed/2019/the-sad-state-of-happiness-in-the-united-states-and-the-role-of-digital-media/

[1941] Larchet, *The New Media Epidemic,* 105.

which they give quick, easy, and unlimited access: online games, sex, compulsive purchases, etc. ... As the psychiatrists Michel Hautefeuille and Dan Velea have remarked: "it [the Internet] is the dream tool for someone drawn to addiction: it can provide whatever attracts the addict."[1942]

The worst kinds of addiction ... cause other tasks and relationships, which make up social life, to be abandoned for much of the day.... The worst kinds of addiction to the new media should not blind us to its milder forms that still have negative effects on psychological life. Nowadays, many users of the new media are addicts without realizing it. They tend to see their dependency as unimportant compared to the worst addictions.... Addiction in all its forms is marked by dependency of different degrees. It consists of a more or less irresistible attraction that indicates a more or less pressing need whose satisfaction brings a more or less conscious pleasure. If left unsatisfied it brings frustration, a feeling of missing out that gives rise to a more or less intense feeling of mental suffering. Apart from these inner gauges, the strength of addiction can be measured by the degree to which it degrades adaption to society and presence therein, first in the family, then in school or work, and finally in relations in general.[1943]

Social media have actually been designed to foster behavioral addictions. As Cal Newport explained:

People don't succumb to [spending inordinate amounts of time on] screens because they're lazy, but instead because billions of dollars have been invested to make this outcome inevitable ... by the high-end device companies and attention economy conglomerates who discovered there are vast fortunes to be made in a culture dominated by gadgets and apps....

Two forces ... repeatedly came up in my own research on how tech companies encourage behavioral addiction: *intermittent positive reinforcement* and *the drive for social approval.*... [Psychological studies have shown] that rewards delivered unpredictably are far more enticing than those delivered with a known pattern. Something about unpredictability releases more dopamine—a key neurotransmitter for regulating our sense of craving.... As whistleblower Tristan Harris explains: "Apps and websites sprinkle intermittent variable rewards all over their products because it's good for business." ... Sean Parker, the founding president of Facebook ... [admitted]: "The thought process that went into building these applications, Facebook being the first of them, ... was all about: 'How do we consume as much of your time and conscious attention as possible?' And that means that we need to sort of give you a little dopamine hit every once in a while, because someone liked or commented on a photo or a post or whatever." ...

The second force that encourages behavioral addiction [is] the drive for social approval. As Adam Alter writes: "We're social beings who can't ever completely ignore what other people think of us.... The technology industry has become adept at exploiting this instinct for approval."[1944]

[1942] Ibid., 106–7.

[1943] Ibid., 107.

[1944] Cal Newport, *Digital Minimalism,* 9, 17–24.

These addictive properties of new technologies are not accidents, but instead carefully engineered design features.... Compulsive use, in this context, is not the result of a character flaw, but instead the realization of a massively profitable business plan.[1945]

In other words, internet companies are taking advantage of the same psychological weakness that casinos do. Whereas casinos use intermittent positive reinforcement to grab our money, the internet uses it to grab our attention and our time.

Even former executives of Facebook admit that its social media platform is harming people. Chamath Palihapitiya, a former vice-president for user growth at Facebook said: "The short-term, dopamine-driven feedback loops that we have created are destroying how society works. No civil discourse, no cooperation, misinformation, mistruth."[1946] Sean Parker, the founding president of Facebook considers himself "something of a conscientious objector" to using social media, for they "exploit a vulnerability in human psychology" by creating a "social-validation feedback loop.... It literally changes your relationship with society, with each other. It probably interferes with productivity in weird ways. God only knows what it's doing to our children's brains."[1947]

One thing it might be doing to children's brains is causing ADHD, according to Simon Sinek, who said: "The number of children diagnosed with attention deficit hyperactivity disorder (ADHD) shot up 66 percent between 2000 and 2010 and continued to rise between 2011 and 2014. Why the sudden and huge spike in a frontal lobe dysfunction over the course of a decade? ... What I believe is likely happening is that more young people are developing an addiction to distraction, or rather, to the dopamine-producing effects of the digital technologies and online activities that are distracting them.[1948]

Digital technologies are creating attention deficits not only in children but also in adults. William Powers remarked:

> Novel psychological conditions and behaviors that some experts attribute to digital overload ... include attention deficit trait.... According to Edward Hallowell, the psychiatrist who first described it ... symptoms include "distractibility, restlessness, a sense of 'gotta go, gotta rush, gotta run around' and impulsive decision-making, because you have so many things to do." Many other [psychological] conditions have been linked to [information] overload, including continuous partial attention, defined as the state of mind in which "most of one's attention is on a primary task, but where one is also monitoring several background tasks just in case something more important or interesting comes up."[1949]

[1945] Ibid., 16–17, 24.

[1946] www.theguardian.com/technology/2017/dec/11/facebook-former-executive-ripping-society-apart

[1947] www.theguardian.com/technology/2017/nov/09/facebook-sean-parker-vulnerability-brain-psychology

[1948] Simon Sinek, *Leaders Eat Last,* 258.

[1949] William Powers, *Hamlet's Blackberry,* 50–51.

Not only does the internet lead to addictions, but it also reduces one's freedom in general. Dr. Larchet observes:

> Because they give everyone the power to communicate immediately and permanently with the whole world, the new media seem to remove two major constraints on our freedom: space and time.... However, as we have seen in the preceding chapters, the new media place a real restraint on personal freedom at several levels: political, through the surveillance and propaganda that they enable; economic, through the surveillance and exploitation of workers that they permit; and social, through the abolition of the boundary between public and private life that they bring about.
>
> Addiction to the new media, be it cyber-dependence or cyber-assisted dependence, is another restriction on freedom in addition to the above. It is worse, since it restricts inner freedom, not simply outer freedom. It gives rise to the same kind of bondage as the passions, both in the modern psychological sense and in the spiritual sense. For these diminish the conscience and the will of the person. They subject the person to the strong attraction of external factors that appear seductive, but in reality are insubstantial, imaginary in the case of the classic passions and virtual for those that attract to the new media. They also act on him through external mechanisms that marshal his energy and disperse his powers in a stream without substance or consistency.[1950]

iv) Cognitive Harm

Finally, using the internet impairs our *cognitive* health by: diminishing our ability to concentrate and think deeply, restricting our inner freedom, hampering creativity, encouraging mental laziness, and leading to cognitive overload. We shall explore each of these problems in this section. Harm of this nature is particularly insidious because it is not immediately evident.

Just as St. Paisios of the Holy Mountain observed that modern appliances make us physically lazy,[1951] Dr. Larchet observes how the internet harms our mental health by enabling the mind to become lazy:

> Computers have changed memory into a mere index, and intelligence into the simple capacity of using this index. In fact, it leaves the memory empty of any significant content.... Rather than memorize information, we now store it digitally and just remember what we stored....
>
> Because this external store of information exists we refer to it every time we need something stored on the web, and so we no longer use our own faculty of memory and recall....
>
> With calculators integrated into every smartphone we often become incapable of the simplest operations of arithmetic, let alone the more complex such as long division or the extraction of square roots that once could be done by anyone who had finished primary school....

[1950] Larchet, *The New Media Epidemic,* 108–9.

[1951] Vid. footnote #1535 on page 287.

This leaves a chasm between our modern digital civilization and the societies of old who valued memory so much that some of them deified it, like the ancient Greeks with their goddess Mnemosyne.[1952]

Nicholas Carr explains the mechanism by which the brain becomes weaker through using the internet:

The extensive activity in the brains of surfers [on the internet] also points to why deep reading and other acts of sustained concentration become so difficult online. The need to evaluate links and make related navigational choices, while also processing a multiplicity of fleeting sensory stimuli, requires constant mental coordination and decision making, distracting the brain from the work of interpreting text or other information. Whenever we, as readers, come upon a link, we have to pause, for at least a split second, to allow our prefrontal cortex to evaluate whether or not we should click on it. The redirection of our mental resources, from reading words to making judgments, may be imperceptible to us—our brains are quick—but it's been shown to impede comprehension and retention, particularly when it's repeated frequently. As the executive functions of the prefrontal cortex kick in, our brains become not only exercised but overtaxed.... In reading online ... we sacrifice the facility that makes deep reading possible.... Our ability to make the rich mental connections that form when we read deeply and without distraction remains largely disengaged.[1953]

The key to memory consolidation is attentiveness. Storing explicit memories and, equally important, forming connections between them requires strong mental concentration, amplified by repetition or by intense intellectual or emotional engagement. The sharper the attention, the sharper the memory.... If we're unable to attend to the information in our working memory, the information lasts only as long as the neurons that hold it maintain their electric charge—a few seconds at best.... The influx of competing messages that we receive whenever we go online not only overloads our working memory; it makes it much harder for our frontal lobes to concentrate our attention on any one thing. The [neurological] process of memory consolidation can't even get started. And, thanks once again to the plasticity of our neuronal pathways, the more we use the Web, the more we train our brain to be distracted—to process information very quickly and very efficiently but without sustained attention. That helps explain why many of us find it hard to concentrate even when we're away from our computers. Our brains become adept at forgetting, inept at remembering.[1954]

As the time we spend hopping across links crowds out the time we devote to quiet reflection and contemplation, the circuits that support those old intellectual functions and pursuits weaken and begin to break apart.[1955]

This means that even if we are reading spiritual texts online, we will be unable to derive the full benefit from them due to the distractions. Moreover, these distractions are compromising the very purpose of reading envisioned by St. Peter of Damascus, who said: "The

---

[1952] Larchet, *The New Media Epidemic,* 126–27.

[1953] Nicholas Carr, *The Shallows,* 122.

[1954] Ibid., 193.

[1955] Ibid., 120.

purpose of spiritual reading is to keep the intellect from distraction and restlessness, for this is the first step toward salvation."[1956]

Dr. Larchet has pointed out other negative aspects of reading from a screen:

> Traditionally, reading was done slowly. The reader took his time. In contrast, reading on the screen is done quickly at a speed imposed by the rhythm of the media, or encouraged by the ambiance of rapidity and reactivity that is theirs, and by the physical and mental frenzy with which they are most often used.... The physical reality of a book gives weight and reality to what is read, while the dematerialized book, read on a digital reader or on-screen as text, makes the [content of the] book seem insignificant. It makes the text lose some of its reality and density, leaving it light and inconsequential.[1957]

A further problem is that reading online enables only superficial learning. Nicholas Carr wrote: "Dozens of studies by psychologists, neurobiologists, educators, and Web designers point to the same conclusion: when we go online, we enter an environment that promotes cursory reading, hurried and distracted thinking, and superficial learning. ... The Net delivers precisely the kind of sensory and cognitive stimuli—repetitive, intensive, interactive, addictive—that have been shown to result in strong and rapid alterations in brain circuits and functions."[1958]

Moreover, a study in 2003 showed that "the digital environment tends to encourage people to explore many topics extensively, but at a more superficial level," and that "hyperlinks [in the text they are reading] distract people from reading and thinking deeply."[1959] As Dr. Larchet wrote:

> Using the new media weakens our ability to reflect, both quantitatively and qualitatively. Reflection is not simply thought, a flow of descriptions, images, and ideas. It is an ordered process that involves the intuition backed by reason, with its logical categories and its rules of organization and argument, and by a critical spirit.... It means stepping back to a certain distance, and taking time. The new media work almost without a pause, pouring forth a continuous flow of information that does not allow our thought to pause and examine itself. Our mental powers go with the flow, almost wholly reduced to dependence and passivity.... Urgency is the hallmark of the new media. Messages must be sent quickly.... This speed prevents reflection, which generally needs time, except in the exceptionally rare case of real urgency.[1960]

A further drawback of internet use is that it naturally encourages the habit of multitasking and frequently shifting our attention. This taxes our mental resources because every time

---

[1956] Palmer, Sherrard, Ware, *The Philokalia,* vol. 3, 155.

[1957] Larchet, *The New Media Epidemic,* 121–22.

[1958] Nicholas Carr, *The Shallows,* 116–17.

[1959] Ziming Liu, "Reading Behavior in the Digital Environment," *Journal of Documentation* 61, no. 6 (2005): 700–12.

[1960] Larchet, *The New Media Epidemic,* 124.

we shift our attention, our brain has to reorient itself. As Maggie Jackson explains in *Distracted,* her book on multitasking, "the brain takes time to change goals, remember the rules needed for the new task, and block out cognitive interference from the previous, still-vivid activity."[1961] A moderate estimate is that "unnecessary interruptions and consequent recovery time now eat up an average of 28 percent of the working day."[1962] The American Psychological Association declared more grimly that "shifting between tasks can cost as much as 40 percent of someone's productive time."[1963] The economic cost of these interruptions in the corporate world was calculated to be $900 billion dollars a year in 2009.[1964] As for how damaging interruptions are for the monastic world and our inner world, this is harder to quantify. Nevertheless, the following points can give us some idea of this.

Nicholas Carr observed: "Many studies have shown that switching between just two tasks can add substantially to our cognitive load, impeding our thinking and increasing the likelihood that we'll overlook or misinterpret important information."[1965] William Powers added: "Recovering focus can take ten to twenty times the length of the interruption. So a one-minute interruption could require fifteen minutes of recovery time. And that's only if you go right back to the original task; jam other tasks in between and the recovery time lengthens further."[1966] Furthermore, Dr. Larchet observes: "On the Net, where we routinely juggle not just two but several mental tasks, the switching costs [of multitasking] are all the higher.... [This] accumulated nervous fatigue leads to decompensations, which can end in depression, but more often take the form of burn out."[1967]

These interruptions turn into a self-perpetuating cycle, as Simon Sinek points out:

> The more external interruptions we experience, like a text or an e-mail alert, the more we engage in self-interruption, that is, interrupting ourselves mid-task to check our e-mail or phones without any notification from a ring or a bing. In other words, interruptions lead to more interruptions. And more interruptions not only reduce opportunities for focused, deep thought, but they also delay the completion of work and increase feelings of pressure and stress.[1968]

[1961] Maggie Jackson, *Distracted: The Erosion of Attention and the Coming Dark Age* (New York, Prometheus, 2008), 79.

[1962] William Powers, *Hamlet's Blackberry,* 60.

[1963] As cited in Simon Sinek, *Leaders Eat Last,* 257.

[1964] Vid. William Powers, *Hamlet's Blackberry,* 62.

[1965] Nicholas Carr, *The Shallows,* 133.

[1966] William Powers, *Hamlet's Blackberry,* 58–59.

[1967] Larchet, *The New Media Epidemic,* 104.

[1968] Simon Sinek, *Leaders Eat Last,* 257.

Part of the problem is that we are like the first-century Athenians who "spend their time in nothing other than telling or hearing something new."[1969] In other words, we are addicted to the short-term pleasure of hearing new things as opposed to appreciating the lasting and satisfying pleasure of what is important. As Nicholas Carr wrote:

> The near-continuous stream of new information pumped out by the Web also plays to our natural tendency to "vastly overvalue what happens to us *right now,*" as Union College psychologist Christopher Chabris explains. We crave the new even when we know that "the new is more often trivial than essential." And so we ask the Internet to keep interrupting us, in ever more and different ways. We willingly accept the loss of concentration and focus, the division of our attention and the fragmentation of our thoughts, in return for the wealth of compelling or at least diverting information we receive. Tuning out is not an option many of us would consider.[1970]

Research by Clifford Nass has revealed that constant attention switching online has a lasting negative effect on your brain. Summarizing his research, he said: "People who multitask all the time can't filter out irrelevancy. They can't manage a working memory. They're chronically distracted. They initiate much larger parts of their brains that are irrelevant to the task at hand.... They're pretty much mental wrecks.... They've developed habits of mind that make it impossible for them to be laser-focused."[1971] Commenting on this finding, Cal Newport wrote: "If every moment of potential boredom in your life … is relieved with a quick glance at your smartphone, then your brain has likely been rewired to a point where, like the 'mental wrecks' in Nass's research, it's not ready for deep work—even if you regularly schedule time to practice this concentration."[1972] What this means for monastics is that the more we indulge in using the internet as a way to relax, the harder we will find it to concentrate in prayer, which should be our primary work.

Although multitasking appears to increase our productivity, what we are really doing is "learning to be skillful at a superficial level,"[1973] according to David Myer, a neuroscientist and leading expert on multitasking. Another neuroscientist, Jordan Grafman, explains that improving our ability to multitask hampers our ability to think deeply and creatively: "The more you multitask, the less deliberative you become; the less able to think

---

[1969] Acts 17:21.

[1970] Nicholas Carr, *The Shallows,* 134.

[1971] As quoted in Cal Newport, *Deep Work: Rules for Focused Success in a Distracted World* (New York: Grand Central Publishing, 2016), 158.

[1972] Ibid., 159.

[1973] As quoted in Sharon Begley and Janeen Interlandi, "The Dumbest Generation? Don't Be Dumb," *Newsweek,* June 2, 2008.

and reason out a problem."[1974] He argues that you become more likely to rely on conventional ideas and solutions than to challenge them with original lines of thought.[1975]

Creativity is also hampered by the distracted state created by the internet, as Nicholas Carr explains: "The constant distractedness that the Net encourages ... is very different from the kind of temporary, purposeful diversion of our mind that refreshes our thinking when we're weighing a decision. The Net's cacophony of stimuli short-circuits both conscious and unconscious thought, preventing our minds from thinking either deeply or creatively."[1976]

Using the internet also reduces the mind's ability to focus because of its continual interruptions. Nicholas Carr wrote:

> The Net seizes our attention only to scatter it. We focus intensively on the medium itself, on the flickering screen, but we're distracted by the medium's rapid-fire delivery of competing messages and stimuli.[1977]
>
> Whenever we turn on our computer, we are plunged into an ecosystem of interruption technologies.[1978]
>
> The Net is, by design, an interruption system, a machine geared for dividing attention. ... Psychological research long ago proved what most of us know from experience: frequent interruptions scatter our thoughts, weaken our memory, and make us tense and anxious. The more complex the train of thought we're involved in, the greater the impairment the distractions cause.[1979]

Dr. Larchet added: "The worst damage caused by the new media is to the faculty of attention, and consequently, to concentration. Their power to distract and disperse make attention more and more difficult, be it to one's own tasks, to others, or to God."[1980]

William Powers elaborates on how digital devices both help and harm the mind:

> Of the mind's many aptitudes, the most remarkable is its power of association, the ability to see new relationships among things.... Digital devices are, in one sense, a tremendous gift to the associative process because they link us to so many sources of information. The potential they hold out for creative insights and synthesis is breathtaking. The best human creativity, however, happens only when we have the time and mental space to take a new thought and follow it wherever it leads. William James once contrasted "the sustained attention of the genius, sticking to his subject for hours together," with the "commonplace mind" that flits from place to place. Geniuses are rare, but by using screens as we do now, constantly jumping around, we're ensuring

---

[1974] As quoted in Don Tapscott, *Grown Up Digital* (New York: McGraw-Hill, 2009), 108–9.

[1975] Nicholas Carr, *The Shallows,* 140.

[1976] Ibid., 119.

[1977] Ibid., 118.

[1978] Ibid., 91.

[1979] Ibid., 131, 132.

[1980] Larchet, *The New Media Epidemic,* 171.

that all of us have fewer ingenious moments and bring less associative creativity to whatever kind of work we do.[1981]

A further problem for the brain caused by internet usage is cognitive overload, which Nicholas Carr explains as follows:

Imagine filling a bathtub with a thimble; that's the challenge involved in transferring information from working memory into long-term memory. By regulating the velocity and intensity of information flow, media exert a strong influence on this process. When we read a book, the information faucet provides a steady drip, which we can control by the pace of our reading. Through our single-minded concentration on the text, we can transfer all or most of the information, thimbleful by thimbleful, into long-term memory and forge the rich associations essential to the creation of schemas. With the Net, we face many information faucets, all going full blast. Our little thimble overflows as we rush from one faucet to the next. We're able to transfer only a small portion of the information to long-term memory, and what we do transfer is a jumble of drops from different faucets, not a continuous, coherent stream from one source.

The information flowing into our working memory at any given moment is called our "cognitive load." When the load exceeds our mind's ability to store and process the information—when the water overflows the thimble—we're unable to retain the information or to draw connections with the information already stored in our long-term memory. We can't translate the new information into schemas. Our ability to learn suffers, and our understanding remains shallow. Because our ability to maintain our attention also depends on our working memory—"we have to remember what it is we are to concentrate on," as Torkel Klingberg says—a high cognitive load amplifies the distractedness we experience. When our brain is over-taxed, we find "distractions more distracting." (Some studies link attention deficit disorder, or ADD, to the overloading of working memory.) Experiments indicate that as we reach the limits of our working memory, it becomes harder to distinguish relevant information from irrelevant information, signal from noise. We become mindless consumers of data.

Difficulties in developing an understanding of a subject or a concept appear to be "heavily determined by working memory load," writes [John] Sweller, and the more complex the material we're trying to learn, the greater the penalty exacted by an overloaded mind. There are many possible sources of cognitive overload, but two of the most important, according to Sweller, are "extraneous problem-solving" and "divided attention." Those also happen to be two of the central features of the Net as an informational medium. Using the Net may, as Gary Small suggests, exercise the brain the way solving crossword puzzles does. But such intensive exercise, when it becomes our primary mode of thought, can impede deep learning and thinking. Try reading a book while doing a crossword puzzle; that's the intellectual environment of the Internet.[1982]

Another reason why interacting with screens is taxing on the brain is because they are unnatural. As William Powers explains:

Among researchers who study how humans interact with technology, there's a theory known as embodied interaction, which says that three-dimensional tools are easier on the mind in certain important ways. This makes intuitive sense. Think of a

---

[1981] William Powers, *Hamlet's Blackberry,* 60–61.

[1982] Nicholas Carr, *The Shallows,* 124–26.

screen with a dozen different documents open, all layered on top of one another, and what a pain it is to try to organize and keep track of them all at once, using just your clicker and keyboard. Sometimes you want to reach in there and grab them, but you can't. Reading and writing on screen, we expend a great deal of mental energy just navigating. Paper's tangibility allows the hands and fingers to take over much of the navigational burden, freeing the brain to think.[1983]

Being exposed to too much information has a detrimental effect on attention. As Herbert Simon, a Nobel laureate, observed: "What information consumes is rather obvious: it consumes the attention of its recipients. Hence a wealth of information creates a poverty of attention."[1984] St. Nicodemos of the Holy Mountain observed this same principle in the spiritual realm. He wrote:

> Just as it is necessary to guard the mind from ignorance, so is it equally necessary to protect it from the opposite, namely from too much knowledge and curiosity. For if we fill it with a quantity of information, ideas, and thoughts, not excluding such as are vain, unsuitable, and harmful, we deprive it of force, so that it is no longer able to understand clearly what is useful for our true self-correction and perfection. Therefore, in relation to the knowledge of earthly things, which is not indispensable, even if it is permissible, your attitude should be as of one already dead. Always collect your mind within yourself, with all the concentration you can, and keep it free of thoughts about all worldly things.[1985]

Considering that St. Nicodemos wrote this two centuries before the "information explosion" of the modern world,[1986] one can only imagine how much more he would have emphasized this point had he lived today.

It should not be too surprising that a powerful tool for the brain such as the internet also has grave, negative effects on the brain, for the philosopher Marshall McLuhan pointed out that our tools end up "numbing" whatever part of our body they "amplify."[1987] As explained by Nicholas Carr:

[1983] William Powers, *Hamlet's Blackberry,* 153–54.

[1984] As cited in Thomas H. Davenport and John C. Beck, *The Attention Economy: Understanding the New Currency of Business* (Boston: Harvard Business School Press, 2001), 1.

[1985] *Unseen Warfare: the* Spiritual Combat *and* Path to Paradise *of Lorenzo Scupoli, edited by Nicodemos of the Holy Mountain, and revised by Theophan the Recluse,* trans. E. Kadloubovsky and G. E. H. Palmer (New York: St. Vladimir's Seminary Press, 1978), 92–93.

[1986] The exponential increase of the *existence* of information is nothing new. Since the 15th century it has been doubling about every three decades, according to Rudolph Hanka of the University of Cambridge. Thus, the information available today is roughly 2^{18} greater (a 262,144-fold increase) than what it was in 1400. The average person's *consumption* of information, however, began increasing exponentially only in recent decades, primarily due to digital media. According to one study, "in 2008, people consumed three times as much information each day as they did in 1960" (www.nytimes.com/2010/06/07/techonology/07brain.html).

[1987] As quoted in Marshall McLuhan, *Understanding the Media: The Extensions of Man,* critical ed., ed. W. Terrence Gordon (Madera: Gingko Press, 2003), 63–70.

When we extend some part of ourselves artificially, we also distance ourselves from the amplified part and its natural functions. … [For example, farmers] lost some of their feel for the soil when they began using mechanical harrows and plows.… When we're behind the wheel of our car … we lose the walker's intimate connection to the land.… The tools of the mind amplify and in turn numb the most intimate, the most human, of our natural capacities—those for reason, perception, memory, emotion.[1988]

+ + +

Now that we have demonstrated how the internet harms us spiritually, physically, psychologically, and cognitively, we must concede that living in our modern world requires that we use the internet in order to function. Facing this predicament, Dr. Larchet concluded: "Our world is so organized that it is extremely hard to abstain entirely from the new media. Realistically, we must compromise. We can limit our use of the new media to what is essential for our way of life, especially for our work."[1989] Similarly, Elder Ephraim was not in favor of his monastics using the internet, but he allowed it only when it was absolutely necessary.

Cal Newport promotes a minimalistic solution to this problem that he explains as follows:

> **Digital Minimalism.** A philosophy of technology use in which you focus your online time on a small number of carefully selected and optimized activities that strongly support things you value, and then happily miss out on everything else.
>
> The so-called digital minimalists who follow this philosophy constantly perform implicitly cost-benefit analyses. If a new technology offers little more than a minor diversion or trivial convenience, the minimalist will ignore it.…
>
> Notice, this minimalist philosophy contrasts starkly with the maximalist philosophy that most people deploy by default—a mind-set in which *any* potential for benefit is enough to start using a technology that catches your attention. A maximalist is very uncomfortable with the idea that anyone might miss out on something that's the least bit interesting or valuable.…
>
> [In contrast, digital minimalists] believe that the best digital life is formed by carefully curating their tools to deliver massive and unambiguous benefits. They tend to be incredibly wary of low-value activities that can clutter up their time and attention and end up hurting more than they help. Put another way: minimalists don't mind missing out on small things; what worries them much more is diminishing the large things they *already know for sure* make a good life good.[1990]

Even though there is sufficient evidence to convince most people that using the internet is harmful in theory, many people may find that putting this theory into practice in their own lives is difficult. The primary reason for this difficulty is because most of us have already

---

[1988] Nicholas Carr, *The Shallows*, 210–11.

[1989] Larchet, *The New Media Epidemic,* 155–56.

[1990] Cal Newport, *Digital Minimalism,* 28–30.

fallen prey to the addictive nature of the internet, at least to some degree. Dr. Larchet recommends some strategies that may help us break this addiction:

> Dependency on the new media is similar to dependency on drugs. So in severe cases, psychotherapy is needed with psychiatrists specialized in addictions. ... However, it must be realized that addiction to the Internet and other new media ... is a response to existential problems that are at its root and that must also be treated urgently. These existential problems most often arise from deep spiritual roots and so require a spiritual therapy.

> Not all the forms of addiction to the new media are grave enough to need a stay in a hospital or even psychotherapy. The firm intention to reduce exposure ... can be effective if there is personal discipline.[1991]

> There are more and more reports of the positive results of ... long-term retreats [from connected devices]. Those who cannot cut themselves off completely for so long, often for professional reasons, are advised to unplug regularly for short periods of at least five days. This radical interruption of all types of connection brings psychological and physical rest.[1992]

> Unplugging [from the internet] is clearly most important for the smartphone, perhaps through time filters, and for emails and text messages. Real-time alerts should be switched off. It is better to look at all the messages at a time of the day or week that is set aside for correspondence.... Online time should be managed so that it remains within set limits.[1993]

> Above all, it is necessary to put into perspective in one's mind the place and importance of the new media. One should realize that there is more to life than information and communication, and that these things should be instruments in the service of the content that precedes and follows them.... [The new media] should also be set against former ways of working, of leisure and relationship, rediscovering the old ways if need be. One will then see that when the media are not absolutely necessary for the work in hand, they do not always improve efficiently or even speed, and that speed is rarely indispensable. It will be seen that the leisure activities proposed by the new media are not always more enriching or relaxing than traditional activities, and that the relationships formed through social networks are not deeper or more satisfying. The pleasure, freedom and depth of the reading of books will be rediscovered. ... The virtue of dead time, of silence, of solitude, of meditation, of contemplation, and of prayer will be ours again.[1994]

15) Success

When striving to achieve something, it isn't enough merely to know what the goal is—it is helpful to know how successfully progress is being made toward that goal. As Abba Benjamin said: "Follow the royal path and count the miles, and thus you do not become

---

[1991] Larchet, *The New Media Epidemic,* 156–57.

[1992] Ibid., 157.

[1993] Ibid., 160.

[1994] Ibid., 158–59.

discouraged."[1995] Commenting on this, Abba Dorotheos explained: "The miles that one covers are the different spiritual states which one must always assess, so as to see where he is.... We have an obligation to examine ourselves, not just every day, but also at regular intervals of time—every year, every month, and every week—and to say, ... 'Last year, I was overcome by that passion to some extent. Where am I now?'"[1996]

Thus, one way of measuring a monk's progress is to assess the intensity of his passions. Another way of measuring progress is to examine the quality of his prayer, since, according to St. John of Sinai, prayer is "the mirror of a monk's progress."[1997] But what criteria can be used to measure the progress and success of a monastery, which is not an individual person but a group of persons and an organization?

For a worldly organization, success can be approximated by measuring specific, tangible variables such as profit margin, capital, number of employees, employee morale, public image, etc. For a monastery, however, assessing success is much more difficult. Some indicators of corporate success may also incidentally be present in a "good" monastery— such as financial well-being, size and quality of buildings, number of monks, morale of the monks, and public opinion of the monastery. History has shown, however, that many excellent brotherhoods even with a saint for their abbot lacked some or all of these attributes for various reasons. For example, the brotherhood of St. Joseph the Hesychast lacked most of those qualities: they were not wealthy, the size and quality of their living quarters left much to be desired, the number of fathers was small, and several others had a low opinion of them, even suspecting that they were deluded.

St. Nilus Sorsky viewed such criteria as worldly and not spiritual. He wrote: "To have the title of the finest monastery in a place and a multitude of brothers—this is the pride of the worldly, the Fathers said— ... or success in worldly reputation ... these are madness."[1998] Therefore, these worldly standards are not very helpful in assessing the state of one's monastery. Besides, the true measure of success for a monastery is how well it is doing God's will, which can be quite different for different monastics and different monasteries. For example, Abba Arsenius was doing God's will by living as a hesychast in silence, whereas Abba Moses in contrast was doing God's will by giving hospitality.[1999]

Since the goal of the monastery is to contribute to the salvation of souls, and since there is a correlation between salvation and spiritual health, one can indirectly assess how

---

[1995] PG 65:145A. Similarly, St. Joseph the Hesychast taught: "Man is meant not only to run but should also count the miles on the road" (Γέροντος Ἰωσήφ, *Ἔκφρασις Μοναχικῆς Ἐμπειρίας*, 202; see also Elder Joseph, *Monastic Wisdom*, 177).

[1996] Metropolitan Chrysostomos, *Our Holy Father Dorotheos of Gaza*, 168–69, 175–76.

[1997] Cf. Holy Transfiguration Monastery, *The Ladder of Divine Ascent*, 212.

[1998] Goldfrank, *Nil Sorsky: The Authentic Writings*, 186–87.

[1999] Vid. Ward, *The Sayings of the Desert Fathers*, 17–18.

"good" a monastery is by evaluating how conducive it is to spiritual health. Bearing this in mind, we can make the following list of attributes, which is nothing but an attempt to distill the essence of monasticism as presented in the foregoing pages of this book. Our hope is that monasteries will find this list to be a helpful aid in critical self-examination, and that postulants may use it to select a monastery that is most likely to help them achieve salvation.

Attributes of a Successful Monastery

1) *How much the monastics love God*—which is evident in how well they keep Christ's commandments, and how strong their faith, prayer, humility, and reverence are;

2) *how much they love their neighbor*—which is evident in the degree of unity in the brotherhood so that "one soul is seen in many bodies,"[2000] and in the degree of genuine, selfless love they have for the other monastics, visitors, and the rest of the world;

3) *how skilled the abbot (or abbess) is in guiding souls,* which entails: inspiring them to love God, helping them to maintain brotherly love (especially in conflicts), selflessly developing their unique personhood,[2001] encouraging them to obey voluntarily instead of enforcing discipline,[2002] and, in general, teaching them through his example, words, and experience to purify their hearts of passions, and ultimately guiding them in noetic prayer to illumination and theosis;

4) *to what degree the abbot has earned the love, trust, and respect[2003] of the fathers*—not merely because of his position but because of his behavior as a person, who as the "good shepherd"[2004] lays down his life for the sheep through sacrificial love, which requires that he have the spiritual and psychological health to tend to his disciples' needs;

5) *how well the monastics are progressing in their struggle against the seven deadly passions* (pride, fornication, jealousy, love of money, gluttony, de-

---

[2000] For the entire quotation of St. Basil the Great, see the text referenced in footnote #1121 on page 206.

[2001] Elder Aimilianos taught that in a monastery "the person should not be stifled, the personality should be cultivated, the individual understood." See page xviii of preface for the full quotation.

[2002] The difference between voluntary obedience and discipline is explained in chapter 3, section 6: "Obedience and Freedom," on page 117.

[2003] Although there have been instances in history where a saintly abbot was not only disrespected but even persecuted by the other monks (because of the latter's passions), such exceptions do not invalidate the general rule that an abbot will receive the trust and respect he has earned.

[2004] Jn. 10:11.

spondency, and anger) as well as other passions, such as laziness, selfishness, impatience, judging, partial love, curiosity, love of power, forgetfulness of death, lying, self-justification, unwillingness to repent and confess, remembrance of wrongs, talkativeness, gossiping, attachment to material items, and the lack of meekness, self-reproach, genuineness, and seriousness;[2005]

6) *how much the monastics and the visitors are helped spiritually and physically by the monastery* because of its location,[2006] external appearance,[2007] cleanliness, and organization.[2008] The concept of "organization" includes having a balanced schedule for worship, prayer, reading, rest, and work (without becoming a "Martha"), as well as creating an atmosphere that encourages love, humility, and repentance. Organization also entails wise stewardship of whatever financial and material resources a monastery may have. A monastery can also foster spiritual growth through poverty and hardships[2009] in moderation, while minimizing luxuries[2010] and internet access;

[2005] "Seriousness" does not mean a gloomy austerity but a level-headed focus and a vigilant stance of self-control. See also the text referenced in footnote #1235 on page 237.

[2006] Many monastic saints have written how inspired they were by the location of their monastic dwelling. For example, St. Joseph the Hesychast wrote: "Ascetical life! Wilderness! Angelic life, full of grace! If only you were here to see us! Oh, if you could only see us! It is an earthly paradise here.... I am the most fortunate of men because I live with no worries, enjoying the honey of hesychia without any interruption. And when grace withdraws, hesychia like another grace shelters me in its bosom. Then the pains and sorrows of this evil and toilsome life seem smaller" (Γέροντος Ἰωσήφ, Ἔκφρασις Μοναχικῆς Ἐμπειρίας, 262, 298; see also Elder Joseph, *Monastic Wisdom*, 226, 255). And Elder Ephraim once predicted with sorrow that a monastery he visited would never make any progress because its location was depressing rather than inspiring. A contemporary theologian observed: "There is an unaccountable solace that fierce landscapes offer to the soul. They heal, as well as mirror, the brokenness we find within.... [There] you experience a crisis of knowing that brings you to the end of yourself, to the only true place where God is met" (Belden C. Lane, *The Solace of Fierce Landscapes: Exploring Desert and Mountain Spirituality* [Oxford: Oxford University Press, 2007], 216). Perhaps it was these factors that made Abba Sisoes lament his departure from the desert and say: "Was not the mere liberty of my thoughts enough for me in the desert?" (PG 65:401A; see also Ward, *The Sayings of the Desert Fathers*, 218).

[2007] St. Paisios of the Holy Mountain explained why the external appearances matter: "The simple buildings and the humble belongings transport the monastics mentally to the caves and the austere dwellings of our holy Fathers, and are of great spiritual benefit." For the entire quotation, see the text referenced in footnote #1583 on page 296.

[2008] When a monastery is disorganized, extra time and effort and worry are spent on secondary matters. Elder Ephraim taught: "Wherever there is order, there is peace, and wherever there is peace, there is God. On the contrary, wherever there is disorder, there is confusion; and wherever there is confusion, there is the devil—not physically present but present in the form of temptations" (cf. Γέροντος Ἐφραίμ, Πατρικαὶ Νουθεσίαι, 165; see also Elder Ephraim, *Counsels from the Holy Mountain*, 124).

[2009] For the spiritual value of hardship, see section VI) 3) on page 283.

[2010] For the spiritual harm of luxury, see section VI) 5) on page 301.

7) *how much equality exists.* Equality means not just holding all possessions in common and behaving as "each others' equal servants,"[2011] but it especially means that they believe so firmly that they are members of the same body that this belief is reflected in their daily lives. Equality also entails showing the same respect and care for the least of the visitors as for the greatest and richest.[2012] Furthermore, equality means having no cliques within or around the monastery;

8) *how well the monastery preserves Orthodox tradition.* This includes dogmatic beliefs, the theory and practice of the spiritual life, the liturgical cycle, and artistic expressions.

It is tempting to include also the following four quantitative attributes as indicative of how successful a monastery is:

9) how many monks live in the monastery and how many pilgrims visit;
10) how many people are benefited by the monastery's alms;
11) how many beneficial things the monastery produces (such as books, icons, newsletters, recordings, candles, handicrafts, etc.);
12) how many buildings the monastery has and their quality.

Although a larger number of monks and pilgrims is often indicative of a good monastery, a monastery in a less populated area might have only a few monks and pilgrims even if its monks are living up to their monastic calling. Likewise, how many alms a monastery can give depends on many factors, several of which are unrelated to its spiritual health, such as: how many pilgrims come and how wealthy they are, how actively donations are sought from people (if at all), how lucrative the monastery's handicrafts are, how frugally the monks live, how great a need they have for constructing new buildings or purchasing expensive medicines, etc.

The benefit ensuing from the monastery's products does not belong on this list, considering that a monastery could be excellent at helping the world through prayer (which is the monk's primary task[2013]) while not being particularly talented at producing "things." As Elder Aimilianos explained in the *Regulations of the Holy Cenobium of the Annunciation*: "The monastic community, living according to its own rhythm, shall live essentially

---

[2011] For the entire quotation of St. Basil, see the text referenced in footnote #1121 on page 206.

[2012] On the evil of favoritism, see James 2:1–7. On numerous occasions the Lord has tested saints by visiting their monasteries in the guise of someone poor and despicable.

[2013] As St. Silouan the Athonite taught: "A monk is someone who prays for the whole world, who weeps for the whole world; and in this lies his main work.... It is not for the monk to serve the world with the work of his hands. That is the layman's business" (Sakharov, *Saint Silouan the Athonite,* 409).

in the Church and for the Church, like the heart or some member of the body and shall not be evaluated for any activity it may undertake but principally for the ardent search for God. The nuns shall thus be perfect images of God and shall in this way attract others to the life divine."[2014]

The number and quality of buildings are unfortunately the primary criteria used by superficial people to evaluate a monastery. Although this aspect usually does contribute positively to the well-being of a monastery, it does so only indirectly, since the main reason why having many buildings is an asset is because this helps the monks and visitors to function more effectively. When an abbot told Elder Paisius of Sihla about the external progress of his own monastery, he replied: "Father Abbot, God will not ask you at the Judgment how many material things you've gathered, how many cells you've built, or how much cattle you have in the monastery. But he will ask us how many souls were gathered there and how many members of the monastic community were saved. And so, we remain here in vain if we are not attending to our souls."[2015]

St. Sophrony of Essex provided a helpful perspective on what a monastery really is:

Recently, I have observed that some people have a very vague idea of what a monastery is. Let us begin with that. When we talk about a monastery, we are referring above all to the people and not to the buildings. Monasteries are created when someone is struggling to live in accordance with the Gospel with his whole being as much as possible, and around this person others gradually begin to gather. In this manner most monasteries—at least the best ones—were established: around St. Athanasios of Athos, or St. Sergius in Russia; in Egypt around St. Anthony, St. Pachomios, and others; in Palestine around St. Savas, etc. Incidentally, I could say that the monasteries that were established by such people were always the best, as history bears witness, because the monks enjoyed spiritual freedom. The monasteries that princes and rich people supported with their care (a common phenomenon in Russia) bore the seal of the benefactor, but they were "second-class" monasteries, so to speak, from a spiritual point of view, even though they were often very well organized by the local hierarchs. Paradoxically, these monasteries always had less depth and were less "productive" on the spiritual level. I do not assert this absolutely, but this is what happens to take place in most of the situations I know. The person around whom we here have gathered is our father [Saint] Silouan. His teaching and the example of his life should be for us a guide that is steady, more or less. And you will ascertain that the desire of our father Silouan coincides with that of Christ Himself, Who said to His disciples: "By this shall all men know that ye are My disciples, if ye have love one to another."[2016] Having this as a basis, the Elder legislated how to live....

All of you—or at least most of you—came and were accepted by me because of the book that mentions the Elder, which is why I am saying that Elder Silouan is the

---

[2014] Elder Aimilianos, *The Authentic Seal,* 162.

[2015] Bălan, *A Little Corner of Paradise,* 165. Likewise, St. Paisios of the Holy Mountain said that when we are judged, Christ "will not ask what buildings we made. He will not even mention them." (For the entire quotation, see the text referenced in footnote #1584 on page 297.)

[2016] Jn. 13:35.

founder of our monastery. So don't lose what he himself says and teaches in his writings; try to find three or five minutes a day to read a few lines from his writings, as well as from those things that I myself have written.[2017]

Thus, a common attribute of many spiritually successful monasteries is that their elder hails from a holy spiritual lineage. In other words, the monastery's elder had himself been under obedience to a holy elder and inherited his grace. This is why St. Daniel of Katounakia said: "Here on the Holy Mountain there is a tradition: you have to bury an elder in order to become an elder."[2018] That is to say, you must be obedient to an elder until his death in order to become an elder yourself. This characteristic is so common to the elders of spiritually successful monasteries that we could cite it as a prerequisite for success. This would be inaccurate, however, since there have been exceptions to this rule—the most notable exception being St. Paisius Velichkovsky.

One final aspect of a "good" monastery not listed here is the amount of grace present in it, in the abbot, and in the brotherhood. We have omitted it not because it is unimportant but because it is the hardest to measure. Yet most people (even the non-Orthodox)[2019] who have visited a holy monastery have a sense of what this grace feels like.

16) Failure

History has shown again and again that people (including saints) attain success usually only after numerous mistakes and failures. We do not expect to be exempt from this law of human nature, and therefore we need to be ready to welcome corrections with humility and gratitude and to have the courage to make a new beginning whenever we realize we have strayed from the true path.

Failure comes in various shapes and sizes. Most of the forms of failure for a monastery are simply the opposites of the forms of success listed in the previous section. A more subtle form of failure is to have "group pride." This is a subtle temptation because just as pride is the most difficult passion to detect in oneself on an individual level, it is also the most difficult passion to detect in one's own group on a collective level.

Abba Dorotheos of Gaza warned about this kind of pride: "When therefore we see ourselves getting vainglorious … because we have a better monastery, or one that is more

---

[2017] Σωφρονίου, *Οἰκοδομῶντας τὸν Ναὸ τοῦ Θεοῦ, Τόμος Α΄,* 34–36.

[2018] Γέροντος Ἐφραίμ, *Ὁ Γέροντάς μου Ἰωσήφ,* 70; see also Elder Ephraim, *My Elder Joseph the Hesychast,* 105.

[2019] When I gave tours of St. Anthony's Monastery in Arizona to non-Orthodox visitors, invariably they would mention how moved they were by the monastery's quietude. One day I gave a tour while someone was using a loud gasoline-powered blower nearby. To my surprise, they still commented how quiet the monastery was! It was then that I realized that what they were perceiving was not an absence of noise but the presence of grace.

convenient, or when we have more brethren, we ought to see that we have reached a high point of this worldly pride."[2020] With this in mind, St. Ignatius Brianchaninov wrote:

> The Fathers forbid postulants to choose a monastery that is famous in the eyes of worldly people. The vainglory which the whole monastery shares must inevitably infect each individual member as well. Experience shows that all the brethren of a community can be infected with the spirit of vainglory, not only on account of the material privileges or superiority of their monastery, but also on account of the high opinion of lay people concerning the special piety of its rule. Hence arises scorn for the brethren of other communities, which implies pride, and this saps the possibility of progress or success in the monastic life which is based on love for our neighbours and humility towards them.[2021]

Fr. Seraphim Rose explained how this temptation could be a challenge for groups establishing new monasteries in America:

> Among the chief temptations to such groups, especially if they are very successful, are: outward success can blind them to inward deficiencies; community solidarity and well-being can cause them to become inflated with a false sense of their own importance; and the appearance of "correctness" can produce spiritual smugness and disdain of those outside the group who are not so "correct." If these temptations are not overcome, a deadly "group pride" can take the place of individual pride and lead the whole community on a fatal path which none of its members can recognize because it is not his *personal* doing; the "renewed" community can become so much out of harmony with the "unrenewed" rest of the Church as to form a virtual "jurisdiction" of its own, and even end in a schism brought about by its own exaggerated feeling of "correctness." The more such groups stay out of the limelight of publicity and church disputes, and the less a point they make of emphasizing their "correctness" and their differences from the older institutions, the better chance they have for remaining spiritually sound.[2022]

The opposite of "group pride" is what one contemporary author called "corporate humility." He observed this kind of humility in a monastery in Greece:

> Having visited literally hundreds of monasteries in my research, I have collected a great number of mementos bearing the insignias of particular monasteries. I have calendars with pictures of abbots with various famous people; I have glossy books filled with pictures of religious treasures and the monastic way of life; and I have CDs of their choirs chanting. I can show friends publicity newsletters and web sites of monasteries I have visited. Many contemporary monasteries seem to excel at self-promotion.
>
> The monastery in Preveza is very different. It has no newsletter, no colorful calendars, no picture books, and no web site. It does not sell a single item in its store bearing its name. It barely has a sign indicating its presence in Flamboura. This anonymity is not due to a lack of organization but rather to a conscious emphasis by Bishop Meletios that one of the primary virtues of the monk should be *afania* (anonymity).... [There is]

[2020] Wheeler, *Abba Dorotheos: Discourses and Sayings,* 97.

[2021] Brianchaninov, *The Arena,* 11–12.

[2022] Rose, *Vita Patrum: The Life of the Fathers by St. Gregory of Tours,* 157.

a conscious recognition that part of the holiness they seek as monks means actively maintaining the obscurity that is nothing more than corporate humility.

This desire for anonymity is grounded also in a historical lesson: the great monastic centers did not begin by seeking out worldly glory or recognition; they did not want to become great. Rather, they sought out authentic holiness. Their rejection of the world was not done out of misanthropy but rather out of their sole desire to seek out holiness here on earth. And it was this holiness that brought them fame, not vice versa. Many modern monasteries seem to reverse this relationship.[2023]

Fr. Seraphim Rose wrote about another pitfall for monasteries in America:

Unfortunately, the awareness of Orthodox monasticism and its ABC's remains largely, even now [in 1975], an outward matter. There is still more *talk* of "elders," "hesychasm," and "prelest" [delusion] than fruitful monastic struggles themselves. Indeed, it is all too possible to accept all the outward marks of the purest and most exalted monastic tradition: absolute obedience to an elder, daily confession of thoughts, long church services or individual rule of Jesus Prayer and prostrations, frequent reception of Holy Communion, reading with understanding of the basic texts of spiritual life, and in doing all this to feel a deep *psychological* peace and ease—and at the same time to remain *spiritually* immature. It is possible to cover over the untreated passions within one by means of a façade or technique of "correct" spirituality, without having true love for Christ and one's brother. The rationalism and coldness of heart of modern men in general make this perhaps the most insidious of the temptations of the monastic aspirant today. Orthodox monastic *forms,* true enough, are being planted in the West; but what about the heart of monasticism and Orthodox Christianity: repentance, humility, love for Christ our God and unquenchable thirst for His Kingdom?

In all humility let us admit the poverty of our Christianity [in America], the coldness of our love for God, the emptiness of our spiritual pretensions; and let us use this confession as the *beginning* of our monastic path, which is a path of correction. Let us, the monks of the last times, realistically aware of our failings and of the pitfalls before us, not lose courage at the sight of them, but let us all the more strenuously offer to God our humble entreaty that he might forgive our sins and heal our wounded souls.[2024]

When an organization is successful, its power naturally increases. This principle applies to monasteries as well. As power increases, however, so does the temptation for corruption. Lord Acton famously quipped: "Power tends to corrupt, and absolute power corrupts absolutely."[2025] Recent studies have shown, however, that it would be more accurate to say that power does not corrupt but rather heightens pre-existing ethical tendencies.[2026] This finding is in line with Abraham Lincoln's maxim: "Nearly all men can stand adversity, but if you

---

[2023] Lloyd-Moffett, *Beauty for Ashes,* 173–74.

[2024] Rose, *Vita Patrum: The Life of the Fathers by St. Gregory of Tours,* 159.

[2025] John Emerich Edward Dalberg-Acton, *Historical Essays & Studies* (London: MacMillan and Co., 1907), 504.

[2026] Vid. K. A. DeCelles, D. S. DeRue, J. D. Margolis, and T. L. Ceranic, "Does Power Corrupt or Enable? When and Why Power Facilitates Self-interested Behavior," *Journal of Applied Psychology* 97, no. 3 (May 2012): 681–89.

want to test a man's character, give him power."[2027] Thus, in a monastery as long as the abbot maintains impeccable ethics, his power will not result in some form of corruption.

17) Legalities

Elder Aimilianos stated in the *Regulations of the Holy Cenobium of the Annunciation:* "A nun whose life is spiritual and whose ardent soul adheres firmly to God shall not have recourse to civil courts, even if she is unjustly treated, suffers or is brought to death itself, but shall live only in God, trusting in Him."[2028] To implement this principle, in some monasteries every novice is required to sign a "release agreement" that expresses his understanding that he will receive no monetary compensation for his work and cannot sue the monastery. Signing this kind of document was a prerequisite for joining some monasteries in the old days. For example, *The Rule of the Master* dictates:

> If the brother chooses to give himself along with his possessions to the monastery and does not wish to sell them, in case he should ever want to leave, subverted and backed by the devil, and make trouble for the monastery by demanding his things, let him first with his own hand draw up a pledge of stability, adding an inventory of his goods. Then let him offer every thing with his soul as a gift to God and to the oratory of the monastery, with religious persons—bishop, priest, and deacon, and the clergy of that area—signing as witnesses. In the document itself let him make this declaration, that should he ever want to quit the monastery he will depart from the monastery without his goods and from God without forgiveness of his sins.... Furthermore, whatever he at any time acquired or made or contributed while in the monastery may absolutely not be given back to him when he leaves.[2029]

When a person wishes to join a monastery, he should read and sign the monastery's typikon. The *Rule of Macarius* states: "If someone from the world should wish to be converted in the monastery, let the rule be read to him when he enters, and let every practice of the monastery be made clear to him. And if he should accept all things suitably, let him thus be fittingly received by the brothers in the cell."[2030]

Likewise, St. Benedict described in more detail how the monastery's rule is to be repeatedly read to a postulant:

> If he [i.e., the postulant] promiseth to remain steadfast, let this Rule be read to him in order after the lapse of two months, and let it be said to him: "Behold the law under which thou desirest to combat. If thou canst keep it, enter; if, however, thou canst not, depart freely." ... And after the lapse of six months let the Rule be read over to him, that he may know for what purpose he entereth. And if he still remaineth firm, let the

---

[2027] Abraham Lincoln, *Quotations of Abraham Lincoln* (Bedford: Applewood Books, 2004), 30.

[2028] Elder Aimilianos, *The Authentic Seal,* 173.

[2029] Eberle, *The Rule of the Master,* 255, 266.

[2030] Franklin, *Early Monastic Rules,* 49.

same Rule be read to him again after four months. And if, after having weighed the matter with himself he promiseth to keep everything, and to do everything that is commanded him, then let him be received into the community, knowing that he is now placed under the law of the Rule, and that from that day forward it is no longer permitted to him to wrest his neck from under the yoke of the Rule, which after so long a deliberation he was at liberty either to refuse or to accept. Let him who is received promise in the oratory, in the presence of all, before God and His saints, stability, the conversion of morals, and obedience, in order that, if he should ever do otherwise, he may know that he will be condemned by God "Whom he mocketh." Let him make a written statement of his promise in the name of the saints whose relics are there, and of the Abbot there present. Let him write this document with his own hand … and with his own hand place it on the altar.[2031]

St. Benedict was continuing the tradition of Galician monasticism, which was known for its "pactualism." As explained by one historian: "The pactum is the name given to a document attached to the end of the Common Rule that constitutes a contract between the novitiate and the abbot, highlighting precisely the expectations of both."[2032] Even before this, in the 4th century Abba Shenoute the Great required new monks to sign a written covenant containing a commitment not to defile the body in any manner, steal, bear false witness, or commit any act of concealed deceit.[2033]

Contemporary monastic typika continue this tradition. For example, the charter that St. Nectarios of Aegina wrote for his monastery required candidates wishing to join it to sign its rules.[2034] Elder Aimilianos wrote that throughout history, "an effort was made [by the monastery] to have the typikon signed by the brotherhood, the Patriarch, the Emperor, and the competent judicial authorities, as well as by the author, in order to ensure and confirm its validity. It thus became the foundation charter of the monastery, respected by all, a guide for the everyday life of the monks, the living voice of God among them."[2035]

Several saints wanted their monastic rules to be read frequently by their disciples. For example, St. Benedict wrote: "We desire that this Rule be read quite often in the community, that none of the brethren may excuse himself of ignorance."[2036] St. Savas of Serbia wrote: "Read these rules at the beginning of every month in the refectory to be reminded of these

---

[2031] *Rule of St. Benedict,* Chapter LVIII.

[2032] Neil Allies, "The Monastic Rules of Visigothic Iberia: A Study of their Text and Language," 79. etheses .bham.ac.uk/787/1/Allies10PhD.pdf

[2033] Vid. Patrich, *Sabas, Leader of Palestinian Monasticism,* 21.

[2034] Vid. *The Charter of the Holy Monastery in Aegina of the Holy Trinity,* Article 8.

[2035] Elder Aimilianos, "On the Preparation of an Internal Regulation for the Holy Monasteries of the Church of Greece," *The Authentic Seal,* 70.

[2036] *Rule of St. Benedict,* Chapter LXVI. St. Athanasios of Athos included this exhortation of St. Benedict nearly verbatim in his own typikon (vid. Thomas and Hero, *Byzantine Monastic Foundation Documents,* 228).

commandments and for the benefit of your souls."[2037] St. Athanasios I, the Patriarch of Constantinople, wrote that his monastic rule should be read every month.[2038] Similarly, the eleventh-century typikon of the Monastery of Evergetis says: "I instruct you to read the present typikon at the beginning of each month during your meal-times, to remind you of your instructions and for the benefit of your souls."[2039] The typikon of the Monastery of Machairas quoted this injunction verbatim, but reduced the frequency to three times a year.[2040] Abba Shenoute the Great ordered: "All the issues, ordinances, and words that we have recorded in all the epistles shall be read four times per year."[2041] Blessed Augustine wrote in his monastic rule: "That you may see yourselves in this little book, as in a mirror, have it read to you once a week so as to neglect no point through forgetfulness."[2042] *The Rule of Paul and Stephen* states: "The Rules of the Fathers also are read constantly for our sake so that by attuning our inner ear to their holy appeals we may grasp the most delightful love of discipline and so that with the help of the Lord we may follow in everything the example of their lives."[2043]

Following in their footsteps, we, too, would benefit by reading our typikon from time to time. This will help us to remain focused on what our monastic goal is, to bear in mind how we intend to reach it by God's grace, and most importantly[2044] to remind us *why* we are choosing to strive in this manner for the Kingdom of Heaven.

[2037] *Charter of Hilandar Monastery,* Article 43.

[2038] Vid. Thomas and Hero, *Byzantine Monastic Foundation Documents,* 1500.

[2039] Ibid., 498.

[2040] Ibid., 1165.

[2041] Layton, *The Canons of Our Fathers: Monastic Rules of Shenoute,* 195.

[2042] Bavel, *The Rule of Saint Augustine,* ch. 7. Reading his rule every week was not very time-consuming, considering that his rule had only 3,000 words.

[2043] Barry Hagan, "The Rule of Paul and Stephen," ch. 41.

[2044] In order to remain connected to his existential purpose in life, St. Arsenios continually asked himself: "Arsenios, why did you leave the world?" (Ward, *The Sayings of the Desert Fathers,* 18). Being aware of one's purpose in life is so crucial that Viktor Frankl emphasized: "Life is never made unbearable by circumstances, but only by lack of meaning and purpose." Along the same lines, Leo Tolstoy observed: "Without knowing what I am and why I am here, life is impossible," and Fyodor Dostoyevsky wrote: "The secret of man's being is not only to live but to have something to live for.... Neither man or nation can exist without a sublime idea."

Chapter Seven:
Monastic Schema

THE ORIGINAL MEANING of the Greek word *schema* is "shape" or "form." By extension, it also meant "fashion" (i.e., "way of life") and "fashion of dress"[2045] or "clothing."[2046] Thus, the term "monastic schema" refers to all the clothes worn by a monk (his "habit"). After the 7th century,[2047] the word *schema* could also mean a specific item of monastic garb, described below on page 418 in section 9).

1) Origins

The origin of the monastic garments (i.e., the monastic "schema") is unknown. After the 9th century,[2048] icons of St. Pachomios the Great (who lived in the 3rd century) often depict an angel wearing the great schema and telling him: "With this schema, everyone shall be saved, O Pachomios." Such icons led to the popular opinion (or perhaps popular opinion led to such icons)[2049] that the angel who gave St. Pachomios a monastic rule was also the first to indicate what garments monks should wear. The problem with this opinion is that prior to this, St. Anthony had already given the schema (i.e., monastic garments) to

---

[2045] Liddell and Scott, *A Greek-English Lexicon,* 1745.

[2046] G. W. H. Lampe, *A Patristic Greek Lexicon* (Oxford: Oxford University Press, 1961), 1359.

[2047] Ζουκόβα, *Γέννηση καὶ Ἐξέλιξη τῆς Ἀκολουθίας τοῦ Μοναχικοῦ Σχήματος,* 297.

[2048] Ibid., 298.

[2049] Ibid., 297.

St. Macarius of Egypt,[2050] and St. Pachomios himself had already received the schema from Abba Palamon.[2051]

Another common misunderstanding with this is that the particular monastic garment known today as the schema was supposedly given to St. Pachomios by the angel. The problem with this notion is that the original accounts of that angelic encounter say nothing of the sort. The part of this encounter recorded in the *Lausiac History* contains only the following instructions from the angel regarding monastic clothing:

> "At night let them [i.e., the monks] wear linen tunics and be belted. Let each of them have a tanned goat-skin without which they may not eat. When they go to Communion on Saturday and Sunday, let them loosen their belts, lay aside their goat skins and go in with the hood only." He [i.e., St. Pachomios] prescribed for them hoods without nap, as for children, and he ordered a sign in the form of a cross to be put on them in purple.[2052]

Commenting on this and other ancient texts, Evgenia Zhoukova wrote:

> These texts clearly show that in the clothing shown to Pachomios by the angel, there was no garment that would be called the schema. Therefore, we must surmise that when we speak of the revelation to Pachomios of the monastic schema, we should understand that the angel revealed to Pachomios primarily the rules of life for the monks of the cenobium as well as the entire monastic outfit, which did not include the *analavos* (known today as the polystavrion) and certainly did not mean the modern "schema" in the sense of a particular garment or the form of the garments of a present-day great-schema monk.[2053]

St. Symeon of Thessalonica taught that the schema (not as a particular garment but as a way of life) is from Christ Himself:

> The first one to write about the angelic and divine monastic schema was the holy Dionysios [the Areopagite], and the Savior Himself handed it down, and this is what His disciples kept. It was not merely from Saints Pachomios and Paul of Thebes and Anthony that this began to be given as a rule (as some say), but it was from the Savior Himself and given to the Apostles. For they lived monastically in terms of chastity and food and garments and poverty and prayers. It increased with those who came after them, and with the holy Fathers it shone forth.[2054]

Elaborating on this, Metropolitan Hierotheos Vlachos observed:

[2050] Vid. Tim Vivian, *Saint Macarius, the Spiritbearer: Coptic Texts Relating to Saint Macarius the Great* (New York: St. Vladimir's Seminary Press, 2004), 168.

[2051] "After the old man [Abba Palamon] had tried him [St. Pachomios] for three full months and had seen his courage and his firm determination, he took a monk's habit with the belt and he placed it before the altar, and they spent the whole night praying over them. Then he clothed him with it at daybreak, and they celebrated the morning prayer together with joy" (Veilleux, *Pachomian Koinonia,* vol. 1, 32).

[2052] Veilleux, *Pachomian Koinonia,* vol. 2, 126.

[2053] Ζουκόβα, *Γέννηση καὶ Ἐξέλιξη τῆς Ἀκολουθίας τοῦ Μοναχικοῦ Σχήματος,* 302.

[2054] PG 155:912CD.

When one carefully reads the Acts of the Apostles as well as the epistles of the Apostles that were sent to the Christians of the first churches, one will notice that the first Christians, who received the Holy Spirit and were members of the Church, were living as monastics do today with an intense spiritual life. The exhortations of the Apostles for thorough repentance, unceasing prayer, keeping the commandments of Christ, expecting the Second Coming of Christ, seeking the heavenly lifestyle, etc., show that the monastic life is actually the Christian life in its fullness.[2055]

Echoing this sentiment, Fr. Theodoros Zeses wrote:

Christ was born of the All-Pure, Ever-Virgin Theotokos in a manner which involved no carnal relations, thus specially honoring the life of virginity. In fact, the Theotokos herself is specially venerated by the monastics, for they see her as a model when it comes to the renunciation of the world, obedience, and purity. At the early age of three the Panagia was dedicated to the temple and there she lived, obedient to the temple priests, and entirely cut off from the world.[2056]

The Church has viewed the Prophet Elias and St. John the Baptist as prototypes of monastic life because they lived alone in the wilderness. This is why the service of the great schema mentions them: "Grant unto him ... to preserve unblemished the Schema ... following in the footsteps of the great Prophet Elijah [Elias], and of the holy Prophet, Forerunner, and Baptist John."[2057] St. Symeon of Thessalonica called the two of them "the leaders of anchoretic life"[2058] and also said: "The Baptist was the first after Elias to prefigure the schema."[2059] This also explains why St. John the Baptist referred to the monastic schema as "*my* schema" in a vision in the following incident related by St. John Moschus:

When a monk who had fallen to temptation was brought before him [i.e., Patriarch John of Jerusalem in 583], he publicly stripped him of his angelic habit [schema], which he put on a pig, and let the pig loose in the streets of the city. That night St. John the Baptist appeared to him: "Man, why have you so treated my habit? I will make suit against you in the dreadful Day of Judgment."[2060]

St. Germanos of Constantinople (in the early 8th century) also attributed the schema to St. John the Baptist: "The monastic schema is in imitation of the desert-dweller John the Baptist whose garment was from camel hairs and had a leather belt around his waist."[2061]

[2055] Ἱεροθέου, *Ὁ Ὀρθόδοξος Μοναχισμός*, 175; Hierotheos, *Orthodox Monasticism*, 163.

[2056] Zisis, *Following the Holy Fathers*, 34.

[2057] *The Great Book of Needs*, vol. 1, 376.

[2058] Συμεὼν Θεσσαλονίκης, *Διάλογος*, κεφ. ΣΟΔ΄, PG 155:501A.

[2059] PG 155:197D. Similarly, St. Gregory Palamas said: "Nor was he just the Forerunner of Christ, but also of His Church and particularly, brethren, of our monastic way of life" (Veniamin, *The Homilies of Saint Gregory Palamas*, vol. 2, 218).

[2060] Chitty, *The Desert a City*, 149.

[2061] PG 98:396B.

2) Levels in Monasticism

The lives and writings of saints clearly show that in the first few centuries of monasticism there was only one kind of monk: he who has been tonsured and given the monastic schema. After the first millennium, however, there have been essentially three different levels of monks:

1) great-schema monks (also called "great monks,"[2062] "great ascetics,"[2063] "first monks,"[2064] and "completely perfect"[2065]),
2) small-schema monks (also called "stavrophore" monks),[2066] and
3) rasophore monks.

In the twelfth century, St. Eustathios of Thessalonica analyzed in detail these three levels of monks, which he called: 1) great-schema monks, 2) "secondary-schema monks with a mantle" (i.e., small-schema monks), and 3) "beginners."[2067] Commenting on this, Protopresbyter Theodoros Zeses wrote: "Whereas the monks of the lowest rank could be called 'rasophores' as they are called in the *Euchologion,* they are also called 'introductory monks' or 'beginners' [by St. Eustathios]."[2068]

In the eleventh century, when the monks of St. Lazaros of Mt. Galesion asked him to explain how the tradition prevailed of dividing the single monastic habit into three, he replied:

> The habit is truly a single thing, even if some have distinguished two ranks in it [i.e., the small and great schema]. The division into three ranks that we now follow has been prescribed primarily because of the slackness and weakness of this present generation, yet at least this has not been done entirely at random or illogically, for this can also represent a greater and more lofty model: such a division seems somehow to echo the heavenly ranking into these three classes, I mean that of the martyrs, apostles, and angels. So the person who has proved suitable for the rank of the first habit can be reckoned with the choirs of the martyrs, the second with those of the apostles, and the third with those of the angels. Indeed this is also clear from the everyday names of

---

[2062] PG 135:796B.

[2063] PG 135:800C.

[2064] PG 135:868A.

[2065] PG 135:900D.

[2066] Although Job, named the Sinner, called a monk with the small schema a rasophore, St. Nicodemos of the Holy Mountain commented: "Note here that he [Job] is the only one who calls the small schema a rasophore, for all the others call the small schema a stavrophore" (trans. Fr. George Dokos, *Exomologetarion: A Manual of Confession,* Nikodemos the Hagiorite [Thessalonica: Uncut Mountain Press, 2006], 284).

[2067] Vid. PG 135:737 (ιβ′ στ. δ′).

[2068] «Αἱ Μοναχικαὶ Τάξεις καὶ αἱ Βαθμίδες τῆς Τελειώσεως κατὰ τὸν Εὐστάθιον Θεσσαλονίκης», *Κληρονομία,* τόμος 7, τεῦχος Α′, Θεσσαλονίκη (1975): 78.

these, as we usually call them the angelic and apostolic habit and the clothing of submission, which is another way of saying martyrdom.[2069]

Fr. Theodoros Zeses explained the difference between a rasophore monk and a novice:

> It must be emphasized that the introductory or beginner monk is different from the novice, who is not a monk at all. Some confusion has arisen regarding this matter for the following reason. The canons demand that the trial period take place with lay clothes and not with monastic clothes.[2070] In certain areas, however, there has been a departure from the canonical path by giving novices a monastic garment—the raso.[2071] But receiving a raso is one of the basic elements of the service for tonsuring an introductory or beginner monk, who for this reason is called a rasophore [literally, a "raso-wearer"]. Furthermore, a crosswise tonsure is also performed on him, which is the primary visible sign of his transition from the rank of a layman to the rank of a monk. Thus, the tonsure radically differentiates the beginner or rasophore monk from the novice, who is not a monk because he has not been tonsured, even though he might be wearing a raso during his trial period.[2072]

The *Life of St. Symeon of Emesa* reveals that there were two levels in monasticism as early as the sixth century. There were monks who had merely been tonsured, and there were monks who had also received the great schema. It narrates:

> Bringing forth the pair of shears and with all due forms of reverence placing them upon the Holy Table, he [the abbot] tonsured them [Sts. John and Symeon]. And taking off their apparel, he clothed them in mean garments—of monastic goats' hair.... And when they were tonsured, John wept greatly.... So after they were tonsured and the Holy Synaxis was celebrated, again the hegoumenos [i.e., the abbot] sat advising them throughout almost the entire day.... Thus he was minded on the next day, it being the Holy Lord's Day, to give them the holy schema also.[2073]

One historian observed: "A distinction is made between a Great and a Little Habit by John the Faster, Patriarch of Constantinople, A.D. 582–595; but the simple tunic, which John the Faster directs to be worn during the time of probation preceding the taking of the Great and

---

[2069] Greenfield, *The Life of Lazaros of Mt. Galesion,* 218.

[2070] Vid. Παναγιωτάκου, *Σύστημα τοῦ Ἐκκλησιαστικοῦ Δικαίου,* 62, σημ. 3, 66, ἑ.

[2071] For example, in the Jerusalem Book of Tonsures there is a special service for a novice's entrance into the monastery which includes dressing with a raso (vid. Michael Wawryk, *Initiatio Monastica in Liturgia Byzantina* [Roma: P. Institutum Orientalium Studiorum, 1968], 56). The custom of novices wearing a raso is also prevalent nowadays in the monasteries of the Church of Greece and the Holy Mountain (vid. Παναγιωτάκου, *Σύστημα τοῦ Ἐκκλησιαστικοῦ Δικαίου,* 100, σημ. 4, 67, σημ. 1).

[2072] Πρωτοπρεσβύτερος Θεόδωρος Ζήσης, *Μοναχισμός: Μορφὲς καὶ Θέματα* (Θεσσαλονίκη: Βρυέννιος Ἐκδόσεις, 1998), 167–68.

[2073] Leontius, Bishop of Neapolis in Cyprus, *Saint Symeon of Emesa, the Fool for Christ's Sake* (Boston: Holy Transfiguration Monastery, 2014), 54–55.

Angelical Habit by a Nun, does not correspond to the Little Habit of the Stavrophore, but rather to the Rason of the Rasophore."[2074]

The earliest mention of the schema being explicitly divided into the small and great schema is found in the eighth century in the testament of St. Theodore the Studite, which states: "You should not grant what they call the little habit and after that the great one, for the habit like baptism is one according to the usages of the fathers."[2075] Similarly, in the 13th century Nikephoros Blemmydes declares in his typikon: "The monastic garb itself, if one considers the matter objectively, allows no difference of grades, even though the speculations of recent thinkers have debased the ancient tradition on this point."[2076] Likewise, St. Gregory Palamas in the 14th century wrote: "This is the great and monastic schema. The Fathers did not know of the small schema nor did they hand down this tradition, but some more recent people thought of dividing the one into two, although they themselves did not divide it truly, for you will find the same vows of renunciation in both of them."[2077] And St. Symeon of Thessalonica taught:

> Just as baptism is one and one only, so too is the habit of monks. For the small schema is an earnest, or pledge, and preamble to the great schema, and was invented by certain later Fathers on account of men's weakness (or even negligence).[2078]
>
> All who are incomplete and imperfect in respect of their schema [i.e., monks who do not have the great schema] ought by all means to become complete and perfect, lest they die incomplete and imperfect, without the most complete and perfect perfection of the schema.... Just as a person who fails to get baptized is not a Christian, so too anyone that fails to become perfected in respect of the schema is not a monk (that is to say, more plainly speaking, he is not perfect).[2079]

Lamenting the division of the schema into small and great, St. Nicodemos of the Holy Mountain wrote:

[2074] N. F. Robinson, *Monasticism in the Orthodox Churches* (London: Society of Saint John the Evangelist, 1916), 52.

[2075] Thomas and Hero, *Byzantine Monastic Foundation Documents,* 78. But since this custom had already become widespread by then, St. Theodore gave his tacit approval of this custom by including it in his *Penitentials*: "If a great-schema monk falls into a passion, let him be without Communion for five years; but if he is a small-schema monk, two years" (Θεοδώρου Στουδίτου, Ἐπιτίμιον 2, 47; PG 99:1753). When St. Athanasios of Athos copied most of St. Theodore's testament verbatim, he omitted St. Theodore's prohibition of the small schema, presumably because he himself had received it before receiving the great schema (vid. Nikodemos, *Exomologetarion: A Manual of Confession,* 288).

[2076] Thomas and Hero, *Byzantine Monastic Foundation Documents,* 1203.

[2077] Γρηγορίου Παλαμᾶ, Ἐπιστολὴ πρὸς τὸν Μοναχὸν Παῦλον, κριτικὴ ἔκδοσις ὑπὸ Ἀλεξάνδρου Λαυριώτου, εἰς τὴν Ἐκκλησιαστικὴν Ἀλήθειαν (1901), 535.

[2078] PG 155:104 as paraphrased by St. Nicodemos in Agapius and Nicodemus, *The Rudder,* 342. St. Nicodemos adds that the *Euchologion* and Patriarch Theodore Balsamon also call the small schema an earnest (ἀρραβῶνα) or foretaste of the great schema.

[2079] As paraphrased by St. Nicodemos in Agapius and Nicodemus, *The Rudder,* 343.

So then, what kind of ignorance is this, when small-schema monks are required to keep the strict lifestyle and perform the works of the great-schema monk through the vows they make to God, and then not to become great-schema monks? Are they merely to endure such labors and be deprived of that grace? Are they to grow old in their monastic life never having become monks? Are they to fight in this arena and in the struggle and then be unworthy to receive the crown? Is there any greater harm to be found than this? Or is there anything more ridiculous than for someone to pass thirty-five years as a small-schema monk, and then, when about to receive the great schema for him to be asked: "Why have you come, brother?" And then for him to reply: "Out of desire for the ascetical life, honorable Father," that is, for him to be dressed as a layman, to be questioned as a layman, and for him to reply as a layman? ...

Therefore it is more exact and more correct and better for monks to become great-schema monks one time, without first becoming small-schema monks, even if the authorities do this. Once because, by this one and only time, the schema of monks is shown in fact to be one in singular, just as the Tradition of the Holy Fathers intends. And also because when the young and healthy receive the schema, they are to cultivate the grace they received and multiply and increase the talent of their Lord, namely, the spiritual strength which the divine schema mystically granted the soul, through struggles against the demons, through conquering the passions, and through the charismata which they will receive from the Holy Spirit.[2080]

St. Sophrony of Essex, however, understood the different levels in monasticism as levels of growth:

As with the three renunciations, it [i.e., passing through the three levels in monasticism] is a case of a steady advancing in spiritual knowledge, since the three vows,[2081] too, have a single aim. Their repetition for the "little schema" and the "great schema" is a sign not of any provisional character but of growth in knowledge of their force and significance. There may be little difference in outward form on the two occasions, but a profound change may have occurred in the monk's inner consciousness. Lest we lose sight of the essence of the Christian life, let me emphasize again that all these monastic dedications and taking of vows are not a *sine qua non* [i.e., an absolute prerequisite] for attaining to the perfection of divine love, which is possible outside the monastic state. But in the same way as St. Luke said of Christ that He "grew, and waxed strong in spirit,"[2082] so every man must develop and grow, and the experience of the Church has proved the value of monasticism.[2083]

St. Eustathios of Thessalonica also viewed the different levels in monasticism as corresponding to different spiritual states:

Now that I have fraternally told these things in a simple manner to you, a beginner monk [i.e., a rasophore], I shall proceed to speak of him who is superior to you [i.e., a small-schema monk], who is not like you—a lightly armed soldier of God—but has

---

[2080] Nikodemos, *Exomologetarion: A Manual of Confession,* 286–87, 288.

[2081] I.e., the three monastic vows of obedience, chastity and poverty, as described below in chapter 7, section 4 on page 397.

[2082] Lk. 10:80.

[2083] Sakharov, *Truth and Life,* 76–77.

been fully armed and has received prayers to have Christ the Savior Himself formed in him through good works. For this reason he has been marked in the name of the Holy Trinity and has cast off superfluous hair as one mourning, and has donned the sacred mantle like mighty armor.

In this way, he has in a sense become someone between men and God. In other words, he is between the divine great-schema monk (who is like God) and those beginner monks below him who are still roaming around the foothills of virtue (who are like men). Because of his middle position, he has the attributes of both extremes mixed in him. On the one hand, he can be proud of having much greater seniority over you who are still a beginner monk, but on the other hand he is quite inferior to the perfect [great-schema] monk and is visibly distinguishable. As long as he remains a mantle-bearing monk [i.e., small-schema monk], he clearly has a middle rank. I could even say that the distance between him and the great-schema monk is the same as the distance between you and him.

If he becomes the leader of a brotherhood, it is no longer possible for him to remain in the same middle rank, since it is as if he has this lofty position in one hand, while in the other he has that which is close to the lowly rank of a beginner monk. Instead, he is ascending past the middle rank and approaching the highest rank. Then he is only slightly beneath the heavenly rank because of the thoroughly spiritual work he is called to perform. Thenceforth, as with the two wings of being a mantle-bearing monk and an abbot, he easily flies up near the great-schema monk. And he has every right to vie with him in terms of his honor and loftiness. In saying that he rivals him, this simply means that he is finding ways to act that make him equal to him. The foremost way is through pastoral work. By doing this, he shows that he has indeed taken up a heavy yoke.

This kind of mantle-bearing abbot who soars high through the sky ascends to heaven in a different way than the great-schema monk does. The important work he does, the excellent ethics, and the godly lifestyle require that he be a great person and not "a little lower than the angels."[2084] We compare the great-schema monk with the angels, since they are an example for men. A great-schema monk is like a true image of an angel. A small-schema monk should also be like that if he is an abbot, since he already has a similar form to that of the great-schema monk.[2085] …

True great-schema monks shine like brilliant lights. In second place is the light emitted by the sacred mantle-bearing monks. The third lights are the beginner monks. And the fourth lights are the virtuous laymen. May this indeed be how things are, and may laymen not be above these three by doing more good than they, which would turn things upside-down. To put it differently, this would make everything backwards. Of course I desire that a layman will progress to the greatest virtue, but I desire the same thing for a monk even more.[2086]

[2084] Ps. 8:5.

[2085] PG 135:876A–C.

[2086] PG 135:900B.

3) The Service of the Great Schema

In its present form the Service of the Great Schema is the result of several centuries of liturgical development. Abbot Tikhon of Stavronikita Monastery explained:

> In the early days of formation of the monastic way of life, no service of monastic tonsure existed, nor was there even a hint of some rudimentary original formulation of it other than the conscious disposition of the person coming to the ascetical, spiritual life. St. Anthony the Great heard the message of the Holy Gospel and began his complete dedication to the monastic/spiritual life without receiving from anyone or from any ecclesiastical authority any kind of tonsure, permission, or approval.

> We also should mention from the Lausiac History the following incident: "When he [i.e., St. Anthony] saw that the old man [i.e., St. Paul the Simple] eagerly followed his way of life, he said to him: 'If you can live like this every day, stay with me.' Paul replied: 'If there is anything more [than the tests you have already subjected me to], I don't know if I can handle them, but I can easily do what I have seen so far.' Then St. Anthony told him, 'Behold, you have become a monk.'"[2087]

> From St. Anthony the Great, St. Pachomios the Great, the lives of the abbas of the desert and onward, the order of the monastic tonsure and confession began to take shape over time and be instituted in terms of its ceremony.[2088]

St. Eustathios of Thessalonica taught that God revealed to the holy Fathers how to tonsure: "The procedure for this Mystery [of tonsure] is found in the sacred books of the most holy Fathers, who prescribed such things by divine revelation."[2089] A Russian historian explained in more detail:

> Historical documents attest that the rules to be followed and the ceremonies to be performed in receiving into the monasteries those who presented themselves to embrace the monastic life, were already fixed in the monastery of St. Pachomios the Great. The candidates were minutely interrogated, and put to the test to see whether they were really capable of practising the austerities and the rude mortifications of Oriental asceticism, and afterwards were admitted to assume the monastic garb. This does not, however, imply the existence of a special ceremonial for admission to the monastery. This ritual, the ceremonial which we find in the liturgical documents of the Byzantine Church, is later than St. Pachomios. Nevertheless, the practice followed in the Egyptian monasteries must have had a great influence in the formation of the Byzantine ritual of monachism.

> At what time this ritual was composed is not definitely known. Neither in the *Regula Patris nostri Pachomii* nor in the *De Institutis* of Johannes Cassianus do we find any trace of a form of monastic vows by which the candidate renounces the world. In his second canonical epistle to Amphilochius, St. Basil declares that he knows nothing of the existence of formulas (ἀνδρῶν ὁμολογίαν) by which the members of the

---

[2087] Παλλαδίου, *Λαυσαϊκὴ Ἱστορία,* «Ἄνθη τῆς Ἐρήμου» 16 (Ἅγιον Ὄρος: Ἰ. Μ. Σταυρονικήτα, 1990), 82. See also W. K. Lowther Clarke, *The Lausiac History of Palladius* (London: Society for Promoting Christian Knowledge, 1918), 99 (Chapter XXII).

[2088] Ἀρχιμανδρίτης Τύχων, *Περὶ τῆς Ἀξίας ἣν Κέκτηται ἐν τῇ Ἐκκλησίᾳ ἡ εἰς Ἀρχάριον Ρασοφοροῦντα Ἱερὰ Ἀκολουθία,* Περιοδικὸν «Γρηγόριος ὁ Παλαμᾶς», Τεῦχος 831, Νοέμ.–Δεκ. 2009.

[2089] PG 135:797BC.

monastic families pledged themselves to celibacy. Professor Palmov supposes accordingly that St. Basil, a zealous propagator and patron of the monastic life, was the first to require of candidates for the monastic life the reading of a formula professing monastic vows. This new custom was speedily followed by the redaction of the ceremonial for the taking of the habit. In the writings of the pseudo-Areopagite, which go back to the first half of the fifth century,[2090] we find the rules to be followed in the taking of the habit already fixed.[2091]

Although the service of tonsure for the great schema nowadays is not generally considered one of the Mysteries (i.e., sacraments) of the Church, it was considered a Mystery by Sts. Dionysius the Areopagite,[2092] Theodore the Studite,[2093] Eustathios of Thessalonica,[2094] and Symeon of Thessalonica.[2095] And St. Sophrony of Essex added: "In his *Feast of the Virgins* St. Methodios of Olympus speaks of virginity as of an 'extraordinarily great work,' a 'sacrament' (μυστήριον). And undoubtedly if marriage is a sacrament, then virginity, too, is a sacrament of the Church."[2096]

[2090] The following seven problematic questions have led the vast majority of both Orthodox and heterodox theologians and scholars to believe that the writings attributed to Dionysius the Areopagite (mentioned in Acts 17:34) do not in fact hail from the first century:

1) Why were these writings of such importance never quoted or even mentioned by a single writer until they suddenly appeared in the sixth century? (This, in fact, was why the Orthodox in AD 532 initially rejected the claim of Severan Monophysites that these writings were authentic.)

2) How could the author describe a developed form of monasticism that would exist in Greece only several centuries later than the time he ostensibly lived in? (According to Fr. Theodoros Zeses, monasticism began in Greece in the fifth century. See *Μοναχισμός: Μορφὲς καὶ Θέματα,* 107.)

3) How could he seem to know about the "Henotikon" of Emperor Zenon (in 482) and use the post-Chalcedon precise theological term "*θεανδρικὴ ἐνέργεια*"?

4) How could he apparently rely so heavily on the works of the neo-Platonic writer Proclus (411–485) and seem to quote him?

5) In his letter to Timothy in *On the Divine Names,* how could he include a quote of Ignatius that was definitely written only *after* Timothy's death?

6) How could he describe liturgical developments (such as the recitation of the Creed in the Liturgy) that would take place only centuries later?

7) Why does a linguistic analysis of the writings indicate that they were most likely written much later than in the first century?

For a detailed examination of this issue, see: "Pseudo-Dionysios the Areopagite and the *Corpus Dionysiacum,*" Archbishop Chrysostomos, *Orthodox Tradition* 35, no. 2 (2018): 3–31.

[2091] Tchokoloff, "The Assumption of the Religious Dress in Monasticism: Ceremonies for the Assumption of the Dress in the Monasticism of the Greek Church," *Studies in History and Archaeology,* Kiev, 1914, as reviewed by Aurelio Palmieri, *Harvard Theological Review* 8 (April 1915): 270–71.

[2092] Vid. Luibhéid, *Pseudo-Dionysius: The Complete Works,* 245 (PG 3:533A).

[2093] Vid. PG 99:1524.

[2094] Vid. PG 135:733D.

[2095] Vid. PG 155:177B, 197A.

[2096] Sakharov, *Truth and Life,* 93.

The *Greek* edition of the service of tonsure for the Great Schema has the following rubrics:

The previous evening, all the garments of him who is to receive the Great and Angelic Schema which are intended for this purpose are brought and placed in the Holy Sanctuary.[2097]

... In the Divine Liturgy, after the entrance of the holy gospel, the priest places the holy gospel before the Beautiful Door just in front of the holy icon of the Master Christ, also placing upon the gospel a pair of scissors. He is who going to receive the Holy Schema, standing before the doors of the Church, puts off his head covering and whatever clothing he is wearing, remaining only in his underclothes. The Abbot receives him there and, holding him by the hand and going before him, makes a gesture to him to make—and he makes—one prostration at the time he enters the Church, one in the middle of the Church, one before the Beautiful Doors, one each to the right and left choirs, three each to the Holy Icons of Christ, the Mother of God and the Saint of the Monastery, and one to the Abbot, whose right hand he kisses. The postulant then stands on the Abbot's left having his arms crossed on his breast.[2098]

The *Slavonic* version of the rubrics adds the following details which are not in the Greek version:

It is fitting that every one who desires to receive the Tonsure should first (before receiving it in Church) confess all his sins to a Confessor-Father, and receive from him full absolution, and be ready for the reception of the most holy mysteries of the Body and Blood of Christ.

During the singing of the Troparion, "Haste thee to open," all the brethren go to the entrance of the Church, at the west end of the Nave, where they form into a procession with lighted candles. While the troparion is being sung softly the brethren advance in procession, two by two, towards the sanctuary, the candidate, supported on either side by the Starets and the ecclesiarch, following in the rear. The candidate, clothed in the Vlasyanitsa [i.e., a long hair-shirt] only, walks between them ungirded, barefooted, and with hands folded upon his breast as though they were bound. On entering into the Nave he makes a low bow of the head towards the east; then coming to the midst of the Nave, in front of the Ambo, he makes a similar prostration; and on approaching the Holy Doors of the Iconostasis he falls to the ground and remains prostrate, praying silently to the Lord that his sins may be forgiven, and that he may be received into the rank of penitents.

When the singing of the troparion is ended, and while the candidate is still lying upon his face, the Hegumen says in a loud voice: "The merciful God, like a loving Father, beholding thy lowliness and true penitence, receiveth thee, my child, as a prodigal son that is penitent and with hearty sorrow falleth down before him." Then, bending, he raises the prostrate candidate, taking him by the right hand. And he, rising

---

[2097] Τάξις καὶ Ἀκολουθία τοῦ Μεγάλου καὶ Ἀγγελικοῦ Σχήματος (Ἅγιον Ὄρος, 1978), 7. St. Eustathios of Thessalonica explained why this is done: "First of all, it is evident that the weapons people take to protect themselves spiritually in the war they have agreed to undertake are weapons from a most holy armory. In accordance with the typikon of weaponry, the holy garments remain within the holy altar and are sanctified throughout the previous night. In this manner it is as if they are dipped like hot iron in water in order to acquire the necessary hardness for protection" (PG 135:741D–744A).

[2098] Τάξις καὶ Ἀκολουθία τοῦ Μεγάλου καὶ Ἀγγελικοῦ Σχήματος, 14–15.

and standing upright, with eyes downcast and hands folded upon the breast, makes a reverent bow of the head towards the Holy Table. The Hegumen then asks the first two questions contained in the Office, receiving the candidate's answer to each. He then says: "Truly a good work," etc. Then follows the exhortation, "Open the ears of thine heart," etc. After which the remaining questions are asked.[2099]

Although most of these Slavonic rubrics are not observed in contemporary Greek practice, they apparently reflect a more ancient Greek practice. For the following rubrics described by St. Symeon of Thessalonica in the fifteenth century are similar to the Slavonic rubrics above:

> He who voluntarily wants to become a monk comes and, having promised to live his life in accordance with God's will, is tried out for a definite time; and having given proof from his life and seeking the perfection of the schema (so as not to appear that he is coerced or forced) he is led to the temple. Since he is offering himself as a gift, he removes himself from the world. And he stands outside the gates [of the temple] because he has not yet been counted among the angels and angelic men. But as one repenting he stands outside paradise and heaven, entreating to be brought inside. When the holy mystagogy [i.e., the Divine Liturgy] has begun, after the first entrance to the altar, which represents the offering up above of our nature, he is brought like the lost sheep that was found and taken up on the Master's shoulders.
>
> He is bare of worldly clothes and his feet and head are bare because, on the one hand, he has cast off everything superfluous and worldly, and on the other hand, because he is poor and a pauper, as one whose wealth has been stolen by the thieves and who is gravely wounded and left naked, lying half-dead (vid. Lk. 10:30), whose possessions have also been taken by the evil citizens and who is afflicted by the famine and the terrible food (vid. Lk. 15:14–16).
>
> Therefore he is brought naked by the good servants as if by messengers of the men who are equal to angels, while the hymn "Make haste to open fatherly arms unto me" is sung out loud. And candles are lit, signifying the grace and illumination and the heavenly joy. And the one brought forth falls down three times (for the sake of the Trinity and the certainty of the offering) and rises three times (for he has risen from his fall). After approaching the holy doors [of the altar] as if approaching heaven, he falls down before the teacher [i.e., the abbot] as if to the heavenly Father, and he is joyfully welcomed like the prodigal son. Then he rises and falls down before the brethren seeking forgiveness, as if begging the older son not to be angry (vid. Lk. 15:28), since he has reviled them as well by living mindlessly. In this manner he is reconciled to them along with the heavenly Father.[2100]

Professor Nenad Milosevic observed: "The manuscript euchologia, dating from the 10th to the 15th centuries, provide evidence that the monastic tonsure was conducted in close association with the Liturgy. Manuscripts and printed euchologia from the 15th century until today demonstrate that this service may be conducted in connection with the Liturgy,

---

[2099] *Slavonic Profession Rites* (Petrograd: Synodical Press, 1909), as translated in Robinson, *Monasticism in the Orthodox Churches,* 144–45).

[2100] PG 155:489D–492C.

though the rubrics of these euchologia also envisage the performance of the rite of the tonsure independently of the Liturgy."[2101]

Elder Aimilianos explained: "In the early days, the service of the monastic tonsure was conducted on the altar table. The monk or the nun would enter into the altar and remain there for eight days. The tonsure is a Mystery performed within the altar. Since we [in recent centuries] have moved it to take place outside the altar, for that moment our Church symbolically brings out the gospel book on a table in front of the royal gate, and from that table we receive the monastic garments."[2102]

In contemporary Athonite practice, the odes of the Orthros canon of the Tonsure Service are usually read instead of being chanted. But St. Eustathios of Thessalonica emphasized the importance of chanting them: "When the Mystery of this work is about to be performed, it is preceded by spiritual odes and psalms, which make a kind of covenant for a joyful soul. An ode is joyful, since a sad animal never sings."[2103]

4) The "Three" Vows

In the Service of the Great Schema, the postulant states that he has come to the Lord of his own free will out of a desire for the life of ascesis. He then vows to:

1) "renounce the world and the things which are in the world,"[2104]
2) "remain in the monastery and in ascesis until his last breath,"[2105]
3) "preserve unto death obedience to the superior and to the whole brotherhood in Christ,"[2106]
4) "endure every affliction and deprivation of the Monastic life for the sake of the Kingdom of the Heavens,"[2107] and
5) "preserve himself in virginity and chastity and piety."[2108]

[2101] Nenad S. Milosevic, *"To Christ and the Church,"* Bishop Maxim Vasiljevic, ed., trans. Fr. Gregory Edwards and Dushan Radosavljevic (Los Angeles: Sebastian Press, 2012), 142.

[2102] Γέροντος Αἰμιλιανοῦ, *Νηπτικὴ Ζωὴ καὶ Ἀσκητικοὶ Κανόνες,* 79.

[2103] PG 135:744A.

[2104] Cf. *The Great Book of Needs,* vol. 1, 363. The monastic understanding of renouncing the world is expounded on in chapter 1) section 3) on page 19.

[2105] *The Great Book of Needs,* vol. 1, 363. For an explanation of the monastic virtue of stability, see chapter 1) section 4) on page 36.

[2106] *The Great Book of Needs,* vol. 1, 363. St. Joseph the Hesychast wrote: "We who have put on the holy schema have clothed ourselves with obedience" (Γέροντος Ἰωσήφ, *Ἔκφρασις Μοναχικῆς Ἐμπειρίας,* 169; see also Elder Joseph, *Monastic Wisdom,* 151).

[2107] *The Great Book of Needs,* vol. 1, 363.

[2108] Ibid., 364.

In the Slavonic version of the service for the great schema, the priest also asks: "Do you vow to remain unto death in non-acquisitiveness and in the voluntary poverty for Christ's sake which belong to the common life; not acquiring or keeping anything for yourself except in accordance with common necessity, and then, only in obedience and not of your own discretion?" And the monk is to reply: "Yes, Reverend Father, I will so remain, God helping me."[2109] Although this explicit vow of poverty is absent from the Greek version of the service of the great schema, it is implicit in the catechism read immediately after the other vows.[2110] Commenting on this part of the catechism, St. Eustathios of Thessalonica wrote: "He is urged to dedicate himself to spiritual struggles and to poverty—which could be understood as being spiritually poor, lacking sins, or as lacking worldly wealth."[2111]

St. Sophrony of Essex explained why the above five vows are considered three:

> "But," we may ask, "if four promises are made for the 'little schema' and five for the great, why do we speak of *three* vows?" Church tradition condenses the substance of monastic dedication into the three vows of obedience, chastity and adherence to the spirit of non-acquisition (poverty).... There is a widespread impression that the main difference between monasticism and ordinary life lies in the celibacy required of the monk or nun. But, in harmony with the Holy Fathers of old and with contemporary ascetics, I would give first importance to obedience, because it often happens that men remain celibate all their lives without becoming monks either in the sacramental sense or even in spirit. Similarly, poverty, understood in the sense of being content with little, is met with among people who are very far from having the monastic spirit.[2112]

St. Sophrony also taught the permanency of these vows:

> [The vow of] remaining in abstinence to one's last breath, gives the monastic vows an irrevocable, inexorable character, extending even beyond the temporal boundaries of this life. The Lord said: "No man, having put his hand to the plough, and looking back, is fit for the kingdom of God."[2113] Here the word "fit" is a translation of the Greek εὔθετος, signifying *suitably prepared for.* And indeed, to make the monastic vows for a certain time only is to misunderstand their real sense and reduce them to a simple exercise of piety, whereas in actual fact they stand for the relinquishment of spiritual childhood for the sake of becoming an adult. St. Paul says: "When I was a child, I spake as a child, I understood as a child, I thought as a child; but when I became

---

[2109] *The Great Book of Needs,* vol. 1, 364.

[2110] The full text of the catechism is presented on the following page, but here are the parts of it that refer to poverty: "Know, therefore, that from the present day you are crucified and dead to the world because of the entire renunciation. For you are renouncing parents, brethren, wife, children, near kinsmen, the customary friendship of others, the tumult of the world, cares, acquisitions, possessions.... If, therefore, you have chosen to follow Him in truth ... be prepared from this present time, not for comfort ... but for spiritual and bodily poverty" (*The Great Book of Needs,* vol. 1, 365).

[2111] PG 135:745A.

[2112] Sakharov, *Truth and Life,* 78, 82.

[2113] Lk. 9:62.

a man I put away childish things."[2114] Childhood is irrecoverable, not so much in the temporal sense as in the sense of a quality of life. How can experience, knowledge, intelligence disappear? Similarly, these promises express another vision of existence, of its meaning, its purpose, its content. What, for instance, distinguishes the vow of chastity from some impermanent abstinence on the part of any other man, if it be considered merely as a temporary exercise? And, if we regard obedience simply as a passing exercise, where is the consciousness that through obedience we are warring against the constricting "narrowness" of self-will and egoism in order to become the bearers of the will of the Heavenly Father? Likewise, if one sees "poverty" only as a temporary state of privation, where is our perception that this vow symbolizes our determination with God's help to master the power of matter over spirit? So, then, he who goes back on his vows is not "fit" for the Kingdom. And we may say that if a monk sets aside his vows it generally means that he pronounced them without having the necessary understanding or being in the right spirit. In other words, he did not keep his vows because he did not take them in the proper fashion.[2115]

Although these vows are given in the presence of other people during the tonsure service, St. Basil the Great pointed out that these people are merely witnesses of vows which are given not to man but to God: "Ecclesiastical officials should be called in as witnesses of the decision, so that through their presence, as well, the consecration of the person as a kind of votive offering to God may be sanctified and the act ratified by their testimony."[2116]

St. Joseph the Hesychast recommended that great-schema monks should read through the Service of the Great Schema again from time to time in order to renew their zeal and to be reminded of their responsibilities and the vows they had given to God.[2117] Likewise, St. Daniel of Katounakia wrote: "Contemplating this [service of the great schema] reminds us of great truths and of our important obligations. Therefore, we monks should as much as possible continually examine these sacred vows with much attention and deep awareness, since a profound study of them inspires the fear of God and obliges us to fulfill our awesome vows as much as possible."[2118]

5) The Catechism

After the postulant has made his vows in the service of tonsure, the priest reads for him the following catechism:

Behold, my child, what manner of promises thou art giving to our Saviour Christ; for Angels are present invisibly, inscribing this thy profession, for which also thou art

---

[2114] 1 Cor. 13:11.

[2115] Sakharov, *Truth and Life*, 104–5.

[2116] *Saint Basil Ascetical Works*, vol. 9, 267 (The *Long Rules*, #15).

[2117] Vid. Elder Ephraim, *My Elder Joseph the Hesychast*, 237.

[2118] Γέροντος Δανιὴλ Κατουνακιώτου, *Ἀγγελικὸς Βίος* (Ἅγιον Ὄρος: Ἔκδοσις Μοναστικῆς Ἀδελφότητος Δανιηλαίων, 1987), 97.

to be held accountable at the Second Coming of our Lord Jesus Christ. I am explaining therefore unto thee this most perfect life, in which, by similitude, our Lord's manner of life is exemplified, testifying what things thou oughtest to embrace, and what things it is necessary to avoid. For the renunciation is nothing else, as concerning him that uttereth it, than a promise of a cross and of a death. Know, then, that from the present day thou art crucified and dead to the world, by reason of the entire renunciation; for thou art renouncing parents, brethren, wife, children, near kindred, companionships, the hubbub of the world, cares, possessions, belongings, and empty and vain pleasures and glory; and thou art abjuring, not only the aforementioned things, but even thine own life also, according to the saying of the Lord, which declareth: "Whosoever will come after Me, let him deny himself, and take up his cross, and follow Me."[2119] If, therefore, thou hast chosen to follow Him in truth, and if thou dost ardently desire to be called, not falsely, His disciple, be prepared from this present time—not for repose, nor for freedom from care, nor for pleasures, nor for any other of the pleasing and delightful things upon earth—but for spiritual conflicts, for continence of flesh, for purity of soul, for strict poverty, for sincere mourning, for all the grievous and painful things of the joy-giving life in God. For thou hast to hunger, and to thirst, and to be naked, and to suffer reproach and ridicule, to be both insulted and persecuted, and to become a prey to many other grievous things, whereby the life in God is distinguished. And when thou hast suffered all these things, "Rejoice," saith the Lord, "for great is your reward in heaven."[2120] With joy, then, rejoice, and exult with exultation, for today the Lord God hath chosen thee, and set thee apart from the life in the world; and He hath placed you, as before His face, in the estate of the Monastic order, in the campaign of the angel-like life, in the loftiness of the imitation of the heavenly citizenship; to worship Him after the manner of angels, to serve Him wholly, to think upon those things which are above, and to seek after them. For our conversation, according to the Apostle, is in Heaven (vid. Phil. 3:20).

Oh, what a vocation! Oh, what a mysterious gift! A second Baptism art thou receiving today, Brother (Sister), in the abundance of the gifts of God who loveth men; and thou shalt be cleansed from thy sins, and become a son (daughter) of light; and Christ Himself, our God, rejoiceth with His holy Angels over thy repentance, killing for thee the fatted calf. Therefore walk worthy of thy vocation, rid thyself of the passion for vanities, hate the desire that draweth thee to the lower things, turn thy whole desire towards the heavenly things; by no means look back to the things that are behind, lest thou become a pillar of salt, like Lot's wife, or like a dog turning to his own vomit again; and lest in thy case the word of the Lord find a fulfilment: "No man, having put his hand to the plough, and looking back, is fit for the Kingdom of God."[2121] For thou art in no small danger, though thou hast now promised to observe all the aforementioned things, of thinking lightly of thy promise; and either of going back again to thy former life, or of separating thyself from the Father and Brethren (Mother and Sisters), who are thy fellow-ascetics; or else, remaining, of spending thy days disorderly. For thou shalt have accounts to render, heavier than before, at the dreadful and unerring tribunal of Christ; in proportion as thou art now rejoicing in greater grace. And better would it be according to the saying, not to vow, than to vow and not to pay (cf. Eccl.

[2119] Mt. 16:24.

[2120] Mt. 5:12.

[2121] Lk. 9:62.

5:5). And again, think not that during the preceding time of thy sojourn here thou hast sufficiently fought against the invisible forces of the enemy; but know that from this time forward greater struggles yet will come upon thee in the conflict against him. But he will in no wise prevail against thee, if he find thee hedged about both by a strong faith in, and a love for, Him who leadeth thee; and also by an integrity of purpose for all obedience and lowliness.

Therefore, put far away from thee unwillingness to listen, gainsaying, pride, strife, jealousy, envy, anger, clamour, blasphemy, stealthy eating, boldness, particular friendships, bragging, quarrelling, grumbling, tale-bearing, private acquisition of some miserable thing, and all other kinds of wickedness; by reason of which the wrath of God cometh on those who do such things, and the seducer of souls beginneth to take root in them. But rather, instead of these, procure for thyself the things that are becoming to Saints—brotherly love, quietness, meekness, meditation on the divine sayings, reading, keeping the heart from unclean thoughts, working according to the ability, continence, endurance until death—under the guidance of a Confession-Father, with whom thou hast first entered into a spiritual relationship, and afterwards hast made a declaration of the secrets of thy heart, in the manner that the Holy Scriptures relate; for "they were baptized," say they, "confessing their sins" (Mt. 3:6).[2122]

Upon hearing this catechism, the postulant "professes all these things in the hope of the strength of God and agrees to persevere in these promises until the end of life, by the grace of Christ."[2123]

6) The Three Prayers

Next, the priest reads three prayers to God for the monk. Presented below are the central parts of those prayers:

1) May the All-compassionate and greatly merciful God, Who openeth up to every one that comes to Him with desire and fervent love, unsearchable goodness from the depths of His own most-pure being, saying, "A woman shall forget the child she has brought forth before ever I will forget thee"; Who also knoweth your desire, and to your good purpose doth lend His own strength for the fulfillment of His commandments, receive, embrace, and shield you; and may He be unto you a firm wall from the face of the enemy, a rock of endurance, a source of consolation, a giver of strength, an inspirer of boldness, a fellow combatant in courage, present with you when you lie down and when you get up, delighting and making glad your heart through the consolation of His own Holy Spirit, and counting you worthy of the portion of our Holy and Venerable Fathers, Anthony, Euthymius, Sabbas, and all the other Venerable Fathers with whom you also shall inherit the Heavenly Kingdom in Christ Jesus our Lord.[2124]

[2122] Robinson, *Monasticism in the Orthodox Churches,* 105–8; see also *The Great Book of Needs,* vol. 1, 364–66.

[2123] Cf. *The Great Book of Needs,* vol. 1, 367.

[2124] Ibid.

2) With a merciful eye, look upon the humility of Thy servant (handmaid) _____,[2125] who has promised and vowed before many witnesses. Join to the gift of adoption and Thy Kingdom, given him (*her*), through Holy Baptism, by his (*her*) first parents, this monastic and angelic vocation, that stands perfectly on the cornerstone and on the spiritual rock that is faith in Thee. Strengthen him (*her*) in the power of Thy might, and put on him (*her*) the whole armor of Thy Holy Spirit, for he (*she*) wars not against flesh and blood but against principalities, against powers, against the rulers of the darkness of this age, against spiritual wickedness. Gird his (*her*) loins with the power of truth, and clothe him (*her*) in the breastplate of righteousness and rejoicing, and put shoes on his (*her*) feet in preparation of the Gospel of peace. Instruct him (*her*) to take the shield of faith, wherewith he (*she*) shall be able to quench all the fiery darts of the evil one, and to take the helmet of salvation and the sword of the Spirit, which is Thy word, helping him (*her*) in the groanings of his (*her*) heart which cannot be uttered. Number him (*her*) with Thine elect, that he (*she*) may become Thy chosen vessel, a son (*daughter*) and heir of Thy Kingdom, a son (*daughter*) of light and of the day, of wisdom, uprightness, sanctification, redemption. Make him (*her*) a harmonious instrument, a sweet psaltery of the Holy Spirit, that henceforth, having progressively put off the old man, corrupted by the seductive deception of the serpent of many forms, he (*she*) may be clothed with the new Adam, which after God is created in holiness and righteousness. Strengthen him (*her*) to bear at all times in his (*her*) body the wounds and the Cross of Jesus by which the world is crucified unto him (*her*), and he (*she*) unto the world. Form in him (*her*) the practicing of true virtue, and not the pleasing of men or the pleasing of self, in patient reverence, and in pious brotherly love and obedience. Grant unto him (*her*), whether awake, working, sleeping, or rising up, in psalmody and hymns and spiritual songs, after the manner of Angels to behold Thee with a pure heart, and to worship Thee, the only living and true God, to his (*her*) ineffable joy.[2126]

3) Do Thou bless Thy servant (*handmaid*) whom Thou hast summoned to Thy spiritual bridal chamber, and make him (*her*) worthy to be Thy holy servant (*handmaid*). Grant wisdom unto him (*her*), and pour out upon him (*her*) the grace and understanding of Thy governing Spirit; strengthen him (*her*) for the warfare against the unseen enemy; cast down by Thy mighty power the uprisings of the flesh; grant him (*her*) to be well-pleasing unto Thee in unceasing hymns and doxologies, in fitting songs, in acceptable prayers, in righteous understanding, in a humble heart, and in the exercise of meekness and truth. And vouchsafe him (*her*) to please Thee in meekness, in love, in perfection, in understanding, in courage; and to offer unto Thee hymns and doxologies and prayers, for an odor of sweet fragrance. Make perfect his (*her*) life in holiness and righteousness, that having an abiding and pure union with Thee, he (*she*) may be counted worthy of the Heavenly Kingdom.[2127]

Commenting on these prayers, Metropolitan Hierotheos Vlachos wrote:

If one reads these three prayers carefully, one can grasp the essence and the "spirit" of Orthodox monasticism, in which there is no place for any kind of individualistic, sentimental, pharisaical, or activistic mindset....

[2125] The name mentioned here is the name that the candidate has had until this time.

[2126] *The Great Book of Needs,* vol. 1, 368–69.

[2127] Ibid., 369.

It is clear from the words of these three prayers that monastic life is an angelic state, living the future life in this life. The monk is trained how to enter into the heavenly life and is taught that he must live constantly in what the Fathers call "illumination of the nous," which in reality is the basis of the spiritual life. When a person is in the state of illumination, he can experience lofty ascents—seeing the uncreated Light—and be initiated into the knowledge of God, in which case he will become an unerring theologian in the Church. Monastic life is the "most perfect life" among human levels and in the realm of corruption and death.[2128]

When a person is tonsured, he receives a new name. St. Nectarios of Aegina explained to his nuns the reasons for this as follows:

The changing of names has become the practice of righteous nuns [and monks] who have professed to live a life according to virtue. There are two very important reasons for this. The first reason is to completely deny the past and constantly remember the change of life, and secondly, so we may hold the saint whose name we bear as an example in our life's struggle. The change of names makes one forget the past and serves as a constant reminder of the change that occurred in the person who has changed his way of life, and of the repeated duties that he ought to fulfill with great love and eagerness.[2129]

Abba Ammonas wrote to his monastic disciples in the fourth century regarding changing names:

When a person changes his life and attains a different life pleasing to God that is more spiritual than the former, his name is changed. When our holy Fathers made progress, their names were changed, and they were given a new name written in the tablets of heaven. For when Sarrah made progress, she was told: "Your name shall not be Sara but Sarrah" (cf. Gen. 17:15). Abram was given the name Abraham, Isac became Isaac,[2130] Jacob became Israel, Saul became Paul, and Simon become Cephas because their life changed and progressed from their former state. This is why you, too, who have become more spiritually mature, should change your names according to your spiritual progress.[2131]

Evgenia Zhoukova (who was apparently unaware of the previous paragraph written by Abba Ammonas) concluded in her dissertation:

A new addition to the reception into monasticism took place in the late eighth or early ninth century: the Service of the Monastic Schema (which by then had already been instituted) mentions the practice of changing of one's name. This practice was unknown until then. In the Lives of the Saints from the fourth to the seventh centuries we encountered a change in name only in the event that barbarians came to monasticism, in which case the change in name clearly took place at baptism....

[2128] Ἱεροθέου, Ὁ Ὀρθόδοξος Μοναχισμός, 536; Hierotheos, *Orthodox Monasticism*, 476–78.

[2129] Strongylis, *St. Nectarios of Pentapolis and the Island of Aegina*, vol. 2, 106 (Letter #39).

[2130] Although three codices of the Greek Septuagint (Alexandrinus, Vaticanus, and Sinaiticus) contain both spellings of Ἰσάκ and Ἰσαάκ, none of them indicate that his name was changed at some point.

[2131] Ἀββᾶς Ἀμμωνᾶς (Ὠρωπὸς Ἀττικῆς: Ἱερὰ Μονὴ Παρακλήτου, 1999), 46–47 (Ἐπιστολὴ ε΄).

Thus it is clear that the change of name that took place when entering monasticism was instituted between the eighth and ninth centuries in order to reinforce the notion that the Service of the Monastic Schema is a second baptism. After witnessing the ancient tradition, however, the modern custom prevailing in some places of changing names twice or three times during the Services at different stages of monastic life seems strange and unacceptable.[2132]

7) **Tonsure**

As with all other Mysteries of the Church, specific actions are taken in conjunction with the prayers. In the case of the monastic tonsure, the first action done after these prayers is for the postulant's hair to be cut. According to St. Eustathios of Thessalonica, this "symbolizes his complete dedication to God, since he gives something of himself to God and thus begins a new life."[2133] When St. Maximos the Confessor was asked what the clipping of the hairs at a monastic tonsure signifies, he replied: "As the head governs all the parts of the body, thus, also, the nous holds the place of the head in the soul. And so, it is necessary to clip off from this all worldly thoughts."[2134]

St. Symeon of Thessalonica described this part of the service as follows:

[The priest] lifts up the one who is lying down, showing that he has risen up from sin and received remission, and that the Father has welcomed him and has restored his sonship to him and gives him the former garment of purification and joins him to the angels. This is why the priest takes him by his right hand when he lifts him up and shows him the Gospel as if it were the Savior and tells him to kiss it, which represents the embrace and kiss of the Father [as in the parable of the prodigal son].

Then he says: "Behold, Christ is invisibly present here," and he orders him to be careful so that he will not fall again, since no one is forcing him to come unwillingly, but he has come voluntarily. He then confesses this to be so, that he has come voluntarily. Then the priest says to him again: "Behold, Christ is invisibly present here, and see to Whom you are approaching (to Christ Himself, that is) and whom you are renouncing (that is, the world itself and things of the world)."

He then gives him the scissors and says: "Take the scissors and give them back to me" in order to demonstrate his volition. And if the priest tonsuring is himself both the sponsor and the Father, he receives it from the monk being tonsured, who kisses it first. Otherwise, the sponsor receives it and gives it to the priest, and the priest gives it again to the one being tonsured, who kisses it again and gives it to the sponsor, who gives it again to the priest. This is done three times, in honor of the Trinity and to certify what is happening.

When the priest gives the scissors to him the third time he says: "Behold, you receive them from the hand of Christ." This is a fearsome saying, instilling awe in

---

[2132] Ζουκόβα, *Γέννηση καὶ Ἐξέλιξη τῆς Ἀκολουθίας τοῦ Μοναχικοῦ Σχήματος,* 277–78.

[2133] Ibid.

[2134] *St. Maximus the Confessor's Questions and Doubts,* trans. Despina D. Prassas (Chicago: Northern Illinois University Press, 2010), 149.

those who hear it. Then he takes the scissors and adds: "Blessed is God Who desires that all be saved," etc. It is proper to thank God for all His salvific works.

Immediately the priest tonsures him in the name of the Trinity in the shape of the cross on the top of his head.[2135] He deposits the hairs in the altar, showing that they (as well as the entire person who has been offered) are the first fruits and a gift to God and a living, well-pleasing sacrifice. Then he dresses him with the garments of the schema, sealing each one of them with the sign of the cross.[2136]

... The tonsure is done in the shape of the cross as a sign of dying to the world and being sealed by Him Who was crucified for us. The removal and cutting of hairs signifies offering to the Lord the first fruits of the body. For the entire person is brought forth and dedicated to Christ, and he sets aside everything superfluous and mundane.[2137]

The second canon of the First-and-Second Council declares that the abbot must be present at the tonsure:

No one at all shall assume the monachal habit without the presence of the person to whom he owes allegiance and who is to act as his superior or abbot ... by which is meant a God-beloved man at the head of a monastery.... For indiscreet and precarious tonsures have both dishonored the monachal habit and caused the name of Christ to be blasphemed.[2138]

For some unknown reason, St. Nicodemos of the Holy Mountain interpreted this canon to mean that the priest tonsuring a monk and the monk's sponsor must be two different people. This is why he was astonished to see that St. Symeon (in the quote on the previous page) permits the priest who is tonsuring a monk to be his sponsor as well. St. Nicodemos concluded that St. Symeon implied that this is only permitted in case of great necessity.[2139]

[2135] In particular, the priest cuts a lock of hair at the front of head while saying: "In the Name of the Father," another lock at the back of head while saying: "and the Son," and one on either side of the head while saying: "and the Holy Spirit."

[2136] PG 155:496B–497A.

[2137] PG 155:493C.

[2138] The full text of this canon is as follows: "In view of the fact that some men pretend to take up the life of solitude, not in order to become purely servants of God, but in order that in addition to and by virtue of the grave appearance of the habit they may acquire the glory and mien of reverence, and find hence a way of enjoying in abundance the pleasures connected therewith, and, only sacrificing their hair, they spend their time in their own homes, without fulfilling any service or status whatever of monks, the holy Council has decreed that no one at all shall assume the monachal habit without the presence of the person to whom he owes allegiance and who is to act as his superior or abbot and to provide for the salvation of his soul, by which is meant a God-beloved man at the head of a monastery and capable of saving a soul that has but recently offered itself to Christ. If anyone be caught tonsuring a person without the presence of the abbot who is to have charge of him, he shall be deposed from office on the ground that he is disobeying the Canons and offending against monachal decorum, while the one who has been illogically and irregularly tonsured shall be consigned to whatever allegiance and monastery the local bishop may see fit. For indiscreet and precarious tonsures have both dishonored the monachal habit and caused the name of Christ to be blasphemed" (Agapius and Nicodemus, *The Rudder,* 457).

[2139] Vid. Agapius and Nicodemus, *The Rudder,* 458.

However, a careful reading of that canon reveals that it is not explicitly saying that the priest and the sponsor must be two different people but merely that the sponsor must be a spiritual elder.

There is a tradition that the priest who tonsures a great-schema monk should also have the great schema. St. Nicodemos discussed this matter as follows:

> As for the requirement that both the sponsor of the monk and the priest tonsuring the latter must wear the same habit as the monk in question is about to take, that of a megaloscheme [i.e., great schema], say, or of a staurophore, this, I say, notwithstanding that we have not received it from any Canon, ought nevertheless to be observed in practice because of the fact that this custom has come to prevail as a matter of tradition. In fact, most holy Patriarch Lucas (or Luke), together with the Synod attending him, in solving certain questions preserved in manuscripts, says about this custom: "As respects the tonsure of a megaloscheme performed by a mandyote (i.e., a staurophore priest) there is always some doubt. Rather lucky, however, I have been in coming across a Canon purporting to be one of Patriarch Nicephoros, in which it is expressly stated that a megaloscheme must be tonsured by a megaloscheme priest, because one can only give what he possesses. To us, however, it appears that it is the part of a priest to tonsure others, not because of his being a monk, but because of his being a priest, no matter of what habit he be. Nevertheless, if the mind of the man who is about to become a monk is shaken by doubts, let him be tonsured by a megaloscheme priest (unless there be some obstacle or necessity to preclude this) as a matter of preventing hesitation, and not as a matter of yielding to necessity.[2140]

There is some confusion regarding whether it is the bishop or the priest who should tonsure monastics. St. Symeon of Thessalonica pointed out that the postulant "does not have the hand of a bishop on him because he is not receiving ordination, but he only has the book of prayers on his head as he receives the prayers from the priest."[2141] Likewise, St. Dionysius the Areopagite wrote: "Hence the sacred ordinance has bestowed a perfecting grace on them [i.e., monks] and has deemed them worthy of a sanctifying invocation which is not the business of the hierarch (he only confers clerical ordination) but of the devout priests who sacredly perform this secondary rite of the hierarchy."[2142] This is why in contemporary practice on Mount Athos and in most men's monasteries in Greece, monastic tonsures are done by a priest rather than by a bishop. Nevertheless, St. Eustathios of Thessalonica taught that either a hierarch or a priest can tonsure a monk.[2143]

[2140] Ibid., 458–59.

[2141] PG 155:496B.

[2142] Luibhéid, *Pseudo-Dionysius: The Complete Works,* 245.

[2143] Vid. Φάνης Καλαϊτζάκης, «Τι φλυαρεί ο μέγας παπάς;» Εὐσταθίου Θεσσαλονίκης: Ἐπίσκεψις Βίου Μοναχικοῦ, (Ἀθήνα: Σαββάλας, 2003), 8; PG 135:733D.

In the fifth century, however, the Council in Carthage declared that "the consecration of virgin girls shall not be done by presbyters"[2144] but only by a bishop. Commenting on this, St. Nicodemos of the Holy Mountain wrote:

> Note that some say that the consecration of these virgins by means of prayers can be performed only by a bishop, and not also by a priest. But as for sponsoring these girls with the monachal habit, and reading to them the rite of bestowing the habit, and tonsuring them, these things may be done by a priest by permission of the bishop. In fact some declare that even the consecration of virgins may be performed by a priest with permission of the bishop.... I am astonished that St. Maximus should have declared that "a Bishop must not bestow a monk's habit, but only a Presbyter may do so," in interpreting ch. 6 of the *Ecclesiastical Hierarchy* of Dionysius the Areopagite. And the reason of this he says is the fact that divine Dionysius speaks of a Priest there tonsuring a monk, and not of a Prelate doing so. I am astonished, I say, that he could have said this at a time when this Council declares that this function is one which is peculiar to the bishop. But perhaps St. Dionysius spoke of a priest as being able to tonsure monks when acting by permission and with the approval of the bishop. That is why special permission is included in the licenses issued to a Spiritual [Father].[2145]

Georgios Apostolakis (a canon law expert) solved this dilemma with the following explanation:

> In the past, the opinion prevailed that the tonsure of women is performed solely by the bishop. This order was based on the custom that resulted from the 6th canon of the Council in Carthage, and it was in regards to the "dedication of girls." It did not survive, however, since the institution of "girls" or "virgins," which is not identical to the institution of women's monasticism, disappeared early on. Laws [in Greece] accept with regularity that "the monastic tonsure of women belongs to the work of both the local bishop as archpriest as well as to that of the presbyter, under the presupposition in regards to this latter one, that her entrance to the monastery for trial was approved of the Bishop."[2146]

The Seventh Ecumenical Council declared that if the abbot of a monastery is a priest and his bishop has laid his hands upon him to be abbot, he may ordain monks of his monastery to be readers.[2147] Commenting on this, Patriarch Theodore Balsamon wrote (in the 12th century): "Based on the ancient tradition prevailing in the place of the law, it seems to me that abbots who are priests may freely tonsure [monks] without the permission of the

---

[2144] Agapius and Nicodemus, *The Rudder,* 608 (Canon VI).

[2145] Ibid., 609.

[2146] Γεώργιος Ἀποστολάκης, *Σχέσεις Μητροπολίτου καὶ Ἱερῶν Μονῶν τῆς Ἐκκλησίας τῆς Ἑλλάδος* (Ἀθήνα: Πρότυπες Θεσσαλικὲς Ἐκδόσεις, 2003), 107–8.

[2147] Canon 14 of the Seventh Ecumenical Council states: "As for the appointment of an Anagnost [or Reader] by imposition of hands, each Abbot is given permission to do this but only in his own Monastery, provided that imposition of hands has been laid upon that very same Abbot himself by a Bishop to enable him to have the presidency of an Abbot—that is to say, more plainly speaking, if he is a Presbyter" (Agapius and Nicodemus, *The Rudder,* 443).

bishop. For if the 14th canon of the Seventh Council permits an abbot to seal a reader in his own monastery without informing his bishop, how much more so is he permitted to tonsure [monks]."[2148] The validity of this interpretation may be inferred from the 2nd Canon of the First-and-Second Council, which states that "if anyone be caught tonsuring a person without the presence of the abbot who is to have charge of him, he shall be deposed from office."[2149] For this canon does not say "without the permission of the bishop" but "without the presence of the abbot."

Historically there have been various traditions regarding how monks' hair should be worn. As one historian explained:

> Both men and women traditionally had their hair cut or removed in specific ways when they entered a monastery or convent. These haircuts symbolized religious devotion, group identity, and humility as well as the renunciation of worldly things and personal vanity. The practice may relate to ancient rites in which people in various cultures offered their hair as a religious sacrifice. Monks and nuns also take a vow of celibacy, and hair has historically been associated with eroticism and sexuality and as a means to attract the opposite sex. Historians say that monastic hairstyles also may relate to the ancient custom of shaving the heads of male slaves. Some early monks who began shaving their heads voluntarily referred to themselves as "slaves of Christ." Such hairstyles thus would show that a person entering religious life intends to subordinate his own will to the will of God.... Some monks cut their hair short, while others shaved it off completely or shaved part of their head.... Some orders of monks who left a narrow crown of hair around their heads said that this signified the crown of thorns placed on Christ's head during his crucifixion.... Three main variations of the tonsure developed among various orders. The eastern style involved shaving the head completely, according to a style attributed to St. Paul, while others shaved just the crown, a style associated with St. Peter and known as the Roman tonsure. A third style, called the Celtic (or transverse tonsure or tonsure of St. John) evolved in the British Isles. Celtic monks shaved the front part of their head from ear to ear but left the hair in the back hanging longer. Some Celtic monks pulled that hair around to form a semi-circle from one ear to the other.[2150]

The "eastern style" of shaving the head completely is mentioned in several ancient texts. For example, in the 4th century St. Pachomios decreed in his monastic rules: "No one shall shave his head without his housemaster's permission; nor shall a man shave another without being ordered; nor shall a man shave another when both are seated."[2151] Also in the 4th

[2148] Vid. Π. Παναγιωτάκου, *Σύστημα τοῦ Ἐκκλησιαστικοῦ Δικαίου*, 82

[2149] Agapius and Nicodemus, *The Rudder*, 457.

[2150] Victoria Sherrow, *Encyclopedia of Hair: A Cultural History* (Santa Barbara: Greenwood Publishing Group, 2006), 272.

[2151] Veilleux, *Pachomian Koinonia*, vol. 2, 161 (Rule #97). Archimandrite Innocent Belyaev suspects that the monastic haircut in the monasteries of St. Pachomios corresponded to the practice of Egyptians who shaved their head completely. Perhaps this is why St. Jerome criticized that haircut as something ethnic and said that keeping the head shaved makes an ascetic look like a servant of the gods Isis and Serapis (vid.

century, St. Ephraim the Syrian mentioned in passing that monastics had cut off their hair.[2152] In the late 4th century, St. Hilarion "shaved his head once a year on the day of holy Pascha."[2153] Venerable Bede wrote: "There was at that time [in the 7th century] in Rome, a monk, called Theodore ... to be ordained bishop.... Theodore, being ordained subdeacon, waited four months for his hair to grow, that it might be shorn into the shape of a crown; for he had before the tonsure of St. Paul, the Apostle, after the manner of the eastern people."[2154] St. Germanos of Constantinople wrote about monks in the 8th century: "Shaving the head entirely is in imitation of the holy Apostle James the Brother of the Lord and the Apostle Paul and the rest."[2155]

This practice was evidently still prevalent in 12th-century Byzantium, since St. Eustathios of Thessalonica mentioned: "A thief or a robber could pass himself off as a monk and fool people, especially if he cuts his hair and shaves his head."[2156] He also said: "If you, O beginner monk who are still far from perfection, desire to follow in the footsteps of those who proceed along the path to God, you have done well to cut off your hair, which symbolizes your good intent.... A monk who does not cut off his hair which is superfluous will only with great difficulty lay aside other worldly cares."[2157]

Not only monks but even nuns shaved their entire head in the early days of Egyptian monasticism. The *Lausiac History* mentions that in St. Pachomios's women's monastery, "all the women are shaved [κεκαρμένων] and have cowls."[2158] Another mention of nuns with shaved heads is found in the following incident told to Abba Pyrros by Sergios. In the days when Scetis in Egypt was still functioning, the ruler of Alexandria arrested seventy nuns in their monastery and ordered his deputy Sergios to bring them to him one day at a

---

Ζουκόβα, *Γέννηση καὶ Ἐξέλιξη τῆς Ἀκολουθίας τοῦ Μοναχικοῦ Σχήματος,* 254; Иннокентий [Беляев] архимандрит, Пострижение в монашество: Опыт историко-литургического изследования обрядов и чинопоследований пострижения в монашество в Греческой и Русской церквах до 17 века включительно [Вильна, 1899]).

[2152] Vid. *Ὁσίου Ἐφραὶμ τοῦ Σύρου: Ἔργα,* Τόμος Γ´ (Θεσσαλονίκη: ἐκδόσεις «Τὸ Περιβόλι τῆς Παναγίας», 1990), 184.

[2153] Παπαδοπούλου-Κεραμέως Ἀθ., *Ἀνάλεκτα Ἱεροσολυμιτικῆς Σταχυολογίας ἢ συλλογὴ ἀνεκδότων καὶ σπανίων ἑλληνικῶν συγγραφῶν περὶ τῶν κατὰ τὴν Ἑῴαν Ὀρθοδόξων Ἐκκλησιῶν καὶ μάλιστα τῆς τῶν Παλαιστινῶν,* τόμος 5 (Πετρούπολις, 1891–98), 88.

[2154] *Bede's Ecclesiastical History of England,* trans. A. M. Sellar (London: George Bell and Sons, 1907), 214.

[2155] PG 98:396B.

[2156] PG 135:805C.

[2157] PG 135:873CD.

[2158] Palladius, *The Lausiac History,* XXXIV.

time so that he could defile them. In order to protect their purity, Sergios hid them somewhere else and paid seventy prostitutes to take their place. In order to deceive the ruler,
though, Sergios had to shave the prostitutes' heads and give them monastic garments.[2159]

Some manuscripts of the Service of the Great Schema until the twelfth century include
rubrics stating that immediately after the new monk's hair has been cut in a crosswise
fashion, "the brethren lead him out to the narthex ... and the abbot or his sponsor takes him
and cuts off all his hair."[2160] In other words, two separate tonsures would take place in the
same service: one with liturgical significance done by the priest, and the other without
liturgical significance done by the abbot or the sponsor.[2161]

Canon XLII of the Sixth Ecumenical Council (AD 680) states that monks who let their
hair grow and associate with laymen in cities should either have their hair cut and live in
monasteries or else dwell in deserts. Commenting on this canon, St. Nicodemos of the Holy
Mountain wrote in the 18th century:

> Note from the present Canon that monks living in monasteries and coenobitic
> communities must cut their hair symmetrically; for it appears that monks affect a
> symmetrical haircut both from this Canon and from the discourse of Athanasius the
> Great concerning virginity, and also from the first *Sermon on Peace* by St. Gregory
> the Theologian, and from many historical narratives of Lausaicus, since the present
> time is (considered to be) a time of mourning among monks, according to divine
> Chrysostom (Homily on the Gospel of St. Matthew, No. 56) and John of the Ladder.
> God, by the way, says through Isaiah that shaving the head is a sign of mourning and
> weeping and of beating the breast (Is. 22:12). And if, as St. Paul says, any man in
> general is ugly when he has [long] hair (and see the footnote to Canon XCVI of the
> present Council), how much more ugly monks are who grow hair! But if all monks in
> general ought to cut their hair symmetrically, how much more ought young monks
> living in monasteries or cells, and deacons, to cut their hair! For such persons scandal-
> ize others with their beardless face as much as they do with their long combed hair.[2162]

St. Eustathios of Thessalonica also criticized monks with long hair in the 12th century:
"Most of you are breaking the rules in this matter by letting your hair grow longer than the
hair of women in the world."[2163] Commenting on this situation, Panagiotis Papaevangelos
wrote in his doctoral thesis:

> Eustathios wrote this apparently having in mind only the monks of Thessalonica
> and the Holy Mountain, and not a generally prevailing situation. This would explain
> the apparent silence regarding this issue of the aforementioned canon law experts who
> lived in Constantinople and Antioch [in the same century]. This would also explain the

---

[2159] Vid. Π. Β. Πάσχου, *Νέον Μητερικόν· Ἄγνωστα καὶ ἀνέκδοτα πατερικὰ καὶ ἀσκητικὰ κείμενα περὶ τιμίων καὶ ἁγίων Γυναικῶν,* Ἁγιολογικὴ βιβλιοθήκη 3 (Ἀθήνα: Ἀκρίτας, 1990), 86 (μβ´).

[2160] Wawryk, *Initiatio Monastica in Liturgia Byzantina,* 31 (*Vat. Gr. 1836*).

[2161] Ζουκόβα, *Γέννηση καὶ Ἐξέλιξη τῆς Ἀκολουθίας τοῦ Μοναχικοῦ Σχήματος,* 252.

[2162] Agapius and Nicodemus, *The Rudder,* 340–41.

[2163] PG 135:873C.

opposite stance mentioned in the typikon of the Monastery of the Holy Great Martyr Mamas in Constantinople, composed in the middle of the 12th century (1159). For in this typikon we see that the complete cutting off of the hair was one of the first and mandatory concerns of the monks. According to it, the hair that a postulant had from the world when he entered the monastery should be cut off on the day of his formal acceptance into the rank of monks in a special service, and he should keep his head shaved for the rest of his life. This is why Chapter 24 in that typikon ordered that whenever monks needed to cut their hair, with the abbot's blessing they could receive permission to go have it cut.[2164]

But it seems that ever since the days of Eustathios's explicit mention of at least some monks who wore their hair long, we find this practice more and more widespread. A homily "On Hair" composed two centuries later by Gavra reveals the extent of this practice, which even became the subject of a special essay. The extent of this practice, however, becomes even more evident from the corresponding reply to Gavra of Gregoras,[2165] in which the latter clearly prefers to side with those who keep their hair long.

Whatever the case may be, both in those days as well as afterwards, it seems that two tendencies coexisted among monks: one group preferred to wear their hair long, and the other—faithful to the ancient practice—continued to shave their head bald. Despite the evident prevalence of the former, it seems that those who shaved their head continued on much longer, even until the days when the *Rudder* was compiled [in the late 18th century].[2166]

Since then, the group of monks who kept their heads shaved has become extinct in the Orthodox Church. Thus, in contemporary Orthodox practice, all monks let their hair grow long; the tonsure as such is not adopted as a hairstyle. The proponents of this monastic practice of letting the hair grow long justify their stance by citing the Old Testament Nazirite tradition: "They must never cut their hair throughout the time of their vow, for they are holy and set apart to the Lord; until the time of their vow has been fulfilled, they must let their hair grow long,"[2167] and the Lord's commandment to Moses: "Priests must not shave their heads or shave off the edges of their beards or cut their bodies."[2168]

[2164] Vid. Thomas and Hero, *Byzantine Monastic Foundation Documents,* 973–1041.

[2165] Νικηφόρου Γρηγορᾶ, *Ἐπιστολὴ 13 τῷ Γαβρᾷ,* κωδ. Lod. Graecus 223, Bavarian State Library, φύλλ. 9.

[2166] Παναγιώτου Σ. Παπαευαγγέλου, *Ἡ Διαμόρφωσις τῆς Ἐξωτερικῆς Ἐμφανίσεως τοῦ Ἀνατολικοῦ καὶ Ἰδίᾳ τοῦ Ἑλληνικοῦ Κλήρου* (Θεσσαλονίκη: Ἀριστοτελείου Πανεπιστημίου Θεσσαλονίκης, 1965), 82–83.

[2167] Num. 6:5.

[2168] Lev. 21:5.

8) Monastic Garments

After cutting the postulant's hair, the priest immediately gives him a cassock (ζωστι-κόν), "the tunic of righteousness and exaltation of the Great and Angelic Schema."[2169] Next, he gives him the schema, "the handkerchief (σουδάριον) of the Great and Angelic Sche-ma"[2170] as well as the polystavrion (πολυσταύριον, which means "many crosses" and con-sists of many woven crosses). The polystavrion is also called the analavos (ἀνάλαβος) because through it he "takes up (ἀναλαμβάνει) his cross on his shoulders and follows the Master Christ."[2171] Then he is given a leather belt to "gird his loins with the power of truth"[2172] and the robe (παλλίον)[2173]—which (since the 9th century)[2174] is usually called a raso (ῥάσον)—"for a garment of incorruption and modesty."[2175] Next, he is given sandals

---

[2169] *Τάξις καὶ Ἀκολουθία τοῦ Μεγάλου καὶ Ἀγγελικοῦ Σχήματος* (Ἅγιον Ὄρος, 1978), 29 and Εὐσταθίου Θεσ-σαλονίκης, *Ἐπίσκεψις Βίου Μοναχικοῦ*, 72, PG 135:789D. The Slavonic version of this prayer is much more elaborate, for it refers to the cassock as "the garment of truth and ... the robe of gladness of the Great and Angelic Schema, in which he (*she*) will remain, for Christ's sake, in full and voluntary poverty both of soul and body; and for the entire avoidance of all acquisition and keeping of personal possessions; and for the putting away and trampling underfoot of all sorrows and troubles proceeding from demons, the flesh, and the world; and for his (*her*) perpetual spiritual joy and gladness in Christ" (*The Great Book of Needs,* vol. 1, 371).

[2170] *Τάξις καὶ Ἀκολουθία τοῦ Μεγάλου καὶ Ἀγγελικοῦ Σχήματος*, 29. Again, the Slavonic version of this prayer is longer and says that the schema is "for a garment of incorruption and purity, both of soul and body, and for a perpetual reminder of his (*her*) taking upon himself Christ's easy yoke, and of bearing His light burden, and for the curbing and restraining of all his (*her*) fleshly lusts and desires" (*The Great Book of Needs,* vol. 1, 371–72).

[2171] *Τάξις καὶ Ἀκολουθία τοῦ Μεγάλου καὶ Ἀγγελικοῦ Σχήματος*, 30. The Slavonic version adds: "and [may] always bear in remembrance His voluntary sufferings and death, which He endured for our sakes; and that he (*she*) may strive as far as possible to imitate them" (*The Great Book of Needs,* vol. 1, 373).

[2172] *Τάξις καὶ Ἀκολουθία τοῦ Μεγάλου καὶ Ἀγγελικοῦ Σχήματος*, 30. The Slavonic version continues: "for mortification of body and renewal of spirit, and for courage and caution in fulfillment of the commandment of Christ" (*The Great Book of Needs,* vol. 1, 372).

[2173] The ancient παλλίον was actually somewhat different from the modern robe. According to Evgenia Zhou-kova: "The παλλίον was a large piece of clothing, a garment covering the monk's entire body that could, if necessary, also cover his head ... and was used as a covering when sleeping" (Ζουκόβα, *Γέννηση καὶ Ἐξέλιξη τῆς Ἀκολουθίας τοῦ Μοναχικοῦ Σχήματος*, 281, 282).

[2174] Συμεὼν Μαγίστρου, *Χρονογραφία*, PG 109:781CD.

[2175] *Τάξις καὶ Ἀκολουθία τοῦ Μεγάλου καὶ Ἀγγελικοῦ Σχήματος*, 30. The Slavonic version refers to the raso as: "the robe of salvation and ... the armor of righteousness, that he (*she*) may withdraw himself (*herself*) from all unrighteousness, and with carefulness put away the vain imaginations of his (*her*) mind and the subtleties of his (*her*) will; that he (*she*) may have the remembrance of his (*her*) own death always in his (*her*) mind and consider himself (*herself*) to be crucified to the world and to be dead to every evil deed, but always alive for the showing forth without laziness of every Christian virtue" (*The Great Book of Needs,* vol. 1, 373).

(σανδάλια) "in preparation for the Gospel of peace,"[2176] the monastic hat (καλυμμαύ-χιον)[2177] and the cowl (κουκούλιον) "of guilelessness for a helmet and hope of salvation."[2178] Finally, he is given the mantle (μανδύας, i.e., a pleated, sleeveless, black robe) "of the Great and Angelic Schema."[2179]

In some traditions, small- and great-schema monks also have a small, square cloth, approximately five inches wide which is attached by ribbons to a wooden cross. It is today called a paramantle (παραμανδύας) or paramand. The cloth is embroidered with a cross and the instruments of the Passion. The wooden cross is worn over the chest (under the cassock), and the ribbons pass over and under the arms like a yoke and hold the square cloth centered on the back. Regarding this, St. Nicodemos of the Holy Mountain wrote:

> That undersized square cloth is today called a paramantle by the unlearned and is worn over both shoulders. I truly wonder for which reason a person invented this and placed it among the monastic garments fixed by the Fathers. This garment, I say, is not only not a paramantle according to its name [since a mantle is a large robe], but neither is it a garment at all.... If, however, someone out of habit also wishes to wear that undersized square cloth over their inner cassock, as a symbol of his carrying the Cross, let him wear it without it being blessed, just as he wears the monastic hat and the hat cover, which are also not blessed, and this does not seem to me improper.[2180]

Another garment worn by monastics is the *κοντό*, which is a sleeveless vest worn over the cassock but under the raso. According to Fr. Emmanuel Kalyvas, "the ancient monastic *ἱμάτιον* (garment) was replaced in approximately the eleventh century by an altered *δαλματική* (robe), which was also called a *κολόβιον* and today is called a *κοντόρασον* or just *κοντό*."[2181] Fr. Evangelos Skordas added: "Apparently there was a difference between the short *κολόβιον* (which was most likely an *ἐπιβαλτάριν* or a *χλαῖνα*) and a *κολόβιον* reaching

---

[2176] *Τάξις καὶ Ἀκολουθία τοῦ Μεγάλου καὶ Ἀγγελικοῦ Σχήματος*, 30. Once again, the Slavonic version of this prayer for the sandals is more elaborate and adds: "that he (*she*) may be swift and diligent in every obedience and in every good deed, but slow and unready for the fulfilling of his (*her*) own will or for any unseemly work; and that he (*she*) may bravely and patiently, by night and by day, engage in standing in prayer" (*The Great Book of Needs*, vol. 1, 373).

[2177] St. Nicodemos of the Holy Mountain pointed out: "The monastic hat (καλυμμαύχιον) and hat covering (ἐπανωκαλυμμαύχιον) do not have separate prayers designated for them, so some recite the prayer and blessing of the cowl for them, because these have been devised to replace the cowl by more recent people" (Nikodemos, *Exomologetarion: A Manual of Confession*, 293–94).

[2178] *Τάξις καὶ Ἀκολουθία τοῦ Μεγάλου καὶ Ἀγγελικοῦ Σχήματος*, 30. The Slavonic version adds that the cowl is for "a silent dwelling in spiritual meditation" and "for cautious taking heed to himself (*herself*)" (*The Great Book of Needs*, vol. 1, 372).

[2179] *Τάξις καὶ Ἀκολουθία τοῦ Μεγάλου καὶ Ἀγγελικοῦ Σχήματος*, 31.

[2180] Nikodemos, *Exomologetarion: A Manual of Confession*, 290.

[2181] Ἀρχιμανδρίτου Ἐμμανουὴλ Καλύβα, *Τὸ Ὀρθόδοξο Ἱερατικὸ Σχῆμα* (Ἀθῆναι: Δόμος Ο.Ε., 1975), 19.

the ankles with wide sleeves (also called a καββάδιν or an ἐπανωφόριν) which is approximately equivalent to the modern raso."[2182]

According to contemporary Athonite tradition, novices usually wear a ζωστικό (cassock), a κοντό (vest), a σκοῦφο (hat), and a simple belt, but they do not wear a κουκούλι (cowl) and a ράσο (robe), which only tonsured monks wear during church. Even though novices wear some monastic clothes, these clothes are given to them without any prayers being read and without a tonsure. Therefore, novices are still laymen, and as such they are free to marry if they decide to leave the monastery.

Elder Ephraim taught us that whenever a novice or a monk is alone in his cell, he should always be wearing at least his cassock on top of his pants and a shirt. Whenever he leaves his cell, he should also be wearing his vest. And if he leaves his building, he must also wear his belt. His hat should also be worn when he is in public.

9) Symbolism of the Garments

St. Symeon of Thessalonica wrote that the garments of the monk "are seven in number—as are the garments of the bishop—because they bear witness to the most perfect life, with the seven graces of the Spirit."[2183]

St. Maximos the Confessor wrote that the **cassock**, "since it protects the entire body and leaves only the hands exposed, signifies that we should put on the ethical way of life, having separated ourselves from the practical activities of sin (for the hands, by general agreement, are a symbol of action and operation)."[2184] St. Symeon of Thessalonica taught that the cassock

> is also called the garment of repentance, since it is mournful, humble, and base, and since it is simple and rejects every human adornment, and since it is not only alien to all worldly thoughts and words and deeds, but it even flees and abolishes worldly things. For it symbolizes the transcendent life and teaches the corruptibility of visible things and the temporality of all human things; it leads to the philosophical contemplation of things above, and it reminds of death and the end of things here. This is why it is also black, since it is a reminder of death and mourning, and of not living in this life but desiring and hastening towards the incorruptible afterlife.[2185]

Although in contemporary practice all monastic garments are black, historically other colors have been used. According to St. Palladios, the monks of St. Pachomios in the 4th

---

[2182] Εὐάγγελου Σκόρδα, Ἡ Ἱστορικὴ Ἐξέλιξις τῆς Ἐνδυμασίας τῶν Ὀρθοδόξων Ἑλλήνων Κληρικῶν (Ἀθῆναι, 1971), 23.

[2183] PG 155:204A. The seven garments he listed are: the cassock, belt, analavos, cowl, raso, sandals, and mantle.

[2184] Prassas, *St. Maximus the Confessor's Questions and Doubts,* 149.

[2185] PG 155:197B.

century wore "a white, worked goatskin cloak" all day except when receiving Communion,[2186] and the monks of Abba Apollos were beautiful to behold "arrayed like an army of angels wearing white in all splendor."[2187] Likewise, St. Matrona in the 5th century was given white garments when she was tonsured.[2188] Synesios of Ptolemais wrote to a novice in the early 5th century: "He also says that you were wearing the coarse, dark mantle. The mantle would lose nothing from being white, for what is clear and luminous to the eyes, would be better suited to the pure character. But if you have given your approval to the dark one out of zeal for any who assumed it before you, I give mine to all that is undertaken from a divine motive."[2189]

In 6th-century Gaul, St. Caesarius of Arles even prohibited his nuns from wearing black clothes:

> All clothing should be very simple and of a good color, never of black nor of a bright color, but only of a plain color or milk-white.... There should be no dyeing done in the monastery, except, as is stated above, of a plain or milk-white, because the other colors do not befit the humility of a virgin.... I admonish especially, as I have already said, that neither bright-colored nor black clothing ever be used, nor with purple trim or beaver, but only of some sober color or milk-white.[2190]

Even though the use of black garments quickly prevailed, some monks continued wearing white for centuries. For when a group of monks from Egypt wearing black garments visited Constantinople in the 12th century, St. Eustathios of Thessalonica wrote how delighted he was to see one of them wearing white garments instead.[2191]

This original preference of white clothing for monastics was perhaps a continuation of the early Church's preference of white clothing for all Christians in general. For Clement of Alexandria wrote to laymen in the 2nd century:

> Dyeing of clothes is also to be rejected. For it is remote both from necessity and truth.... But, for those who are white and unstained within, it is most suitable to use white and simple garments. Clearly and plainly, therefore, Daniel the Prophet says, "Thrones were set, and upon them sat one like the Ancient of days, and His vesture was white as snow."[2192] The Apocalypse says also that the Lord Himself appeared wearing such a robe. It says also, "I saw the souls of those that had witnessed, beneath the altar, and there was given to each a white robe."[2193] ...

[2186] PG 34:1009D.

[2187] PG 34:1139C.

[2188] *Βίος καὶ πολιτεία τῆς ὁσίας καὶ ἁγίας Ματρώνης*, 51, ἐν: *Acta Sanctorum,* Antverpiae-Bruxellis, Novembris, III (1910): 812F.

[2189] PG 66:1544A.

[2190] McCarthy, *The Rule for Nuns of St. Caesarius of Arles,* 185, 189.

[2191] Vid. PG 135:816BC.

[2192] Dan. 7:9.

[2193] Rev. 7:9,11.

The Instructor permits us, then, to use simple clothing, and of a white colour, as we said before. So that, accommodating ourselves not to variegated art, but to nature as it is produced, and pushing away whatever is deceptive and belies the truth, we may embrace the uniformity and simplicity of the truth.… And white colours well become gravity.… To men of peace and of light, therefore, white is appropriate.[2194]

Nevertheless, grey and black clothes also began quite early to be worn by monastics. According to the church historian Archimandrite Vasileios Stefanides, "The spreading of monasticism to colder regions farther north brought about a change in the aforementioned monastic clothing of Pachomios. A larger cassock [completely covering the arms and legs] was worn which was not made of linen, and the color was made black, as mentioned by Libanius."[2195] In the 4th century, Libanius (a pagan teacher of St. John Chrysostom) objected to the destruction of the temples of idols by monks "clad in black."[2196] Also in the 4th century, St. Gregory the Theologian described monks as wearing a black robe.[2197] Zosimos the Historian mentioned that the monks slaughtered in a church after the condemnation of St. John Chrysostom in 403 were wearing grey garments.[2198] In 6th-century Sinai, St. John of Sinai wrote to monks: "Let your very dress urge you to the work of mourning, because all who lament the dead are dressed in black."[2199] In 7th-century Constantinople, St. Maximos the Confessor wrote: "The [monastic] garments being black signifies that it is necessary for us to be invisible in the world since we have 'our citizenship in heaven.'"[2200] Later in the 7th century in the same region, the fathers of the Sixth Ecumenical Council mentioned in Canon XLV that nuns wear black robes. Commenting on this canon, St. Nicodemos of the Holy Mountain wrote:

> The divine Athanasius in his discourse concerning virginity says, "Let thy coat be black, not dyed with a dye, but of material naturally of that color."[2201] It is not only black clothing, however, that befits monks and nuns, but also gray clothing that is neither very dark nor very light in color, but of a color compounded of black and white. That is why Chrysostom, in his discourse concerning virginity, says that "virginity does not consist in gray clothes and colors."[2202] Zonaras the Historian also notes this

---

[2194] *Fathers of the Second Century: Hermas, Tatian, Athenagoras, Theophilus, and Clement of Alexandria,* 265, 284.

[2195] Βασίλειος Στεφανίδης, *Ἐκκλησιαστικὴ Ἱστορία* (Ἀθήνα: Παπαδημητρίου-Ἀστήρ, 1998), 160.

[2196] Ἰωάννου Χρυσοστόμου, *Πρὸς Θεοδόσιον τὸν βασιλέα. Ὑπὲρ τῶν ἱερῶν, λόγος* 30 (ἢ 29), 6, τόμος 3 (Λειψία, 1906), 91.

[2197] Γρηγορίου τοῦ Θεολόγου, *Εἰς ἑαυτὸν* 1, 44, PG 36:1351.

[2198] *Νέα Ἱστορία* (Nova Historia) 5, 23, ἔκδοσις Λειψίας, 1887 (ἐπανέκδοσις Olms, 1963), 244.

[2199] Holy Transfiguration Monastery, *The Ladder of Divine Ascent,* 73.

[2200] Prassas, *St. Maximus the Confessor's Questions and Doubts,* 150.

[2201] Μ. Ἀθανασίου, *Περὶ Παρθενίας* 11, PG 28:264.

[2202] Μ. Ἀθανασίου, *Περὶ Παρθενίας* 7, 1.

fact. But the color black also denotes mourning and grief, which every monk and nun ought to be engrossed in.[2203]

Paraphrasing St. Dionysius Areopagite, George Pachymeres wrote in the 13th century that the black color emphasizes the need for keeping one's monastic vows, since other colors "easily become other colors and all can become black, whereas black never becomes another color.[2204] St. Nicodemos of the Holy Mountain added to this that the black color is a reminder for monks "to live solitarily and to have their senses and nous gathered into themselves, just as black gathers light into itself."[2205]

St. Eustathios of Thessalonica elaborated on the significance of the black color:

The black color of the robes lets monks be distinguished among themselves because of their virtue like luminous stars on dark nights. Just as some stars stand out at night due to their bright light, likewise the true, shining virtue among these holy men wearing black should clearly stand out. Another symbolism of the black is that an ascetic who lives virtuously should conceal himself rather than show off.[2206] ...

You [monastics] ought to be light indeed—but a hidden light resembling God Who is surrounded by a cloud and darkness.[2207] You will certainly not be typical darkness, but darkness will be round about you, hiding the light of your virtue, which—although concealed—shines out inadvertently.[2208] ...

Furthermore, you should view the blackness of your garments as a symbol of a life in obscurity devoid of all publicity. I assume you recall that when you were tonsured you renounced all seeking of publicity, as we mentioned earlier, so that by giving up such worldly pursuits you may attain a godly life....

You are crucified—as you vowed to be when you were tonsured. So if [worldly] things or people shout at you: "Come down now from the cross,"[2209] do not come down. Await not your descent but your true ascent through your spiritual unnailing. Otherwise you will grievously scandalize others. Do not seek to live a double life, since you have chosen the singular way.[2210]

The *General Regulations of the Holy Mountain* approved by the Holy Community in 1911 declared: "All the monks without exception should wear black. Garments of various colors—even different shades of black—are forbidden as unbecoming."[2211] Criticizing this

---

[2203] Agapius and Nicodemus, *The Rudder,* 345.

[2204] PG 3:548A.

[2205] Nikodemos, *Exomologetarion: A Manual of Confession,* 291f.

[2206] Εὐσταθίου Θεσσαλονίκης, Ἐπίσκεψις Βίου Μοναχικοῦ, 138 (PG 135:804B).

[2207] "Clouds and darkness are round about Him" (Ps. 96:2).

[2208] Εὐσταθίου Θεσσαλονίκης, Ἐπίσκεψις Βίου Μοναχικοῦ, 146 (PG 135:808D).

[2209] Cf. Mt. 27:42.

[2210] Εὐσταθίου Θεσσαλονίκης, Ἐπίσκεψις Βίου Μοναχικοῦ, 160–64 (PG 135:818D–820C).

[2211] Ἀπόστολος Χρήστου Παπάζογου, Γενικοὶ Κανονισμοὶ Ἁγίου Ὄρους (Κωνσταντινούπολις: τύποις Μισαηλιδῶν, 1912), 37 (ἄρθρον 230).

decree, Protopresbyter Theodoros Zeses wrote: "The general prohibition of shades of black by these regulations is an innovation, since it is clear from the [ancient] sources that this used to be permitted in monastic dress."[2212]

The **schema** is a black piece of cloth that is worn around the neck and drapes down in the front and the back, similar in shape to a priest's stole (πετραχήλι). In the Greek tradition, it has a red cross and letters embroidered on it. It also depicts some items from the Passion of Christ, which almost always include a spear, a sponge on a reed, and a skull. It sometimes also has a crown of thorns, nails, hammer, pliers, a rooster, a pillar, and a ladder. Traditions vary as to which letters are embroidered. Here are the most common combinations of letters along with the phrases they abbreviate:

ΟΒΤΔ	Ὁ Βασιλεὺς τῆς Δόξης	The King of Glory
IC XC NIKA	Ἰησοῦς Χριστὸς νικᾷ	Jesus Christ conquers
ΤΤΔΦ	Τετιμημένον τρόπαιον δαιμόνων φρίκη	The honored trophy [the cross] is the terror for demons
ΡΡΔΡ	Ῥητορικοτέρα ῥημάτων δακρύων ῥοή	A flow of tears is more eloquent than words
ΧΧΧΧ	Χριστὸς Χριστιανοῖς χαρίζει χάριν	Christ bestows grace upon Christians
ξΓΘΗ	Ξύλου γεῦσις θάνατον ἤγαγεν	The tasting of the tree brought death
ϹξζϹ	Σταυροῦ ξύλῳ ζωὴν εὕρομεν	We have found life through the wood of the Cross
ϹϹϹϹ	Ἑλένης εὕρημα εὕρηκεν Ἐδέμ OR:	The discovery of Helen has uncovered Eden OR:
	Ἑλένης εὕρεσις Ἑβραίων ἔλεγχος OR:	The discovery of Helen is the censure of the Hebrews OR:
	Ἑωσφόρος ἔπεσεν, εὕρομεν Ἐδέμ	Lucifer has fallen; we have found Eden
ΦΧΦΠ	Φῶς Χριστοῦ φαίνει πᾶσι	The light of Christ shines on all
ΘΘΘΘ	Θεοῦ θέα θεῖον θαῦμα	The vision of God is a divine miracle
ΤϹΔΦ	Τύπον Σταυροῦ δαίμονες φρίττουσιν OR:	Demons dread the sign of the Cross OR:
	Τοῦτο τὸ σχῆμα δαίμονες φρίττουσιν	Demons dread this schema
ΑΔΑΜ	Ἀδάμ	Adam
ΤΚΠΓ	Τόπος κρανίου Παράδεισος γέγονε	The place of the skull has become Paradise
ξζ	Ξύλον Ζωῆς OR:	The Tree of Life OR:
	Ξένη Ζωή	Foreign Life[2213]

[2212] Ζήσης, *Μοναχισμός: Μορφὲς καὶ Θέματα*, 151.

[2213] Commenting on this, St. Porphyrios of Kafsokalyvia taught: "The life of a monk is life in a foreign land. This is embroidered into the monastic schema worn by the monk. A large letter Ξ is joined to the letter Ζ,

The cross has a prominent place on the schema because ever since the early days of monasticism, the monastic life has been viewed as the "cross-bearing life."[2214] St. Dionysius the Areopagite taught that in monastic tonsure "the sign of the cross proclaims ... the death of all fleshly desire."[2215]

> Abba Dorotheos wrote that the **polystavrion**
>
>> is worn in the form of a cross on our shoulders. This means that we carry the symbol of the cross on our shoulders, as it says, 'Take up your cross and follow Me' (Mt. 16:24). But what is the cross if not the total mortification that is realised in ourselves through faith in Christ? ... A man puts to death in himself the affection for the things of this world. He has given up parents, possessions, riches, all that a man can give up to take up the contest; let him also renounce self-will and the desire for these things. This is what we mean by perfect renunciation.[2216]

Similarly, St. Maximos the Confessor taught[2217] that the polystavrion has crosses on both the front and the back to symbolize the monk's two-fold crucifixion (i.e., mortification) to the world, as St. Paul said: "in the cross of our Lord Jesus Christ, by whom the world is crucified to me, and I to the world."[2218] Abba Dorotheos clarified the difference between the two as follows:

> The world is crucified for a man when he denies the world and becomes a monastic, when he leaves parents, money, personal properties and affairs, and his professional dealings. It is thus that the world is crucified, for he abandons it. This is what the Apostle meant when he says, "The world has been crucified in me." Afterwards he adds, "and I to the world." But how is a man crucified to the world? He is crucified when, having been liberated from external things, he struggles against enjoyments themselves, against his very desires for material objects, against what he wills, and puts the passions to death.[2219]

St. Maximos the Confessor explained: "We avoid pleasures, not because they are evil, but because the sinful man is easily captivated by pleasures and becomes their slave.... O monk, take care that no one should beguile you into believing that it is possible to be saved while you are enslaved to pleasure and vainglory."[2220]

---

standing for Ξένη Ζωή, which means 'foreign life.' I have experienced this living in a foreign land [in the desert of the Holy Mountain] far from everyone and everything. You work and you pray, and only God sees you. I loved the desert very much" (Chrysopigi, *Wounded by Love*, 160–61).

[2214] Vid. Wagner, *Saint Basil: Ascetical Works*, vol. 9, 15.

[2215] Luibhéid, *Pseudo-Dionysius: The Complete Works*, 247.

[2216] Scouteris, *Abba Dorotheos: Practical Teaching on the Christian Life*, 81; see also Wheeler, *Dorotheos of Gaza: Discourses and Sayings*, 87.

[2217] Vid. Μαξίμου Ὁμολογητοῦ, *Πεύσεις καὶ Ἀποκρίσεις καὶ Ἐρωτήσεις καὶ Ἐκλογαί, ΞΖ´*, PG 90:841A.

[2218] Gal. 6:14.

[2219] Metropolitan Chrysostomos, *Our Holy Father Dorotheos of Gaza*, 37.

[2220] Chrysostomos, *The Evergetinos, Book I*, 277, and http://www.livejournal.com/users/abbatus-mozdok

Abba Dorotheos explained the **belt** as follows:

> The belt which we wear symbolises firstly that we are ready for work, since everyone who wants to work puts on his belt and then starts his work, as it says, "Let your waist be girded."[2221] Again, as the belt is from the leather of a dead animal, so we have to mortify our desire for pleasure. We put the belt around our waist where the kidneys are, and it is said that the kidneys are the centre of the soul's desire and this is what the Apostle says, "Put to death the members which are on the earth: fornication, uncleanness,"[2222] and so on.[2223]

Similarly, St. Maximos the Confessor taught:

> The belt, because it is made from dead skins and binds the loins and the navel, signifies mortification through self-control, and it is necessary for self-control to have authority over the power and activity of evil. For "the power" of the opposing authority of the wicked one is, according to Job, "in the navel of the belly" (Job 40:16), and "the loins" according to the blessed David are filled with demonic "mockings" (Ps. 37:8). And "mockings" are the different activities of sexual impurity.[2224]

Abba Dorotheos further explained that the **cowl** is

> the symbol of humility. Innocent infants wear cowls or bonnets but adults do not. Thus, we wear it for that reason, to be infants in malice, as the Apostle says, "Do not be children in understanding, but be babes in malice."[2225] What does "be babes in malice" mean? An infant is free from evil. If it is dishonoured it does not become angry, and if it is honoured it does not become proud. If somebody takes its things, it is not troubled. It is innocent of evil. It does not want to satisfy its passion and neither does it strive after glory. Again, the cowl is a symbol of God's grace, because, as the cowl covers the child's head and keeps it warm, so God's grace covers our nous, as the *Sayings of the Fathers*[2226] state.[2227]

Likewise, St. Maximos said: "The cowl represents the grace of God guarding and protecting our nous."[2228] St. Eustathios of Thessalonica called the cowl "a helmet of hope and salvation."[2229] Similarly, St. Symeon of Thessalonica taught: "With the cowl he dons

---

[2221] Lk. 12:35.

[2222] Col. 3:5.

[2223] Scouteris, *Abba Dorotheos: Practical Teaching on the Christian Life,* 80.

[2224] Prassas, *St. Maximus the Confessor's Questions and Doubts,* 149.

[2225] 1 Cor. 14:20.

[2226] Vid. Evagrius, *Praktikos to Anatolios,* PG 40:1.

[2227] Scouteris, *Abba Dorotheos: Practical Teaching on the Christian Life,* 80–81.

[2228] Prassas, *St. Maximus the Confessor's Questions and Doubts,* 150; PG 90:841B.

[2229] Εὐσταθίου Θεσσαλονίκης, Ἐπίσκεψις Βίου Μοναχικοῦ, PG 135:789D.

humility for salvation, so that with his governing mind he thinks humbly and trains his senses well. This is why it is also called the helmet of salvation."[2230]

The cowl also has two lappets (i.e., flaps) hanging down on the right and left sides. Their origin is explained as follows by one historian:

> The lappets, or wings, of the veil [i.e., cowl] are said to date from the time of St. Methodius (†A.D. 846), Patriarch of Constantinople, who was wounded in the face during the reign of the iconoclast Emperor Theophilus. In order to conceal his wounds the Saint wore lappets with his veil, and fastened them about the lower part of his face, where he had been wounded. The use of veils with lappets became universal, in memory of the sufferings of St. Methodius at the hands of the iconoclasts, and it has so continued down to the present day.[2231]

St. Maximos the Confessor explained: "**Sandals** have this meaning: since they are made from dead skins, and they are situated beneath a small part of the body, in the same way that the whole body is related to the soles of its sandal, so the soul must make use of the body, and the body with this is dead to the unnatural passions."[2232] St. Symeon of Thessalonica taught that the sandals empower the monk "to proceed along the way leading to salvation and peace, since he ought to go in peace (according to the Gospel) and spread the Gospel."[2233]

St. Eustathios of Thessalonica explained that the **mantle** "symbolizes the spiritual armor of the mantle-wearing monks."[2234] St. Germanos of Constantinople taught: "The mantle with its flowing spread represents and imitates the wings of the angels, for the schema is called angelic."[2235] According to St. Symeon of Thessalonica, however, it symbolizes the grave[2236] of the body,[2237] or the protective power of God.[2238] Abba Dorotheos wrote the following about the mantle:

[2230] Συμεὼν Θεσσαλονίκης, *Διάλογος,* κεφ. ΣΟΔ΄, PG 155:500D. Professor K. Kalokyres conjectured that the cowl is a simplified version of the ancient Egyptian "nemes" (i.e., striped headcloth), which "Coptic Christians and especially Coptic monks adopted, and from them it was passed on to other monks of the East and has prevailed until today" (as quoted in Παπαευαγγέλου, *Ἡ Διαμόρφωσις τῆς Ἐξωτερικῆς Ἐμφανίσεως τοῦ Ἀνατολικοῦ καὶ Ἰδίᾳ τοῦ Ἑλληνικοῦ Κλήρου,* 129).

[2231] Vid. Th. A. v. Maltzew, *Begräbniss-Ritus,* ii, 206, 207 (as cited in Robinson, *Monasticism in the Orthodox Churches,* 42); see also Παπαευαγγέλου, *Ἡ Διαμόρφωσις τῆς Ἐξωτερικῆς Ἐμφανίσεως τοῦ Ἀνατολικοῦ καὶ Ἰδίᾳ τοῦ Ἑλληνικοῦ Κλήρου,* 128.

[2232] Prassas, *St. Maximus the Confessor's Questions and Doubts,* 150.

[2233] Συμεὼν Θεσσαλονίκης, *Διάλογος,* κεφ. ΣΟΔ΄, PG 155:501A.

[2234] PG 135:895B; see also Γ. Θεοδωρούδη, *Ὁ Μοναχισμὸς κατὰ τὸν Εὐστάθιον Θεσσαλονίκης,* (Διατριβὴ ἐπὶ διδακτορίᾳ), Ἀριστοτέλειο Πανεπιστήμιο Θεσσαλονίκης, 1983, 49.

[2235] Γερμανοῦ Κωνσταντινουπόλεως, *Ἐκκλησιαστικὴ Ἱστορία καὶ Μυστικὴ Θεωρία,* PG 98:396.

[2236] Συμεὼν Θεσσαλονίκης, *Διάλογος,* κεφ. ΣΟΔ΄, PG 155:500B.

[2237] Συμεὼν Θεσσαλονίκης, *Ἀποκρίσεις πρὸς τὸν Πενταπόλεως Γαβριήλ, Ξ΄,* PG 155:916A.

[2238] Ibid.

Why do we wear a sleeveless garment? While all the other men wear sleeves, why do we not wear them? Sleeves symbolize the hands and we use our hands for doing things. When a thought or temptation comes to us to do something according to the "old man," for example, to steal or to hit someone or any other sin using our hands, we should pay attention to our monastic habit and consider that we do not have sleeves. That is to say, we do not have hands to do the work of the "old man."[2239]

Abbot Philaret of the Glinsk Hermitage in the 19th-century added the following interpretation of the mantle:

> Our mantia [i.e., mantle] reminds us of the royal purple. Just as soldiers wear a wide cloak, which resembles the royal purple, and indicates that they serve a king, so also do we wear a mantia as a sign of the fact that we have become warriors of Christ. Jesus Christ was clothed in a purple garment as a king, for truly He was the King of Kings and the Lord of Lords. He was also clothed in purple as one reviled by the impious. We, too, when we wear the mantia must imitate the Lord and bear all sufferings. As a soldier may not desert his military service in order to engage in trade or to till the land, so as not to lose his calling,[2240] so also we must struggle in diligent service to the one God without caring about anything worldly.[2241]

Ever since the Turkish occupation of Greece, Greek great-schema monks have no longer worn the mantle except during their tonsure.[2242] St. Nicodemos of the Holy Mountain, however, criticized this practice. He wrote:

> Those great-schema monks from among us Grecians should wear the mantle, if not always, then at least during the *synaxis,* or Church gatherings, and during the Divine Liturgy, just as it is worn by the great-schema monks from among the pious Russians[2243] and Romanians, being that the mantle is the most characteristic garment of great-schema monks. But we (barring a few) have changed the order, being satisfied with just the outer cassock or *exorason* [i.e., raso], as we have said, which should not have been done and is incorrect.[2244]

After the monk has been clothed with these monastic garments, two other prayers are read for him, in which the priest asks God to strengthen him who has been tonsured. After a reading from the epistle and the gospel, the priest gives the newly tonsured monk a **cross** with a **prayer-rope**. Upon doing so, according to the Greek rubrics the priest says to him only: "The Lord said, 'He who would come after Me, let him deny himself and take up his

---

[2239] Scouteris, *Abba Dorotheos: Practical Teaching on the Christian Life,* 79.

[2240] 2 Tim. 2:4.

[2241] Fr. Theodosius Clare, *Glinsk Patericon* (Wildwood: St. Xenia Skete, 1984), 52–53.

[2242] Ζουκόβα, Γέννηση καὶ Ἐξέλιξη τῆς Ἀκολουθίας τοῦ Μοναχικοῦ Σχήματος, 282.

[2243] For example, St. Theodore of Sanaxar, a contemporary of St. Nicodemos in Russia, wrote in the rule of his monastery: "The monks come to church in their mantles to every service" (St. Herman of Alaska Brotherhood, *Little Russian Philokalia, Volume V: Saint Theodore of Sanaxar,* 163).

[2244] Nikodemos, *Exomologetarion: A Manual of Confession,* 294.

cross and follow Me.'"[2245] But in the Slavonic version of the service, the priest also tells him: "Take, Brother (*Sister*) *N.*, the shield of faith, the Cross of Christ, with which you will be able to put out the flaming darts of the Evil One."[2246] And when the priest gives him the prayer-rope, according to the Slavonic rubrics he tells him: "Take, Brother (*Sister*) *N.*, the sword of the Spirit, which is the word of God, for continual prayer to Jesus; for you must always have the Name of the Lord Jesus in mind, in heart, and on your lips, ever saying, 'O Lord Jesus Christ, Son of God, have mercy on me, a sinner.' And know that, henceforth, you must have the word of God ceaselessly upon your lips, in prayer, in psalms and hymns and spiritual songs; and may no vain words go forth out of your mouth."[2247] According to St. Symeon of Thessalonica, if the person being tonsured is a priest, he is given the gospel instead of a cross.[2248]

Thereafter, the priest gives the monk a lit **candle** and tells him: "Let your light so shine before men that they may see your good works and glorify your Father Who is in Heaven."[2249] But in the Slavonic version, the priest additionally says to him: "Take, Brother (*Sister*) *N.*, this candle, and know that from henceforth you must, by a pure and virtuous life and by a good character and by word and deed and by a humble demeanor, by a gentle and silent taking heed to yourself, and by an ever-strict abstinence, bear light unto the world."[2250] Regarding this candle, St. Eustathios of Thessalonica wrote:

> One could say that these candles are like wedding candles, since they are reminiscent of the wedding service, as mentioned earlier. For these lit candles symbolize the fire and light of this kind of wedding.... A [beeswax] candle is exceptional because it is collected from thousands of beautiful flowers.... When a candle is burned, it is completely consumed and leaves no trace of itself after it has gone out; it leaves no ash or smoke or unpleasant odor. Likewise, a man who undergoes this spiritual tonsure strives to be perfect as he has promised. He himself becomes a light that burns, reaching for God with intense impetus, striving to approach the greatest Light and, in a sense, to be united with Him without leaving any material trace behind down below that would emit an odor, but instead to be offered to God as a fragrant scent. This is because he has ascended spotless from the filth of the world to the immaculate and supremely holy God.[2251]

[2245] *Τάξις καὶ Ἀκολουθία τοῦ Μεγάλου καὶ Ἀγγελικοῦ Σχήματος*, 36.

[2246] *The Great Book of Needs,* vol. 1, 374.

[2247] Ibid.

[2248] "Then, while the deacon is holding the holy gospel, the priest takes it and says: 'He who would come after Me, let him deny himself and take up his cross and follow Me.' And he gives it to him [who is being tonsured] if he is a priest. Otherwise, he gives him a cross" (PG 155:501C).

[2249] *Τάξις καὶ Ἀκολουθία τοῦ Μεγάλου καὶ Ἀγγελικοῦ Σχήματος*, 37.

[2250] *The Great Book of Needs,* vol. 1, 375.

[2251] PG 135:800C–801C.

Finally, in the Slavonic version of the service (but not in the Greek version) the priest then says: "Our Brother (*Sister*) N. has received the Great Angelic Schema and has been clothed in the whole armor of God, that he (*she*) may be able to vanquish all the power and warfare of principalities and powers, and rulers of the darkness of this age, of evil spirits under the heavens, in silence giving heed to himself (*herself*), in the Name of the Father and of the Son and of the Holy Spirit. Let us all say for him (*her*), 'Lord, have mercy.'"[2252]

According to an ancient tradition expressed in a 13th-century manuscript, the newly tonsured monk "enters the house of prayer and remains there for seven days resting in prayer and reading and psalmody until the eighth day, wearing the cowl and not taking it off, nor removing any other part of the schema."[2253] Another medieval *Euchologion* with slightly different rubrics states: "On the following six days he stays in the diakonikon [i.e., the south side of the altar], eating dry food and resting from work, remaining in the church."[2254]

After the monk has spent a week in the church, the priest reads over him the following Prayer for the Removal of the Cowl:

> O Most-merciful Lord, Who by the taking of the Angelic Schema hast bestowed upon Thy servant (*handmaid*), N., the cowl for a helmet of the hope of salvation: Do Thou preserve, therefore, such a grace of Thine from being taken from his (*her*) head, maintaining and keeping fervent his (*her*) thoughts, ruling them, unshaken from the wiles of the adversaries, that he (*she*), trampling underfoot the head of the all-evil serpent—who has been permitted to lie in wait for his (*her*) heel—may lift up the eyes of his (*her*) mind to Thee, the dread and only Head of all things.[2255]

In accordance with the contemporary practice in some places, instead of having the monk stay in the church for a week and then reading this prayer, it is read at the end of the tonsuring service, and the monk exits the church.

The service of tonsure to the Great Schema was originally done preceding the Trisagion during the Divine Liturgy so that the newly tonsured monk could receive Holy Communion.[2256] The option of tonsuring a monk separately from the Divine Liturgy first appears in Athonite codices of the fourteenth century. St. Symeon of Thessalonica taught that the tonsure should take place during the Divine Liturgy because "Holy Communion [which is received during the Liturgy] is the consummation of every rite and the seal of

---

[2252] *The Great Book of Needs,* vol. 1, 375.

[2253] Ἀκολουθία καὶ νουθεσία εἰς τὸ ἀποκουκούλισμα, Mosq. Syn. B - cae 396. This rubric is based on an even older tradition, since in the *Penitentiale* of Theodore of Tarsus (A.D. 668–690), it is stated that the monk covers his head with his cowl for seven days, and on the seventh day the abbot removes it (vid. *Penitentiale Theodori,* lib. ii, cap. iii, in *Councils and Ecclesiastical Documents,* Haddan and Stubbs, iii, 192).

[2254] A. Dmitrievskij, *Euchologia* (Kiev, 1901), 243.

[2255] *The Great Book of Needs,* vol. 1, 384.

[2256] Evidence for this is found in Sts. Dionysius the Areopagite (vid. PG 3:533AB, 536B) and Theodore the Studite (PG 99:1333BC) as well as in codices containing *Euchologia* from the tenth century and onwards.

every divine mystery [i.e., sacrament]."[2257] Metropolitan Hierotheos Vlachos explains this in more detail:

> The service of the Great and Angelic Schema is connected to the holy Eucharist, and subsequently the monk communes the Body and Blood of Christ. For without Christ no one can accomplish these lofty goals and by grace attain theosis, which is the ultimate goal of the spiritual and monastic life....
>
> Monastic life, as it is described in the service of tonsure to the Great and Angelic Schema, presupposes a hesychastic monasticism, a monasticism in accordance with the Gospel. Everyone who has ever become a monk has passed through this service and has given these vows. And, of course, this service has been well-tried in practice, in the sense that thousands and millions of monastics throughout the ages have gone through this service, heard the same words that are repeated in it, and given the same confessions and vows. This means that the monks who through this whole service have received the Great and Angelic Schema must live in the spirit of this holy service. Any who want to live a different kind of monasticism that is contrary to the spirit of the service we have briefly analyzed should not accept being made monks through this service that has stood the test of time, but should come up with another service that will be in harmony with the "spirit" of the monasticism that they want to live—that is, a monasticism with worldly comforts, commerce, business ventures, worldly publicity, insubordination to the Church and the Bishop, satisfaction of the senses, and pleasures. For it is not possible for them to accept this service and give these vows, and then to live a Frankish, worldly monasticism, that is anti-traditional, anti-hesychastic, anti-Patristic, and anti-ecclesiastical.[2258]

St. Symeon of Thessalonica described how the remainder of the Divine Liturgy is conducted following a tonsure:

> Then the priest sets him [i.e., the tonsured monk] before the holy doors as one who has reached the gates of heaven and has been reconciled with the Master. The monk holds the Gospel and the lit candle because he ought to live in an evangelical and luminous way for the glory of God Who has called him to His wondrous light. Then the priest embraces him for the love and union in Christ. This represents the embrace of the heavenly Father when He found the lost [prodigal] son and received him with great joy. The priest sets him beside him since he has approached God.
>
> The brethren along with the Father [i.e., the abbot] are all holding candles (showing the joyfulness, the grace of God, and the joy of the angels) and depart. Each of them kisses the holy Gospel, the priest (who preserves the image of Christ) as well as his cross, and the one who has received the schema, and they all sing joyously. What they sing is: "Brethren, let us understand the power of the Mystery...."[2259] What mystery is this? "That the all-good Father has gone out to meet and kiss him who has returned from sin to the Father's house." And after restoring him to his former rank, with delight he joins him with those above and sacrifices the fatted calf.
>
> This is why, after the embrace, the service of the living calf [i.e., the rest of the Divine Liturgy] is conducted. And according to the proper order, the epistle and gospel

---

[2257] PG 155:512D.

[2258] Ἱεροθέου, Ὁ Ὀρθόδοξος Μοναχισμός, 543–44; Hierotheos, *Orthodox Monasticism,* 484–85.

[2259] Vid. *The Great Book of Needs,* vol. 1, 377–78.

are read. And he who received the schema goes out in front of the gospel and the holy ones bearing candles [during the great entrance] as one who has been made a soldier and servant of Christ. He is counted worthy of being commemorated in the petitions as one who has been written in the heavens and enrolled in the choir of the brethren. And finally he is counted fully worthy to commune the most holy gifts, having been made a communicant of the heavenly, living table.

In this manner, while all are singing joyfully and wishing him to be made perfect as a vine of the Lord,[2260] they proceed to the physical table [i.e., the refectory] rejoicing along with those of equal rank. From then on, he quietly spends time in prayers and obedience and serving, running the course of life in humility and following Christ.[2261]

St. Eustathios of Thessalonica also emphasized the festive character of a tonsure:

He who has been tonsured is greatly applauded with hymns, as if those present were celebrating his salvation or as if they were escorting him on to greater things. For he is renouncing this life, just as the departed leave things on earth behind. Many candles are lit, as if he were abandoning the darkness of this life and entering the light, where it is appropriate for angels to live, as well as for men who have chosen the angelic way of life.[2262]

One historian observed: "After the tonsure service, a festal dinner frequently followed for the brothers of the monastery and for others present."[2263] When St. Joseph the Hesychast tonsured someone, he celebrated the event by making *loukoumades* [doughnut balls].[2264]

Yet this festive atmosphere should not detract from the monk's χαρμολύπη [joy-making sorrow]. St. Ephraim of Katounakia once related: "I was displeased with the behavior of Fr. X after receiving the great schema. After the service, we all went to the sitting room for a snack, and there for two hours he waxed eloquent about Stalin and others. He hardly let anyone get a word in edgewise. He was babbling so much, whereas he should have had silence and tears after receiving the schema."[2265]

[2260] Cf. Ps. 79:15.

[2261] PG 155:501C–504B.

[2262] PG 135:792D–793A.

[2263] Καλαϊτζάκης, Ἐπίσκεψις Βίου Μοναχικοῦ, 301.

[2264] Vid. Elder Ephraim, *My Elder Joseph the Hesychast*, 434.

[2265] Βίος καὶ Πολιτεία τοῦ Ὁσίου καὶ Θεοφόρου Πατρὸς ἡμῶν Ἰωσὴφ τοῦ Ἡσυχαστοῦ, (the Greek title of my rough draft of Elder Ephraim, *My Elder Joseph the Hesychast*), 484.

10) A Second Baptism

The service of tonsure has numerous similarities to the service of baptism. In particular:[2266]

1) In the service of baptism, a person "renounces Satan and all his works and all his service and all his pride,"[2267] whereas in the service of tonsure one "renounces the world and the things which are in the world."[2268]

2) In both services, the hair is cut while the priest says exactly the same words: "_____ is shorn in the Name of the Father, and of the Son, and of the Holy Spirit."[2269]

3) In both services, the garment worn is called a "robe of righteousness."[2270]

4) In the service of baptism, the priest prays, "Preserve his (*her*) pledge inviolate,"[2271] whereas in the service of tonsure, one receives the "pledge of the Great and Angelic Schema."[2272]

5) In the service of tonsure there is no physical chrismation as in baptism. There is, however, a spiritual "chrismation" through the invocation of the Holy Spirit, according to what St. Neilos wrote to Monk Amphilochios: "But you were invisibly chrismated by coming to the honorable schema. A divine chrismation is what I call the grace of the Holy Spirit that came upon you."[2273] This grace is mentioned in the canon before the service of tonsure: "Renew unto us from on high the tokens of Thine adoption, through the operation and grace of Thy Divine Spirit";[2274] and "by the renewal of the Divine Spirit do Thou instruct me who have become inveterate,[2275] adorning me with the beauty of holiness."[2276]

[2266] This list is a paraphrase of Στεφανίας Ντύρου, *Τὸ Μέγα καὶ Ἀγγελικὸ Σχῆμα ὡς Δεύτερο Βάπτισμα* μεταπτυχιακὴ μελέτη (Θεσσαλονίκη: Ἀριστοτέλειο Πανεπιστήμιο Θεσσαλονίκης, 2008), 93–97.

[2267] *The Great Book of Needs,* vol. 1, 24.

[2268] *Τάξις καὶ Ἀκολουθία τοῦ Μεγάλου καὶ Ἀγγελικοῦ Σχήματος,* 19; cf. *The Great Book of Needs,* vol. 1, 363.

[2269] *The Great Book of Needs,* vol. 1, 50.

[2270] Ibid., 38.

[2271] Ibid., 48.

[2272] *Τάξις καὶ Ἀκολουθία τοῦ Μεγάλου καὶ Ἀγγελικοῦ Σχήματος,* 28.

[2273] *Ἐπιστολαί,* βιβλ. 2, 4β΄, PG 79:241BC.

[2274] *The Great Book of Needs,* vol. 1, 357.

[2275] Since the phrase "having grown old" (παλαιωθέντα) in the translation found in *The Great Book of Needs* could be misunderstood in this context to mean "having become advanced in age," we replaced it with the more precise "having become inveterate," which means "having become settled in a [bad] habit."

[2276] *The Great Book of Needs,* vol. 1, 356.

6) In both services, the sponsor plays a vital role. He testifies that the person being baptized or tonsured has come of his own free will; he acts as his guide; and he is responsible for his future progress in Christ.

7) In both services there is a catechism, on which the renunciation and enrollment are based.

8) The meaning of the changing of clothes during the service of tonsure is analogous to the same thing in baptism. As St. Dionysius the Areopagite wrote regarding the service of tonsure: "The removal of the clothing of old and the putting on of something else indicate the switch from the sacred life of the middle order to one of greater perfection. For the rite of divine birth includes the changing of the clothes to signify the uplifting of a purified life toward the higher reaches of contemplation and of illumination."[2277]

9) Both services are traditionally done during the Divine Liturgy and conclude with the reception of Holy Communion.[2278]

10) The service of tonsure contains slightly altered phrases of prayers from the service of baptism.[2279]

11) The hymn "As many of you as were baptized into Christ have put on Christ" is chanted instead of the Trisagion in both services.

12) A new name is given in both services.

More connections between tonsure and baptism may be found in the writings of the holy Fathers. For example, St. Symeon of Thessalonica wrote (condemning the Roman Catholic practice of having different monastic orders): "All [the Fathers] say that the monastic schema is one and only one, just as baptism."[2280] St. Photios the Great commented: "Not everyone who is baptized has been saved but he who does the works of God—that is to say, neither has everyone who is tonsured been saved but he who keeps what is proper for

---

[2277] Luibhéid, *Pseudo-Dionysius: The Complete Works,* 247.

[2278] Vid. ibid., 248.

[2279] For example, the service of baptism says: "The Angelic Powers serve Thee. The choirs of Archangels worship Thee. The many-eyed Cherubim and the six-winged Seraphim, standing and flying round about, cover themselves with fear at Thine unapproachable glory" (*The Great Book of Needs,* vol. 1, 33–34). Similarly, the service of tonsure says: "O God, Who sittest upon the Cherubim and art ceaselessly hymned by the thrice-holy voice of the Seraphim, before Whom stand a thousand thousands and ten thousand times ten thousand of holy Angels and hosts of Archangels" (ibid., 368). In the same prayer, the priest says: "That henceforth, having progressively put off the old man, corrupted by the seductive deception of the serpent of many forms, he (*she*) may be clothed with the new Adam, which after God is created in holiness and righteousness" (ibid.), which is very similar to the prayer in baptism: "Grant that he (*she*) that is to be baptized may be transformed therein to the putting away of the old man, which is corrupt according to the deceitful lusts, and to the putting on of the new, which is renewed according to the image of Him that created him (*her*)" (ibid., 35).

[2280] PG 155:104C.

monks."[2281] St. John of Sinai wrote: "No one who foreknew his death would at once proceed to baptism or the monastic life; but everyone would spend all his days in iniquities, and only on the day of his death would he approach baptism and repentance."[2282] Thus, the reception of the schema is a baptism of repentance.

11) Forgiveness of Sins

Another crucial similarity between tonsure and baptism is that in both of them a person is cleansed from all prior sins and is reborn, while promising to avoid them in the future. This is clearly seen in the service of tonsure, in troparia and prayers such as these:

> Thou hast given us the power to renew the grace of Baptism, through confession, purification of life, the shedding of tears, and genuine repentance, O Lover of Mankind.[2283]
>
> Having received regeneration and redemption in the mystical Fountain of Regeneration [i.e., in Baptism], yet having wasted my life in laziness and falls into sin, now I cry out unto Thee, O Good One: Grant me a fountain of tears of repentance, and wash the filth of my transgressions, O Almighty and Greatly-merciful Savior.[2284]
>
> O, the mystery of the gift! A second Baptism you are receiving today, Brother (*Sister*), in the riches of the gifts of God, the Lover of Mankind. And you shall be cleansed of your sins, and become a son (*daughter*) of the Light.[2285]
>
> Grant that this divine Schema may be the change and transformation of life, and the cleansing of iniquities, to Thy faithful servant (*handmaid*) who comes unto Thee.[2286]

The same understanding is also found in the writings of the holy Fathers. In the sixth century, the monks of the monastery of Abba Gerasimou "said in passing, in the hearing of [Saints] Symeon [the Fool for Christ] and John, that tomorrow [at their tonsure] they would be regenerated and purged of sin as on the day of their baptisms."[2287] St. Theodore

---

[2281] PG 88:648D (Comment #15 on Step 1:9 in *The Ladder*). In the same spirit, St. George Karslidis wrote to a pious widow who wanted to become a nun: "Continue living as you are. Don't think that the robes and the holy schema save a person. No; it is primarily godly good works, humility, obedience, love, almsgiving" (as cited in Καββαδία, *Γέροντας καὶ Γυναικεῖος Μοναχισμός*, 399).

[2282] Holy Transfiguration Monastery, *The Ladder of Divine Ascent*, 67.

[2283] *The Great Book of Needs*, vol. 1, 357 (2nd troparion of the 8th ode). Likewise, St. John of Sinai taught that "repentance is the renewal of baptism" (Holy Transfiguration Monastery, *The Ladder of Divine Ascent*, 54).

[2284] *The Great Book of Needs*, vol. 1, 360 (second antiphon).

[2285] Ibid., 365.

[2286] Ibid., 353.

[2287] *The Great Synaxaristes of the Orthodox Church: July* (Buena Vista: Holy Apostles Convent, 2008), 872.

the Studite called the monastic tonsure a "second baptism"[2288] which is "high and lofty, and cleanses every sin."[2289] This is why he also taught that "removing the schema from a monk is equivalent to unbaptizing someone."[2290] Commenting on this, St. Sophrony of Essex wrote: "The phrase 'second baptism' must be understood in the sense that monastic tonsure is similar to the Mystery of baptism in terms of its grandeur and rich outpouring of the Holy Spirit upon man. Yet the Mystery of baptism always remains 'one,' just as we confess [in the Creed]."[2291]

St. Symeon of Thessalonica addressed the monks of the Great Lavra, calling them "sanctified in Christ ... by the sacred bathing and second baptism of the angelic and salvific schema."[2292] St. Symeon also taught: "This schema wipes out the disobedience [of Adam], the curse of death, and the fleshliness of man conceived by a flow of defilement and pleasure. It opens paradise and heaven itself, it bestows immortality, and it is the first-fruit of eternal life."[2293] Likewise, St. Eustathios taught:

> All these things I mentioned [regarding the service of tonsure], O brother, are awesome. But the thing in the divine service book of renunciation that makes me tremble most of all is that, just like a catechumen [who is baptized], the postulant who hears these things immediately receives a baptism by which he not only begins a new, different life and a transformed being—or rather, a salvific regeneration—but also he is cleansed of his sins and becomes a son of the light.[2294]

St. Symeon the New Theologian also taught that receiving the schema forgives sins:

> If you have received the remission of all your sins—whether through confession or by donning the holy and angelic schema—how much love and gratitude and humility this will produce for you! For even though you deserve thousands of punishments,

---

[2288] Vid. Θεοδώρου Στουδίτου, *Μεγάλη Κατήχησις*, Βιβλίον Β΄ (Θεσσαλονίκη: Ὀρθόδοξος Κυψέλη, 1987), 55.

[2289] PG 99:1816C.

[2290] Θεοδώρου Στουδίτου, *Ἐπιστολὴ* 56, PG 99:1521B. When St. Theodore wrote this, he probably had in mind what had happened nearby a few decades earlier. An imposter had convinced St. Stephen the New to tonsure him, whereupon he immediately returned to the iconoclastic emperor who had sent him for this purpose. After the impious crowd removed all his monastic garments and trampled upon them, "they brought a vessel full of water and poured it over his head to undo (so to speak) his baptism [i.e., his tonsure]" (PG 100:1137). An English translation of the complete life of St. Stephen the New may be found in *The Great Synaxaristes of the Orthodox Church: November*, 969–1001, although it lacks this detail found in the *Patrologia Graeca*.

[2291] Ἀρχιμανδρίτου Σωφρονίου, *Ἄσκησις καὶ Θεωρία* (Ἔσσεξ: Ἱερὰ Μονὴ Τιμίου Προδρόμου, 1996), 40, ὑποσημείωσις.

[2292] As quoted in Ἀρχ. Γεωργίου Καψάνη, *Πρακτικὰ Λειτουργικοῦ Συνεδρίου*, «Ὁ Μοναχισμὸς κατὰ τὸν Ἅγιο Συμεὼν Θεσσαλονίκης» (ἔκδοσις Ἱ.Μ. Ἁγίας Θεοδώρας, 1983), 164.

[2293] PG 155:916AB.

[2294] PG 135:745B.

you have not only been freed from them but have also been counted worthy of sonship and glory and the Kingdom of Heaven.[2295]

Practical evidence that all one's sins are indeed forgiven when becoming a monk is found in the life of St. Anthony when the demons were not allowed to criticize him for sins he had committed before becoming a monk.[2296]

Repentance is at the core of monastic life. This is why St. Paisios of the Holy Mountain declared: "The work of a monk is repentance."[2297] Elaborating on this concept Stephania Dyros observed:

> The element of repentance is so essential for a great-schema monk that he seeks to "please the Lord for the rest of his life in repentance"[2298]—in other words, to be continually rebaptized through repentance. The monastery in which he receives the schema and lives for the rest of his life is called his "monastery of repentance," and the procedure of receiving the schema[2299] is called "repentance."[2300]

This explains why the service of tonsure is replete with references to the repentance of the prodigal son. It was this central importance of repentance in monasticism that led St. Symeon the New Theologian to lament: "I am worthy of double punishment; for having failed much in my earlier life [i.e., prior to monasticism], I promised to repent thoroughly [in monasticism].[2301]

Repentance is so essential to monasticism that Michael Glykas, a scholarly monk in 12th-century Constantinople, believed that the forgiveness of sins when receiving the schema is not automatic but is contingent on one's repentance. He explained:

> We, too, know that a clairvoyant and divine man maintained: "The power I saw during a baptism I also saw at the vesting of a monk."[2302] We also know that the holy

---

[2295] PG 120:657AB, ֱμθʹ.

[2296] St. Athanasios the Great wrote: "Once, when about to eat, having risen up to pray about the ninth hour, St. Anthony perceived that he was caught up in the spirit, and, wonderful to tell, he stood and saw himself, as it were, from outside himself, and that he was led in the air by certain ones. Next certain bitter and terrible beings stood in the air and wished to hinder him from passing through. But when his guides opposed them, they demanded to know whether he was not accountable to them. And when they wished to sum up the account from his birth, Anthony's guides stopped them, saying, 'The Lord hath wiped out the sins from his birth, but from the time he became a monk, and devoted himself to God, it is permitted you to make a reckoning'" (*Athanasius: Select Works and Letters,* 213).

[2297] Chamberas, *Saint Paisios the Athonite,* 201.

[2298] Cf. *The Great Book of Needs,* vol. 1, 360.

[2299] "Our God rejoices with His holy Angels over your repentance" (*The Great Book of Needs,* vol. 1, 365).

[2300] Ντύρου, *Τὸ Μέγα καὶ Ἀγγελικὸ Σχῆμα ὡς Δεύτερο Βάπτισμα,* 97.

[2301] Griggs, *Divine Eros: Hymns of Saint Symeon the New Theologian,* 193.

[2302] He is probably referring to the following incident: "There was once a great clairvoyant Elder who maintained that the power of grace which he saw during a baptism, near at hand to the person being baptized, he *also* saw at the time that a monk was receiving the angelic schema" (Chrysostomos, *The Evergetinos, Book I,* 262).

Fathers called this a second baptism (even though we are not particularly learned in sacred writings). For the holy service conducted nowadays for those who are dressed [with monastic clothes] is in imitation of the divine baptism in terms of its vows of renunciation and its composition, not to mention that it is usually much more toilsome and awesome. For there [in baptism], one says: "I renounce Satan," "I believe in one God," etc., but here [in the tonsure]: "I renounce parents and all my family as well as all empty and vain pleasure and glory. Not only do I renounce these things but even my own soul, and I will keep myself in purity and poverty for the sake of the Kingdom of Heaven."

That clairvoyant man said he maintained this view regarding the monastic schema. But I do not know if it has the same power as baptism in every way, or if it immediately bestows forgiveness of sins upon those who come to it. For the divine bath [i.e., baptism] is able to remit sins even without tears and any other laborious behavior. Not only this, but it even immediately makes those illumined [through baptism] to be partakers of the Holy Spirit. For if this were not the case, those who were baptized then [vid. Acts 19:6] would not have immediately received the gift of speaking in tongues. Therefore, the pool near the Sheep Gate[2303]—which immediately cured the sick people put in it—was also symbolic of this divine bath. Indeed, one who was guilty even of many sins but received illumination [i.e., was baptized] is not hindered from being elevated at once to a clerical rank, inasmuch as the wounds of his soul were cleansed in baptism. Whether or not the monastic clothing and the removal of hair is likewise able to accomplish these things, let those who are experts in these matters say. For we are doubtful about this, since we have Gregory the great Theologian indicating the laboriousness of repentance by saying: "How many tears must we shed in order to replace the baptismal font? For even if our tears were so many that they would drown our sins, we would not be found above them."[2304] This is also what the divine David indicated by saying: "Except in a flood of many waters, they shall not come nigh unto him."[2305]

Thus it is evident that the monastic schema by itself does not give remission of sins unless pains also accompany it. For if this were not the case, this divine man would not have called the baptism of tears a laborious baptism.... By calling it laborious, he clearly showed that without toil and tears it is unable to remit sins. For the divine Fathers confess *one* baptism free of labor that grants remission of sins. This is what John Chrysostom also shows in his interpretation of the gospel according to Matthew verbatim: "Was any guilty of fornication after the laver [of baptism]? In this case not even a consolation is left for the sin any more."[2306]

Therefore, do not let the sacred service of the monastic schema entice those of us who are negligent. I, too, have already agreed that it counts the tonsured monk worthy of divine wisdom and fills him with much courage against the noetic enemies. But if it is able to remit the sins of the one being tonsured, I do not know at all. For if this were the case, all the more so a person being ordained [to the priesthood] should certainly be completely freed of his sins because of the service conducted for him and the overshadowing of the All-holy Spirit, and he should not still be dragging his sins

---

[2303] Vid. Jn. 5:2.

[2304] Schaff, *Cyril of Jerusalem, Gregory Nazianzen,* 362 (Oration 40, *On Holy Baptism,* IX).

[2305] Ps. 31:6.

[2306] *St. Chrysostom: Homilies on the Gospel of St. Matthew,* 437 (Homily 75).

behind him like a long rope after the most holy bishop has sung for him the holy songs and called upon the grace of the All-holy Spirit.

Furthermore, St. Gregory of Nyssa allowed some people who had fallen into grave crimes to partake of Holy Communion at the time of their departure, but when they unexpectedly recovered, he said they were barred from Communion. This apparently shows that coming to repentance without toil does not give remission of sins. For if this were immediately given, as it certainly is in the divine bath [of baptism], he would not have prohibited those who recovered from receiving the holy Mysteries of Christ.[2307]

Michael Glykas then cites the life of the Prophet David as an example of the necessity of laborious repentance and adds:

[The monastic schema] is called a promise of repentance. Indeed, he who wears it promises to repent of his former sins. He who promises to do something is not considered one who has already accomplished it. When one has not done what he has promised but will do it in the future, how can he receive the reward as if he has already done it? Thus the promise would be pointless if he does not proceed to execute what he promised.

For if you see some young man dressed with the usual military garb, and he promises henceforth to proceed and engage in battle with the enemies and endure wounds and blows and despise life itself and face death, but he does not reach the point of fulfilling his promises, how would the judge of the contest be disposed towards such a person? Would he perhaps welcome him with honor and count him worthy of a higher rank and reward him with royal gifts? No, not at all, not at all! But he will give these things to him who has reached the point of fulfilling all his promises.

Therefore, the more negligent ones among us should not be enticed by the mere wearing of the schema, inasmuch as it is a second baptism. The fact that only the divine bath of rebirth [i.e., baptism]—and not this monastic schema—is able to renew and regenerate and restore those who come to it, making them new instead of old, is shown by Gregory the Theologian, who said verbatim: "There is no second regeneration [i.e., no second baptism], or re-creation, or restoration to our former state, even though we seek it with all our might, and with many sighs and tears, by which it is cicatrized [i.e., healed by scar formation] over (with great difficulty in my opinion, though we all believe that it may be cicatrized). Yet if we might wipe away even the scars I should be glad, since I too have need of mercy."[2308]

From this it is evident that this garment does not without toil bestow healing of the wounds and blows of evil. I consider this kind of garment sacred and indeed very much so, for it is both a path to salvation and a promise of repentance as well as a symbol of mortification. But this by itself is not able to grant forgiveness unless it is accompanied by pains, fountains of tears, and the working of virtues. For if these with difficulty bestow healing (as the aforementioned holy man said), what can be said if we lack these things due to limited time? The Lord is merciful, but they who call upon Him for mercy need great labor. This is what the divine David said, indicating the toil of repentance: "I humbled my soul with fasting,"[2309] and: "My flesh is changed for want of

---

[2307] PG 158:936D–940C (Ἐπιστολὴ 25).

[2308] Schaff, *Cyril of Jerusalem, Gregory Nazianzen*, 362.

[2309] Ps. 34:16.

oil,"[2310] and immediately: "Because I kept silence, my bones are waxed old through my crying all the day long."[2311]

Therefore, the most holy Ephraim [the Syrian] correctly said: "It is not the tonsure and the clothing that make the monk, but the longing for heavenly things and a life in accordance with the will of God."[2312] By this we are given to understand that it was because of how easily we slip that this kind of clothing was shown to Pachomios the Great by an angel. Why? In order to restrain as with a bridle those who come to repentance and not let them consider any change of attitude. And this is made much clearer by what he said: "O monk, behold the schema you are wearing and be aware that it stands apart from this world and completely attracts you to spiritual work instead." In the same vein the most holy John of the Ladder said: "Let your very dress urge you to the work of mourning, because all who lament the dead are dressed in black."[2313]

Thus, it was because of how easily we slip that the sacred service of [monastic] clothing was given to us. For if this were not the case, they who desire to be monks would not need such a thing. See how Anthony the Great, the most divine Paul of Thebes, and those who lived monastically in those days did not have this schema, since their souls were firm because they had reached the loftiest height of holiness.

So true repentance is not wearing black clothes and cutting the hair but returning to the Lord, living a life of rejecting things not good, as well as abstaining from former evils, and shedding hot tears afterwards for those things. Scripture says: "My son, hast thou sinned? Do so no more, but ask pardon for thy former sins."[2314] For as Chrysostom says, merely ceasing to sin is not enough to be counted as repentance, but one must also have fruits worthy of repentance. For in terms of wounds it is not sufficient merely to remove the arrow, but they must also put the appropriate medicines on the wound. This is the kind of repentance the author of *The Ladder* indicated by saying: "Repentance is reconciliation with the Lord by the practice of good deeds contrary to the sins."[2315]

Hence it is evident that this schema alone does not give remission of sins except through much labor and by practicing the virtues. If things were like that and it immediately gave remission of sins to those who voluntarily come to it, then how indeed would we need so many tears afterwards that they would equal the fount of baptism according to the great Theologian Gregory? How could it give release of sins to those who involuntarily (in a sense) and by coercion resort to the schema? I fear that the sacred service of the schema might be completely unsuitable for such people. For I do not know what such a person who has worn it will be able to do, since he is already breathing his last. He is preparing for battle [by receiving the schema], yet his hands are bound. He is donning the full armor and weaponry, yet there is no more time for war. He vows to remain in the monastery, yet he is being seized from this world. He solemnly promises to obey the superior, yet the tyranny of death forbids him. He vows to renounce wives and children, and he immediately gives up his soul. He testifies that

---

[2310] Ps. 108:23.

[2311] Ps. 31:3.

[2312] Chrysostomos, *The Evergetinos, Book I,* 268.

[2313] Holy Transfiguration Monastery, *The Ladder of Divine Ascent,* 73.

[2314] Sir. 21:1.

[2315] Holy Transfiguration Monastery, *The Ladder of Divine Ascent,* 54.

he is not approaching the schema by coercion, yet pneumonia is on its way and forces him to have his hair tonsured. He gives to the needy everything here that he unwillingly leaves behind. And he vows many other things, namely, to endure reproach, ridicule, and everything else like that, yet he does none of them because the remaining time of his life is extremely brief. The rewards are prepared for him, but it seems to me that such a person receives none of them....

We are saying these things not to prevent a person at the end of his life from receiving the divine transformation [of the schema] and the sacred service conducted for it. How could we, considering that even the small sighs [of repentance] are not rejected, especially for those whose lives were not corrupt. But we are saying these things to convince ourselves not to disregard completely God's commandments, relying on our last entreaty for help, as if this final clothing could help those who have spent their lives like this in indolence.

On the one hand, the divine bath [of baptism], as we have said above, does bestow remission of sins even without tears. Why? Not only because this kind of power is given to this bath, but also because the sins committed before baptism deserve great leniency since they were done out of ignorance, whereas sins after illumination [i.e., baptism] definitely call for tears ... because we commit them in knowledge, which is why we will receive "many lashes"[2316] for them....

I wish and deeply desire that those who come to this sacred garment will find remission of sins even at their last breath. But I am afraid and made doubtful by what the Lord said through the prophet: "Do thou first confess thy transgressions that thou mayest be justified."[2317] This prophetic statement makes me afraid that someone who comes in the hour of death by force and is also coerced into revealing his secret sins is not "first confessing." Without first confessing, one is not at all able to be justified, according to God's words. Take a look at Cain; since he did not confess first but only after he was censured by the Lord, he said: "My crime is too great for me to be forgiven!" He did not attain forgiveness because this kind of statement was not even a confession, as John Chrysostom says.

Furthermore, what Basil the Great says makes me afraid: "The thanks belong to death, not to you. If you were immortal, you would never have remembered the commandments."[2318] And what that preacher of repentance says also makes me afraid: "It is not almsgiving to bestow it upon this man and upon that man when one dies, and is no longer master of it. Thou art then no longer giving of thine own, but of absolute necessity: thanks to death, not to thee."[2319]

... I am terrified more by this story from the Fathers than by everything else. It is written that an elder was going to some city to sell his wares, and suddenly he was seated at the gate of some rich man who was about to die. While he was sitting there watching, he saw some black men with fiery cudgels in their hands and riding horses

---

[2316] "And that slave who knew his master's will and did not get ready or act in accord with his will, will receive many lashes" (Lk. 12:47).

[2317] Is. 43:26.

[2318] *St. Basil the Great: On Social Justice,* trans. C. Paul Schroeder (New York: St. Vladimir's Seminary Press, 2009), 56–57.

[2319] A Select Library of the Nicene and Post-Nicene Fathers of the Christian Church, *St. Chrysostom: Homilies on Galatians, Ephesians, Philippians, Colossians, Thessalonians, Timothy, Titus, and Philemon,* vol. 13, 135 (Homily 18).

that were also black. When they reached the gates, they left their horses outside and went inside. When the sick man saw them, he began crying out in a loud voice: "Lord, have mercy on me and help me." Then they said to him: "Are you remembering God only now that the sun has set? Why didn't you seek Him when the sun was high in the sky? Now there is no more hope for salvation." Then they violently ripped out his soul and departed.

If this is how things are, what shall we do who hope to show repentance at our final breath? So the baptism of repentance is truly a second baptism that renews the first, as we have said, but it requires many tears.[2320]

12) The Grace of the Schema

Regarding the grace one receives along with the schema, Elder Ephraim taught:

When people are tonsured, grace visits some of them greatly, while others less. This, however, does not foretell the monk's future spiritual life. Some do not feel the grace of the angelic schema at all, and yet they make much progress thereafter, whereas the opposite happens with others. Regardless, the goal of monasticism is purity of heart, from which perfect love is attained. This is what should preoccupy us and what we should pay attention to: whether or not we have patience and bravery in our battles with the devil, pure love, a tongue free of criticism and backbiting, etc. A monk has two joys: one when he becomes a monk and one when he approaches death. What is the life of a monk but a constant martyrdom? This is why death is joyful, because he realizes that he will escape the torments and battles of the tempter.[2321]

Elder Ephraim also taught that the grace of the schema strengthens monastics in their struggle for chastity: "Strengthened by the angelic schema's grace, a nun [or a monk] courageously struggles against the rough waves of the flesh while ceaselessly calling upon Jesus until He comes and rebukes the sea: 'Peace, be still' (Mk. 4:39)."[2322]

The grace that accompanies the great schema is also evident from the following incident in the life of Sts. John and Symeon the Fool for Christ:

Nikon bade the newly-tonsured monk to come forward, so that Symeon and John might see him. When this took place, a vision was granted to those who were accounted pure and unpolluted. The all-good God vouchsafed Symeon and John the following sight. They beheld the newly-tonsured monk approach, at which point they both kneeled at the feet of Abba Nikon. They felt enjoined to say to him, "If we are about to receive such honor and glory, do thou garb us this very evening. For we fear lest during the night we, the miserable ones, should expire from some demonic illusion; and thereby, we would be deprived of such a precious crown and the splendid escort which accompanies this new monk."

[2320] PG 158:941C–952A (Ἐπιστολὴ 25).

[2321] Γέροντος Ἐφραίμ, *Πατρικαὶ Νουθεσίαι,* 122; see also Elder Ephraim, *Counsels from the Holy Mountain,* 84.

[2322] Γέροντος Ἐφραίμ, *Πατρικαὶ Νουθεσίαι,* 107; see also Elder Ephraim, *Counsels from the Holy Mountain,* 73.

The hegumen, hearing this description, understood that the two young men were beholding a vision. Nikon then dismissed the newly-tonsured man to return to his cell. The youths of Christ were saddened exceedingly and said as much to the abbot: "Happy should we be were we to be vouchsafed such honor, that we might wear upon our brows such a splendid crown, and be escorted by a multitude of monastics bearing lamps in their hands and rejoicing." By these words, the hegumen was assured that the young men had seen a vision....

[After they received the holy schema][2323] their countenances possessed such light and their heads were donned with precious crowns, even as the aforementioned newly-tonsured monk at that monastery, that Symeon and John could see each other's faces that night as though it were day....

The great Symeon, afterward, related to Hierodeacon John about that early period of his life, saying that "Our souls experienced such joy that we had no desire to take either food or drink for the reverence we felt."[2324]

Evidently, this special grace lasts only seven days, for this instructive narrative continues:

As it happened, two days later Symeon and John caught sight of the monk who had received the Schema just days before they had. They observed that he was engaged in some obediences. He was dressed in other garb and there was no longer a crown about his brow. Indeed, he was no longer escorted by monks bearing lights as they had seen only a few days earlier. Symeon made a remark to John, saying, "Believe me, brother, after we fulfil our seven days, we, too, shall possess no longer either such grace or such majesty. Therefore, if thou wilt hear me, be ready to follow me. Let us go to a solitary and calm place, where we can labor for our souls. Indeed, brother most beloved, even as we have renounced all that is in the world, let us also forsake every earthly provision and care that we might meditate solely on heavenly things. When we had received this holy Schema, I want you to know that I beheld strange and wondrous things. When the slave of God, Abba Nikon, garbed us, I was sensing a fire which was consuming my inward parts. Moreover, I now find that my soul no longer seeks either to behold men or to speak to anyone anymore."[2325]

Then St. Symeon and John decided to sneak out of the monastery at night in order to become ascetics:

The pure bridegrooms of the Master Christ were just then coming toward the gate in order to leave. Nikon caught sight of them, but he also observed that others [i.e., angels]—some bearing lamps and some holding a scepter in one hand—were advancing with them....

Symeon and John were about to make a prostration before Abba Nikon when he forbade them, saying that on account of the Angelic Schema which had been bestowed upon them, it was not permitted that week to make prostrations.... [After expressing their deep gratitude to Abba Nikon and] entreating him to keep them in remembrance,

---

[2323] This phrase is missing from this English translation but is found in PG 93:1688B.

[2324] *The Great Synaxaristes of the Orthodox Church: July,* 872–73.

[2325] Ibid., 873.

the venerable Nikon wondered at the former simpletons made wise so quickly after their tonsure.[2326]

Another description of receiving much grace along with the great schema is found in the life of St. Akakios of Kafsokalyvia:

> On the very night [St. Akakios] received the holy schema, he was counted worthy of seeing a divine vision. He saw in his sleep—or rather in a waking state—that he was holding a lit candle with a brilliant light that shone and illumined the whole place there. (This, I think [writes the author of his life], represented his future virtuous way of life, which would shine and illumine not just Mount Athos by the grace given to him by God but also—even though it is bold to say—the entire world of the Orthodox Church.) When this holy man saw this miraculous sign, he correctly reasoned that in this manner the holy virtues of Christ (and especially "uplifting humility") must illumine a monk.[2327]

Gerondissa Makrina also experienced tremendous grace when receiving the great schema:

> The tonsuring [of Gerondissa Makrina] took place during the service of Compline. Gerondissa beheld a light as if the sun were rising from the Holy Altar of the church, illuminating everything as if it were daytime. She was in a state of theoria and she beheld Christ crucified and His immaculate blood flowing from His wounds into her heart. For forty days her mind was full of light and joy, and she shed endless tears. Her radiant spiritual state affected all those around her. Because of this spiritual transformation, Gerondissa desired to go up to a high mountaintop—as she would later say many times—and proclaim the grandeur of God, crying out for all people to become monastics in order to glorify God. Throughout the first days after her tonsure, whenever she saw the icon of the Last Judgment outside her cell, she would go into theoria, as if she were in the flames of hell. This transformation from the grace of the Great and Angelic Schema lasted for some time. For many days, she did not want to taste any food, and for an entire year, she was not occupied by any earthly thoughts.[2328]

Furthermore, Gerondissa Makrina taught: "Those of us with the Great Schema have two angels: the guardian angel of our soul and the angel of the Schema."[2329] She spoke from personal experience, for after receiving the great schema she had been counted worthy of seeing both of her angels on several occasions. For example, she once told her nuns:

> When I was in the hospital for my surgery, I saw my guardian angel and the angel of my Schema guarding me. They came hand in hand and were looking at me. They gave me joy, life, and gladness. They enriched my soul with their glance, as if they were telling me, "We are here, don't worry; we won't abandon you." Oh, how much joy I had when they were close to me! How I felt their presence! This is why we should

---

[2326] Ibid., 874–75 and PG 93:1692B.

[2327] Παταπίου Καυσοκαλυβίτου, *Ἅγιος Ἀκάκιος ὁ Καυσοκαλυβίτης*, Ἐρημοπολίτες 7 (Ἅγιον Ὄρος, 2001), 62–67.

[2328] Panagia Odigitria Monastery, *Words of the Heart: Gerondissa Makrina Vassopoulou,* (Goldendale: St. John the Forerunner Greek Orthodox Monastery, 2018), 60–61.

[2329] Ibid., 376.

not embitter our guardian angel and the angel of our Schema, but we should respect them. They are always close to us, next to us. What a joyous truth![2330]

One of the nuns of Gerondissa Makrina was counted worthy of both seeing and even touching the angel she was given at her tonsure. As Gerondissa Makrina related:

> When her own tonsure came, that same sister saw her angel embracing her with her two huge wings wrapped around her, holding her tightly. At that moment, she felt a great transformation in her soul and an abundance of grace. She felt such majesty! She told me, "I touched the wings, Gerondissa! They were like a peacock's; that's what they felt like in my hands. He had large brown wings, with green on the inside and a little red. That's what they looked like. The angel standing over me was very tall!"[2331]

13) The Rank of Monastics

St. Dionysius the Areopagite wrote the following about the grace and rank that God bestows on monastics:

> But of all the initiates [i.e., those who are not clergymen] the most exalted order is the sacred rank of the monks which has been purified of all stain and possesses full power and complete holiness in its own activities. To the extent that is permissible, it has entered upon sacred contemplative activity and has achieved intellectual contemplation and communion. This order is entrusted to the perfecting power of those men of God, the hierarchs, whose enlightening activities and hierarchal traditions have introduced it, according to capacity, to the holy operations of the sacred sacraments it has beheld. Thanks to their sacred understanding it has been uplifted into the most complete perfection proportionate to this order. This is why our blessed leaders considered such men to be worthy of several sacred designations; some gave them the name of "therapeutae," or servants, and sometimes "monks," because of the purity of their duty and service to God and because their lives, far from being scattered, are monopolized by their unifying and sacred recollection which excludes all distraction and enables them to achieve a singular mode of life conforming to God and open to the perfection of God's love. Hence the sacred ordinance has bestowed a perfecting grace on them and has deemed them worthy of a sanctifying invocation which is not the business of the hierarch (he only confers clerical ordination) but of the devout priests who sacredly performed this secondary rite of the hierarchy.[2332]

This special rank given to monastics is evident also in the following incident from the life of St. Alypios:

> Among these holy women dwelled the mother of St. Alypios. She practiced the same rule as the others, but she could not be persuaded to receive the monastic schema, even though her virtue was certainly remarkable, as we said in another place. She constantly refused to obey the many persistent entreaties of her son, maintaining that in the monastery the servant is the same as the nun. However, it happened that a divine

---

[2330] Ibid., 382–83.

[2331] Ibid., 240.

[2332] Luibhéid, *Pseudo-Dionysius: The Complete Works,* 244–45.

dream brought her into immediate obedience to her son's entreaty, so that she now began to beg him fervently in this regard. It seemed to her, in this revealing dream, that she was hearing certain holy women chanting in melodious psalmody. She was so delighted by this chanting, that she wanted to enter the room where this wonderful choir was singing and to be united, herself, with the chanting women. But when she tried to enter, a guard prevented her, saying: "She who is not wearing the same schema as the servants of God may not communicate with them."[2333]

Nevertheless, despite the importance of receiving the schema, St. Ephraim the Syrian reminds us:

It is not the tonsure and the clothing that make the monk, but the longing for heavenly things and a life in accordance with the will of God; the true monk is recognized by the latter. In the same way, the worldly man is not known by his hairstyle and clothing, but by his evil manner of life and his greed for worldly and material luxuries; for it is by these that the soul is made sinful. If you have renounced the world, be attentive to your spiritual labor, that you might acquire the pearl that you were seeking. For many have renounced the world and withdrawn from it; yet others have set aside military rank and have scorned their riches. But since in the end they were seduced by their own wills, they fell; for there is no worse sin than for one to be taken captive by his own will and to bypass what he judges to be correct.[2334]

In the same spirit, Elder Ephraim said:

Therefore, since we have put on the angelic schema, aren't we also obliged to live in an angelic manner? How can you be considered to be living an angelic life when I see you talking back, complaining, displaying self-will, enmity, and, worst of all, disobedience? By doing so, aren't you doing the opposite of what you have been counseled to do by my lowliness? Won't you receive a greater condemnation by doing the opposite, according to the saying in scripture that "he who knows and does not do shall be beaten with many blows" (Lk. 12:47)? In other words, he will be strictly chastised with many terrible blows and punishments.[2335]

St. John (Alexeev) of Valaam related the following incident revealing that it is more important to be a monk inwardly than outwardly: "In Kiev this happened: a schema-monk and a novice had been buried at the same time. When their graves were opened, the novice was wearing the habit and the schema-monk was wearing the novice's dress. There's a schema-monk for you! Poor fellow, you wore a schema and it served not for your salvation but for your condemnation."[2336]

[2333] Chrysostomos, *The Evergetinos, Book I,* 262.

[2334] Ibid., 268.

[2335] Γέροντος Ἐφραίμ, *Πατρικαὶ Νουθεσίαι,* 302; see also Elder Ephraim, *Counsels from the Holy Mountain,* 241–42.

[2336] Father John, *Christ Is in Our Midst: Letters from a Russian Monk* (New York: St. Vladimir's Seminary Press, 1980), 87 (Letter #76).

St. Eustathios of Thessalonica reproached monks who thought that the grace they would receive along with the schema was so powerful that they could afford to live negligently until then:

> These [lazy] monks believe that even though they have never done anything good, they will automatically be able to do so as soon as they have received the great tonsure. This approach is foolish because it resembles in an evil way the saying: "Let us eat and drink, for tomorrow we die."[2337] In other words, "Let's sin without restraint, since tomorrow by receiving the schema that brings us close to God we will die to the corruptible and corrupting life and world, and we will stand before God no longer as sinners but as His angels."[2338]

St. Symeon of Thessalonica taught that a monk who has received the schema has become heavenly: "Thus, a monk is no longer earthly and of this world but above this world and heavenly, and his 'citizenship is truly in the heavens,' together with Paul (vid. Phil. 3:20), and this is how he promises to live. Therefore, every monk should know that he no longer belongs to this present life but has been mortified towards this life and is an incorruptible and heavenly man."[2339]

> St. Sophrony of Essex also spoke of the heavenly nature of monasticism:

> The idea that the world must be renounced has led the majority of people to regard the monastic state as something sombre and uncomfortable. But those who have chosen monasticism see it differently. St. Theodore the Studite, for instance, in his enthusiasm for the life of a monk, called it "the third grace." The first grace was the law of Moses; the second, "the grace for grace"[2340] which we have all received of the fulness of Christ; and now the third, the monastic life, understood as celestial life, as the descent to earth of the angelic world, as the attainment and realization in history of what by its very essence lies beyond the confines of history.[2341]

St. Theodore the Studite viewed monks who have been "perfected in the divine mystagogy" (i.e., tonsured) as "surpassing many [laymen] in terms of knowledge and rank."[2342] Elaborating on this, St. Symeon of Thessalonica compared the priesthood with monasticism:

> Which is greater: the priesthood or the monastic schema? In terms of order, the priesthood is much greater than the monastic schema, for the works of the priesthood are the works of God, and without the priesthood no one would be a Christian, nor would anyone have sanctification or communion with God. Yet the monastic order is greater than a priest in the world (as Dionysios says) not in terms of the priesthood but

---

[2337] Is. 22:13.

[2338] PG 135:877B.

[2339] PG 155:913CD.

[2340] Jn. 1:16.

[2341] Sakharov, *Truth and Life,* 67.

[2342] Vid. Προκοπίῳ μονάζοντι, PG 99:1437D.

in terms of his life. Therefore, a monk who is also a priest is superior to a priest in the world. A simple monk, however, is not superior to a priest in the world, as we have said. For the priesthood is the work of God, but a simple monk is superior in terms of his life. Through the priesthood, a priest always blesses and sanctifies a monk who is superior to him in terms of his life. This is why Anthony [the Great] bent down and bowed his head not only to bishops but to every clergyman. Therefore, let every priest (as one having great worth) live a holy life and struggle to live like a monk; in some instances, let him even hasten to become a monk.[2343]

St. John Chrysostom also viewed priests as superior to monks:

> Great is the conflict which recluses undergo, and much their toil. But if any one compare their exertions with those which the right exercise of the priesthood involves, he will find the difference as great as the distance between a king and a commoner.... If any one were to give me my choice whether I would rather gain distinction in the oversight of the Church, or in the life of the recluse, I would vote a thousand times over for accepting the former.[2344]

St. Symeon of Thessalonica also wrote: "The schema is in the likeness of angels and of Jesus Christ Himself, Who prayed to His Father, 'Not My will but Thine be done' (Lk. 22:42). This is why Dionysios [the Areopagite] said that this schema is superior in purity even to the life of bishops in the world."[2345] Even though St. Symeon apparently misunderstood what Dionysius the Areopagite was saying,[2346] this perhaps explains why St. Symeon (who was both a monk and an archbishop) preferred to sign his name as "Monk Symeon" rather than "Archbishop Symeon."

With the same understanding, St. Nectarios of Aegina (who was also a bishop) wrote:

> The rank [of a bishop] is great indeed, but only in and of itself. Due to its inherent value, this rank truly honors the one who holds it, but it in no way alters the relations of those counted worthy of this rank towards his brothers, the brothers of the Lord; these relations remain always the same. This is why there is no difference and therefore no inequality between them.... The rank honors the one who has it but does not distinguish him from among the brothers of the Lord. Among the brothers of the Lord, the ones who imitate Christ are distinguished regardless of rank, since they bear the original image and the grace of the Holy Spirit.... He who has been perfected in virtue is superior to him who is not yet perfected, and he who has not at all become virtuous is very inferior to him who lives virtuously. Someone who is negligent and lazy—even if he happens to be a bishop—is miles behind someone who is diligent and vigilant—

[2343] PG 155:881C–884A.

[2344] *Chrysostom: On the Priesthood, Ascetic Treatises, Select Homilies and Letters, Homilies on the Statues,* 77–78.

[2345] PG 155:489C.

[2346] Dionysius the Areopagite did write: "Of all the *initiates* [emphasis added] the most exalted order is the sacred rank of the monks," but on the previous page he stated: "These, therefore, are the clerical orders.... Something must now be said of the three orders of initiates who are subordinate to them [i.e., subordinate to the clerical orders, which include all bishops and priests]" (Luibhéid, *Pseudo-Dionysius: The Complete Works,* 244, 243).

even if he happens to be some lowly and insignificant monk.... So please tell me now who is superior in virtue: he who lives in comfort and abundance or a hermit lacking even the smallest consolation; he who is worldly or he who is dedicated to God? ... Thus, it is virtue and virtue alone that matters, and virtue depends on one's way of life.... Behold what my conviction is, beloved brother, because of which I consider the ascetic superior to the bishop, and which I confess in all sincerity.[2347]

On the other hand, St. Eustathios of Thessalonica (who likewise was both a monk and a bishop) presented a different comparison of how bishops and monks differ in rank:

[Great-schema monks] are obliged to acknowledge seniority only to one holy rank—the lofty and holy rank of bishops. Great-schema monks are superior to all the rest in both form and figure. For of all the human ranks on earth (which of course are inferior to those in heaven), the first and foremost for man's salvation are they who are symbolic of the first and great Bishop of our salvation [i.e., Christ]. Since they [i.e., bishops] bring straight down from God every good thing, they do nothing but lead every person to Him, as is their duty. The light that these bishops emit is inferior to the light of God Himself. There are three sources of light: first, the light of God which is incomparably brighter than the sun; then, the light of the angels which resembles the sun and is the light that the bishop emits; and then follows the light which is like moonlight (in a sense) which the great-schema monks emit. After this come all the other godly stars around the earth [i.e., other spiritual people] who illumine with light and give warmth to lowly people with their vivifying energy, in the same way rich earth is made fruitful. Such monks (and those who are like them) are offered to God as the first fruits of this spiritual crop, but bishops are superior to them. They are similar to each other since they both belong to a sacred rank, but the bishops are superior due to the loftiness of being a bishop, which is a "royal priesthood."[2348] And since it is superior, from this do monks (who are clearly inferior) receive their blessings, even though they might be displeased to hear me saying so. This is something I have deduced from my own personal experience. But this behavior of theirs is completely senseless, since they are unable to justify their displeasure if someone were to ask them for an explanation.

All liturgical sanctifications—for example, in holy baptism and in all the other services done in the lives of those who have been baptized, as well as all the priestly ranks and the service of tonsure by which monks are dedicated to God—are performed spiritually and symbolically by the Holy Spirit but visibly by the bishop or by priests whom the bishops have appointed to perform such holy services. So then, considering that the bishops themselves sanctify monks in the Mystery of tonsure, how can a monk dare to object and say that he is not subject to the authority of the bishop who is superior to him, to whom he is clearly inferior? These ignorant monks raise their head and try to become autonomous not only from the bishop who in the beginning blessed and dedicated them but also from anyone else they might meet later. They think that they are autocephalous, whereas in reality they are just necks without heads, and out of their arrogance they end up being something molded that answers back to their molders.[2349] They do not understand that their difference from the rank of bishop is

---

[2347] Ματθαιάκη, *Ὁ Ὅσιος Νεκτάριος Κεφαλᾶς*, «Ἐπιστολὴ πρὸς Μοναχόν», 260.

[2348] 1 Pet. 2:9.

[2349] Cf. Rom. 9:20, "Who are you, O man, who answers back to God? The thing molded will not say to the molder, 'Why did you make me like this,' will it?"

that they are merely fathers, whereas a bishop is the father of fathers. Nor do they comprehend that although they are shepherds and sometimes also abbots, the arch-shepherd is the bishop, since the position he has been given is superior to that of the abbots, especially when the bishop is an archbishop of many. Furthermore, they do not realize that, if they want to and exert themselves systematically in their hard monastic duties, they can ascend to the rank of bishop. And this, of course, does not mean that they will fall from some lofty position into a precipice, but they will ascend to a much higher place, as if from earth to Mt. Olympus.[2350] …

You are certainly not unaware that God is rightly called the Bishop [ἀρχιερεύς][2351] of our salvation, and that Scripture calls Him the Bishop [ἐπίσκοπος][2352] Who oversees His chosen, but nowhere is He called an elder [καλόγερος] or a monk [μοναχός] of any kind.[2353]

The council held in the Temple of Holy Wisdom in 879 explained why a monk is inferior to a bishop: "If any bishop or anyone else with a prelatical office is desirous of descending to monastic life and of replenishing the region of penitence and of penance, let him no longer cherish any claim to prelatical dignity. For the monks' conditions of subordination represent the relationship of pupilship, and not of teachership or of presidency; nor do they undertake to pastor others, but are to be content with being pastored."[2354]

14) When to Receive the Schema

In the Byzantine era, a person would receive the schema after three years of trial. For example, the First-and-Second Council in Constantinople decreed in 861:

No one shall lay claim to the monastic habit [i.e., the schema] until, after the expiration of the term of three years allowed them to prove their worthiness, they turn out to be adequate and fit to take up such a mode of life in earnest … unless … some grave disease has overtaken the person … or unless, there should be anywhere a man so reverent as to lead a monastic life even in a worldly habit—for in the case of such a man even a six months' period of trial is sufficient for a thorough test.[2355]

Commenting on this canon, St. Nicodemos of the Holy Mountain expressed the opinion: "It may be inferred, too, from this Canon that anyone that fails to become a monk by the end of three years while living in a monastery will thereafter if he stays there be dwelling with the brethren in the monastery illegally and unlawfully, and ought either to become a

---

[2350] PG 135:733B–735A.

[2351] Ever since at least the second century (vid. 1 Clem. 40:5), the word ἀρχιερεύς (which was used a dozen times in Hebrews in reference to Christ the "High Priest") has been used to refer to bishops.

[2352] 1 Pet. 2:25. The literal meaning of ἐπίσκοπος is "overseer."

[2353] PG 135:841A.

[2354] Agapius and Nicodemus, *The Rudder,* 478 (Canon II).

[2355] Ibid., 460 (Canon V).

monk or to depart."[2356] Although Elder Ephraim agreed that after a certain time period a novice should either become a monk or depart, his experience with novices in America showed him that three years is often not a long enough trial period.

Notwithstanding this minimum trial period of three years, "when death is imminent the holy habit will be granted without delay to those who are leaving this world,"[2357] according to the 13th-century typikon of Nikephoros Blemmydes and several others, including Canon XXV of St. Nicephoros the Confessor (9th century),[2358] Patriarch Theodore Balsamon (12th century), and St. Symeon of Thessalonica (14th century).[2359]

In contemporary practice there are varying traditions regarding when a person should receive the great schema. Monasteries in the Russian tradition typically wait until a monk is on his deathbed. But in some places on the Holy Mountain, after a person has been a novice for 5–10 years he is immediately given the great schema without first becoming a rasophore or small-schema monk. Elder Ephraim had a more moderate approach and typically waited 20–30 years before giving the great schema to rasophores. His reasoning was that since a tremendous amount of grace is given with the great schema, it should not be given to someone who might lose that grace through inattentiveness. In the case of monks living negligently, he would wait until their deathbed before giving them the great schema.

St. Ephraim the Syrian also believed that one should patiently wait to receive the schema at the proper time. He wrote:

> Brother, be not impatient to receive the angelic schema; for the Enemy implants in some people the unreasonable desire to demand the monastic schema when the time is not yet ripe. But as for you, my beloved, as one striving to please God, be patient and hear what the Apostle says: "If thou mayest be made free, use slavery rather."[2360] Cast your gaze over the past generations and see that it was through forbearance and patience that all the saints received promises from God, and goad yourself daily to be a fellow-heir with them in the Kingdom of Heaven.
>
> Have you considered that the Patriarch Jacob worked as a slave in Mesopotamia for fourteen years next to Laban the Syrian, enduring the heat of the day and the frost of the night, for the sake of Rachel? Likewise, did not the beloved Joseph remain for several years as a slave in a foreign country? In this regard Scripture says: "Joseph was seventeen years old, feeding the sheep with his brethren."[2361] Later on it says: "Joseph was thirty years old when he stood before Pharaoh."[2362] Moses, the servant of the Lord, remained as a refugee in the land of Madiam for forty years. The Hebrews entered into the Promised Land after a journey of forty years. Prior to all of this, think how many

---

[2356] Ibid., 462.

[2357] Thomas and Hero, *Byzantine Monastic Foundation Documents,* 1203.

[2358] Vid. Agapius and Nicodemus, *The Rudder,* 967.

[2359] Ibid., 343.

[2360] 1 Cor. 7:21.

[2361] Gen. 37:1.

[2362] Gen. 41:46.

years it was before Abraham received what had been promised to him by God. In general, all the saints gained the Divine promises through ungrudging waiting. Therefore, you, too, should wait patiently on the Lord with humility, and He will exalt you in the proper time, "and He shall bring forth thy righteousness as the light and thy judgment as the noonday" (Ps. 36:6).[2363]

St. Symeon of Thessalonica emphasized how important it is for monks to receive the great schema:

> Just as he who has not been baptized is not a Christian, so, too, he who has not been perfected by receiving the schema will not be considered a monk.... He who has not attained to becoming a monk should become one at the end of his life. For the gift is tremendous! The seal is royal! It is a second baptism! It purges sins! It gives gifts and graces! It arms and marks him! It delivers him from enemies! It presents him to the King and makes him his friend![2364]

St. Sophrony of Essex taught: "No one ought to ask for the priesthood, whereas one ought to ask for the monastic schema, because monasticism is the search for repentance."[2365] Likewise, the *Ascetical Discourse* attributed to St. Basil states: "An ascetic should not desire to become a clergyman or the superior of brethren. For this illness is diabolical, and it is the transgression of loving authority, which is characteristic of the devil's supreme cunning."[2366]

St. Eustathios of Thessalonica compared progress in monasticism with progress climbing a mountain and said that a monk is ready to receive the great schema after reaching a certain level:

> ... [A small-schema monk] wearing black has not yet completely attained greatness, nor has he ascended to the loftiest point of perfection, but he has just recently stopped being a lowly pedestrian and has come to the mountain to climb it as his strength permits. Now that he has left behind the level plain and the smog engulfing it, he has passed into a clearer atmosphere with refreshing air. Moreover, he has a different view of the earth and of things on earth, and he ponders on those things that had previously ruined his true human form. And he is afraid lest he fall down from this height and suffer something worse.
>
> When he has felt this genuine fear, he will spread his wings early in the morning with vigilance and prayers that God hears. He will close his eyes and every other sense as a person who no longer wants to be a man of the world at all but a man transcending the heavens. And he will keep himself steady to stand on the pinnacle of virtue, and will leave behind the stagnant air and the darkness engulfing it and the various tempests in order to reach the cloudless place where the sun always shines. And he will certainly achieve such a goal of illumination and will approach God after coming to this lofty

---

[2363] Παύλου Μοναχοῦ, *Εὐεργετινός,* Τόμος Α΄, ἔκδοσις ἑβδόμη (Ἡλίας Μπακόπουλος Μοναχός: Ἀθῆναι, 2001), 446; see also Chrysostomos, *The Evergetinos, Book I,* 264.

[2364] PG 155:673B.

[2365] Hierotheos, *"I Know a Man in Christ,"* 385.

[2366] Μ. Βασιλείου, *Ἀσκητικαὶ Διατάξεις* 9, PG 31:1369D.

place from where the Lord Himself has a panoramic view of all the sons of men. That is, he will in a sense bend down his head along with God and will be able to see people who need his help and he, too, will do whatever he desires [as God also does]. Then, having risen above the small schema (it is not possible to describe how much so), he has reached the great schema, glorying in a bright and great face, beholding the face of our great God and Savior, Jesus Christ, Who is one of the superbrilliant Trinity. He also sees the other two Persons [of the Trinity] with his spirit, which makes up for this lack with the grandeur appropriate to the unity of God. In this manner he is true to the great schema he has received, which could have been called the greatest schema [μέγιστον σχῆμα, i.e., the greatest "form" of being], if the holy Fathers—who did well—hadn't chosen to give this title to the One and Only Bearer of the greatest form of being [i.e., God]. In comparison to this eternal form of being, the other forms of being are like shadows.

So the life of the great-schema monk has these three stages as we have said. He is the refuge of pious Christians when they want to hide from the enemies [i.e., the demons] who are attacking them from above. Blessed is he who truly has this form (σχῆμα) and has been divinely transformed and has taken the form of God and has henceforth acquired this greatness as a natural trait of his. Furthermore, he perfects those who are inferior to the great schema [i.e., small-schema and rasophore monks], and thus the great-schema monk holds a primary position because of his philosophy. He is able to make up for their deficiencies with a divine and discursive method by which the knowledge of virtue is reached. Simultaneously he guides them to imitate those in heaven, as we shall elaborate hereafter. Thus, such a monk who completed these three stages is blessed, since he has ascended to the rank of the great schema. He has become as light as a feather and has ascended to the third heaven.[2367] ...

A great-schema monk should be proud [in a good sense] that he has been made erudite in spiritual matters by both doing and teaching them, not as a mental exercise. By obeying the Holy Spirit, he helps the inferior monastic ranks attain perfection and please the only wise God.[2368] ...

It would be proper to mention first the leaders of the group of monastics, who are perfect and make others perfect. This is the right order, since they are like gods (according to the scriptural reference) and ought to help all the others in every small matter. These are the ones who have the great and angelic schema, who because of it are indeed great like angels, in accordance with the provisions of the rules and also according to the vows they gave during the sacramental rite. For they have turned their backs to the world, primarily by flying away from it with their spiritual wings to God Himself. Now they have the responsibility (if they want it) to look down from these divine heights and help others.[2369] ...

The monastic order is not just any order but a truly divine order. It is a sacred army, a brigade of God, chosen by the Lord, the glorious ones of heaven who have withdrawn from every worldly glorious thing—which would be sinful for them. They are soldiers against the devil, the rebellious apostate. They imitate the angels, which is why they are the protectors not only of people's souls but also of their bodies, which they keep healthy, releasing them from sins that often disintegrate the harmonious elements of

---

[2367] PG 135:740C–741C.

[2368] PG 135:737B.

[2369] PG 135:733AB.

our nature. They are vessels of virtue, as long as they keep themselves suitable and open to it. They are containers of divine myrrh, when they have nothing filthy in themselves. They are imprints of the Apostles, as long as they do not fail to learn things about God. They are gardens of salvation, inaccessible to the serpents' whisperings, by which the devil tries to speak to those who open their ears to him. This magnificent order (which the episcopal order surpasses) boasts that its leaders are those who have the truly great schema, who must neither fail to be great literally nor be unworthy of this compound title [i.e., of being a "great-schema" monk, which means having a great form].[2370] ...

I remind great-schema monks that they have been taught to yearn after the form [σχῆμα] of angels so that they may play the role of an angel. Therefore, the reverence shown to them should not be viewed as being excessive, since they are superior even to angels, as we are taught by the sacred ascetical writings, which say that if they want to, they can cover the small distance that separates them from the angels according to the psalm[2371] and even surpass them. So bear this in mind, you monk who do not live in the world, who are a saint at least by intention.[2372] ...

A true great-schema monk (as well as all true Christians) should always be ready to serve a friend in all ways and help him with whatever he needs.[2373] ...

It is through them [i.e., great-schema monks] that the world is saved, for they are always devoted to God alone and are closer to Him than the angels. They do not turn to the world except to remember us in prayer.[2374]

St. Paisios of the Holy Mountain objected to the practice of intentionally waiting until old age to receive the great schema:

> Those who receive the Angelic Schema at a young age and humbly struggle with *philotimo* greatly move God. If the Angelic Schema has externally become a bit dusty (with the passing of years), I still think it is cleaner than the Schema of monks who were intentionally tonsured in their old age, that they might live a little slothfully. They gloat over their brand-new Schema at the hour of death (fresh from the tailor) and give their vows on their deathbed with a half-gone voice, promising to keep virginity, poverty, and obedience. Where? In the grave? Let us not set our mind to rest with these kinds of illusions.[2375]

As for the time of year for becoming a monk, St. Theodore the Studite wrote in the 8th century: "It should be known that on the Tuesday of Renovation [Easter Week] we grant the great habit to those brothers who have been designated to receive it."[2376] The life of St.

[2370] PG 135:736B–D.

[2371] "Thou hast made him a little lower than the angels, with glory and honour hast Thou crowned him" (Ps. 8:6).

[2372] PG 135:764BC.

[2373] PG 135:772B.

[2374] PG 135:793D.

[2375] Elder Paisios, *Epistles,* 195.

[2376] Thomas and Hero, *Byzantine Monastic Foundation Documents,* 101.

Symeon the Fool for Christ mentions that in the 6th century someone received the schema on the day of the Holy Cross, although it was also given on other days.[2377] The 11th-century *Strategios Euchologion*[2378] describes the service of tonsure along with the prayers of the Washing of the Feet, which implies that monks were tonsured on Holy Thursday. St. Symeon of Thessalonica taught in the 15th century: "Though any time may be considered fitting for one to become a monk, yet the period of the forty days of Lent is more fitting than any other because it is a time of mournful repentance."[2379] Elder Ephraim agreed that any time of year is fitting to receive the great schema, but he had a slight preference for tonsuring on feast days. In contrast, St. Sophrony of Essex taught: "Monastic professions are not festive services, so they ought to take place in a contrite atmosphere of repentance and prayer. The monastic life is a cross and spiritual burial. A bright and festive atmosphere removes the monk from the essence of the monastic life."[2380]

15) When to Wear the Schema

In the early days of monasticism, "the Egyptian fathers had the custom of keeping the cloak and cowl in which they took the holy habit until their death, only wearing them on Sundays for the Holy Communion and taking them off immediately afterwards."[2381] Similarly, in Athonite tradition, great-schema monks wear their schema only when they receive Communion. When they are not wearing the full version of the great schema on top of their cassock, they always wear a small version of it under their cassock hanging from their neck on their chest. This is because St. Symeon of Thessalonica taught that a monk "should always be wearing all the symbols of the schema"[2382] since it helps to effect "an unforgettable remembrance of God and union with Him and boldness and courage towards Him."[2383]

St. Paisios of the Holy Mountain cautioned monks not to display their schema vaingloriously:

> Some monks, for example, make broad and long great schemas reaching down to their feet, with red crosses, roses, red branches and many letters…. And they open their cassock to reveal the schema, like the Pharisees who "make broad their phylacteries,

---

[2377] Vid. Holy Transfiguration Monastery *Saint Symeon of Emesa*, 56; PG 93:1685CD.

[2378] Vid. J. Duncan, *Coislin 213. Euchologe de la Grande Eglise. Dissertatio ad Lauream* (Rome, 1983).

[2379] Reply #25, as paraphrased by St. Nicodemos in Agapius and Nicodemus, *The Rudder,* 343.

[2380] Hierotheos, *"I Know a Man in Christ,"* 305.

[2381] Vid. Ward, *The Sayings of the Desert Fathers,* 241.

[2382] PG 155:916C.

[2383] Balfour, Ἁγίου Συμεὼν Θεσσαλονίκης: Ἔργα Θεολογικά, 176.

and enlarge the borders of their garments,"[2384] to show that they pray a lot! But in the past one could barely see the schema under the cassock of a monk as he walked. In fact, many wore a small schema underneath to hide it altogether.[2385]

St. Symeon of Thessalonica gave the following details of how a monk should be buried:

> After [the corpse] is wiped in the shape of the cross, they dress him with the garments of the schema, and they sew him up in his mantle, which is like his tomb. They make crosses on the top for the sake of Christ for Whom he was crucified. And an icon of Him Whom he loved is placed on top of him.[2386] After the priest says the prayer, they lift him up and take him to the holy temple with candles.[2387]

St. Symeon explained the reason why monks are buried with the garments of the schema:

> [It is] not because these [garments] will be raised along with them, but because they are symbolic of divine things and because he who wore them lived with their power. But even if he did not live in this manner, he did come and submit himself in obedience. Therefore, since each person will be in his own rank [in heaven], both the monk and the priest are dressed in this life [at their burial] with the things belonging to their schema and order, and they are offered to God with these things along with whatever else there is in the schema or in the priesthood. And since this present life is a time for work whereas the future life is for a reward, each person shows in this life that in whatever rank he was found here he will also be enrolled there. This is why one must be buried with the schema appropriate to one's rank, so that one does not think that one casts it off in death.[2388]

[2384] Mt. 23:5.

[2385] Elder Paisios, *Spiritual Awakening,* 365. Interestingly, though, whenever the holy elder of St. Paisios, Papa Tikhon, was asked to be photographed, he would first don his schema for the photo. Clearly, there are both passionate and dispassionate reasons why a monk would want to be seen wearing his schema.

[2386] In contemporary Athonite practice, the icon placed on the monk's chest is an icon of the Resurrection, with the top of the icon close to the monk's chin. The icon is removed from his chest after the funeral service before he is buried.

[2387] PG 155:676CD.

[2388] PG 155:916CD.

Appendix:
The Benefit of Heterodox Writings According to the Holy Fathers

I N THIS BOOK we have included some insights of wise men who were not Orthodox. Since, however, the heterodox lack the fulness of grace of Orthodox Christians, it may seem inappropriate to derive benefit from heterodox sources. To address such concerns, the first half of this appendix will demonstrate that this approach is in fact justified because the greatest Church Fathers throughout the centuries have unanimously declared that Christians should take advantage of whatever wisdom is to be found in the writings of the heterodox. The second half of this appendix will attempt to explain how the grace of God can work through those outside the Church.

+ + +

In the 2nd century, St. Justin the Philosopher and Martyr taught that God can be discovered through the writings of Hellenic philosophers, and he attributed their wisdom to a "seed" of God the Word. He wrote:

> I confess that I both boast and with all my strength strive to be found a Christian; not because the teachings of Plato are different from those of Christ, but because they are not in all respects similar, as neither are those of the others, Stoics, and poets, and historians. For each man spoke well in proportion to the share he had of the spermatic divine Logos, seeing what was related to it.... Whatever things were rightly said among all men are the property of us Christians.[2389]

A contemporary of his, St. Irenaeus of Lyons, agreed: "The Word of God has never ceased to be present in the race of man."[2390] Another contemporary of his, St. Athenagoras of Athens, believed that the Hellenic poets and philosophers were moved to religious knowledge by the "breath of God" within them.[2391] Similarly, Blessed Augustine taught: "What

---

[2389] Justin Martyr, *Apologia,* II, 13; PG 6:465B.

[2390] *Adversus Haereses,* III, 16, 1 (as quoted in Jean Daniélou, *Holy Pagans of the Old Testament,* trans. Felix Faber [London: Longmans, Green & Co., 1957], 4).

[2391] PG 6:904B (*Πρεσβεία 7*).

is now called the Christian religion existed even among the ancients and was not lacking from the beginning of the human race until 'Christ came in the flesh' (cf. 1 Jn. 4:2)."[2392]

St. Justin also said: "Christ, Whom Socrates knew in part (for He is the Word everywhere present), swayed not only philosophers and lettered men but even workmen and ignorant folk, to such effect that they scorned public opinion, fear and death; for the Word is the power (δύναμις) of the Father and not a product of human reason."[2393] Commenting on this passage, Fr. Jean Daniélou wrote: "The last phrase is to be noted. Justin definitely means by his words a supernatural action of grace (δύναμις) and not a simple exercise of reason."[2394]

In the late 2nd (or perhaps early 3rd) century, Clement of Alexandria in his *Stromata* expounded extensively on "the importance and uses of Greek [i.e., pagan] philosophy for the Christian."[2395] He wrote:

> For clearly, as I think, he [i.e., Peter] showed that the one God was known by the Greeks in pagan fashion, to the Jews in Jewish fashion, and to us [Christians] in a new and spiritual way.[2396] ...
>
> It is He who also gave philosophy to the Greeks by means of the inferior angels.... He is Saviour; not [the Saviour] of some, and of others not. But in proportion to the adaptation possessed by each, He has dispensed His beneficence both to Greeks and Barbarians.[2397] ...
>
> The Greek preparatory culture, therefore, with philosophy itself, is shown to have come down from God to men.[2398] ...
>
> [Pagan] philosophy does not ruin life ... although some have calumniated it, though it be the clear image of truth, a divine gift to the Greeks; nor does it drag us away from the faith, as if we were bewitched by some delusive art, but rather, so to speak, by the use of an ampler circuit, obtains a common exercise demonstrative of the faith. Further, the juxtaposition of doctrines, by comparison, saves the truth, from which follows knowledge.[2399] ...
>
> Before the advent of the Lord, philosophy was necessary to the Greeks for righteousness. And now it becomes conducive to piety.[2400] ...

[2392] *St. Augustine: The Retractations,* The Fathers of the Church, vol. 60, trans. Sister M. Inez Bogan (Washington, D.C.: Catholic University of America Press, 1968), 52 (Retractiones, book 1, chapter 12).

[2393] Justin Martyr, *Apologia,* II, 10, 4–5 (as translated in Daniélou, *Holy Pagans of the Old Testament,* 19–20); PG 6:461AB.

[2394] Daniélou, *Holy Pagans of the Old Testament,* 20.

[2395] Frank Leslie Cross, *The Early Christian Fathers* (London: B. Duckworth, 1960), 121.

[2396] *Fathers of the Second Century: Hermas, Tatian, Athenagoras, Theophilus, and Clement of Alexandria,* 489 (*Stromata,* Book 6, Chapter 5; PG 9:261AB).

[2397] Ibid., 522 (*Stromata,* Book 7, Chapter 2; PG 9:409B).

[2398] Ibid., 308 (*Stromata,* Book 1, Chapter 7; PG 8:732B).

[2399] Ibid., 303–4 (*Stromata,* Book 1, Chapter 2; PG 8:709B).

[2400] Ibid., 305 (*Stromata,* Book 1, Chapter 5; PG 8:717C).

> Since, therefore, truth is one ... so the sects both of barbarian and Hellenic philosophy have done with truth, and each vaunts as the whole truth the portion which has fallen to its lot. But all, in my opinion, are illuminated by the dawn of Light.... So, then, the barbarian and Hellenic philosophy has torn off a fragment of eternal truth not from the mythology of Dionysus, but from the theology of the ever-living Word. And he who brings again together the separate fragments, and makes them one, will without peril, be assured, contemplate the perfect Word, the truth.[2401]

Thus, Clement demonstrates that the wisdom in barbarian and Hellenic philosophy are fragments of truth acquired by the grace of God, and therefore we can (as he said above) "without peril bring together the separate fragments."

This gathering of fragments of truth from the heterodox is what St. Basil the Great in the 4th century recommended:

> For just as bees know how to extract honey from flowers, which to men are agreeable only for their fragrance and color, even so here also those who look for something more than pleasure and enjoyment in such writers may derive profit for their souls. Now, then, altogether after the manner of bees must we use these writings, for the bees do not visit all the flowers without discrimination, nor indeed do they seek to carry away entire those upon which they light, but rather, having taken so much as is adapted to their needs, they let the rest go. So we, if wise, shall take from heathen books whatever befits us and is allied to the truth, and shall pass over the rest. And just as in culling roses we avoid the thorns, from such writings as these we will gather everything useful, and guard against the noxious. So, from the very beginning, we must examine each of their teachings, to harmonize it with our ultimate purpose, according to the Doric proverb, "testing each stone by the measuring-line."[2402]

Nevertheless, St. Basil also wrote with regret: "Much time had I spent in vanity, and had wasted nearly all my youth in the vain labour which I underwent in acquiring the [pagan] wisdom made foolish by God."[2403] Elsewhere, St. Basil added that people "should apply discernment to the studies they make, seeking out useful studies and rejecting what is unintelligent or harmful."[2404] These quotes show that St. Basil thinks that when we read heterodox books, we must be careful not only to avoid the "thorns" but also to avoid spending an inordinate amount of time reading them.

In the same century, St. Gregory the Theologian expressed his stance toward pagan Greek culture in the apothegm: "Avoid the thorns, pluck the roses."[2405] He wrote:

[2401] Ibid., 313 (*Stromata*, Book 1, Chapter 13; PG 8:753C–756B).

[2402] St. Basil the Great, *Address to Young Men on the Right Use of Greek Literature*, as quoted in Frederick Morgan Padelford, *Essays on the Study and Use of Poetry by Plutarch and Basil the Great*, Yale Studies in English 15 (1902): 105 (PG 31:569C).

[2403] *Basil: Letters and Select Works*, 263 (Letter 223).

[2404] Homily XII on Proverbs 1:6 (PG 31:397BC) as quoted by St. Gregory Palamas in Amis, *The Triads in Defence of the Holy Hesychasts: Book 1*, 39 (Triad 1.1.8).

[2405] Vid. Frederick Norris, "Of Thorns and Roses," *Church History* 53 (December 1984): 455–64.

External culture [i.e., the culture of the heathen] which many Christians by an error of judgment scorn as treacherous and dangerous and as turning away from God.... we select from them what is useful both for life and enjoyment and we avoid what is dangerous.... Even from certain reptiles we have at times compounded salutary medicines. So also from the pagans we have received principles of inquiry and speculation, while we have rejected whatever leads to demons, and error, and the abyss of perdition. And from such material we have drawn profit for piety, by learning to distinguish from the worse, and from its weakness we have made our own doctrine strong.[2406]

Also in the 4th century, St. Gregory of Nyssa interpreted anagogically Moses's instruction to the Israelites in Exodus 11:2 to take the wealth of Egypt with them as follows:

The loftier meaning [of Moses's instruction]... commands those participating through virtue in the free life also to equip themselves with the wealth of pagan learning by which foreigners to the faith beautify themselves. Our guide in virtue commands someone who "borrows" from wealthy Egyptians to receive such things as moral and natural philosophy, geometry, astronomy, dialectic, and whatever else is sought by those outside the Church, since these things will be useful when in time the divine sanctuary of mystery must be beautified with the riches of reason.[2407] ...

There are certain things derived from profane education which should not be rejected when we propose to give birth to virtue. Indeed moral and natural philosophy may become at certain times a comrade, friend, and companion of life to the higher way, provided that the offspring of this union introduce nothing of a foreign defilement.[2408]

The attitude of St. John Chrysostom (in the 4th century) towards pagan philosophers was in general unenthusiastic.[2409] He did acknowledge, however, that some of their writings are instructive: "Read, if you will, both our own books and those without [i.e., both Christian and heathen books]: for they also abound in such examples. If you despise ours, and this from pride; if you admire the works of [pagan] philosophers, go even to them. They will instruct thee."[2410] Elsewhere he said: "I do not say this to prevent your teaching him these things [of pagan philosophy], but to prevent your attending to them exclusively."[2411]

In the 5th century, Blessed Augustine (who was by no means complacent towards paganism) taught that the pagan philosophers were saved: "From the beginning of the

---

[2406] *Funeral Orations by S Gregory Nazianzen and S Ambrose,* Fathers of the Church, vol. 22, trans. Leo P. McCauley (Washington, D.C.: Catholic University of America Press, 1953), 35–36 (PG 36:508B).

[2407] *Gregory of Nyssa: The Life of Moses,* trans. Abraham J. Malherbe and Everett Ferguson, (New York: Paulist Press, 1978), 81, §115 (PG 44:360B).

[2408] Ibid., 62–63 (PG 44:336D–337A).

[2409] Vid. Θεοδωρούδη, *Θεία καὶ Ἀνθρωπίνη Σοφία κατὰ τὴν Πατερικὴν Παράδοσιν τῆς Ὀρθοδόξου Ἐκκλησίας,* 75–78.

[2410] *St. Chrysostom: Homilies on Galatians, Ephesians, Philippians, Colossians, Thessalonians, Timothy, Titus, and Philemon,* 379 (Homily 1 on Second Thessalonians).

[2411] Ibid., 155 (Homily 21 on Ephesians 6:1–3).

human race, there were people who believed in Jesus Christ, knew Him and lived a good and devout life according to His commandments. No matter when or where they lived, they without doubt were saved by Him."[2412] St. Anastasios of Antioch and St. Nectarios of Aegina also believed that the pagan philosophers were saved, for the latter wrote:

> Jesus said: "I did not come to call the righteous, but sinners to repentance" (Mt. 9:13). These words of Jesus clearly show that the righteous [before Christ] had a part in the salvation of the human race that would come through Jesus Christ. Since those who were under the law had a part in salvation, why would the Gentiles—who have the law written in their hearts and keep it—be excluded from salvation? Is God a respecter of persons? Or is He the God only of Jews? Nonsense! God is a just God and the Father of every nation and race of man. So if He promised salvation to those under the law if they keep the law, He will also save the uncircumcised who kept the law written in their hearts.
>
> St. Anastasios the Patriarch of Antioch assured us that the salvation of the righteous Gentiles was revealed to him by revelation. He mentioned that the wise Plato appeared to an Orthodox monk while awake who was reviling him for some of his errors. Plato informed him about his salvation in Jesus Christ, and he admonished him to stop reviling him and sinning in doing so. Even if this testimony were not taken into consideration—although it is trustworthy since it comes from a trustworthy source—the belief regarding the salvation of the Gentiles is based on sound reasoning and is true by itself.[2413]

Moreover, it may be inferred that the Athonite fathers since at least the 13th century also concurred with this positive stance toward pagan philosophers, considering that at Vatopaidi and Iveron Monasteries there are frescoes of them holding statements akin to those contained in Christian teaching. But to indicate that these pagans did not reach the same levels of illumination and theosis as the Christian saints did, the pagan philosophers are accordingly depicted without halos.[2414]

In the 5th century, St. Nilus of Ancyra (and/or an anonymous contemporary of his)[2415] found the *Enchiridion* of Epictetus (a pagan Greek philosopher) so beneficial that he presented it as a Christian treatise by replacing the word "gods" with "God" in it[2416] and by removing sections inapplicable for Christians.[2417] Ever since then, it has been embraced as a spiritually edifying text by Christians, and it was even included in the Patristic series

---

[2412] Saint Augustine, *Letters,* vol. 2 (83–130), The Fathers of the Church: A New Translation, vol. 18, trans. Sister Wilfrid Parsons (Washington, D.C.: Catholic University of America Press, 1953), 155–56 (Epistle 102).

[2413] Ζιόμπολα, *Ὁ Ἅγιος Νεκτάριος, ὁ κορυφαῖος καὶ λαοφιλὴς τῶν καιρῶν μας,* 243–44.

[2414] Vid. Constantine Cavarnos, *Anchored in God,* second edition (Boston: Institute for Byzantine and Modern Greek Studies, 1975), 68–70.

[2415] Regarding the person responsible for the Christian revision of this document, see: http://en.wikipedia.org/wiki/Enchiridion_of_Epictetus

[2416] For example, compare Chapter 31:1 of the *Enchiridion* with PG 79:1301B.

[2417] For example, Chapter 32 of the *Enchiridion* regarding divination is absent from PG 79:1301D.

"Φιλοκαλία τῶν Νηπτικῶν καὶ Ἀσκητικῶν" published in Greece in 1972.[2418] This shows that the content of some heterodox writings does not conflict with Orthodoxy and can even be helpful to the Orthodox.

In fact, the content of some heterodox writings can be so close to Orthodox texts that even excellent theologians can fail to distinguish between the two, as is evident from the following amusing incident with Metropolitan Anthony Bloom and the renowned theologian Vladimir Lossky:

> At one time, Lossky's opinion was that the Eastern [non-Christian] religions had no proper knowledge or experience of God. Andrei [Metropolitan Anthony's name as a layman] did not dare to argue openly with such a distinguished person, about a somewhat controversial topic. "But what courage couldn't achieve, cunning could," he later said, and he decided to make his point in a way that his friend could not fail to respond to.
>
> Andrei slipped home and wrote out eight quotations from the Upanishads [a collection of ancient texts containing central religious concepts of Hinduism]. He took them back to Lossky with an apparently innocent query. "Could you help me? I have some sayings of the Fathers here and I can't remember who said what. Can you identify them for me, please?"
>
> Lossky went through the list and without hesitation wrote beside each quotation the relevant name: St. John Chrysostom, St. Basil the Great and so on. When the theologian had attributed them all, Andrei dropped his bombshell. "It's the Upanishads."
>
> "From then on," he said, "Lossky began to look much more sympathetically at other faiths and came to find in them truths he had never before been able to acknowledge."[2419]

In the 6th century, a monk asked St. John the Prophet: "Should we not, then, read even the works of Evagrios?" (Note that Evagrios the Solitary was considered a heretic because he had espoused some *theoretical* speculations of Origen that were later condemned at the Second Ecumenical Council. The *practical* teachings of Evagrios, however, were held in high regard, which is why several of his apothegms appear in the *Vitae Patrum,* and St. Nicodemos of the Holy Mountain included some writings of Evagrios in the *Philokalia.*) St. John the Prophet replied: "Do not accept such doctrines from his works; but go ahead and read, if you like, those works that are beneficial for the soul, according to the parable about the net in the Gospel. For it has been written: 'They placed the good into baskets, but threw out the bad.'[2420] You, too, should do the same."[2421] Thus we see that St. John had the

---

[2418] Νείλου τοῦ Μοναχοῦ, *Ἅπαντα τὰ Ἔργα,* ΕΠΕ, Φιλοκαλία 11Γ, 172 ἑπ.

[2419] Gillian Crow, *This Holy Man: Impressions of Metropolitan Anthony* (New York: St. Vladimir's Seminary Press, 2006), 84–85.

[2420] Mt. 13:48.

[2421] Chryssavgis, *Barsanuphius and John, Letters,* vol. 2, 183 (letter 602).

same approach towards *Christian* heretics that St. Basil the Great and others had towards *pagan* heretics: "Avoid the thorns, pluck the roses."

St. John the Damascene in the 8th century had the same mindset. For he wrote in the preface to his *Fount of Knowledge:*

> First of all I shall set forth the best contributions of the philosophers of the Greeks, because whatever there is of good has been given to men from above by God, since 'every best gift and every perfect gift is from above, coming down from the Father of lights.'[2422] ... In imitation of the method of the bee, I shall make my composition from those things which are conformable with the truth and from our enemies themselves gather the fruit of salvation. But all that is worthless and falsely labeled as knowledge I shall reject.[2423]

Also in the 8th century, St. Theodore the Studite studied pagan philosophy and (in the words of his biographer) "did not hold on to its mythology but kept what is edifying, while perceiving and detecting what is superfluous."[2424] Furthermore, "St. Theodore, emphasizing that the faith forms the most secure foundation, encouraged the faithful to gather from [pagan] philosophy whatever agrees with the faith and to censure those who are against it."[2425] Similarly, St. Photios the Great in the 9th century, having mastered all secular learning,[2426] taught that it acquires value and becomes useful only when it "guides the mind towards piety."[2427]

In the 12th century, St. Eustathios of Thessalonica wrote: "I would prefer that monks make anthologies also of secular writings, opinions, and sayings. The most holy Fathers in the old days selected these things ... and pleased God by working in this manner. I myself would love to have such monks here. But instead, the monks here scorn non-Christian books as well as Christian books.... I hope they acquire some prudence and stop behaving foolishly like this."[2428] Although this stance of St. Eustathios may appear at first glance to be the same as the heretical stance that Barlaam the Calabrian would take in the 14th century (since he also urged monks to occupy themselves with worldly learning),[2429] there is a

---

[2422] Jas. 1:17.

[2423] *Saint John of Damascus: Writings,* The Fathers of the Church, vol. 37, trans. Frederic H. Chase, Jr. (Washington, D.C.: Catholic University of America Press, 1958), 5, [PG 94:524C]).

[2424] PG 99:117CD.

[2425] Θεοδωρούδη, *Θεία καὶ Ἀνθρωπίνη Σοφία κατὰ τὴν Πατερικὴν Παράδοσιν τῆς Ὀρθοδόξου Ἐκκλησίας,* 97.

[2426] Vid. PG 105:509.

[2427] PG 102:597C.

[2428] For the entire quotation of St. Eustathios and its context, see the paragraphs referenced in footnote #956 on page 179.

[2429] Barlaam believed "that monks also should pursue secular wisdom, and that if they do not possess this wisdom, it is impossible for them to avoid ignorance and false opinion, even if they have achieved the highest level of impassibility; and that one cannot acquire perfection and sanctity without seeking knowledge from

fundamental difference: St. Eustathios made a clear distinction between human and divine wisdom and their corresponding benefits (as did other Church Fathers),[2430] whereas "Barlaam, being influenced by the unifying methodology of scholastic theology, equated the objects, method, and accomplishments of human and divine wisdom,"[2431] which resulted in his overemphasizing the value of human wisdom.

St. Gregory Palamas in the 14th century made a distinction similar to that of St. Eustathios and "differentiated between philosophy and theology, human reason and [divine] revelation, the created and the uncreated, and he taught that the two kinds of wisdom (human and divine) are clearly distinct and that the purpose of each of them determines its value."[2432] St. Gregory criticized Barlaam's overemphasis of human wisdom and his attribution of soteriological value to pagan philosophy. Nevertheless, St. Gregory added:

> Is there then anything of use to us in this philosophy? Certainly. For just as there is much therapeutic value even in substances obtained from the flesh of serpents, and the doctors consider there is no better and more useful medicine than that derived from this source, so there is something of benefit to be had even from the profane philosophers—but somewhat as in a mixture of honey and hemlock. So it is most needful that those who wish to separate out the honey from the mixture should beware that they do not take the deadly residue by mistake.[2433] ...
>
> Studying them [i.e., the various branches of human knowledge] is a good thing, but only to the measure that through it they develop sharpness of vision in the eye of the psyche [i.e., in the nous].[2434]

Nevertheless, St. Gregory described how difficult it is to extract benefit from pagan philosophy:

> In the case of secular wisdom, you must first kill the serpent, in other words, overcome the pride that arises from this philosophy. How difficult that is! "The arrogance of philosophy has nothing in common with humility," as the saying goes. Having overcome it, then, you must separate and cast away the head and tail, for these things are evil in the highest degree. By the head, I mean manifestly wrong opinions concerning things intelligible and divine and primordial; and by the tail, the fabulous stories concerning created things. As to what lies in between the head and tail, that is, discourses on nature, you must separate out useless ideas by means of the faculties of examination and inspection possessed by the soul, just as pharmacists purify the flesh of serpents with fire and water. Even if you do all this, and make good use of what has been properly set aside, how much trouble and circumspection will be required for the

---

all quarters, above all from Greek culture" (*Gregory Palamas: The Triads,* Classics of Western Spirituality, trans. John Meyendorff [New York: Paulist Press, 1983], 25, [1:1:4]).

[2430] Vid. Θεοδωρούδη, *Ὁ μοναχισμὸς κατὰ τὸν Εὐστάθιον Θεσσαλονίκης,* 69.

[2431] Θεοδωρούδη, *Θεία καὶ Ἀνθρωπίνη Σοφία κατὰ τὴν Πατερικὴν Παράδοσιν τῆς Ὀρθοδόξου Ἐκκλησίας,* 146.

[2432] Ibid., 154.

[2433] Meyendorff, *Gregory Palamas: The Triads,* 28.

[2434] Amis, *The Triads in Defence of the Holy Hesychasts: Book 1,* 37 (Triad 1.1.6).

task! Nonetheless, if you put to good use that part of the profane wisdom which has been well excised, no harm can result, for it will naturally have become an instrument for good.[2435]

St. Gregory himself, of course, had this discernment to extract the good from the harmful, which is why in his homilies he could quote non-Orthodox philosophers such as Pythagoras.[2436]

In the late 18th century St. Nicodemos of the Holy Mountain warned *others* to avoid the writings of the heterodox,[2437] but he himself quoted them in his books, and occasionally he even translated and published large portions of what they had written, such as Lorenzo Scupoli's *Spiritual Combat,* Ignatius Loyola's *Spiritual Exercises* with Giovanni Pietro Pinamonti's Italian commentary, and Paolo Segneri's *Il Confessore Istruito* and *Il Penitence Istruito.*[2438] Perhaps St. Nicodemos was so critical of the heterodox because he was simply trying to protect his audience—the largely uneducated Greek people under the Turkish yoke—who would not have had the discernment to separate "the honey from the hemlock." We would also say that anyone today who has not thoroughly acquired a patristic mindset is likely to consume some "hemlock" unwittingly if he tries to find the "honey" of the heterodox.

St. Athanasios Parios in the early 19th century sharply criticized heterodox teachings from Western Europe. Nevertheless, he acknowledged that using the beneficial insights of the heterodox "is something that the divine and foremost holy Fathers cultivated very much throughout their lives. They, too, selected whatever good they found in others and passed it on to benefit the public"[2439] This is why, according to Protopresbyter Theodoros Zeses:

> [Saint] Athanasios did not forbid the use of other [non-Orthodox] books. He himself used them and taught them to his students, just as the Fathers also did. He correctly believed that worldly wisdom does not lead to perfection and sanctity and the acquisition of the good things of the Kingdom of God, and that their usefulness is limited to life here on earth. Nevertheless, it is useful even in theology, as he wrote in *Epitome.*[2440]

[2435] Meyendorff, *Gregory Palamas: The Triads,* 29.

[2436] Vid. Veniamin, *Saint Gregory Palamas: The Homilies,* 371, n. 724.

[2437] For example, St. Nicodemos of the Holy Mountain wrote: "Be careful not to read the books of heretics. Avoid the books of atheists like fire. Do not even accept to take them into your hands" (Chamberas, *Nicodemos of the Holy Mountain: A Handbook of Spiritual Counsel,* 190).

[2438] According to Metropolitan Kallistos Ware, the *Exomologetarion* written by St. Nicodemos is "mostly a direct translation" of those two books by Paolo Segneri (vid. Dimitri Conomos, Graham Speake "St. Nikodimos and the Philokalia," in *Mount Athos, the Sacred Bridge: The Spirituality of the Holy Mountain* [Oxford: Bern, 2010], 91).

[2439] As quoted in Ζήσης, *Μοναχισμός: Μορφὲς καὶ Θέματα,* 196.

[2440] Ibid., 197.

Fr. Constantine Cavarnos added that St. Athanasios Parios

> emphasizes the inferiority of "external" or "human philosophy" compared with the "internal philosophy" or "philosophy from God." Throughout the book he is concerned with making his compatriots understand these two things: (a) The great importance of preserving in Greece the true order of the two philosophies, placing "Divine" philosophy above "human philosophy," Christianity above secular systems of knowledge. (b) The real danger involved in sending their sons to Europe for higher education, because in Europe this hierarchal order has been inverted....
>
> [But] he was not altogether closed to Western European thought. This is clearly testified to by the fact that he translated the book of the Italian philosopher Antonio Genovesi, *Elements of Metaphysics,* and used it as a handbook in his course on metaphysics.[2441]

In the late 19th century, St. Nectarios of Aegina wrote dozens of books and articles in which he frequently included inspiring quotes of non-Christians. Specifically, Fr. Constantine Cavarnos observed:

> Of the ancient Greek philosophers, the one from whom our Saint [Nectarios] draws most often is Plato. Next come, in order, Plutarch, Socrates, Aristotle, Epictetos, Pythagoras, and some others. Of other ancient Greek writers, the most frequently quoted are Xenophon, Isocrates, Euripides, Menander, Homer, Aesop, Demosthenes, Herodotos, Sophocles, Theognis, and Thucydides.[2442]

Furthermore, when St. Nectarios published the second edition of the book *Sketch Concerning Religious Tolerance* by Eugenios Voulgaris, he "contributed eighteen pages of notes taken from a [non-Orthodox] French work which Voulgaris used as a basis for his treatment of the subject. He selected some of the notes contained in the French work, translated them and appended them in order to help the readers understand in a more precise manner certain parts of Voulgaris' work."[2443]

St. Nikolai Velimirovich (1880–1956) expressed in poetry the benefit his own soul had gained from heterodox prophets:

> All the prophets have from the beginning cried out to my soul, imploring her to make herself a virgin and prepare herself to receive the Divine Son into her immaculate womb....
>
> The wise man of China admonishes my soul to be peaceful and still, and to wait for Tao to act within her. Glory be the memory of Lao-tse, the teacher and prophet of his people!
>
> The wise man of India teaches my soul not to be afraid of suffering, but through arduous and relentless drilling in purification and prayer to elevate herself to the One

---

[2441] Cavarnos, *Saint Athanasios Parios,* 67–69.

[2442] Cavarnos, *St. Nectarios of Aegina,* 37. St. Nectarios also published a book in 1896 entitled *Epic and Elegiac Maxims of Minor Greek Poets,* consisting entirely of spiritually edifying sayings of non-Christians (Ibid., 39).

[2443] Ibid., 22–23.

on high, who will come out to greet her and manifest to her His face and His power. Glorious be the memory of Krishna, the teacher and prophet of his people!

The royal son of India teaches my soul to empty herself completely of every seed and crop of the world, to abandon all the serpentine allurements of frail and shadowy matter, and then—in vacuity, tranquillity, purity, and bliss—to await nirvana. Blessed be the memory of Buddha, the royal son and inexorable teacher of his people!

The thunderous man of Persia tells my soul that there is nothing in the world except light and darkness, and that the soul must break free from the darkness as the day does from the night. For the sons of light are conceived from the light, and the sons of darkness are conceived from darkness. Glorious be the memory of Zoroaster, the great prophet of his people.

The prophet of Israel cries out to my soul: Behold, the virgin will conceive and bear a son, whose name will be—the God-man. Glorious be the memory of Isaiah, the clairvoyant prophet of my soul!

O heavenly Lord, open the hearing of my soul, lest she become deaf to the counsels of Your messenger.

Do not slay the prophets sent to you, my soul, for their graves contain not them, but those who slew them.[2444]

Furthermore, St. Nikolai Velimirovich believed that God was using Mahatma Gandhi (a Hindu) to teach the Christian world lessons in fasting, prayer, and silence. St. Nikolai wrote:

A warning from God—that is surely the meaning of the leader of the great Indian nation.... Gandhi's political method is very simple and obvious—he does not require anything except the man who cries out and the God who hearkens. Against weapons, ammunition and army, Gandhi places fasting; against skill, wiliness and violence—prayer; and against political quarrel—silence. Fasting, prayer and silence! Providence has chosen Gandhi, an unbaptized man, to serve as a warning to the baptized....

Providence sometimes uses such warnings for the good of the people. The Gospel also tells us that Providence sometimes uses such warnings for the good of the people.... I am alluding to the Roman captain from Capernaum (Mt. ch. 8). On the one hand, you see the elders of Israel who, as chosen monotheists of the time, boasted of their faith, meanwhile rejecting Christ, and on the other hand and you see the despised Roman pagan who came to Christ with great faith and humility, and asked Him to heal his servant. And when Jesus heard it, He was astonished and said to those who followed Him, "Truly I say to you, not even in Israel have I found faith like this." The Christian world is the new, baptized Israel. Listen! Is Christ not telling the same words today to the consciences of the Christian elders by pointing to today's captain of India?[2445]

In the 20th century, St. John Maximovitch also had the same openness to non-Orthodox sources, according to Fr. Seraphim Rose, who wrote:

[2444] Nikolaj Velimirović, *Prayers by the Lake,* A Treasury of Serbian Orthodox Spirituality, vol. 5, trans. Archimandrite Todor Mika and Stevan Scott (Grayslake: The Free Serbian Orthodox Diocese of the United States of America and Canada, 1989), 86–87.

[2445] Saint Nikolai Velimirovich, *Missionary Letters of Saint Nikolai Velimirovich, Part 1,* A Treasury of Serbian Orthodox Spirituality, vol. 6 (Grayslake: New Gracanica Monastery, 2008), 171–73.

> In 1640 or so, a [Roman Catholic] man in France named Ardenon wrote a book called *On Frequent Communion.*... At about the same time in Spain, someone named Miguel De Molinos also wrote about frequent Communion. It is very likely, although we cannot prove it right now, that St. Macarius [of Corinth] read one or both of these books, and that he even translated whole chapters from them for his own book. We do not need to get upset that he may have been taking a Western spiritual practice, however, if we realize that St. Macarius was adapting from the West something which can be important for us in our corrupted state; therefore there is nothing wrong with it at all. In fact, this is what we may call a true theological wisdom: when one is not afraid of something foreign just because it is foreign. One can take something foreign, having a higher wisdom which the Church gives, and adapt for one's own what is useful and throw out what is not useful. This kind of theological wisdom is precisely what we find in Archbishop [Saint] John [Maximovitch]. He was in the full tradition of Orthodoxy, and in the full tradition of those who adapted from wherever they could find sources for spiritual profit.[2446] ...
>
> A person who has prudence and discernment can read these [heterodox] texts and find out where they are right or they are wrong and use them properly.... Today we are in a situation where everyone who is Orthodox is totally immersed in this Western world, this Western understanding; and therefore we had better know how to take wisdom from it, what to accept and what to reject.[2447]

The spiritual forefathers of our monastic community continued this Patristic understanding of how edifying the wisdom of the heterodox can be. For example, St. Joseph the Hesychast in a pastoral epistle of his cited an edifying incident from the life of Philip of Macedonia and remarked that "the truth of things made the pagans wise."[2448] Elder Ephraim believed that also contemporary heterodox writings can be beneficial. One day (in 2009) one of his monks told me that he had read a non-Christian book[2449] about ethical behavior and benefitted greatly from the author's insights. This puzzled him, and he asked Elder Ephraim: "How is it possible to derive such great benefit from an author who is not even Christian?" Elder Ephraim replied: "Of course we can benefit from the writings of the heterodox. I, too, read some books of theirs."

Elder Ephraim not only read some heterodox books but he even referred to them in his homilies. For example, in his homily "Enthusiasm and Fanaticism: Two Completely Opposite Concepts," he cited the opinion of an Anglican regarding Islam. Even more boldly, several times Elder Ephraim mentioned in his homilies the story of how Napoleon Bonaparte convinced someone of God's existence by using a teleological argument (i.e., an "argument from design"). It is such a strong argument that Elder Ephraim even managed

---

[2446] *The Orthodox Word,* no. 175–6 (March–June 1994), 155.

[2447] Ibid., 152, 155–56.

[2448] Γέροντος Ἰωσήφ, Ἔκφρασις Μοναχικῆς Ἐμπειρίας, 298; see also Elder Joseph, *Monastic Wisdom,* 256.

[2449] The book was *The 7 Habits of Highly Effective Families* by Stephen R. Covey, who was a Mormon theologian. Covey does not touch on theological matters in this book of his.

to convert someone to Orthodoxy with the help of this insight, despite the fact that Napoleon was not even Christian. What he said was the following:

> Napoleon was a pious man of faith, but he had a general who did not believe in God. The emperor knew him well and made many attempts to convince his general, but he objected and refused to believe. One day the emperor invited him to lunch but had previously placed a ball on the dinner table. The emperor said to him: "I believe this ball on its own appeared here out of thin air."
> "Your Highness, you must be joking. Do you think I'm a fool to believe this?"
> "Yes, you are a fool," Napoleon replied. "If you believe this insignificant ball was made by someone, how can you not believe that the entire universe which operates with such precision was not created by God?"[2450]

+ + +

The reason why it is possible to benefit from the insights of the heterodox is because, according to the holy Fathers, their wisdom can be attributed to the grace of the Holy Spirit acting on them externally. In particular, St. John Chrysostom said:

> If He "lighteth every man that cometh into the world,"[2451] how is it that so many continue unenlightened? For not all have known the majesty of Christ. How then doth He "light every man"? He lighteth all as far as in Him lies. But if some, willfully closing the eyes of their mind, would not receive the rays of that Light, their darkness arises not from the nature of the Light, but from their own wickedness, who willfully deprive themselves of the gift. For the grace is shed forth upon all, turning itself back neither from Jew, nor Greek, nor Barbarian, nor Scythian, nor free, nor bond, nor male, nor female, nor old, nor young, but admitting all alike, and inviting with an equal regard.[2452]

St. Athanasios the Great spoke of the same thing: "The Saviour is working mightily among men, every day He is invisibly persuading numbers of people all over the world, both within and beyond the Greek-speaking world, to accept His faith and be obedient to His teaching."[2453]

St. Maximos the Confessor also taught that the grace of the Holy Spirit works in all people:

> The Holy Spirit is not absent from any created being, especially not from those which in any way participate in intelligence. For being God and God's Spirit, He embraces in unity the spiritual knowledge of all created things, providentially permeating all things with His power, and vivifying their inner essences in accordance with their nature. In this way He makes men aware of things done sinfully against the law

---

[2450] Vid. Γέροντος Ἐφραίμ, *Ἡ Τέχνη τῆς Σωτηρίας*, Τόμος Γ΄, ὁμιλία κθ΄ (ἀνέκδοτο).

[2451] Jn. 1:9.

[2452] *A Select Library of the Nicene and Post-Nicene Fathers of the Christian Church*, vol. 14, trans. Philip Schaff, Homily 8: John 1:9 (New York: Christian Literature Company, 1886), 29; PG 59:65.

[2453] *St. Athanasius, On the Incarnation*, trans. "A Religious of C.S.M.V." (New York: St. Vladimir's Orthodox Theological Seminary Press, 1993), 61.

of nature, and renders them capable of choosing principles which are true and in conformity with nature. Thus we find many barbarians and nomadic peoples turning to a virtuous way of life and setting aside the savage laws which they had kept among themselves from time immemorial.[2454]

Likewise, St. John Cassian stated: "The grace of Christ then is at hand every day, which, while it 'willeth all men to be saved and to come to the knowledge of the truth,' calleth all without any exception, saying: 'Come unto Me, all ye that labor and are heavy laden, and I will refresh you (Mt. 11:28).'"[2455]

St. Diadochos of Photiki made a distinction between how grace works on those who are baptized (i.e., Christians) and on those who have not been baptized (i.e., people outside the Church): "Before holy baptism, grace encourages the soul towards good things from the outside, while Satan lurks in its depths, trying to block all the ways of the nous from approaching the divine. But from the moment that we are reborn [through baptism], the demon is outside, and grace is within."[2456]

St. Seraphim of Sarov elaborated further on this external action of grace. Commenting on the Scripture that "the Spirit of God was not yet in the world" (Jn. 7:39), he said:

> That does not mean that the Spirit of God was not in the world at all, but His presence was not so apparent as in Adam or in us Orthodox Christians. It was manifested only externally.... The grace of the Holy Spirit acting externally was also reflected in all the Old Testament prophets and Saints of Israel.... Though not with the same power as in the people of God, nevertheless, the presence of the Spirit of God also acted in the pagans who did not know the true God, because even among them God found for Himself chosen people.... Though the pagan philosophers also wandered in the darkness of ignorance of God, yet they sought the truth which is beloved by God, and on account of this God-pleasing seeking, they could partake of the Spirit of God, for it is said that the nations who do not know God practice by nature the demands of the law and do what is pleasing to God (cf. Rom. 2:14).[2457]

St. Sophrony of Essex concurred: "Many people have received grace, and not only those in the Church but outside the Church, too, for 'God is no respecter of persons' (Acts 10:34)."[2458]

[2454] Μαξίμου τοῦ Ὁμολογητοῦ, «Ἑκατοντὰς τρίτη, κεφάλαια διάφορα θεολογικά τε καὶ οἰκονομικὰ καὶ περὶ ἀρετῆς καὶ κακίας» ἐν *Φιλοκαλία τῶν Ἱερῶν Νηπτικῶν*, τόμος β΄ (1991), 103–4 (κεφ. οβ΄); see also Palmer, Sherrard, Ware, *The Philokalia*, vol. 2, 180 (ch. 72).

[2455] *Nicene and Post-Nicene Fathers*, vol. 11, trans. Edgar C. S. Gibson, 2nd sermon (New York: Christian Literature Company, 1895), 425.

[2456] Διαδόχου Φωτικῆς, «Λόγος Ἀσκητικός» ἐν *Φιλοκαλία*, τόμος α΄ (1893), 155, κεφ. ος΄; see also Palmer, Sherrard, Ware, *The Philokalia*, vol. 1, 279 (St. Diadochos of Photiki 76).

[2457] *A Conversation of St. Seraphim of Sarov with N. A. Motovilov* (Blanco: New Sarov Press), 12–13.

[2458] Sakharov, *Saint Silouan the Athonite*, 127.

St. Gregory the Theologian held that the character of some people outside the Church can be more Christian than that of many inside the Church. In the funeral oration for his father's death he stated:

> Even before he was of our fold, he was ours. His character made him one of us. For, as many of our own are not with us, whose life alienates them from the common body, so, many of those without are on our side, whose character [τρόπῳ] anticipates their faith, and need only the name of that which indeed they possess. My father was one of these, an alien shoot, but inclined by his life towards us.[2459]

There are several instances of holy people who were not part of Abraham's covenant with God in the Old Testament, or were outside the Church in the New Testament, who were nevertheless enlightened by the grace of God. For example, St. Justin the Philosopher and Martyr pointed out that Adam, Abel, Enoch, Noah, Lot, and Melchizedek were amongst those "who did not observe the Sabbath, yet nevertheless were pleasing to God."[2460] Commenting on this, Fr. Jean Daniélou wrote that St. Justin "is thus a witness to the fact that, in the natural order, certain men were able to know the true God and to serve Him."[2461] And St. Gregory the Dialogist wrote apropos of Job: "It is not without cause that the life of a just pagan is set before us as a model side by side with the life of the Israelites. Our Saviour, coming for the redemption of Jews and Gentiles, willed also to be foretold by the voice of Jews and Gentiles."[2462]

Blessed Theodoret of Cyrus wrote about the Queen of the South: "That is where that wonderful woman was queen, whose eagerness Christ the Master lauded in the holy gospels (vid. Mt. 12:42).... I remember the teaching of the Apostle who praised those that were justified without the law: 'When the Gentiles, who have not the law, do by nature those things that are of the law, these not having the law are a law unto themselves' (Rom. 2:14)."[2463] St. Isidore of Seville added: "Not only is she blessed with the reward of heavenly resurrection, but she is declared worthy, by the voice of the Judge Himself, of the apostolic power to judge the adulterous Jews."[2464]

An example from the New Testament of a Christian being benefitted by a non-Christian after the coming of Christ is found in chapter ten of Acts. It tells of Cornelius the Italian, who because of his piety, almsgiving, and prayers was counted worthy to speak with an angel, even though he was not Christian or even Jewish. The Holy Spirit then used

---

[2459] Schaff, *Cyril of Jerusalem, Gregory Nazianzen*, 256 (Oration 18:6).

[2460] PG 6:517A.

[2461] Daniélou, *Holy Pagans of the Old Testament*, 112.

[2462] *Moral. super Job*. Proem; Sources Chrétiennes, 128 (as translated in Daniélou, *Holy Pagans of the Old Testament*, 4).

[2463] *Quaest Reg*. III, 10, 33; PG 80:697C–700A.

[2464] *Quaest Reg*. III, 5; PL 83:417.

him to teach the chief Apostle Peter something he had not yet understood. Upon learning this lesson, St. Peter declared: "I most certainly understand now that God is not one to show partiality, but in every nation the man who fears Him and does what is right is welcome to Him."[2465]

Another noteworthy observation from the New Testament is that the Apostle Paul quoted pagan writers several times as a means of strengthening his points by demonstrating that his message contains universal truths, as St. Basil pointed out: "The Apostle [Paul] often was not above using even pagan utterances which were congruent with his special purpose."[2466] Thus, in Acts 17:28 St. Paul quoted Arstus of Tarsus[2467] and Cleanthes of Asses:[2468] "'In Him we live and move and exist,' as even some of your own poets have said, 'For we also are His children.'" In First Corinthians 15:33, St. Paul quoted Menander: "Bad company corrupts good morals." Furthermore, in Titus 1:12–13 St. Paul quoted Epimenides and even called him a prophet: "One of themselves, a prophet of their own, said, 'Cretans are always liars, evil beasts, lazy gluttons.' This testimony is true." Most surprising of all is that, according to St. Paul in Acts 26:14, *Jesus Himself* quoted a heathen proverb to him: "It is hard for you to kick against the goads."[2469]

Several biblical scholars[2470] believe that St. Paul wrote the following words to the Phillipians (heirs of Hellenistic culture) as a way to suggest that they continue implementing the ideals of Hellenistic virtue: "Finally, brethren, whatsoever things are true,

---

[2465] Acts 10:34–35.

[2466] Wagner, *Saint Basil: Ascetical Works,* vol. 9, 58.

[2467] In *Phaenomena,* 1.

[2468] Vid. *Fabricii Biblioth.* Gr. l. 3. c. 18. 453.

[2469] Acts 26:14. According to a biblical scholar: "There is no Jewish use of this proverbial expression; it is entirely classical, and is of frequent occurrence in the Greek and Latin Poets" (John William Donaldson, *Christian Orthodoxy Reconciled with the Conclusions of Modern Biblical Learning: A Theological Essay with Critical and Controversial Supplements* [London, 1857], 293).

[2470] For example, one contemporary biblical scholar wrote: "The list of virtues in verse 8 is not uniquely Christian nor even Jewish in character. Rather, the list 'espouses the highest ideals of Hellenistic virtue' (White 1990: 221). The appropriation of Hellenistic virtues by Paul has troubled some (e.g., Martin 1976: 157–58), but Paul makes no attempt to 'Christianize' them. Instead he accepts what was considered ethically commendable in Hellenistic culture and tells Christians to reflect on this as a norm for their own behavior" (*Eerdmans Commentary on the Bible,* James D. G. Dunn, ed. [Grand Rapids: Wm. B. Eerdmans Publishing Co., 2003], 1401). The 19th-century *Pulpit Commentary* observed: "This word ['virtue' in Phil. 4:8], so very common in the Greek moralists, occurs nowhere else in St. Paul. Nor does any other of the New Testament writers use it except St. Peter (1 Peter 2:9 [in the Greek]; 2 Peter 1:3, 5). Bishop Lightfoot says, 'The strangeness of the word, combined with the change of expression, εἴ τις, will suggest another explanation: "Whatever value may reside in your old heathen conception of virtue, whatever consideration is due to the praise of men"; as if the apostle were anxious not to omit any possible ground of appeal'" (Henry Donald Maurice Spence-Jones, *The Pulpit Commentary: Galatians, Ephesians, Philippians, Colossians,* vol. 20 [New York: Anson D. F. Randolph, 1895]).

whatsoever things are honest, whatsoever things are just, whatsoever things are pure, whatsoever things are lovely, whatsoever things are of good report; if there be any virtue, and if there be any praise, think on these things."[2471] Likewise, St. Paul's advice to the Thessalonians: "Examine everything carefully; hold fast to that which is good,"[2472] was understood by St. John the Damascene to mean: "Let us examine also the words of non-Christian wise men [τῶν ἔξω σοφῶν], that we may find something in them worth carrying away and reap some fruit that will be of profit to our soul."[2473]

Regarding this issue of the presence of God's grace among the heterodox, St. Sophrony of Essex wrote: "Only the one and only [Orthodox] Church can possess the fullness of grace. All the other [heterodox] churches have grace due to their faith in Christ, although not the fullness of grace."[2474] A contemporary Orthodox author explained this in more detail:

> In any attempt to elucidate an Orthodox position on dogmatic issues, it is also important to consult the texts of the Divine Services. A brief look at some frequently used prayers will help to illustrate the concept of the Holy Spirit's general ministry. The first example introduces the Trisagion and is recited at almost every Orthodox service: "O Heavenly King, the Comforter, the Spirit of Truth, Who art everywhere present and fillest all things, the Treasury of good things and Giver of life." Here one can see an affirmation of the Holy Spirit's general ministry towards all of creation in which He fills all things with the energies of God in His rôle as the Divine Agent of Him by Whom "all things consist."[2475] The second example is the prayer which concludes the First Hour. Based on Saint John 1:9, it is a good example of the Orthodox understanding of the Economy of God towards His creation: "O Christ the True Light, Who enlightenest and sanctifiest every man that cometh into the world: Let the light of Thy countenance be signed upon us, that in it we may see the Unapproachable Light." ...
>
> There are innumerable examples of [non-Orthodox] believers who clearly appear to have had a deep relationship with Christ, as attested by their words and deeds.[2476] Some famous ones readily come to mind: C. S. Lewis—a Christian apologist whose thinking was close to Orthodoxy in many ways—is a "hero" to innumerable Christians

---

[2471] Phil. 4:8.

[2472] 1 Thes. 5:21.

[2473] PG 94:532A; see also Chase, *Saint John of Damascus: Writings,* 9.

[2474] Σωφρονίου, *Ἀγώνας Θεογνωσίας,* 161–62 (Ἐπιστολὴ 11).

[2475] Col. 1:17.

[2476] The author of this book added the following footnote: "Caution is required here, however. Occasionally one will find misguided Orthodox Christians who have adopted as their own one or more 'saints' of Roman Catholicism (post-Great Schism), Francis of Assisi being the most common. Although we do not wish to cast judgment upon Francis, to uphold such a person as a model is a grave error, as the following studies clearly bear out: *Unseen Light* (Blanco: New Sarov Press, 1999, forthcoming); Father George Macris, 'A Comparison of the Mysticism of Francis of Assisi with that of St. Seraphim of Sarov,' *Synaxis,* vol. 2, 39–56; "Francis of Assisi," *Orthodox Tradition,* Vol. XII, No. 2, 41–42. The divergence of Roman Catholic spirituality from that of Orthodoxy will become readily apparent after reading these."

of every variety. His writings have been instrumental in leading many to faith in Christ. Then there is Mother Theresa, who is revered by thousands as a model of Christian charity. One also recalls William Law, who wrote the challenging Anglican classic on the spiritual life, *A Serious Call to a Devout and Holy Life.* And we cannot forget Cardinal John Henry Newman, whose love for God in his intellectual biography, *Apologia pro vita sua,* is most evident. Of course, Orthodox Christians would readily disagree with many things these people wrote and did. Nevertheless—recognizing in them true feeling, piety, and love for God—, we can rightly thank God for their lives and work, not presuming to know how He will judge them. In such people it is obvious that God has found hearts that are open to Him. But Orthodox Christians should also say that this openness is in reality the reception of the *external* influence of God's Grace (Divine Energies) upon their lives, which is not the same thing as the *internal* working of ecclesial Grace given only through Baptism.[2477]

Based on all the foregoing, it follows that not only the pagan philosophers who lived *before* Christ were enlightened by the grace of the Holy Spirit, but even non-Christians who lived *after* the economia of Christ in the flesh "could partake of the Spirit of God on account of their God-pleasing seeking," as St. Seraphim of Sarov said.[2478] Therefore, since the grace of God has been at work even in non-Christians who "sought the truth which is beloved by God,"[2479] it makes sense that the holy Fathers would be able to appreciate the "spermatic divine Logos" present in some heterodox writings and would encourage others to benefit from them as well.

It is interesting to note that prior to the 18th century, the only non-Orthodox authors quoted by the saints of the Church were the Hellenic philosophers. After the 18th century, however, the saints began to quote contemporary non-Orthodox wise men as well (as cited above on pages 459–463). One explanation for this phenomenon would be to claim that these recent saints were an aberration from the norm and departed from the stance of the holy Fathers. However, this explanation has two problems: 1) it assumes that a number of saints was making a mistake, and 2) it implies that the grace of God ceased to act in the non-Orthodox after Hellenistic times, which is an implication that contradicts the patristic understanding of grace explained above on pages 463–465. Perhaps a more accurate explanation for this phenomenon can be found through an understanding of the historical context. Until the Byzantine Empire fell in the 15th century, it was the epitome of civilization and culture in the world. As such, it had very little to learn from its less civilized neighbors. But after a few centuries of suppression under the Ottoman yoke, and after Western Europe had emerged from its Dark Ages, the Orthodox Christians in the former Byzantine Empire were no longer at the forefront of worldly civilization and education. As

---

[2477] Patrick Barnes, *The Non-Orthodox: The Orthodox Teaching on Christians Outside of the Church* (Salisbury: Regina Orthodox Press, 1999), Chapter II.

[2478] *A Conversation of St. Seraphim of Sarov with N. A. Motovilov,* 13.

[2479] Ibid.

a result, they could thenceforth benefit from some aspects of "human philosophy" (as St. Athanasios Parios called it) of heterodox Western Europe.

In his book *Orthodox Monasticism,* Professor Christos Krikonis observed that Orthodox monasteries have traditionally appreciated the value of books written by non-Christians as well as books regarding non-spiritual matters:

> The contribution of monks is also typical in all the higher cultural values, such as the development of literacy and science. This contribution of theirs instills awe and admiration for the open-mindedness with which the monks preserved in their libraries the works of the ancient Greeks and of other authors, which they display with pride. Thus, among the thousands of old monastery manuscripts (which are vital for the preservation and study of the texts' history) are found entire or partial works that the ancient writers have bequeathed on us (such as: Aesop, Aeschylus, Aristotle, Aristophanes, Galen, Demosthenes, Epictetus, Euripides, Herodotus, Hesiod, Thucydides, Hippocrates, Isocrates, Josephus, Lucian, Homer, Horace, Pindar, Solon, Sophocles, Philo, and innumerable others).
>
> Among the thousands of manuscripts and printed books that are kept in the monastery libraries, all branches of knowledge and everything known to man are found: grammar, syntax, rhetoric, logic, metaphysics, psychology, geography, botany, medicine, physics, mathematics, meteorology, physiology.[2480]

Some people, however, might reason that heterodox writings are superfluous, considering that there have been countless saints throughout the history of the Church who have attained holiness without ever being exposed to such writings. Their reasoning appears to be supported by St. Irenaeus of Lyons who said: "Since therefore we have such proofs, it is not necessary to seek the truth among others which it is easy to obtain from the Church; since the apostles, like a rich man [depositing his money] in a bank, lodged in her hands most copiously all things pertaining to the truth: so that every man, whosoever will, can draw from her the water of life (Rev. 22:17). For she is the entrance to life; all others are thieves and robbers."[2481] St. Irenaeus, however, was speaking of *theological* truth, not scientific and ethical truths.

Although we can agree that heterodox writings are superfluous in the sense that it would be blasphemous to assert that the teachings of Jesus Christ were deficient, nevertheless, it is clear from what the holy Fathers demonstrated in word and deed that we Orthodox Christians should "beautify the faith with the riches of reason of those outside the Church,"[2482] as St. Gregory of Nyssa put it. And, according to St. Basil the Great, doing so is not merely optional, but "we *must* use these writings."[2483] St. Gregory the Theologian

---

[2480] Χρίστου Θ. Κρικώνη, *Ὁ Ὀρθόδοξος Μοναχισμός: Φορέας πνευματικότητος, κοινωνικῆς προσφορᾶς καὶ παράγων πολιτισμοῦ ἢ ἄρνηση ζωῆς;* (Ἀθήνα: Ἀποστολικὴ Διακονία, 2010), 40.

[2481] *Ante-Nicene Fathers,* vol. 1, Adversus Haereses, III, (New York: Christian Literature Company, 1885), 4.

[2482] For the entire quotation of St. Gregory of Nyssa, see the text referenced in footnote #2407 on page 454.

[2483] For the entire quotation of St. Basil the Great, see the text referenced in footnote #2402 on page 453.

even lamented that "many Christians by an error of judgment scorn [heterodox writings] as treacherous and dangerous and as turning away from God,"[2484] just as St. Eustathios of Thessalonica lamented the "foolish behavior" of monks who "scorn non-Christian books."[2485]

St. Gregory of Nyssa enumerated some of the fields of knowledge that we ought to borrow from the heterodox: "moral and natural philosophy, geometry, astronomy, dialectic, and whatever else is sought by those outside the Church, since these things will be useful."[2486] This is why we have included in this book insightful examples of moral and natural philosophy from the heterodox as well as some of their scientific findings. But we have avoided referring to the dogmas, theology, and ontology of the heterodox because they are incompatible with Orthodoxy.

It is important to make this distinction between the harmful *theological* teachings of the heterodox and their beneficial *moral* and *scientific* teachings. Failing to do so would result in "throwing out the baby with the bathwater," or to put it more patristically, "throwing out the roses with the thorns." Making this distinction enables us to see why some of the holy Fathers would approve of reading heterodox writings while others would prohibit this. The prohibitions were always in regards to books that specifically contain heresies— i.e., the *theological* teachings of the heterodox. The following passage of St. Paisius Velichkovsky in the 18th century is a good example of such a prohibition:

Can a true Christian have and read books forbidden by the Church which are being secretly reprinted in a sacrilegious manner by schismatics and being distributed by them among the people, or should this be not done? My answer is that the Divine Church forbids reading heretical books and holding discussions with heretics. In a book on the profession of the Orthodox faith, there is a question asking what is the fifth commandment of the Church. The answer is that those who are unlearned in the Holy Scriptures and other necessary fields should not read heretical books or listen to the harmful teachings of heretics, or even speak and have dealings with them, as the psalm-singer prophet says: "Blessed is the man who walks not in the counsel of the wicked, nor stands in the way of sinners" (Ps. 1:1). Elsewhere the Holy Scripture says: "As for a man who is factious, after admonishing him once or twice, have nothing more to do with him" (Titus 3:10). Watch carefully and note that the Divine Church does not command everyone not to read heretical books and not to hold discussions with heretics, but only those who are unlearned in the Holy Scriptures and the various fields of learning. It is very easy for the latter, as they read heretical books and get acquainted with their teachings, or carelessly enter into conversations with heretics, to succumb to their ungodly and perverted sophistry. In the eyes of ignorant people, heretical teaching often appears to be truthful, while actually being unquestionably

---

[2484] For the entire quotation of St. Gregory the Theologian, see the text referenced in footnote #2406 on page 454.

[2485] For the entire quotation of St. Eustathios of Thessalonica, see the text referenced in footnote #956 on page 179.

[2486] For the entire quotation of St. Gregory of Nyssa, see the text referenced in footnote #2407 on page 454.

false. Just as Satan, being darkness, becomes transformed into a radiant angel, so do heretical teachings, being darkness and totally alienated from the light of God's Truth, often appear to people who are unlearned in the Holy Scriptures and various fields to be somewhat similar to the truth. This is why the Church forbids whose who are unlearned in the Holy Scriptures and the other fields to read heretical books, and to have discussions with heretics, so that they will not, due to their unsophistication, be harmed by their teachings. Those who have studied the Holy Scriptures and the other fields are exempt from this commandment. Such are the Holy Fathers, the pastors, and the teachers of the Church. Not only were they instructed to perfection in the Holy Scriptures by the grace of God, but they also mastered the other fields of knowledge, surpassing in worldly wisdom not only their instructors, but also all the ancient philosophers. These God-bearing Fathers of ours saw how various heretics, proud of their worldly wisdom, would turn the Divine Scriptures into a weapon of their philosophy, interpreting them in an erroneous and perverted sense through philosophical proofs and bringing constant strife into the Church of Christ through their teachings. Thus the Fathers would read their false heretical teachings, and subordinating their philosophies to the Divine Scriptures in every respect, would perceive the heretics' errors clearer than the sun, and through the invincible double weapon, i.e., theology and philosophical proof, would rend asunder all their heretical stratagems as a spider web and would defend God's Church by the word of truth from all heretical attacks. For philosophy, too, if used correctly, as the Holy and Apostolic Church teaches us, corresponds to God's truth to such an extent that it cannot be surpassed by any heretical verbal stratagems. If used contrary to the true sense of the Holy Scriptures and the Holy Church, as is done by the heretics, it becomes opposed to God's truth, and since it upholds lies it gets vanquished by truthful evidence. Thus, one who starts reading schismatic books must lack neither theological knowledge nor worldly learning. For the one who does not have the appropriate knowledge, it is better to obey God and the Church commandment which says: "Do not read heretical books and do not take part in discussions with heretics."[2487]

Panayiotis Nellas, a contemporary theologian, called for discernment in dealing with such matters:

The task of contemporary Orthodox theology does not consist in theologians identifying themselves with scientific research or political action, with the idea of corroborating these things, nor does it consist in trying to overthrow the achievements of these things on the basis of a supposedly evangelical or patristic teaching. The Gospel teaches that the struggle of the faithful is "not against flesh and blood"[2488]—that struggle within the framework created by science, politics, and the other dimensions of the "garments of skin," because such a framework is not of its own nature evil—but it is a struggle "against principalities, against powers, against world rulers of this present darkness,"[2489] against the devil and sin. Orthodox theology ought to practice a discernment of spirits. Its aim should be to liberate whatever good exists among the fruits of scientific research, technological development, etc., from lawless autonomy, which

---

[2487] Chetverikov, *Starets Paisii Velichkovskii,* 253–55.

[2488] Eph. 6:12.

[2489] Ibid.

is slavery to corruption and the devil, the ultimate sin, and to assign to this good element an ordered place within its own catholic truth, because that is where it belongs by virtue of its own nature; for [according to St. Justin][2490] "whatever is called good by all men belongs to us Christians."[2491]

+ + +

Today we live in an age of syncretism, nihilism, globalization, and general confusion. Thus, the average Orthodox Christian nowadays has been exposed to various unorthodox teachings and is usually trying to fit Orthodoxy into an already made, but quite distorted, framework. For example, he has been taught that "there are many paths up the mountain," that there is a "transcendental unity of all religions," that "what matters is that one does good works, not what one believes," and many other such heretical ideas. Therefore, we want to make it perfectly clear that despite our inclusion of select quotes from the heterodox, we believe that "no man cometh unto the Father but by Me [Jesus]."[2492] We certainly do not endorse all or even many teachings of the heterodox authors quoted, nor do we disregard the Patristic warnings regarding the harm that can ensue from indiscriminately reading the writings of heretics. Therefore we urge all Orthodox Christians to flee from the *spiritual, theological,* and *dogmatic* writings of the heterodox "as from fire," but to learn only from their *ethical* and *scientific* insights, as we did in this book. Furthermore, we believe that it is crucial to keep all such ethical and scientific approaches in their proper place, that is, subordinate to Orthodox spiritual life, which is why they occupy only a small part of this book. We have completely avoided any dogmatic opinions of the heterodox, since we believe that the Church is indeed "the pillar and ground of the truth."[2493]

The End

Glory be to God for all things.

[2490] For the entire quotation of St. Justin, see the text referenced in footnote #2389 on page 451.

[2491] Panayiotis Nellas, *Deification in Christ* (New York: St. Vladimir's Seminary Press, 1987), 102–3.

[2492] Jn. 14:6.

[2493] 1 Tim. 3:15.

Index of Persons

B

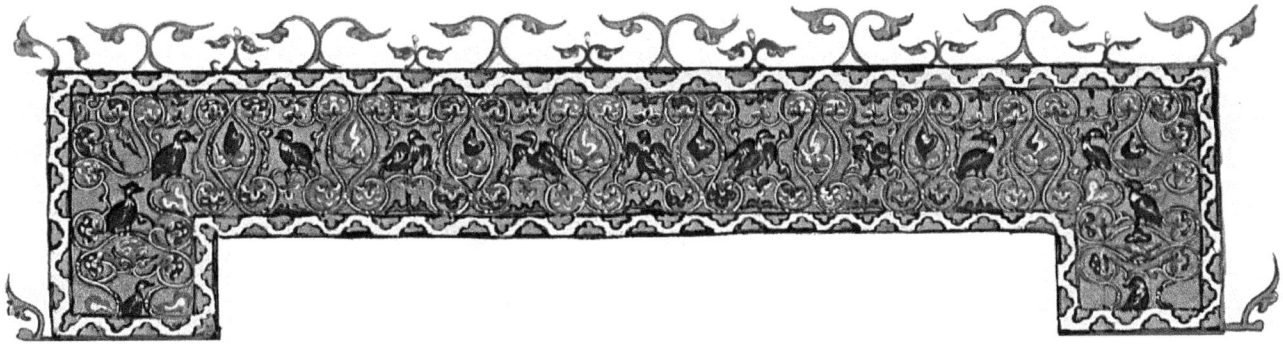

Index of Subjects

of the Canons of Marūtā, 7, 150, 264

of the Monastery of Evergetis, 82, 83, 248, 384

of the Monastery of Machairas, 245, 246, 384

of the Monastery of Petritzonitissa, 67, 258

of the Monastery of St. John the Forerunner (Serres), 70, 199

of the Monastery of St. John the Forerunner of Phoberos, 245, 247

of the Monastery of St. Mamas, 411

of the Monastery of the Archangel Michael, 297

of the Regulations of Horsiesios, 197, 238

of the Rule for the Monastery of Compludo, 61, 82, 151, 201, 234, 245, 264, 320

of the Rule of Carthage, 302

of the Rule of Macarius, 18, 63, 178, 382

of the Rule of St. Ailbe, 86, 197, 230, 340

of the Rule of St. Comghall, 44

of the Rule of Tallaght, 190, 252, 322

of the Rule of Tarn, 87, 90, 175, 210, 243, 246, 250, 281

of the Rule of the Four Fathers, 239

of the Rule of the Master, 64, 69, 86, 94, 100, 114, 190, 191, 199, 239, 243, 251, 272, 325, 382

of the Rules Attributed to Ephrēm, 272

of the Rules for the Monks in Persia, 90

of the Rules of Bābai, 253

of the Rules of Rabbūlā for the Monks, 243

of the Rules of Rabbūlā for the Qeiāmā, 294

of the Third Rule of the Fathers, 10, 317

reading of, 382, 383

schedule of services, 333–39

signed by monastics, 382

U

unacquisitiveness. *See* poverty

uncreated Light, 403

understanding

hampered by excessive information, 370

need to receive, 216

of God's works, 2

of Koine Greek, 180

of life, 305

of self, 31

opinions produces shallow connection, 215

others, 74, 204, 217, 219, 220, 318

renunciation of, 107, 123

singing with, 151, 168, 182, 183

through books, 179, 180

unhappiness. *See* depression

union

Christ born without conjugal, 139

of Christ with Church, 127

of mind and heart, 165

with God, 402, 449

unity

abbot labors to preserve, 73

acting with counsel preserves, 69

cenobium fosters, 206

importance of preserving, xviii, 77, 103, 318, 375

novices not tonsured who disrupt, 16

obedience to abbot ensures, 70, 77, 107

of all religions a heresy, 472

of faculties dispersed by internet, 346

of wills, 77

overcoming one's desires necessary for, 93

primary goal, 89, 209, 229, 314

rules help preserve, 335

unmarried. *See also* virginity

better to be, 137

superiority of being, 126

Upanishads, 456

V

vainglory, 21, 34, 269, 309, 345, 380, 408, 419

vest, 413, 414

vices. *See* passions

vigil, 166–75

aid in chastity, 147

as core of monastic life, 172

bodily stance in, 169

duration of, 173

fruits of, 172

power of prayer in, 167

reading during, 174

spiritual gifts in, 167

struggle of, 168

time for, 166

www.ingramcontent.com/pod-product-compliance
Lightning Source LLC
Chambersburg PA
CBHW062000090426
42811CB00006B/995

9 781733 884907